STUDY GUIDE

STUDY GUIDE

Richard O. Straub

University of Michigan, Dearborn

to accompany

SEVENTH EDITION

The Developing Person
Through the Life Span

Kathleen Stassen Berger

WORTH PUBLISHERS

Study Guide
by Richard O. Straub
to accompany
Berger: **The Developing Person Through the Life Span**, Seventh Edition

ISBN 10: 0-7167-6092-4
ISBN 13: 978-0-7167-6092-4

First printing

Worth Publishers
41 Madison Avenue
New York, NY 10010
www.worthpublishers.com

Contents

Preface

This Study Guide is designed for use with *The Developing Person Through the Life Span*, Seventh Edition, by Kathleen Stassen Berger. It is intended to help you to evaluate your understanding of that material, and then to review any problem areas. "How to Manage Your Time Efficiently, Study More Effectively, and Think Critically" provides detailed instructions on how to use the textbook and this Study Guide for maximum benefit. It also offers additional study suggestions based on principles of time management, effective note-taking, evaluation of exam performance, and an effective program for improving your comprehension while studying from textbooks.

Each chapter of the Study Guide includes a Chapter Overview, a set of Guided Study questions to pace your reading of the text chapter, a Chapter Review section to be completed after you have read the text chapter, and three review tests. One chapter in each section of the text includes a crossword puzzle that provides an alternative way of testing your understanding of the terms and concepts. The review tests are of two types: Progress Tests that consist of questions focusing on facts and definitions and a test titled Developmental Psychology Applied that evaluates your understanding of the text chapter's broader conceptual material and its application to real-world situations. For all three review tests, the correct answers are given, followed by textbook page references (so you can easily go back and reread the material), and complete explanations not only of why the answer is correct but also of why the other choices are incorrect.

I would like to thank Betty and Don Probert of The Special Projects Group for their exceptional work in all phases of this project. My thanks also to Sharon Merritt, Jenny Chiu, and Stacey Alexander for their skillful assistance in the preparation of this Study Guide. We hope that our work will help you to achieve your highest level of academic performance in this course and to acquire a keen appreciation of human development.

Richard O. Straub
October 2007

How to Manage Your Time Efficiently, Study More Effectively, and Think Critically

How effectively do you study? Good study habits make the job of being a college student much easier. Many students, who *could* succeed in college, fail or drop out because they have never learned to manage their time efficiently. Even the best students can usually benefit from an in-depth evaluation of their current study habits.

There are many ways to achieve academic success, of course, but your approach may not be the most effective or efficient. Are you sacrificing your social life or your physical or mental health in order to get A's on your exams? Good study habits result in better grades *and* more time for other activities.

Evaluate Your Current Study Habits

To improve your study habits, you must first have an accurate picture of how you currently spend your time. Begin by putting together a profile of your present living and studying habits. Answer the following questions by writing *yes* or *no* on each line.

_____ 1. Do you usually set up a schedule to budget your time for studying, recreation, and other activities?

_____ 2. Do you often put off studying until time pressures force you to cram?

_____ 3. Do other students seem to study less than you do, but get better grades?

_____ 4. Do you usually spend hours at a time studying one subject, rather than dividing that time between several subjects?

_____ 5. Do you often have trouble remembering what you have just read in a textbook?

_____ 6. Before reading a chapter in a textbook, do you skim through it and read the section headings?

_____ 7. Do you try to predict exam questions from your lecture notes and reading?

_____ 8. Do you usually attempt to paraphrase or summarize what you have just finished reading?

_____ 9. Do you find it difficult to concentrate very long when you study?

_____ 10. Do you often feel that you studied the wrong material for an exam?

Thousands of college students have participated in similar surveys. Students who are fully realizing their academic potential usually respond as follows: (1) yes, (2) no, (3) no, (4) no, (5) no, (6) yes, (7) yes, (8) yes, (9) no, (10) no.

Compare your responses to those of successful students. The greater the discrepancy, the more you could benefit from a program to improve your study habits. The questions are designed to identify areas of weakness. Once you have identified your weaknesses, you will be able to set specific goals for improvement and implement a program for reaching them.

Manage Your Time

Do you often feel frustrated because there isn't enough time to do all the things you must and want to do? Take heart. Even the most productive and successful people feel this way at times. But they establish priorities for their activities and they learn to budget time for each of them. There's much in the saying "If you want something done, ask a busy person to do it." A busy person knows how to get things done.

If you don't now have a system for budgeting your time, develop one. Not only will your academic accomplishments increase, but you will actually find more time in your schedule for other activities. And you won't have to feel guilty about "taking time off," because all your obligations will be covered.

Establish a Baseline

As a first step in preparing to budget your time, keep a diary for a few days to establish a summary, or baseline, of the time you spend in studying, socializing, working, and so on. If you are like many students, much of your "study" time is nonproductive; you may sit at your desk and leaf through a book, but the time is actually wasted. Or you may procrastinate. You are always getting ready to study, but you rarely do.

Besides revealing where you waste time, your time-management diary will give you a realistic picture of how much time you need to allot for meals, commuting, and other fixed activities. In addition, careful records should indicate the times of the day when you are consistently most productive. Table 1 shows a sample time-management diary.

Plan the Term

Having established and evaluated your baseline, you are ready to devise a more efficient schedule. Buy a calendar that covers the entire school term and has ample space for each day. Using the course outlines provided by your instructors, enter the dates of all exams, term paper deadlines, and other important academic obligations. If you have any long-range personal plans (concerts, weekend trips, etc.), enter the dates on the calendar as well. Keep your calendar up to date and refer to it often. I recommend carrying it with you at all times.

Develop a Weekly Calendar

Now that you have a general picture of the school term, develop a weekly schedule that includes all of your activities. Aim for a schedule that you can live with for the entire school term. A sample weekly schedule, incorporating the following guidelines, is shown in Table 2.

1. Enter your class times, work hours, and any other fixed obligations first. *Be thorough.* Using information from your time-management diary, allow plenty of time for such things as commuting, meals, laundry, and the like.

Table 1   Sample Time-Management Diary

| Activity | Monday | |
	Time Completed	Duration Hours: Minutes
Sleep	7:00	7:30
Dressing	7:25	:25
Breakfast	7:45	:20
Commute	8:20	:35
Coffee	9:00	:40
French	10:00	1:00
Socialize	10:15	:15
Videogame	10:35	:20
Coffee	11:00	:25
Psychology	12:00	1:00
Lunch	12:25	:25
Study Lab	1:00	:35
Psych. Lab	4:00	3:00
Work	5:30	1:30
Commute	6:10	:40
Dinner	6:45	:35
TV	7:30	:45
Study Psych.	10:00	2:30
Socialize	11:30	1:30
Sleep		

Prepare a similar chart for each day of the week. When you finish an activity, note it on the chart and write down the time it was completed. Then determine its duration by subtracting the time the previous activity was finished from the newly entered time.

2. Set up a study schedule for each of your courses. The study habits survey and your time-management diary will direct you. The following guidelines should also be useful.

(a) Establish regular study times for each course. The 4 hours needed to study one subject, for example, are most profitable when divided into shorter periods spaced over several days. If you cram your studying into one 4-hour block, what you attempt to learn in the third or fourth hour will interfere with what you studied in the first 2 hours. Newly acquired knowledge is like wet cement. It needs some time to "harden" to become memory.

(b) Alternate subjects. The type of interference just mentioned is greatest between similar topics. Set up a schedule in which you spend time on several *different* courses during each study session. Besides reducing the potential for interference, alternating subjects will help to prevent mental fatigue with one topic.

(c) Set weekly goals to determine the amount of study time you need to do well in each course. This will

Table 2   Sample Weekly Schedule

Time	Mon.	Tues.	Wed.	Thurs.	Fri.	Sat.
7–8	Dress Eat	Dress Eat	Dress Eat	Dress Eat	Dress Eat	
8–9	Psych.	Study Psych.	Psych.	Study Psych.	Psych.	Dress Eat
9–10	Eng.	Study Eng.	Eng.	Study Eng.	Eng.	Study Eng.
10–11	Study French	Free	Study French	Open Study	Study French	Study Stats.
11–12	French	Study Psych. Lab	French	Open Study	French	Study Stats.
12–1	Lunch	Lunch	Lunch	Lunch	Lunch	Lunch
1–2	Stats.	Psych. Lab	Stats.	Study or Free	Stats.	Free
2–3	Bio.	Psych. Lab	Bio.	Free	Bio.	Free
3–4	Free	Psych.	Free	Free	Free	Free
4–5	Job	Job	Job	Job	Job	Free
5–6	Job	Job	Job	Job	Job	Free
6–7	Dinner	Dinner	Dinner	Dinner	Dinner	Dinner
7–8	Study Bio.	Study Bio.	Study Bio.	Study Bio.	Free	Free
8–9	Study Eng.	Study Stats.	Study Psych.	Open Study	Open Study	Free
9–10	Open Study	Open Study	Open Study	Open Study	Free	Free

This is a sample schedule for a student with a 16-credit load and a 10-hour-per-week part-time job. Using this chart as an illustration, make up a weekly schedule, following the guidelines outlined here.

depend on, among other things, the difficulty of your courses and the effectiveness of your methods. Many professors recommend studying at least 1 to 2 hours for each hour in class. If your time-management diary indicates that you presently study less time than that, do not plan to jump immediately to a much higher level. Increase study time from your baseline by setting weekly goals [see (4)] that will gradually bring you up to the desired level. As an initial schedule, for example, you might set aside an amount of study time for each course that matches class time.

(d) Schedule for maximum effectiveness. Tailor your schedule to meet the demands of each course. For the course that emphasizes lecture notes, schedule time for a daily review soon after the class. This will give you a chance to revise your notes and clean up any hard-to-decipher shorthand while the material is still fresh in your mind. If you are evaluated for class participation (for example, in a language course), allow time for a review just before the class meets. Schedule study time for your most difficult (or least motivat-

ing) courses during hours when you are the most alert and distractions are fewest.

(e) Schedule open study time. Emergencies, additional obligations, and the like could throw off your schedule. And you may simply need some extra time periodically for a project or for review in one of your courses. Schedule several hours each week for such purposes.

3. After you have budgeted time for studying, fill in slots for recreation, hobbies, relaxation, household errands, and the like.

4. Set specific goals. Before each study session, make a list of specific goals. The simple note "7–8 PM: study psychology" is too broad to ensure the most effective use of the time. Formulate your daily goals according to what you know you must accomplish during the term. If you have course outlines with advance assignments, set systematic daily goals that will allow you, for example, to cover fifteen chapters before the exam. And be realistic: Can you actually expect to cover a 78-page chapter in one session? Divide large tasks into smaller units; stop at the most logical resting points. When you complete a specific goal, take a 5- or 10-minute break before tackling the next goal.

5. Evaluate how successful or unsuccessful your studying has been on a daily or weekly basis. Did you reach most of your goals? If so, reward yourself immediately. You might even make a list of five to ten rewards to choose from. If you have trouble studying regularly, you may be able to motivate yourself by making such rewards contingent on completing specific goals.

6. Finally, until you have lived with your schedule for several weeks, don't hesitate to revise it. You may need to allow more time for chemistry, for example, and less for some other course. If you are trying to study regularly for the first time and are feeling burned out, you probably have set your initial goals too high. Don't let failure cause you to despair and abandon the program. Accept your limitations and revise your schedule so that you are studying only 15 to 20 minutes more each evening than you are used to. The point is to identify a regular schedule with which you can achieve some success. Time management, like any skill, must be practiced to become effective.

Techniques for Effective Study

Knowing how to put study time to best use is, of course, as important as finding a place for it in your schedule. Here are some suggestions that should enable you to increase your reading comprehension and improve your note-taking. A few study tips are included as well.

Using SQ3R to Increase Reading Comprehension

How do you study from a textbook? If you are like many students, you simply read and reread in a *passive* manner. Studies have shown, however, that most students who simply read a textbook cannot remember more than half the material ten minutes after they have finished. Often, what is retained is the unessential material rather than the important points upon which exam questions will be based.

This *Study Guide* employs a program known as SQ3R (*Survey*, *Question*, *Read*, *Recite*, and *Review*) to facilitate, and allow you to assess, your comprehension of the important facts and concepts in *The Developing Person Through the Life Span*, Seventh Edition, by Kathleen Stassen Berger.

Research has shown that students using SQ3R achieve significantly greater comprehension of textbooks than students reading in the more traditional passive manner. Once you have learned this program, you can improve your comprehension of any textbook.

Survey Before reading a chapter, determine whether the text or the study guide has an outline or list of objectives. Read this material and the summary at the end of the chapter. Next, read the textbook chapter fairly quickly, paying special attention to the major headings and subheadings. This survey will give you an idea of the chapter's contents and organization. You will then be able to divide the chapter into logical sections in order to formulate specific goals for a more careful reading of the chapter.

In this Study Guide, the *Chapter Overview* summarizes the major topics of the textbook chapter. This section also provides a few suggestions for approaching topics you may find difficult.

Question You will retain material longer when you have a use for it. If you look up a word's definition in order to solve a crossword puzzle, for example, you will remember it longer than if you merely fill in the letters as a result of putting other words in. Surveying the chapter will allow you to generate important questions that the chapter will proceed to answer. These question correspond to "mental files" into which knowledge will be sorted for easy access.

As you survey, jot down several questions for each chapter section. One simple technique is to generate questions by rephrasing a section heading. For example, the "Preoperational Thought" head could be turned into "What is preoperational thought?" Good questions will allow you to focus on the important points in the text. Examples of good questions are those that begin as follows: "List two examples of . . .." "What is the function of . . .?" "What is the significance of . . .?" Such questions give a purpose to your reading. Similarly, you can formulate questions based on the chapter outline.

The *Guided Study* section of this Study Guide provides the types of questions you might formulate while surveying each chapter. This section is a detailed set of objectives covering the points made in the text.

Read When you have established "files" for each section of the chapter, review your first question, begin reading, and continue until you have discovered its answer. If you come to material that seems to answer an important question you don't have a file for, stop and write down the question.

Using this Study Guide, read the chapter one section at a time. First, preview the section by skimming it, noting headings and boldface items. Next, study the appropriate section objectives in the *Guided Study*. Then, as you read the chapter section, search for the answer to each objective.

Be sure to read everything. Don't skip photo or art captions, graphs, marginal notes. In some cases, what may seem vague in reading will be made clear by a simple graph. Keep in mind that test questions are sometimes drawn from illustrations and charts.

Recite   When you have found the answer to a question, close your eyes and mentally recite the question and its answer. Then *write* the answer next to the question. It is important that you recite an answer in your own words rather than the author's. Don't rely on your short-term memory to repeat the author's words verbatim.

In responding to the objectives, pay close attention to what is called for. If you are asked to identify or list, do just that. If asked to compare, contrast, or do both, you should focus on the similarities (compare) and differences (contrast) between the concepts or theories. Answering the objectives carefully will not only help you to focus your attention on the important concepts of the text, but it will also provide excellent practice for essay exams.

Recitation is an extremely effective study technique, recommended by many learning experts. In addition to increasing reading comprehension, it is useful for review. Trying to explain something in your own words clarifies your knowledge, often by revealing aspects of your answer that are vague or incomplete. If you repeatedly rely upon "I know" in recitation, you really may not know.

Recitation has the additional advantage of simulating an exam, especially an essay exam; the same skills are required in both cases. Too often students study without ever putting the book and notes aside, which makes it easy for them to develop false confidence in their knowledge. When the material is in front of you, you may be able to recognize an answer, but will you be able to recall it later, when you take an exam that does not provide these retrieval cues?

After you have recited and written your answer, continue with your next question. Read, recite, and so on.

Review   When you have answered the last question on the material you have designated as a study goal, go back and review. Read over each question and your written answer to it. Your review might also include a brief written summary that integrates all of your questions and answers. This review need not

take longer than a few minutes, but it is important. It will help you retain the material longer and will greatly facilitate a final review of each chapter before the exam.

In this Study Guide, the *Chapter Review* section contains fill-in and one- or two-sentence essay questions for you to complete after you have finished reading the text and have written answers to the objectives. The correct answers are given at the end of the chapter. Generally, your answer to a fill-in question should match exactly (as in the case of important terms, theories, or people). In some cases, the answer is not a term or name, so a word close in meaning will suffice. You should go through the Chapter Review several times before taking an exam, so it is a good idea to mentally fill in the answers until you are ready for a final pretest review. Textbook page references are provided with each section title, in case you need to reread any of the material.

Also provided to facilitate your review are two *Progress Tests* that include multiple-choice questions and, where appropriate, matching or true–false questions. These tests are not to be taken until you have read the chapter, written answers to the objectives, and completed the *Chapter Review*. Correct answers, along with explanations of why each alternative is correct or incorrect, are provided at the end of the chapter. The relevant text page numbers for each question are also given. If you miss a question, read these explanations and, if necessary, review the text pages to further understand why. The *Progress Tests* do not test every aspect of a concept, so you should treat an incorrect answer as an indication that you need to review the concept.

Following the two Progress Tests is *Developmental Psychology Applied*, a test that should be taken just prior to an exam. It includes questions that test your ability to analyze, integrate, and apply the concepts in the chapter. As with the *Progress Tests*, answers for *Developmental Psychology Applied* are provided at the end of each chapter, along with relevant page numbers.

The chapter concludes with *Key Terms*, either in list form only or also in a crossword puzzle. In either form, as with the *Guided Study* objectives, it is important that the answers be written from memory, and in list form, in your own words. The *Answers* section at the end of the chapter gives a definition of each term, sometimes along with an example of its usage and/or a tip to help you remember its meaning.

One final suggestion: Incorporate SQ3R into your time-management calendar. Set specific goals for completing SQ3R with each assigned chapter. Keep a record of chapters completed, and reward yourself for being conscientious. Initially, it takes more time and effort to "read" using SQ3R, but with practice, the steps will become automatic. More importantly, you will comprehend significantly more material and retain what you have learned longer than passive readers do.

Taking Lecture Notes

Are your class notes as useful as they might be? One way to determine their worth is to compare them with those taken by other good students. Are yours as thorough? Do they provide you with a comprehensible outline of each lecture? If not, then the following suggestions might increase the effectiveness of your note-taking.

1. Keep a separate notebook for each course. Use standard notebook pages. Consider using a ring binder, which would allow you to revise and insert notes while still preserving lecture order.

2. Take notes in the format of a lecture outline. Use roman numerals for major points, letters for supporting arguments, and so on. Some instructors will make this easy by delivering organized lectures and, in some cases, by outlining their lectures on the board. If a lecture is disorganized, you will probably want to reorganize your notes soon after the class.

3. As you take notes in class, leave a wide margin on one side of each page. After the lecture, expand or clarify any shorthand notes while the material is fresh in your mind. Use this time to write important questions in the margin next to notes that answer them. This will facilitate later review and will allow you to anticipate similar exam questions.

Evaluate Your Exam Performance

How often have you received a grade on an exam that did not do justice to the effort you spent preparing for the exam? This is a common experience that can leave one feeling bewildered and abused. "What do I have to do to get an A?" "The test was unfair!" "I studied the wrong material!"

The chances of this happening are greatly reduced if you have an effective time-management schedule and use the study techniques described here. But it can happen to the best-prepared student and is most likely to occur on your first exam with a new professor.

Remember that there are two main reasons for studying. One is to learn for your own general academic development. Many people believe that such knowledge is all that really matters. Of course, it is possible,

though unlikely, to be an expert on a topic without achieving commensurate grades, just as one can, occasionally, earn an excellent grade without truly mastering the course material. During a job interview or in the workplace, however, your A in Cobol won't mean much if you can't actually program a computer.

In order to keep career options open after you graduate, you must know the material and maintain competitive grades. In the short run, this means performing well on exams, which is the second main objective in studying.

Probably the single best piece of advice to keep in mind when studying for exams is to *try to predict exam questions.* This means ignoring the trivia and focusing on the important questions and their answers (with your instructor's emphasis in mind).

A second point is obvious. How well you do on exams is determined by your mastery of both lecture and textbook material. Many students (partly because of poor time management) concentrate too much on one at the expense of the other.

To evaluate how well you are learning lecture and textbook material, analyze the questions you missed on the first exam. If your instructor does not review exams during class, you can easily do it yourself. Divide the questions into two categories: those drawn primarily from lectures and those drawn primarily from the textbook. Determine the percentage of questions you missed in each category. If your errors are evenly distributed and you are satisfied with your grade, you have no problem. If you are weaker in one area, you will need to set future goals for increasing and/or improving your study of that area.

Similarly, note the percentage of test questions drawn from each category. Although exams in most courses cover both lecture notes and the textbook, the relative emphasis of each may vary from instructor to instructor. While your instructors may not be entirely consistent in making up future exams, you may be able to tailor your studying for each course by placing additional emphasis on the appropriate area.

Exam evaluation will also point out the types of questions your instructor prefers. Does the exam consist primarily of multiple-choice, true–false, or essay questions? You may also discover that an instructor is fond of wording questions in certain ways. For example, an instructor may rely heavily on questions that require you to draw an analogy between a theory or concept and a real-world example. Evaluate both your instructor's style and how well you do with each format. Use this information to guide your future exam preparation.

Important aids, not only in studying for exams but also in determining how well prepared you are, are the Progress and Thinking Critically Tests provided in this Study Guide. If these tests don't include all of the types of questions your instructor typically writes, make up your own practice exam questions. Spend extra time testing yourself with question formats that are most difficult for you. There is no better way to evaluate your preparation for an upcoming exam than by testing yourself under the conditions most likely to be in effect during the actual test.

A Few Practical Tips

Even the best intentions for studying sometimes fail. Some of these failures occur because students attempt to work under conditions that are simply not conducive to concentrated study. To help ensure the success of your time-management program, here are a few suggestions that should assist you in reducing the possibility of procrastination or distraction.

1. If you have set up a schedule for studying, make your roommate, family, and friends aware of this commitment, and ask them to honor your quiet study time. Close your door and post a "Do Not Disturb" sign.

2. Set up a place to study that minimizes potential distractions. Use a desk or table, not your bed or an extremely comfortable chair. Keep your desk and the walls around it free from clutter. If you need a place other than your room, find one that meets as many of the above requirements as possible—for example, in the library stacks.

3. Do nothing but study in this place. It should become associated with studying so that it "triggers" this activity, just as a mouth-watering aroma elicits an appetite.

4. Never study with the television on or with other distracting noises present. If you must have music in the background in order to mask outside noise, for example, play soft instrumental music. Don't pick vocal selections; your mind will be drawn to the lyrics.

5. Study by yourself. Other students can be distracting or can break the pace at which your learning is most efficient. In addition, there is always the possibility that group studying will become a social gathering. Reserve that for its own place in your schedule.

If you continue to have difficulty concentrating for very long, try the following suggestions.

6. Study your most difficult or most challenging subjects first, when you are most alert.

7. Start with relatively short periods of concentrated study, with breaks in between. If your attention starts to wander, get up immediately and take a break. It is better to study effectively for 15 minutes and then take a break than to fritter away 45 minutes out of an hour. Gradually increase the length of study periods, using your attention span as an indicator of successful pacing.

Critical Thinking

Having discussed a number of specific techniques for managing your time efficiently and studying effectively, let us now turn to a much broader topic: What exactly should you expect to learn as a student of developmental psychology?

Most developmental psychology courses have two major goals: (1) to help you acquire a basic understanding of the discipline's knowledge base, and (2) to help you learn to think like a psychologist. Many students devote all of their efforts to the first of these goals, concentrating on memorizing as much of the course's material as possible.

The second goal—learning to think like a psychologist—has to do with critical thinking. Critical thinking has many meanings. On one level, it refers to an attitude of healthy skepticism that should guide your study of psychology. As a critical thinker, you learn not to accept any explanation or conclusion about behavior as true until you have evaluated the evidence. On another level, critical thinking refers to a systematic process for examining the conclusions and arguments presented by others. In this regard, many of the features of the SQ3R technique for improving reading comprehension can be incorporated into an effective critical thinking system.

To learn to think critically, you must first recognize that psychological information is transmitted through the construction of persuasive arguments. An argument consists of three parts: an assertion, evidence, and an explanation (Mayer and Goodchild, 1990).

An assertion is a statement of relationship between some aspect of behavior, such as intelligence, and another factor, such as age. Learn to identify and evaluate the assertions about behavior and mental processes that you encounter as you read your textbook, listen to lectures, and engage in discussions with classmates. A good test of your understanding of an assertion is to try to restate it in your own words. As you do so, pay close attention to how important terms and concepts are defined. When a researcher asserts that "intelligence declines with age," for example, what does he or she mean by "intelligence"? Assertions such as this one may be true when a critical term ("intelligence") is defined one way (for example, "speed of thinking"), but not when defined in another way (for example, "general knowledge"). One of the strengths of psychology is the use of *operational* definitions that specify how key terms and concepts are measured, thus eliminating any ambiguity about their meaning. "Intelligence," for example, is often operationally defined as performance on a test measuring various cognitive skills. Whenever you encounter an assertion that is ambiguous, be skeptical of its accuracy.

When you have a clear understanding of an argument's assertion, evaluate its supporting evidence, the second component of an argument. Is it *empirical*? Does it, in fact, support the assertion? Psychologists accept only *empirical (observable) evidence* that is based on direct measurement of behavior. Hearsay, intuition, and personal experiences are not acceptable evidence. Chapter 1 discusses the various research methods used by developmental psychologists to gather empirical evidence. Some examples include surveys, observations of behavior in natural settings, and experiments.

As you study developmental psychology, you will become aware of another important issue in evaluating evidence—determining whether or not the research on which it is based is faulty. Research can be faulty for many reasons, including the use of an unrepresentative sample of subjects, experimenter bias, and inadequate control of unanticipated factors that might influence results. Evidence based on faulty research should be discounted.

The third component of an argument is the explanation provided for an assertion, which is based on the evidence that has been presented. While the argument's assertion merely *describes* how two things (such as intelligence and age) are related, the explanation tells *why*, often by proposing some theoretical mechanism that causes the relationship. Empirical evidence that thinking speed slows with age (the assertion), for example, may be explained as being caused by age-related changes in the activity of brain cells (a physiological explanation).

Be cautious in accepting explanations. In order to think critically about an argument's explanation, ask yourself three questions: (1) Can I restate the explanation in my own words?; (2) Does the explanation make sense based on the stated evidence?; and (3) Are there alternative explanations that adequately

explain the assertion? Consider this last point in relation to our sample assertion: It is possible that the slower thinking speed of older adults is due to their having less recent experience than younger people with tasks that require quick thinking (a disuse explanation).

Because psychology is a relatively young science, its theoretical explanations are still emerging, and often change. For this reason, not all psychological arguments will offer explanations. Many arguments will only raise additional questions for further research to address.

Some Suggestions for Becoming a Critical Thinker

1. Adopt an attitude of healthy skepticism in evaluating psychological arguments.

2. Insist on unambiguous operational definitions of an argument's important concepts and terms.

3. Be cautious in accepting supporting evidence for an argument's assertion.

4. Refuse to accept evidence for an argument if it is based on faulty research.

5. Ask yourself if the theoretical explanation provided for an argument "makes sense" based on the empirical evidence.

6. Determine whether there are alternative explanations that adequately explain an assertion.

7. Use critical thinking to construct your own effective arguments when writing term papers, answering essay questions, and speaking.

8. Polish your critical-thinking skills by applying them to each of your college courses, and to other areas of life as well. Learn to think critically about advertising, political speeches, and the material presented in popular periodicals.

Some Closing Thoughts

I hope that these suggestions help make you more successful academically, and that they enhance the quality of your college life in general. Having the necessary skills makes any job a lot easier and more pleasant. Let me repeat my warning not to attempt to make too drastic a change in your life-style immediately. Good habits require time and self-discipline to develop. Once established they can last a lifetime.

1

Introduction

Chapter Overview

The first chapter introduces the study of human development. The first two sections define development, identify five characteristics of the scientific study of human development, and explain different aspects of the overlapping contexts in which people develop. The story of David illustrates the effects of these contexts. The ecological-systems approach—Bronfenbrenner's description of how the individual is affected by, and affects, many other individuals, groups of individuals, and larger systems in the environment—can be used with any research strategy or any combination of strategies.

The next section discusses the strategies developmentalists use in their research, beginning with the scientific method and including scientific observation, experiments, surveys, and case studies. To study people over time, developmentalists have created several research designs: cross-sectional, longitudinal, and cross-sequential.

The final section discusses several common mistakes that can be made in interpreting research, including the mistake of confusing correlation with causation and the ethics of research with humans. In addition to ensuring confidentiality and safety, developmentalists who study children are especially concerned that the benefits of research outweigh the risks.

NOTE: Answer guidelines for all Chapter 1 questions begin on page 11.

Guided Study

The text chapter should be studied one section at a time. Before you read, preview each section by skimming it, noting headings and boldface items. Then read the appropriate section objectives from the following outline. Keep these objectives in mind and, as you read the chapter section, search for the information that will enable you to meet each objective. Once you have finished a section, write out answers for its objectives.

Defining Development (pp. 3–6)

1. Define development, focusing on three elements of its scientific study and noting how dynamic-systems theory highlights the interactive nature of development.

2. Describe the ecological-systems approach to the study of human development, and explain how this approach leads to an understanding of the overlapping contexts in which people develop.

Five Characteristics of Development (pp. 7–16)

3. Identify five characteristics of development.

4. Explain what it means to say development is multidirectional, and describe two aspects of the social context that affect development.

5. Discuss the multicultural nature of human development.

6. Define and differentiate culture, ethnicity, and race.

7. Discuss the multidisciplinary approach to the study of development, noting the three domains into which human development is often separated.

8. Discuss the implications of mirror-neuron research.

9. Explain the importance of plasticity in human development.

Developmental Study as a Science (pp. 16–25)

10. List and describe the basic steps of the scientific method.

11. Describe scientific observation as a research strategy, noting at least one advantage (or strength) and one disadvantage (or weakness).

12. Describe the components of an experiment, and discuss the main advantage of this research method.

13. Describe surveys and case studies, noting at least one advantage (or strength) and one disadvantage (or weakness) of each.

14. Describe three basic research designs used by developmental psychologists.

Cautions from Science (pp. 25–29)

15. Describe two common mistakes made in the interpretation of research.

16. Briefly summarize some of the ethical issues involved in conducting research with humans.

Chapter Review

When you have finished reading the chapter, work through the material that follows to review it. Complete the sentences and answer the questions. As you proceed, evaluate your performance for each section by consulting the answers on page 11. Do not continue with the next section until you understand each answer. If you need to, review or reread the appropriate section in the textbook before continuing.

Defining Development (pp. 3–6)

1. The scientific study of human development can be defined as the science that seeks to understand

_____

_____.

2. Developmental science is _____ , meaning that it is based on data and facts.

3. The theory that stresses fluctuations and transitions in development is _____-_____ theory. The word _____ captures the idea that _____ .

4. The approach that emphasizes the influence of the systems that support the developing person is called the _____-_____

approach. This approach was emphasized by _____ .

5. According to this model, the family, the peer group, and other aspects of the immediate social setting constitute the _____ .

6. Community institutions such as school and church make up the _____ .

7. Cultural values, political philosophies, economic patterns, and social systems make up the

_____ .

8. The system that emphasizes the importance of historical time on development is the

_____ .

9. Systems that link one microsystem to another constitute the _____ .

Five Characteristics of Development (pp. 7–16)

10. The five developmental characteristics embodied within the science of development are that development is

a. _____

b. _____

c. _____

d. _____

e. _____

11. Three important insights emerging from the fact that development is multidirectional are that

a. human development is _____ .

b. each aspect of life is _____ .

c. even a tiny change in one system can have a profound effect on the other systems of development, called the

_____ _____ .

12. A group of people born within a few years of each other is called a _____ . These people tend to be affected by history in _____ (the same way/different ways).

13. A contextual influence that is determined by a person's income, education, place of residence, and occupation is called _____ _____ , which is often abbreviated _____ .

14. The "patterns of behavior that are passed from one generation to the next" constitute a _____ .

15. Cultures are _____ , always changing as circumstances change. Also, people are influenced by _____ (only one/more than one) culture.

16. A collection of people who share certain attributes, such as ancestry, national origin, religion, and language, is called a(n) _____ _____ .

17. A group of people who are regarded as _____ distinct on the basis of physical appearance constitute a _____ .

18. Although race was once thought to be a _____ category, it is actually an idea created by _____ . Thus, it is a _____ _____ .

19. The study of human development can be divided into three domains: _____ , _____ , and _____ .

20. Multiple disciplines are needed to understand development because people develop in several _____ , multifaceted _____ , and diverse _____ .

21. The value of an interdisciplinary approach to understanding human development can be seen in research on _____ _____—brain cells that respond to _____ .

22. One of the most encouraging aspects of the science of development is that development is characterized by _____ , or the ability to change.

23. (A Case to Study) Because his mother contracted the disease _____ during her pregnancy, David was born with a heart defect and cataracts over both eyes. Thus, his immediate problems centered on _____ problems. However, because he was born at a particular time, he was already influenced by the larger _____ context. David's continuing development of his skills is a testament to _____ .

Developmental Study as a Science (pp. 16–25)

24. In order, the basic steps of the scientific method are
    a. _____
    b. _____
    c. _____
    d. _____
    e. _____

25. A specific, testable prediction that forms the basis of a research project is called a _____ .

26. To repeat an experimental test procedure and obtain the same results is to _____ the test of the hypothesis.

27. In designing research studies, scientists are concerned with four issues: _____ , or whether a study measures what it purports to measure; _____ , or whether its measurements are accurate; _____ , or whether the study applies to other populations and situations; and _____ , or whether it solves real-life problems.

28. When researchers observe and record, in a systematic and objective manner, what research participants do, they are using _____ .

29. In the science of human development, people may be observed in a _____ setting or in a _____ .

30. A chief limitation of observation is that it does not indicate the _____ of the behavior being observed.

31. The method that allows a scientist to determine cause and effect is the _____ . In

this method, researchers manipulate a(n) _____ variable to determine its effect on a(n) _____ variable. Sometimes, results are reported by _____ size, and sometimes tests of _____ are used to indicate whether the results might have occurred by chance.

32. In an experiment, the participants who receive a particular treatment constitute the _____ _____ ; the participants who do not receive the treatment constitute the _____ _____ .

33. In a(n) _____ , scientists collect information from a large group of people by personal interview, written questionnaire, or some other means.

34. Potential problems with this research method are that those being questioned are not _____ of the group of interest, the _____ and _____ of the questions may influence people's answers, and respondents may give answers that make them seem wise or good.

35. An intensive study of one individual is called a(n) _____ _____ . An advantage of this method is that it makes it possible to understand a particular individual very well. Other important uses are that it provides a good _____ _____ for other research and that it can illustrate _____ .

36. Research that involves the comparison of people of different ages is called a _____- _____ research design.

37. With cross-sectional research, it is very difficult to ensure that the various groups differ only in their _____ . In addition, every cross-sectional study will, to some degree, reflect _____ _____ in addition to age effects.

38. Research that follows the same people over a relatively long period of time is called a _____ research design.

State three drawbacks of this type of research design.

39. The research method that combines the longitudinal and cross-sectional methods is the _____-_____ research method.

Cautions from Science (pp. 25–29)

40. A number that indicates the degree of relationship between two variables is a _____ . To say that two variables are related in this way _____ (does/ does not) necessarily imply that one caused the other. A correlation is _____ if both variables tend to _____ together; a correlation is _____ if one variable tends to _____ when the other _____ ; a correlation is _____ if there is no evident connection between the two variables.

41. Because numbers can be easily summarized and compared, scientists often rely on data produced by _____ research. This method may be particularly limiting when researchers describe _____ , and so many developmental researchers use _____ research that asks _____- _____ questions.

42. Developmental researchers work from a set of moral principles that constitute their _____ _____ _____ . Researchers who study humans must obtain _____ _____ , which refers to written permission, and ensure that their participants are not _____ and that they are allowed to stop at any time.

43. To ensure that research is not unintentionally slanting, scientific _____ , _____ , and replication are crucial.

Progress Test 1

Multiple-Choice Questions

Circle your answers to the following questions and check them against the answers on page 12. If your answer is incorrect, read the explanation for why it is incorrect and then consult the appropriate pages of the text (in parentheses following the correct answer).

1. The scientific study of human development is defined as the study of:
   a. how and why people change or remain the same over time.
   b. psychosocial influences on aging.
   c. individual differences in learning over the life span.
   d. all of the above.

2. The research method that involves the use of open-ended questions and obtains answers that are not easily translated into categories is:
   a. the case study.
   b. qualitative research.
   c. cross-sectional study.
   d. quantitative research.

3. Which of the following is *not* an important aspect of the social context mentioned in the text?
   a. historical
   b. socioeconomic
   c. cultural
   d. racial

4. Dynamic-systems theory emphasizes the idea(s) that:
   a. human development is always changing and that change in one area affects all others.
   b. developmental science should emphasize quantitative data.
   c. a person's position in society is determined primarily by social factors such as income and education.
   d. concepts such as race are based on social perceptions.

5. The ecological-systems approach to developmental psychology focuses on the:
   a. biochemistry of the body systems.
   b. macrosystems only.
   c. internal thinking processes.
   d. overall environment of development.

6. The science of development focuses on:
   a. the sources of continuity from the beginning of life to the end.
   b. the sources of discontinuity throughout life.
   c. the "nonlinear" character of human development.
   d. all of the above.

7. Brain cells that respond to actions performed by another person are called:
   a. cohort neurons.
   b. mirror neurons.
   c. butterfly cells.
   d. premotor cells.

8. A hypothesis is a:
   a. conclusion.
   b. prediction to be tested.
   c. statistical test.
   d. correlation.

9. A developmentalist who is interested in studying the influences of a person's immediate environment on his or her behavior is focusing on which system?
   a. mesosystem   c. microsystem
   b. macrosystem   d. exosystem

10. Socioeconomic status is determined by a combination of variables, including:
    a. age, education, and income.
    b. income, ethnicity, and occupation.
    c. income, education, and occupation.
    d. age, ethnicity, and occupation.

11. To say that developmental science is empirical means that it is:
    a. theoretical in nature.
    b. hypothetical in nature.
    c. based on observation, experience, or experiment.
    d. characterized by all of the above.

12. In an experiment that tests the effects of group size on individual effort in a tug-of-war task, the number of people in each group is the:
    a. hypothesis.
    b. independent variable.
    c. dependent variable.
    d. level of significance.

13. Which research method would be most appropriate for investigating the relationship between parents' religious beliefs and their attitudes toward middle-school sex education?
    a. experimentation
    b. longitudinal research
    c. naturalistic observation
    d. the survey

14. To establish cause, which type of research study would an investigator conduct?
    a. an experiment
    b. a survey
    c. scientific observation
    d. a case study

15. Developmentalists who carefully observe the behavior of schoolchildren during recess are using a research method known as:
    a. the case study.
    b. cross-sectional research.
    c. scientific observation.
    d. cross-sequential research.

True or False Items

Write T (*true*) or F (*false*) on the line in front of each statement.

_____ 1. Scientists rarely repeat an experiment.

_____ 2. (A Case to Study) The case study of David clearly demonstrates that for some children only nature (or heredity) is important.

_____ 3. Observation usually indicates a clear relationship between cause and effect.

_____ 4. Each social context influences development independently.

_____ 5. Cohort differences are an example of the impact of the social context on development.

_____ 6. Every trait of an individual can be molded into different forms and shapes.

_____ 7. Because of its limitations, qualitative research is rarely used in developmental research.

_____ 8. The influences between and within Bronfenbrenner's systems are unidirectional and independent.

_____ 9. People of different ethnic groups can all share one culture.

_____ 10. Longitudinal research is particularly useful in studying development over a long age span.

Progress Test 2

Progress Test 2 should be completed during a final chapter review. Answer the following questions after you thoroughly understand the correct answers for the Chapter Review and Progress Test 1.

Multiple-Choice Questions

1. An individual's personal sphere of development refers to his or her:
    a. microsystem and mesosystem.
    b. exosystem.
    c. macrosystem.
    d. microsystem, mesosystem, exosystem, macrosystem, and chronosystem.

2. Developmental psychologists explore three domains of development:
    a. physical, cognitive, psychosocial.
    b. physical, biosocial, cognitive.
    c. biosocial, cognitive, psychosocial.
    d. biosocial, cognitive, emotional.

3. The most important principle of the developmental research code of ethics is:
    a. never physically or psychologically harm those who are involved in research.
    b. maintain confidentiality at all costs.
    c. obtain informed consent from all participants.
    d. ensure that participants do not understand the true purpose of their research study.

4. When developmentalists speak of the "butterfly effect," they are most directly referring to the idea that:
    a. a small event may have a powerful impact on development.
    b. development is fundamentally a nonlinear event.
    c. each context of development is a dynamic system.
    d. each context of development interacts with the others.

5. According to the ecological-systems approach, the macrosystem would include:
    a. the peer group.   c. cultural values.
    b. the community.   d. the family.

6. An idea that is built more on shared perceptions than on objective reality is a:
    a. cohort effect.
    b. butterfly effect.
    c. social construction.
    d. hypothesis.

7. Professor Cohen predicts that because "baby boomers" grew up in an era that promoted independence and assertiveness, people in their 40s and 50s will respond differently to a political survey than will people in their 20s and 30s. The professor's prediction regarding political attitudes is an example of a(n):
   a. replication.
   b. hypothesis.
   c. independent variable.
   d. dependent variable.

8. A cohort is defined as a group of people:
   a. of similar national origin.
   b. who share a common language.
   c. born within a few years of each other.
   d. who share the same religion.

9. In a test of the effects of noise, groups of students performed a proofreading task in a noisy or a quiet room. To what group were students in the noisy room assigned?
   a. experimental   c. randomly assigned
   b. comparison   d. dependent

10. In differentiating ethnicity and culture, we note that:
    a. ethnicity is an exclusively biological phenomenon.
    b. an ethnic group is a group of people who were born within a few years of each other.
    c. people of many ethnic groups can share one culture, yet maintain their ethnic identities.
    d. racial identity is always an element of culture.

11. If developmentalists discovered that poor people are happier than wealthy people, this would indicate that wealth and happiness are:
    a. unrelated.
    b. correlated.
    c. examples of nature and nurture, respectively.
    d. causally related.

12. The plasticity of development refers to the fact that:
    a. development is not always linear.
    b. each human life must be understood as embedded in many contexts.
    c. there are many reciprocal connections between childhood and adulthood.
    d. human characteristics can be molded into different forms and shapes.

13. In an experiment that tests the effects of noise level on mood, mood is the:
    a. hypothesis.
    b. independent variable.
    c. dependent variable.
    d. scientific observation.

14. Research on mirror neurons has revealed:
    a. that when experts in dance watch a performance, their brains are activated as if they themselves were performing.
    b. a possible connection between a lack of mirror neurons and autism.
    c. new possible explanations for why children whose parents fight often learn less in school.
    d. all of the above.

15. Which of the following statements concerning ethnicity and culture is *not* true?
    a. Ethnicity is determined genetically.
    b. Race is a social construction.
    c. Racial identity is an element of ethnicity.
    d. Ethnic identity provides people with shared values and beliefs.

Matching Items

Match each definition or description with its corresponding term.

Terms

_____ **1.** independent variable
_____ **2.** dependent variable
_____ **3.** culture
_____ **4.** replicate
_____ **5.** chronosystem
_____ **6.** exosystem
_____ **7.** mesosystem
_____ **8.** socioeconomic status
_____ **9.** cohort
_____ **10.** ethnic group
_____ **11.** cross-sectional research
_____ **12.** longitudinal research

Definitions or Descriptions

a. group of people born within a few years of each other
b. determined by a person's income, education, occupation, and so on
c. research study comparing people of different ages at the same time
d. the historical conditions that affect development
e. collection of people who share certain attributes, such as national origin
f. shared values, patterns of behavior, and customs maintained by people in a specific setting
g. local institutions such as schools
h. the variable manipulated in an experiment
i. connections between microsystems
j. to repeat a study and obtain the same findings
k. the variable measured in an experiment
l. research study retesting one group of people at several different times

Developmental Psychology Applied

Answer these questions the day before an exam as a final check on your understanding of the chapter's terms and concepts.

1. Dr. Ahmed is conducting research that takes into consideration the relationship between the individual and the environment. Evidently, Dr. Ahmed is using the:
   a. ecological-systems approach.
   b. longitudinal method.
   c. cross-sectional method.
   d. case study method.

2. To study the effects of temperature on mood, Dr. Sanchez had students fill out questionnaires in very warm or very cool rooms. In this study, the independent variable consisted of:
   a. the number of students assigned to each group.
   b. the students' responses to the questionnaire.
   c. the room temperature.
   d. the subject matter of the questions.

3. Jahmal is writing a paper on the role of the social context in development. He would do well to consult the writings of:
   a. Piaget.   **c.** Bronfenbrenner.
   b. Freud.   **d.** Skinner.

4. Summarizing her presentation on race and biology, Trisha notes that:
   a. a racial group is a collection of people who share ancestral heritage.
   b. race is a biological construction defined by the genetic traits of a group of people.
   c. social scientists recognize that all racial categories are imprecise.
   d. all of the above are true.

5. Esteban believes that high doses of caffeine slow a person's reaction time. To test his belief, he has five friends each drink three 8-ounce cups of coffee and then measures their reaction time on a learning task. What is wrong with Esteban's research strategy?
   a. No independent variable is specified.
   b. No dependent variable is specified.
   c. There is no comparison condition.
   d. There is no provision for replication of the findings.

6. In an experiment testing the effects of group size on individual effort in a tug-of-war task, the amount of individual effort is the:
   a. hypothesis.
   b. independent variable.
   c. dependent variable.
   d. level of significance.

7. Concluding her presentation on ethnicity and race, Maya notes that experts today view race as a social construction. By this, she means that race is:
   a. a valid biological category.
   b. a meaningless concept.
   c. an idea created by society.
   d. none of the above.

8. Professor Jorgenson believes development is plastic. By this she means that:
   a. change in development occurs in every direction, not always in a straight line.
   b. human lives are embedded in many different contexts.
   c. many cultures influence development.
   d. every individual, and every trait within each individual, can be altered at any point in the life span.

9. Karen's mother is puzzled by the numerous discrepancies between the developmental psychology textbook she used in 1976 and her daughter's contemporary text. Karen explains that the differences are the result of:
   a. the lack of regard by earlier researchers for the scientific method.
   b. changing social conditions and cohort effects.
   c. the widespread use of cross-sectional research today.
   d. the widespread use of longitudinal research today.

10. If height and body weight are correlated, which of the following is true?
    a. There is a cause-and-effect relationship between height and weight.
    b. Knowing a person's height, one can predict his or her weight.
    c. Both a. and b. are true.
    d. Neither is true.

11. An example of longitudinal research would be when an investigator compares the performance of:
    a. several different age groups on a memory test.
    b. the same group of people, at different ages, on a test of memory.
    c. an experimental group and a comparison group on a test of memory.
    d. several different age groups on a test of memory as each group is tested repeatedly over a period of years.

12. For her developmental psychology research project, Lakia decides she wants to focus primarily on qualitative data. You advise her to conduct:
    a. a survey.
    b. an experiment.
    c. a cross-sectional study.
    d. a case study.

13. Professor Johnson warns her students to be skeptical of the results of a controversial study because it has not been replicated. By this, she means that:
    a. there was no experimental group.
    b. there was no comparison group.
    c. the study has not yet been repeated by other researchers in order to verify the original findings.
    d. the results are statistically insignificant.

14. Dr. Weston is comparing research findings for a group of 30-year-olds with findings for the same individuals at age 20, as well as with findings for groups who were 30 in 1990. Which research method is she using?
    a. longitudinal research
    b. cross-sectional research
    c. case study
    d. cross-sequential research

15. To find out whether people's attitudes regarding an issue vary with their ages, Karen distributes the same survey to groups of people in their 20s, 30s, 40s, 50s, and 60s. Karen is evidently conducting:
    a. longitudinal research.
    b. cross-sectional research.
    c. cross-sequential research.
    d. a case study.

Key Terms

Using your own words, write a brief definition or explanation of each of the following terms on a separate piece of paper.

1. science of human development
2. empirical
3. dynamic-systems theory
4. ecological-systems approach
5. butterfly effect
6. cohort
7. socioeconomic status (SES)
8. ethnic group
9. race
10. social construction
11. mirror neurons
12. scientific method
13. hypothesis
14. replication
15. scientific observation
16. experiment
17. independent variable
18. dependent variable
19. experimental group
20. comparison group/control group
21. survey
22. case study
23. cross-sectional research
24. longitudinal research
25. cross-sequential research
26. correlation
27. quantitative research
28. qualitative research
29. code of ethics

ANSWERS

CHAPTER REVIEW

1. how and why people—all people, everywhere—change or remain the same over time
2. empirical
3. dynamic-systems; systems; change in one part of a person, or family, or society will affect all other aspects of development.
4. ecological-systems; Urie Bronfenbrenner
5. microsystem
6. mesosystem
7. macrosystem
8. chronosystem
9. exosystem
10. a. multidirectional
    b. multicontextual
    c. multicultural
    d. multidisciplinary
    e. plastic
11. a. dynamic
    b. multidirectional
    c. butterfly effect
12. cohort; the same way
13. socioeconomic status; SES
14. culture
15. dynamic; more than one
16. ethnic group
17. genetically; race
18. biological; society; social construction
19. biosocial; cognitive; psychosocial
20. domains; contexts; cultures
21. mirror neurons; actions performed by someone else
22. plasticity
23. rubella; physical; historical; plasticity
24. a. ask a question
    b. develop a hypothesis
    c. test the hypothesis
    d. draw conclusions
    e. make the findings available
25. hypothesis
26. replicate
27. validity; reliability; generalizability; usefulness
28. scientific observation
29. naturalistic; laboratory
30. cause
31. experiment; independent; dependent; effect; significance
32. experimental group; comparison group (control group)
33. survey
34. representative; wording; sequence
35. case study; starting point; more general truths
36. cross-sectional
37. ages; cohort effects
38. longitudinal

Over time, some participants may leave the study. Some people may "improve" simply because they are familiar with the goals of the study. The biggest problem is the changing historical context.

39. cross-sequential
40. correlation; does not; positive; increase; negative; increase; decreases; zero
41. quantitative; children; qualitative; open-ended
42. code of ethics; informed consent; harmed
43. training; collaboration

PROGRESS TEST 1

Multiple-Choice Questions

1. **a.** is the answer. (p. 3)

   b. & c. The study of development is concerned with a broader range of phenomena, including physical aspects of development, than these answers specify.

2. **b.** is the answer. (p. 27)

   a. In this research method, one individual is studied intensively.

   c. In this research method, groups of people who differ in age are compared.

   d. This type of research provides data that can be expressed with numbers.

3. **d.** is the answer. (pp. 9–10)

4. **a.** is the answer. (p. 5)

5. **d.** is the answer. This approach sees development as occurring within five interacting levels, or environments. (p. 5)

6. **d.** is the answer. (pp. 3–4)

7. **b.** is the answer. (p. 14)

8. **b.** is the answer. (p. 17)

9. **c.** is the answer. (p. 5)

   a. This refers to systems that link one microsystem to another.

   b. This refers to cultural values, political philosophies, economic patterns, and social conditions.

   d. This includes the community structures that affect the functioning of smaller systems.

10. **c.** is the answer. (p. 9)

11. **c.** is the answer. (p. 14)

12. **b.** is the answer. (p. 18)

    a. A possible hypothesis for this experiment would be that the larger the group, the less hard a given individual will pull.

    c. The dependent variable is the measure of individual effort.

    d. Significance level refers to the numerical value specifying the possibility that the results of an experiment could have occurred by chance.

13. **d.** is the answer. (p. 20)

    a. Experimentation is appropriate when one is seeking to uncover cause-and-effect relationships; in this example, the researcher is only interested in determining whether the parents' beliefs *predict* their attitudes.

    b. Longitudinal research would be appropriate if the researcher sought to examine the development of these attitudes over a long period of time.

    c. Mere observation would not allow the researcher to determine the attitudes of the participants.

14. **a.** is the answer. (p. 18)

    b., c., & d. These research methods do not indicate what causes people to do what they do.

15. **c.** is the answer. (pp. 17–18)

    a. In this method, *one* person is studied over a period of time.

    b. & d. In these research methods, two or more *groups* of participants are studied and compared.

True or False Items

1. F   Just the opposite. Scientists always try to replicate their or other people's work. (p. 17)

2. F   The case study of David shows that both nature and nurture are important in affecting outcome. (pp. 15–16)

3. F   A disadvantage of observation is that the variables are numerous and uncontrolled, and therefore cause-and-effect relationships are difficult to pinpoint. (p. 18)

4. F   Each social context affects the way a person develops, and each is affected by the other contexts. (p. 5)

5. T (p. 9)

6. T (p. 15)

7. F   Qualitative research often reveals information that would be lost if an observation were expressed in numbers. (p. 27)

8. F   Quite the reverse is true. (pp. 5–6)

9. T (p. 11)

10. T (pp. 22–23)

PROGRESS TEST 2

Multiple-Choice Questions

1. **d.** is the answer. (p. 5)

2. **c.** is the answer. (p. 13)

3. **a.** is the answer. (p. 28)

   b. & c. Although these are important aspects of the code of ethics, protecting participants from harm is the most important.

4. **a.** is the answer. (p. 8)

b., c., & d. Although these are true, they are not the butterfly effect.

5. **c.** is the answer. (p. 5)

   a. & d. These are part of the microsystem.

   b. This is part of the exosystem.

6. **c.** is the answer. (p. 11)

7. **b.** is the answer. (p. 17)

   a. Replication refers to the repetition of a scientific study.

   c. & d. Variables are treatments (independent) or behaviors (dependent) in *experiments*, which this situation clearly is not.

8. **c.** is the answer. (p. 9)

   a., b., & d. These are attributes of an ethnic group.

9. **a.** is the answer. The experimental group is the one in which the variable or treatment—in this case, noise—is present. (p. 19)

   b. Students in the quiet room would be in the comparison condition.

   c. Presumably, all students in both groups were randomly assigned to their groups.

   d. The word *dependent* refers to a kind of variable in experiments; groups are either experimental or control.

10. **c.** is the answer. (p. 11)

    a. & d. Ethnicity refers to shared attributes, such as ancestry, national origin, religion, and language.

    b. This describes a cohort.

11. **b.** is the answer. (p. 25)

    a. Wealth and happiness clearly *are* related.

    c. For one thing, poverty is clearly an example of nurture, not nature.

    d. Correlation does not imply causation.

12. **d.** is the answer. (p. 15)

13. **c.** is the answer. (p. 18)

    a. Hypotheses make *specific*, testable predictions.

    b. Noise level is the independent variable.

    d. Scientific observation is a research method in which participants are watched, while their behavior is recorded unobtrusively.

14. **d.** is the answer. (p. 14)

15. **a.** is the answer. Ethnic identity is a product of the social environment and the individual's consciousness. (p. 11)

Matching Items

1. h (p. 18)   5. d (p. 5)   9. a (p. 9)
2. k (p. 18)   6. g (p. 5)   10. e (p. 11)
3. f (p. 10)   7. i (p. 5)   11. c (p. 22)
4. j (p. 17)   8. b (p. 9)   12. l (p. 22)

DEVELOPMENTAL PSYCHOLOGY APPLIED

1. **a.** is the answer. (p. 5)

2. **c.** is the answer. Room temperature is the variable being manipulated. (p. 18)

   a. & d. These answers are incorrect because they involve aspects of the experiment other than the variables.

   b. This answer is the dependent, not the independent, variable.

3. **c.** is the answer. (p. 5)

   a. Piaget is notable in the area of cognitive development.

   b. Freud was a pioneer of psychoanalysis.

   d. Skinner is notable in the history of learning theory.

4. **c.** is the answer. (p. 11)

   a. This is an ethnic group.

   b. Race is a social construction.

5. **c.** is the answer. In order to determine the effects of caffeine on reaction time, Esteban needs to measure reaction time in a comparison group that does not receive caffeine. (p. 19)

   a. Caffeine is the independent variable.

   b. Reaction time is the dependent variable.

   d. Whether or not Esteban's experiment can be replicated is determined by the precision with which he reports his procedures, which is not an aspect of research strategy.

6. **b.** is the answer. (p. 18)

   a., b., & d. The hypothesis would probably be that group size reduces individual effort in a tug-of-war task. Individual effort is the dependent variable. Level of significance is related to results, not to experimental set-up.

7. **c.** is the answer. (p. 11)

8. **d.** is the answer. (p. 15)

   a. This describes the multidirectional nature of development.

   b. This describes the multicontextual nature of development.

   c. This describes the multicultural nature of development.

9. **b.** is the answer. (pp. 9–10)

   a. Earlier developmentalists had no less regard for the scientific method.

   c. & d. Both cross-sectional and longitudinal research were widely used in the 1970s.

10. **b.** is the answer. (p. 25)

    a. Correlation does not imply causation.

11. **b.** is the answer. (p. 22)

    a. This is an example of cross-sectional research.

    c. This is an example of an experiment.

    d. This is an example of cross-sequential research.

12. **d.** is the answer. (pp. 20–21, 27)

    a., b., & c. These research methods generally yield *quantitative,* rather than qualitative, data.

13. **c.** is the answer. (p. 17)

    a., b., & c. Although any of these may be true, none has anything to do with replication.

14. **d.** is the answer. (p. 24)

    a. & c. In these research methods, only one group of people is studied.

    b. Dr. Weston's design includes comparison of groups of people of different ages *over time.*

15. **b.** is the answer. (p. 22)

    a. In longitudinal research, the same individuals are studied over a long period of time.

    c. In cross-sequential research, groups of people of different ages are followed over a long period of time.

    d. In a case study, one person is studied intensively.

KEY TERMS

1. The **science of human development** seeks to understand how and why all people, everywhere, change or remain the same over time. (p. 3)

2. To say that the science of human development is **empirical** means that it is based on observation and experimentation, rather than theory alone. (p. 4)

3. **Dynamic-systems theory** views human development as in a constant state of flux (dynamic), and as the product of the interaction between systems within the person and the environment. (p. 5)

4. The **ecological-systems approach** to developmental research takes into consideration the relationship between the individual and the environment. (p. 5)

5. The **butterfly effect** is the insight that even a small event or thing (such as the breeze created by the flap of a butterfly's wings) may set off a series of changes that create a major event. (p. 8)

6. A **cohort** is a group of people who, because they were born within a few years of each other, experience many of the same historical changes. (p. 9)

7. An individual's **socioeconomic status (SES)** is determined by his or her income, education, place of residence, occupation, and other factors. (p. 9)

8. An **ethnic group** is a collection of people whose ancestors were born in the same region, usually sharing a language and religion. (p. 11)

9. **Race** is a misleading social construction for a group of people who are regarded (by themselves or others) as genetically distinct on the basis of physical appearance. (p. 11)

10. **Social constructions** are ideas that are based more on shared perceptions than on objective reality. (p. 11)

11. **Mirror neurons** are cells in a person's brain that respond to the observed actions of others. (p. 14)

12. The **scientific method** is a way to answer questions that requires empirical research and data-based conclusions. The five basic steps of the scientific method are (1) formulate a research question; (2) develop a hypothesis; (3) test the hypothesis; (4) draw conclusions; and (5) make the findings available. (pp. 16–17)

13. In the scientific method, a **hypothesis** is a specific, testable prediction. (p. 17)

14. **Replication** means to repeat a test of a research hypothesis and to try to obtain the same results using a different but related group of participants or procedures in order to test the study's validity. (p. 17)

15. **Scientific observation** is the unobtrusive watching and recording of participants' behavior in a systematic and objective manner, either in the laboratory or in a natural setting. (p. 17)

16. The **experiment** is the research method designed to untangle cause from effect by manipulating one variable to observe the effect on another variable. (p. 18)

17. The **independent variable** is the variable that is manipulated in an experiment to observe what effect it has on the dependent variable. (p. 18)

18. The **dependent variable** is the variable that may change as a result of whatever new condition or situation is added in an experiment. (p. 18)

    Example: In the study of the effects of a new drug on memory, the participants' memory is the dependent variable.

19. The **experimental group** of an experiment is one in which participants are exposed to the independent variable being studied. (p. 19)

20. The **comparison group/control group** of an experiment is one in which the treatment of interest, or independent variable, is withheld so that comparisons to the experimental group can be made. (p. 19)

21. The **survey** is the research method in which information is collected from a large number of people, either through written questionnaires, personal interviews, or some other means. (p. 20)

22. The **case study** is the research method involving the intensive study of one person. (p. 20)

23. In **cross-sectional research,** groups of people who differ in age but share other important characteristics are compared with regard to the variable under investigation. (p. 22)

24. In **longitudinal research,** the same group of individuals is studied over a period of time to measure both change and stability as they age. (p. 22)

25. **Cross-sequential research** follows a group of people of different ages over time, thus combining the strengths of the cross-sectional and longitudinal methods. (p. 24)

26. **Correlation** is a number indicating the degree of relationship between two variables, such that one is likely (or unlikely) to occur when the other occurs or one is likely to increase (or decrease) when the other increases (or decreases). (p. 25)

27. **Quantitative research** collects data that are expressed with numbers. (p. 26)

28. **Qualitative research** collects non-numerical descriptions of participants' characteristic behaviors and ideas. (p. 27)

29. Developmental psychologists and other scientists work from a **code of ethics,** which is a set of moral principles that guide their research. (p. 27)

2

Theories of Development

Chapter Overview

Developmental theories are systematic statements of principles and generalizations that provide a coherent framework for studying and explaining development. Many such theories have influenced our understanding of human development. This chapter describes and evaluates five broad theories—psychoanalytic theory, behaviorism, cognitive theory, sociocultural theory, and epigenetic theory—that will be used throughout the book to present information and to provide a framework for interpreting events and issues in human development. Each of the theories has developed a unique vocabulary with which to describe and explain events as well as to organize ideas into a cohesive system of thought.

Three of the theories presented—psychoanalytic theory, behaviorism, and cognitive theory—are "grand theories" that are comprehensive in scope but inadequate in the face of recent research findings. Two of the theories—sociocultural and epigenetic—are considered "emergent theories" because they may become the comprehensive theories of the future. Rather than adopt any one theory exclusively, most developmentalists take an eclectic perspective and use many or all of the theories.

As you study this part of the chapter, consider what each of the theories has to say about your own development, as well as that of friends and relatives in other age groups. It is also a good idea to keep the following questions in mind as you study each theory: Which of the theory's principles are generally accepted by contemporary developmentalists? How has the theory been criticized? In what ways does this theory agree with the other theories? In what ways does it disagree?

NOTE: Answer guidelines for all Chapter 2 questions begin on page 29.

Guided Study

The text chapter should be studied one section at a time. Before you read, preview each section by skimming it, noting headings and boldface items. Then read the appropriate section objectives from the following outline. Keep these objectives in mind and, as you read the chapter section, search for the information that will enable you to meet each objective. Once you have finished a section, write out answers for its objectives.

What Theories Do (pp. 33–34)

1. Define developmental theory, and describe how developmental theories help explain human behavior and development, noting the differences between grand theories and emergent theories.

Grand Theories (pp. 34–46)

2. Discuss the major focus of psychoanalytic theories, and describe the conflicts that occur during Freud's psychosexual stages.

3. Describe the crises of Erikson's theory of psychosocial development, and contrast them with Freud's stages.

4. Discuss the major focus of behaviorism, and explain the basic principles of classical and operant conditioning.

5. (Thinking Like a Scientist) Discuss Harlow's research with infant monkeys, and explain how it contributed to revisions of psychoanalytic theory and behaviorism, while also demonstrating the importance of testing theories.

6. Discuss social learning theory as an extension of behaviorism.

7. Identify the primary focus of cognitive theory, and briefly describe Piaget's periods of cognitive development.

8. Discuss the process that, according to Piaget, guides cognitive development.

Emergent Theories (pp. 46–54)

9. Discuss the primary focus of sociocultural theory.

10. Discuss the basic concepts and techniques proposed by Vygotsky in his sociocultural theory of development.

11. Discuss the basic ideas of epigenetic theory, giving examples of how genes and environment interact in human development.

12. (In Person) Discuss the role of selective adaptation in infant and caregiver attachments.

What Theories Contribute (pp. 54–57)

13. Summarize the contributions and criticisms of the major developmental theories, and describe the eclectic perspective of contemporary developmentalists.

14. Explain the nature–nurture controversy as it pertains to hyperactivity and sexual orientation.

Chapter Review

When you have finished reading the chapter, work through the material that follows to review it. Complete the sentences and answer the questions. As you proceed, evaluate your performance for each section by consulting the answers beginning on page 29.

Do not continue with the next section until you understand each answer. If you need to, review or reread the appropriate section in the textbook before continuing.

What Theories Do (pp. 33–34)

1. A systematic statement of principles and generalizations that provides a coherent framework for understanding how and why people change as they grow older is called a(n)

   _____ _____ .

2. Developmental theories form the basis for educated guesses, or _____ , about behavior; they generate _____ , and they offer _____ guidance.

3. Developmental theories fall into three categories: _____ theories, which traditionally offer a comprehensive view of development; _____ theories, which explain a specific area of development; and _____ theories, which may become the comprehensive theories of the future.

Grand Theories (pp. 34–46)

4. Psychoanalytic theories interpret human development in terms of inner _____ and _____ , many of which are _____ (conscious/unconscious) and _____ .

5. According to Freud's _____ theory, children experience sexual pleasures and desires during the first six years as they pass through three stages. From infancy to early childhood to the preschool years, these stages are the _____ stage, the _____ stage, and the _____ stage. One of Freud's most influential ideas was that each stage includes its own potential _____ between child and parent.

Specify the focus of sexual pleasure and the major developmental need associated with each of Freud's stages.

oral   _____

    _____

anal   _____

    _____

phallic   _____

    _____

genital   _____

    _____

6. Erik Erikson's theory of development, which focuses on social and cultural influences, describes _____ (number) developmental stages, each characterized by a particular developmental _____ related to the person's relationship to the social environment. Unlike Freud, Erikson proposed stages of development that _____ (span/do not span) a person's lifetime.

Complete the following chart regarding Erikson's stages of psychosocial development.

Age Period	Stage
Birth to 1 yr.	trust vs. _____
1–3 yrs.	autonomy vs. _____
3–6 yrs.	initiative vs. _____
6–11 yrs.	_____ vs. inferiority
Adolescence	identity vs. _____
Young adulthood	_____ vs. isolation
Middle adulthood	_____ vs. stagnation
Older adulthood	_____ vs. despair

7. A major theory in American psychology, which directly opposed psychoanalytic theory, was _____ . This theory, which emerged early in the twentieth century under the influence of _____ , is also called _____ theory because of its emphasis on how we learn specific behaviors.

8. Behaviorists have formulated laws of behavior that are believed to apply _____ (only at certain ages/at all ages). The learning process, which is called _____ , takes two forms: _____ _____ and _____ _____ .

9. In classical conditioning, which was discovered by the Russian scientist _____ and is also called _____ conditioning, a person or an animal learns to associate a(n) _____ stimulus with a meaningful one.

10. According to _____ , the learning of more complex responses is the result of _____ conditioning, in which a person learns that a particular behavior produces a particular _____ , such as a reward. This type of learning is also called _____ conditioning.

11. The process of repeating a consequence to make it more likely that the behavior in question will recur is called _____ .

12. (Thinking Like a Scientist) The behavior of infant monkeys separated from their mothers led researcher _____ to investigate the origins of _____ in infant monkeys. These studies, which demonstrated that infant monkeys clung more often to "surrogate" mothers that provided _____ (food/contact comfort), disproved _____ theory's idea that infants seek to satisfy oral needs and _____ view that reinforcement directs behavior.

13. The extension of behaviorism that emphasizes the ways that people learn new behaviors by observing others is called _____ _____ theory. The process whereby a child patterns his or her behavior after a parent or teacher, for example, is called _____ .

14. This process is most likely to occur when an observer is _____ or

_____ and when the model is

_____ .

This type of learning is also affected by the individual's _____ and

_____ . Human social learning is related to _____ ,

_____ _____ ,

and _____ .

15. The structure and development of the individual's thought processes and the way those thought processes affect the person's understanding of the world are the focus of

_____ theory. An important pioneer of cognitive theory is _____ .

16. In Piaget's first stage of development, the

_____ stage, children experience the world through their senses and motor abilities. This stage occurs between birth and age

_____ .

17. According to Piaget, during the preschool years (up to age _____), children are in the _____ stage. A hallmark of this stage is that children begin to think magically and poetically. Another hallmark is that sometimes the child's thinking is _____ , or focused on seeing the world solely from his or her own perspective.

18. Piaget believed that children begin to think logically in a consistent way at about

_____ years of age. At this time, they enter the _____

_____ stage.

19. In Piaget's final stage, the _____

_____ stage, reasoning expands from the purely concrete to encompass

_____ thinking. Piaget believed most children enter this stage by age

_____ .

20. According to Piaget, cognitive development is guided by the need to maintain a state of mental balance, called _____

_____ .

21. When new experiences challenge existing understanding, creating a kind of imbalance, the individual experiences _____

_____ , which eventually leads to mental growth.

22. According to Piaget, people adapt to new experiences either by reinterpreting them to fit into, or _____ with, old ideas. Some new experiences force people to revamp old ideas so that they can _____ new experiences.

Emergent Theories (pp. 46–54)

23. In contrast to the grand theories, the two emergent theories draw from the findings of

_____ (one/many) discipline(s).

24. Sociocultural theory sees human development as the result of _____

_____ between developing persons and their surrounding _____ .

25. A major pioneer of this perspective was

_____ , who was primarily interested in the development of

_____ competencies.

26. Vygotsky believed that these competencies result from the interaction between _____ and more skilled members of the society, acting as _____ .

27. In Vygotsky's view, the best way to accomplish the goals of apprenticeship is through

_____ _____ , also called _____ _____

_____ , in which the tutor engages the learner in joint activities.

28. According to Vygotsky, a tutor draws a child into the _____ _____ _____ _____ , which is defined as the range of skills that a person can acquire with _____ but cannot master independently.

Cite a contribution and a criticism of sociocultural theory.

29. The newest of the emergent theories, _____ theory, emphasizes the interaction between _____ and the _____ . This idea contrasts sharply with the idea of _____ , according to which everything is set in advance by genes.

30. The prefix "epi" refers to the various _____ factors that affect the expression of _____ _____ . These include _____ factors such as injury, temperature, and crowding. Others are _____ factors such as nourishing food and freedom to play.

31. Development proceeds within the range of possible outcomes set by earlier _____– _____ interactions. This range of outcomes is called the _____ _____ .

32. Some epigenetic factors are the result of the evolutionary process called _____ _____ , in which, over generations, genes for useful traits that promote survival of the species become more prevalent.

33. "Everything that seems to be genetic is actually epigenetic." This statement highlights the fact that _____ (some/most/all) genetic expressions are affected by the environment.

34. (In Person) Newborn animals and human infants are genetically programmed for _____ _____ and forming _____ _____ _____ as a means of survival. Similarly, adult animals and humans are genetically programmed to _____ _____ .

What Theories Contribute (pp. 54–57)

35. Which major theory of development emphasizes:
    a. the importance of culture in fostering development? _____
    b. the ways in which thought processes affect actions? _____
    c. environmental influences? _____
    d. the impact of unconscious impulses on development? _____
    _____
    e. the interaction of genes and environment? ____
    _____

36. Which major theory of development has been criticized for:
    a. being too mechanistic?
    _____
    b. undervaluing cultural diversity?
    _____
    c. being too subjective?
    _____
    d. neglecting the human spirit?
    _____
    e. neglecting individual initiative?
    _____

37. Because no one theory can encompass all human behavior, most developmentalists have a(n) _____ perspective, which capitalizes on the strengths of all the theories.

38. The debate over the relative influence of heredity and environment in shaping personal traits and characteristics is called the _____–_____ controversy. Traits inherited at the moment of conception give evidence of the influence of _____ ; those that emerge in response to learning and environmental influences give evidence of the effect of _____ .

39. Developmentalists agree that, at every point, the _____ between nature and nurture is the crucial influence on any particular aspect of development.

40. Children who are especially impulsive, restless, and unable to attend to anything for more than a moment may be suffering from _____-_____/ _____ _____ . This disorder is more common in _____ (girls/boys).

State several pieces of evidence that genetic inheritance is responsible for ADHD.

41. Most social scientists once considered homosexuality to be the product of _____ (nature/nurture). However, new research suggests that it is at least partly due to _____ (nature/nurture). This has also led researchers to draw a distinction between _____ _____ , which encompasses erotic _____ and _____ , and _____ _____ , which encompasses sexual _____ .

Progress Test 1

Multiple-Choice Questions

Circle your answers to the following questions and check them with the answers on page 30. If your answer is incorrect, read the explanation for why it is incorrect and then consult the appropriate pages of the text (in parentheses following the correct answer).

1. The purpose of a developmental theory is to:
   a. provide a broad and coherent view of the complex influences on human development.
   b. offer guidance for practical issues encountered by parents, teachers, and therapists.
   c. generate testable hypotheses about development.
   d. do all of the above.

2. Which developmental theory emphasizes the influence of unconscious drives and motives on behavior?
   a. psychoanalytic   c. cognitive
   b. behaviorism   d. sociocultural

3. Which of the following is the correct order of the psychosexual stages proposed by Freud?
   a. oral stage; anal stage; phallic stage; latency; genital stage
   b. anal stage; oral stage; phallic stage; latency; genital stage
   c. oral stage; anal stage; genital stage; latency; phallic stage
   d. anal stage; oral stage; genital stage; latency; phallic stage

4. Erikson's psychosocial theory of human development describes:
   a. eight crises all people are thought to face.
   b. four psychosocial stages and a latency period.
   c. the same number of stages as Freud's, but with different names.
   d. a stage theory that is not psychoanalytic.

5. Which of the following theories does *not* belong with the others?
   a. psychoanalytic   c. sociocultural
   b. behaviorism   d. cognitive

6. An American psychologist who explained complex human behaviors in terms of operant conditioning was:
   a. Lev Vygotsky.   c. B. F. Skinner.
   b. Ivan Pavlov.   d. Jean Piaget.

7. Pavlov's dogs learned to salivate at the sound of a bell because they associated the bell with food. Pavlov's experiment with dogs was an early demonstration of:
   a. classical conditioning.
   b. operant conditioning.
   c. positive reinforcement.
   d. social learning.

8. The nature–nurture controversy considers the degree to which traits, characteristics, and behaviors are the result of:
   a. early or lifelong learning.
   b. genes or heredity.
   c. heredity or experience.
   d. different historical concepts of childhood.

9. Modeling, an integral part of social learning theory, is so called because it:
   a. follows the scientific model of learning.
   b. molds character.
   c. follows the immediate reinforcement model developed by Bandura.
   d. involves people's patterning their behavior after that of others.

10. Which developmental theory suggests that each person is born with genetic possibilities that must be nurtured in order to grow?
    a. sociocultural   c. behaviorism
    b. cognitive   d. epigenetic

11. Vygotsky's theory has been criticized for neglecting:
    a. the role of genes in guiding development.
    b. developmental processes that are not primarily biological.
    c. the importance of language in development.
    d. social factors in development.

12. Which is the correct sequence of stages in Piaget's theory of cognitive development?
    a. sensorimotor, preoperational, concrete operational, formal operational
    b. sensorimotor, preoperational, formal operational, concrete operational
    c. preoperational, sensorimotor, concrete operational, formal operational
    d. preoperational, sensorimotor, formal operational, concrete operational

13. When an individual's existing understanding no longer fits his or her present experiences, the result is called:
    a. a psychosocial crisis.
    b. equilibrium.
    c. disequilibrium.
    d. negative reinforcement.

14. In explaining the origins of homosexuality, most social scientists have traditionally emphasized:
    a. nature over nurture.
    b. nurture over nature.
    c. a weak father and overbearing mother.
    d. the individual's voluntary choice.

15. The zone of proximal development refers to:
    a. a stage during which the child exhibits preoperational thinking.
    b. the influence of a pleasurable stimulus on behavior.
    c. the range of skills a learner can exercise with assistance but cannot perform independently.
    d. the tendency of a child to model an admired adult's behavior.

True or False Items

Write T (*true*) or F (*false*) on the line in front of each statement.

_____ 1. Behaviorists study what people actually do, not what they might be thinking.

_____ 2. Erikson's eight developmental stages are centered not on a body part but on each person's relationship to the social environment.

_____ 3. Most developmentalists agree that the nature–nurture controversy has been laid to rest.

_____ 4. Few developmental theorists today believe that humans have instincts or abilities that arise from our species' biological heritage.

_____ 5. Of the major developmental theories, cognitive theory gives the most emphasis to the interaction of genes and experience in shaping development.

_____ 6. According to Piaget, a state of cognitive equilibrium must be attained before cognitive growth can occur.

_____ 7. In part, cognitive theory examines how an individual's understandings and expectations affect his or her behavior.

_____ 8. According to Piaget, children begin to think only when they reach preschool age.

_____ 9. Most contemporary researchers have adopted an eclectic perspective on development.

_____ 10. Sexual orientation and sexual expression are the same thing. .

Progress Test 2

Progress Test 2 should be completed during a final chapter review. Answer the following questions after you thoroughly understand the correct answers for the Chapter Review and Progress Test 1.

Multiple-Choice Questions

1. Which developmental theorist has been criticized for suggesting that every child, in every culture, in every nation, passes through certain fixed stages?
   a. Freud
   b. Erikson
   c. Piaget
   d. all of the above.

2. Of the following terms, the one that does *not* describe a stage of Freud's theory of childhood sexuality is:
   a. phallic.
   b. oral.
   c. anal.
   d. sensorimotor.

3. We are more likely to imitate the behavior of others if we particularly admire and identify with them. This belief finds expression in:
   a. stage theory.
   b. sociocultural theory.
   c. social learning theory.
   d. Pavlov's experiments.

4. How do minitheories differ from grand Theories?
   a. Unlike the more comprehensive grand theories, minitheories explain only a part of development.
   b. Unlike grand theories, which usually reflect the thinking of many researchers, minitheories tend to stem from one person.
   c. Only the recency of the research on which they are based keeps minitheories from having the sweeping influence of grand theories.
   d. They differ in all the above ways.

5. According to Erikson, an adult who has difficulty establishing a secure, mutual relationship with a life partner might never have resolved the crisis of:
   a. initiative versus guilt.
   b. autonomy versus shame and doubt.
   c. intimacy versus isolation.
   d. identity versus role confusion.

6. Who would be most likely to agree with the statement, "anything can be learned"?
   a. Jean Piaget
   b. Lev Vygotsky
   c. John Watson
   d. Erik Erikson

7. Classical conditioning is to _____ as operant conditioning is to _____ .
   a. Skinner; Pavlov
   b. Watson; Vygotsky
   c. Pavlov; Skinner
   d. Vygotsky; Watson

8. Behaviorists have found that they can often solve a person's seemingly complex psychological problem by:
   a. analyzing the patient.
   b. admitting the existence of the unconscious.
   c. altering the environment.
   d. administering well-designed punishments.

9. According to Piaget, an infant first comes to know the world through:
   a. senses and motor abilities.
   b. naming and counting.
   c. preoperational thought.
   d. instruction from parents.

10. According to Piaget, the stage of cognitive development that generally characterizes preschool children (2 to 6 years old) is the:
    a. preoperational stage.
    b. sensorimotor stage.
    c. oral stage.
    d. psychosocial stage.

11. In Piaget's theory, cognitive equilibrium refers to:
    a. a state of mental balance.
    b. a kind of imbalance that leads to cognitive growth.
    c. the ultimate stage of cognitive development.
    d. the first stage in the processing of information.

12. You teach your dog to "speak" by giving her a treat each time she does so. This is an example of:
    a. classical conditioning.
    b. respondent conditioning.
    c. reinforcement.
    d. modeling.

13. A child who must modify an old idea in order to incorporate a new experience is using the process of:
   a. assimilation.
   b. accommodation.
   c. cognitive equilibrium.
   d. guided participation.

14. Which of the following is a common criticism of sociocultural theory?
   a. It places too great an emphasis on unconscious motives and childhood sexuality.
   b. Its mechanistic approach fails to explain many complex human behaviors.
   c. Development is more gradual than its stages imply.
   d. It neglects developmental processes that are not primarily social.

15. A major pioneer of the sociocultural perspective was:
   a. Jean Piaget.
   b. Albert Bandura.
   c. Lev Vygotsky.
   d. Ivan Pavlov.

Matching Items

Match each theory or term with its corresponding description or definition.

Theories or Terms
_____ 1. psychoanalytic theory
_____ 2. nature
_____ 3. behaviorism
_____ 4. social learning theory
_____ 5. cognitive theory
_____ 6. nurture
_____ 7. sociocultural theory
_____ 8. conditioning
_____ 9. emergent theories
_____ 10. modeling
_____ 11. epigenetic theory

Descriptions or Definitions
a. emphasizes the impact of the immediate environment on behavior
b. relatively new, comprehensive theories
c. emphasizes that people learn by observing others
d. environmental influences that affect development
e. a process of learning, as described by Pavlov or Skinner
f. emphasizes the "hidden dramas" that influence behavior
g. emphasizes the cultural context in development
h. emphasizes how our thoughts shape our actions
i. the process whereby a person learns by imitating someone else's behavior
j. emphasizes the interaction of genes and environmental forces
k. traits that are inherited

Developmental Psychology Applied

Answer these questions the day before an exam as a final check on your understanding of the chapter's terms and concepts.

1. Many songbirds inherit a genetically programmed species song that enhances their ability to mate and establish a territory. The evolution of such a trait is an example of:
   a. selective adaptation.
   b. epigenetic development.
   c. accommodation.
   d. assimilation.

2. When a pigeon is rewarded for producing a particular response, and so learns to produce that response to obtain rewards, psychologists describe this chain of events as:
   a. operant conditioning.
   c. modeling.
   b. classical conditioning.
   d. reflexive actions.

3. Professor Swenson, who believes that a considerable amount of development involves the developing person coming to associate neutral stimuli with meaningful stimuli, would most likely agree with the writings of:
   a. Freud.
   c. Vygotsky.
   b. Erikson.
   d. Pavlov.

4. Dr. Ivey's research focuses on the biological forces that shape each child's characteristic way of reacting to environmental experiences. Evidently, Dr. Ivey is working from a(n) _____ perspective.
   a. psychoanalytic
   b. cognitive
   c. sociocultural
   d. epigenetic

5. Which of the following is the best example of guided participation?
   a. After watching her mother change her baby sister's diaper, 4-year-old Brandy changes her doll's diaper.
   b. To help her son learn to pour liquids, Sandra engages him in a bathtub game involving pouring water from cups of different sizes.
   c. Seeing his father shaving, 3-year-old Kyle pretends to shave by rubbing whipped cream on his face.
   d. After reading a recipe in a magazine, Jack gathers ingredients from the cupboard.

6. A child who calls all furry animals "doggie" will experience cognitive _____ when she encounters a hairless breed for the first time. This may cause her to revamp her concept of "dog" in order to _____ the new experience.
   a. disequilibrium; accommodate
   b. disequilibrium; assimilate
   c. equilibrium; accommodate
   d. equilibrium; assimilate

7. A confirmed neo-Freudian, Dr. Thomas strongly endorses the views of Erik Erikson. She would most likely disagree with Freud regarding the importance of:
   a. unconscious forces in development.
   b. irrational forces in personality formation.
   c. early childhood experiences.
   d. sexual urges in development.

8. After watching several older children climbing around a new junglegym, 5-year-old Jennie decides to try it herself. Which of the following best accounts for her behavior?
   a. classical conditioning
   b. modeling
   c. guided participation
   d. reinforcement

9. I am 8 years old, and although I understand some logical principles, I have trouble thinking about hypothetical concepts. According to Piaget, I am in the _____ stage of development.

   a. sensorimotor
   b. preoperational
   c. concrete operational
   d. formal operational

10. Two-year-old Jamail has a simple understanding for "dad," and so each time he encounters a man with a child, he calls him "dad." When he learns that these other men are not "dad," Jamail experiences:
    a. conservation.
    b. cognition.
    c. equilibrium.
    d. disequilibrium.

11. (In Person) Most adults become physiologically aroused by the sound of an infant's laughter. These interactive reactions, in which caregivers and babies elicit responses in each other:
    a. help ensure the survival of the next generation.
    b. do not occur in all human cultures.
    c. are the result of conditioning very early in life.
    d. are more often found in females than in males.

12. The school psychologist believes that each child's developmental needs can be understood only by taking into consideration the child's broader social and cultural background. Evidently, the school psychologist is working within the _____ perspective.
    a. psychoanalytic
    b. epigenetic
    c. social learning
    d. sociocultural

13. Four-year-old Bjorn takes great pride in successfully undertaking new activities. Erikson would probably say that Bjorn is capably meeting the psychosocial challenge of:
    a. trust vs. mistrust.
    b. initiative vs. guilt.
    c. industry vs. inferiority.
    d. identity vs. role confusion.

14. Dr. Cleaver's developmental research draws upon insights from several theoretical perspectives. Evidently, Dr. Cleaver is working from a(n) _____ perspective.
    a. cognitive
    b. behaviorist
    c. eclectic
    d. sociocultural

15. Dr. Bazzi believes that development is a lifelong process of gradual and continuous growth. Based on this information, with which of the following theories would Dr. Bazzi most likely agree?
    a. Piaget's cognitive theory
    b. Erikson's psychosocial theory
    c. Freud's psychoanalytic theory
    d. behaviorism

Key Terms

Writing Definitions

Using your own words, write a brief definition or explanation of each of the following terms on a separate piece of paper.

1. developmental theory
2. grand theories
3. emergent theories
4. psychoanalytic theory
5. behaviorism
6. conditioning
7. classical conditioning
8. operant conditioning
9. reinforcement
10. social learning theory
11. modeling
12. self-efficacy
13. cognitive theory
14. cognitive equilibrium
15. sociocultural theory
16. guided participation
17. zone of proximal development
18. epigenetic theory
19. selective adaptation
20. eclectic perspective
21. nature
22. nurture
23. sexual orientation

Cross-Check

After you have written the definitions of the key terms in this chapter, you should complete the crossword puzzle to ensure that you can reverse the process—recognize the term, given the definition.

ACROSS

2. Behaviorism focuses on the sequences and processes involved in the _____ of behavior.
8. An instinctive or learned behavior that is elicited by a specific stimulus.
11. All the genetic influences on development.
12. Developmental perspective that accepts elements from several theories.
14. Influential theorist who developed a stage theory of cognitive development.
17. All the environmental (nongenetic) influences on development.
19. Type of theory that brings together information from many disciplines into a comprehensive model of development but is not yet established enough to be considered a grand theory.

DOWN

1. Theory that focuses on some specific area of development.
3. Theory that emphasizes the interaction of genetic and environmental factors in development.
4. The process by which the consequences of a behavior make the behavior more likely to occur.

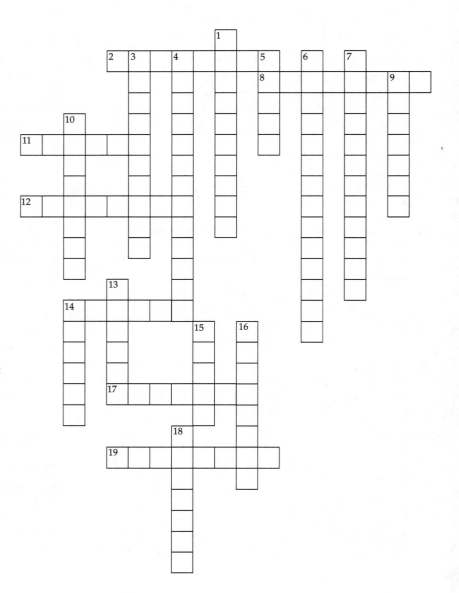

5. Comprehensive theory of development that has proven to be inadequate in explaining the full range of human development.

6. Theory of personality and development that emphasizes unconscious forces.

7. Learning process that occurs through the association of two stimuli or through the use of reinforcement.

9. Influential theorist who outlined the principles of operant conditioning.

10. The study of animals in their natural environments.

13. An early and especially strong proponent of learning theory in America.

14. Russian scientist who outlined the principles of classical conditioning.

15. The developer of psychoanalytic theory.

16. The process of learning by imitating another person's behavior.

18. Psychoanalytic theorist who viewed development as a series of psychosocial crises.

ANSWERS

CHAPTER REVIEW

1. developmental theory

2. hypotheses; discoveries; practical

3. grand; mini; emergent

4. motives; drives; unconscious; irrational

5. psychoanalytic; oral; anal; phallic; conflicts

Oral stage: The mouth is the focus of pleasurable sensations as the baby becomes emotionally attached to the person who provides the oral gratifications derived from sucking.

Anal stage: Pleasures related to control and self-control, initially in connection with defecation and toilet training, are paramount.

Phallic stage: Pleasure is derived from genital stimulation.

Genital stage: Mature sexual interests that last throughout adulthood emerge.

6. eight; crisis (challenge); span

Age Period	Stage
Birth to 1 yr.	trust vs. **mistrust**
1–3 yrs.	autonomy vs. **shame and doubt**
3–6 yrs.	initiative vs. **guilt**
6–11 yrs.	**industry** vs. inferiority
Adolescence	identity vs. **role confusion**
Young adulthood	**intimacy** vs. isolation
Middle adulthood	**generativity** vs. stagnation
Older adulthood	**integrity** vs. despair

7. behaviorism; John B. Watson; learning

8. at all ages; conditioning; classical conditioning; operant conditioning

9. Ivan Pavlov; respondent; neutral

10. B. F. Skinner; operant; consequence; instrumental

11. reinforcement

12. Harry Harlow; attachment; contact comfort; psychoanalytic; behaviorism's

13. social learning; modeling

14. uncertain; inexperienced; admirable and powerful, nurturing, or similar to the observer; perceptions; interpretations; self-understanding; social reflection; self-efficacy

15. cognitive; information-processing; Jean Piaget

16. sensorimotor; 2

17. 6; preoperational; egocentric

18. 6; concrete operational

19. formal operational; abstract (hypothetical); 12

20. cognitive equilibrium

21. cognitive disequilibrium

22. assimilate; accommodate

23. many

24. dynamic interaction; society

25. Lev Vygotsky; cognitive

26. novices; tutors

27. guided participation; apprenticeship in thinking

28. zone of proximal development; assistance

Sociocultural theory has emphasized the need to study development in the specific cultural context in which it occurs. The theory has been criticized for neglecting the importance of developmental processes that are not primarily social, such as the role of biological maturation in development.

29. epigenetic; genes; environment; preformism

30. environmental; genetic influences; stress; facilitating

31. genetic–environmental; reaction range

32. selective adaptation

33. all

34. accepting help; attachments to caregivers; nurture babies

35. a. sociocultural
    b. cognitive
    c. behaviorism
    d. psychoanalytic
    e. epigenetic

36. **a.** behaviorism
    b. cognitive
    c. psychoanalytic
    d. epigenetic
    e. sociocultural
37. eclectic
38. nature–nurture; genes (nature); nurture
39. interaction
40. attention-deficit/hyperactivity disorder (ADHD); boys

    ADHD children:
    - often have close male relatives with the same problem
    - are overactive in every context
    - calm down when they take stimulants
41. nurture; nature; sexual orientation; inclinations; thoughts; sexual expression; behavior

PROGRESS TEST 1

Multiple-Choice Questions

1. **d.** is the answer (pp. 33–34)
2. **a.** is the answer. (p. 35)

    b. Behaviorism emphasizes the influence of the immediate environment on behavior.

    c. Cognitive theory emphasizes the impact of *conscious* thought processes on behavior.

    d. Sociocultural theory emphasizes the influence on development of social interaction in a specific cultural context.
3. **a.** is the answer. (pp. 35, 36)
4. **a.** is the answer. (pp. 36–37)

    b. & c. Whereas Freud identified four stages of psychosexual development, Erikson proposed eight psychosocial stages.

    d. Although his theory places greater emphasis on social and cultural forces than Freud's did, Erikson's theory is nevertheless classified as a psychoanalytic theory.
5. **c.** is the answer. Sociocultural theory is an emergent theory. (p. 46)

    a., b., & d. Each of these is an example of a grand theory.
6. **c.** is the answer. (p. 39)
7. **a.** is the answer. In classical conditioning, a neutral stimulus—in this case, the bell—is associated with a meaningful stimulus—in this case, food. (p. 39)

b. In operant conditioning, the consequences of a voluntary response determine the likelihood of its being repeated. Salivation is an involuntary response.

c. & d. Positive reinforcement and social learning pertain to voluntary, or operant, responses.

8. **c.** is the answer. (p. 55)

    a. These are both examples of nurture.

    b. Both of these refer to nature.

    d. The impact of changing historical concepts of childhood on development is an example of how environmental forces (nurture) shape development.
9. **d.** is the answer. (p. 43)

    a. & c. These can be true in all types of learning.

    b. This was not discussed as an aspect of developmental theory.
10. **d.** is the answer. (p. 49)

    a. & c. Sociocultural theory and behaviorism focus almost entirely on environmental factors (nurture) in development.

    b. Cognitive theory emphasizes the developing person's own mental activity but ignores genetic differences in individuals.
11. **a.** is the answer. (p. 49)

    b. Vygotsky's theory does not emphasize biological processes.

    c. & d. Vygotsky's theory places considerable emphasis on language and social factors.
12. **a.** is the answer. (pp. 43, 44)
13. **c.** is the answer. (p. 45)

    a. This refers to the core of Erikson's psychosocial stages, which deals with people's interactions with the environment.

    b. Equilibrium occurs when existing schemes *do* fit a person's current experiences.

    d. Negative reinforcement is the removal of a stimulus as a consequence of a desired behavior.
14. **b.** is the answer. (p. 56)

    c. This is only true of psychoanalytic theory.

    d. Although the grand theories have emphasized nurture over nature in this matter, no theory suggests that sexual orientation is voluntarily chosen.
15. **c.** is the answer. (p. 48)

    a. This is a stage of Piaget's cognitive theory.

    b. This describes positive reinforcement.

    d. This is an aspect of social learning theory.

True or False Items

1. T (p. 38)

2. T (pp. 36, 37)

3. F   Although most developmentalists believe that nature and nurture interact in shaping development, the practical implications of whether nature or nurture plays a greater role in certain abilities keep the controversy alive. (pp. 55–57)

4. F   This assumption lies at the heart of epigenetic theory. (p. 49)

5. F   Epigenetic theory emphasizes the interaction of genes and experience. (p. 49)

6. F   On the contrary, *dis*equilibrium often fosters greater growth. (p. 45)

7. T (p. 43)

8. F   The hallmark of Piaget's theory is that, at every age, individuals think about the world in unique ways. (p. 43)

9. T (p. 55)

10. F   Sociocultural theorists first distinguished between sexual orientation and expression to point out that nurture affects expression, not orientation. (p. 56)

PROGRESS TEST 2

Multiple-Choice Questions

1. **d.** is the answer. (pp. 35, 36, 43)

2. **d.** is the answer. This is one of Piaget's stages of cognitive development. (pp. 36, 44)

3. **c.** is the answer. (p. 42)

4. **a.** is the answer. (p. 34)

   b. *Grand* theories, rather than minitheories, usually stem from one person.

   c. This describes emergent theories.

5. **d.** is the answer. (p. 36)

6. **c.** is the answer. (p. 38)

   a. Piaget formulated a cognitive theory of development.

   b. Vygotsky formulated a sociocultural theory of development.

   d. Erikson formulated a psychoanalytic theory of development.

7. **c.** is the answer. (p. 39)

8. **c.** is the answer. (pp. 38–40)

a. & b. These are psychoanalytic approaches to treating psychological problems.

d. Behaviorists generally do not recommend the use of punishment.

9. **a.** is the answer. These behaviors are typical of infants in the sensorimotor stage. (p. 44)

   b., c., & d. These are typical of older children.

10. **a.** is the answer. (p. 44)

    b. The sensorimotor stage describes development from birth until 2 years of age.

    c. This is a psychoanalytic stage described by Freud.

    d. This is not the name of a stage; "psychosocial" refers to Erikson's stage theory.

11. **a.** is the answer. (p. 44)

    b. This describes *dis*equilibrium.

    c. This is formal operational thinking.

    d. Piaget's theory does not propose stages of information processing.

12. **c.** is the answer. (p. 39)

    a. & b. Teaching your dog in this way is an example of operant, rather than classical (respondent), conditioning.

    d. Modeling involves learning by imitating others.

13. **b.** is the answer. (p. 45)

    a. Assimilation occurs when new experiences do *not* clash with existing ideas.

    c. Cognitive equilibrium is mental balance, which occurs when ideas and experiences do *not* clash.

    d. This is Vygotsky's term for the process by which a mentor engages a child in shared learning activities.

14. **d.** is the answer. (p. 49)

    a. This is a common criticism of psychoanalytic theory.

    b. This is a common criticism of behaviorism.

    c. This is a common criticism of psychoanalytic and cognitive theories that describe development as occurring in a sequence of stages.

15. **c.** is the answer. (p. 47)

Matching Items

1. f (p. 35)	**5.** h (p. 43)	**9.** b (p. 34)
2. k (p. 55)	**6.** d (p. 55)	**10.** i (p. 43)
3. a (p. 38)	**7.** g (p. 46)	**11.** j (p. 49)
4. c (p. 42)	**8.** e (p. 39)	

DEVELOPMENTAL PSYCHOLOGY APPLIED

1. **a.** is the answer. (p. 51)

   b. This term was not used to describe development.

   c. & d. These terms describe the processes by which cognitive concepts incorporate (assimilate) new experiences or are revamped (accommodated) by them.

2. **a.** is the answer. This is an example of operant conditioning because a response recurs due to its consequences. (p. 39)

   b. & d. In classical conditioning, the individual learns to associate a neutral stimulus with a meaningful stimulus.

   c. In modeling, learning occurs through the observation of others, rather than through direct exposure to reinforcing consequences, as in this example.

3. **d.** is the answer. In classical conditioning, an organism comes to associate a neutral stimulus with a meaningful one and then responds to the former stimulus as if it were the latter. (p. 39)

4. **d.** is the answer. (p. 49)

   a. Psychoanalytic theorists focus on the role of unconscious forces in development.

   b. Cognitive theorists emphasize how the developing person actively seeks to understand experiences.

   c. Sociocultural theorists focus on the social context, as expressed through people, language, and customs.

5. **b.** is the answer. (p. 47)

   a. & c. These are both examples of modeling.

   d. Guided participation involves coaching by a tutor. In this example, Jack is simply following written directions.

6. **a.** is the answer. (p. 45)

   b. Because the dog is not furry, the child's concept of dog cannot incorporate (assimilate) the discrepant experience without being revamped.

   c. & d. Equilibrium exists when ideas (such as what a dog is) and experiences (such as seeing a hairless dog) do *not* clash.

7. **d.** is the answer. (p. 37)

8. **b.** is the answer. Evidently, Jennie has learned by observing the other children at play. (p. 43)

   a. Classical conditioning is concerned with the association of stimuli, not with complex responses, as in this example.

   c. Guided participation involves the interaction of a tutor and a learner.

   d. Reinforcement is a process for getting a response to recur.

9. **c.** is the answer. (p. 44)

10. **d.** is the answer. When Jamail experiences something that conflicts with his existing understanding, he experiences disequilibrium. (p. 45)

    a. Conservation is the ability to recognize that objects do not change when their appearances change.

    b. Cognition refers to all mental activities associated with thinking.

    c. If Jamail's thinking were in equilibrium, all men would be "dad"!

11. **a.** is the answer. (p. 53)

    b. & c. Infant social reflexes and adult caregiving impulses occur in all cultures (b), which indicates that they are the product of nature rather than nurture (c).

    d. The text does not address the issue of gender differences in infant reflexes or caregiving impulses.

12. **d.** is the answer. (p. 46)

13. **b.** is the answer. (p. 36)

    a. According to Erikson, this crisis concerns younger children.

    c. & d. In Erikson's theory, these crises concern older children.

14. **c.** is the answer. (p. 55)

    a., b., & d. These are three of the many theoretical perspectives upon which someone working from an eclectic perspective might draw.

15. **d.** is the answer. (p. 38)

    a., b., & c. Each of these theories emphasizes that development is a discontinuous process that occurs in stages.

KEY TERMS

Writing Definitions

1. A **developmental theory** is a systematic statement of principles and generalizations that provides a coherent framework for understanding how and why people change as they grow older. (p. 33)

2. **Grand theories** are comprehensive theories of psychology, which have traditionally inspired

and directed psychologists' thinking about child development. Examples of grand theories are psychoanalytic and cognitive theories and behaviorism. (p. 34)

3. **Emergent theories,** such as sociocultural theory and epigenetic theory, are newer comprehensive theories that bring together information from many disciplines but are not yet a systematic and comprehensive whole. (p. 34)

4. **Psychoanalytic theory,** a grand theory, interprets human development in terms of inner drives and motives, many of which are irrational and unconscious. (p. 35)

5. **Behaviorism,** a grand theory, emphasizes the laws and processes by which behavior is learned; also called *learning theory.* (p. 38)

6. **Conditioning** is the learning process that occurs either through the association of two stimuli (classical conditioning) or through the use of positive or negative reinforcement or punishment (operant conditioning). (p. 39)

7. **Classical conditioning** is the process by which a neutral stimulus becomes associated with a meaningful one so that both are responded to in the same way. (p. 39)

8. **Operant conditioning** is the process by which a response is gradually learned through reinforcement or punishment. (p. 39)

9. **Reinforcement** is the process by which the consequences of a particular behavior make it more likely that the behavior will be repeated. (p. 39)

10. An extension of behaviorism, **social learning theory** emphasizes that people often learn new behaviors through observation and imitation of other people. (p. 42)

11. **Modeling** refers to the process by which we observe other people's behavior and then pattern our own after it. (p. 43)

12. In social learning theory, **self-efficacy** is the belief that one is effective. (p. 43)

13. **Cognitive theory,** a grand theory, emphasizes that the way people think and understand the world shapes their attitudes, beliefs, and behaviors. (p. 43)

14. In Piaget's theory, **cognitive equilibrium** is a state of mental balance, in which a person's thoughts about the world seem not to clash with each other or with his or her experiences. (p. 44)

15. **Sociocultural theory,** an emergent theory, seeks to explain development as the result of a dynamic interaction between developing persons and the surrounding social and cultural forces. (p. 46)

16. In sociocultural theory, **guided participation** is a learning process in which the learner is tutored, or mentored, through social interaction with a skilled teacher. (p. 47)

17. According to Vygotsky, developmental growth occurs when mentors draw children into the **zone of proximal development,** which is the range of skills, knowledge, and concepts the child can acquire with assistance but cannot master independently. (p. 48)

18. **Epigenetic theory,** an emergent theory, emphasizes the genetic origins of behavior but also stresses that genes, over time, are directly and systematically affected by environmental forces. (p. 49)

19. **Selective adaptation** is the evolutionary process through which useful genes that enhance survival become more common within individuals. (p. 51)

20. Developmentalists who work from an **eclectic perspective** accept elements from several theories, instead of adhering to only a single perspective. (p. 55)

21. **Nature** refers to all the traits, capacities, and limitations that a person inherits from his or her parents at the moment of conception. (p. 55)

22. **Nurture** refers to all the environmental influences that affect a person's development following the moment of conception. (p. 55)

23. **Sexual orientation** refers to a person's impulses and personal direction regarding sexual interest toward persons of the same sex, of the other sex, or of both sexes. (p. 56)

Cross-Check

ACROSS

2. learning
8. response
11. nature
12. eclectic
14. Piaget
17. nurture
19. emergent

DOWN

1. minitheory
3. epigenetic
4. reinforcement
5. grand
6. psychoanalytic
7. conditioning
9. Skinner
10. ethology
13. Watson
14. Pavlov
15. Freud
16. modeling
18. Erikson

3

Heredity and Environment

Chapter Overview

Conception occurs when the male and female reproductive cells—the sperm and ovum, respectively—come together to create a new, one-celled zygote with its own unique combination of genetic material. The genetic material furnishes the instructions for development—not only for obvious physical characteristics, such as sex, coloring, and body shape but also for certain psychological characteristics, such as bashfulness, moodiness, and vocational aptitude.

Every year, scientists make new discoveries and reach new understandings about genes and their effects on the development of individuals. This chapter presents some of their findings, including that most human characteristics are polygenic and multifactorial—the result of the interaction of many genetic and environmental influences. Perhaps the most important findings have come from research into the causes of genetic and chromosomal abnormalities. The chapter discusses the most common of these abnormalities and concludes with a section on genetic counseling. Genetic testing before and after conception can help predict whether a couple will have a child with a genetic problem.

Many students find the technical material in this chapter difficult to master, but it *can* be done with a great deal of rehearsal. Working through the Chapter Review several times and mentally reciting terms are both useful techniques for rehearsing this type of material.

NOTE: Answer guidelines for all Chapter 3 questions begin on page 46.

Guided Study

The text chapter should be studied one section at a time. Before you read, preview each section by skimming it, noting headings and boldface items. Then read the appropriate section objectives from the following outline. Keep these objectives in mind and, as you read the chapter section, search for the information that will enable you to meet each objective. Once you have finished a section, write out answers for its objectives.

The Genetic Code (pp. 61–66)

1. Identify the mechanisms of heredity.

2. Describe the process of conception and the first hours of development of the zygote.

3. Explain how sex is determined.

From One Cell to Many (pp. 66–72)

4. Differentiate genotype from phenotype, and describe the processes of duplication, division, and differentiation.

5. Explain the polygenic and multifactorial nature of human traits, and discuss how the Human Genome Project is attempting to uncover the mechanisms of genetic interaction.

6. Describe the additive and nonadditive patterns of genetic interaction, giving examples of the traits that result from each type of interaction.

7. Discuss X-linked genes in terms of genotype and phenotype.

8. Distinguish between monozygotic and dizygotic twins and between monozygotic twins and clones.

9. (text and In Person) Discuss issues related to the use of assisted reproductive technology for infertile couples.

From Genotype to Phenotype (pp. 73–78)

10. Discuss the interaction of genes and environment, focusing on the development of addiction and visual acuity.

11. Discuss the practical implications of research on nature–nurture interactions.

Chromosomal and Genetic Abnormalities (pp. 79–87)

12. Describe the most common chromosomal abnormalities, including abnormalities involving the sex chromosomes.

13. Identify two common genetic disorders, and discuss reasons for their relatively low incidence of occurrence.

14. Describe four situations in which couples should seek genetic testing and counseling.

15. (text and Thinking Like a Scientist) Give several examples of why sharing genetic information with concerned parents and other family members can be a difficult matter for genetic counselors.

Chapter Review

When you have finished reading the chapter, work through the material that follows to review it. Complete the sentences and answer the questions. As you proceed, evaluate your performance for each section by consulting the answers beginning on page 46. Do not continue with the next section until you understand each answer. If you need to, review or reread the appropriate section in the textbook before continuing.

The Genetic Code (pp. 61–66)

1. The work of body cells is done by _____ , under the direction of instructions stored in molecules of _____ , each of which is called a _____ .

2. Each normal person inherits _____ chromosomes, _____ from each parent. The genetic instructions in chromosomes are organized into units called _____ , each of which contains instructions for a specific _____ , which in turn is composed of chemical building blocks called _____ _____ . These instructions are transmitted to cells via four chemical _____ that include _____ . _____ , _____ , and _____ . The sum total of these genetic instructions for a given species is called its _____ .

3. The human reproductive cells, which are called _____ , include the male's _____ and the female's _____ .

4. When the gametes' nuclei fuse, a living cell called a _____ is formed.

5. This new cells receives _____ chromosomes from the father and _____ from the mother.

6. An organism's entire genetic inheritance is called its _____ .

7. The chromosomes in a pair are generally identical or similar. The 44 chromosomes that are independent of the sex chromosomes are called _____ . If a gene from one parent is exactly like that from the other parent, the gene pair is said to be _____ . If the match is not perfect, the gene pair is said to be _____ . Some genes come in several slight, normal variations called _____ .

8. The developing person's sex is determined by the _____ pair of chromosomes. In the female, this pair is composed of two _____-shaped chromosomes and is designated _____ . In the male, this pair includes one _____ and one _____ chromosome and is therefore designated _____ .

9. The critical factor in the determination of a zygote's sex is which _____ (sperm/ovum) reaches the other gamete first. The natural sex ratio at birth is about _____ . In a stressful pregnancy, _____ (XX/XY) embryos are more likely to be expelled in a miscarriage, or _____ _____ . The sex ratio can also be affected by _____ _____ .

10. (text and Issues and Applications) At birth, the overall sex ratio has always _____ (favored males/favored females/been roughly equal). In countries such as China, prenatal tests that show the sex of the child have been used to _____ .

From One Cell to Many (pp. 66–72)

11. The actual appearance and manifest behavior of the person is called the _____ .

12. Within hours after conception, the zygote begins to _____ and _____ . At about the eight-cell stage, the cells start to _____ , with various cells beginning to specialize and reproduce at different rates. Specific genes affect this process as they _____ on at particular times.

_____ (how many?) of all human genes affect the brain.

13. Most human characteristics are affected by many genes, and so they are _____ ; and by many factors, and so they are _____ .

14. The international effort to map the complete human genetic code is referred to as the _____ _____ _____ . This effort found most importantly that all living creatures _____ (have different/share) genes. The differences among species are due to the actions of the _____ genes.

15. A phenotype that reflects the sum of the contributions of all the genes involved in its determination illustrates the _____ pattern of genetic interaction. Examples include genes that affect _____ and _____ _____ .

16. Less often, genes interact in a _____ fashion. In one example of this pattern, some genes are more influential than others; this is called the _____–_____ pattern. In this pattern, the more influential gene is called _____ , and the weaker gene is called _____ .

17. Some recessive genes are located only on the X chromosome and so are called _____-_____ . Examples of such genes are the ones that determine _____ . Because they have only one X chromosome, _____ (females/males) are more likely to have these characteristics in their phenotype.

18. Although females always inherit two _____ chromosomes, one of these is relatively _____ .

19. Identical twins, who develop from one _____ , _____ (are/are not) genetically identical. This occurs about once in every _____ (how many?) conceptions. When such twins differ in a genetic trait, this signifies a developmental effect that is _____ .

20. Twins who begin life as two separate zygotes created by the fertilization of two ova are called _____ twins. Such twins have approximately _____ percent of their genes in common.

21. The incidence of dizygotic births varies by the mother's _____ and _____ .

22. An artificially created organism that is exactly the same genotype as another organism that is already alive is called a _____ . Although human cloning is _____ , it would technically be possible via _____ _____ _____ , which involves fertilization in a laboratory dish.

23. Couples that have been unable to produce a baby after at least one year of trying are troubled by _____ . For such couples, _____ _____ _____ can help in conceiving and then sustaining a pregnancy.

24. One simple treatment for infertility is to use _____ to cause ovulation. If the male partner is infertile, donor sperm may be inserted into the female's uterus in a process called _____ _____ .

From Genotype to Phenotype (pp. 73–78)

25. State four general principles of genetic influences on development that virtually all developmentalists accept.

    a. _____

    _____

    b. _____

    _____

    c. _____

    _____

    d. _____

    _____

26. Genetic influences _____ (increase/decrease) during adulthood.

27. A person who has a gene in his or her genotype that is not expressed in the phenotype but that can be passed on to the person's offspring is said to be a _____ of that gene.

28. Some people's inherited biochemistry makes them highly susceptible to each kind of _____ . Certain _____ traits are also correlated with addiction, including _____ . Two other factors in alcohlism are _____ and _____ . Women become drunk on _____ (less/more) alcohol than men do.

29. The most common vision problem in children is _____ , also called _____ . This problem may be caused by genes, by physical _____ or _____ , and by poor _____ . The alarming increase in the rate of this vision problem among children in some parts of the world has been attributed to the increasing amount of time spent by children in the _____ .

30. On a practical level, knowing that a particular genetic disorder runs in the family can help parents take _____ measures to reduce their children's vulnerability. For instance, type 2 diabetes does not begin unless a person is _____ vulnerable and has more _____ _____ than is ideal for his or her age and height.

Chromosomal and Genetic Abnormalities (pp. 79–87)

31. Researchers study genetic and chromosomal abnormalities for three major reasons. State them.

    a. _____

    _____

    b. _____

    _____

    c. _____

    _____

32. Chromosomal abnormalities occur during the formation and _____ of the _____ , producing a sperm or ovum that does not have the normal complement of chromosomes.

33. The variable that most often correlates with chromosomal abnormalities is _____ _____ . When cells in a zygote end up with more or fewer than 46 chromosomes, the result is a person who is _____ .

34. Most fetuses with chromosomal abnormalities are _____ _____ . Nevertheless, about 1 in every _____ newborns has one chromosome too few or one too many, leading to a cluster of characteristics called a _____ .

35. The most common extra-chromosome syndrome is _____ _____ , which is also called _____-_____ . People with this syndrome age _____ (faster/more slowly) than other adults. By middle age, people with Down syndrome almost invariably develop _____ _____ , which severely impairs their already limited _____ skills.

List several of the physical and psychological characteristics associated with Down syndrome.

36. About 1 in every 500 infants is either missing a _____ chromosome or has two or more such chromosomes. One resulting syndrome is _____ , in which a girl inherits only one _____ chromosome; another is _____ _____ , in which a boy inherits the _____ chromosome pattern.

37. Most of the known genetic disorders are _____ (dominant/recessive). Genetic disorders usually _____ (are/are not) seriously disabling. Severe dominant disorders are _____ (common/rare) because people with these disorders usually _____ (do/do not) have children.

38. Two exceptions are the central nervous system disease called _____ and the disorder that causes its victims to exhibit uncontrollable tics and explosive outbursts, called _____ .

39. In some individuals, part of the X chromosome is attached by such a thin string of molecules that it seems about to break off; this abnormality is called _____ _____ syndrome.

40. Three common recessive disorders that are not sex-linked are _____ , _____ , and _____-_____ _____ .

41. Through _____ _____ , couples today can learn more about their genes and about their chances of conceiving a child with chromosomal or other genetic abnormalities.

42. List four situations in which genetic counseling is strongly recommended.

    a. _____

    b. _____

    c. _____

    d. _____

43. In the United States and many other nations, every newborn is tested for _____ , a recessive condition that will result in severe retardation if the common food substance _____ is consumed.

Progress Test 1

Circle your answers to the following questions and check them against the answers beginning on page 47. If your answer is incorrect, read the explanation for why it is incorrect and then consult the appropriate pages of the text (in parentheses following the correct answer).

Multiple-Choice Questions

1. When a sperm and an ovum merge, a one-celled _____ is formed.
   a. zygote
   b. reproductive cell
   c. gamete
   d. monozygote

2. Genes are separate units that provide the chemical instructions that each cell needs to become:
   a. a zygote.
   b. a chromosome.
   c. a specific part of a functioning human body.
   d. deoxyribonucleic acid.

3. In the male, the 23rd pair of chromosomes is designated _____ ; in the female, this pair is designated _____.
   a. XX; XY
   b. XY; XX
   c. XO; XXX
   d. XXY; XO

4. Because the 23rd pair of chromosomes in females is XX, each ovum carries an:
   a. XX zygote.
   b. X zygote.
   c. XY zygote.
   d. X chromosome.

5. When a zygote splits, the two identical, independent clusters that develop become:
   a. dizygotic twins.
   b. monozygotic twins.
   c. fraternal twins.
   d. trizygotic twins.

6. During adulthood, genetic influences on development:
   a. generally increase.
   b. generally decrease.
   c. remain steady.
   d. vary from individual to individual.

7. Most of the known genetic disorders are:
   a. dominant.
   b. recessive.
   c. seriously disabling.
   d. sex-linked.

8. When we say that a characteristic is multifactorial, we mean that:
   a. many genes are involved.
   b. many environmental factors are involved.
   c. many genetic and environmental factors are involved.
   d. the characteristic is polygenic.

9. Genes are segments of molecules of:
   a. genotype.
   b. deoxyribonucleic acid (DNA).
   c. karyotype.
   d. phenotype.

10. In the United States, newborns are tested for the recessive genetic disorder:
    a. phenylketonuria.
    b. Alzheimer's disease.
    c. Down syndrome.
    d. fragile X syndrome.

11. A chromosomal abnormality that affects males only involves a(n):
    a. X0 chromosomal pattern.
    b. XXX chromosomal pattern.
    c. YY chromosomal pattern.
    d. XXY chromosomal pattern.

12. Some developmentalists believe that the epidemic increase in myopia among children in Hong Kong, Singapore, and Japan is partly the result of:
    a. the recent epidemic of rubella.
    b. vitamin A deficiency.
    c. the increasing amount of time spent by children in close study of books and papers.
    d. mutations in the Pax6 gene.

13. Babies born with trisomy-21 (Down syndrome) are often:
    a. born to older parents.
    b. unusually aggressive.
    c. abnormally tall by adolescence.
    d. blind.

14. To say that a trait is polygenic means that:
    a. many genes make it more likely that the individual will inherit the trait.
    b. several genes must be present in order for the individual to inherit the trait.
    c. the trait is multifactorial.
    d. most people carry genes for the trait.

15. Some genetic diseases are recessive, so the child cannot inherit the condition unless both parents:
    a. have Klinefelter syndrome.
    b. carry the same recessive gene.
    c. have X0 chromosomes.
    d. have the disease.

Matching Items

Match each term with its corresponding description or definition.

Terms

_____   **1.** gametes
_____   **2.** chromosome
_____   **3.** genotype
_____   **4.** phenotype
_____   **5.** monozygotic
_____   **6.** dizygotic
_____   **7.** additive
_____   **8.** fragile X syndrome
_____   **9.** carrier
_____   **10.** zygote
_____   **11.** alleles
_____   **12.** XX
_____   **13.** XY

Descriptions or Definitions

a. chromosome pair inherited by genetic females
b. identical twins
c. sperm and ovum
d. the first cell of the developing person
e. a person who has a recessive gene in his or her genotype that is not expressed in the phenotype
f. fraternal twins
g. a pattern in which each gene in question makes an active contribution to the final outcome
h. a DNA molecule
i. the behavioral or physical expression of genetic potential
j. a chromosomal abnormality
k. alternate versions of a gene
l. chromosome pair inherited by genetic males
m. a person's entire genetic inheritance

Progress Test 2

Progress Test 2 should be completed during a final chapter review. Answer the following questions after you thoroughly understand the correct answers for the Chapter Review and Progress Test 1.

1. Which of the following provides the best broad description of the relationship between heredity and environment?
   a. Heredity is the primary influence, with environment affecting development only in severe situations.
   b. Heredity and environment contribute equally to development.
   c. Environment is the major influence on physical characteristics.
   d. Heredity directs the individual's potential, and environment determines whether and to what degree the individual reaches that potential.

2. The recent increase in type 2 diabetes among children in the United States is the result of:
   a. unknown factors.
   b. genes acting alone.
   c. vitamin deficiencies among certain ethnic groups.
   d. genetic vulnerability coupled with increasing obesity.

3. Males with fragile X syndrome are:
   a. feminine in appearance.
   b. less severely affected than females.
   c. frequently retarded intellectually.
   d. likely to have fatty deposits around the breasts.

4. With the exception of sperm and egg cells, each human cell contains:
   a. 23 genes.   **c.** 46 genes.
   b. 23 chromosomes.   **d.** 46 chromosomes.

5. The disorder in which a genetic female inherits only one X chromosome (X0 pattern) is called:
   a. trisomy-21.
   b. Down syndrome.
   c. Turner syndrome.
   d. Klinefelter syndrome.

6. Dizygotic twins result when:
   a. a single egg is fertilized by a sperm and then splits.
   b. a single egg is fertilized by two different sperm.
   c. two eggs are fertilized by two different sperm.
   d. either a single egg is fertilized by one sperm or two eggs are fertilized by two different sperm.

7. Molecules of DNA that in humans are organized into 23 complementary pairs are called:
   a. zygotes.   c. chromosomes.
   b. genes.   d. ova.

8. Shortly after the zygote is formed, it begins the processes of duplication and division. Each resulting new cell has:
   a. the same number of chromosomes as was contained in the zygote.
   b. half the number of chromosomes as was contained in the zygote.
   c. twice, then four times, then eight times the number of chromosomes as was contained in the zygote.
   d. all the chromosomes except those that determine sex.

9. If an ovum is fertilized by a sperm bearing a Y chromosome:
   a. a female will develop.
   b. cell division will result.
   c. a male will develop.
   d. spontaneous abortion will occur.

10. When the male cells in the testes and the female cells in the ovaries divide to produce gametes, the process differs from that in the production of all other cells. As a result of the different process, the gametes have:
    a. one rather than both members of each chromosome pair.
    b. 23 chromosome pairs.
    c. X but not Y chromosomes.
    d. chromosomes from both parents.

11. Most human traits are:
    a. polygenic.
    b. multifactorial.
    c. determined by dominant–recessive patterns.
    d. both a. and b.

12. Genotype is to phenotype as _____ is to _____ .
    a. genetic potential; physical expression
    b. physical expression; genetic potential
    c. sperm; ovum
    d. gamete; zygote

13. The genes that influence height and skin color interact according to the _____ pattern.
    a. dominant–recessive   c. additive
    b. X-linked   d. nonadditive

14. X-linked recessive genes explain why some traits seem to be passed from:
    a. father to son.
    b. father to daughter.
    c. mother to daughter.
    d. mother to son.

15. In vitro fertilization is a technique:
    a. in which sperm are mixed with ova that have been surgically removed from a woman's ovary.
    b. in which sperm from a donor are inserted into the woman's uterus via a syringe.
    c. for helping infertile couples conceive a pregnancy.
    d. for helping infertile couples sustain a pregnancy.

True or False Items

Write T (*true*) or F (*false*) on the line in front of each statement.

_____ 1. Most human characteristics are multifactorial, caused by the interaction of genetic and environmental factors.

_____ 2. Chromosomal abnormalities can occur only for genetic reasons.

_____ 3. Research suggests that susceptibility to alcoholism is at least partly the result of genetic inheritance.

_____ 4. The human reproductive cells (ova and sperm) are called gametes.

_____ 5. Only a very few human traits are polygenic.

_____ 6. The zygote contains all the biologically inherited information—the genes and chromosomes—that a person will have during his or her life.

_____ 7. A couple should probably seek genetic counseling if several earlier pregnancies ended in spontaneous abortion.

_____ 8. Many genetic conditions are recessive; thus, a child will have the condition even if only the mother carries the gene.

_____ 9. Two people who have the same phenotype may have a different genotype for a trait such as eye color.

_____ 10. When cells divide to produce reproductive cells (gametes), each sperm or ovum receives only 23 chromosomes, half as many as the original cell.

_____ 11. Most genes have only one function.

Developmental Psychology Applied

Answer these questions the day before an exam as a final check on your understanding of the chapter's terms and concepts.

1. Randy's son was born with an XXY chromosomal pattern. It is likely that his son's condition will:
   a. go undetected until puberty.
   b. benefit from hormone supplements.
   c. develop some female sex characteristics at puberty.
   d. be characterized by all of the above.

2. Concluding her presentation on the hazards of multiple births, Kirsten notes that, "the more embryos that develop together, the":
   a. larger each is.
   b. less mature and more vulnerable each is.
   c. less vulnerable each is.
   d. larger and less vulnerable each is.

3. Which of the following is an inherited abnormality that quite possibly could develop into a recognizable syndrome?
   a. Just before dividing to form a sperm or ovum, corresponding gene segments of a chromosome pair break off and are exchanged.
   b. Just before conception, a chromosome pair splits imprecisely, resulting in a mixture of cells.
   c. A person inherits an X chromosome in which part of the chromosome is attached to the rest of it by a very slim string of molecules.
   d. A person inherits a recessive gene on his Y chromosome.

4. Some men are color-blind because they inherit a particular recessive gene from their mothers. That recessive gene is carried on the:
   a. X chromosome.
   b. XX chromosome pair.
   c. Y chromosome.
   d. X or Y chromosome.

5. If your mother is much taller than your father, it is most likely that your height will be:
   a. about the same as your mother's, because the X chromosome determines height.
   b. about the same as your father's, because the Y chromosome determines height.
   c. somewhere between your mother's and father's heights because the genes for height are additive.
   d. greater than both your mother's and father's because of your grandfather's dominant gene.

6. If a dizygotic twin develops schizophrenia, the likelihood of the other twin experiencing serious mental illness is much lower than is the case with monozygotic twins. This suggests that:
   a. schizophrenia is caused by genes.
   b. schizophrenia is influenced by genes.
   c. environment is unimportant in the development of schizophrenia.
   d. monozygotic twins are especially vulnerable to schizophrenia.

7. A person's skin turns yellow-orange as a result of a carrot-juice diet regimen. This is an example of:
   a. an environmental influence.
   b. an alteration in genotype.
   c. polygenic inheritance.
   d. incomplete dominance.

8. Jason has an inherited, dominant disorder that causes him to exhibit uncontrollable tics and explosive outbursts. Jason most likely would be diagnosed with:
   a. Klinefelter syndrome.
   b. Huntington's disease.
   c. Fragile X syndrome.
   d. Tourette syndrome.

9. If a man carries the recessive gene for cystic fibrosis and his wife does not, the chances of their having a child with cystic fibrosis is:
   a. one in four.
   b. fifty-fifty.
   c. zero.
   d. dependent upon the wife's ethnic background.

10. One reason scientists are skeptical of research that attempts to distinguish genetic influences from environmental ones is that:
    a. genes elicit responses from other people that shape each child's development.
    b. there are too few monozygotic twins available for research studies.
    c. twin research is compromised by the fact that most environmental influences on children raised in the same household are shared.
    d. dizygotic twins raised together share both genes and environment.

11. The attending physician explains that a young couple's new baby was born with a mixture of cells, some normal and some with too few or too many chromosomes. Evidently, this baby has the condition called:
    a. Down syndrome.   c. mosaic.
    b. fragile X syndrome.   d. PKU.

12. Laurie and Brad, who both have a history of alcoholism in their families, are concerned that the child they hope to have will inherit a genetic predisposition to alcoholism. Based on information presented in the text, what advice should you offer them?

    a. "Stop worrying, alcoholism is only weakly genetic."
    b. "It is almost certain that your child will become alcoholic."
    c. "Social influences, such as the family and peer environment, play a critical role in determining whether alcoholism is expressed."
    d. "Wait to have children until you are both middle aged, in order to see if the two of you become alcoholic."

13. Sixteen-year-old Joey experiences some mental slowness and hearing and heart problems, yet he is able to care for himself and is unusually sweet-tempered. Joey probably:

    a. has Tourette syndrome.
    b. has Alzheimer's disease.
    c. has Klinefelter syndrome.
    d. has Down syndrome.

14. Genetically, Claude's potential height is 6'0. Because he did not receive a balanced diet, however, he grew to only 5'9". Claude's actual height is an example of a:

    a. recessive gene.
    b. dominant gene.
    c. genotype.
    d. phenotype.

15. Winona inherited a gene from her mother that, regardless of her father's contribution to her genotype, will be expressed in her phenotype. Evidently, the gene Winona received from her mother is a(n) _____ gene.

    a. polygenic   c. dominant
    b. recessive   d. X-linked

Key Terms

Writing Definitions

Using your own words, write on a separate piece of paper a brief definition or explanation of each of the following terms.

1. DNA
2. chromosome
3. gene
4. genome
5. gamete
6. zygote
7. genotype
8. allele
9. 23rd pair
10. XX
11. XY
12. spontaneous abortion
13. induced abortion
14. phenotype
15. polygenic
16. multifactorial
17. Human Genome Project
18. additive gene
19. dominant—recessive pattern
20. X-linked
21. monozygotic (MZ) twins
22. dizygotic (DZ) twins
23. clone
24. in vitro fertilization
25. infertility
26. assisted reproductive technology (ART)
27. carrier
28. type 2 diabetes
29. mosaic
30. Down syndrome
31. fragile X syndrome
32. genetic counseling
33. phenylketonuria (PKU)

Cross-Check

After you have written the definitions of the key terms in this chapter, you should complete the crossword puzzle to ensure that you can reverse the process—recognize the term, given the definition.

ACROSS

2. Cluster of distinct characteristics that tend to occur together in a given disorder.
7. An organism's entire genetic inheritance.
9. The single cell formed from the fusing of an ovum and a sperm.
12. The stronger gene in an interacting pair of genes.
13. All the genetic traits that are expressed in a person.
15. Genes that are on the X chromosome.
16. The sequence of chemical bases held within DNA molecules that directs development.
17. One of 46 in each normal human cell.
18. A disease that nearly always develops in middle age in people with Down syndrome.
19. The genes that affect height, hair curliness, and skin color are of this type.

DOWN

1. A genetic disorder in which part of the X chromosome is attached to the rest of it by a very slim string of molecules.
3. Fraternal twins.
4. All the nongenetic factors that can affect development.
5. The growth process in which cells begin to specialize, taking different forms and dividing at different rates.
6. The basic unit of genetic instruction.
8. A spontaneous abortion.
10. The international project to map the complete human genetic code.
11. Type of trait produced by the interaction of many genes (rather than by a single gene).
12. The most common extra-chromosome syndrome (also called trisomy-21).
14. The weaker gene in an interacting pair of genes.

ANSWERS

CHAPTER REVIEW

1. proteins; DNA; chromosome
2. 46; 23; genes; protein; amino acids; genome
3. gametes; sperm; ova
4. zygote
5. 23; 23
6. genotype
7. autosomes; homozygous; heterozygous; alleles
8. 23rd; X; XX; X; Y; XY
9. sperm; 50/50; XY; spontaneous abortion; induced abortion
10. been roughly equal; abort female fetuses
11. phenotype
12. duplicate; divide; differentiate; switch; almost half
13. polygenic; multifactorial
14. Human Genome Project; share; regulator
15. additive; height; skin color (or hair curliness)
16. nonadditive; dominant–recessive; dominant; recessive
17. X-linked; color blindness, many allergies, several diseases, and some learning disabilities; males
18. X; inactive
19. zygote; are; 250; nongenetic

20. dizygotic; 50
21. ethnicity; age
22. clone; illegal; in vitro fertilization
23. infertility; assisted reproductive technology
24. drugs; artificial insemination
25. **a.** Genes affect every aspect of human behavior.

    b. Most environmental influences on children raised in the same household are not shared.

    c. Genes elicit responses from other people that shape each child's development.

    d. People of all ages choose environments that are compatible with their genes.
26. increase
27. carrier
28. addiction; personality; a quick temper, a readiness to take risks, and a high level of anxiety; gender; culture; less
29. nearsightedness; myopia; trauma; illness; nutrition; Vitamin A; close study of books and papers
30. protective; genetically; body fat
31. **a.** They provide insight into the complexities of genetic interactions.

    b. Knowledge about their origins suggests how to limit their harmful consequences.

    c. Misinformation and prejudice compound the problems of people who are affected by such abnormalities.
32. duplication; gametes
33. maternal age; mosaic
34. spontaneously aborted; 200; syndrome
35. Down Syndrome; trisomy-21; faster; Alzheimer's disease; communication

Most people with Down syndrome have certain facial characteristics—a thick tongue, round face, slanted eyes—as well as distinctive hands, feet, and fingerprints. Many also have hearing problems, heart abnormalities, muscle weakness, and short stature. Almost all experience some mental slowness, especially in language.

36. sex; Turner syndrome; X; Klinefelter syndrome; XXY
37. dominant; are not; rare; do not
38. Huntington's disease; Tourette syndrome
39. fragile X
40. cystic fibrosis, thalassemia, sickle-cell anemia
41. genetic counseling
42. Genetic counseling is recommended for (a) those who have a parent, sibling, or child with a serious genetic condition; (b) those who have a history of spontaneous abortions, stillbirths, or infertility; (c) couples who are from the same ethnic group or subgroup; and (d) women over age 35 and men age 40 or older.
43. phenylketonuria (PKU); phenylalanine

PROGRESS TEST 1

Multiple-Choice Questions

1. **a.** is the answer. (p. 63)

    b. & c. The reproductive cells (sperm and ova), which are also called gametes, are individual entities.

    d. Monozygote refers to one member of a pair of identical twins.

2. **c.** is the answer. (p. 61)

    a. The zygote is the first cell of the developing person.

    b. Chromosomes are molecules of DNA that *carry* genes.

    d. DNA molecules contain genetic information.

3. **b.** is the answer. (p. 64)

4. **d.** is the answer. When the gametes are formed, one member of each chromosome pair splits off; because in females both are X chromosomes, each ovum must carry an X chromosome. (p. 64)

    a., b., & c. The zygote refers to the merged sperm and ovum that is the first new cell of the developing individual.

5. **b.** is the answer. *Mono* means "one." Thus, monozygotic twins develop from one zygote. (p. 69)

    a. & c. Dizygotic, or fraternal, twins develop from two (*di*) zygotes.

    d. A trizygotic birth would result in triplets (*tri*), rather than twins.

6. **a.** is the answer. (p. 73)

7. **a.** is the answer. (p. 81)

    c. & d. Most dominant disorders are neither seriously disabling nor sex-linked.

8. **c.** is the answer. (p. 67)

    a., b., & d. *Polygenic* means "many genes"; *multifactorial* means "many factors," which are not limited to either genetic or environmental factors.

9. **b.** is the answer. (p. 61)

    a. Genotype is a person's genetic potential.

    c. A karyotype is a picture of a person's chromosomes.

d. Phenotype is the actual expression of a genotype.

10. a. is the answer. (p. 86)

11. d. is the answer. (p. 81)

a. & b. These chromosomal abnormalities affect females.

c. There is no such abnormality.

12. c. is the answer. (pp. 76–77)

a. Although nearsightedness is associated with rubella, there has not been an increase in rubella in these countries.

b. Vitamin A deficiencies may be a factor in the vision problems of children among certain African ethnic groups.

d. The rapid changes in the prevalence of myopia suggest that an environmental factor is the culprit.

13. a. is the answer. (p. 79)

14. b. is the answer. (p. 67)

15. b. is the answer. (p. 84)

a. & c. These abnormalities involve the sex chromosomes, not genes.

d. For an offspring to inherit a recessive condition, the parents need only be carriers of the recessive gene in their genotypes; they need not actually have the disease.

Matching Items

1. c (p. 63)	**6.** f (p. 70)	**11.** k (p. 64)
2. h (p. 61)	**7.** g (p. 67)	**12.** a (p. 64)
3. m (p. 63)	**8.** j (p. 81)	**13.** l (p. 64)
4. i (p. 66)	**9.** e (p. 73)	
5. b (p. 69)	**10.** d (p. 63)	

PROGRESS TEST 2

Multiple-Choice Questions

1. d. is the answer. (pp. 73–74)

2. d. is the answer. (pp. 77–78)

3. c. is the answer. (p. 81)

a. Physical appearance is usually normal in this syndrome.

b. Males are more frequently and more severely affected.

d. This is true of the XXY chromosomal abnormality, but not the fragile X syndrome.

4. d. is the answer. (p. 61)

a. & c. Human cells contain thousands of genes.

5. c. is the answer. (p. 81)

a. This syndrome involves inheriting an *extra* chromosome.

d. This syndrome involves inheriting three sex chromosomes in an XXY pattern.

6. c. is the answer. (p. 70)

a. This would result in monozygotic twins.

b. Only one sperm can fertilize an ovum.

d. A single egg fertilized by one sperm would produce a single offspring or monozygotic twins.

7. c. is the answer. (p. 61)

a. Zygotes are fertilized ova.

b. Genes are the smaller units of heredity that are organized into sequences on chromosomes.

d. Ova are female reproductive cells.

8. a. is the answer. (p. 66)

9. c. is the answer. The ovum will contain an X chromosome; with the sperm's Y chromosome, it will produce the male XY pattern. (p. 64)

a. Only if the ovum is fertilized by an X chromosome from the sperm will a female develop.

b. Cell division will occur regardless of whether the sperm contributes an X or a Y chromosome.

d. Spontaneous abortions are likely to occur when there are chromosomal or genetic abnormalities; the situation described is perfectly normal.

10. a. is the answer. (p. 63)

b. & d. These are true of all body cells *except* the gametes.

c. Gametes have either X or Y chromosomes.

11. d. is the answer. (p. 67)

12. a. is the answer. Genotype refers to the sum total of all the genes a person inherits; phenotype refers to the actual expression of the individual's characteristics. (pp. 63, 66)

13. c. is the answer. (p. 67)

14. d. is the answer. X-linked genes are located only on the X chromosome. Because males inherit only one X chromosome, they are more likely than females to have these characteristics in their phenotype. (p. 68)

15. a. is the answer. (p. 71)

b. This describes artificial insemination.

c. & d. These answers, which are too general, describe all forms of assisted reproductive technology.

True or False Items

1. T (p. 67)
2. F Chromosomal abnormalities may be environmentally caused, as with parents' exposure to excessive radiation. (p. 79)
3. T (pp. 74, 75)
4. T (p. 63)
5. F Most traits are polygenic. (p. 67)
6. T (p. 63)
7. T (p. 85)
8. F A trait from a recessive gene will be part of the phenotype only when the person has two recessive genes for that trait. (p. 84)
9. T (p. 66)
10. T (p. 63)
11. F Most genes have several functions. (p. 67)

DEVELOPMENTAL PSYCHOLOGY APPLIED

1. **d.** is the answer. (p. 81)
2. **b.** is the answer. (p. 72)
3. **c.** is the answer. This describes the fragile X syndrome. (p. 81)

   a. This phenomenon, which is called *crossing over,* merely contributes to genetic diversity.

   b. This is merely an example of a particular non-additive gene interaction pattern.

   d. For a recessive gene to be expressed, both parents must pass it on to the child.
4. **a.** is the answer. (p. 68)

   b. The male genotype is XY, not XX.

   c. & d. The mother contributes only an X chromosome.
5. **c.** is the answer. (p. 67)

   a., b., & d. It is unlikely that these factors account for height differences from one generation to the next.
6. **b.** is the answer. Because monozygotic twins are genetically identical, while dizygotic twins share only 50 percent of their genes, greater similarity of traits between monozygotic twins suggests that genes are an important influence. (pp. 69–70)

a. & c. Even though schizophrenia has a strong genetic component, it is not the case that if one twin has schizophrenia the other also automatically does. Therefore, the environment, too, is an important influence.

d. This does not necessarily follow.

7. **a.** is the answer. (p. 73)

   b. Genotype is a person's genetic potential, established at conception.

   c. Polygenic inheritance refers to the influence of many genes on a particular trait.

   d. Incomplete dominance refers to the phenotype being influenced primarily, but not exclusively, by the dominant gene.
8. **d.** is the answer. (p. 81)
9. **c.** is the answer. Cystic fibrosis is a recessive-gene disorder; therefore, for a child to inherit this disease, he or she must receive the recessive gene from both parents. (p. 84)
10. **a.** is the answer. (p. 73)

    b. Although identical twins are not common, there have been a number of studies of their traits.

    c. In fact, most environmental influences on children raised in the same household are not shared.
11. **c.** is the answer. (p. 79)
12. **c.** is the answer. (pp. 74, 75)

    a. Some people's inherited biochemistry makes them highly susceptible to alcoholism.

    b. Despite a strong genetic influence on alcoholism, the environment also plays a critical role.

    d. Not only is this advice unreasonable, but it might increase the likelihood of chromosomal abnormalities in the parents' sperm and ova.
13. **d.** is the answer. (pp. 79–80)
14. **d.** is the answer. (p. 66)

    a. & b. Genes are separate units of a chromosome.

    c. Genotype refers to genetic potential.
15. **c.** is the answer. (p. 68)

    a. There is no such thing as a "polygenic gene." *Polygenic* means "many genes."

    b. A recessive gene paired with a dominant gene will not be expressed in the phenotype.

    d. X-linked genes may be dominant or recessive.

KEY TERMS

Writing Definitions

1. **DNA (deoxyribonucleic acid)** is the molecule that contains the chemical instructions for cells to manufacture various proteins. (p. 61)

2. **Chromosomes** are molecules of DNA that contain the genes organized in precise sequences. (p. 61)

3. **Genes** are segments of a chromosome, which is a DNA molecule; they are the basic units for the transmission of hereditary instructions. (p. 61)

4. The **genome** is the full set of 25,000 or so genes that are the instructions to make a member of a certain species. (p. 62)

5. **Gametes** are the human reproductive cells. (p. 63)

6. The **zygote** is the one-celled organism formed during conception by the union of sperm and ovum. (p. 63)

7. The total of all the genes a person inherits—his or her genetic potential—is called the **genotype.** (p. 63)

8. An **allele** is one of the normal versions of a gene that has several possible sequences of base pairs. (p. 64)

9. The **23rd pair** of chromosomes, in humans, determines the individual's sex. (p. 64)

10. **XX** is the 23rd chromosome pair that, in humans, determines that the developing fetus will be female. (p. 64)

11. **XY** is the 23rd chromosome pair that, in humans, determines that the developing fetus will be male. (p. 64)

12. Also known as a miscarriage, a **spontaneous abortion** is the natural termination of a pregnancy before the fetus is fully developed. (p. 64)

13. An **induced abortion** is the intentional termination of a pregnancy. (p. 64)

14. The actual physical or behavioral expression of a genotype, the result of the interaction of the genes with each other and with the environment, is called the **phenotype.** (p. 66)

15. Most human traits are **polygenic;** that is, they are affected by many genes. (p. 67)

16. Most human traits are also **multifactorial**—that is, influenced by many factors, including genetic and environmental factors. (p. 67)

    Memory aid: The roots of the words polygenic and multifactorial give their meaning: *poly* means "many" and genic means "of the genes"; *multi* means "several" and factorial obviously refers to factors.

17. **The Human Genome Project** is an international effort to map the complete human genetic code. (p. 67)

18. When a trait is determined by **additive genes,** the phenotype reflects the sum of the contributions of all the genes involved. The genes affecting height, for example, interact in this fashion. (p. 67)

19. The **dominant–recessive** pattern is the interaction of a gene's alleles in such a way that one, the dominant gene, has a stronger influence than the other, recessive gene. (p. 68)

20. **X-linked** genes are genes that are located only on the X chromosome. Because males have only one X chromosome, they are more likely than females to have the characteristics determined by these genes in their phenotype. (p. 68)

21. **Monozygotic (MZ) twins** develop from one zygote that splits apart, producing genetically identical zygotes; also called *identical twins.* (p. 69)

    Memory aid: Mono means "one"; **monozygotic twins** develop from one fertilized ovum.

22. **Dizygotic (DZ) twins** develop from two separate ova fertilized by different sperm at roughly the same time, and therefore are no more genetically similar than ordinary siblings; also called **fraternal twins** (p. 70)

    Memory aid: A fraternity is a group of two (*di*) or more nonidentical individuals.

23. A **clone** is an artificially created organism that has exactly the same genotype as another living organism. (p. 70)

24. **In vitro fertilization (IVF)** is a form of ART in which ova surgically removed from a woman are mixed with sperm. If a zygote is produced, it is inserted in the woman's uterus after three duplications. (p. 71)

25. **Infertility** is the inability to produce a baby after at least one year of trying. (p. 71)

26. **Assisted reproductive technology (ART)** refers to the various techniques available to help infertile couples conceive and sustain a pregnancy. (p. 71)

27. A person who has a recessive gene that is not expressed in his or her genotype but that can be passed on to the person's offspring is called a **carrier** of that gene. (p. 73)

28. **Type 2 diabetes** is a chronic illness in which the body doesn't produce sufficient insulin to metabolize glucose. (p. 77)

29. **Mosaic** refers to the condition in which a person has a mixture of cells, some normal and some with too few or too many chromosomes. (p. 79)

30. **Down syndrome** (*trisomy-21*) is the most common extra-chromosome condition. People with Down syndrome age faster than others, often have unusual facial features and heart abnormalities, and invariably develop Alzheimer's disease. (p. 79)

31. The **fragile X syndrome** is a single-gene disorder in which part of the X chromosome is attached by such a thin string of molecules that it seems about to break off. Although the characteristics associated with this syndrome are quite varied, some mental deficiency is relatively common. (p. 81)

32. **Genetic counseling** involves a variety of tests through which couples can learn more about their genes, and can thus make informed decisions about their childbearing and child-rearing future. (p. 84)

33. **Phenylketonuria (PKU)** is a genetic disorder in which the body cannot metabolize the common food substance phenylalanine. (p. 86)

Cross-Check

ACROSS
2. syndrome
7. genotype
9. zygote
12. dominant
13. phenotype
15. X-linked
16. genetic code
17. chromosome
18. Alzheimer's
19. additive

DOWN
1. fragile X
3. dizygotic
4. environment
5. differentiation
6. gene
8. miscarriage
10. Human Genome
11. polygenic
12. Down syndrome
14. recessive

4

Prenatal Development and Birth

Chapter Overview

Prenatal development is complex and startlingly rapid—more rapid than any other period of the life span. During prenatal development, the individual changes from a one-celled zygote to a complex human baby. This development is outlined in Chapter 4, along with some of the problems that can occur—among them prenatal exposure to disease, drugs, and other hazards—and the factors that moderate the risks of teratogenic exposure.

For the developing person, birth marks the most radical transition of the entire life span. No longer sheltered from the outside world, the fetus becomes a separate human being who begins life almost completely dependent upon his or her caregivers. Chapter 4 also examines the birth process and its possible variations and problems.

The chapter concludes with a discussion of the significance of the parent–infant bond, including factors that affect its development.

NOTE: Answer guidelines for all Chapter 4 questions begin on page 63.

Guided Study

The text chapter should be studied one section at a time. Before you read, preview each section by skimming it, noting headings and boldface items. Then read the appropriate section objectives from the following outline. Keep these objectives in mind and, as you read the chapter section, search for the information that will enable you to meet each objective. Once you have finished a section, write out answers for its objectives.

From Zygote to Newborn (pp. 91–96)

1. Describe the significant developments of the germinal period.

2. Describe the significant developments of the embryonic period.

3. Describe the significant developments of the fetal period, noting the importance of the age of viability.

Risk Reduction (pp. 97–108)

4. Explain the main goal of teratology, and discuss several factors that determine whether a specific teratogen will be harmful.

5. (text and Thinking Like a Scientist) Discuss protective steps that may be taken to prevent the damaging effects of teratogens, emphasizing the effects of alcohol use by the expectant mother.

6. (Table 4.4) Identify at least five teratogens, and describe their effects on the developing embryo or fetus.

7. (text and Table 4.5) Discuss the benefits of prenatal care, and describe methods of postconception testing.

The Birth Process (pp. 108–119)

8. Describe the birth process, the possible need for medical intervention during this process, and the test used to assess the new born's condition at birth.

9. Explain the causes and effects of anoxia and low birthweight, and distinguish the various forms of low-birthweight (LBW) babies from preterm and small-for-gestational-age (SGA) infants.

10. Discuss the importance of social support, a strong parental alliance, and parent–infant bonding to a healthy start for the baby.

Chapter Review

When you have finished reading the chapter, work through the material that follows to review it. Complete the sentences and answer the questions. As you proceed, evaluate your performance for each section by consulting the answers beginning on page 63. Do not continue with the next section until you understand each answer. If you need to, review or reread the appropriate section in the textbook before continuing.

From Zygote to Newborn (pp. 91–96)

1. Prenatal development is divided into _____ main periods. The first two weeks of development are called the _____ period; from the _____ week through the _____ week is known as the _____ period; and from this point until birth is the _____ period.

2. Once clusters of cells begin to take on distinct characteristics, the cell mass is called a _____ . About one week after conception, the multiplying cells separate into outer cells that will become the _____ and inner cells that will become the _____ .

3. The next significant event is the burrowing of the zygote into the lining of the uterus, a process called _____ . This process _____ (is/is not) automatic.

4. At the beginning of the period of the embryo, a thin line down the middle of the developing individual forms a structure that will become the _____ _____ , which becomes the _____ _____ and eventually will develop into the _____ _____ _____ .

Briefly describe the major features of development during the second month.

5. Eight weeks after conception, the embryo weighs about _____ and is about _____ in length. From the ninth week after conception until birth, the organism is called the _____ .

6. The genital organs are fully formed by week _____ . If the fetus has a(n) _____ chromosome, the _____ gene on this chromosome sends a signal that triggers development of the _____ (male/female) sex organs. Without that gene, no signal is sent and the fetus begins to develop _____ (male/female) sex organs.

7. By the end of the _____ month, the fetus is fully formed, weighs approximately _____ , and is about _____ long. These figures _____ (vary/do not vary) from fetus to fetus.

8. During the fourth, fifth, and sixth months, the brain increases in size by a factor of _____ . The brain develops new neurons in a process called _____ and new connections between them in a process called _____ . This neurological maturation is essential to the regulation of such basic body functions as _____ and _____ .

9. The age at which a fetus has at least some chance of surviving outside the uterus is called the _____ _____ _____ , which occurs _____ weeks after conception. This barrier _____ (has/has not) been reduced by advances in neonatal care, probably because maintaining life depends on some _____ response.

10. At about _____ weeks after concep- tion, brain-wave patterns begin to resemble the _____–_____ cycles of a newborn.

11. A 28-week-old fetus typically weighs about _____ and has about a _____ percent chance of survival.

12. Three crucial aspects of development in the last months of prenatal life are maturation of the _____ , _____ , and _____ systems.

13. By full term, brain growth is so extensive that the brain's advanced outer areas, called the _____ , must _____ _____ in order to fit into the skull.

14. In the final _____ (how many?) months, the fetus hears many sounds, including the mother's _____ and _____ .

Risk Reduction (pp. 97–108)

15. The scientific study of birth defects is called _____ . Harmful agents that can cause birth defects, called _____ , include _____ _____ .

16. Substances that impair the child's action and intellect by harming the brain are called _____ _____ .

    Approximately _____ percent of all children are born with behavioral difficulties that could be connected to behavioral teratogens.

17. Teratology is a science of _____ _____ , which attempts to evaluate the factors that can make prenatal harm more or less likely to occur.

18. Three crucial factors that determine whether a specific teratogen will cause harm, and of what nature, are the _____ of exposure, the _____ of exposure, and the developing organism's _____ _____ to damage from the substance.

19. The time when a particular part of the body is most susceptible to teratogenic damage is called its _____ _____ . For physical structure and form, this is the entire period of the _____ . However, for _____ teratogens, the entire prenatal period is critical.

20. Some teratogens have a _____ effect—that is, the substances are harmless until exposure reaches a certain frequency or amount. Others have an _____ effect, which occurs when some teratogens taken together make them more harmful at lower dosage levels than when taken separately.

21. Cleft palate, cleft lip, and club foot result from a combination of _____ _____ , _____ , and inadequate _____ .

22. When the mother-to-be's diet is deficient in _____ _____ , neural- tube defects such as _____ _____ or _____ may result. These defects occur more commonly in certain _____ groups.

23. Genetic vulnerability is also related to the sex of the developing organism. Generally, _____ (male/female) embryos and fetuses are more vulnerable to teratogens. This sex not only has more frequent _____ _____ and a higher rate of terato- genic birth defects, _____ _____ , and other behavioral problems.

24. Women are advised to avoid all
_____ before becoming pregnant,
especially _____
_____ . Prenatal
development can also be impaired by
_____ .

25. (Thinking Like a Scientist) High doses of alcohol
during pregnancy may cause _____
_____ _____ .

26. One advantage of early prenatal care is protection
against _____ . An image of the
fetus, called a _____ , allows doc-
tors to see if the fetus is developing normally.

27. (Table 4.5) There are a number of tests to determine whether a pregnancy is problematic.
Among them are the _____-
_____ _____ , which
tests for neural-tube defects; the
_____ , which shows body malfor-
mations; and _____ , which shows
chromosomal abnormalities and other genetic
and prenatal problems.

28. Although pediatric AIDS has almost disappeared
from _____ _____ and
_____ , it is still on the rise in
_____ .

The Birth Process (pp. 108–119)

29. About _____ (how many?) weeks
after conception, the fetal brain signals the release
of certain _____ into the mother's
bloodstream, which trigger her
_____ _____
to contract and relax. The normal birth process
begins when these contractions become regular.
The average length of labor is
_____ hours for first births and
_____ hours for subsequent births.

30. The newborn is usually rated on the
_____ _____ , which
assigns a score of 0, 1, or 2 to each of the following five characteristics: _____
_____ . A
score below _____ indicates that the
newborn is in critical condition and requires
immediate attention; if the score is
_____ or better, all is well. This rat-
ing is made twice, at _____
minute(s) after birth and again at
_____ minutes.

31. The birth experience is influenced by several
factors, including _____
_____ .

32. In about 28 percent of U.S. births, a surgical
procedure called a _____
_____ is performed.

33. A growing number of North American mothers
today use a professional birth coach, or
_____ , to assist them.

34. The disorder _____
_____ , which affects motor centers
in the brain, often results from
_____ vulnerability, worsened by
exposure to _____ and a preterm
birth that involves _____ , a temporary lack of _____ during birth.

35. Newborns who weigh less than
_____ are classified as
_____-_____ babies.
Below 3 pounds, 5 ounces, they are called
_____-_____-
_____ babies; at less than 2 pounds,
3 ounces, they are _____-
_____-_____ babies.
Worldwide, rates of this condition
_____ (vary/do not vary) from
nation to nation.

36. Babies who are born 3 or more weeks early are
called _____ .

37. Infants who weigh substantially less than they should, given how much time has passed since conception, are called _____ _____ _____ .

38. About 25 percent of all low-birthweight (LBW) births are linked to maternal use of _____ .

39. Another other common reason for low birth-weight is maternal _____ . In addition, _____ births are more likely to result in LBW. Consequently, the rate of LBW has increased dramatically with the use of _____ _____ _____ .

40. LBW babies are more likely to become adults who are _____ and have health problems, especially affecting the _____ .

41. Providing extra soothing stimulation to vulnerable infants in the hospital _____ (does/does not) aid weight gain and _____ (does/does not) increase overall alertness. One example of this is _____ _____ , in which mothers of low-birthweight infants spend extra time holding their infants between their breasts.

42. The deficits related to low birthweight usually _____ (can/cannot) be overcome. Especially important is the role played by a supportive _____ , who can help _____ _____ .

43. A crucial factor in the birth experience is the formation of a strong _____ _____ between the prospective parents.

44. Some new mothers experience a profound feeling of sadness called _____ .

45. The term used to describe the close relationship that begins within the first hours after birth is the _____ – _____ _____ .

Progress Test 1

Multiple-Choice Questions

Circle your answers to the following questions and check them with the answers on page 64. If your answer is incorrect, read the explanation for why it is incorrect and then consult the appropriate pages of the text (in parentheses following the correct answer).

1. The third through the eighth week after conception is called the:
   a. embryonic period.
   b. ovum period.
   c. fetal period.
   d. germinal period.

2. The primitive streak develops into the:
   a. respiratory system.
   b. umbilical cord.
   c. brain and spinal column.
   d. circulatory system.

3. To say that a teratogen has a "threshold effect" means that it is:
   a. virtually harmless until exposure reaches a certain level.
   b. harmful only to low-birthweight infants.
   c. harmful to certain developing organs during periods when these organs are developing most rapidly.
   d. harmful only if the pregnant woman's weight does not increase by a certain minimum amount during her pregnancy.

4. By the eighth week after conception, the embryo has almost all the basic organs except the:
   a. skeleton.   c. sex organs.
   b. elbows and knees. d. fingers and toes.

5. The most critical factor in attaining the age of viability is development of the:
   a. placenta.   c. brain.
   b. eyes.   d. skeleton.

6. An important nutrient that many women do not get in adequate amounts from the typical diet is:
   a. vitamin A.   c. guanine.
   b. zinc.   d. folic acid.

7. An embryo begins to develop male sex organs if _____ , and female sex organs if _____ .
   a. genes on the Y chromosome send a signal; no signal is sent from an X chromosome
   b. genes on the Y chromosome send a signal; genes on the X chromosome send a signal

c. genes on the *X* chromosome send a signal; no signal is sent from an *X* chromosome

d. genes on the *X* chromosome send a signal; genes on the *Y* chromosome send a signal

8. A teratogen:

a. cannot cross the placenta during the period of the embryo.

b. is usually inherited from the mother.

c. can be counteracted by good nutrition most of the time.

d. may be a virus, a drug, a chemical, radiation, or environmental pollutants.

9. (Thinking Like A Scientist) Among the characteristics of babies born with fetal alcohol syndrome are:

a. slowed physical growth and behavior problems.

b. addiction to alcohol and methadone.

c. deformed arms and legs.

d. blindness.

10. The birth process begins:

a. when the fetus moves into the right position.

b. when the uterus begins to contract at regular intervals to push the fetus out.

c. about eight hours (for firstborns) after the uterus begins to contract at regular intervals.

d. when the baby's head appears at the opening of the vagina.

11. The Apgar scale is administered:

a. only if the newborn is in obvious distress.

b. once, just after birth.

c. twice, one minute and five minutes after birth.

d. repeatedly during the newborn's first hours.

12. Most newborns weigh about:

a. 5 pounds. **c.** $7^1/_2$ pounds.

b. 6 pounds. **d.** $8^1/_2$ pounds.

13. Low-birthweight babies born near the due date but weighing substantially less than they should:

a. are classified as preterm.

b. are called small for gestational age.

c. usually have no sex organs.

d. show many signs of immaturity.

14. Approximately one out of every four low-birthweight births in the United States is caused by maternal use of:

a. alcohol. **c.** crack cocaine.

b. tobacco. **d.** household chemicals.

15. The idea of a parent–infant bond in humans arose from:

a. observations in the delivery room.

b. data on adopted infants.

c. animal studies.

d. studies of disturbed mother–infant pairs.

Matching Items

Match each definition or description with its corresponding term.

Terms

_____ **1.** embryonic period
_____ **2.** fetal period
_____ **3.** placenta
_____ **4.** preterm
_____ **5.** teratogens
_____ **6.** anoxia
_____ **7.** doula
_____ **8.** critical period
_____ **9.** primitive streak
_____ **10.** fetal alcohol syndrome
_____ **11.** germinal period

Definitions or Descriptions

a. term for the period during which a developing baby's body parts are most susceptible to damage

b. external agents and conditions that can damage the developing organism

c. the age when viability is attained

d. the precursor of the central nervous system

e. lack of oxygen, which, if prolonged during the birth process, may lead to brain damage.

f. characterized by abnormal facial characteristics, slowed growth, behavior problems, and mental retardation

g. a woman who helps with the birth process

h. the life-giving organ that nourishes the embryo and fetus

i. when implantation occurs

j. the prenatal period when all major body structures begin to form

k. a baby born 3 or more weeks early

Progress Test 2

Progress Test 2 should be completed during a final chapter review. Answer the following questions after you thoroughly understand the correct answers for the Chapter Review and Progress Test 1.

Multiple-Choice Questions

1. A 35-year-old woman who is pregnant is most likely to undergo which type of test for the detection of prenatal chromosomal or genetic abnormalities?
   a. pre-implantation testing
   b. ultrasound
   c. amniocentesis
   d. alpha-fetoprotein assay

2. In order, the correct sequence of prenatal stages of development is:
   a. embryo; germinal; fetus
   b. germinal; fetus; embryo
   c. germinal; embryo; fetus
   d. ovum; fetus; embryo

3. Monika is preparing for the birth of her first child. If all proceeds normally, she can expect that her labor will last about:
   a. 7 hours.   c. 10 hours.
   b. 8 hours.   d. 12 hours.

4. (Table 4.4) Tetracycline and retinoic acid:
   a. can be harmful to the human fetus.
   b. have been proven safe for pregnant women after the embryonic period.
   c. will prevent spontaneous abortions.
   d. are safe when used before the fetal period.

5. (Table 4.4) The teratogen that, if not prevented by immunization, could cause deafness, blindness, and brain damage in the fetus is:
   a. rubella (German measles).
   b. anoxia.
   c. acquired immune deficiency syndrome (AIDS).
   d. neural-tube defect.

6. Kangaroo care refers to:
   a. the rigid attachment formed between mothers and offspring in the animal kingdom
   b. the fragmented care that the children of single parents often receive.
   c. a program of increased involvement by mothers of low-birthweight infants.
   d. none of the above.

7. Among the characteristics rated on the Apgar scale are:
   a. shape of the newborn's head and nose.
   b. presence of body hair.
   c. interactive behaviors.
   d. muscle tone and color.

8. A newborn is classified as low birthweight if he or she weighs less than:
   a. 7 pounds.   c. 5^1/$_2$ pounds.
   b. 6 pounds.   d. 4 pounds.

9. A critical problem for preterm babies is:
   a. the immaturity of the sex organs—for example, undescended testicles.
   b. spitting up or hiccupping.
   c. infection from intravenous feeding.
   d. breathing difficulties.

10. (Thinking Like a Scientist) Which of the following is *not* true regarding alcohol use and pregnancy?
    a. Alcohol in high doses is a proven teratogen.
    b. Not every pregnant woman who drinks heavily has a newborn with fetal alcohol syndrome.
    c. Most doctors in the United States advise pregnant women to use alcohol in moderation during pregnancy.
    d. Only after a fetus is born does fetal alcohol syndrome become apparent.

11. Neurogenesis refers to the process by which:
    a. the fetal brain develops new neurons.
    b. new connections between neurons develop.
    c. the neural tube forms during the middle trimester.
    d. the cortex folds into layers in order to fit into the skull.

12. Which Apgar score indicates that a newborn is in normal health?
    a. 4   c. 6
    b. 5   d. 7

13. Synaptogenesis refers to the process by which:
    a. the fetal brain develops new neurons.
    b. new connections between neurons develop.
    c. the neural tube forms during the middle trimester.
    d. the cortex folds into layers in order to fit into the skull.

14. When there is a strong parental alliance:
    a. mother and father cooperate because of their mutual commitment to their children.
    b. the parents agree to support each other in their shared parental roles.
    c. children are likely to thrive.
    d. all of the above are true.

15. The critical period for preventing physical defects appears to be the:
    a. zygote period.
    b. embryonic period.
    c. fetal period.
    d. entire pregnancy.

True or False Items

Write T (*true*) or F (*false*) on the line in front of each statement.

_____ 1. Newborns can recognize some of what they heard while in the womb.

_____ 2. Eight weeks after conception, the embryo has formed almost all the basic organs.

_____ 3. Only 1 percent of births in the United States take place in the home.

_____ 4. In general, behavioral teratogens have the greatest effect during the embryonic period.

_____ 5. The effects of cigarette smoking during pregnancy remain highly controversial.

_____ 6. The Apgar scale is used to measure vital signs such as heart rate, breathing, and reflexes.

_____ 7. Newborns usually cry on their own, moments after birth.

_____ 8. Research has shown that immediate mother–infant contact at birth is necessary for the normal emotional development of the child.

_____ 9. Low birthweight is often correlated with maternal malnutrition.

_____ 10. Cesarean sections are rarely performed in the United States today because of the resulting danger to the fetus.

Developmental Psychology Applied

Answer these questions the day before an exam as a final check on your understanding of the chapter's terms and concepts.

1. (Table 4.4 and Thinking Like a Scientist) Babies born to mothers who are powerfully addicted to a psychoactive drug are *most* likely to suffer from:
   a. structural problems.
   b. behavioral problems.
   c. both a. and b.
   d. neither a. nor b.

2. I am about 1 inch long and 1 gram in weight. I have all the basic organs (except sex organs) and features of a human being. What am I?
   a. a zygote   c. a fetus
   b. an embryo   d. ovum

3. Karen and Brad report to their neighbors that, 5 weeks after conception, a sonogram of their child-to-be revealed female sex organs. The neighbors are skeptical of their statement because:
   a. sonograms are never administered before the ninth week.
   b. sonograms only reveal the presence or absence of male sex organs.
   c. the fetus does not begin to develop female sex organs until about the eighth week.
   d. it is impossible to determine that a woman is pregnant until six weeks after conception.

4. Five-year-old Benjamin can't sit quietly and concentrate on a task for more than a minute at a time. Dr. Simmons, who is a teratologist, suspects that Benjamin may have been exposed to _____ during prenatal development.
   a. human immunodeficiency virus
   b. a behavioral teratogen
   c. rubella
   d. lead

5. Sylvia and Stan, who are of British descent, are hoping to have a child. Dr. Caruthers asks for a complete nutritional history and is particularly concerned when she discovers that Sylvia may have a deficiency of folic acid in her diet. Dr. Caruthers is probably worried about the risk of _____ in the couple's offspring.
   a. FAS
   b. brain damage
   c. neural-tube defects
   d. respiratory problems

6. Three-year-old Kenny was born underweight and premature. Today, he is small for his age. His doctor suspects that:
   a. Kenny is a victim of fetal alcohol syndrome.
   b. Kenny suffers from fetal alcohol effects.
   c. Kenny's mother smoked heavily during her pregnancy.
   d. Kenny's mother used cocaine during her pregnancy.

7. Which of the following is an example of an inter-action effect?
   a. Some teratogens are virtually harmless until exposure reaches a certain level.
   b. Maternal use of alcohol and tobacco together does more harm to the developing fetus than either teratogen would do alone.
   c. Some teratogens cause damage only on specific days during prenatal development.
   d. All of the above are examples of interaction effects.

8. Fetal alcohol syndrome is common in newborns whose mothers were heavy drinkers during pregnancy, whereas newborns whose mothers were moderate drinkers may suffer fetal alcohol effects. This finding shows that to assess and understand risk we must know:
   a. the kind of alcoholic beverage (for example, beer, wine, or whiskey).
   b. the level of exposure to the teratogen.
   c. whether the substance really is teratogenic.
   d. the timing of exposure to the teratogen.

9. Your sister and brother-in-law, who are about to adopt a 1-year-old, are worried that the child will never bond with them. What advice should you offer?
   a. Tell them that, unfortunately, this is true; they would be better off waiting for a younger child who has not yet bonded.
   b. Tell them that, although the first year is a biologically determined critical period for attachment, there is a 50/50 chance that the child will bond with them.
   c. Tell them that bonding is a long-term process between parent and child that is determined by the nature of interaction throughout infancy, childhood, and beyond.
   d. Tell them that if the child is female, there is a good chance that she will bond with them, even at this late stage.

10. Which of the following newborns would be most likely to have problems in body structure and functioning?
    a. Anton, whose Apgar score is 6
    b. Debora, whose Apgar score is 7
    c. Sheila, whose Apgar score is 3
    d. Simon, whose Apgar score is 5

11. At birth, Clarence was classified as small for gestational age. It is likely that Clarence:
    a. was born in a rural hospital.
    b. suffered several months of prenatal malnutrition.
    c. was born in a large city hospital.
    d. comes from a family with a history of such births.

12. Of the following, who is *most* likely to give birth to a low-birthweight child?
    a. 21-year-old Janice, who was herself a low-birthweight baby
    b. 25-year-old May Ling, who gained 25 pounds during her pregnancy
    c. 16-year-old Donna, who diets frequently despite being underweight
    d. 30-year-old Maria, who has already given birth to 4 children

13. An infant born 38 weeks after conception, weighing 4 pounds, would be designated a _____ infant.
    a. preterm
    b. low-birthweight
    c. small-for-gestational-age
    d. b. & c.

14. An infant who was born at 35 weeks, weighing 6 pounds, would be called a _____ infant.
    a. preterm
    b. low-birthweight
    c. small-for-gestational-age
    d. premature

15. The five characteristics evaluated by the Apgar scale are:
    a. heart rate, length, weight, muscle tone, and color.
    b. orientation, muscle tone, reflexes, interaction, and responses to stress.
    c. reflexes, breathing, muscle tone, heart rate, and color.
    d. pupillary response, heart rate, reflex irritability, alertness, and breathing.

Key Terms

Using your own words, write a brief definition or explanation of each of the following terms on a separate piece of paper.

1. germinal period
2. embryonic period
3. fetal period
4. blastocyst
5. placenta
6. implantation
7. embryo
8. fetus
9. age of viability
10. teratogens
11. behavioral teratogens
12. risk analysis
13. critical period
14. threshold effect
15. interaction effect
16. fetal alcohol syndrome (FAS)
17. Apgar scale
18. cesarean section
19. doula
20. anoxia
21. cerebral palsy
22. low birthweight (LBW)
23. very low birthweight (VLBW)
24. extremely low birthweight (ELBW)
25. preterm birth
26. small for gestational age (SGA)
27. kangaroo care
28. parental alliance
29. postpartum depression
30. parent–infant bond

ANSWERS

CHAPTER REVIEW

1. three; germinal; third; eighth; embryonic; fetal
2. blastocyst; placenta; embryo
3. implantation; is not

4. primitive streak; neural tube; central nervous system

The head begins to take shape as the eyes, ears, nose, and mouth start to form. A tiny blood vessel that will become the heart begins to pulsate. The upper arms, then the forearms, palms, and webbed fingers appear. Legs, feet, and webbed toes follow. At eight weeks, the embryo's head is more rounded, and the facial features are formed. The embryo has all the basic organs and body parts (except sex organs).

5. $1/30$ ounce (1 gram); 1 inch (2.5 centimeters); fetus
6. 12; Y; SRY; male; female
7. third; 3 ounces (87 grams); 3 inches (7.5 centimeters); vary
8. six; neurogenesis; synaptogenesis; breathing; sucking
9. age of viability; 22; has not; brain
10. 28; sleep–wake
11. 3 pounds (1.3 kilograms); 95
12. neurological; respiratory; cardiovascular
13. cortex; fold into layers
14. three; heartbeat; voice
15. teratology; teratogens; viruses, drugs, chemicals, pollutants, stressors, and malnutrition
16. behavioral teratogens; 20
17. risk analysis
18. timing; amount; genetic vulnerability
19. critical period; embryo; behavioral
20. threshold; interaction
21. genetic vulnerability; stress; nutrition
22. folic acid; spina bifida; microcephaly; ethnic
24. male; spontaneous abortions; learning disabilities
25. fetal alcohol syndrome
26. teratogens; sonogram
27. alpha-fetoprotein assay; sonogram; amniocentesis
28. North America; Europe; Africa
29. 38; hormones; uterine muscles; 12; 7
30. Apgar scale; heart rate, breathing, muscle tone, color, and reflexes; 4; 7; one; five
31. the parents' preparation for birth, the physical and emotional support provided by birth attendants, the position and size of the fetus, the customs of the culture
32. cesarean section
33. doula
34. cerebral palsy; genetic; teratogens; anoxia; oxygen

35. 2,490 grams (5½ pounds); low-birthweight; very-low-birthweight; extremely-low-birthweight; vary

36. preterm

37. small for gestational age

38. tobacco

39. malnutrition; multiple; assisted reproductive technology

40. overweight; heart

41. does; does; kangaroo care

42. can; father; the mother-to-be stay healthy, well nourished, and drug-free.

43. parental alliance

44. postpartum depression

45. parent–infant bond

PROGRESS TEST 1

Multiple-Choice Questions

1. **a.** is the answer. (p. 91)

    b. This term, which refers to the germinal period, is not used in the text.

    c. The fetal period is from the ninth week until birth.

    d. The germinal period covers the first two weeks.

2. **c.** is the answer. (p. 93)

3. **a.** is the answer. (p. 98)

    b., c., & d. Although low birthweight (b), critical periods of organ development (c), and maternal malnutrition (d) are all hazardous to the developing person during prenatal development, none is an example of a threshold effect.

4. **c.** is the answer. The sex organs do not begin to take shape until the fetal period. (pp. 93–94)

5. **c.** is the answer. (p. 95)

6. **d.** is the answer. (p. 100)

7. **a.** is the answer. (p. 94)

8. **d.** is the answer. (p. 97)

    a. In general, teratogens can cross the placenta at any time.

    b. Teratogens are agents in the environment, not heritable genes (although *susceptibility* to individual teratogens has a genetic component).

c. Although nutrition is an important factor in healthy prenatal development, the text does not suggest that nutrition alone can usually counteract the harmful effects of teratogens.

9. **a.** is the answer. (p. 102)

10. **b.** is the answer. (p. 108)

11. **c.** is the answer. (p. 110)

12. **c.** is the answer. (p. 94)

13. **b.** is the answer. (p. 114)

14. **b.** is the answer. (p. 114)

15. **c.** is the answer. (p. 119)

Matching Items

1. j (p. 91)
2. c (p. 91)
3. h (p. 92)
4. k (p. 114)
5. b (p. 97)
6. e (p. 112)
7. g (p. 112)
8. a (p. 98)
9. d (p. 93)
10. f (p. 102)
11. i (p. 91)

PROGRESS TEST 2

Multiple-Choice Questions

1. **c.** is the answer. (p. 105)

2. **c.** is the answer. (p. 91)

3. **d.** is the answer. (p. 109)

    a. The average length of labor for subsequent births is 7 hours.

4. **a.** is the answer. (p. 103)

5. **a.** is the answer. (p. 103)

6. **c.** is the answer. (p. 117)

7. **d.** is the answer. (p. 110)

8. **c.** is the answer. (p. 113)

9. **d.** is the answer. (p. 96)

10. **c.** is the answer. Most doctors in the United States advise pregnant women to abstain completely from alcohol. (p. 102)

11. **a.** is the answer. (p. 95)

12. **d.** is the answer. (p. 110)

13. **b.** is the answer. (p. 95)

14. **d.** is the answer. (p. 118)

15. **b.** is the answer. (p. 98)

True or False Items

1. T (p. 96)
2. T (p. 94)
3. T (p. 109)
4. F   Behavioral teratogens can affect the fetus at any time during the prenatal period. (p. 98)
5. F   There is no controversy about the damaging effects of smoking during pregnancy. (p. 114)
6. T (p. 110)
7. T (p. 109)
8. F   Though highly desirable, mother–infant contact at birth is not necessary for the child's normal development or for a good parent–child relationship. Many opportunities for bonding occur throughout childhood. (p. 119)
9. T (pp. 114–115)
10. F   About 28 percent of births in the United States are now cesarean. (p. 110)

DEVELOPMENTAL PSYCHOLOGY APPLIED

1. **c.** is the answer. (pp. 102, 104)
2. **b.** is the answer. (p. 93)

    a. The zygote is the fertilized ovum.

    c. The developing organism is designated a fetus starting at the ninth week.

    d. The ovum is the female egg that is fertilized by the sperm.

3. **c.** is the answer. (p. 94)
4. **b.** is the answer. (p. 97)

    a. This is the virus that causes AIDS.

    c. Rubella may cause blindness, deafness, and brain damage.

    d. In small doses, it may be harmless; large doses may produce brain damage in the fetus.

5. **c.** is the answer. (p. 100)

    a. FAS is caused in infants by the mother-to-be drinking high doses of alcohol during pregnancy.

    b. Brain damage is caused by the use of social drugs during pregnancy.

    d. Respiratory problems do not result from a lack of folic acid.

6. **c.** is the answer. (p. 114)
7. **b.** is the answer. (p. 99)
8. **b.** is the answer. (pp. 98–99, 102)

9. **c.** is the answer. (p. 119)

    a. & b. Bonding in humans is not a biologically determined event limited to a critical period, as it is in many other animal species.

    d. There is no evidence of any gender differences in the formation of the parent–infant bond.

10. **c.** is the answer. If a neonate's Apgar score is below 4, the infant is in critical condition and needs immediate medical attention. (p. 110)

11. **b.** is the answer. (p. 114)

    a., c., & d. Prenatal malnutrition is the most common cause of a small-for-dates baby.

12. **c.** is the answer. Donna's risk factor for having an LBW baby is her weight (teens tend not to eat well and can be undernourished). (pp. 114–115)

    a. & d. Neither of these has been linked to increased risk of having LBW babies.

    b. In fact, based only on her age and normal weight gain, May Ling's baby would *not* be expected to be LBW.

13. **d.** is the answer. (pp. 113–114)

    a. & c. At 38 weeks, this infant is full term.

14. **a.** is the answer. (p. 114)

    b. Low birthweight is defined as weighing less than 5¹⁄₂ pounds.

    c. Although an infant can be both preterm and small for gestational age, this baby's weight is within the normal range of healthy babies.

    d. This term is no longer used to describe early births.

15. **c.** is the answer. (p. 110)

KEY TERMS

1. The first two weeks of development after conception, characterized by rapid cell division and the beginning of cell differentiation, are called the **germinal period.** (p. 91)

    Memory aid: A *germ cell* is one from which a new organism can develop. The **germ**inal period is the first stage in the development of the new organism.

2. The **embryonic period** is approximately the third through the eighth week of prenatal development, when the basic forms of all body structures develop. (p. 91)

3. From the ninth week after conception until birth is the **fetal period,** when the organs grow in size and mature in functioning. (p. 91)

4. During the germinal period, once the developing cell mass begins to take on distinct characteristics it is called a **blastocyst**. (p. 91)

5. The **placenta** is the organ that develops in the uterus to protect and nourish the developing person. (p. 92)

6. **Implantation** is the process by which the zygote burrows into the uterine lining, where it can be nourished and protected during growth. (p. 92)

7. **Embryo** is the name given to the developing organism from the third through the eighth week after conception. (p. 93)

8. **Fetus** is the name for the developing organism from eight weeks after conception until birth. (p. 94)

9. About 22 weeks after conception, the fetus attains the **age of viability,** at which point it has at least some slight chance of survival outside the uterus if specialized medical care is available. (p. 95)

10. **Teratogens** are external agents and conditions, such as viruses, drugs, chemicals, stressors, and malnutrition, that can impair prenatal development and lead to birth defects and even death. (p. 97)

11. **Behavioral teratogens** tend to damage the brain, impairing the future child's intellectual and emotional functioning. (p. 97)

12. The science of teratology is a science of **risk analysis**, meaning that it attempts to evaluate what factors make prenatal harm more or less likely to occur. (p. 98)

13. In prenatal development, a **critical period** is the time when a particular organ or other body part is most susceptible to teratogenic damage. (p. 98)

14. A **threshold effect** is the harmful effect of a substance that occurs when exposure to it reaches a certain level. (p. 98)

15. An **interaction effect** occurs when one teratogen intensifies the harmful effects of another. (p. 99)

16. Prenatal alcohol exposure may cause **fetal alcohol syndrome (FAS)**, which includes abnormal facial characteristics, slow physical growth, behavior problems, and mental retardation. Likely victims are those who are genetically vulnerable and whose mothers drink three or more drinks daily during pregnancy. (p. 102)

17. Newborns are rated at one and then at five minutes after birth according to the **Apgar scale**. This scale assigns a score of 0, 1, or 2 to each of five characteristics: heart rate, breathing, muscle tone, color, and reflexes. A score of 7 or better indicates that all is well. (p. 110)

18. In a **cesarean section**, the fetus is removed from the mother surgically. (p. 110)

19. A **doula** is a woman who works alongside medical staff to assist a woman through labor and delivery. (p.112)

20. **Anoxia** is a temporary lack of fetal oxygen during the birth process that, if prolonged, can cause brain damage or even death. (p. 112)

21. **Cerebral palsy** is a muscular control disorder caused by damage to the brain's motor centers during or before birth. (p. 113)

22. A birthweight of less than $5^1/2$ pounds (2.5 kilograms) is called **low birthweight (LBW)**. Low-birthweight infants are at risk for many immediate and long-term problems. (p. 113)

23. A birthweight of less than 3 pounds (1.3 kilograms) is called **very low birthweight (VLBW)**. (p. 113)

24. A birthweight of less than 2 pounds (1 kilogram) is called **extremely low birthweight (ELBW)**. (p. 113)

25. When an infant is born three or more weeks before the due date, it is said to be a **preterm birth.** (p. 114)

26. Infants who weigh substantially less than they should, given how much time has passed since conception, are called **small for gestational age (SGA),** or small for dates. (p. 114)

27. **Kangaroo care** occurs when the mother of a low-birthweight infant spends at least one hour a day holding her infant between her breasts. (p. 117)

28. **Parental alliance** refers to the cooperation and mutual support between mother and father because of their commitment to their children. (p. 118)

29. **Postpartum depression** is a profound feeling of sadness, inadequacy, and hopelessness sometimes experienced by new mothers. (p. 118)

30. The term **parent–infant bond** describes the strong feelings of attachment between parent and child in the early moments of their relationship together. (p. 119)

5

The First Two Years: Biosocial Development

Chapter Overview

Chapter 5 is the first of a three-chapter unit that describes the developing person from birth to age 2 in terms of biosocial, cognitive, and psychosocial development. Physical development is the first to be examined.

The chapter begins with observations on the overall growth and health of infants, including information on infant sleep patterns. Following is a discussion of brain growth and development and the importance of experience in brain development. The chapter then turns to a discussion of sensory, perceptual, and motor abilities and the ages at which the average infant acquires them. Preventive medicine, the importance of immunizations during the first two years, and the possible causes of sudden infant death syndrome (SIDS) are discussed next. The final section explains the importance of nutrition during the first two years and the consequences of severe malnutrition and undernutrition.

NOTE: Answer guidelines for all Chapter 5 questions begin on page 78.

Guided Study

The text chapter should be studied one section at a time. Before you read, preview each section by skimming it, noting headings and boldface items. Then read the appropriate section objectives from the following outline. Keep these objectives in mind and, as you read the chapter section, search for the information that will enable you to meet each objective. Once you have finished a section, write out answers for its objectives.

Body Changes (pp. 125–128)

1. Describe the infant's height and weight, including how they change during the first two years.

2. Describe the infant's changing sleep patterns.

3. Discuss the attitudes of different cultures about where infants sleep.

Brain Development (pp. 125–135)

4. Describe the ways in which the brain changes or matures during infancy.

5. (text and Thinking Like a Scientist) Discuss the role of experience in brain development.

Senses and Motor Skills (pp. 136–143)

6. Distinguish among sensation, perception, and cognition.

7. Describe the development of an infant's sensory and perceptual abilities in terms of the senses of hearing, vision, taste, smell, and touch.

8. Describe the basic reflexes of the newborn, and distinguish between gross motor skills and fine motor skills.

9. Describe the basic pattern of motor-skill development, and discuss variations in the timing of motor-skill acquisition.

Public Health Measures (pp. 143–151)

10. Identify key factors in the worldwide decline in childhood mortality over the past century, and discuss the importance of childhood immunizations.

11. Identify risk factors for sudden infant death syndrome, and discuss possible explanations for ethnic group variations in the incidence of this situation.

12. Describe the nutritional needs of infants.

13. Discuss the causes and effects of malnutrition in the first years.

Chapter Review

When you have finished reading the chapter, work through the material that follows to review it. Complete the sentences and answer the questions. As you proceed, evaluate your performance for each section by consulting the answers on page 78. Do not continue with the next section until you understand each answer. If you need to, review or reread the appropriate section in the textbook before continuing.

Body Changes (pp. 125–128)

1. The average North American newborn measures _____ and weighs about

   _____ .

2. By age 2, the typical child weighs about _____ and measures

   _____ . The typical 2-year-old is almost _____ percent of his or her adult weight and

   _____ percent of his or her adult height.

3. A standard, or average, of physical development that is derived for a specific group or population is a _____ .

4. To compare a child's growth to that of other children, we determine a

   _____ , a point on a ranking scale of

   _____ (what number?) to

   _____ (what number?).

5. The phenomenon in which inadequate nutrition causes the body to stop growing but not the brain is called _____-_____ .

6. Throughout childhood, regular and ample

   _____ correlates with

   _____ maturation,

   _____ , _____ regulation, and _____ adjustment in school and within the family.

7. Over the first months of life, the relative amount of time spent in the different _____ of sleep changes. The stage of sleep characterized by flickering eyes behind closed lids and

   _____ is called _____

   _____ . During this stage of sleep,

brain waves are fairly _____ (slow/rapid). This stage of sleep _____ (increases/decreases) over the first months, as does the dozing stage called _____

_____ . Slow-wave sleep, also called

_____ , increases markedly at about

_____ months of age.

8. In most Western cultures, children _____ (do/do not) sleep with their parents. In contrast, parents in _____ , _____ , and _____ _____ traditionally practice _____ with their infants. This practice _____ (does/does not) seem to be harmful unless the adult is _____ .

Brain Development (pp. 129–135)

9. At birth, the brain has attained about

   _____ percent of its adult weight; by age 2, the brain is about _____ percent of its adult weight. In comparison, body weight at age 2 is about _____ percent of what it will be in adulthood.

10. The brain's communication system consists primarily of nerve cells called _____ , which are connected by intricate networks of nerve fibers, called _____ and

    _____ . About _____ percent of these cells are in the brain's outer layer called the _____ . This area takes up about _____ percent of human brain material and is the site of

    _____ , _____ , and

    _____ .

11. Each neuron has many _____ but only a single _____ .

12. Neurons communicate with one another at intersections called _____ . After traveling down the length of the

    _____ , electrical impulses excite chemicals called _____ that carry information across the _____

    _____ to the _____ of

a "receiving" neuron. Most of the nerve cells _____ (are/are not) present at birth, whereas the fiber networks _____ (are/are not) rudimentary.

13. During the first months of life, brain development is most noticeable in the _____ .

14. From birth until age 2, the density of dendrites in the cortex _____ (increases/decreases) by a factor of _____ . The phenomenal increase in neural connections over the first two years has been called _____ _____ .

    Following this growth process, neurons in some areas of the brain wither in the process called _____ , because _____ does not activate those brain areas. The importance of early experience is seen in the brain's production of stress hormones such as _____ .

15. Brain functions that require basic common experiences in order to develop are called _____-_____ brain functions; those that depend on particular, and variable, experiences in order to develop are called _____-_____ brain functions. The last part of the brain to mature is the _____ _____ , which is the area for _____ , _____ , and _____ _____ .

16. A life-threatening condition that occurs when an infant is held by the shoulders and quickly shaken back and forth is _____ _____ _____ . Crying stops because of ruptured _____ in the brain and broken _____ connections.

17. An important implication of brain development for caregivers is that early brain growth is _____ and reflects _____ . Another is that each part of the brain has its own _____ for _____ , _____ , and _____ .

The inborn drive to remedy any deficit that may occur in development is called _____ .

18. (text and Thinking Like a Scientist) Neuroscientists once believed that brains were entirely formed by _____ and _____ _____ ; today, most believe in _____ , which is the concept that personality, intellect, habits, and emotions change throughout life for _____ (one/a combination of) reason(s). Specific times when particular kinds of development are primed to occur are called _____ _____ . Marion Diamond, William Greenough, and colleagues discovered that the brains of rats who were raised in stimulating environments were better developed, with more _____ branching, than the brains of rats raised in barren environments. Orphaned Romanian children who were isolated and deprived of stimulation showed signs of _____ damage. Placed in healthier environments, these children _____ (improved/did not improve); years later, persistent deficits in these children _____ (were/were not) found.

Senses and Motor Skills (pp. 136–143)

19. The process by which the visual, auditory, and other sensory systems detect stimuli is called _____ ; _____ occurs when the brain tries to make sense out of a stimulus so that the individual becomes aware of it. At birth, only _____ is apparent; _____ requires experience. In the process called _____ , a person thinks about and interprets what he or she has perceived. This process _____ (can/cannot) occur without either sensation or perception.

20. Generally speaking, newborns' hearing _____ (is/is not) very acute at birth. Newborns _____ (can/cannot) perceive differences in voices, rhythms, and language. The brain is especially good at detecting differences in sound that are _____ .

21. The least mature of the senses at birth is
_____ . Newborns' visual focusing
is best for objects between _____
and _____ inches away.

22. Increasing maturation of the visual cortex
accounts for improvements in other visual abilities, such as the infant's ability to _____
on an object and _____ to its critical
areas. The ability to use both eyes in a coordinated manner to focus on one object, which is called
_____ _____ , devel-
ops at about _____ of age.

23. Taste, smell, and touch _____ (func-
tion/do not function) at birth. The ability to be
comforted by the human _____ is a
skill tested in the _____ Neonatal
Behavioral Assessment Scale.

24. The infant's early sensory abilities seem organized for two goals: _____
_____ and _____ .

25. The most visible and dramatic body changes of
infancy involve _____
_____ .

26. An involuntary response to a stimulus is called a
_____ .

27. The involuntary response that causes the newborn to take the first breath even before the
umbilical cord is cut is called the
_____ _____ . Because
breathing is irregular during the first few days,
other reflexive behaviors, such as
_____ , _____ ,
and _____ , are common.

28. Shivering, crying, and tucking the legs close to
the body are examples of reflexes that help to
maintain _____
_____ _____ .

29. A third set of reflexes manages _____ .
One of these is the tendency of the newborn to
suck anything that touches the lips; this is the
_____ reflex. Another is the tenden-
cy of newborns to turn their heads and start to
suck when something brushes against their
cheek; this is the _____ reflex.

Identify each reflex by filling in the missing information in the chart below.

Name of reflex	Description
a. _____	Toes fan upward when infants' feet are stroked
b. _____	Infants move their legs as if to walk when they are held upright and their feet touch a flat surface
c. _____	Infants stretch out their arms and legs when they are held on their stomachs
d. _____	Infants grip things that touch their palms
e. _____	Infants fling their arms outward and then clutch them against their chests in response to a loud noise

30. Large movements such as running and climbing
are called _____
_____ skills.

31. Most infants are able to crawl on all fours (sometimes called creeping) between _____
and _____ months of age. Three factors in the development of walking are
_____ _____ ,
_____ , and _____
_____ .

List the major hallmarks in children's mastery of
walking.

32. Abilities that require more precise, small movements, such as picking up a coin, are called
_____ _____ skills. By
_____ of age, most babies can reach
for, grab, and hold onto almost any object of the
right size.

33. Although the _____ in which motor skills are mastered is the same in all healthy infants, the _____ of acquisition of skills varies greatly.

34. The average ages, or _____ , at which most infants master major motor skills are based on a large sample of infants drawn from _____ (a single/many) ethnic group(s).

35. Motor skill norms vary from one _____ group to another.

36. Motor skill acquisition in identical twins _____ (is/is not) more similar than in fraternal twins, suggesting that genes _____ (do/do not) play an important role. Another influential factor is the _____ .

Public Health Measures (pp. 143–151)

37. Globally, today most children _____ (do/do not) live to adulthood. A key factor in reducing the childhood death rate was the development of _____—a process that stimulates the body's _____ system to defend against contagious diseases. This process has met with stunning success in eradicating or reducing diseases such as _____ , _____ , _____ , and _____ .

38. Another reason for lower infant mortality worldwide is a decrease in _____ _____ _____ , in which seemingly healthy infants die unexpectedly in their _____ .

39. A key factor in SIDS is _____ background. In ethnically diverse nations, babies of _____ descent are less likely to succumb to SIDS than are babies of _____ or _____ descent.

Identify several practices that may explain why certain ethnic groups have a low incidence of SIDS.

40. The ideal infant food is _____ _____ , beginning with the thick, high-calorie fluid called _____ . The only situations in which formula may be healthier for the infant than breast milk are when _____ _____ .

State several advantages of breast milk over cow's milk for the developing infant.

41. Most doctors recommend exclusive breast-feeding for the first _____ (how many?) months.

42. The most serious nutritional problem of infancy is _____-_____ _____ .

43. Chronically malnourished infants suffer in three ways: Their _____ may not develop normally; they may have no _____ _____ to protect them against disease, and they may develop the diseases _____ or _____ .

44. Severe protein-calorie deficiency in early infancy causes _____ . If malnutrition begins after age 1, protein-calorie deficiency is more likely to cause the disease called _____ , which involves swelling or bloating of the face, legs, and abdomen.

Progress Test 1

Multiple-Choice Questions

Circle your answers to the following questions and check them with the answers beginning on page 78. If your answer is incorrect, read the explanation for why it is incorrect and then consult the appropriate pages of the text (in parentheses following the correct answer).

1. The average North American newborn:
   a. weighs approximately 6 pounds.
   b. weighs approximately 7½ pounds.
   c. is "overweight" because of the diet of the mother.
   d. weighs 10 percent less than what is desirable.

2. Compared to the first year, growth during the second year:
   a. proceeds at a slower rate.
   b. continues at about the same rate.
   c. includes more insulating fat.
   d. includes more bone and muscle.

3. The major motor skill most likely to be mastered by an infant before the age of 6 months is:
   a. sitting without support.
   b. sitting with head steady.
   c. turning the head in search of a nipple.
   d. grabbing an object with thumb and forefinger.

4. Norms suggest that the earliest walkers in the world are infants from:
   a. Western Europe.   c. Uganda.
   b. the United States.   d. Denver.

5. Head-sparing is the phenomenon in which:
   a. the brain continues to grow even though the body stops growing as a result of malnutrition.
   b. the infant's body grows more rapidly during the second year.
   c. axons develop more rapidly than dendrites.
   d. dendrites develop more rapidly than axons.

6. Dreaming is characteristic of:
   a. slow-wave sleep.   c. REM sleep.
   b. transitional sleep. d. quiet sleep.

7. For a pediatrician, the most important factor in assessing a child's healthy growth is:
   a. height in inches.
   b. weight in pounds.
   c. body fat percentage.
   d. the percentile rank of a child's height or weight.

8. Brain functions that depend on babies' having things to see and hear, and people to feed and carry them, are called:
   a. experience-dependent.
   b. experience-expectant.
   c. pruning functions.
   d. transient exuberance.

9. Compared with formula-fed infants, breast-fed infants tend to have:
   a. greater weight gain.
   b. fewer allergies and digestive upsets.
   c. less frequent feedings during the first few months.
   d. more social approval.

10. Marasmus and kwashiorkor are caused by:
    a. bloating.
    b. protein-calorie deficiency.
    c. living in a developing country.
    d. poor family food habits.

11. The infant's first "motor skills" are:
    a. fine motor skills.   c. reflexes.
    b. gross motor skills. d. unpredictable.

12. Which of the following is said to have had the greatest impact on human mortality reduction and population growth?
    a. improvements in infant nutrition
    b. oral rehydration therapy
    c. medical advances in newborn care
    d. childhood immunization

13. Which of the following is true of motor-skill development in healthy infants?
    a. It follows the same basic sequence the world over.
    b. It occurs at different rates from individual to individual.
    c. It follows norms that vary from one ethnic group to another.
    d. All of the above are true.

14. All the nerve cells a human brain will ever need are present:
    a. at conception.
    b. about 1 month following conception.
    c. at birth.
    d. at age 5 or 6.

15. Chronically malnourished children suffer in which of the following ways?

    a. They have no body reserves to protect them.

    b. Their brains may not develop normally.

    c. They may die from marasmus.

    d. All of the above are true of malnourished children.

Matching Items

Match each definition or description with its corresponding term.

Terms

_____ **1.** neurons

_____ **2.** dendrites

_____ **3.** kwashiorkor

_____ **4.** marasmus

_____ **5.** gross motor skill

_____ **6.** fine motor skill

_____ **7.** reflex

_____ **8.** protein-calorie malnutrition

_____ **9.** transient exuberance

_____ **10.** prefrontal cortex

_____ **11.** self-righting

Definitions or Descriptions

a. protein deficiency during the first year in which growth stops and body tissues waste away

b. picking up an object

c. the most common serious nutrition problem of infancy

d. protein deficiency during toddlerhood

e. communication networks among nerve cells

f. running or climbing

g. an involuntary response

h. the phenomenal increase in neural connections over the first 2 years

i. nerve cells

j. the brain area that specializes in anticipation, planning, and impulse control

k. the inborn drive to correct a developmental deficit

Progress Test 2

Progress Test 2 should be completed during a final chapter review. Answer the following questions after you thoroughly understand the correct answers for the Chapter Review and Progress Test 1.

Multiple-Choice Questions

1. Dendrite is to axon as neural _____ is to neural _____ .

    a. input; output   **c.** myelin; synapse

    b. output; input   **d.** synapse; myelin

2. A reflex is best defined as a(n):

    a. fine motor skill.

    b. motor ability mastered at a specific age.

    c. involuntary response to a given stimulus.

    d. gross motor skill.

3. A norm is:

    a. a standard, or average, that is derived for a specific group or population.

    b. a point on a ranking scale of 0 to 100.

    c. a milestone of development that all children reach at the same age.

    d. all of the above.

4. Most babies can reach for, grasp, and hold onto an object by about the _____ month.

    a. second   **c.** ninth

    b. sixth   **d.** fourteenth

5. Regarding the brain's cortex, which of the following is *not* true?

    a. The cortex houses about 70 percent of the brain's neurons.

    b. The cortex is the brain's outer layer.

    c. The cortex is the location of most thinking, feeling, and sensing.

    d. Only primates have a cortex.

6. During the first weeks of life, babies seem to focus reasonably well on:
   a. little in their environment.
   b. objects at a distance of 4 to 30 inches.
   c. objects at a distance of 1 to 3 inches.
   d. objects several feet away.

7. Which sleep stage increases markedly at about 3 or 4 months?
   a. REM
   b. transitional
   c. fast-wave
   d. slow-wave

8. An advantage of breast milk over formula is that it:
   a. is always sterile and at body temperature.
   b. contains traces of medications ingested by the mother.
   c. can be given without involving the father.
   d. contains more protein and vitamin D than does formula.

9. Synapses are:
   a. nerve fibers that receive electrical impulses from other neurons.
   b. nerve fibers that transmit electrical impulses to other neurons.
   c. intersections between the axon of one neuron and the dendrites of other neurons.
   d. chemical signals that transmit information from one neuron to another.

10. Transient exuberance and pruning demonstrate that:
    a. the pace of acquisition of motor skills varies markedly from child to child.
    b. Newborns sleep more than older children because their immature nervous systems cannot handle the higher, waking level of sensory stimulation.
    c. The specifics of brain structure and growth depend partly on the infant's experience.
    d. Good nutrition is essential to healthy biosocial development.

11. Climbing is to using a crayon as _____ is to _____ .
    a. fine motor skill; gross motor skill
    b. gross motor skill; fine motor skill
    c. reflex; fine motor skill
    d. reflex; gross motor skill

12. Some infant reflexes are critical for survival. Hiccups and sneezes help the infant maintain the _____ and leg tucking maintains _____ .
    a. feeding; oxygen supply
    b. feeding; a constant body temperature
    c. oxygen supply; feeding
    d. oxygen supply; a constant body temperature

13. (Thinking Like a Scientist) Compared with the brains of laboratory rats that were raised in barren cages, those of rats raised in stimulating, toy-filled cages:
    a. were better developed and had more dendritic branching.
    b. had fewer synaptic connections.
    c. showed less transient exuberance.
    d. displayed all of the above characteristics.

14. In determining a healthy child's growth, a pediatrician focuses on
    a. the child's past growth.
    b. the growth of the child's brothers and sisters.
    c. the stature of other children.
    d. all of the above.

15. Infant sensory and perceptual abilities appear to be especially organized for:
    a. obtaining adequate nutrition and comfort.
    b. comfort and social interaction.
    c. looking.
    d. touching and smelling.

True or False Items

Write T (*true*) or F (*false*) on the line in front of each statement.

_____ 1. Imaging studies have identified a specific area of the brain that specializes in recognizing faces.

_____ 2. Putting babies to sleep on their stomachs increases the risk of SIDS.

_____ 3. Reflexive hiccups, sneezes, and thrashing are signs that the infant's reflexes are not functioning properly.

_____ 4. Infants of all ethnic backgrounds develop the same motor skills at approximately the same age.

_____ 5. The typical 2-year-old is almost one-fifth its adult weight and one-half its adult height.

_____ 6. Vision is better developed than hearing in most newborns.

_____ 7. Today, most infants in industrialized nations are breast-fed up to 6 months.

_____ 8. Certain basic sensory experiences seem necessary to ensure full brain development in the human infant.

_____ 9. Dendrite growth is the major reason that brain weight increases so dramatically in the first two years.

_____ 10. The only motor skills apparent at birth are reflexes.

_____ 11. The prefrontal cortex is one of the first brain areas to mature.

Developmental Psychology Applied

Answer these questions the day before an exam as a final check on your understanding of the chapter's terms and concepts.

1. Newborns cry, shiver, and tuck their legs close to their bodies. This set of reflexes helps them:
   a. ensure proper muscle tone.
   b. learn how to signal distress.
   c. maintain constant body temperature.
   d. communicate serious hunger pangs.

2. I am a chemical that carries information between nerve cells in the brain. What am I?
   a. a synapse.
   b. a dendrite
   c. a neurotransmitter
   d. a neuron

3. (Thinking Like a Scientist) Research studies of the more than 100,000 Romanian children orphaned and severely deprived in infancy reported all of the following except:
   a. all of the children were overburdened with stress.
   b. after adoption, the children gained weight quickly.
   c. during early childhood, many still showed signs of emotional damage.
   d. most of the children placed in healthy adoptive homes eventually recovered.

4. The Farbers, who are first-time parents, are wondering whether they should be concerned because their 12-month-old daughter, who weighs 22 pounds and measures 30 inches, is not growing quite as fast as she did during her first year. You should tell them that:
   a. any slowdown in growth during the second year is a cause for immediate concern.
   b. their daughter's weight and height are well below average for her age.

   c. growth patterns for a first child are often erratic.
   d. physical growth is somewhat slower in the second year.

5. Regarding body size, a child generally is said to be average if he or she is:
   a. at the 25th percentile.
   b. between the 25th and 40th percentiles.
   c. at the 50th percentile.
   d. at the 75th percentile or greater.

6. Concluding her presentation on sleep, Lakshmi notes each of the following except:
   a. dreaming occurs during REM sleep.
   b. quiet sleep increases markedly at about 3 or 4 months.
   c. the dreaming brain is characterized by slow brain waves.
   d. regular and ample sleep is an important factor in a child's emotional regulation.

7. Michael can focus on objects between 4 and 30 inches from him and is able to discriminate subtle sound differences. Michael most likely:
   a. is a preterm infant.
   b. has brain damage in the visual processing areas of the cortex.
   c. is a newborn.
   d. is slow-to-mature.

8. A baby turns her head and starts to suck when her receiving blanket is brushed against her cheek. The baby is displaying the:
   a. sucking reflex.
   b. rooting reflex.
   c. thrashing reflex.
   d. tucking reflex.

9. The pediatrician notices that Freddy seems indifferent to everything. Knowing that Freddy was abused as an infant, she suspects that:
   a. because of pruning, his brain's neuronal reaction has lost the capacity to react normally to stress.
   b. Freddy has a learning disability.
   c. Freddy has developed a personality disorder.
   d. as a result of the early abuse, Freddy is now mentally retarded.

10. Sensation is to perception as _____ is to _____ .
    a. hearing; seeing
    b. detecting a stimulus; making sense of a stimulus
    c. making sense of a stimulus; detecting a stimulus
    d. tasting; smelling

11. Sharetta's pediatrician informs her parents that Sharetta's 1-year-old brain is exhibiting transient exuberance. In response to this news, Sharetta's parents:

   a. smile, because they know their daughter's brain is developing new neural connections.

   b. worry, because this may indicate increased vulnerability to a later learning disability.

   c. know that this process, in which axons become coated, is normal.

   d. are alarmed, because this news indicates that the frontal area of Sharetta's cortex is immature.

12. (Thinking Like a Scientist) To say that most developmentalists are multidisciplinary and believe in plasticity means they believe personality, intellect, and emotions:

   a. change throughout life as a result of biological maturation.

   b. change throughout life for a combination of reasons.

   c. remain stable throughout life.

   d. more strongly reveal the impact of genes as people get older.

13. Like all newborns, Serena is able to:

   a. differentiate one sound from another.

   b. see objects more than 30 inches from her face quite clearly.

   c. use her mouth to recognize objects by taste and touch.

   d. do all of the above.

14. Three-week-old Nathan should have the *least* difficulty focusing on the sight of:

   a. stuffed animals on a bookshelf across the room from his crib.

   b. his mother's face as she holds him in her arms.

   c. the checkerboard pattern in the wallpaper covering the ceiling of his room.

   d. the family dog as it dashes into the nursery.

15. Trying to impress his professor, Erik notes that the reason humans have a critical period for learning certain skills might be due to the fact that the brain cannot form new synapses after age 13. Should the professor be impressed with Erik's knowledge of biosocial development?

   a. Yes, although each neuron may have already formed as many as 15,000 connections with other neurons.

   b. Yes, although the branching of dendrites and axons does continue through young adulthood.

   c. No. Although Erik is correct about neural development, the brain attains adult size by about age 7.

   d. No. Synapses form throughout life.

Key Terms

Using your own words, write a brief definition or explanation of each of the following terms on a separate piece of paper.

1. norm
2. percentile
3. head-sparing
4. REM sleep
5. co-sleeping
6. neuron
7. cortex
8. axon
9. dendrite
10. synapse
11. transient exuberance
12. experience-expectant
13. experience-dependent
14. prefrontal cortex
15. shaken baby syndrome
16. self-righting
17. sensitive period
18. sensation
19. perception
20. binocular vision
21. motor skill
22. reflex
23. gross motor skills
24. fine motor skills
25. immunization
26. sudden infant death syndrome (SIDS)
27. protein-calorie malnutrition
28. marasmus
29. kwashiorkor

ANSWERS

CHAPTER REVIEW

1. 20 inches (51 centimeters); 7½ pounds (3,400 grams)

2. 30 pounds (13½ kilograms); between 32 and 36 inches (81–91 centimeters); 15 to 20; 50

3. norm

4. percentile; 0; 100

5. head-sparing

6. sleep; brain; learning, emotional, psychological

7. stages; dreaming; REM sleep; rapid; decreases; transitional sleep; quiet sleep; 3 or 4

8. do not; Asia; Africa; Latin America; co-sleeping; does not; drugged or drunk

9. 25; 75; 15 to 20

10. neurons; axons; dendrites; 70; cortex; 80; thinking; feeling; sensing

11. dendrites; axon

12. synapses; axon; neurotransmitters; synaptic gap; dendrite; are; are

13. cortex

14. increases; five; transient exuberance; pruning; experience; cortisol

15. experience-expectant; experience-dependent; prefrontal cortex; anticipation; planning; impulse control

16. shaken baby syndrome; blood vessels; neural

17. rapid; experience; sequence; growth; connecting; pruning; self-righting

18. genes; prenatal influences; plasticity; a combination of; sensitive periods; dendritic; emotional; improved; were

19. sensation; perception; sensation; perception; cognition; can

20. is; can; meaningful

21. vision; 4; 30

22. focus; scan; binocular vision; 14 weeks

23. function; touch; Brazelton

24. social interaction; comfort

25. motor skills

26. reflex

27. breathing reflex; hiccups; sneezes; thrashing

28. constant body temperature

29. feeding; sucking; rooting

    a. Babinski reflex

    b. stepping reflex

    c. swimming reflex

    d. Palmar grasping reflex

    e. Moro reflex

30. gross motor

31. 8; 10; muscle strength; practice; brain maturation within the motor cortex

On average, a child can walk while holding a hand at 9 months, can stand alone momentarily at 10 months, and can walk well, unassisted, at 12 months.

32. fine motor; 6 months

33. sequence; age

34. norms; many

35. ethnic

36. is; do; pattern of infant care

37. do; immunization; immune; smallpox; polio; measles; rotovirus

38. sudden infant death syndrome (SIDS); sleep

39. ethnic; Asian; European; African

Chinese parents tend to their babies periodically as they sleep, which makes them less likely to fall into a deep, nonbreathing sleep. Bangladeshi infants are usually surrounded by many family members in a rich sensory environment, making them less likely to sleep deeply for very long.

40. breast milk; colostrum; the mother is HIV-positive or using toxic or addictive drugs

Breast milk is always sterile and at body temperature; it contains more iron, vitamin C, and vitamin A; it contains antibodies that provide the infant some protection against disease; it is more digestible than any formula; and it decreases the frequency of almost every infant illness and allergy.

41. four to six

42. protein-calorie malnutrition

43. brains; body reserves; marasmus; kwashiorkor

44. marasmus; kwashiorkor

PROGRESS TEST 1

Multiple-Choice Questions

1. **b.** is the answer. (p. 125)

2. **a.** is the answer. (p. 125)

3. **b.** is the answer. (p. 141)

   a. The age norm for this skill is 6–7 months.

c. This is a reflex, not an acquired motor skill.

d. This skill is acquired between 9 and 14 months.

4. **c.** is the answer. (p. 141)

5. **a.** is the answer. (p. 127)

6. **c.** is the answer. (p. 127)

7. **d.** is the answer. (p. 126)

8. **b.** is the answer. (p. 132)

   a. Experience-dependent functions depend on particular, and variable, experiences in order to develop.

   c. Pruning refers to the process by which some neurons wither because experience does not activate them.

   d. This refers to the great increase in the number of neurons, dendrites, and synapses that occurs in an infant's brain over the first two years of life.

9. **b.** is the answer. This is because breast milk is more digestible than cow's milk or formula. (p. 149)

   a., c., & d. Breast- and bottle-fed babies do not differ in these attributes.

10. **b.** is the answer. (p. 151)

11. **c.** is the answer. (p. 138)

    a. & b. These motor skills do not emerge until somewhat later; reflexes are present at birth.

    d. On the contrary, reflexes are quite predictable.

12. **d.** is the answer. (p. 144)

13. **d.** is the answer. (pp. 141–142)

14. **c.** is the answer. (p. 131)

15. **d.** is the answer. (pp. 150–151)

Matching Items

1. i (p. 129) 6. b (p. 140) 11. k (p. 134)
2. e (p. 130) 7. g (p. 138)
3. d (p. 151) 8. c (p. 150)
4. a (p. 151) 9. h (p. 131)
5. f (p. 140) 10. j (p. 133)

PROGRESS TEST 2

Multiple-Choice Questions

1. **a.** is the answer. (p. 130)

2. **c.** is the answer. (p. 138)

   a., b., & d. Each of these refers to voluntary responses that are acquired only after a certain amount of practice; reflexes are involuntary responses that are present at birth and require no practice.

3. **a.** is the answer. (p. 126)

   b. This defines percentile.

4. **b.** is the answer. (p. 141)

5. **d.** is the answer. All mammals have a cortex. (p. 129)

6. **b.** is the answer. (p. 137)

   a. Although focusing ability seems to be limited to a certain range, babies do focus on many objects in this range.

   c. This is not within the range at which babies *can* focus.

   d. Babies have very poor distance vision.

7. **d.** is the answer. (p. 127)

8. **a.** is the answer. (p. 149)

   b. If anything, this is a potential *disadvantage* of breast milk over formula.

   c. So can formula.

   d. Breast milk contains more iron, vitamin C, and vitamin A than cow's milk; it does not contain more protein and vitamin D, however.

9. **c.** is the answer. (p. 130)

   a. These are dendrites.

   b. These are axons.

   d. These are neurotransmitters.

10. **c.** is the answer. (p. 131)

11. **b.** is the answer. (pp. 140–141)

    c. & d. Reflexes are involuntary responses; climbing and using a crayon are both voluntary responses.

12. **d.** is the answer. (p. 139)

13. **a.** is the answer. (p. 134)

14. **d.** is the answer. (p. 126)

15. **b.** is the answer. (p. 138)

True or False Items

1. T (p. 130)

2. T (p. 148)

3. F Hiccups, sneezes, and thrashing are common during the first few days, and they are entirely normal reflexes. (p. 139)

4. F Although all healthy infants develop the same motor skills in the same sequence, the age at which these skills are acquired can vary greatly from infant to infant. (pp. 141–142)

5. T (p. 126)

6. F Vision is relatively poorly developed at birth, whereas hearing is well developed. (p. 137)

7. F Only one-third of all babies are breast-fed up to 6 months. (p. 150)

8. T (pp. 132–133)

9. T (p. 131)

10. T (p. 138)

11. F   In fact, the prefrontal cortex is probably the last area of the brain to attain maturity. (p. 133)

DEVELOPMENTAL PSYCHOLOGY APPLIED

1. **c.** is the answer. (p. 139)

2. **c.** is the answer. (pp. 130–131)

   a. A synapse is the intersection between the axon of one neuron and the dendrites of other neurons.

   b. Dendrites are nerve fibers that receive electrical impulses transmitted from other neurons.

   d. Neurons are nerve cells.

3. **d.** is the answer. Although all the children improved, persistent deficits remained in many of them. (pp. 134–135)

4. **d.** is the answer. (p. 125)

   a. & b. Although slowdowns in growth during infancy are often a cause for concern, their daughter's weight and height are typical of 1-year-old babies.

   c. Growth patterns are no more erratic for first children than for later children.

5. **c.** is the answer. (p. 126)

6. **c.** is the answer. The dreaming brain is characterized by rapid brain waves. (p. 127)

7. **c.** is the answer. (p. 137)

8. **b.** is the answer. (p. 139)

   a. This is the reflexive sucking of newborns in response to anything that touches their *lips.*

   c. This is the response that infants make when their feet are stroked.

   d. This is part of the reflex when the infant is cold.

9. **a.** is the answer. (p. 132)

   b., c., & d. Freddy's indifference and history point to an abnormal capacity to react to stress, not a learning disability, personality disorder, or mental retardation.

10. **b.** is the answer. (p. 136)

    a. & d. Sensation and perception operate in all of these sensory modalities.

11. **a.** is the answer. Transient exuberance results in a proliferation of neural connections during infancy, some of which will disappear because they are not used; that is, they are not needed to process information. (p. 131)

b. & d. Transient exuberance is a normal developmental process that occurs in all healthy infants.

c. This describes the coating of axons with myelin, which speeds neural transmission.

12. **b.** is the answer. (pp. 134–135)

13. **a.** is the answer. (p. 137)

    b. Objects at this distance are out of focus for newborns.

    c. This ability does not emerge until about one month of age.

14. **b.** is the answer. This is true because, at birth, focusing is best for objects between 4 and 30 inches away. (p. 137)

    a., c., & d. Newborns have very poor distance vision; each of these situations involves a distance greater than the optimal focus range.

15. **d.** is the answer. (p. 131)

KEY TERMS

1. A **norm** is an average, or standard, developed for a specific population. (p. 126)

2. A **percentile** is any point on a ranking scale of 0 to 100; percentiles are often used to compare a child's development to group norms and to his or her own prior development. (p. 126)

3. **Head-sparing** is the phenomenon by which the brain continues to grow even though the body stops growing in a malnourished child. (p. 127)

4. **REM sleep,** or rapid eye movement sleep, is a stage of sleep characterized by flickering eyes behind closed eyelids, dreaming, and rapid brain waves. (p. 127)

5. **Co-sleeping** is the custom in which parents and their infants sleep together. (p. 128)

6. A **neuron,** or nerve cell, is the main component of the central nervous system. (p. 129)

7. The **cortex** is the outer layers of the brain that is involved in most thinking, feeling, and sensing. (p. 129)

   Memory aid: Cortex in Latin means "bark." As bark covers a tree, the cortex is the "bark of the brain."

8. An **axon** is the nerve fiber that sends electrical impulses from one neuron to the dendrites of other neurons. (p. 130)

9. A **dendrite** is a nerve fiber that receives the electrical impulses transmitted from other neurons via their axons. (p. 130)

10. A **synapse** is the point at which the axon of a sending neuron meets the dendrites of a receiving neuron. (p. 130)

11. **Transient exuberance** is the dramatic increase in the number of dendrites that occurs in an infant's brain over the first two years of life. (p. 131)

12. **Experience-expectant** brain functions are those that require basic common experiences (such as having things to see and hear) in order to develop. (p. 132)

13. **Experience-dependent** brain functions are those that depend on particular, and variable, experiences (such as experiencing language) in order to develop. (p. 132)

14. The **prefrontal cortex** is the brain area that specializes in anticipation, planning, and impulse control. (p. 133)

15. **Shaken baby syndrome** is a life-threatening condition in which blood vessels in an infant's brain have been ruptured because the infant has been forcefully shaken back and forth. (p. 133)

16. **Self-righting** is the inborn drive to correct a deficit in development. (p. 134)

17. A **sensitive period** is a time when a specific kind of development is most likely to take place. (p. 134)

18. **Sensation** is the process by which a sensory system detects a particular stimulus. (p. 136)

19. **Perception** is the process by which the brain tries to make sense of a stimulus such that the individual becomes aware of it. (p. 136)

20. **Binocular vision** is the ability to use both eyes in a coordinated fashion in order to see one image. (p. 137)

Memory aid: Bi- indicates "two"; ocular means something pertaining to the eye. Binocular vision is vision for "two eyes."

21. **Motor skills** are learned abilities to move specific parts of the body. (p. 138)

22. A **reflex** is an involuntary physical response to a specific stimulus. (p. 138)

23. **Gross motor skills** are physical abilities that demand large body movements, such as climbing, jumping, or running. (p. 140)

24. **Fine motor skills** are physical abilities that require precise, small movements, such as picking up a coin. (p. 140)

25. **Immunization** is the process through which the body's immune system is stimulated (as by a vaccine) to defend against attack by a particular contagious disease. (p. 144)

26. **Sudden infant death syndrome (SIDS)** is a set of circumstances in which a seemingly healthy infant, at least 2 months of age, dies unexpectedly in his or her sleep. (p. 146)

27. **Protein-calorie malnutrition** results when a person does not consume enough food to thrive. (p. 150)

28. **Marasmus** is a disease caused by severe protein-calorie deficiency during the first year of life. Growth stops, body tissues waste away, and the infant dies. (p. 151)

29. **Kwashiorkor** is a disease caused by protein-calorie deficiency during childhood. The child's face, legs, and abdomen swell with water, sometimes making the child appear well fed; the child becomes more vulnerable to other diseases. Other body parts are degraded, including the hair, which becomes thin, brittle, and colorless. (p. 151)

6

The First Two Years: Cognitive Development

Chapter Overview

Chapter 6 explores the ways in which the infant comes to learn about, think about, and adapt to his or her surroundings. It focuses on the various ways in which infant intelligence is revealed: through sensorimotor intelligence, perception, memory, and language development. The chapter begins with a description of Jean Piaget's theory of sensorimotor intelligence, which maintains that infants think exclusively with their senses and motor skills. Piaget's six stages of sensorimotor intelligence are examined.

The second section discusses the information-processing theory, which compares cognition to the ways in which computers analyze data. Eleanor and James Gibson's influential theory is also described. Central to this theory is the idea that infants gain cognitive understanding of their world through the affordances of objects, that is, the activities they can do with them.

The text also discusses the key cognitive elements needed by the infant to structure the environment discovered through his or her newfound perceptual abilities. Using the habituation procedure, researchers have found that the speed with which infants recognize familiarity and seek something novel is related to later cognitive skill. It points out the importance of memory to cognitive development.

Finally, the chapter turns to the most remarkable cognitive achievement of the first two years: the acquisition of language. Beginning with a description of the infant's first attempts at language, the chapter follows the sequence of events that leads to the child's ability to utter two-word sentences. The chapter concludes with an examination of three classic theories of language acquisition and a fourth, hybrid theory that combines aspects of each.

NOTE: Answer guidelines for all Chapter 6 questions begin on page 93.

Guided Study

The text chapter should be studied one section at a time. Before you read, preview each section by skimming it, noting headings and boldface items. Then read the appropriate section objectives from the following outline. Keep these objectives in mind and, as you read the chapter section, search for the information that will enable you to meet each objective. Once you have finished a section, write out answers for its objectives.

Sensorimotor Intelligence (pp. 155–161)

1. Identify and describe Piaget's first two stages of sensorimotor intelligence.

2. Identify and describe stages 3 and 4 of Piaget's theory of sensorimotor intelligence.

3. (text and Thinking Like a Scientist) Explain what object permanence is, how it is tested in infancy, and what these tests reveal.

4. Identify and describe stages 5 and 6 of Piaget's theory of sensorimotor intelligence.

5. Describe some major advances in the scientific investigation of infant cognition.

Information Processing (pp. 161–167)

6. Explain the information-processing theory of cognition.

7. Discuss the Gibsons' view of perception, focusing on the idea of affordances and giving examples of the affordances perceived by infants.

8. Discuss research findings on infant memory.

Language: What Develops in the First Two Years? (pp. 167–175)

9. Identify the main features of child-directed speech, and explain its importance.

10. Describe language development during infancy, and identify its major hallmarks.

11. Differentiate three theories of language learning, and explain current views on language learning.

Chapter Review

When you have finished reading the chapter, work through the material that follows to review it. Complete the sentences and answer the questions. As you proceed, evaluate your performance for each section by consulting the answers beginning on page 93. Do not continue with the next section until you understand each answer. If you need to, review or reread the appropriate section in the textbook before continuing.

Sensorimotor Intelligence (pp. 155–161)

1. Cognition involves _____
_____ .

2. The first major theorist to realize that infants are active learners was _____ .

3. When infants begin to explore the environment through sensory and motor skills, they are displaying what Piaget called
_____ intelligence. In number,

Piaget described _____ stages of development of this type of intelligence.

4. The first two stages of sensorimotor intelligence are examples of _____ _____ _____ . Stage one begins with newborns' reflexes, such as _____ and _____ , and also the _____ , which are very responsive at birth. It lasts from birth to _____ of age.

5. Stage two begins when newborns show signs of _____ of their _____ and senses to the specifics of the environment.

Describe the development of the sucking reflex during stages one and two.

6. In stages three and four, development switches to _____ _____ _____ , involving the baby with an object or with another person. During stage three, which occurs between _____ and _____ months of age, infants repeat a specific action that has just elicited a pleasing response.

Describe a typical stage-three behavior.

7. In stage four, which lasts from _____ to _____ months of age, infants can better _____ events. At this stage, babies also engage in purposeful actions, or _____-_____ behavior.

8. (text and Thinking Like a Scientist) A major cognitive accomplishment of infancy is the ability to understand that objects exist even when they are _____ . This awareness is called _____ _____ . To test for this awareness, Piaget devised a procedure to observe whether an

infant will _____ for a hidden object. Using this test, Piaget concluded that this awareness does not develop until about _____ of age. More recent research studies have shown that this ability actually begins to emerge at _____ months.

9. During stage five, which lasts from _____ to _____ months, infants begin experimenting in thought and deed. They do so through _____ _____ _____ , which involve taking in experiences and trying to make sense of them.

Explain what Piaget meant when he described the stage-five infant as a "little scientist."

10. Stage six, which lasts from _____ to _____ months, is the stage of achieving new means by using _____ _____ .

11. One sign that children have reached stage six is _____ _____ , which is their emerging ability to imitate behaviors they noticed earlier.

12. Two research tools that have become available since Piaget's time are _____ studies and _____ , which reveals brain activity as cognition occurs.

Information Processing (pp. 161–167)

13. A perspective on human cognition that is modeled on how computers analyze data is the _____-_____ theory. Two aspects of this theory as applied to human development are _____ , which concern perception and so are analogous to computer input, and _____ , which involves storage and retrieval of ideas, or output.

14. Much of the current research in perception and cognition has been inspired by the work of the Gibsons, who stress that perception is a(n)

_____ (active/passive/automatic) cognitive phenomenon.

15. According to the Gibsons, any object in the environment offers diverse opportunities for interaction; this property of an object is called an

_____ .

16. Which of these properties an individual perceives in an object depends on the individual's

_____ _____ and

_____ _____ , on his

or her _____ _____ ,

and on his or her _____

_____ of what the object might be used for.

17. A firm surface that appears to drop off is called a

_____ _____ .

Although perception of this drop off was once linked to _____ maturity, later research found that infants as young as

_____ are able to perceive the drop off, as evidenced by changes in their

_____ _____ and their wide open eyes.

18. Perception that is primed to focus on movement and change is called _____

_____ . Another universal principle of infant perception is _____

_____ , which may have evolved because humans _____ by learning to attend to, and rely on, one another.

19. Babies have great difficulty storing new memories in their first _____ (how long?).

20. Research has shown, however, that babies can show that they remember when three conditions are met:

(a) _____

(b) _____

(c) _____

21. When these conditions are met, infants as young as _____ months "remembered" events from two weeks earlier if they experienced a _____ _____ prior to retesting.

22. After about _____ months, infants become capable of retaining information for longer periods of time, with less reminding.

23. Most researchers believe there _____ (is one type of memory/are many types of memory). Memory for routines that remains hidden until a stimulus triggers it is called

_____ _____ .

Memories that can be recalled on demand are referred to as _____

_____ .

Language: What Develops in the First Two Years? (pp. 167–175)

24. Children the world over _____ (follow/do not follow) the same sequence of early language development. The timing of this sequence and depth of ability _____ (varies/does not vary).

25. Newborns show a preference for hearing _____ over other sounds, including the high-pitched, simplified adult speech called

_____-_____ speech, which is sometimes called

_____ _____ .

26. By 4 months of age, most babies' verbal repertoire consists of _____

_____ .

27. Between _____ and

_____ months of age, babies begin to repeat certain syllables, a phenomenon referred to as _____ .

28. Deaf babies begin oral babbling _____ (earlier/later) than hearing babies do. Deaf babies may also use _____

_____ to babble, with this behavior emerging _____ (earlier than/at the same time as/later than) hearing infants begin oral babbling.

29. The average baby speaks a few words at about _____ of age. When vocabulary reaches approximately 50 words, it suddenly begins to build rapidly, at a rate of

_____ or more words a month. This language spurt is called the _____ _____ because toddlers learn a disproportionate number of _____ .

30. Language acquisition may be shaped by our _____ , as revealed by the fact that English-speaking infants learn more _____ than Chinese or Korean infants, who learn more _____ . Alternatively, the entire _____ _____ may determine language acquisition.

31. Another characteristic is the use of the _____ , in which a single word expresses a complete thought. Variations of tone and pitch, called _____ , are extensive in babbling.

32. Children begin to produce their first two-word sentences at about _____ months, showing a clearly emerging understanding of _____ , which refers to all the methods that languages use to communicate meaning, apart from the words themselves.

33. Reinforcement and other conditioning processes account for language development, according to the learning theory of _____ . Support for this theory comes from the fact that there are wide variations in language _____ , especially when children from different cultures are compared. One study that followed mother–infant pairs over time found that the frequency of early _____ _____ predicted the child's rate of language acquisition many months later.

34. The theorist who stressed that language is too complex to be mastered so early and easily through conditioning is _____ . Because all young children _____ (master/do not master) basic grammar at about the same age, there is, in a sense, a _____ _____ . This

theorist also maintained that all children are born with a LAD, or _____ _____ _____ , that enables children to quickly derive the rules of grammar from the speech they hear.

Summarize the research support for theory two.

35. A third, _____-_____ , theory of language proposes that _____ _____ foster infant language.

36. A new hybrid theory, based on a model called an _____ _____ , combines aspects of several theories. A fundamental aspect of this theory is that _____ _____ .

Progress Test 1

Multiple-Choice Questions

Circle your answers to the following questions and check them with the answers beginning on page 94. If your answer is incorrect, read the explanation for why it is incorrect and then consult the appropriate pages of the text (in parentheses following the correct answer).

1. In general terms, the Gibsons' concept of affordances emphasizes the idea that the individual perceives an object in terms of its:
   a. economic importance.
   b. physical qualities.
   c. function or use to the individual.
   d. role in the larger culture or environment.

2. According to Piaget, when a baby repeats an action that has just triggered a pleasing response from his or her caregiver, a stage _____ behavior has occurred.
   a. one   c. three
   b. two   d. six

3. Sensorimotor intelligence begins with a baby's first:
   a. attempt to crawl.
   b. reflex actions.
   c. auditory perception.
   d. adaptation of a reflex.

4. Piaget and the Gibsons would most likely agree that:
   a. perception is largely automatic.
   b. language development is biologically predisposed in children.
   c. learning and perception are active cognitive processes.
   d. it is unwise to "push" children too hard academically.

5. By the end of the first year, infants usually learn how to:
   a. accomplish simple goals.
   b. manipulate various symbols.
   c. solve complex problems.
   d. pretend.

6. When an infant begins to understand that objects exist even when they are out of sight, she or he has begun to understand the concept of object:
   a. displacement.   c. permanence.
   b. importance.   d. location.

7. Today, most cognitive psychologists view language acquisition as:
   a. primarily the result of imitation of adult speech.
   b. a behavior that is determined primarily by biological maturation.
   c. a behavior determined entirely by learning.
   d. determined by both biological maturation and learning.

8. Despite cultural differences, children all over the world attain very similar language skills:
   a. according to ethnically specific timetables.
   b. in the same sequence according to a variable timetable.
   c. according to culturally specific timetables.
   d. according to timetables that vary from child to child.

9. The average baby speaks a few words at about:
   a. 6 months.   c. 12 months.
   b. 9 months.   d. 24 months.

10. A single word used by toddlers to express a complete thought is:
    a. a holophrase.
    b. child-directed speech.
    c. babbling.
    d. an affordance.

11. A distinctive form of language, with a particular pitch, structure, etc., that adults use in talking to infants is called:
    a. a holophrase.
    b. the LAD.
    c. child-directed speech.
    d. conversation.

12. Habituation studies reveal that most infants detect the difference between a pah sound and a bah sound at:
    a. birth.   c. 3 months.
    b. 1 month.   d. 6 months.

13. The imaging technique in which the brain's magnetic properties indicate activation in various parts of the brain is called a(n):
    a. PET scan.   c. fMRI.
    b. EEG.   d. CAT scan.

14. A toddler who taps on the computer's keyboard after observing her mother sending e-mail the day before is demonstrating:
    a. assimilation.   c. deferred imitation.
    b. accommodation.   d. dynamic perception.

15. In Piaget's theory of sensorimotor intelligence, reflexes that involve the infant's own body are examples of:
    a. primary circular reactions.
    b. secondary circular reactions.
    c. tertiary circular reactions.
    d. none of the above.

Matching Items

Match each definition or description with its corresponding term.

Terms

_____ **1.** people preference
_____ **2.** affordances
_____ **3.** object permanence
_____ **4.** Noam Chomsky
_____ **5.** B. F. Skinner
_____ **6.** sensorimotor intelligence
_____ **7.** babbling
_____ **8.** holophrase
_____ **9.** habituation
_____ **10.** deferred imitation
_____ **11.** dynamic perception

Definitions or Descriptions

a. getting used to an object or event after repeated exposure to it
b. repetitive utterance of certain syllables
c. perception that focuses on movement and change
d. the ability to witness, remember, and later copy a behavior
e. the realization that something that is out of sight continues to exist
f. the innate attraction of human babies to humans
g. opportunities for interaction that an object offers
h. theorist who believed that verbal behavior is conditioned
i. a single word used to express a complete thought
j. theorist who believed that language ability is innate
k. thinking through the senses and motor skills

Progress Test 2

Progress Test 2 should be completed during a final chapter review. Answer the following questions after you thoroughly understand the correct answers for the Chapter Review and Progress Test 1.

Multiple-Choice Questions

1. Stage five (12 to 18 months) of sensorimotor intelligence is best described as:
   a. first acquired adaptations.
   b. the period of the "little scientist."
   c. procedures for making interesting sights last.
   d. new means through symbolization.

2. Which of the following is *not* evidence of dynamic perception during infancy?
   a. Babies prefer to look at things in motion.
   b. Babies form simple expectations of the path that a moving object will follow.
   c. Babies use movement cues to discern the boundaries of objects.
   d. Babies quickly grasp that even though objects look different when seen from different viewpoints, they are the same objects.

3. (text and Thinking Like a Scientist) Research suggests that the concept of object permanence:
   a. fades after a few months.
   b. is a skill some children never acquire.
   c. may occur earlier and more gradually than Piaget recognized.
   d. involves pretending as well as mental combinations.

4. Which of the following is an example of a secondary circular reaction?
   a. 1-month-old infant staring at a mobile suspended over her crib
   b. a 2-month-old infant sucking a pacifier
   c. realizing that rattles make noise, a 4-month-old infant laughs with delight when his mother puts a rattle in his hand
   d. a 12-month-old toddler licks a bar of soap to learn what it tastes like

5. Eighteen-month-old Colin puts a collar on his stuffed dog, then pretends to take it for a walk. Colin's behavior is an example of a:
   a. primary circular reaction.
   b. secondary circular reaction.
   c. tertiary circular reaction.
   d. first acquired adaptation.

6. According to Piaget, the use of deferred imitation is an example of stage _____ behavior.
   a. three   **c.** five
   b. four   **d.** six

7. For Noam Chomsky, the language acquisition device refers to:
   a. the human predisposition to acquire language.
   b. the portion of the human brain that processes speech.
   c. the vocabulary of the language to which the child is exposed.
   d. all of the above.

8. The first stage of sensorimotor intelligence lasts until:
   a. infants can anticipate events that will fulfill their needs.
   b. infants begin to adapt their reflexes to the environment.
   c. infants interact with objects to produce exciting experiences.
   d. infants are capable of thinking about past and future events.

9. Whether or not an infant perceives certain characteristics of objects, such as "suckability" or "graspability," seems to depend on:
   a. his or her prior experiences.
   b. his or her needs.
   c. his or her sensory awareness.
   d. all of the above.

10. (Thinking Like a Scientist) Piaget was *incorrect* in his belief that infants do not have:
    a. object permanence.
    b. intelligence.
    c. goal-directed behavior.
    d. all of the above.

11. The purposeful actions that begin to develop in sensorimotor stage four are called:
    a. reflexes.
    b. affordances.
    c. goal-directed behaviors.
    d. mental combinations.

12. What is the correct sequence of stages of language development?
    a. crying, babbling, cooing, first word
    b. crying, cooing, babbling, first word
    c. crying, babbling, first word, cooing
    d. crying, cooing, first word, babbling

13. Compared with hearing babies, deaf babies:
    a. are less likely to babble.
    b. are more likely to babble.
    c. begin to babble vocally at about the same age.
    d. begin to babble manually at about the same age as hearing babies begin to babble vocally.

14. According to Skinner, children acquire language:
    a. as a result of an inborn ability to use the basic structure of language.
    b. through reinforcement and other aspects of conditioning.
    c. mostly because of biological maturation.
    d. in a fixed sequence of predictable stages.

15. A fundamental idea of the emergentist coalition model of language acquisition is that:
    a. all humans are born with an innate language acquisition device.
    b. some aspects of language are best learned in one way at one age, others in another way at another age.
    c. language development occurs too rapidly and easily to be entirely the product of conditioning.
    d. imitation and reinforcement are crucial to the development of language.

Matching Items

Match each definition or description with its corresponding term. **5 and 7 OK to replace assimilation and accommodation. see b and c also**

Terms

_____ 1. goal-directed behavior
_____ 2. visual cliff
_____ 3. primary circular reaction
_____ 4. child-directed speech
_____ 5. new adaptation and anticipation
_____ 6. "little scientist"
_____ 7. mental combinations
_____ 8. secondary circular reaction
_____ 9. tertiary circular reaction
_____ 10. LAD
_____ 11. grammar

Definitions or Descriptions

a. a device for studying depth perception
b. understanding how to reach a goal
c. able to put two ideas together
d. a feedback loop involving the infant's own body
e. a feedback loop involving people and objects
f. a hypothetical device that facilitates language development
g. also called baby talk or motherese
h. Piaget's term for the stage-five toddler
i. purposeful actions
j. a feedback loop involving active exploration and experimentation
k. all the methods used by a language to communicate meaning

Developmental Psychology Applied

Answer these questions the day before an exam as a final check on your understanding of the chapter's terms and concepts.

1. A 9-month-old repeatedly reaches for his sister's doll, even though he has been told "no" many times. This is an example of:
   a. primary circular reactions.
   b. habituation.
   c. delayed imitation.
   d. goal-directed behavior.

2. If a baby sucks harder on a nipple, evidences a change in heart rate, or stares longer at one image than at another when presented with a change of stimulus, the indication is that the baby:
   a. is annoyed by the change.
   b. is both hungry and angry.
   c. has become habituated to the new stimulus.
   d. perceives some differences between stimuli.

3. As an advocate of the social-pragmatic theory, Professor Robinson believes that:
   a. infants communicate in every way they can because they are social beings.
   b. biological maturation is a dominant force in language development.
   c. infants' language abilities mirror those of their primary caregivers.
   d. language develops in many ways for many reasons.

4. According to Skinner's theory, an infant who learns to delight his father by saying "da-da" is probably benefiting from:
   a. social reinforcers, such as smiles and hugs.
   b. modeling.
   c. learning by imitation.
   d. an innate ability to use language.

5. Before putting her dolly to bed, 18-month-old Jessica sings her a song. According to Piaget, Jessica's behavior is an example of the use of:
   a. new means through active experimentation.
   b. mental combinations.
   c. new adaptation and anticipation.
   d. first acquired adaptations.

6. At about 21 months, the typical child will:
   a. have a vocabulary of between 250 and 350 words.
   b. begin to speak in holophrases.
   c. put words together to form rudimentary sentences.
   d. do all of the above.

7. A 20-month-old girl who is able to try out various actions mentally without having to actually perform them is learning to solve simple problems by using:
   a. dynamic perception.
   b. object permanence.
   c. affordances.
   d. mental combinations.

8. A baby who attempts to interact with a smiling parent is demonstrating an ability that typically occurs in which stage of sensorimotor development?
   a. one   c. three
   b. two   d. four

9. Piaget referred to the shift in an infant's behavior from reflexes to deliberate actions as the shift from:
   a. secondary circular reactions to primary circular reactions.
   b. first acquired adaptations to secondary circular reactions.
   c. primary circular reactions to tertiary circular reactions.
   d. stage one primary circular reactions to stage two primary circular reactions.

10. A baby who realizes that a rubber duck that has fallen out of the tub must be somewhere on the floor has achieved:
    a. object permanence.
    b. deferred imitation.
    c. mental combinations.
    d. goal-directed behavior.

11. As soon as her babysitter arrives, 21-month-old Christine holds on to her mother's legs and, in a questioning manner, says "bye-bye." Because Christine clearly is "asking" her mother not to leave, her utterance can be classified as:
    a. babbling.
    b. a noun.
    c. a holophrase.
    d. subject-predicate order.

12. The 6-month-old infant's continual repetition of sound combinations such as "ba-ba-ba" is called:
    a. cooing.   c. a holophrase.
    b. babbling.   d. crooning.

13. Nine-month-old Akshay, who looks out of his crib for a toy that has fallen, is clearly demonstrating:
    a. object permanence.
    b. goal-directed behavior.
    c. a secondary circular reaction.
    d. all of the above.

14. Monica firmly believes that her infant daughter "taught" herself language because of the seemingly effortless manner in which she has mastered new words and phrases. Monica is evidently a proponent of the theory proposed by:
    a. B. F. Skinner.
    b. Noam Chomsky.
    c. social pragmatic theorists.
    d. the emergentist coalition.

15. Like most Korean toddlers, Noriko has acquired a greater number of _____ in her vocabulary than her North American counterparts, who tend to acquire more _____ .
    a. verbs; nouns
    b. nouns; verbs
    c. adjectives; verbs
    d. adjectives; nouns

Key Terms

Writing Definitions

Using your own words, write a brief definition or explanation of each of the following terms on a separate piece of paper.

1. sensorimotor intelligence
2. primary circular reactions
3. secondary circular reactions
4. object permanence
5. tertiary circular reactions
6. "little scientist"
7. deferred imitation
8. habituation
9. fMRI
10. information-processing theory
11. affordance
12. visual cliff
13. dynamic perception
14. people preference

15. reminder session
16. child-directed speech
17. babbling
18. naming explosion

19. holophrase
20. grammar
21. language acquisition device (LAD)

Cross-Check
After you have written the definitions of the key terms in this chapter, you should complete the crossword puzzle to ensure that you can reverse the process—recognize the term, given the definition.

ACROSS

6. a brain-imaging technique
7. a circular reaction involving the infant's own body
8. a circular reaction involving people and objects
9. a type of perception primed to focus on movement
11. the process of getting used to an object
12. child-directed speech
14. a sudden increase in an infant's vocabulary

DOWN

1. the methods used by languages to communicate meaning
2. a type of circular reaction that involves active exploration
3. a single word used to express a complete thought
4. Piaget's term for the stage-five toddler
5. an opportunity for perception
9. imitation of something that occurred earlier
10. extended repetition of syllables
13. Chomsky's term for a brain structure that enables language

ANSWERS

CHAPTER REVIEW

1. intelligence, learning, memory, and language
2. Piaget
3. sensorimotor; six
4. primary circular reactions; sucking; grasping; senses; 1 month
5. adaptation; reflexes

Stage-one infants suck everything that touches their lips. At about 1 month, they start to adapt their suck-ing to specific objects. After several months, they have organized the world into objects to be sucked for nourishment, objects to be sucked for pleasure, and objects not to be sucked at all.

6. secondary circular reactions; 4; 8

A stage-three infant may squeeze a duck, hear a quack, and squeeze the duck again.

7. 8; 12; anticipate; goal-directed
8. no longer in sight; object permanence; search; 8 months; 4½
9. 12; 18; tertiary circular reactions

Having discovered some action or set of actions that is possible with a given object, stage-five "little scientists" seem to ask, "What else can I do with this?"

10. 18; 24; mental combinations

11. deferred imitation
12. habituation; fMRI
13. information-processing; affordances; memory
14. active
15. affordance
16. past experiences; current development; immediate motivation; sensory awareness
17. visual cliff; visual; 3 months; heart rate
18. dynamic perception; people preference; survived
19. year
20. (a) experimental conditions are similar to real life; (b) motivation is high; (c) special measures aid memory retrieval
21. 3 months; reminder session
22. 6
23. are many types of memory; implicit memory; explicit memory
24. follow; varies
25. speech; child-directed; baby talk (or motherese)
26. squeals, growls, gurgles, grunts, croons, and yells, as well as some speechlike sounds
27. 6; 9; babbling
28. later; hand gestures; at the same time as
29. 1 year; 50 to 100; naming explosion; nouns
30. culture; nouns; verbs; social context
31. holophrase; intonation
32. 21; grammar
33. B. F. Skinner; fluency; maternal responsiveness
34. Noam Chomsky; master; universal grammar; language acquisition device

Support for this theory comes from the fact that all babies babble ma-ma and da-da sounds at about 6 to 9 months. No reinforcement is needed. All they need is for dendrites to grow, mouth muscles to strengthen, neurons to connect, and speech to be heard.

35. social-pragmatic; social impulses
36. emergentist coalition; some aspects of language are best learned in one way at one age, others in another way at another age

PROGRESS TEST 1

Multiple-Choice Questions

1. **c.** is the answer. (p. 162)
2. **c.** is the answer. (pp. 156, 157)
3. **b.** is the answer. This was Piaget's most basic contribution to the study of infant cognition—that

intelligence is revealed in behavior at every age. (p. 156)

4. **c.** is the answer. (pp. 155, 162)

   b. This is Chomsky's position.

   d. This issue was not discussed in the text.

5. **a.** is the answer. (pp. 156, 157–158)

   b. & c. These abilities are not acquired until children are much older.

   d. Pretending is associated with stage six (18 to 24 months).

6. **c.** is the answer. (p. 158)

7. **d.** is the answer. (pp. 174–175)

8. **b.** is the answer. (p. 168)

   a., c., & d. Children the world over follow the same sequence, but the timing of their accomplishments may vary considerably.

9. **c.** is the answer. (pp. 168, 169)

10. **a.** is the answer. (p. 170)

    b. Child-directed speech is the speech adults use with infants.

    c. Babbling refers to the first syllables a baby utters.

    d. An affordance is an opportunity for perception and interaction.

11. **c.** is the answer. (p. 168)

    a. A holophrase is a single word uttered by a toddler to express a complete thought.

    b. According to Noam Chomsky, the LAD, or language acquisition device, is an innate ability in humans to acquire language.

    d. These characteristic differences in pitch and structure are precisely what distinguish child-directed speech from regular conversation.

12. **b.** is the answer. (p. 160)

13. **c.** is the answer. (p. 160)

14. **c.** is the answer (p. 159)

    a. & b. In Piaget's theory, these refer to processes by which mental concepts incorporate new experiences (assimilation) or are modified in response to new experiences (accommodation).

    d. Dynamic perception is perception that is primed to focus on movement and change.

15. **a.** is the answer. (p. 156)

    b. Secondary circular reactions involve the baby with an object or with another person.

c. Tertiary circular reactions involve active exploration and experimentation, rather than mere reflexive action.

Matching Items

1. f (p. 164)	**5.** h (p. 171)	**9.** a (p. 160)
2. g (p. 162)	**6.** k (p. 155)	**10.** d (p. 159)
3. e (p. 158)	**7.** b (p. 169)	**11.** c (p. 164)
4. j (p. 173)	**8.** i (p. 170)	

PROGRESS TEST 2

Multiple-Choice Questions

1. **b.** is the answer. (pp. 156, 159)

   a. & c. These are stages two and three.

   d. This is not one of Piaget's stages of sensorimotor intelligence.

2. **d.** is the answer. This is an example of perceptual constancy. (p. 164)

3. **c.** is the answer. (pp. 158–159)

4. **c.** is the answer. (p. 157)

   a. & b. These are examples of primary circular reactions.

   d. This is an example of a tertiary circular reaction.

5. **c.** is the answer. (p. 159)

6. **d.** is the answer. (p. 159)

7. **a.** is the answer. Chomsky believed that this device is innate. (p. 173)

8. **b.** is the answer. (p. 156)

   a. & c. Both of these occur later than stage one.

   d. This is a hallmark of stage six.

9. **d.** is the answer. (p. 162)

10. **a.** is the answer. (pp. 158–159)

11. **c.** is the answer. (pp. 156, 157–158)

    a. Reflexes are involuntary (and therefore unintentional) responses.

    b. Affordances are perceived opportunities for interaction with objects.

    d. Mental combinations are actions that are carried out mentally, rather than behaviorally. Moreover, mental combinations do not develop until a later age, during sensorimotor stage six.

12. **b.** is the answer. (pp. 168–169)

13. **d.** is the answer. (p. 169)

    a. & b. Hearing and deaf babies do not differ in the overall likelihood that they will babble.

c. Deaf babies begin to babble vocally several months later than hearing babies do.

14. **b.** is the answer. (pp. 171–172)

    a., c., & d. These views on language acquisition describe the theory offered by Noam Chomsky.

15. **b.** is the answer. (p. 174)

    a. & c. These ideas are consistent with Noam Chomsky's theory.

    d. This is the central idea of B. F. Skinner's theory.

Matching Items

1. i (p. 157)	**5.** b (p. 157)	**9.** j (p. 159)
2. a (p. 163)	**6.** h (p. 159)	**10.** f (p. 173)
3. d (p. 156)	**7.** c (p. 159)	**11.** k (p. 171)
4. g (p. 168)	**8.** e (p. 157)	

DEVELOPMENTAL PSYCHOLOGY APPLIED

1. **d.** is the answer. The baby is clearly behaving purposefully, which is the hallmark of goal-directed behavior. (pp. 157–158)

   a. This is a stage-four behavior, not stages one or two.

   b. He is clearly not getting used to the stimulus.

   c. Delayed imitation is the ability to imitate actions seen in the past.

2. **d.** is the answer. (p. 160)

   a. & b. These changes in behavior indicate that the newborn has perceived an unfamiliar stimulus, not that he or she is hungry, annoyed, or angry.

   c. Habituation refers to a *decrease* in physiological responsiveness to a familiar stimulus.

3. **a.** is the answer. (pp. 173–174)

   b. This idea is more consistent with Noam Chomsky's theory.

   c. This idea is more consistent with B. F. Skinner's theory.

   d. This expresses the emergentist coalition theory.

4. **a.** is the answer. The father's expression of delight is a reinforcer in that it has increased the likelihood of the infant's vocalization. (pp. 171–173)

   b. & c. Modeling, or learning by imitation, would be implicated if the father attempted to increase the infant's vocalizations by repeatedly saying "da-da" himself, in the infant's presence.

   d. This is Chomsky's viewpoint; Skinner maintained that language is acquired through learning.

5. **b.** is the answer. (p. 159)

    a. This is an example of stage-5 behavior.

    c. This is a stage-4 behavior.

    d. This is a stage-2 behavior.

6. **c.** is the answer. (p. 171)

    a. At 21 months of age, most children have much smaller vocabularies.

    b. Speaking in holophrases is typical of younger infants.

7. **d.** is the answer. (p. 159)

    a. Dynamic perception is perception primed to focus on movement and change.

    b. Object permanence is the awareness that objects do not cease to exist when they are out of sight.

    c. Affordances are the opportunities for perception and interaction that an object or place offers to any individual.

8. **c.** is the answer. (p. 157)

9. **d.** is the answer. (p. 157)

10. **a.** is the answer. Before object permanence is attained, an object that disappears from sight ceases to exist for the infant. (p. 158)

    b. Deferred imitation is the ability to witness, remember, and later copy a particular behavior.

    c. Mental combinations are actions that are carried out mentally.

    d. Goal-directed behavior refers to purposeful actions initiated by infants in anticipation of events that will fulfill their needs and wishes.

11. **c.** is the answer. (p. 170)

    a. Because Christine is expressing a complete thought, her speech is much more than babbling.

    b. "Bye-bye" is not a noun.

    d. The ability to understand subject-predicate order emerges later, when children begin forming two-word sentences.

12. **b.** is the answer. (p. 169)

    a. & d. Cooing and crooning are the pleasant-sounding utterances of the infant by about 4 months.

    c. The holophrase occurs later and refers to the toddler's use of a single word to express a complete thought.

13. **d.** is the answer. (pp. 157–158)

14. **b.** is the answer. (p. 173)

15. **a.** is the answer. (p. 170)

KEY TERMS

1. Piaget's stages of **sensorimotor intelligence** (from birth to about 2 years old) are based on his theory that infants think exclusively with their senses and motor skills. (p. 155)

2. In Piaget's theory, **primary circular reactions** are a type of feedback loop involving the infant's own body, in which infants take in experiences (such as sucking and grasping) and try to make sense of them. (p. 156)

3. **Secondary circular reactions** are a type of feedback loop involving the infant's responses to objects and other people. (p. 157)

4. **Object permanence** is the understanding that objects continue to exist even when they cannot be seen, touched, or heard. (p. 158)

5. In Piaget's theory, **tertiary circular reactions** are the most sophisticated type of infant feedback loop, involving active exploration and experimentation. (p. 159)

6. **"Little scientist"** is Piaget's term for the stage-five toddler who learns about the properties of objects in his or her world through active experimentation. (p. 159)

7. **Deferred imitation** is the ability of infants to witness, remember, and later copy a behavior they noticed hours or days earlier. (p. 159)

8. **Habituation** is the process of getting used to an object or event through repeated exposure to it. (p. 160)

9. **fMRI** (functional magnetic resonance imaging) is an imaging technique in which the brain's magnetic properties are measured to reveal changes in activity levels in various parts of the brain. (p. 160)

10. **Information-processing theory** is a theory of human cognition that compares thinking to the ways in which a computer analyzes data, through the processes of sensory input, connections, stored memories, and output. (p. 161)

11. **Affordances** are perceived opportunities for interacting with people, objects, or places in the environment. Infants perceive sucking, grasping, noisemaking, and many other affordances of objects at an early age. (p. 162)

12. A **visual cliff** is an experimental apparatus that provides the illusion of a sudden drop between one surface and another. (p. 163)

13. **Dynamic perception,** a universal principle of infant perception, is perception that is primed to focus on movement and change. (p. 164)

14. **People preference,** a universal principle of infant perception, is the innate attraction that human babies have to other humans. (p. 164)

15. A **reminder session** is any perceptual experience of some aspect of an event that triggers the entire memory of the event. (p. 165)

16. **Child-directed speech** is a form of speech used by adults when talking to infants. It is simplified, it has a higher pitch, and it is repetitive; it is also called *baby talk* or *motherese.* (p. 168)

17. **Babbling,** which begins between 6 and 9 months of age, is characterized by the extended repetition of certain syllables (such as "ma-ma"). (p. 169)

18. The **naming explosion** refers to the dramatic increase in the infant's vocabulary that begins at about 18 months of age. (p. 169)

19. Another characteristic of infant speech is the use of the **holophrase,** in which a single word is used to convey a complete thought. (p. 170)

20. The **grammar** of a language includes rules of word order, verb forms, and all other methods used to communicate meaning apart from words themselves. (p. 171)

21. According to Chomsky, children possess an innate **language acquisition device (LAD),** which is a hypothesized mental structure that enables them to acquire language, including the basic aspects of grammar. (p. 173)

Cross-Check

ACROSS

6. fMRI
7. primary
8. secondary
9. dynamic
11. habituation
12. baby talk
14. naming explosion

DOWN

1. grammar
2. tertiary
3. holophrase
4. little scientist
5. affordance
9. deferred
10. babbling
13. LAD

7

The First Two Years: Psychosocial Development

Chapter Overview

Chapter 7 describes the emotional and social life of the developing person during the first two years. It begins with a description of the infant's emerging emotions and how they reflect mobility and social awareness. Two emotions, contentment and distress, are apparent at birth and are soon joined by anger and fear. As self-awareness develops, many new emotions emerge, including embarrassment, shame, guilt, and pride.

The second section explores the psychoanalytic theories of Freud and Erikson along with behaviorist, cognitive, epigenetic systems, and sociocultural theories, which help us understand how the infant's emotional and behavioral responses begin to take on the various patterns that form personality. Temperament, which affects later personality and is primarily inborn, is influenced by the individual's interactions with the environment.

The third section explores the social context in which emotions develop. By referencing their caregivers' signals, infants learn when and how to express their emotions. Emotions and relationships are then examined from a different perspective—that of parent–infant interaction. Videotaped studies of parents and infants, combined with laboratory studies of attachment, have greatly expanded our understanding of psychosocial development. This section concludes by exploring the impact of day care on infants.

NOTE: Answer guidelines for all Chapter 7 questions begin on page 109.

Guided Study

The text chapter should be studied one section at a time. Before you read, preview each section by skimming it, noting headings and boldface items. Then read the appropriate section objectives from the following outline. Keep these objectives in mind and, as you read the chapter section, search for the information that will enable you to meet each objective. Once you have finished a section, write out answers for its objectives.

Emotional Development (pp. 180–183)

1. Describe the basic emotions expressed by infants during the first days and months.

2. Describe the main developments in the emotional life of the child between 6 months and 2 years.

3. Discuss the links between the infant's emerging self-awareness and his or her continuing emotional development.

Theories About Infant Psychosocial Development
(pp. 183–191)

4. Describe Freud's psychosexual stages of infant development.

5. Describe Erikson's psychosocial stages of infant development.

6. Contrast the perspectives of behaviorism and cognitive theory regarding psychosocial development in the first two years of life.

7. Discuss the epigenetic theory explanation of the roles of temperament and infant–caregiver interaction in the child's psychosocial development.

8. Discuss the sociocultural view regarding the influence of culture on development, focusing on two different parenting practices.

The Development of Social Bonds (pp. 191–199)

9. (text and Thinking Like a Scientist) Discuss the importance of synchrony in caregiver–infant interaction during the first year, and describe the still-face technique for measuring synchrony.

10. Define attachment, explain how it is measured and how it is influenced by context, and identify factors that predict secure or insecure attachment.

11. Discuss the concept of social referencing, noting the difference in how the infant interacts with mother and father.

12. Discuss the impact of nonrelative care on young children, and identify the factors that define high-quality day care.

Conclusions in Theory and Practice (pp. 199–201)

13. State several conclusions that can be drawn from research on early psychosocial development.

Chapter Review

When you have finished reading the chapter, work through the material that follows to review it. Complete the sentences and answer the questions. As you proceed, evaluate your performance for each section by consulting the answers beginning on page 109. Do not continue with the next section until you understand each answer. If you need to, review or reread the appropriate section in the textbook before continuing.

Introduction and *Emotional Development* (pp. 179–183)

1. Psychosocial development includes
_____ development and
_____ development.

2. The first emotions that can be reliably discerned in infants are _____ and
_____ . Other early infant emotions include _____ ,
_____ , and _____ .
Infants' pleasure in seeing faces is first expressed by the _____ _____ ,
which appears at about _____
weeks.

3. Anger becomes evident at about _____
months. During infancy, anger _____
(is/is not) a healthy response, and usually occurs in response to _____ . In contrast,
sadness indicates _____ and is accompanied by an increase in the stress hormone _____ .

4. Fully formed fear emerges at about
_____ . One expression of this new emotion is _____ _____ ;
another is _____
_____ , or fear of abandonment,
which is normal at age _____ year(s)
and intensifies by age _____
year(s). During the second year, anger and fear typically _____ (increase/decrease)
and become more _____ toward specific things.

5. Toward the end of the second year, the new emotions of _____ , _____ ,
_____ , and _____

become apparent. These emotions require an awareness of _____
_____ .

6. An important foundation for emotional growth is
_____ ; very young infants have no sense of _____ . This emerging sense of "me" and "mine" leads to a new
_____ of others.

Briefly describe the nature and findings of the classic rouge-and-mirror experiment on self-awareness in infants.

7. Pride and shame are strongly linked with
_____ . Important in this development is children's ability to form their own positive _____ . The best way to build self-esteem is not to _____ young children but to allow them to
_____ .

Theories About Infant Psychosocial Development (pp. 183–191)

8. In Freud's theory, development begins with the
_____ stage, so named because the
_____ is the infant's prime source of gratification and pleasure.

9. According to Freud, in the second year, the prime focus of gratification comes from stimulation and control of the bowels. Freud referred to this period as the _____ stage.

Describe Freud's ideas on the importance of early oral experiences to later personality development.

10. The theorist who believed that development occurs through a series of psychosocial crises is _____ . According to his theory, the crisis of infancy is one of

_____ ,

whereas the crisis of toddlerhood is one of

_____ .

11. According to the perspective of _____ , personality is molded through the processes of _____ and _____ of the child's spontaneous behaviors. A strong proponent of this position was _____ .

12. Later theorists incorporated the role of _____ learning, that is, infants' tendencies to observe and _____ the personality traits of their parents. The theorist most closely associated with this type of learning is _____ .

13. According to cognitive theory, a person's

_____ , _____ ,

_____ , and _____

determine his or her perspective on the world. More specifically, infants use their early relationships to build a _____

_____ that becomes a frame of reference for organizing perceptions and experiences.

14. According to _____ theory, each infant is born with a _____ predisposition to develop certain emotional traits. Among these are the traits of _____ .

15. These traits are similar to _____ . Although these traits are not learned, their expression is influenced by the _____ .

16. The classic long-term study of children's temperament is the _____ . The study found that by 3 months, infants can be clustered into one of four types: _____ ,

_____ , _____ ,

and _____ .

17. The "Big Five" personality traits include

_____ , _____ ,

_____ , _____ , and

_____ .

18. An important factor in healthy psychosocial development is _____

_____ _____ between the developing child and the caregiving context.

19. According to _____ theory, the entire _____ context can have a major impact on infant–caregiver relationships and the infant's development. An _____ is a theory of child rearing that is specific to a culture or _____ group. As an example, researchers have found that physically close, _____ parenting predicts toddlers who later are more _____ and _____ , in comparison to physically far, _____ parenting, which produces children with the opposite traits.

The Development of Social Bonds (pp. 191–199)

20. The coordinated interaction of response between infant and caregiver is called _____ . Partly through this interaction, infants learn to _____ _____ and to develop some of the basic skills of _____ _____ . It also helps infants express their own _____ . Synchrony usually begins with _____ (infants/ parents) imitating _____ (infants/ parents).

21. (Thinking Like a Scientist) To study the importance of synchrony to development, researchers use an experimental device, called the _____-_____ technique, in which the caregiver _____ (does/does not) respond to the infant's movements.

22. The emotional bond that develops between slightly older infants and their caregivers is called _____ .

23. Approaching, following, and climbing onto the caregiver's lap are signs of _____-_____ behaviors, while snuggling

and holding are signs of _____-_____ behaviors.

24. An infant who derives comfort and confidence from the secure base provided by the caregiver is displaying _____ _____ (type B). In this type of relationship, the caregiver acts as a _____ _____ _____ from which the child is willing to venture forth.

25. By contrast, _____ _____ is characterized by an infant's fear, anger, or seeming indifference to the caregiver. Two extremes of this type of relationship are _____-_____ (type A) and _____-_____/_____ (type C).

(text and Table 7.3) Briefly describe the two types of insecure attachment as well as disorganized attachment.

26. The procedure developed by Mary Ainsworth to measure attachment is called the

_____ _____ .

Approximately _____ (what proportion?) of all normal infants tested with this procedure demonstrate secure attachment. When infant–caregiver interactions are inconsistent, infants are classified as _____ .

27. The most troubled infants may be those who are type _____ . Attachment status _____ (can/cannot) change.

State several conditions that promote secure attachment.

State several conditions that promote insecure attachment.

28. The search for information about another person's feelings is called _____ _____ .

29. Although early research on psychosocial development focused on _____– _____ relationships, it is clear that other relatives and unrelated people are crucial to the child's development.

30. The social information from fathers tends to be more _____ than that from mothers, who are more _____ and _____ . Fathers are more _____ (proximal/distal) in their parenting than mothers.

31. Infant day care programs include _____ day care, in which children of various ages are cared for in a paid caregiver's home, and _____ day care, in which several paid providers care for children in a designated place.

32. Regarding the impact of nonmaternal care on young children, recent research studies have generally found that children _____ _____ .

33. The best predictor of a child's social skills is _____.

34. One benefit of day care is the opportunity for toddlers to learn to _____ _____ .

35. (Table 7.5) Researchers have identified five factors that are essential to high-quality day care:

    a. _____

    b. _____

    c. _____

    d. _____

    e. _____

36. Early day care may be detrimental when the mother is _____ and the infant spends more than _____ (how many?) hours each week in a poor-quality program.

Conclusions in Theory and Practice (pp. 199–201)

37. Regarding the major theories of development, _____ _____ theory stands out as the best interpretation. Although the first two years are important, early _____ and _____ development is influenced by the _____ behavior, the support provided by the _____ , the quality of _____ _____ , patterns within the child's _____ , and traits that are _____ .

Progress Test 1

Multiple-Choice Questions

Circle your answers to the following questions and check them with the answers on page 110. If your answer is incorrect, read the explanation for why it is incorrect and then consult the appropriate pages of the text (in parentheses following the correct answer).

1. Newborns have two identifiable emotions:
    a. shame and distress.
    b. pleasure and pain.
    c. anger and joy.
    d. pride and guilt.

2. Parenting that focuses more on children's intellectual development than on their physical development is called:
    a. proximal parenting.
    b. distal parenting.
    c. synchrony.
    d. scaffolding.

3. An infant's fear of being left by the mother or other caregiver, called _____ , is most obvious at about _____ .
    a. separation anxiety; 2 to 4 months
    b. stranger wariness; 2 to 4 months
    c. separation anxiety; 9 to 14 months
    d. stranger wariness; 9 to 14 months

4. Social referencing refers to:
    a. parenting skills that change over time.
    b. changes in community values regarding, for example, the acceptability of using physical punishment with small children.
    c. the support network for new parents provided by extended family members.
    d. the infant response of looking to trusted adults for emotional cues in uncertain situations.

5. A key difference between temperament and personality is that:
    a. temperamental traits are learned.
    b. personality includes traits that are primarily learned.
    c. personality is more stable than temperament.
    d. personality does not begin to form until much later, when self-awareness emerges.

6. The concept of a working model is most consistent with:
    a. psychoanalytic theory.
    b. behaviorism.
    c. cognitive theory.
    d. sociocultural theory.

7. Freud's oral stage corresponds to Erikson's crisis of:
    a. orality versus anality.
    b. trust versus mistrust.
    c. autonomy versus shame and doubt.
    d. secure versus insecure attachment.

8. Erikson believed that the development of a sense of trust in early infancy depends on:
    a. the quality of the infant's food.
    b. the child's genetic inheritance.
    c. consistency, continuity, and sameness of experience.
    d. the introduction of toilet training.

9. Keisha is concerned that her 15-month-old daughter, who no longer seems to enjoy face-to-face play, is showing signs of insecure attachment. You tell her:
   a. not to worry; face-to-face play almost disappears toward the end of the first year.
   b. she may be right to worry, because face-to-face play typically increases throughout infancy.
   c. not to worry; attachment behaviors are unreliable until toddlerhood.
   d. that her child is typical of children who spend more than 20 hours in day care each week.

10. "Easy," "slow to warm up," and "difficult" are descriptions of different:
    a. forms of attachment.
    b. types of temperament.
    c. types of parenting.
    d. toddler responses to the Strange Situation.

11. The more physical play of fathers has been described as:
    a. proximal parenting.
    b. distal parenting.
    c. disorganized parenting.
    d. insecure parenting.

12. *Synchrony* is a term that describes:
    a. the carefully coordinated interaction between caregiver and infant.
    b. a mismatch of the temperaments of caregiver and infant.
    c. a research technique involving videotapes.
    d. the concurrent evolution of different species.

13. The emotional tie that develops between an infant and his or her primary caregiver is called:
    a. self-awareness.   c. affiliation.
    b. synchrony.   d. attachment.

14. Research studies using the still-face technique have demonstrated that:
    a. a parent's responsiveness to an infant aids development.
    b. babies become more upset when a parent leaves the room than when the parent's facial expression is not synchonized with the infant's.
    c. beginning at about 2 months, babies become very upset by a still-faced caregiver.
    d. beginning at about 10 months, babies become very upset by a still-faced caregiver.

15. Interest in people, as evidenced by the social smile, appears for the first time when an infant is _____ weeks old.
    a. 3   c. 9
    b. 6   d. 12

True or False Items

Write T (*true*) or F (*false*) on the line in front of each statement.

_____ 1. The major developmental theories all agree that maternal care is better for children than nonmaternal care.

_____ 2. Approximately 25 percent of infants display secure attachment.

_____ 3. A baby at 11 months is likely to display both stranger wariness and separation anxiety.

_____ 4. Emotional development is affected by maturation of conscious awareness.

_____ 5. A securely attached toddler is most likely to stay close to his or her mother even in a familiar environment.

_____ 6. Current research shows that the majority of infants in day care are slow to develop cognitive and social skills.

_____ 7. Infants use their fathers for social referencing when they look for encouragement.

_____ 8. Temperament is genetically determined and is unaffected by environmental factors.

_____ 9. Self-awareness enables toddlers to feel pride as well as guilt.

_____ 10. The expression of genetic tendencies in temperament are influenced by the environment throughout life.

Progress Test 2

Progress Test 2 should be completed during a final chapter review. Answer the following questions after you thoroughly understand the correct answers for the Chapter Review and Progress Test 1.

Multiple-Choice Questions

1. Infant–caregiver interactions that are marked by inconsistency are usually classified as:
   a. disorganized.
   b. insecure-avoidant.
   c. insecure-resistant.
   d. insecure-ambivalent.

2. Freud's anal stage corresponds to Erikson's crisis of:
   a. autonomy versus shame and doubt.
   b. trust versus mistrust.
   c. orality versus anality.
   d. identity versus role confusion.

3. Not until the sense of self begins to emerge do babies realize that they are seeing their own faces in the mirror. This realization usually occurs:
   a. shortly before 3 months.
   b. at about 6 months.
   c. between 15 and 24 months.
   d. after 24 months.

4. When there is goodness of fit, the parents of a slow-to-warm-up boy will:
   a. give him extra time to adjust to new situations.
   b. encourage independence in their son by frequently leaving him for short periods of time.
   c. put their son in regular day care so other children's temperaments will "rub off" on him.
   d. do all of the above.

5. Emotions such as shame, guilt, embarrassment, and pride emerge at the same time that:
   a. the social smile appears.
   b. aspects of the infant's temperament can first be discerned.
   c. self-awareness begins to emerge.
   d. parents initiate toilet training.

6. Research by the NYLS on temperamental characteristics indicates that:
   a. temperament is probably innate.
   b. the interaction of parent and child determines later personality.
   c. parents pass their temperaments on to their children through modeling.
   d. self-awareness contributes to the development of temperament.

7. In the second six months, stranger wariness is a:
   a. result of insecure attachment.
   b. result of social isolation.
   c. normal emotional response.
   d. setback in emotional development.

8. The caregiving environment can affect a child's temperament through:
   a. the child's temperamental pattern and the demands of the home environment.
   b. parental expectations.
   c. both a. and b.
   d. neither a. nor b.

9. While observing mothers playing with their infants in a playroom, you notice one mother who often teases her son, ignores him when he falls down, and tells him to "hush" when he cries. Mothers who display these behaviors usually have infants who exhibit which type of attachment?
   a. secure
   b. insecure-avoidant
   c. insecure-resistant
   d. disorganized

10. The later consequences of secure attachment and insecure attachment for children are:
    a. balanced by the child's current rearing circumstances.
    b. irreversible, regardless of the child's current rearing circumstances.
    c. more significant in girls than in boys.
    d. more significant in boys than in girls.

11. The attachment pattern marked by anxiety and uncertainty is:
    a. insecure-avoidant.
    b. insecure-resistant/ambivalent.
    c. disorganized.
    d. type B.

12. Compared with mothers, fathers are more likely to:
    a. engage in noisier, more boisterous play.
    b. encourage intellectual development in their children.
    c. encourage social development in their children.
    d. read to their toddlers.

13. Like Freud, Erikson believed that:
    a. problems arising in early infancy last a lifetime.
    b. inability to resolve a conflict in infancy may result in later fixation.
    c. human development can be viewed in terms of psychosexual stages.
    d. all of the above are true.

14. Which of the following is an example of social learning?
    a. Sue discovers that a playmate will share a favorite toy if she asks politely.
    b. Jon learns that other children are afraid of him when he raises his voice.
    c. Zach develops a hot temper after seeing his father regularly display anger and, in turn, receive respect from others.
    d. All of these are examples of social learning.

15. Which of the following is *not* true regarding synchrony?
    a. There are wide variations in the frequency of synchrony from baby to baby.
    b. Synchrony appears to be uninfluenced by cultural differences.
    c. The frequency of mother–infant synchrony has varied over historical time.
    d. Parents and infants spend about one hour a day in face-to-face play.

Matching Items

Match each theorist, term, or concept with its corresponding description or definition.

Theorists, Terms, or Concepts

_____ 1. temperament
_____ 2. Erikson
_____ 3. the Strange Situation
_____ 4. synchrony
_____ 5. trust versus mistrust
_____ 6. Freud
_____ 7. social referencing
_____ 8. autonomy versus shame and doubt
_____ 9. self-awareness
_____ 10. Ainsworth
_____ 11. proximity-seeking behaviors
_____ 12. contact-maintaining behaviors

Descriptions or Definitions

a. looking to caregivers for emotional cues
b. the crisis of infancy
c. the crisis of toddlerhood
d. approaching, following, and climbing
e. theorist who described psychosexual stages of development
f. researcher who devised a laboratory procedure for studying attachment
g. laboratory procedure for studying attachment
h. the relatively consistent, basic dispositions inherent in a person
i. clinging and resisting being put down
j. coordinated interaction between parent and infant
k. theorist who described psychosocial stages of development
l. a person's sense of being distinct from others

Developmental Psychology Applied

Answer these questions the day before an exam as a final check on your understanding of the chapter's terms and concepts.

1. In laboratory tests of attachment, when the mother returns to the playroom after a short absence, a securely attached infant is most likely to:
   a. cry and protest the mother's return.
   b. climb into the mother's arms, then leave to resume play.
   c. climb into the mother's arms and stay there.
   d. continue playing without acknowledging the mother.

2. After a scary fall, 18-month-old Miguel looks to his mother to see if he should cry or laugh. Miguel's behavior is an example of:
   a. proximity-seeking behavior.
   b. social referencing.
   c. insecure attachment.
   d. the crisis of trust versus mistrust.

3. Which of the following is a clear sign of an infant's attachment to a particular person?
   a. The infant turns to that person when distressed.
   b. The infant protests when that person leaves a room.
   c. The infant may cry when strangers appear.
   d. They are all signs of infant attachment.

4. If you had to predict a newborn baby's personality "type" solely on the basis of probability, which classification would be the most likely?
   a. easy
   b. slow-to-warm-up
   c. difficult
   d. hard to classify

5. Professor Kipketer believes that infants' emotions are molded as their parents reinforce or punish their behaviors. Professor Kipketer evidently is a proponent of:
   a. cognitive theory.
   c. epigenetic theory.
   b. behaviorism.
   d. sociocultural theory.

6. Monica, who recently read a newspaper headline stating that "low-income infants are more likely to be insecurely attached to their mothers," is concerned that her own state of poverty will adversely influence any children she might have. You wisely tell her that:
   a. attachment status is determined by a mother's overt responses to an infant's attempts at synchrony and attachment.
   b. the correlation between income and attachment is due to the fact that most low-income mothers are clinically depressed.
   c. insecure attachment has not been shown to adversely influence a child's later development.
   d. all of the above are true.

7. Concluding her report on the impact of day care on young children, Deborah notes that infants are likely to become insecurely attached if:
   a. their own mothers are insensitive caregivers.
   b. the quality of day care is poor.
   c. more than 20 hours per week are spent in day care.
   d. all of the above are true.

8. Mashiyat, who advocates epigenetic theory in explaining the origins of personality, points to research evidence that:
   a. infants are born with definite and distinct temperaments that can change.
   b. early temperamental traits almost never change.
   c. an infant's temperament does not begin to clearly emerge until 2 years of age.
   d. temperament appears to be almost completely unaffected by the social context.

9. Kalil's mother left him alone in the room for a few minutes. When she returned, Kalil seemed indifferent to her presence. According to Mary Ainsworth's research with children in the Strange Situation, Kalil is probably:
   a. a normal, independent infant.
   b. an abused child.
   c. insecurely attached.
   d. securely attached.

10. Connie and Lev, who are first-time parents, are concerned because their 1-month-old baby is difficult to care for and hard to soothe. They are worried that they are doing something wrong. You inform them that their child is probably that way because:
    a. they are reinforcing the child's tantrum behaviors.
    b. they are not meeting some biological need of the child's.
    c. of his or her inherited temperament.
    d. at 1 month of age, all children are difficult to care for and hard to soothe.

11. Two-year-old Anita and her mother visit a day care center. Seeing an interesting toy, Anita runs a few steps toward it, then stops and looks back to see if her mother is coming. Anita's behavior illustrates:
    a. the crisis of autonomy versus shame and doubt.
    b. synchrony.
    c. dyssynchrony.
    d. social referencing.

12. Felix has a biting, sarcastic manner. Freud would probably say that Felix is:
    a. anally expulsive.
    b. anally retentive.
    c. fixated in the oral stage.
    d. experiencing the crisis of trust versus mistrust.

13. A researcher at the child development center places a dot on an infant's nose and watches to see if the infant reacts to her image in a mirror by touching her nose. Evidently, the researcher is testing the child's:
    a. attachment.
    c. self-awareness.
    b. temperament.
    d. social referencing.

14. Four-month-old Carl and his 13-month-old sister Carla are left in the care of a babysitter. As their parents are leaving, it is to be expected that:
    a. Both Carl and Carla will become very upset as their parents leave.
    b. Carl will become more upset over his parents' departure than will Carla.
    c. Carla will become more upset over her parents' departure than will Carl.
    d. Neither Carl nor Carla will become very upset as their parents leave.

15. Dr. Hidalgo believes that infants use their early relationships to develop a set of assumptions that become a frame of reference for later experiences. Dr. Hidalgo evidently is a proponent of:

    a. cognitive theory.
    c. epigenetic theory.
    b. behaviorism.
    d. sociocultural theory.

Key Terms

Using your own words, write a brief definition or explanation of each of the following terms on a separate piece of paper.

1. social smile
2. stranger wariness
3. separation anxiety
4. self-awareness
5. trust versus mistrust
6. autonomy versus shame and doubt
7. social learning
8. working model
9. temperament
10. goodness of fit
11. ethnotheory
12. proximal parenting
13. distal parenting
14. synchrony
15. still-face technique
16. attachment
17. secure attachment
18. insecure-avoidant attachment
19. insecure-resistant/ambivalent attachment
20. disorganized attachment
21. Strange Situation
22. social referencing
23. family day care
24. center day care

ANSWERS

CHAPTER REVIEW

1. emotional; social
2. pleasure; pain; curiosity; happiness; anger; social smile; 6

3. 6; is; frustration; withdrawal; cortisol
4. 9 months; stranger wariness; separation anxiety; 1; 2; decrease; targeted
5. pride, shame, embarrassment, guilt; other people
6. self-awareness; self; consciousness

In the classic self-awareness experiment, babies look in a mirror after a dot of rouge is put on their nose. If the babies react to the mirror image by touching their noses, it is clear they know they are seeing their own faces. Most babies demonstrate this self-awareness between 15 and 24 months of age.

7. self-concept; self-evaluations; praise; accomplish things that make them feel proud
8. oral; mouth
9. anal

Freud believed that the oral and anal stages are fraught with potential conflict that can have long-term consequences for the infant. If nursing is a hurried or tense event, for example, the child may become fixated at the oral stage, excessively eating, drinking, chewing, biting, or talking in quest of oral satisfaction. Similarly, if toilet training is overly strict or begins too soon, the child may become fixated and, as an adult, have an unusually strong need for self-control and regularity.

10. Erikson; trust versus mistrust; autonomy versus shame and doubt
11. behaviorism; reinforcement; punishment; John Watson
12. social; imitate; Albert Bandura
13. beliefs; thoughts; perceptions; memories; working model
14. epigenetic; genetic; temperament
15. personality; environment
16. New York Longitudinal Study (NYLS); easy; difficult; slow to warm up; hard to classify
17. openness; conscientiousness; extroversion; agreeableness; neuroticism
18. goodness of fit
19. sociocultural; social; ethnotheory; ethnic; proximal; self-aware; compliant; distal
20. synchrony; read other people's emotions; social interaction; feelings; parents; infants
21. still-face; does not
22. attachment
23. proximity-seeking; contact-maintaining
24. secure attachment; base for exploration

25. insecure attachment; insecure-avoidant; insecure-resistant/ambivalent

Some infants are avoidant: They engage in little interaction with their mothers before and after her departure. Others are anxious and resistant: They cling nervously to their mothers, are unwilling to explore, cry loudly when she leaves, and refuse to be comforted when she returns. Others are disorganized: They show an inconsistent mixture of behaviors toward their mothers.

26. Strange Situation; two-thirds; disorganized

27. D; can

Secure attachment is more likely if the parent is sensitive and responsive to the infant's needs, the relationship is high in synchrony, the infant has an "easy" temperament, the parents are not highly stressed, and the parents have a "working model" of secure attachment from their own parents.

Insecure attachment is more likely if the child is mistreated or has a "difficult" or "slow-to-warm-up" temperament; the mother is mentally ill; or the parents are highly stressed, intrusive, controlling, or actively alcoholic.

28. social referencing

29. mother–infant

30. encouraging; cautious; protective; proximal

31. family; center

32. are not harmed by, and sometimes benefit from, professional day care

33. the mother's warmth and sensitivity

34. express emotions

35. (a) adequate attention to each child; (b) encouragement of sensorimotor and language development; (c) attention to health and safety; (d) well-trained and professional caregivers; (e) warm and reponsive caregivers

36. insensitive; 20

37. no single; emotional; social; mother's; father; day care; culture; inborn

PROGRESS TEST 1

Multiple-Choice Questions

1. b. is the answer. (p. 180)

a., c., & d. These emotions emerge later in infancy, at about the same time as self-awareness emerges.

2. b. is the answer. (pp. 189)

3. c. is the answer. (p. 181)

4. d. is the answer. (p. 196)

5. b. is the answer. (p. 185)

6. c. is the answer. (p. 184)

7. b. is the answer. (pp. 183–184)

a. Orality and anality refer to personality traits that result from fixation in the oral and anal stages, respectively.

c. According to Erikson, this is the crisis of toddlerhood, which corresponds to Freud's anal stage.

d. This is not a developmental crisis in Erikson's theory.

8. c. is the answer. (p. 183)

9. a. is the answer. (p. 192)

c. Attachment behaviors are reliably found during infancy.

d. There is no indication that the child attends day care.

10. b. is the answer. Another type is "hard to classify." (p. 186)

a. "Secure" and "insecure" are different forms of attachment.

c. The chapter does not describe different types of parenting.

d. The Strange Situation is a test of attachment rather than of temperament.

11. a. is the answer. (pp. 189, 197)

c. & d. These terms were not used to describe parenting styles.

12. a. is the answer. (p. 191)

13. d. is the answer. (p. 192)

a. Self-awareness refers to the infant's developing sense of "me and mine."

b. Synchrony describes the coordinated interaction between infant and caregiver.

c. Affiliation describes the tendency of people at any age to seek the companionship of others.

14. a. is the answer. (p. 192)

b. In fact, just the opposite is true.

c. & d. Not usually at 2 months, but clearly at 6 months, babies become very upset by a still-faced caregiver.

15. b. is the answer. (p. 180)

True or False Items

1. F   Sociocultural theorists contend that the entire social context can have an impact on the infant's development. (p. 188)

2. F   Almost two-thirds of infants display secure attachment. (p. 194)

3. T (p. 181)

4. T (p. 182)

5. F   A securely attached toddler is most likely to explore the environment, with the mother's presence being enough to give him or her the courage to do so. (pp. 194–195)

6. F   Researchers believe that high-quality day care is not likely to harm the child. In fact, it is thought to be beneficial to the development of cognitive and social skills. (pp. 197–199)

7. T (p. 197)

8. F   Temperament is a product of both nature and nurture. (p. 185)

9. T (p. 182)

10. T (p. 185)

PROGRESS TEST 2

Multiple-Choice Questions

1. **a.** is the answer. (p. 194)

2. **a.** is the answer. (pp. 183–184)

3. **c.** is the answer. (p. 182)

4. **a.** is the answer. (p. 187)

5. **c.** is the answer. (p. 182)

   a. & b. The social smile, as well as temperamental characteristics, emerge well before the first signs of self-awareness.

   d. Contemporary developmentalists link these emotions to self-consciousness, rather than any specific environmental event such as toilet training.

6. **a.** is the answer. (p. 186)

   b. & c. Although environment, especially parents, affects temperamental tendencies, the study noted that temperament was established within 3 months of birth.

   d. Self-awareness is not a temperamental characteristic.

7. **c.** is the answer. (p. 181)

8. **c.** is the answer. (pp. 187–188)

9. **d.** is the answer. (p. 194)

10. **a.** is the answer. (p. 196)

    c. & d. The text does not suggest that the consequences of secure and insecure attachment differ in boys and girls.

11. **b.** is the answer. (p. 194)

    a. Insecure-avoidant attachment is marked by behaviors that indicate an infant is uninterested in a caregiver's presence or departure.

    c. Disorganized attachment is marked only by the inconsistency of infant–caregiver behaviors.

    d. Type B, or secure attachment, is marked by behaviors that indicate an infant is using a caregiver as a base from which to explore the environment.

12. **a.** is the answer. (p. 197)

13. **a.** is the answer. (p. 184)

    b. & c. Freud alone would have agreed with these statements.

14. **c.** is the answer. (p. 184)

    a. & b. Social learning involves learning by observing others. In these examples, the children are learning directly from the consequences of their own behavior.

15. **b.** is the answer. (pp. 191–192)

Matching Items

1. h (p. 185)	5. b (p. 183)	9. l (p. 182)
2. k (p. 183)	6. e (p. 183)	10. f (p. 193)
3. g (p. 194)	7. a (p. 196)	11. d (p. 193)
4. j (p. 191)	8. c (p 184)	12. i (p. 193)

DEVELOPMENTAL PSYCHOLOGY APPLIED

1. **b.** is the answer. (pp. 194–195)

   a., c., & d. These responses are more typical of insecurely attached infants.

2. **b.** is the answer. (p. 196)

3. **d.** is the answer. (pp. 194–195)

4. **a.** is the answer. About 40 percent of young infants can be described as "easy." (p. 186)

   b. About 15 percent of infants are described as "slow to warm up."

   c. About 10 percent of infants are described as "difficult."

   d. About 35 percent are described as "hard to classify."

5. **b.** is the answer. (p. 184)

   a. Cognitive theorists focus on a person's thoughts and values.

b. Epigenetic theory explores the relative effects of nature and nurture on behavior.

d. Sociocultural theory explores the entire social context.

6. **a.** is the answer. (pp. 195–196)

7. **d.** is the answer. (pp. 197–199)

8. **a.** is the answer. (p. 185)

b. Although temperament is genetic in origin, early temperamental traits *can* change.

c. Temperament is apparent shortly after birth.

d. As the person develops, the social context exerts a strong effect on temperament.

9. **c.** is the answer. (pp. 194–195)

a. & d. When their mothers return following an absence, securely attached infants usually re-establish social contact (with a smile or by climbing into their laps) and then resume playing.

b. There is no evidence in this example that Kalil is an abused child.

10. **c.** is the answer. (p. 186)

a. & b. There is no evidence in the question that the parents are reinforcing tantrum behavior or failing to meet some biological need of the child's.

d. On the contrary, about 50 percent of infants are "easy" in temperamental style.

11. **d.** is the answer. (p. 196)

a. According to Erikson, this is the crisis of toddlerhood.

b. This describes a moment of coordinated and mutually responsive interaction between a parent and an infant.

c. Dyssynchrony occurs when the coordinated pace and timing of a synchronous interaction are temporarily lost.

12. **c.** is the answer. (p. 183)

a. & b. In Freud's theory, a person who is fixated in the anal stage exhibits messiness and disorganization or compulsive neatness.

d. Erikson, rather than Freud, proposed crises of development.

13. **c.** is the answer. (p. 182)

14. **c.** is the answer. The fear of being left by a caregiver (separation anxiety) is most obvious at 9 to 14 months. For this reason, 4-month-old Carl can be expected to become less upset than his older sister. (p. 181)

15. **a.** is the answer. (pp. 184–185)

KEY TERMS

1. A **social smile** occurs when an infant smiles in response to a human face. (p. 180)

2. A common early fear, **stranger wariness** (also called fear of strangers) is first noticeable at about 9 months. (p. 181)

3. **Separation anxiety**, which is the infant's fear of being left by the mother or other caregiver, is usually strongest at 9 to 14 months. (p. 181)

4. **Self-awareness** refers to a person's realization that he or she is a distinct individual whose body, mind, and actions are separate from other people. Self-awareness makes possible many new self-conscious emotions, including shame, guilt, embarrassment, and pride. (p. 182)

5. In Erikson's theory, the crisis of infancy is one of **trust versus mistrust**, in which the infant learns whether the world is essentially a secure place in which basic needs will be met. (p. 183)

6. In Erikson's theory, the crisis of toddlerhood is one of **autonomy versus shame and doubt**, in which toddlers strive to rule their own actions and bodies. (p. 184)

7. **Social learning** is learning by observing others. (p. 184)

8. According to cognitive theory, infants use social relationships to develop a set of assumptions called a **working model** that organizes their perceptions and experiences. (p. 184)

9. **Temperament** refers to the "constitutionally based individual differences" in emotions, activity, and self-control. (p. 185)

10. **Goodness of fit** is the pattern of smooth interaction between the individual and the social context. (p. 187)

11. An **ethnotheory** is a theory of child rearing that reflects a specific ethnic group or culture. (p. 188)

12. **Proximal parenting** practices involve close physical contact between child and parent. (p. 189)

13. **Distal parenting** practices focus more on intellectual development than on physical development. (p. 189)

14. **Synchrony** refers to the coordinated, rapid, and smooth interaction between caregiver and infant that helps infants learn to express and read emotions. (p. 191)

15. The **still-face technique** is an experimental device in which an adult keeps his or her face unmoving and without expression in face-to-face interaction with an infant. (p. 192)

16. According to Mary Ainsworth, **attachment** is the enduring emotional tie that a person forms with another. (p. 192)

17. A **secure attachment** is one in which the infant derives comfort and confidence from the base of exploration provided by a caregiver. (p. 193)

18. **Insecure-avoidant attachment** is the pattern of attachment in which the infant seems uninterested in the caregiver's presence or departure. (p. 194)

19. **Insecure-resistant/ambivalent attachment** is the pattern of attachment in which an infant resists active exploration, becomes very upset when the caregiver leaves, and both resists and seeks contact when the caregiver returns. (p. 194)

20. **Disorganized attachment** is the pattern of attachment that is neither secure nor insecure and is marked by inconsistent infant–caregiver interactions. (p. 194)

21. The **Strange Situation** is a laboratory procedure developed by Mary Ainsworth for assessing attachment. Infants are observed in a playroom, in several successive episodes, while the caregiver (usually the mother) and a stranger move in and out of the room. (p. 194)

22. When infants engage in **social referencing,** they are looking to trusted adults for emotional cues on how to interpret uncertain situations. (p. 196)

23. **Family day care** is regular care provided for six or fewer children in a paid caregiver's home. (p. 197)

24. **Center day care** is regular care provided for children by several paid caregivers in a place designed for that purpose. (p. 197)

8

The Play Years: Biosocial Development

Chapter Overview

Chapter 8 introduces the developing person between the ages of 2 and 6. This period is called the play years, emphasizing the central importance of play to the biosocial, cognitive, and psychosocial development of preschoolers.

The chapter begins by outlining growth rates and the changes in shape that occur from ages 2 through 6, as well as the toddler's eating habits. This is followed by a look at brain growth and development and its role in the development of physical and cognitive abilities. The developing limbic system is also described, along with its role in the expression and regulation of emotions during the play years. A description of the acquisition of gross and fine motor skills follows, noting that mastery of such skills develops steadily during the play years along with intellectual growth. The section concludes with a discussion of the important issues of injury control and accidents, the major cause of childhood death except in times of famine.

The last section is an in-depth exploration of child maltreatment, including its prevalence, contributing factors, consequences for future development, treatment, and prevention.

NOTE: Answer guidelines for all Chapter 8 questions begin on page 124.

Guided Study

The text chapter should be studied one section at a time. Before you read, preview each section by skimming it, noting headings and boldface items. Then read the appropriate section objectives from the following outline. Keep these objectives in mind and, as you read the chapter section, search for the information that will enable you to meet each objective. Once you have finished a section, write out answers for its objectives.

Body Changes (pp. 207–209)

1. Describe normal physical growth during the play years, and account for variations in height and weight.

2. Describe changes in eating habits during the preschool years.

Brain Development (pp. 210–218)

3. Discuss the processes of myelination and lateralization and their effects on development during the play years.

4. Describe the development of the prefrontal cortex during the play years and its role in impulse control and appropriate focus.

5. Describe the development of the limbic system during the play years and its role in the expression and regulation of emotions.

6. Distinguish between gross and fine motor skills, and discuss the development of each during the play years.

7. Discuss the significance of artistic expression during the play years.

Injuries and Abuse (pp. 218–228)

8. Briefly discuss the risk of accidental injury among children.

9. Explain what is meant by "injury control," and describe some measures that have significantly reduced accidental death rates for children.

10. Identify the various categories of child maltreatment.

11. Describe warnings signs of child maltreatment.

12. Discuss the consequences of maltreatment.

13. Discuss foster care, kinship care, and adoption as intervention options in cases of child maltreatment.

Chapter Review

When you have finished reading the chapter, work through the material that follows to review it. Complete the sentences and answer the questions. As you proceed, evaluate your performance for each section by consulting the answers on page 124. Do not continue with the next section until you understand each answer. If you need to, review or reread the appropriate section in the textbook before continuing.

Body Changes (pp. 207–209)

1. During the preschool years, from age _____ to _____ , children add almost _____ in height and gain about _____ in weight per year. By age 6, the average child in a developed nation weighs about _____ and measures _____ in height.

2. In multiethnic countries, children of _____ descent tend to be tallest, followed by _____ , then _____ , and then _____ .

3. Height differences _____ (between/within) groups are greater than the average differences _____ (between/within) groups.

4. Household _____ also affects physical growth. In Brazil, for instance, whereas low income once correlated with _____ , today it also correlates with more _____ .

5. During the preschool years, children need _____ (fewer/more) calories per pound than they did as infants.

6. The most prevalent nutritional problem in early childhood is an insufficient intake of _____ , _____ , and _____ . An additional problem for American children is that they consume too many _____ .

7. Young children generally insist that a particular experience occur in an exact sequence and manner, a phenomenon called _____ _____ . By age _____ , this rigidity fades.

Brain Development (pp. 210–218)

8. By age 2, most pruning of the brain's _____ has occurred, and the brain weighs _____ percent of its adult weight. By age 5, the brain has attained about _____ percent of its adult weight.

9. Part of the brain's increase in size during childhood is due to the continued proliferation of _____ pathways and the ongoing process of _____ .

10. The band of nerve fibers that connects the right and left sides of the brain, called the _____ _____ , grows and _____ rapidly during the play years. This helps children better coordinate functions that involve _____ _____ .

11. The two sides of the body and brain _____ (are/are not) identical. The specialization of the two sides of the body and brain is called _____ . Throughout the world, societies are organized to favor _____-handedness. Developmentalists _____ (advise against/advise) trying to switch a child's handedness.

12. Adults who are _____ (right-/left-) handed tend to have thicker corpus callosa, which may enable better _____ of both sides of the body.

13. The left hemisphere of the brain controls the _____ side of the body and contains areas dedicated to _____ , _____ , and _____ . The right hemisphere controls the _____ side of the body and contains brain areas dedicated to _____ and _____ impulses.

14. In older children, the corpus callosum is more _____ , which partly explains why their behaviors sometimes are less clumsy.

15. The part of the brain that shows the most prolonged period of postnatal development is the

    _____ _____ .

    Development of this brain area increases throughout _____ . This area is sometimes called the _____ because all other areas of the brain are ruled by its decisions.

16. Two signs of an undeveloped prefrontal cortex are _____ and _____ , which is the tendency to stick to a thought or action even after it has become inappropriate.

17. The part of the brain that plays a crucial role in the expression and regulation of emotions is the

    _____ _____ . Within this system is the _____ , which registers emotions, particularly _____ and _____ . Next to this area is the _____ , which is a central processor of _____ , especially of _____ . Another structure in this brain region is the _____ , which produces _____ that activate other parts of the brain and body.

18. Memory of when, where, and how a fact was learned is called _____

    _____ .

19. Large body movements such as running, climbing, jumping, and throwing are called

    _____ _____ skills. These skills, which improve dramatically during the preschool years, require guided

    _____ , as well as a certain level of _____ _____ and

    _____ .

20. Most children learn these skills from _____ (other children/parents).

21. Skills that involve small body movements, such as pouring liquids and cutting food, are called _____ _____ skills.

Preschoolers have greater difficulty with these skills primarily because they have not developed the _____ control, patience, or _____ needed—in part because of the immaturity of the _____ and

_____ .

22. Fine motor skills are useful in almost all forms of _____ _____ , yet such skills are far from perfect. Fortunately, young children tend not to be _____ . The pictures children draw often reveal their unique _____ and

_____ .

Injuries and Abuse (pp. 218–228)

23. Except in famine, the leading cause of childhood death is _____ _____ .

24. Not until age _____ does any disease become a greater cause of mortality.

25. Instead of "accident prevention," many experts speak of _____ _____ (or _____ _____), an approach based on the belief that most accidents _____ (are/are not) preventable.

26. Preventive community actions that reduce everyone's chance of injury are called

    _____ _____ .

    Preventive actions that avert harm in the immediate situation constitute _____

    _____ . Actions aimed at minimizing the impact of an adverse event that has already occurred constitute _____

    _____ .

27. Until about 1960, the concept of child maltreatment was mostly limited to rare and

    _____ outbursts of a mentally disturbed stranger. Today, it is known that most perpetrators of maltreatment are the child's

    _____ .

28. Intentional harm to, or avoidable endangerment of, someone under age 18 defines child

    _____ . Actions that are deliberately harmful to a child's well-being are classified as

_____ . A failure to act appropriately to meet a child's basic needs is classified as _____ .

29. Since 1993, the ratio of the number of cases of _____ _____ , in which authorities have been officially notified, to cases of _____ _____ , which have been reported, investigated, and verified, has been about _____ (what ratio?).

30. Signs of maltreatment may be symptoms of _____-_____ _____ _____ , which was first described in combat victims.

31. Abused and neglected children are more often _____ , _____ , and _____ .

Describe other deficits of children who have been maltreated.

32. Public policy measures and other efforts designed to prevent maltreatment from ever occurring are called _____ _____ . An approach that focuses on spotting and treating the first symptoms of maltreatment is called _____ _____ . Last-ditch measures, such as removing a child from an abusive home, jailing the perpetrator, and so forth, constitute _____ _____ .

33. Once maltreatment has been substantiated, the first priority is _____ _____ for the child's long-term care.

34. Some children are officially removed from their biological parents and placed in a _____ _____ arrangement with another adult or family who is paid to nurture them.

35. In another type of foster care, called _____ _____ , a relative of the maltreated child becomes the approved caregiver. A final option is _____ .

Progress Test 1

Multiple-Choice Questions

Circle your answers to the following questions and check them with the answers beginning on page 124. If your answer is incorrect, read the explanation for why it is incorrect and then consult the appropriate pages of the text (in parentheses following the correct answer).

1. During the preschool years, the most common disease of young children in developed nations is:
   a. undernutrition.
   b. malnutrition.
   c. tooth decay.
   d. diabetes.

2. The brain center for speech is usually located in the:
   a. right hemisphere.
   b. left hemisphere.
   c. corpus callosum.
   d. space just below the right ear.

3. Which of the following is an example of tertiary prevention of child maltreatment?
   a. removing a child from an abusive home
   b. home visitation of families with infants by a social worker
   c. new laws establishing stiff penalties for child maltreatment
   d. public policy measures aimed at creating stable neighborhoods

4. The brain area that registers emotions is the:
   a. hippocampus.
   b. hypothalamus.
   c. amygdala.
   d. prefrontal cortex.

5. Children tend to have too much _____ in their diet, which contributes to _____ .
   a. iron; anemia
   b. sugar; tooth decay
   c. fat; delayed development of fine motor skills
   d. carbohydrate; delayed development of gross motor skills

6. Skills that involve large body movements, such as running and jumping, are called:
   a. activity-level skills.
   b. fine motor skills.
   c. gross motor skills.
   d. left-brain skills.

7. The brain's ongoing myelination during childhood helps children:
   a. control their actions more precisely.
   b. react more quickly to stimuli.
   c. control their emotions.
   d. do all of the above.

8. The leading cause of death in childhood is:
   a. accidents.
   b. untreated diabetes.
   c. malnutrition.
   d. iron deficiency anemia.

9. Regarding lateralization, which of the following is *not* true?
   a. Some cognitive skills require only one side of the brain.
   b. Brain centers for generalized emotional impulses can be found in the right hemisphere.
   c. The left hemisphere contains brain areas dedicated to spatial reasoning.
   d. The right side of the brain controls the left side of the body.

10. In young children, perseveration is a sign of:
    a. immature brain functions.
    b. maltreatment.
    c. abuse.
    d. neglect.

11. The area of the brain that directs and controls the other areas is the:
    a. corpus callosum.
    b. myelin sheath.
    c. prefrontal cortex.
    d. temporal lobe.

12. (A Case to Study) The relationship between physical abuse and neglect and income can be described as:
    a. a positive correlation.
    b. a negative correlation.
    c. curvilinear.
    d. no correlation.

13. Which of the following is true of the corpus callosum?
    a. It enables short-term memory.
    b. It connects the two halves of the brain.
    c. It must be fully myelinated before gross motor skills can be acquired.
    d. All of the above are correct.

14. The improvements in eye–hand coordination that allow preschoolers to catch and then throw a ball occur, in part, because:
    a. the brain areas associated with this ability become more fully myelinated.
    b. the corpus callosum begins to function.
    c. fine motor skills have matured by age 2.
    d. gross motor skills have matured by age 2.

15. During the school years, inadequate lateralization of the brain and immaturity of the prefrontal cortex may contribute to deficiencies in:
    a. cognition.
    b. peer relationships.
    c. emotional control.
    d. all of the above.

True or False Items

Write T (*true*) or F (*false*) on the line in front of each statement.

_____ 1. Growth between ages 2 and 6 results in body proportions more similar to those of an adult.

_____ 2. During childhood, the legs develop faster than any other part of the body.

_____ 3. For most people, the brain center for speech is located in the left hemisphere.

_____ 4. During the play years, children are more likely to be underweight than overweight.

_____ 5. Memories of when, where, and how a certain fact was learned are quite inaccurate in preschoolers.

_____ 6. Fine motor skills are usually easier for preschoolers to master than are gross motor skills.

_____ 7. Most serious childhood injuries truly are "accidents."

_____ 8. Children often fare as well in kinship care as they do in conventional foster care.

_____ 9. (In Person) Laws are generally more effective than educational campaigns in preventing childhood injuries.

_____ 10. Myelination is essential for basic communication between neurons.

Progress Test 2

Progress Test 2 should be completed during a final chapter review. Answer the following questions after you thoroughly understand the correct answers for the Chapter Review and Progress Test 1.

Multiple-Choice Questions

1. Each year from ages 2 to 6, the average child gains and grows, respectively:
   a. 2 pounds and 1 inch.
   b. 3 pounds and 2 inches.
   c. 4½ pounds and 3 inches.
   d. 6 pounds and 6 inches.

2. The center for perceiving various types of visual configurations is usually located in the brain's:
   a. right hemisphere.
   b. left hemisphere.
   c. right or left hemisphere.
   d. corpus callosum.

3. Regarding handedness, which of the following is not true?
   a. Sleeping newborns show a preference for turning their heads rightward or leftward.
   b. Some societies favor left-handed people.
   c. Experience can influence hand development.
   d. Language, customs, tools, and taboos all illustrate social biases toward right-handedness.

4. The most prevalent disease or condition of young children in developed nations is:
   a. obesity.
   b. tooth decay.
   c. measles.
   d. muscular dystrophy.

5. Seeing her toddler reach for a brightly glowing burner on the stove, Sheila grabs his hand and says, "No, that's very hot." Sheila's behavior is an example of:
   a. primary prevention.
   b. secondary prevention.
   c. tertiary prevention.
   d. none of the above.

6. When parents or caregivers do not meet a child's basic physical, educational, or emotional needs, it is referred to as:
   a. abuse.   c. endangering.
   b. neglect.   d. maltreatment.

7. Which of the following is true of a developed nation in which many ethnic groups live together?
   a. Ethnic variations in height and weight disappear.
   b. Ethnic variations in stature persist, but are substantially smaller.
   c. Children of African descent tend to be tallest, followed by Europeans, Asians, and Latinos.
   d. Cultural patterns exert a stronger-than-normal impact on growth patterns.

8. Which of the following is an example of perseveration?
   a. 2-year-old Jason sings the same song over and over
   b. 3-year-old Kwame falls down when attempting to kick a soccer ball
   c. 4-year-old Kara pours water very slowly from a pitcher into a glass
   d. None of the above is an example.

9. Which of the following is an example of a fine motor skill?
   a. kicking a ball
   b. running
   c. drawing with a pencil
   d. jumping

10. Children who have been maltreated often:
    a. regard other children and adults as hostile and exploitative.
    b. are less friendly and more aggressive.
    c. are more isolated than other children.
    d. are all of the above.

11. The left half of the brain contains areas dedicated to all of the following except:
    a. language.
    b. logic.
    c. analysis.
    d. creative impulses.

12. Most gross motor skills can be learned by healthy children by about age:
    a. 2.   c. 5.
    b. 3.   d. 7.

13. Andrea is concerned because her 3-year-old daughter has been having nightmares. Her pediatrician tells her:
    a. not to worry, because nightmares are often caused by increased activity in the amygdala, which is normal during early childhood.
    b. nightmares are a possible sign of an overdeveloped prefrontal cortex.
    c. to monitor her daughter's diet, because nightmares are often caused by too much sugar.
    d. to consult a neurologist, because nightmares are never a sign of healthy development.

14. The brain area that is a central processor for memory is the:
    a. hippocampus.   c. hypothalamus.
    b. amygdala.   d. prefrontal cortex.

15. During the play years, children's appetites seem _____ they were in the first two years of life.
    a. larger than
    b. smaller than
    c. about the same as
    d. erratic, sometimes smaller and sometimes larger than

Matching Items

Match each term or concept with its corresponding description or definition.

Terms or Concepts

_____ 1. corpus callosum
_____ 2. gross motor skills
_____ 3. fine motor skills
_____ 4. kinship care
_____ 5. foster care
_____ 6. injury control
_____ 7. right hemisphere
_____ 8. left hemisphere
_____ 9. child abuse
_____ 10. child neglect
_____ 11. primary prevention
_____ 12. secondary prevention
_____ 13. tertiary prevention

Descriptions or Definitions

a. brain area that is primarily responsible for processing language
b. brain area that is primarily responsible for recognizing visual shapes
c. legal placement of a child in the care of someone other than his or her biological parents
d. a form of care in which a relative of a maltreated child takes over from the biological parents
e. procedures to prevent unwanted events or circumstances from ever occurring
f. running and jumping
g. actions that are deliberately harmful to a child's well-being
h. actions for averting harm in the immediate situation
i. painting a picture or tying shoelaces
j. failure to appropriately meet a child's basic needs
k. an approach emphasizing accident prevention
l. actions aimed at reducing the harm that has occurred
m. band of nerve fibers connecting the right and left hemispheres of the brain

Developmental Psychology Applied

Answer these questions the day before an exam as a final check on your understanding of the chapter's terms and concepts.

1. Left-handed adults tend to have:
    a. thinner corpus callosa.
    b. thicker corpus callosa.
    c. delayed maturation of the prefrontal cortex.
    d. accelerated maturation of the prefrontal cortex.

2. Two-year-old Carrie is hyperactive, often confused between fantasy and reality, and jumps at any sudden noise. Her pediatrician suspects that she is suffering from:
    a. perseveration.
    b. child abuse.
    c. post-traumatic stress disorder.
    d. child neglect.

3. Following an automobile accident, Amira developed severe problems with her speech. Her doctor believes that the accident injured the _____ of her brain.
   a. left side
   b. right side
   c. communication pathways
   d. corpus callosum

4. Two-year-old Ali is quite clumsy, falls down frequently, and often bumps into stationary objects. Ali most likely:
   a. has a neuromuscular disorder.
   b. has an underdeveloped right hemisphere of the brain.
   c. is suffering from an iron deficiency.
   d. is a normal 2-year-old whose gross motor skills will improve dramatically during the preschool years.

5. Climbing a fence is an example of a:
   a. fine motor skill.
   b. gross motor skill.
   c. circular reaction.
   d. launching event.

6. To prevent accidental death in childhood, some experts urge forethought and planning for safety and measures to limit the damage of such accidents when they do occur. This approach is called:
   a. protective analysis.
   b. safety education.
   c. injury control.
   d. childproofing.

7. After his daughter scraped her knee, Ben gently cleansed the wound and bandaged it. Ben's behavior is an example of:
   a. primary prevention.
   b. secondary prevention.
   c. tertiary prevention.
   d. none of the above.

8. Which of the following activities would probably be the most difficult for a 5-year-old child?
   a. climbing a ladder
   b. catching a ball
   c. throwing a ball
   d. pouring juice from a pitcher without spilling it

9. (A Case to Study) Of the following children, the child with the greatest risk of physical abuse and neglect is:
   a. 5-year-old Brandon, whose family lives below the poverty line.
   b. 6-year-old Stacey, whose mother is a high school graduate.
   c. 3-year-old Daniel, who comes from an affluent family.

d. 3-year-old Bonita, whose father lives in the home.

10. Child maltreatment typically is characterized as:
    a. ongoing abuse and neglect by a child's own parents.
    b. a rare outburst from the perpetrator.
    c. abuse by neighbor or friend of the child's family.
    d. abuse by a mentally ill perpetrator.

11. A mayoral candidate is calling for sweeping policy changes to help ensure the well-being of children by promoting home ownership, high-quality community centers, and more stable neighborhoods. If these measures are effective in reducing child maltreatment, they would be classified as:
    a. primary prevention.
    b. secondary prevention.
    c. tertiary prevention.
    d. differential response.

12. A factor that would figure very little into the development of fine motor skills, such as drawing and writing, is:
    a. strength.
    b. muscular control.
    c. judgment.
    d. short, fat fingers.

13. Jason is a 3-year-old child, whose hyperactivity and hypervigilance may be symptoms of:
    a. post-traumatic stress disorder.
    b. an immature corpus callosum.
    c. an immature prefrontal cortex.
    d. normal development.

14. Which aspect of brain development during the play years contributes *most* to enhancing communication among the brain's various specialized areas?
    a. increasing brain weight
    b. proliferation of dendrite networks
    c. myelination
    d. increasing specialization of brain areas

15. Three-year-old Kyle's parents are concerned because Kyle, who generally seems healthy, doesn't seem to have the hefty appetite he had as an infant. Should they be worried?
    a. Yes, because appetite normally increases throughout the preschool years.
    b. Yes, because appetite remains as good during the preschool years as it was earlier.
    c. No, because caloric need is less during the preschool years than during infancy.
    d. There is not enough information to determine whether Kyle is developing normally.

Key Terms

Using your own words, write a brief definition or explanation of each of the following terms on a separate piece of paper.

1. myelination
2. corpus callosum
3. lateralization
4. perseveration
5. amygdala
6. hippocampus
7. hypothalamus
8. injury control/harm reduction
9. primary prevention
10. secondary prevention
11. tertiary prevention
12. child maltreatment
13. child abuse
14. child neglect
15. reported maltreatment
16. substantiated maltreatment
17. post-traumatic stress disorder
18. permanency planning
19. foster care
20. kinship care

ANSWERS

CHAPTER REVIEW

1. 2; 6; 3 inches (about 7 centimeters); 4½ pounds (2 kilograms); 46 pounds (21 kilograms); 46 inches (117 centimeters)
2. African; Europeans; Asians; Latinos
3. within; between
4. income; underweight; overweight
5. fewer
6. iron; zinc; calcium; sweetened cereals and drinks
7. just right (just so); 6
8. dendrites; 75; 90
9. communication; myelination
10. corpus callosum; myelinates; both sides of the brain and body
11. are not; lateralization; right; advise against
12. left-; coordination
13. right; logic; analysis; language; left; emotional; creative

14. myelinated
15. prefrontal cortex; adolescence; executive
16. impulsiveness; perseveration
17. limbic system; amygdala; fear; anxiety; hippocampus; memory; locations; hypothalamus; hormones
18. source memory
19. gross motor; practice; brain maturation; motivation
20. other children
21. fine motor; muscular; judgment; corpus callosum; prefrontal cortex
22. artistic expression; self-critical; perception; cognition
23. accidental injury
24. 40
25. injury control; harm reduction; are
26. primary prevention; secondary prevention; tertiary prevention
27. sudden; own parents
28. maltreatment; abuse; neglect
29. reported maltreatment; substantiated maltreatment; 3-to-1
30. post-traumatic stress disorder
31. injured; sick; hospitalized

Maltreated children tend to regard other people as hostile and exploitative, and thus are less friendly, more aggressive, and more isolated than other children. As adolescents and adults, they often use drugs or alcohol, choose unsupportive relationships, become victims or aggressors, sabotage their own careers, eat too much or too little, and generally engage in self-destructive behavior.

32. primary prevention; secondary prevention; tertiary prevention
33. permanency planning
34. foster care
35. kinship care; adoption

PROGRESS TEST 1

Multiple-Choice Questions

1. **c.** is the answer. (p. 208)

   a.. b., & d. All of these conditions are much more likely to occur in infancy or in adolescence than in early childhood.

2. b. is the answer. (p. 211)

a. & d. The right brain is the location of areas associated with generalized emotional and creative impulses.

c. The corpus callosum helps integrate the functioning of the two halves of the brain; it does not contain areas specialized for particular skills.

3. a. is the answer. (p. 226)

b. This is an example of secondary prevention.

c. & d. These are examples of primary prevention.

4. c. is the answer. (p. 213)

a. The hippocampus is a central processor of memory.

b. The hypothalamus produces hormones that activate other parts of the brain and body.

c. The prefrontal cortex is responsible for regulating attention, among other things. It makes formal education more possible in children.

5. b. is the answer. (p. 208)

6. c. is the answer. (p. 216)

7. d. is the answer. (p. 210)

8. a. is the answer. (p. 219)

9. a. is the answer. (pp. 211–212)

10. a. is the answer. (p. 213)

b., c., & d. Although maltreatment, whether in the form of abuse or neglect, may cause brain injury, perseveration is not necessarily a symptom of brain injury from those sources.

11. c. is the answer. (p. 212)

a. The corpus callosum is the band of fibers that link the two halves of the brain.

b. The myelin sheath is the fatty insulation that surrounds some neurons in the brain.

d. The temporal lobes of the brain contain the primary centers for hearing.

12. b. is the answer. Children who live in poor neighborhoods have *higher* rates of abuse and neglect. (p. 225)

13. b. is the answer. (p. 210)

a. The corpus callosum is not directly involved in memory.

c. Myelination of the central nervous system is important to the mastery of *fine* motor skills.

14. a. is the answer. (p. 210)

b. The corpus callosum begins to function long before the play years.

c. & d. Neither fine nor gross motor skills have fully matured by age 2.

15. d. is the answer. (p. 213)

True or False Items

1. T (p. 207)

2. F   During childhood, the brain develops faster than any other part of the body. (p. 210)

3. T (pp. 211–212)

4. T (p. 207)

5. T (pp. 213–214)

6. F   Fine motor skills are more difficult for preschoolers to master than are gross motor skills. (p. 216)

7. F   Most serious accidents involve someone's lack of forethought. (p. 219)

8. T (p. 227)

9. T (p. 221)

10. F   Although myelination is not essential for basic communication between neurons, it is essential for fast and complex communication (p. 210)

PROGRESS TEST 2

Multiple-Choice Questions

1. c. is the answer. (p. 207)

2. a. is the answer. (pp. 211–212)

b. & c. The left hemisphere of the brain contains areas associated with language development.

d. The corpus callosum does not contain areas for specific behaviors.

3. b. is the answer. All societies favor right-handed people. (pp. 210–211)

4. b. is the answer. (p. 208)

5. b. is the answer. (p. 220)

6. b. is the answer. (p. 222)

a. Abuse is deliberate, harsh injury to the body.

c. Endangerment was not discussed.

d. Maltreatment is too broad a term.

7. c. is the answer. (p. 208)

8. a. is the answer. (p. 213)

b. Kicking a ball is a gross motor skill.

c. Pouring is a fine motor skill.

9. c. is the answer. (pp. 216–217)

a., b., & d. These are gross motor skills.

10. d. is the answer. (pp. 223; 224)

11. **d.** is the answer. Brain areas that control generalized creative and emotional impulses are found in the right hemisphere. (pp. 211–212)

12. **c.** is the answer. (p. 216)

13. **a.** is the answer. (p. 213)

   b. Nightmares generally occur when activity in the amygdala overwhelms the slowly developing prefrontal cortex.

   c. There is no indication that nightmares are caused by diet.

   d. Increased activity in the amygdala is normal during early childhood, as are the nightmares that some children experience.

14. **a.** is the answer. (p. 213)

   b. The amygdala is responsible for registering emotions.

   c. The hypothalamus produces hormones that activate other parts of the brain and body.

   d. The prefrontal cortex is involved in planning and goal-directed behavior.

15. **b.** is the answer. (p. 208)

Matching Items

1. m (p. 210)
2. f (p. 216)
3. i (p. 216)
4. d (p. 227)
5. c (p. 227)
6. k (p. 219)
7. b (p. 211)
8. a (p. 211)
9. g (p. 222)
10. j (p. 222)
11. e (p. 220)
12. h (p. 220)
13. l (p. 220)

DEVELOPMENTAL PSYCHOLOGY APPLIED

1. **a.** is the answer. (p. 211)

2. **c.** is the answer. (p. 223)

   a. Perseveration is the tendency to stick to thoughts or actions, even after they have become useless.

   b. & d. Child neglect refers to failure to meet a child's basic needs. Child abuse refers to deliberate attempts to harm the child, which is not evident in this example. Carrie's specific symptoms may be caused by neglect or maltreatment, but they are most directly signs of PTSD.

3. **a.** is the answer. In most people, the left hemisphere of the brain contains centers for language, including speech. (p. 211)

4. **d.** is the answer. (p. 216)

5. **b.** is the answer. (p. 216)

   a. Fine motor skills involve small body movements, such as the hand movements used in painting.

c. & d. These events were not discussed in this chapter.

6. **c.** is the answer. (p. 219)

7. **c.** is the answer. (pp. 220–221)

8. **d.** is the answer. (pp. 216–217)

   a., b., & c. Preschoolers find these gross motor skills easier to perform than fine motor skills such as that described in d.

9. **a.** Children who live in a poor neighborhood are more likely to be physically abused or neglected. (pp. 224–225)

10. **a.** is the answer. (p. XX)

11. **a.** is the answer. (p. 220)

   b. Had the candidate called for measures to spot the early warning signs of maltreatment, this answer would be true.

   c. Had the candidate called for jailing those who maltreat children or providing greater counseling and health care for victims, this answer would be true.

   d. Differential response is not discussed in the chapter; however, it refers to separate reporting procedures for high- and low-risk families.

12. **a.** is the answer. Strength is a more important factor in the development of gross motor skills. (pp. 216–217)

13. **a.** is the answer. (p. 223)

14. **b.** is the answer. (p. 210)

15. **c.** is the answer. (p. 208)

KEY TERMS

1. **Myelination** is the process by which axons become coated with myelin, which speeds up the transmission of nerve impulses between neurons. (p. 210)

2. The **corpus callosum** is a long band of nerve fibers that connects the right and left hemispheres of the brain. (p. 210)

3. **Lateralization** refers to the differentiation of the two sides of the brain so that each serves specific, specialized functions. (p. 210)

4. **Perseveration** is the tendency to stick to thoughts or actions, even after they have become useless or inappropriate. In young children, perseveration is a normal product of immature brain functions. (p. 213)

   Memory Aid: To *persevere* is to continue, or persist, at something.

5. A part of the brain's limbic system, the **amygdala** registers emotions, particularly fear and anxiety. (p. 213)

6. The **hippocampus** is the part of the brain's limbic system that is a central processor of memory. (p. 213)

7. The **hypothalamus** is the brain structure that produces hormones that activate other parts of the brain and body. (p. 214)

8. **Injury control/harm reduction** is the practice of limiting the extent of injuries by anticipating, controlling, and preventing dangerous activities. (p. 219)

9. **Primary prevention** refers to actions that change overall background conditions to prevent some unwanted event or circumstance. (p. 220)

10. **Secondary prevention** involves actions that avert harm in the immediate situation. (p. 220)

11. **Tertiary prevention** involves actions taken after an adverse event occurs, aimed at reducing the harm or preventing disability. (p. 220)

12. **Child maltreatment** is intentional harm to, or avoidable endangerment of, anyone under age 18. (p. 222)

13. **Child abuse** refers to deliberate actions that are harmful to a child's physical, emotional, or sexual well-being. (p. 222)

14. **Child neglect** refers to failure to appropriately meet a child's basic physical, educational, or emotional needs. (p. 222)

15. Child maltreatment that has been officially reported to the police or other authorities is called **reported maltreatment**. (p. 222)

16. Child maltreatment that has been officially reported to authorities, investigated, and verified is called **substantiated maltreatment**. (p. 222)

17. **Post-traumatic stress disorder (PTSD)** is a syndrome triggered by exposure to an extreme traumatic stressor. In maltreated children, symptoms of PTSD include hyperactivity and hypervigilance, sleeplessness, sudden terror or anxiety, and confusion between fantasy and reality. (p. 223)

18. **Permanency planning** is planning for the long-term care of a child who has experienced substantiated maltreatment. (p. 227)

19. **Foster care** is a legally sanctioned, publicly supported arrangement in which children are removed from their biological parents and temporarily given to another adult to nurture. (p. 227)

20. **Kinship care** is a form of foster care in which a relative of a maltreated child becomes the child's approved caregiver. (p. 227)

9

The Play Years: Cognitive Development

Chapter Overview

In countless everyday instances, as well as in the findings of numerous research studies, young children reveal themselves to be remarkably thoughtful, insightful, and perceptive thinkers whose grasp of the causes of everyday events, memory of the past, and mastery of language are sometimes astonishing. Chapter 9 begins with Piaget's and Vygotsky's views of cognitive development at this age. According to Piaget, young children's thought is prelogical: Between the ages of 2 and 6, they are unable to perform many logical operations and are limited by irreversible, centered, and static thinking. Lev Vygotsky, a contemporary of Piaget's, saw learning as a social activity more than as a matter of individual discovery. Vygotsky focused on the child's "zone of proximal development" and the relationship between language and thought.

The next section focuses on what preschoolers can do, including their emerging abilities to theorize about the world. This leads into a section on language development during the play years. Although young children demonstrate rapid improvement in vocabulary and grammar, they have difficulty with comparisons and certain rules of grammar. A discussion of whether bilingualism in young children is useful concludes the section on language.

The chapter ends with a discussion of preschool education, including a description of "quality" preschool programs and an evaluation of their impact on children.

NOTE: Answer guidelines for all Chapter 9 questions begin on page 138.

Guided Study

The text chapter should be studied one section at a time. Before you read, preview each section by skimming it, noting headings and boldface items. Then read the appropriate section objectives from the following outline. Keep these objectives in mind and, as you read the chapter section, search for the information that will enable you to meet each objective. Once you have finished a section, write out answers for its objectives.

Piaget and Vygotsky (pp. 231–236)

1. Describe and discuss the major characteristics of Piaget's stage of preoperational thought, and identify the major limitations of Piaget's research.

2. Explain Vygotsky's views on cognitive development, focusing on the concepts of guided participation and scaffolding in promoting cognitive growth.

3. Describe Vygotsky's view of the role of language in cognitive growth.

Children's Theories (pp. 236–239)

4. Describe how theory-theory supports the idea that children are active learners.

5. Explain the typical preschool child's theory of mind, noting how it is affected by context and culture.

Language (pp. 240–245)

6. (text and In Person) Describe the development of vocabulary in children, and explain the role of fast-mapping in this process.

7. Describe the development of grammar during the play years, noting limitations in the young child's language abilities.

8. Discuss the advantages and disadvantages of bilingualism at an early age.

Early-Childhood Education (pp. 245–251)

9. Discuss variations in early-childhood education programs.

10. Identify the characteristics of a high-quality pre-school intervention program, and briefly discuss the costs and benefits of preschool education.

Chapter Review

When you have finished reading the chapter, work through the material that follows to review it. Complete the sentences and answer the questions. As you proceed, evaluate your performance for each section by consulting the answers beginning on page 138. Do not continue with the next section until you understand each answer. If you need to, review or reread the appropriate section in the textbook before continuing.

1. Young children are sometimes _____ , understanding only their own perspective. As a result of their experiences with others, however, they also acquire a _____

   _____ _____ that reflects their understanding of how minds work.

Piaget and Vygotsky (pp. 231–236)

2. Piaget referred to cognitive development between the ages of 2 and 6 as _____ intelligence.

3. Young children's tendency to contemplate the world exclusively from their personal perspective is referred to as _____ . Their ten-

dency think about one aspect of a situation at a time is called _____ . This tendency _____ (is/is not) equated with selfishness. Children also tend to focus on _____ to the exclusion of other attributes of objects and people.

4. Preschoolers' understanding of the world tends to focus on _____ (static/dynamic) reasoning, which means that they tend to think of their world as _____ . A closely related characteristic is _____—the inability to recognize that reversing a process will restore the original conditions from which the process began.

5. The idea that amount is unaffected by changes in appearance is called _____ . In the case of _____ _____ _____ , preschoolers who are shown pairs of checkers in two even rows and who then observe one row being spaced out will say that the spaced-out row has more checkers.

6. Researchers now believe that Piaget _____ (overestimated/underestimated) conceptual ability during early childhood.

7. Much of the research from the sociocultural perspective on the young child's emerging cognition is inspired by the Russian psychologist _____ . According to this perspective, a child is an _____ _____ _____ , whose intellectual growth is stimulated by more skilled members of society.

8. Vygotsky believed that adults can most effectively help a child solve a problem by presenting _____ , by offering _____ , by providing _____ , and by encouraging _____ . This emphasizes that children's intellectual growth is stimulated by their _____ _____ in _____ experiences of their environment. The critical element in this process is that the mentor and the child _____ to accomplish a task.

9. Vygotsky suggested that for each developing individual there is a _____ _____ _____ _____ , a range of skills that the person can exercise with assistance but is not yet able to perform independently.

10. How and when new skills are developed depends, in part, on the willingness of tutors to _____ the child's participation in learning encounters.

11. Vygotsky believed that language is essential to the advancement of thinking in two crucial ways. The first is through the internal dialogue in which a person talks to himself or herself, called _____ _____ . In preschoolers, this dialogue is likely to be _____ (expressed silently/uttered aloud).

12. According to Vygotsky, another way language advances thinking is as the _____ of the social interaction.

Children's Theories (pp. 236–239)

13. The term _____-_____ highlights the idea that children attempt to construct theories to explain everything they see and hear.

14. At about _____ years, young children acquire an understanding of others' thinking, or a _____ _____ _____ .

Describe the theory of mind of children between the ages of 3 and 6.

15. Most 3-year-olds _____ (have/do not have) difficulty realizing that a belief can be false.

16. Research studies reveal that theory-of-mind development depends partly on _____ maturation, particularly of the brain's _____ _____ . General _____ ability is also important in strengthening preschoolers' theory of mind. A third helpful factor is having at least one

    _____ .

    Finally, _____ may be a factor.

Language (pp. 240–245)

17. Two aspects of development that make ages 2 to 6 the prime time for learning language are _____ and _____ in the language areas of the brain.

18. Although early childhood does not appear to be a _____ period for language development, it does seem to be a _____ period for the learning of vocabulary, grammar, and pronunciation.

19. During the preschool years, a dramatic increase in language occurs, with _____ increasing exponentially.

20. Through the process called _____- _____ , preschoolers often learn words after only one or two hearings. A closely related process is _____ _____ , by which children are able to apply newly learned words to other objects in the same category.

21. Because preschool children tend to think in absolute terms, they have difficulty with words that express _____ , as well as words expressing relationships of _____ and _____ .

22. The structures, techniques, and rules that a language uses to communicate meaning define its _____ .

23. Two factors that affect how well young children use language are _____ input and encouragement and _____ .

24. Preschoolers' tendency to apply rules of grammar when they should not is called

    _____ .

Give an example of this tendency.

25. Most developmentalists agree that bilingualism _____ (is/is not necessarily) an asset to children in today's world. Even so, language-minority children are at a(n) _____ (advantage/disadvantage) in most ways.

26. Children who speak two languages by age 5 often are less _____ in their understanding of language and more advanced in their _____ _____ _____ . Advocates of monolingualism point out that bilingual proficiency comes at the expense of _____ in one or both languages, slowing down the development of _____ and other linguistic skills.

27. Some immigrant parents are saddened when their children make a _____ _____ and become more fluent in their new language than that of their home culture. The best solution is for children to become _____ _____ , who are fluent in both languages.

Early-Childhood Education (pp. 245–251)

28. Compared to a hundred years ago, when children didn't start school until _____ _____ , today most _____- to _____-year-olds are in school.

29. Many new programs use an educational model inspired by _____ that allows children to _____ .
Many programs are also influenced by _____ , who believed that children learn from other _____ under the watchful guidance of adults.

30. One type of preschool was opened by _____ for poor children in Rome. This _____-_____ school was based on the belief that children needed structured, individualized projects in order to give them a sense of _____ .

31. Another new early-childhood curriculum called _____ _____ encourages children to master skills not usually seen in American schools until about age _____ .

32. Other preschool programs are more _____-directed. These programs explicitly teach basic _____ skills, including _____ , _____ , and _____ , typically using _____ _____ by a teacher.

33. In 1965, _____ _____ _____ was inaugurated to give low-income children some form of compensatory education during the preschool years. Longitudinal research found that graduates of similar but more intensive, well-evaluated programs scored _____ (higher/no higher) on achievement tests and were more likely to attend college and less likely to go to jail.

List several characteristics of high-quality early childhood education.

Progress Test 1

Multiple-Choice Questions

Circle your answers to the following questions and check them with the answers on on page 139. If your answer is incorrect, read the explanation for why it is incorrect and then consult the appropriate pages of the text (in parentheses following the correct answer).

1. Piaget believed that children are in the preoperational stage from ages:
   a. 6 months to 1 year.   c. 2 to 6 years.
   b. 1 to 3 years.   d. 5 to 11 years.

2. Which of the following is *not* a characteristic of preoperational thinking?
   a. focus on appearance
   b. static reasoning
   c. abstract thinking
   d. centration

3. Which of the following provides evidence that early childhood is a sensitive period, rather than a critical period, for language learning?
   a. People can and do master their native language after early childhood.
   b. Vocabulary, grammar, and pronunciation are acquired especially easily during early childhood.
   c. Neurological characteristics of the young child's developing brain facilitate language acquisition.
   d. All of the above provide evidence.

4. According to Vygotsky, children learn because adults do all of the following except:
   a. present challenges.
   b. offer assistance.
   c. encourage motivation.
   d. provide reinforcement.

5. Reggio Emilia is:
   a. the educator who first opened nursery schools for poor children in Rome.
   b. the early-childhood curriculum that allows children to discover ideas at their own pace.
   c. a new form of early-childhood education that encourages children to master skills not usually seen until age 7 or so.
   d. the Canadian system for promoting bilingualism in young children.

6. The vocabulary of preschool children consists primarily of:
   a. metaphors.
   b. self-created words.
   c. abstract nouns.
   d. verbs and concrete nouns.

7. Preschoolers sometimes apply the rules of grammar even when they shouldn't. This tendency is called:
   a. overregularization.   c. practical usage.
   b. literal language.   d. single-mindedness.

8. The Russian psychologist Vygotsky emphasized that:
   a. language helps children form ideas.
   b. children form concepts first, then find words to express them.
   c. language and other cognitive developments are unrelated at this stage.
   d. preschoolers learn language only for egocentric purposes.

9. Private speech can be described as:
   a. a way of formulating ideas to oneself.
   b. fantasy.
   c. an early learning difficulty.
   d. the beginnings of deception.

10. The child who has not yet grasped the principle of conservation is likely to:
   a. insist that a tall, narrow glass contains more liquid than a short, wide glass, even though both glasses actually contain the same amount.
   b. be incapable of egocentric thought.
   c. be unable to reverse an event.
   d. do all of the above.

11. In later life, High/Scope graduates showed:
   a. better report cards, but more behavioral problems.
   b. significantly higher IQ scores.
   c. higher scores on math and reading achievement tests.
   d. alienation from their original neighborhoods and families.

12. The best preschool programs are generally those that provide the most:
   a. behavioral control.
   b. positive social interactions among children and adults.
   c. instruction in conservation and other logical principles.
   d. demonstration of toys by professionals.

13. Many preschool programs that are inspired by Piaget stress _____ , in contrast to alternative programs that stress _____ .
   a. academics; school readiness
   b. readiness; academics
   c. child development; school readiness
   d. academics; child development

14. Preschoolers can succeed at tests of conservation when:
   a. they are allowed to work cooperatively with other children.
   b. the test is presented as a competition.
   c. they are informed that they are being observed by their parents.
   d. the test is presented in a simple, nonverbal, and gamelike way.

15. Through the process called fast-mapping, children:
   a. immediately assimilate new words by connecting them through their assumed meaning to categories of words they have already mastered.
   b. acquire the concept of conservation at an earlier age than Piaget believed.
   c. are able to move beyond egocentric thinking.
   d. become skilled in the practical use of language.

True or False Items

Write *T (true)* or *F (false)* on the line in front of each statement.

_____ 1. Early childhood is a prime learning period for every child.

_____ 2. In conservation problems, many preschoolers are unable to understand the transformation because they focus exclusively on appearances.

_____ 3. Preschoolers use private speech more selectively than older children.

_____ 4. Children typically develop a theory of mind at about age 7.

_____ 5. Preoperational children tend to focus on one aspect of a situation to the exclusion of all others.

_____ 6. Piaget focused on what children cannot do rather than what they can do.

_____ 7. With the beginning of preoperational thought, most preschoolers can understand abstract words.

_____ 8. A preschooler who says "You comed up and hurted me" is demonstrating a lack of understanding of English grammar.

_____ 9. Successful preschool programs generally have a low adult/child ratio.

_____ 10. Vygotsky believed that cognitive growth is largely a social activity.

_____ 11. *Theory-theory* refers to the tendency of young children to see the world as an unchanging reflection of their current construction of reality.

Progress Test 2

Progress Test 2 should be completed during a final chapter review. Answer the following questions after you thoroughly understand the correct answers for the Chapter Review and Progress Test 1.

Multiple-Choice Questions

1. Children who speak two languages by age 5:
   a. are less egocentric in their understanding of language.
   b. are more advanced in their theory of mind.
   c. have somewhat slower vocabulary development in one or both languages.
   d. are characterized by all of the above.

2. Piaget believed that preoperational children fail conservation of liquid tests because of their tendency to:
   a. focus on appearance.
   b. fast-map.
   c. overregularize.
   d. do all of the above.

3. A preschooler who focuses his or her attention on only one feature of a situation is demonstrating a characteristic of preoperational thought called:
   a. centration.   c. reversibility.
   b. overregularization. d. egocentrism.

4. One characteristic of preoperational thought is:
   a. the ability to categorize objects.
   b. the ability to count in multiples of 5.
   c. the inability to perform logical operations.
   d. difficulty adjusting to changes in routine.

5. The zone of proximal development represents the:
   a. skills or knowledge that are within the potential of the learner but are not yet mastered.
   b. influence of a child's peers on cognitive development.

   c. explosive period of language development during the play years.
   d. normal variations in children's language proficiency.

6. According to Vygotsky, language advances thinking through private speech, and by:
   a. helping children to privately review what they know.
   b. helping children explain events to themselves.
   c. serving as a mediator of the social interaction that is a vital part of learning.
   d. facilitating the process of fast-mapping.

7. Irreversibility refers to the:
   a. inability to understand that other people view the world from a different perspective than one's own.
   b. inability to think about more than one idea at a time.
   c. failure to understand that changing the arrangement of a group of objects doesn't change their number.
   d. failure to understand that undoing a process will restore the original conditions.

8. According to Piaget:
   a. it is impossible for preoperational children to grasp the concept of conservation, no matter how carefully it is explained.
   b. preschoolers fail to solve conservation problems because they center their attention on the transformation that has occurred and ignore the changed appearances of the objects.
   c. with special training, even preoperational children are able to grasp some aspects of conservation.
   d. preschoolers fail to solve conservation problems because they have no theory of mind.

9. Scaffolding of a child's cognitive skills can be provided by:
   a. a mentor.
   b. the objects or experiences of a culture.
   c. the child's past learning.
   d. all of the above.

10. Which theorist would be most likely to agree with the statement, "Adults should focus on helping children learn rather than on what they cannot do"?
    a. Piaget   c. both a. and b.
    b. Vygotsky   d. neither a. nor b.

11. Children first demonstrate some understanding of grammar:
    a. as soon as the first words are produced.
    b. once they begin to use language for practical purposes.
    c. through the process called fast-mapping.
    d. in their earliest sentences.

12. Seeing his cousin Jack for the first time in several months, 3-year-old Zach notices how long Jack's hair has become. "You're turning into a girl," he exclaims. Zach's comment reflects the preoperational child's:
    a. egocentrism.
    b. tendency to focus on appearance.
    c. static reasoning.
    d. irreversibility.

13. Most 5-year-olds have difficulty understanding comparisons because:
    a. they have not yet begun to develop grammar.
    b. they don't understand that meaning depends on context.
    c. of their limited vocabulary.
    d. of their tendency to overregularize.

14. Overregularization indicates that a child:
    a. is clearly applying rules of grammar.
    b. persists in egocentric thinking.
    c. has not yet mastered the principle of conservation.
    d. does not yet have a theory of mind.

15. Regarding the value of preschool education, most developmentalists believe that:
    a. most disadvantaged children will not benefit from an early preschool education.
    b. most disadvantaged children will benefit from an early preschool education.
    c. the early benefits of preschool education are likely to disappear by grade 3.
    d. the relatively small benefits of antipoverty measures such as Head Start do not justify their huge costs.

Matching Items

Match each term or concept with its corresponding description or definition.

Terms or Concepts

_____ 1. static reasoning
_____ 2. scaffold
_____ 3. theory of mind
_____ 4. zone of proximal development
_____ 5. overregularization
_____ 6. fast-mapping
_____ 7. irreversibility
_____ 8. centration
_____ 9. conservation
_____ 10. private speech
_____ 11. guided participation

Descriptions or Definitions

a. the idea that amount is unaffected by changes in shape or placement
b. the tendency to see the world as an unchanging place
c. the cognitive distance between a child's actual and potential levels of development
d. the tendency to think about one aspect of a situation at a time
e. the process whereby the child learns through social interaction with a mentor
f. our understanding of mental processes in ourselves and others
g. the process by which words are learned after only one hearing
h. an inappropriate application of rules of grammar
i. the internal use of language to form ideas
j. the inability to understand that original conditions are restored by the undoing of some process
k. to structure a child's participation in learning encounters

Developmental Psychology Applied

Answer these questions the day before an exam as a final check on your understanding of the chapter's terms and concepts.

1. An experimenter first shows a child two rows of checkers that each have the same number of checkers. Then, with the child watching, the experimenter elongates one row and asks the child if each of the two rows still has an equal number of checkers. This experiment tests the child's understanding of:
   a. reversibility.
   b. conservation of matter.
   c. conservation of number.
   d. centration.

2. A preschooler believes that a "party" is the one and only attribute of a birthday. She says that Daddy doesn't have a birthday because he never has a party. This thinking demonstrates the tendency Piaget called:
   a. egocentrism.
   b. centration.
   c. conservation of events.
   d. mental representation.

3. A child who understands that 6 + 3 = 9 means that 9 − 6 = 3 has had to master the concept of:
   a. reversibility.
   b. number.
   c. conservation.
   d. egocentrism.

4. A 4-year-old tells the teacher that a clown should not be allowed to visit the class because "Pat is 'fraid of clowns." The 4-year-old thus shows that he can anticipate how another will feel. This is evidence of the beginnings of:
   a. egocentrism.
   b. deception.
   c. a theory of mind.
   d. conservation.

5. When asked "Where do dreams come from?," a 5-year-old child is likely to answer:
   a. "from God."
   b. "from the sky."
   c. "from my pillow."
   d. "from inside my head."

6. A nursery school teacher is given the job of selecting holiday entertainment for a group of preschool children. If the teacher agrees with the ideas of Vygotsky, she is most likely to select:
   a. a simple TV show that every child can understand.
   b. a hands-on experience that requires little adult supervision.
   c. brief, action-oriented play activities that the children and teachers will perform together.
   d. holiday puzzles for children to work on individually.

7. Which of the following terms does *not* belong with the others?
   a. focus on appearances
   b. static reasoning
   c. reversibility
   d. centration

8. That a child produces sentences that follow such rules of word order as "the initiator of an action precedes the verb, the receiver of an action follows it" demonstrates a knowledge of:
   a. grammar.
   b. conservation.
   c. centration.
   d. phrase structure.

9. The 2-year-old child who says, "We goed to the store," is making a grammatical:
   a. centration.
   b. overregularization.
   c. extension.
   d. fast map.

10. An experimenter who makes two balls of clay of equal amount, then rolls one into a long, skinny rope and asks the child if the amounts are still the same, is testing the child's understanding of:
    a. conservation.
    b. reversibility.
    c. perspective-taking.
    d. centration.

11. Dr. Jones, who believes that children's language growth greatly contributes to their cognitive growth, evidently is a proponent of the ideas of:
    a. Piaget.
    b. Chomsky.
    c. Flavell.
    d. Vygotsky.

12. Comparing the views of Piaget with those of Vygotsky, active learning is to guided participation as egocentrism is to:
    a. apprenticeship.
    b. structure.
    c. scaffold.
    d. fast-mapping.

13. In describing the limited logical reasoning of pre-schoolers, a developmentalist is *least* likely to emphasize:
    a. irreversibility.   c. its action-bound nature.
    b. centration.   d. its static nature.

14. A preschooler fails to put together a difficult puzzle on her own, so her mother encourages her to try again, this time guiding her by asking questions such as, "For this space, do we need a big piece or a little piece?" With Mom's help, the child successfully completes the puzzle. Lev Vygotsky would attribute the child's success to:
    a. additional practice with the puzzle pieces.
    b. imitation of her mother's behavior.
    c. the social interaction with her mother that restructured the task to make its solution more attainable.
    d. modeling and reinforcement.

15. Mark is answering an essay question that asks him to "discuss the positions of major developmental theorists regarding the relationship between language and cognitive development." To help organize his answer, Mark jots down a reminder that _____ contended that language is essential to the advancement of thinking, as private speech, and as a _____ of social interactions.
    a. Piaget; mediator   c. Piaget; theory
    b. Vygotsky; mediator   d. Vygotsky; theory

Key Terms

Using your own words, write a brief definition or explanation of each of the following terms on a separate piece of paper.

1. preoperational intelligence
2. centration
3. egocentrism
4. focus on appearance
5. static reasoning
6. irreversibility
7. conservation
8. apprentice in thinking
9. guided participation
10. zone of proximal development
11. scaffolding
12. private speech
13. social mediation

14. theory-theory
15. theory of mind
16. critical period
17. sensitive period
18. fast-mapping
19. overregularization
20. balanced bilingual

ANSWERS
CHAPTER REVIEW

1. egocentric; theory of mind
2. preoperational
3. egocentrism; centration; is not; appearance
4. static; unchanging; irreversibility
5. conservation; conservation of number
6. underestimated
7. Lev Vygotsky; apprentice in thinking
8. challenges; assistance; instruction; motivation; guided participation; social; interact
9. zone of proximal development
10. scaffold
11. private speech; uttered aloud
12. mediator
13. theory-theory
14. 4; theory of mind

Between the ages of 3 and 6, young children come to realize that mental phenomena may not reflect reality and that individuals can believe various things and, therefore, can be deliberately deceived or fooled.

15. have
16. neurological; prefrontal cortex; language; brother or sister; culture
17. maturation; myelination
18. critical; sensitive
19. vocabulary
20. fast-mapping; logical extension
21. comparisons; time; place
22. grammar
23. parental; genes
24. overregularization

Many preschoolers overapply the rule of adding "s" to form the plural. Thus, preschoolers are likely to say "foots" and "snows."

25. is; disadvantage

26. egocentric; theory of mind; fluency; reading

27. language shift; balanced bilinguals

28. first grade; 3; 5

29. Piaget; discover ideas at their own pace; Vygotsky; children

30. Maria Montessori; child-centered; accomplishment

31. Reggio Emilia; 7

32. teacher; reading; writing; arithmetic; direct instruction

33. Project Head Start; higher

In Chapter 7, high-quality preschools were described as being characterized by (a) a low adult/child ratio, (b) a trained staff (or educated parents) who are unlikely to leave the program, (c) positive social interactions among children and adults, (d) adequate space and equipment, and (e) safety. Continuity also helps, and curriculum is important.

PROGRESS TEST 1

Multiple-Choice Questions

1. **c.** is the answer. (p. 231)

2. **c.** is the answer. Preoperational children have great difficulty understanding abstract concepts. (p. 232)

3. **d.** is the answer. (p. 240)

4. **d.** is the answer. (p. 234)

5. **c.** is the answer. (pp. 247–248)

    a. This describes Maria Montessori.

    b. This refers to Piaget's approach.

    d. The program originated in Italy.

6. **d.** is the answer. (p. 240)

    a. & c. Preschoolers generally have great difficulty understanding, and therefore using, metaphors and abstract nouns.

    b. Other than the grammatical errors of overregularization, the text does not indicate that preschoolers use a significant number of self-created words.

7. **a.** is the answer. (p. 243)

    b. & d. These terms are not identified in the text and do not apply to the use of grammar.

    c. Practical usage, which also is not discussed in the text, refers to communication between one person and another in terms of the overall context in which language is used.

8. **a.** is the answer. (p. 235)

    b. This expresses the views of Piaget.

    c. Because he believed that language facilitates thinking, Vygotsky obviously felt that language and other cognitive developments are intimately related.

    d. Vygotsky did not hold this view.

9. **a.** is the answer. (p. 235)

10. **a.** is the answer. (pp. 232, 233)

    b., c., & d. Failure to conserve is the result of thinking that is centered on appearances. Egocentrism and irreversibility are also examples of centered thinking.

11. **c.** is the answer. (p. 250)

    b. This is not discussed in the text.

    a. & d. There was no indication of greater behavioral problems or alienation in graduates of this program.

12. **b.** is the answer. (p. 251)

13. **c.** is the answer. (pp. 246, 248)

14. **d.** is the answer. (pp. 232–234)

15. **a.** is the answer. (pp. 240–241)

True or False Items

1. T (p. 231)

2. T (pp. 232, 233)

3. F In fact, just the opposite is true. (p. 235)

4. F Children develop a theory of mind between the ages of 3 and 6. (p. 238)

5. T (p. 232)

6. T (p. 234)

7. F Preschoolers have difficulty understanding abstract words; their vocabulary consists mainly of concrete nouns and verbs. (p. 242)

8. F In adding "ed" to form a past tense, the child has indicated an understanding of the grammatical rule for making past tenses in English, even though the construction in these two cases is incorrect. (p. 243)

9. T (p. 251)

10. T (p. 234)

11. F This describes static reasoning; theory-theory is the idea that children attempt to construct a theory to explain all their experiences. (p. 236)

PROGRESS TEST 2

Multiple-Choice Questions

1. **d.** is the answer. (p. 244)

2. **a.** is the answer. (pp. 232, 233)

   b. & c. Fast-mapping and overregularization are characteristics of language development during the play years; they have nothing to do with reasoning about volume.

3. **a.** is the answer. (p. 232)

   b. Overregularization is the child's tendency to apply grammatical rules even when he or she shouldn't.

   c. Reversibility is the concept that reversing an operation, such as addition, will restore the original conditions.

   d. This term is used to refer to the young child's belief that people think as he or she does.

4. **c.** is the answer. This is why the stage is called *pre*operational. (p. 231)

5. **a.** is the answer. (p. 235)

6. **c.** is the answer. (pp. 235–236)

   a. & b. These are both advantages of private speech.

   d. Fast-mapping is the process by which new words are acquired, often after only one hearing.

7. **d.** is the answer. (p. 232)

   a. This describes egocentrism.

   b. This is the opposite of centration.

   c. This defines conservation of number.

8. **a.** is the answer. (p. 232)

   b. According to Piaget, preschoolers fail to solve conservation problems because they focus on the *appearance* of objects and ignore the transformation that has occurred.

   d. Piaget did not relate conservation to a theory of mind.

9. **d.** is the answer. (p. 235)

10. **b.** is the answer. (pp. 234–235)

    a. Piaget focused on what children cannot do.

11. **d.** is the answer. Preschoolers almost always put subject before verb in their two-word sentences. (p. 242)

12. **b.** is the answer. (p. 232)

    a., c., & d. Egocentrism, static reasoning, and irreversibility are all characteristics of preoperational thinking, but noticing the long hair is a matter of attending to appearances.

13. **b.** is the answer. (p. 242)

    a. By the time children are 3 years old, their grammar is quite impressive.

    c. On the contrary, vocabulary develops so rapidly that, by age 5, children seem to be able to understand and use almost any term they hear.

    d. This tendency to make language more logical by overapplying certain grammatical rules has nothing to do with understanding comparisons.

14. **a.** is the answer. (p. 243)

    b., c., & d. Overregularization is a *linguistic* phenomenon rather than a characteristic type of thinking (b. and d.), or a logical principle (c.).

15. **b.** is the answer. (p. 249)

Matching Items

1. b (p. 232)
2. k (p. 235)
3. f (p. 238)
4. c (p. 235)
5. h (p. 243)
6. g (p. 240)
7. j (p. 232)
8. d (p. 232)
9. a (p. 232)
10. i (p. 235)
11. e (p. 234)

DEVELOPMENTAL PSYCHOLOGY APPLIED

1. **c.** is the answer. (p. 233)

   a. A test of reversibility would ask a child to perform an operation, such as adding 4 to 3, and then reverse the process (subtract 3 from 7) to determine whether the child understood that the original condition (the number 4) was restored.

   b. A test of conservation of matter would transform the appearance of an object, such as a ball of clay, to determine whether the child understood that the object remained the same.

   d. A test of centration would involve the child's ability to see various aspects of a situation.

2. **b.** is the answer. (p. 232)

   a. Egocentrism is thinking that is self-centered.

   c. This is not a concept in Piaget's theory.

   d. Mental representation is an example of symbolic thought.

3. **a.** is the answer. (p. 232)

4. **c.** is the answer. (p. 238)

   a. Egocentrism is self-centered thinking.

   b. Although deception provides evidence of a theory of mind, the child in this example is not deceiving anyone.

   d. Conservation is the understanding that the amount of a substance is unchanged by changes in its shape or placement.

5. **d.** is the answer. (p. 238)

a., b., & c. These answers are typical of younger children, who have not yet developed a theory of mind.

6. **c.** is the answer. In Vygotsky's view, learning is a social activity. Thus, social interaction that provides motivation and focuses attention facilitates learning. (p. 246)

   a., b., & d. These situations either provide no opportunity for social interaction (b. & d.) or do not challenge the children (a.).

7. **c.** is the answer. (p. 232)

   a., b., & d. These are all characteristics of preoperational thinking.

8. **a.** is the answer. (pp. 242–243)

   b. & c. Conservation and centration are both aspects of preoperational thinking, not language.

   d. The text does not discuss this aspect of language.

9. **b.** is the answer. (p. 243)

10. **a.** is the answer. (pp. 232, 233)

11. **d.** is the answer. (pp. 235–236)

   a. Piaget believed that cognitive growth precedes language development.

   b. & c. Chomsky focused on the *acquisition* of language, and Flavell emphasizes cognition.

12. **a.** is the answer. Piaget emphasized the preschooler's egocentric tendency to perceive everything from his or her own perspective; Vygotsky emphasized the preschooler's tendency to look to others for insight and guidance. (pp. 232, 234)

13. **c.** is the answer. This is typical of cognition during the first two years, when infants think exclusively with their senses and motor skills. (p. 232)

14. **c.** is the answer. (pp. 234–235)

15. **b.** is the answer. (p. 235)

KEY TERMS

1. According to Piaget, thinking between ages 2 and 6 is characterized by **preoperational intelligence,** meaning that children cannot yet perform logical operations; that is, they cannot use logical principles. (p. 231)

2. **Centration** is the tendency of preoperational children to focus only on a single aspect of a situation or object. (p. 232)

3. **Egocentrism** is Piaget's term for a type of centration in which the preoperational child views the world exclusively from his or her own perspective. (p. 232)

4. **Focus on appearance** refers to the preoperational child's tendency to focus only on apparent attributes and ignore all others. (p. 232)

5. Preoperational thinking is characterized by **static reasoning,** in which the young child sees the world as unchanging. (p. 232)

6. **Irreversibility** is the characteristic of preoperational thought in which the young child fails to recognize that a process can be reversed to restore the original conditions of a situation. (p. 232)

7. **Conservation** is the understanding that the amount or quantity of a substance or object is unaffected by changes in its appearance. (p. 232)

8. According to Vygotsky, a young child is an **apprentice in thinking,** whose intellectual growth is stimulated and directed by more skilled members of society. (p. 234)

9. According to Vygotsky, **guided participation** is the process by which young children learn to think by having social experiences and by exploring their universe. As mentors, parents, siblings, and peers present challenging tasks, offer assistance (not taking over), maintain enthusiasm, provide instructions, and support the child's interest and motivation. (p. 234)

10. According to Vygotsky, each individual has a **zone of proximal development (ZPD),** which represents the skills that are within the potential of the learner but cannot be performed independently. (p. 235)

11. Tutors who utilize **scaffolding** structure children's learning experiences in order to foster their emerging capabilities. (p. 235)

12. **Private speech** is Vygotsky's term for the internal dialogue in which a person talks to himself or herself. Private speech, which often is uttered aloud, helps preschoolers to think, review what they know, and decide what to do. (p. 235)

13. In Vygotsky's theory, **social mediation** is a function of speech by which a person's cognitive skills are refined and extended through both formal instruction and casual conversation (p. 235)

14. **Theory-theory** is Gopnik's term for the tendency of young children to attempt to construct theories to explain everything they experience. (p. 236)

15. A **theory of mind** is an understanding of human mental processes, that is, of one's own or another's emotions, beliefs, intentions, motives, and thoughts. (p. 238)

16. A **critical period** is a time when a specific type of development must happen if the individual is to develop normally. (p. 240)

17. A **sensitive period** is a time when a specific type of development is most likely to happen, and when it happens most easily. (p. 240)

18. **Fast-mapping** is the not very precise process by which children rapidly learn new words by quickly connecting them to words and categories that they already understand. (p. 240)

19. **Overregularization** occurs when children apply rules of grammar when they should not. It is seen in English, for example, when children add "s" to form the plural even in irregular cases that form the plural in a different way. (p. 243)

20. A **balanced bilingual** is a person who is equally fluent in two languages. (p. 245)

10

The Play Years:
Psychosocial Development

Chapter Overview

Chapter 10 explores the ways in which young children begin to relate to others in an ever-widening social environment. The chapter begins where social understanding begins, with emotional development and the emergence of the sense of self. With their increasing social awareness, children become more concerned with how others evaluate them and better able to regulate their emotions. This section also explores the origins of helpful, prosocial behaviors in young children, as well as antisocial behaviors such as the different forms of aggressive behavior.

The next section discusses Baumrind's parenting patterns and their effects on the developing child. The usefulness of the different forms of punishment is also explored, as are the effects of the media on parenting and family life in general.

The chapter concludes with a description of children's emerging awareness of male–female differences and gender identity. Five major theories of gender-role development are considered.

NOTE: Answer guidelines for all Chapter 10 questions begin on page 153.

Guided Study

The text chapter should be studied one section at a time. Before you read, preview each section by skimming it, noting headings and boldface items. Then read the appropriate section objectives from the following outline. Keep these objectives in mind and, as you read the chapter section, search for the information that will enable you to meet each objective. Once you have finished a section, write out answers for its objectives.

Emotional Development (pp. 255–263)

1. Explain the relationship between Erik Erikson's third stage and the development of the self-concept.

2. Discuss the development during early childhood of emotional regulation, focusing on how it is determined by both nature and nurture.

3. Explain how and why children develop empathy or antipathy, and describe the behaviors produced by each type of emotion.

4. Differentiate four types of aggression during the play years, and describe the pattern of aggression throughout childhood.

Parents (pp. 264–271)

5. Compare and contrast three classic patterns of parenting and their effect on children.

6. Discuss the pros and cons of punishment, and describe effective methods for disciplining a child.

7. Discuss how exposure to the electronic media contributes to the development of violence in children and interferes with family life.

Becoming Boys and Girls (pp. 271–277)

8. Describe the developmental progression of gender awareness in young children.

9. Summarize five theories of gender-role development during the play years, noting important contributions of each.

Chapter Review

When you have finished reading the chapter, work through the material that follows to review it. Complete the sentences and answer the questions. As you proceed, evaluate your performance for each section by consulting the answers beginning on page 153. Do not continue with the next section until you understand each answer. If you need to, review or reread the appropriate section in the textbook before continuing.

Emotional Development (pp. 255–263)

1. The major psychosocial accomplishment of the play years is learning _____
   _____ .
   This ability is called _____
   _____ .

2. Between 3 and 6 years of age, according to Erikson, children are in the stage of
   _____ _____
   _____ . As they acquire skills and competencies, children develop
   _____ , a belief in their own abilities. In the process, they develop a positive
   _____ and feelings of
   _____ in their accomplishments.

3. Unlike the earlier stage of
   _____ _____
   _____ , children in this stage want to begin *and* _____ something. Children also develop a longer
   _____ span that enables concentration, greater _____ , and a willingness to _____ .

4. Erikson also believed that during this stage, children begin to feel _____ when their efforts result in failure or criticism. Many people believe that _____ is a more mature emotion than _____ , because the former emotion is _____ .

5. For the most part, preschool children enjoy learning, playing, and practicing for their own joy; that is, they are _____ _____ .

6. An illness or disorder that involves the mind is called _____ . Children who have _____ problems and lash out at other people or things are said to be "_____" (overcontrolled/undercontrolled). Children who have _____ problems tend to be inhibited, fearful, and withdrawn.

7. Neurological advances in the brain's _____ _____ are partly responsible for the greater capacity for self-control that occurs at about age _____ .

8. Girls generally are better at regulating their _____ (internalizing/externalizing) emotions, but less successful with _____ (internalizing/externalizing) ones than boys.

9. Repeated exposure to extreme stress can kill _____ and make some children physiologically unable to regulate their emotions.

10. Another set of influences on emotional regulation is the child's early and current _____ _____ . Neglect or abuse in the first two years of life is likely to cause later _____ or _____ problems.

11. The ability to truly understand the emotions of another, called _____ , often leads to sharing, helping, and other examples of _____ _____ . In contrast, dislike for others, or _____ , may lead to actions that are destructive or deliberately hurtful. Such actions are called _____ _____ .

12. By age _____ , most children can be deliberately prosocial or antisocial. This occurs as a result of _____ maturation, _____ regulation, _____ _____ _____ , and interactions with _____ .

13. Preschool children are capable of identifying with and being proud of their own group without being _____ against other groups.

14. The most antisocial behavior of all is active _____ . Developmentalists distinguish four types of physical aggression: _____ , used to obtain or retain an object or privilege; _____ , used in angry retaliation against an intentional or accidental act committed by a peer; _____ , which takes the form of insults or social rejection; and _____ , used in an unprovoked attack on a peer.

15. (Table 10.1) The form of aggression that is most likely to increase from age 2 to 6 is _____ _____ . Of greater concern are _____ _____ , because it can indicate a lack of _____ _____ ; and _____ _____ , which is most worrisome overall.

Parents (pp. 264–271)

16. A significant influence on early psychosocial growth is the style of _____ that characterizes a child's family life.

17 The early research on parenting styles, which was conducted by _____ , found that parents varied in four dimensions: their expressions of _____ ; their strategies for _____ ; their _____ ; and their expectations for _____ .

18. Parents who adopt the _____ style demand unquestioning obedience from their children. In this style of parenting, nurturance tends to be _____ (low/high), maturity demands are _____ (low/high), and parent–child communication tends to be _____ (low/high).

19. Parents who adopt the _____ style make few demands on their children and are lax in discipline. Such parents _____ (are/are not very) nurturant, communicate _____ (well/poorly), and make _____ (few/extensive) maturity demands.

20. Parents who adopt the _____ style set limits and enforce rules but also listen to their children. Such parents make _____ (high/low) maturity demands, communicate _____ (well/poorly), and _____ (are/are not) nurturant.

21. Follow-up studies indicate that children raised by _____ parents are likely to be obedient but unhappy and those raised by _____ parents are likely to lack self-control. Those raised by _____ parents are more likely to be successful, happy with themselves, and generous with others.

22. An important factor in the effectiveness of parenting style is the child's _____ . All parents _____ (do/do not) neatly fit into one of Baumrind's three major categories of parenting.

23. Culture _____ (exerts/does not exert) a strong influence on disciplinary techniques. Japanese mothers tend to use _____ _____ as disciplinary techniques more often than do North American mothers.

24. The first step in choosing an appropriate punishment for a child is to clarify what is _____ . The second step is to remember what the child is _____ to do. Punishment _____ (should/should not) be rare and reserved for behaviors that the child _____ and can reasonably _____ .

(Table 10.3) State four specific recommendations for the use of punishment that are derived from developmental research findings.

a. _____

b. _____

c. _____

d. _____

25. Six major organizations concerned with the well-being of children urge parents to avoid exposing their children to _____ _____ .

26. Most young children in the United States spend more than _____ (how many?) hours each day using some sort of media.

27. Longitudinal research demonstrates that children who watched educational programs as young children became teenagers who had _____ _____ . This finding was especially true for _____ (boys/girls). Teenagers who, as children watched violent television programs, had _____ , especially if they were _____ (boys/girls).

28. Children who watch violence on television _____ (do/do not) become more violent themselves.

29. The more media a family uses, the less time they spend _____ .

Becoming Boys and Girls (pp. 271–277)

30. Social scientists distinguish between biological, or _____ , differences between males and females, and cultural, or _____ , differences in the _____ and behavior of males and females.

31. By age _____ , children can consistently apply gender labels and have a rudimentary understanding of the permanence of their own gender. By age _____ , children are convinced that certain toys and roles are appropriate for one gender but not the other.

Awareness that sex is a fixed biological characteristic does not become solid until about age _____ .

32. Freud called the period from age 3 to 6 the _____ _____ . According to his view, boys in this stage develop sexual feelings about their _____ and become jealous of their _____ . Freud called this phenomenon the _____ _____ .

33. In Freud's theory, preschool boys resolve their guilty feelings defensively through _____ with their father. Boys also develop, again in self-defense, a powerful conscience called the _____ .

34. During the phallic stage, little girls may experience the _____ _____ , in which they want to get rid of their mother and become intimate with their father.

35. According to behaviorism, preschool children develop gender-role ideas by being _____ for behaviors deemed appropriate for their sex and _____ for behaviors deemed inappropriate.

36. Behaviorists also maintain that children learn gender-appropriate behavior not only through direct reinforcement but also by _____ .

37. Cognitive theorists focus on children's _____ of male–female differences.

38. Gender education varies by region, socioeconomic status, and historical period, according to the _____ theory. Gender distinctions are emphasized in many _____ cultures. This theory points out that children can maintain a balance of male and female characteristics, or _____ , only if their culture promotes that idea.

39. According to _____ theory, gender attitudes and roles are the result of interaction between _____ and _____ _____ .

40. The idea that is supported by recent research is that some gender differences are _____ based because of differences between male and female _____ .

41. These differences probably result from the differing _____ _____ that influence brain development. However, the theory maintains that the manifestations of biological origins are shaped, enhanced, or halted by _____ _____ . One example of such a factor is that prehistorically, female brains apparently favored _____ , which may have created a genetically inclined tendency for girls to _____ earlier than boys.

Progress Test 1

Multiple-Choice Questions

Circle your answers to the following questions and check them with the answers beginning on page 154. If your answer is incorrect, read the explanation for why it is incorrect and then consult the appropriate pages of the text (in parentheses following the correct answer).

1. Preschool children have a clear (but not necessarily accurate) concept of self. Typically, the preschooler believes that she or he:
   a. owns all objects in sight.
   b. is great at almost everything.
   c. is much less competent than peers and older children.
   d. is more powerful than her or his parents.

2. According to Freud, the third stage of psychosexual development, during which the penis is the focus of psychological concern and pleasure, is the:
   a. oral stage.   c. phallic stage.
   b. anal stage.   d. latency period.

3. Girls generally are better than boys at regulating their:
   a. internalizing emotions.
   b. externalizing emotions.
   c. internalizing and externalizing emotions.
   d. prosocial behaviors.

4. The three *basic* patterns of parenting described by Diana Baumrind are:
   a. hostile, loving, and harsh.
   b. authoritarian, permissive, and authoritative.
   c. positive, negative, and punishing.
   d. indulgent, neglecting, and traditional.

5. Authoritative parents are receptive and loving, but they also normally:
   a. set limits and enforce rules.
   b. have difficulty communicating.
   c. withhold praise and affection.
   d. encourage aggressive behavior.

6. Children who watch a lot of violent television or play violent video games:
   a. are more likely to be violent.
   b. do less reading.
   c. tend to have lower grades in school.
   d. have all of the above characteristics.

7. (Table 10.1) Between 2 and 6 years of age, the form of aggression that is most likely to increase is:
   a. reactive   c. relational
   b. instrumental   d. bullying

8. During the play years, a child's self-concept is defined largely by his or her:
   a. expanding range of skills and competencies.
   b. physical appearance.
   c. gender.
   d. relationship with family members.

9. Behaviorists emphasize the importance of _____ in the development of the preschool child.
   a. identification   c. initiative
   b. praise and blame   d. a theory of mind

10. Children apply gender labels and have definite ideas about how boys and girls behave as early as age:
    a. 2.   c. 5.
    b. 4.   d. 7.

11. Developmentalists agree that punishment should be:
    a. avoided at all costs.
    b. immediate and harsh.
    c. delayed until emotions subside.
    d. rare and limited to behaviors the child understands and can control.

12. Six-year-old Leonardo has superior verbal ability rivaling that of most girls his age. Dr. Laurent believes this is due to the fact that although his sex is predisposed to slower language development, Leonardo's upbringing in a linguistically rich home enhanced his biological capabilities. Dr. Laurent is evidently a proponent of:
    a. cognitive theory.
    b. psychoanalytic theory.
    c. sociocultural theory.
    d. epigenetic theory.

13. Three-year-old Jake, who lashes out at the family pet in anger, is displaying signs of _____ problems, which suggests that he is emotionally _____ .
    a. internalizing; overcontrolled
    b. internalizing; undercontrolled
    c. externalizing; overcontrolled
    d. externalizing; undercontrolled

14. Compared to North American mothers, Japanese mothers are more likely to:
    a. use reasoning to control their preschoolers' social behavior.
    b. use expressions of disappointment to control their preschoolers' social behavior.
    c. express empathy for the child.
    d. do all of the above.

15. (Table 10.1) When her friend hurts her feelings, Maya shouts that she is a "mean old stinker!" Maya's behavior is an example of:
    a. instrumental aggression.
    b. reactive aggression.
    c. bullying aggression.
    d. relational aggression.

True or False Items

Write *T (true) or F (false)* on the line in front of each statement.

_____ 1. According to Diana Baumrind, only authoritarian parents make maturity demands on their children.

_____ 2. Children of authoritative parents tend to be successful, happy with themselves, and generous with others.

_____ 3. Not until age 4 can children apply gender labels.

_____ 4. Throughout the world, cultures do not vary in how much they encourage prosocial behavior during the play years.

_____ 5. Many gender differences are genetically based.

_____ 6. Children can be truly androgynous only if their culture promotes such ideas and practices.

_____ 7. Developmentalists do not agree about how children acquire gender roles.

_____ 8. By age 4, most children have definite ideas about what constitutes appropriate masculine and feminine roles.

_____ 9. Identification was defined by Freud as a means of defending one's self-concept by taking on the attitudes and behaviors of another person.

_____ 10. By adolescence, undercontrolled boys may become delinquents.

Progress Test 2

Progress Test 2 should be completed during a final chapter review. Answer the following questions after you thoroughly understand the correct answers for the Chapter Review and Progress Test 1.

Multiple-Choice Questions

1. Children of permissive parents are *most* likely to lack:

   a. social skills.   c. initiative and guilt.
   b. self-control.   d. care and concern.

2. The major psychosocial accomplishment of the play years is:

   a. learning when and how to express emotions.
   b. developing an internalized sense of initiative.
   c. developing an identity.
   d. forging positive self-esteem.

3. Which area of the brain plays an important role in the child's greater capacity for self-control that appears at age 4 or 5?

   a. temporal lobe   c. prefrontal cortex
   b. occipital lobe   d. hippocampus

4. Generally speaking, the motivation of preschool children is:

   a. intrinsic.
   b. extrinsic.
   c. the desire to gain praise or some other reward from someone else.
   d. varies too much from country to country to be characterized.

5. Which of the following best summarizes the current view of developmentalists regarding gender differences?

   a. Developmentalists disagree on the proportion of gender differences that are biological in origin.
   b. Most gender differences are biological in origin.
   c. Nearly all gender differences are cultural in origin.
   d. There is no consensus among developmentalists regarding the origin of gender differences.

6. According to Freud, a young boy's jealousy of his father's relationship with his mother, and the guilt feelings that result, are part of the:

   a. Electra complex.
   b. Oedipus complex.
   c. phallic complex.
   d. penis envy complex.

7. The style of parenting in which the parents make few demands on children, the discipline is lax, and the parents are nurturant and accepting is:

   a. authoritarian.
   b. authoritative.
   c. permissive.
   d. traditional.

8. Cooperating with a playmate is to _____ as insulting a playmate is to _____ .

   a. antisocial behavior; prosocial behavior
   b. prosocial behavior; antisocial behavior
   c. emotional regulation; antisocial behavior
   d. prosocial behavior; emotional regulation

9. Antipathy refers to a person's:

   a. understanding of the emotions of another person.
   b. self-understanding.
   c. feelings of anger or dislike toward another person.
   d. tendency to internalize emotions or inhibit their expression.

10. Which of the following theories advocates the development of gender identification as a means of avoiding guilt over feelings for the opposite-sex parent?

    a. behaviorism   c. psychoanalytic
    b. sociocultural   d. social learning

11. A parent who wishes to use a time-out to discipline her son for behaving aggressively on the playground would be advised to:

    a. have the child sit quietly indoors for a few minutes.

    b. tell her son that he will be punished later at home.

    c. tell the child that he will not be allowed to play outdoors for the rest of the week.

    d. choose a different disciplinary technique because time-outs are ineffective.

12. The preschooler's readiness to learn new tasks and play activities reflects his or her:

    a. emerging competency and self-awareness.

    b. theory of mind.

    c. relationship with parents.

    d. growing identification with others.

13. Emotional regulation is in part related to maturation of a specific part of the brain in the:

    a. prefrontal cortex.   **c.** temporal lobe.

    b. parietal cortex.   **d.** occipital lobe.

14. In which style of parenting is the parents' word law and misbehavior strictly punished?

    a. permissive   **c.** authoritarian

    b. authoritative   **d.** traditional

15. Erikson noted that preschoolers eagerly begin many new activities but are vulnerable to criticism and feelings of failure; they experience the crisis of:

    a. identity versus role confusion.

    b. initiative versus guilt.

    c. basic trust versus mistrust.

    d. efficacy versus helplessness.

Matching Items

Match each term or concept with its corresponding description or definition.

Terms or Concepts

    _____ **1.** empathy
    _____ **2.** androgyny
    _____ **3.** antipathy
    _____ **4.** prosocial behavior
    _____ **5.** antisocial behavior
    _____ **6.** Electra complex
    _____ **7.** Oedipus complex
    _____ **8.** authoritative
    _____ **9.** authoritarian
    _____ **10.** identification
    _____ **11.** instrumental aggression

Descriptions or Definitions

    a. forceful behavior that is intended to get or keep something that another person has

    b. Freudian theory that every daughter secretly wishes to replace her mother

    c. parenting style associated with high maturity demands and low parent–child communication

    d. an action performed for the benefit of another person without the expectation of reward

    e. Freudian theory that every son secretly wishes to replace his father

    f. parenting style associated with high maturity demands and high parent–child communication

    g. understanding the feelings of others

    h. an action that is intended to harm someone else

    i. dislike of others

    j. a defense mechanism through which children cope with their feelings of guilt during the phallic stage

    k. a balance of traditional male and female characteristics in an individual

Developmental Psychology Applied

Answer these questions the day before an exam as a final check on your understanding of the chapter's terms and concepts.

1. Bonita eventually copes with the fear and anger she feels over her hatred of her mother and love of her father by:
   a. identifying with her mother.
   b. copying her brother's behavior.
   c. adopting her father's moral code.
   d. competing with her brother for her father's attention.

2. A little girl who says she wants her mother to go on vacation so that she can marry her father is voicing a fantasy consistent with the _____ described by Freud.
   a. Oedipus complex
   b. Electra complex
   c. theory of mind
   d. crisis of initiative versus guilt

3. According to Erikson, before the preschool years, children are incapable of feeling guilt because:
   a. guilt depends on a sense of self, which is not sufficiently established in preschoolers.
   b. they do not yet understand that they are male or female for life.
   c. this emotion is unlikely to have been reinforced at such an early age.
   d. guilt is associated with the resolution of the Oedipus complex, which occurs later in life.

4. Parents who are strict and aloof are *most* likely to make their children:
   a. cooperative and trusting.
   b. obedient but unhappy.
   c. violent.
   d. withdrawn and anxious.

5. When 4-year-old Seema grabs for Vincenzo's Beanie Baby, Vincenzo slaps her hand away, displaying an example of:
   a. bullying aggression.
   b. reactive aggression.
   c. instrumental aggression.
   d. relational aggression.

6. The belief that almost all sexual patterns are learned rather than inborn would find its strongest adherents among:
   a. cognitive theorists.
   b. behaviorists.
   c. psychoanalytic theorists.
   d. epigenetic theorists.

7. In explaining the origins of gender distinctions, Dr. Christie notes that every society teaches its children its values and attitudes regarding preferred behavior for men and women. Dr. Christie is evidently a proponent of:
   a. behaviorism.
   b. sociocultural theory.
   c. epigenetic theory.
   d. psychoanalytic theory.

8. Three-year-old Ali, who is fearful and withdrawn, is displaying signs of _____ problems, which suggests that he is emotionally _____ .
   a. internalizing; overcontrolled
   b. internalizing; undercontrolled
   c. externalizing; overcontrolled
   d. externalizing; undercontrolled

9. Summarizing her report on neurological aspects of emotional regulation, Alycia notes that young children who have internalizing problems tend to have greater activity in the:
   a. right temporal lobe.
   b. left temporal lobe.
   c. right prefrontal cortex.
   d. left prefrontal cortex.

10. Concerning children's concept of gender, which of the following statements is true?
    a. By age 3, children have a rudimentary understanding that sex distinctions are lifelong.
    b. Children as young as 1 year have a clear understanding of the physical differences between girls and boys and can consistently apply gender labels.
    c. Not until age 5 or 6 do children show a clear preference for gender-typed toys.
    d. All of the above are true.

11. Which of the following is *not* a feature of parenting used by Baumrind to differentiate authoritarian, permissive, and authoritative parents?
    a. maturity demands for the child's conduct
    b. efforts to control the child's actions
    c. nurturance
    d. adherence to stereotypical gender roles

12. Seeking to discipline her 3-year-old son for snatching a playmate's toy, Cassandra gently says, "How would you feel if Juwan grabbed your car?" Developmentalists would probably say that Cassandra's approach:
   a. is too permissive and would therefore be ineffective in the long run.
   b. would probably be more effective with a girl.
   c. will be effective in increasing prosocial behavior because it promotes empathy.
   d. will backfire and threaten her son's self-confidence.

13. Five-year-old Curtis, who is above average in height and weight, often picks on children who are smaller than he is. Curtis' behavior is an example of:
   a. bullying aggression.
   b. reactive aggression.
   c. instrumental aggression.
   d. relational aggression.

14. Which of the following is *not* true regarding children's exposure to media?
   a. Experts recommend no television for children before age 2.
   b. Most young children in the United States spend about 1 hour each day using some sort of media.
   c. The "good guys" in most media tend to be male and White.
   d. Women are usually portrayed as victims, not as leaders.

15. Four-year-old Eboni shows signs of distrust toward strangers. Eboni's behavior is an example of:
   a. prosocial behavior.
   b. antisocial behavior.
   c. instrumental aggression.
   d. antipathy.

Key Terms

Writing Definitions

Using your own words, write a brief definition or explanation of each of the following terms on a separate piece of paper.

1. emotional regulation
2. initiative versus guilt
3. self-esteem
4. self-concept
5. intrinsic motivation
6. extrinsic motivation
7. externalizing problems
8. internalizing problems
9. empathy
10. antipathy
11. prosocial behavior
12. antisocial behavior
13. instrumental aggression
14. reactive aggression
15. bullying aggression
16. authoritarian parenting
17. permissive parenting
18. authoritative parenting
19. psychological control
20. time-out
21. sex differences
22. gender differences
23. phallic stage
24. Oedipus complex
25. superego
26. Electra complex
27. identification
28. gender schema
29. androgyny

Cross-Check

After you have written the definitions of the key terms in this chapter, you should complete the crossword puzzle to ensure that you can reverse the process—recognize the term, given the definition.

ACROSS

1. A balance of traditionally male and female characteristics.
3. A behavior, such as cooperating or sharing, performed to benefit another person without the expectation of a reward.
8. In psychoanalytic theory, the self-critical and judgmental part of personality that internalizes the moral standards set by parents and society.
12. Behavior that takes the form of insults or social rejection is called _____ aggression.
14. Act intended to obtain or retain an object desired by another is called _____ aggression.
15. Style of parenting in which parents make few demands on their children, yet are nurturant and accepting and communicate well with their children.

DOWN

2. Cultural differences in the roles and behaviors of males and females.
4. Defense mechanism through which a person takes on the role and attitudes of a person more powerful than himself or herself.
5. Ability to manage and modify one's feelings, particularly feelings of fear, frustration, and anger.
6. In Freud's phallic stage of psychosexual development, a boy's sexual attraction toward the mother and resentment of the father.
7. Style of child rearing in which the parents show little affection or nurturance for their children, maturity demands are high, and parent–child communication is low.
9. In Freud's phallic stage of psychosexual development, a girl's sexual attraction toward the father and resentment of the mother.
10. Style of parenting in which the parents set limits and enforce rules but do so more democratically than do authoritarian parents.
11. Form of aggression involving an unprovoked attack on another child.
13. Aggressive behavior that is an angry retaliation for some intentional or incidental act by another person.

ANSWERS

CHAPTER REVIEW

1. when and how to express emotions; emotional regulation; impulses
2. initiative versus guilt; self-esteem; self-concept; pride
3. autonomy versus shame; complete; attention; persistence; try new experiences
4. guilt; guilt; shame; internalized
5. intrinsically motivated
6. psychopathology; externalizing; undercontrolled; internalizing
7. prefrontal cortex; 4 or 5
8. externalizing; internalizing
9. neurons
10. care experiences; internalizing; externalizing
11. empathy; prosocial behaviors; antipathy; antisocial behavior
12. 4 or 5; brain; emotional; theory of mind; caregivers

13. prejudiced
14. aggression; instrumental; reactive; relational; bullying
15. instrumental aggression; reactive aggression; emotional regulation; bullying aggression
16. parenting
17. Diana Baumrind; warmth; discipline; communication; maturity
18. authoritarian; low; high; low
19. permissive; are; well; few
20. authoritative; high; well; are
21. authoritarian; permissive; authoritative
22. temperament; do not
23. exerts; reasoning, empathy, and expressions of disappointment
24. expected; able; should; understands; control
   a. Remember theory of mind.
   b. Remember emerging self-concept.
   c. Remember the language explosion and fast-mapping.
   d. Remember that young children are not yet logical.
25. video violence
26. 3
27. higher grades; boys; lower grades; girls
28. do
29. together
30. sex; gender; roles
31. 2; 4; 8
32. phallic stage; mothers; fathers; Oedipus complex
33. identification; superego
34. Electra complex
35. reinforced; punished
36. modeling
37. understanding
38. sociocultural; traditional; androgyny
39. epigenetic; genes; early experience
40. biologically; brains
41. sex hormones; environmental factors; language; speak

PROGRESS TEST 1

Multiple-Choice Questions

1. **b.** is the answer. (p. 256)
2. **c.** is the answer. (p. 272)

a. & b. In Freud's theory, the oral and anal stages are associated with infant and early childhood development, respectively.

d. In Freud's theory, the latency period is associated with development during the school years.

3. **b.** is the answer. (p. 259)
4. **b.** is the answer. (pp. 264–265)

d. Traditional is a variation of the basic styles uncovered by later research. Indulgent and neglecting are abusive styles and clearly harmful, unlike the styles initially identified by Baumrind.

5. **a.** is the answer. (p. 264)

b. & c. Authoritative parents communicate very well and are quite affectionate.

d. This is not typical of authoritative parents.

6. **d.** is the answer. (p. 270)
7. **b.** is the answer. (p. 262)
8. **a.** is the answer. (p. 256)
9. **b.** is the answer. (p. 274)

a. This is the focus of Freud's phallic stage.

c. This is the focus of Erikson's psychosocial theory.

d. This is the focus of cognitive theorists.

10. **a.** is the answer. (p. 271)
11. **d.** is the answer. (p. 267)
12. **d.** is the answer. In accounting for Leonardo's verbal ability, Dr. Laurent alludes to both genetic and environmental factors, a giveaway for epigenetic theory. (pp. 276–277)

a., b., & c. These theories do not address biological or genetic influences on development.

13. **d.** is the answer. (p. 258)

a. & b. Children who display internalizing problems are withdrawn and bottle up their emotions.

c. Jake is displaying an inability to control his negative emotions.

14. **d.** is the answer. (p. 265)
15. **d.** is the answer. (p. 262)

True or False Items

1. F All parents make some maturity demands on their children; maturity demands are high in both the authoritarian and authoritative parenting styles. (pp. 264, 265)
2. T (p. 265)

3. F Children can apply gender labels by age 2. (p. 271)

4. F Cultures vary in how much they encourage prosocial behavior. (p. 260)

5. T (p. 276)

6. T (p. 276)

7. T (pp. 272–277)

8. T (p. 271)

9. T (p. 273)

10. T (p. 259)

PROGRESS TEST 2

Multiple-Choice Questions

1. **b.** is the answer. (p. 265)

2. **a.** is the answer. (p. 255)

    b. & d. Developing a sense of initiative and positive self-esteem are aspects of emotional regulation.

    c. Developing a sense of identity is the task of adolescence.

3. **c.** is the answer. (p. 259)

4. **a.** is the answer. (p. 258)

5. **a.** is the answer. (p. 272)

6. **b.** is the answer. (p. 272)

    a. & d. These are Freud's versions of phallic-stage development in little girls.

    c. There is no such thing as the "phallic complex."

7. **c.** is the answer. (p. 264)

    a. & b. Both authoritarian and authoritative parents make high demands on their children.

    d. This is not one of the three parenting styles. Traditional parents could be any one of these types.

8. **b.** is the answer. (p. 260)

9. **c.** is the answer. (p. 259)

    a. This describes empathy.

    b. This describes self-concept.

    d. This describes an internalizing problem.

10. **c.** is the answer. (p. 273)

    a. & d. Behaviorism, which includes social learning theory, emphasizes that children learn about gender by rewards and punishments and by observing others.

    b. Sociocultural theory focuses on the impact of the environment on gender identification.

11. **a.** is the answer. (p. 268)

b. & c. Time-outs involve removing a child from a situation in which misbehavior has occurred. Moreover, these threats of future punishment would likely be less effective because of the delay between the behavior and the consequence.

d. Although developmentalists stress the need to prevent misdeeds instead of punishing them and warn that time-outs may have unintended consequences, they nevertheless can be an effective form of discipline.

12. **a.** is the answer. (pp. 256–257)

    b. This viewpoint is associated only with cognitive theory.

    c. Although parent–child relationships are important to social development, they do not determine readiness.

    d. Identification is a Freudian defense mechanism.

13. **a.** is the answer. (p. 259)

14. **c.** is the answer. (p. 264)

15. **b.** is the answer. (p. 256)

    a. & c. According to Erikson, these are the crises of adolescence and infancy, respectively.

    d. This is not a crisis described by Erikson.

Matching Items

1. g (p. 259)
2. k (p. 276)
3. i (p. 259)
4. d (p. 260)
5. h (p. 260)
6. b (p. 273)
7. e (p. 272)
8. f (p. 264)
9. c (p. 264)
10. j (p. 273)
11. a (p. 261)

DEVELOPMENTAL PSYCHOLOGY APPLIED

1. **a.** is the answer. (p. 273)

2. **b.** is the answer. (p. 273)

    a. According to Freud, the Oedipus complex refers to the male's sexual feelings toward his mother and resentment toward his father.

    c. & d. These are concepts introduced by cognitive theorists and Erik Erikson, respectively.

3. **a.** is the answer. (p. 256)

    b. Erikson did not equate gender constancy with the emergence of guilt.

    c. & d. These reflect the viewpoints of learning theory and Freud, respectively.

4. **b.** is the answer. (p. 265)

5. **c.** is the answer. The purpose of Vincenzo's action is clearly to retain the Beanie Baby, rather than to retaliate (b) or bully Seema (a). (pp. 261, 262)

d. Relational aggression takes the form of a verbal insult.

6. **b.** is the answer. (p. 274)

7. **b.** is the answer. (p. 275)

8. **a.** is the answer. (p. 258)

9. **c.** is the answer. (p. 259)

   a. & b. The temporal lobes are involved in speech and hearing rather than emotional regulation.

   d. Children who have externalizing problems tend to have greater activity in this area.

10. **a.** is the answer. (p. 271)

    b. Not until about age 2 can children consistently apply gender labels.

    c. By age 4, children prefer gender-typed toys.

11. **d.** is the answer. (p. 264)

12. **c.** is the answer. (p. 260)

13. **a.** is the answer. (pp. 261–262)

14. **b.** Most young children in the United States spend about three hours each day using some sort of media. (p. 269)

15. **d.** is the answer. (p. 259)

KEY TERMS

Writing Definitions

1. **Emotional regulation** is the ability to inhibit, enhance, direct, and modulate emotions. (p. 255)

2. According to Erikson, the crisis of the preschool years is **initiative versus guilt**. In this crisis, young children eagerly take on new tasks and play activities and feel guilty when their efforts result in failure or criticism. (p. 256)

3. **Self-esteem** is the belief in one's own ability. (p. 256)

4. **Self-concept** refers to people's understanding of who they are. (p. 256)

5. **Intrinsic motivation** is the internal goals or drives to accomplish something for the joy of doing it. (p. 257)

6. **Extrinsic motivation** is the need for rewards from outside, such as material possessions. (p. 257)

7. Young children who have **externalizing problems** tend to experience emotions outside themselves and uncontrollably lash out at other people or things. (p. 258)

8. Children who have **internalizing problems** tend to be fearful and withdrawn as a consequence of their tendencies to keep their emotions bottled up inside themselves. (p. 258)

9. **Empathy** is a person's true understanding of the emotions of another person. (p. 259)

10. **Antipathy** is a person's feelings of anger, distrust, dislike, or even hatred toward another person. (p. 259)

11. **Prosocial behavior** is an action, such as helping or sharing, that is performed for another person without any obvious benefit. (p. 260)

12. **Antisocial behavior** is an action, such as hitting or insulting, that is deliberately hurtful or destructive. (p. 260)

13. **Instrumental aggression** is hurtful behavior that is intended to get or keep something that another person has. (p. 261)

14. **Reactive aggression** is impulsive retaliation for some intentional or accidental act, verbal or physical, by another person. (p. 261)

    Memory aid: Instrumental aggression is behavior that is *instrumental* in allowing a child to retain a favorite toy. **Reactive aggression** is a *reaction* to another child's behavior.

15. An unprovoked, repeated physical or verbal attack on another person is an example of **bullying aggression**. (p. 261)

16. **Authoritarian parenting** is Baumrind's term for a style of child rearing in which the parents show little affection or nurturance for their children, maturity demands are high, and parent–child communication is low. (p. 264)

    Memory aid: Someone who is an **authoritarian** demands unquestioning obedience and acts in a dictatorial way.

17. **Permissive parenting** is Baumrind's term for a style of child rearing in which the parents make few demands on their children, yet are nurturant and accepting and communicate well with their children. (p. 264)

18. **Authoritative parenting** is Baumrind's term for a style of child rearing in which the parents set limits and enforce rules but are willing to listen to the child's ideas and to make compromises. (p. 264)

    Memory aid: **Authoritative parents** act as *authorities* do on a subject—by discussing and explaining why certain family rules are in place.

19. **Psychological control** is a form of discipline that involves threatening to withdraw love and support from a child. (p. 267)

20. A **time-out** is a form of discipline in which a child is required to stop all activity and sit quietly apart from other people for a few minutes. (p. 268)

21. **Sex differences** are biological differences between females and males. (p. 271)

22. **Gender differences** are cultural differences in the roles and behavior of males and females. (p. 271)

23. In psychoanalytic theory, the **phallic stage** is the third stage of psychosexual development, in which the penis becomes the focus of concern and pleasure. (p. 272)

24. According to Freud, boys in the phallic stage of psychosexual development develop a collection of feelings, known as the **Oedipus complex**, that center on sexual attraction to the mother and resentment of the father. (p. 272)

25. In psychoanalytic theory, the **superego** is the self-critical and judgmental part of personality that internalizes the moral standards of the parents. (p. 272)

26. Girls in Freud's phallic stage may develop a collection of feelings, known as the **Electra complex**, that center on sexual attraction to the father and resentment of the mother. (p. 273)

27. In Freud's theory, **identification** is a means of defending one's self-concept by taking on the roles and attitudes of another person. (p. 273)

28. In cognitive theory, **gender schema** is the child's understanding of sex differences.

29. **Androgyny** is a balance of traditionally female and male psychological characteristics in a person. (p. 276)

Cross-Check

ACROSS

1. androgyny
3. prosocial
8. superego
12. relational
14. instrumental
15. permissive

DOWN

2. gender difference
4. identification
5. emotional regulation
6. Oedipus complex
7. authoritarian
9. Electra complex
10. authoritative
11. bullying
13. reactive

11

The School Years: Biosocial Development

Chapter Overview

This chapter introduces middle childhood, the years from 7 to 11. Changes in physical size and shape are described, and the problem of obesity is addressed. The discussion then turns to the continuing development of intellectual skills during the school years, culminating in an evaluation of intelligence testing. A final section examines the experiences of children with special needs, such as children with attention-deficit/hyperactivity disorder, those with learning disabilities, and children with autism. The causes of and treatments for these problems are discussed, with emphasis placed on insights arising from the developmental psychopathology perspective. This perspective makes it clear that the manifestations of any special childhood problem will change as the child grows older and that treatment must often focus on all three domains of development.

NOTE: Answer guidelines for all Chapter 11 questions begin on page 168.

Guided Study

The text chapter should be studied one section at a time. Before you read, preview each section by skimming it, noting headings and boldface items. Then read the appropriate section objectives from the following outline. Keep these objectives in mind and, as you read the chapter section, search for the information that will enable you to meet each objective. Once you have finished a section, write out answers for its objectives.

A Healthy Time (pp. 283–290)

1. Describe normal physical growth and development during middle childhood, and account for the usual variations among children.

2. Discuss the problems of obese children in middle childhood, and describe possible causes of obesity.

3. Discuss the benefits and hazards of play activity and physical exercise for 6- to 11-year-olds.

4. Discuss the physical and psychological impact of chronic illness, especially asthma, during middle childhood.

Children with Special Needs (pp. 295–303)

8. Explain the developmental psychopathology perspective, and discuss its value in treating children with special needs.

Brain Development (pp. 290–295)

4. Discuss advances in brain functioning during middle childhood.

9. (text and Thinking Like a Scientist) Describe the symptoms and treatment of attention-deficit disorder and attention-deficit/hyperactivity disorder, and discuss the use and misuse of prescription drugs in treating these disorders.

6. Explain how achievement and aptitude tests are used in evaluating individual differences in cognitive growth, and discuss why use of such tests is controversial.

10. Discuss the characteristics of learning disabilities.

7. Describe Sternberg's and Gardner's theories of multiple intelligences, and explain the significance of these theories.

11. Identify the symptoms and possible causes of autism, and describe its most effective treatment.

12. Describe techniques that have been tried in efforts to educate children with special needs.

Chapter Review

When you have finished reading the chapter, work through the material that follows to review it. Complete the sentences and answer the questions. As you proceed, evaluate your performance for each section by consulting the answers beginning on page 168. Do not continue with the next section until you understand each answer. If you need to, review or reread the appropriate section in the textbook before continuing.

1. The biggest influence on development from age 7 to 11 is the changing _____ .

A Healthy Time (pp. 283–290)

2. Compared with biosocial development during other periods of the life span, biosocial development during this time, known as _____ _____ , is _____ (relatively smooth/often fraught with problems). For example, disease and death during these years are _____ (more common/rarer) than during any other period.

3. Children grow at a _____ (faster/slower) rate during middle childhood than they did earlier.

Describe several other features of physical development during the school years.

4. Children are said to be overweight when their body mass index is above the _____ (what number?) percentile of the growth chart for their age. Obesity is defined as having a BMI above the _____ (what number?) percentile.

5. Childhood obesity, which is _____ (increasing/decreasing) in the United States, is hazardous to children's health because it reduces _____ and increases _____ _____ , both of which are associated with serious health prob-

lems in middle adulthood. School achievement and self-esteem _____ (increase/decrease) as weight increases.

6. People who inherit a gene allele called _____ are more likely to be obese.

7. Children who watch more than _____ hours of television and drink more than _____ servings of _____ each day are more often overweight than those who do neither.

State some of the benefits and hazards of childhood sports.

8. Compared to the past, middle childhood is now a healthier time _____ (in every nation of the world/only in developed nations).

9. About _____ percent of children have special health needs. Among those that often get worse during the school years are _____ , _____ , and _____ .

10. Most poor children today live in _____ (rural areas/cities).

11. A chronic inflammatory disorder of the airways is called _____ . This disorder is _____ (more common/less common) today than in the past.

12. The causes or triggers of asthma include _____ , _____ , and exposure to _____ such as pet hair.

13. The use of injections, inhalers, and pills to treat asthma is an example of _____ prevention. Less than _____ (how many?) of all asthmatic children in the United States benefit from this type of treatment. The best approach to treating childhood diseases is _____ _____ , which in the case of asthma includes proper _____ of homes and schools, decreased _____ , eradication of cockroaches, and safe outdoor _____ _____ .

State two important strategies for preventing asthma and many other adult health problems in children.

Brain Development (pp. 290–295)

14. Advances in brain development during early childhood enable emerging _____ regulation and _____ _____ _____ . Left–right coordination emerges in middle childhood as the _____ _____ strengthens connections between the brain's two _____ . The executive functions of the brain also develop, along with maturation of the _____ _____ .

15. The length of time it takes a person to respond to a particular stimulus is called _____ _____ .

16. Two other advances in brain function at this time include the ability to _____ _____ , called _____ _____ , and the _____ of thoughts and actions that are repeated in sequence.

17. The potential to learn a particular skill or body of knowledge is a person's _____ . The most commonly used tests of this type are _____ _____ . In the original version of the most commonly used test of this type, a person's score was calculated as a _____ (the child's _____ _____ divided by the child's _____ _____ and multiplied by 100 to determine his or her _____).

18. Tests that are designed to measure what a child has learned are called _____ tests. Tests that are designed to measure learning potential are called _____ tests.

19. The average IQ scores of nations have _____ (increased/decreased), a phenomenon called the _____ _____ .

20. Two highly regarded IQ tests are the _____ _____ _____ _____ _____ and the _____-_____ .

21. To be classified as _____ _____ , children must have IQs below _____ and be unusually low in _____ .

22. IQ testing is controversial in part because no test can measure _____ without also measuring _____ or without reflecting the _____ . Another reason is that a child's intellectual potential _____ (changes/does not change) over time.

23. Robert Sternberg believes that there are three distinct types of intelligence: _____ , _____ , and _____ . Similarly, Howard Gardner describes _____ (how many?) distinct intelligences.

Children with Special Needs (pp. 295–303)

24. Among the conditions that give rise to "special needs" are _____ _____ _____ _____ .

25. Down syndrome and other conditions that give rise to "special needs" begin with a _____ anomaly.

26. The field of study that is concerned with childhood psychological disorders is _____ _____ . This perspective has provided several lessons that apply to all children. Three of these are that _____ is normal; disability _____ (changes/does not change) over time; and adolescence and adulthood may be _____ .

27. This perspective also has made diagnosticians much more aware of the _____ _____ of childhood problems. This awareness is reflected in the official diagnostic guide of the American Psychiatric Association, which is the _____ _____ .

28. A condition that manifests itself in a difficulty in concentrating for more than a few moments is called _____-_____ _____ .

29. The most common type of this disorder, which includes a need to be active, often accompanied by excitability and impulsivity, is called _____-_____/ _____ _____ . Children suffering from this disorder can be _____ , _____ , and _____ .

30. Other disorders often occur together with ADHD. Examples of these _____ conditions include _____ .

31. In childhood, the most effective forms of treatment for ADHD are _____ , _____ , and _____ for parents and teachers.

32. Certain drugs that stimulate adults, such as _____ and _____ , have a reverse effect on many hyperactive children.

33. Children who have difficulty acquiring a particular skill that others acquire easily are said to have a _____ _____ . These deficits usually _____ (do/do not) result in lifelong impediments.

34. A disability in reading is called_____ .

35. The most severe disturbance of early childhood is _____ , which is used to describe children who have extremely inadequate _____ skills. Children who are less withdrawn are usually diagnosed with _____ _____ .

36. In early childhood autism, severe deficiencies appear in three areas: _____ ability, _____ _____ , and _____ .

37. Children who have autistic symptoms that are less severe than those in the classic syndrome are sometimes diagnosed with _____ _____ , also called _____-_____ _____ .

State three possible reasons for the increased incidence of autistic spectrum disorder.

38. Another possibility is that some new _____ harms their developing brains. One suspected toxin was the antiseptic _____ , which is used in childhood _____ . Other possible toxins are _____ _____ .

39. The process of formally identifying a child with special needs usually begins with a teacher _____ , which may ultimately lead to agreement on an _____ _____ _____ for the child.

40. In response to a 1975 act requiring that children with special needs be taught in the _____ _____ _____ , the strategy of not separating special-needs children into special classes, called _____ , emerged. More recently, some schools have developed a _____ _____ , in which such children spend part of each day with a teaching specialist. In the most recent approach, called _____ , learning-disabled children receive targeted help within the setting of a regular classroom.

Progress Test 1

Multiple-Choice Questions

Circle your answers to the following questions and check them with the answers beginning on page 169. If your answer is incorrect, read the explanation for why it is incorrect and then consult the appropriate pages of the text (in parentheses following the correct answer).

1. As children move into middle childhood:
   a. the rate of accidental death increases.
   b. sexual urges intensify.
   c. the rate of weight gain increases.
   d. biological growth slows and steadies.

2. Ongoing maturation of which brain area contributes most to left–right coordination?
   a. corpus callosum
   b. prefrontal cortex
   c. brainstem
   d. temporal lobe

3. The ability to filter out distractions and concentrate on relevant details is called:
   a. automatization.
   b. reaction time.
   c. selective attention.
   d. inclusion.

4. Dyslexia is a learning disability that affects the ability to:
   a. do math.   c. write.
   b. read.   d. speak.

5. The developmental psychopathology perspective is characterized by its:
   a. contextual approach.
   b. emphasis on the unchanging nature of developmental disorders.
   c. emphasis on the cognitive domain of development.
   d. concern with all of the above.

6. The time—usually measured in fractions of a second—it takes for a person to respond to a particular stimulus is called:
   a. the interstimulus interval.
   b. reaction time.
   c. the stimulus–response interval.
   d. response latency.

7. The underlying problem in attention-deficit/hyperactivity disorder appears to be:
   a. low overall intelligence.
   b. a neurological difficulty in paying attention.
   c. a learning disability in a specific academic skill.
   d. the existence of a conduct disorder.

8. Healthy 6-year-olds tend to have:
   a. the lowest body mass index of any age group.
   b. the highest body mass index of any age group.
   c. more short-term illnesses than any other age group.
   d. fewer short-term illnesses than any other age group.

9. Autistic children generally have severe deficiencies in all but which of the following?
   a. social skills
   b. imaginative play
   c. echolalia
   d. communication ability

10. Although asthma has genetic origins, several environmental factors contribute to its onset, including:
    a. urbanization.
    b. airtight windows.
    c. dogs and cats living inside the house.
    d. all of the above.

11. Psychoactive drugs are most effective in treating attention-deficit/hyperactivity disorder when they are administered:
    a. before the diagnosis becomes certain.
    b. for several years after the basic problem has abated.
    c. as part of the labeling process.
    d. with psychotherapy and training of parents and teachers.

12. Tests that measure a child's potential to learn a new subject are called _____ tests.
    a. aptitude   c. vocational
    b. achievement   d. intelligence

13. In the earliest aptitude tests, a child's score was calculated by dividing the child's _____ age by his or her _____ age to find the _____ quotient.
    a. mental; chronological; intelligence
    b. chronological; mental; intelligence
    c. intelligence; chronological; mental
    d. intelligence; mental; chronological

14. Selective attention refers to the ability to:
    a. choose which of many stimuli to concentrate on.
    b. control emotional outbursts.
    c. persist at a task.
    d. perform a familiar action without much conscious thought.

15. Ongoing maturation of which brain area enables schoolchildren to more effectively analyze the potential consequences of their actions?
    a. corpus callosum
    b. prefrontal cortex
    c. brainstem
    d. temporal lobe

True or False Items

Write *T (true)* or *F (false)* on the line in front of each statement.

_____ 1. The rate of growth in school-age children continues at a rapid pace.

_____ 2. Genes and hereditary differences in taste preferences are the most important factors in promoting childhood obesity.

_____ 3. Childhood obesity increases the risk for serious health problems in adulthood.

_____ 4. The quick reaction time that is crucial in some sports can be readily achieved with practice.

_____ 5. The intellectual performance of children with Asperger syndrome is poor in all areas.

_____ 6. The incidence of children with autistic characteristics is decreasing.

_____ 7. Despite the efforts of teachers and parents, most children with learning disabilities can expect their disabilities to persist and even worsen as they enter adulthood.

_____ 8. Stressful living conditions are an important consideration in diagnosing a learning disability.

_____ 9. The drugs sometimes given to children to reduce hyperactive behaviors have a reverse effect on adults.

_____ 10. Mainstreaming is the most effective educational method for children with special needs.

Progress Test 2

Progress Test 2 should be completed during a final chapter review. Answer the following questions after you thoroughly understand the correct answers for the Chapter Review and Progress Test 1.

Multiple-Choice Questions

1. During the years from 7 to 11, the average child:
   a. becomes slimmer.
   b. gains about 12 pounds a year.
   c. has decreased lung capacity.
   d. is more likely to become obese than at any other period in the life span.

2. Comorbidity refers to the presence of:
   a. two or more unrelated disease conditions in the same person.
   b. abnormal neurons in the prefrontal cortex.
   c. developmental delays in physical development.
   d. any of several disorders characterized by inadequate social skills.

3. A specific learning disability that becomes apparent when a child experiences unusual difficulty in learning to read is:
   a. dyslexia.   c. ADHD.
   b. Asperger syndrome. d. ADD.

4. Marked delays in particular areas of learning are collectively referred to as:
   a. learning disabilities.
   b. attention-deficit/hyperactivity disorder.
   c. hyperactivity.
   d. dyslexia.

5. Aptitude and achievement testing are controversial in part because:
   a. most tests are unreliable with respect to the individual scores they yield.
   b. a child's intellectual potential often changes over time.
   c. they often fail to identify serious learning problems.
   d. of all of the above reasons.

6. The most effective form of help for children with ADHD is:
   a. medication.
   b. psychotherapy.
   c. training parents and teachers.
   d. a combination of some or all of the above.

7. A key factor in reaction time is:
   a. whether the child is male or female.
   b. brain maturation.
   c. whether the stimulus to be reacted to is an auditory or visual one.
   d. all of the above.

8. The first noticeable symptom of autism is usually:
   a. the lack of spoken language.
   b. abnormal social responsiveness.
   c. both a. and b.
   d. unpredictable.

9. Which of the following is true of children with a diagnosed learning disability?
   a. They may have an average or above-average IQ.
   b. They often have a specific physical handicap, such as hearing loss.
   c. They often lack basic educational experiences.
   d. All of the above are true.

10. A key factor in the automatization of children's thoughts and actions is:
    a. the continuing myelination of neurons.
    b. diet.
    c. activity level.
    d. all of the above.

11. Which approach to education may best meet the needs of learning-disabled children in terms of both skill remediation and social interaction with other children?
    a. mainstreaming   c. inclusion
    b. special education   d. resource rooms

12. Asperger syndrome is a disorder in which:
    a. body weight fluctuates dramatically over short periods of time.
    b. verbal skills seem normal, but social perceptions and skills are abnormal.
    c. an autistic child is extremely aggressive.
    d. a child of normal intelligence has difficulty mastering a specific cognitive skill.

13. Which of the following is *not* evidence of ADHD?
    a. inattentiveness   c. impulsivity
    b. poor language skills   d. overreactivity

14. Tests that measure what a child has already learned are called _____ tests.
    a. aptitude   c. achievement
    b. vocational   d. intelligence

15. Which of the following is *not* a type of intelligence identified in Robert Sternberg's theory?
    a. academic   c. achievement
    b. practical   d. creative

Matching Items

Match each term or concept with its corresponding description or definition.

Terms or Concepts

_____ 1. dyslexia
_____ 2. automatization
_____ 3. Asperger syndrome
_____ 4. attention-deficit/hyperactivity disorder
_____ 5. asthma
_____ 6. Flynn Effect
_____ 7. autism
_____ 8. developmental psychopathology
_____ 9. *DSM-IV-R*
_____ 10. learning disability
_____ 11. mainstreaming

Descriptions or Definitions

a. set of symptoms in which a child has impaired social skills despite having normal speech and intelligence
b. the rise in IQ score averages that has occurred in many nations
c. the diagnostic guide of the American Psychiatric Association
d. process by which thoughts and actions become routine and no longer require much thought
e. system in which learning-disabled children are taught in general education classrooms
f. disorder characterized by self-absorption
g. chronic inflammation of the airways
h. behavior problem involving difficulty in concentrating, as well as excitability and impulsivity
i. applies insights from studies of normal development to the study of childhood disorders
j. an unexpected difficulty with one or more academic skills
k. difficulty in reading

Developmental Psychology Applied

Answer these questions the day before an exam as a final check on your understanding of the chapter's terms and concepts.

1. According to developmentalists, the benefits of sports include:
   a. better overall health.
   b. appreciation of fair play.
   c. improved problem-solving abilities.
   d. all of the above.

2. Dr. Rutter, who believes that knowledge about normal development can be applied to the study and treatment of psychological disorders, evidently is working from which of the following perspectives?
   a. clinical psychology
   b. developmental psychopathology
   c. behaviorism
   d. psychoanalysis

3. Summarizing physical development during middle childhood, Professor Wilson notes each of the following except that:
   a. it is the healthiest period of the life span.
   b. mortal injuries are unusual during this time.
   c. most fatal childhood diseases occur during middle childhood.
   d. growth is slower than during early childhood.

4. Angela was born in 1984. In 1992, she scored 125 on an intelligence test. Using the original formula, what was Angela's mental age when she took the test?
   a. 6
   b. 8
   c. 10
   d. 12

5. Ten-year-old Clarence is quick-tempered, easily frustrated, and is often disruptive in the classroom. Clarence may be suffering from:
   a. dyslexia.
   b. Asperger syndrome.
   c. attention-deficit disorder.
   d. attention-deficit/hyperactivity disorder.

6. Because 11-year-old Wayne is obese, he runs a greater risk of developing:
   a. heart problems.
   b. diabetes.
   c. psychological problems.
   d. all of the above.

7. Of the following individuals, who is likely to have the fastest reaction time?
   a. a 7-year-old
   b. a 9-year-old
   c. an 11-year-old
   d. an adult

8. Harold weighs about 20 pounds more than his friend Jay. During school recess, Jay can usually be found playing soccer with his classmates, while Harold sits on the sidelines by himself. Harold's rejection is likely due to his:
   a. being physically different.
   b. being dyslexic.
   c. intimidation of his schoolmates.
   d. being hyperactive.

9. In determining whether an 8-year-old has a learning disability, a teacher looks primarily for:
   a. exceptional performance in a subject area.
   b. the exclusion of other explanations.
   c. a family history of the learning disability.
   d. both a. and b.

10. Although 9-year-old Carl has severely impaired social skills, his intelligence and speech are normal. Carl is evidently displaying symptoms of:
    a. autism.
    b. ADD.
    c. ADHD.
    d. Asperger syndrome.

11. Concluding his presentation on the Flynn Effect, Kwame notes that the reasons for this trend include all of the following except:
    a. better health.
    b. genetic vulnerability.
    c. more schooling.
    d. smaller families.

12. Jennifer displays inadequate social skills and is extremely self-absorbed. It is likely that she suffers from:
    a. autism.
    b. ADHD.
    c. dyslexia.
    d. asthma.

13. Danny has been diagnosed as having attention-deficit/hyperactivity disorder. Every day, his parents make sure that he takes the proper dose of Ritalin. His parents should:
    a. continue this behavior until Danny is an adult.
    b. try different medications when Danny seems to be reverting to his normal overactive behavior.
    c. also make sure that Danny has psychotherapy and that they and Danny's teachers receive training.
    d. not worry about Danny's condition; he will outgrow it.

14. Concluding her presentation on "Asthma During Middle Childhood," Amanda mentions each of the following *except* that:
    a. asthma is much more common today than 20 years ago.
    b. genetic vulnerability is rarely a factor in a child's susceptibility to developing asthma.
    c. the incidence of asthma continues to increase.
    d. carpeted floors, airtight windows, and less outdoor play increase the risk of asthma attacks.

15. Howard Gardner and Robert Sternberg would probably be most critical of traditional aptitude and achievement tests because they:
    a. inadvertently reflect certain nonacademic competencies.
    b. do not reflect knowledge of cultural ideas.
    c. measure only a limited set of abilities.
    d. underestimate the intellectual potential of disadvantaged children.

Key Terms

Using your own words, write a brief definition or explanation of each of the following terms on a separate piece of paper.

1. middle childhood
2. overweight
3. obesity
4. asthma
5. reaction time
6. selective attention
7. automatization
8. aptitude
9. IQ test
10. achievement test
11. Flynn Effect
12. Wechsler Intelligence Scale for Children (WISC)
13. mental retardation
14. child with special needs
15. developmental psychopathology
16. *Diagnostic and Statistical Manual of Mental Disorders (DSM-IV-R)*
17. attention-deficit/hyperactivity disorder (ADHD)
18. comorbidity
19. learning disability
20. dyslexia
21. autism
22. autistic spectrum disorder
23. Asperger syndrome
24. individual education plan (IEP)
25. least restrictive environment (LRE)
26. resource room
27. inclusion

ANSWERS
CHAPTER REVIEW

1. context
2. middle childhood; relatively smooth; rarer
3. slower

During the school years, children generally become slimmer, muscles become stronger, and lung capacity increases.

4. 85th; 95th
5. increasing; exercise; blood pressure; decrease
6. FTO
7. two; two; soda (pop)

The benefits of sports include better overall health, less obesity, an appreciation of cooperation and fair play, improved problem-solving ability, and respect for teammates and opponents. The hazards may include loss of self-esteem as a result of criticism, injuries, reinforcement of existing prejudices, increased stress, and time taken away from learning academic skills.

8. in every nation of the world
9. 13; Tourette syndrome; stuttering; allergies
10. cities
11. asthma; more common
12. genes; infections; allergens
13. tertiary; half; primary prevention; ventilation; pollution; play spaces

Parents must be diligent in providing regular preventive care, and children must develop the habit of taking care of their health.

14. emotional; theory of mind; corpus callosum; hemispheres; prefrontal cortex

15. reaction time

16. pay special heed to one source of information among many; selective attention; automatization

17. aptitude; IQ tests; quotient; mental age; chronological age; IQ

18. achievement; aptitude

19. increased; Flynn Effect

20. Wechsler Intelligence Scale for Children (WISC); Stanford-Binet

21. mentally retarded; 70; adaptation to daily life

22. potential; achievement; culture; changes

23. academic; creative; practical; eight

24. anxiety disorder, autism, conduct disorder, clinical depression, developmental delay, learning disability, Down syndrome, attachment disorder, attention-deficit disorder, bipolar disorder, and Asperger syndrome

25. biological

26. developmental psychopathology; abnormality; changes; better or worse

27. social context; *Diagnostic and Statistical Manual of Mental Disorders* (*DSM-IV-R*)

28. attention-deficit disorder

29. attention-deficit/hyperactivity disorder; inattentive; impulsive; overactive

30. comorbid; conduct disorder, depression, anxiety, Tourette syndrome, dyslexia, bipolar disorder, autism, and schizophrenia

31. medication; psychotherapy; training

32. amphetamines; methylphenidate (Ritalin)

33. learning disability; do not

34. dyslexia

35. autism; social; autistic spectrum disorder

36. language; social interaction; play

37. Asperger syndrome; high-functioning autism
The increase may reflect an expanded definition of the condition, earlier diagnosis, and the greater availability of special education.

38. teratogen; thimerosal; immunizations; pesticides, cleaning chemicals, and some ingredients in nail polish

39. referral; individual education plan (IEP)

40. least restrictive environment (LRE); mainstreaming; resource room; inclusion

PROGRESS TEST 1

Multiple-Choice Questions

1. **d.** is the answer. (p. 284)

2. **a.** is the answer. (p. 290)

3. **c.** (pp. 290–291)

   a. Automatization is the process in which repetition of a sequence of thoughts and actions makes the sequence routine.

   b. Reaction time is the length of time it takes to respond to a stimulus.

   d. Inclusion is an approach in which children with special needs are educated in regular classrooms along with all the other children.

4. **b.** is the answer. (p. 299)

   a. Though not defined in the text, this is called dyscalcula.

   c. & d. The text does not give labels for learning disabilities in writing or speaking.

5. **a.** is the answer. (p. 296)

   b. & c. Because of its contextual approach, developmental psychopathology emphasizes *all* domains of development. Also, it points out that behaviors change over time.

6. **b.** is the answer. (p. 290)

7. **b.** is the answer. (p. 297)

8. **a.** is the answer. (p. 284)

9. **c.** is the answer. Echolalia *is* a type of communication difficulty, a characteristic form of speech of many autistic children. (p. 299)

10. **d.** is the answer. (p. 289)

11. **d.** is the answer. (p. 297)

12. **a.** is the answer. (p. 292)

    b. Achievement tests measure what has already been learned.

    c. Vocational tests, which, as their name implies, measure what a person has learned about a particular trade, are achievement tests.

    d. Intelligence tests measure general aptitude, rather than aptitude for a specific subject.

13. **a.** is the answer. (p. 292)

14. **a.** is the answer. (pp. 290–291)

    b. This is emotional regulation.

    d. This is automatization.

15. **b.** is the answer. (p. 290)

    a. Maturation of the corpus callosum contributes to left–right coordination.

    c. & d. These brain areas, which were not discussed in this chapter, play important roles in regulating sleep–waking cycles (brain stem) and hearing and language abilities (temporal lobe).

True or False Items

1. F   The rate of growth slows down during middle childhood. (p. 284)
2. F   Environmental factors are more important in promoting obesity during middle childhood. (p. 285)
3. T   (p. 285)
4. F   Reaction time depends on brain maturation and is not readily affected by practice. (p. 290)
5. F   Children with Asperger syndrome show isolated areas of remarkable skill. (p. 300)
6. F   Just the opposite is true, possibly because of better diagnoses. (p. 301)
7. F   Some children find ways to compensate for their deficiencies, and others are taught effective strategies for learning. (p. 299)
8. F   Stressful living conditions must be excluded before diagnosing a learning disability. (p. 299)
9. T (pp. 297–298)
10. F   Mainstreaming did not meet all children's educational needs. (p. 303)

PROGRESS TEST 2
Multiple-Choice Questions

1. **a.** is the answer. (p. 284)
   b. & c. During this period, children gain 5 to 7 pounds per year and experience increased lung capacity.
   d. Although childhood obesity is a common problem, the text does not indicate that a person is more likely to become obese at this age than at any other.
2. **a.** is the answer. (p. 297)
3. **a.** is the answer. (p. 299)
   b., c. & d. These disorders do not manifest themselves in a particular academic skill but instead appear in psychological processes that affect learning in general.
4. **a.** is the answer. (p. 299)
   b. & c. ADHD is a disorder that usually does not manifest itself in specific subject areas. Hyperactivity is a facet of this disorder.
   d. Dyslexia is a learning disability in reading only.
5. **b.** is the answer. (pp. 293–294)

6. **d.** is the answer. (p. 297)
7. **b.** is the answer. (p. 290)
8. **c.** is the answer. (p. 299)
9. **a.** is the answer. (p. 299)
10. **a.** is the answer. (p. 291)
11. **c.** is the answer. (p. 303)
    a. Many general education teachers are unable to cope with the special needs of some children.
    b. & d. These approaches undermined the social integration of children with special needs.
12. **b.** is the answer. (p. 300)
13. **b.** is the answer. (p. 297)
14. **c.** is the answer. (p. 292)
15. **c.** is the answer. (p. 294)

Matching Items

1. k (p. 299)   5. g (p. 288)   9. c (p. 296)
2. d (p. 291)   6. b (p. 292)   10. j (p. 299)
3. a (p. 300)   7. f (p. 299)   11. e (p. 303)
4. h (p. 297)   8. i (p. 296)

DEVELOPMENTAL PSYCHOLOGY APPLIED

1. **d.** is the answer. (p. 286)
2. **b.** is the answer. (p. 296)
3. **c.** is the answer. Most fatal childhood diseases occur before age 7. (p. 283)
4. **c.** is the answer. At the time she took the test, Angela's chronological age was 8. Knowing that her IQ was 125, we can solve the equation to yield a mental age value of 10. (p. 292)
5. **d.** is the answer. (p. 297)
6. **d.** is the answer. (p. 285)
7. **d.** is the answer. (p. 290)
8. **a.** is the answer. (p. 285)
   b., c., & d. Obese children are no more likely to be dyslexic, physically intimidating, or hyperactive than other children.
9. **d.** is the answer. (p. 299)
10. **d.** is the answer. (p. 300)
11. **b.** is the answer. (p. 292)
12. **a.** is the answer. (p. 299)
    b. Children with ADHD are inattentive, impulsive, and overactive.
    c. Dyslexia is a learning disability
    d. Asthma is a chronic inflammatory disorder.

13. **c.** is the answer. Medication alone cannot ameliorate all the problems of ADHD. (p. 297)

14. **b.** is the answer. Genes typically *do* play a role in a child's susceptibility to asthma. (p. 288)

15. **c.** is the answer. Both Sternberg and Gardner believe that there are multiple intelligences rather than the narrowly defined abilities measured by traditional aptitude and achievement tests. (p. 294)

   a., b., & d. Although these criticisms are certainly valid, they are not specifically associated with Sternberg or Gardner.

KEY TERMS

1. **Middle childhood** is the period from roughly age 6 or 7 to 10 or 11. (p. 283)

2. A child whose body mass index (BMI) falls above the 85th percentile for children of a specific age and height is designated as **overweight.** (p. 284)

3. **Obesity** is a body mass index (BMI) above the 95th percentile for children of a specific age and height. (p. 284)

4. **Asthma** is a disorder in which the airways are chronically inflamed. (p. 288)

5. **Reaction time** is the length of time it takes a person to respond to a particular stimulus. (p. 290)

6. **Selective attention** is the ability to concentrate on one stimulus while ignoring others. (p. 290)

7. **Automatization** is the process by which thoughts and actions that are repeated often enough to become routine no longer require much conscious thought. (p. 291)

8. **Aptitude** is the potential to learn a particular skill or body of knowledge. (p. 292)

9. **IQ tests** are aptitude tests, which were originally designed to yield a measure of intelligence and calculated as mental age divided by chronological age, multiplied by 100. (p. 292)

10. **Achievement tests** measure what a child has already learned in a particular academic subject or subjects. (p. 292)

11. The **Flynn Effect** refers to the rise in average IQ scores that has occurred recently in many nations. (p. 292)

12. The **Wechsler Intelligence Scale for Children (WISC)** is a widely used IQ test for school-age children that assesses vocabulary, general knowledge, memory, and spatial comprehension. (p. 293)

13. People are considered **mentally retarded** if their IQs fall below 70 and they are unusually low in adaptation to daily life. (p. 293)

14. A **child with special needs** is one who, because of physical or mental disability, requires extra help in order to learn. (p. 295)

15. **Developmental psychopathology** is a field that applies the insights from studies of typical development to the study and treatment of childhood disorders, and vice versa. (p. 296)

16. The fourth edition of the *Diagnostic and Statistical Manual of Mental Disorders (DSM-IV-R),* developed by the American Psychiatric Association, is the leading means of diagnosing mental disorders. (p. 296)

17. **Attention-deficit/hyperactivity disorder (ADHD)** is a behavior problem in which the individual has great difficulty concentrating and is often inattentive, impulsive, and overactive. (p. 297)

18. **Comorbidity** is the presence of two or more unrelated diseases at the same time in the same person. (p. 297)

19. A **learning disability** is a difficulty in a particular area of learning that is not attributable to overall intellectual slowness, a physical handicap, or a severely stressful living condition. (p. 299)

20. **Dyslexia** is a learning disability in reading. (p. 299)

21. **Autism** is a severe disturbance of early childhood characterized by an inability to communicate with others in an ordinary way, by extreme self-absorption, and by an inability to learn normal speech. (p. 299)

22. **Autistic spectrum disorder** is any of several disorders characterized by deficient social skills, unusual communication, and abnormal play. (p. 299)

23. **Asperger syndrome** is a type of autistic spectrum disorder characterized by extreme attention to details and poor social skills. (p. 300)

24. An **individual education plan (IEP)** is a legal document that specifies a set of educational goals for a child with special needs. (p. 302)

25. A **least restrictive environment (LRE)** is a legally required school setting that offers special-needs children as much freedom as possible to benefit from the instruction available to other children, often in a mainstreamed classroom. (p. 303)

26. A **resource room** is a classroom equipped with special material, in which children with special needs spend part of their day working with a trained specialist in order to learn basic skills. (p. 303)

27. **Inclusion** is an educational approach in which children with special needs receive individualized instruction within a regular classroom setting. (p. 303)

12

The School Years: Cognitive Development

Chapter Overview

Chapter 12 examines the development of cognitive abilities in children from ages 7 to 11. The first section discusses the views of Piaget and Vygotsky regarding cognitive development, which involves the child's growing ability to use logic and reasoning (as emphasized by Piaget) and to benefit from social interactions with skilled mentors (as emphasized by Vygotsky). It also explores information-processing theory, which focuses on changes in the child's processing speed and capacity, control processes, knowledge base, and metacognition.

The second section looks at language development during middle childhood. During this time, children develop a more analytic understanding of words and show a marked improvement in their language skills. This section also discusses the problems of children who speak a minority language.

The third section covers educational and environmental conditions that are conducive to learning by schoolchildren, including how reading, math, and science are best taught.

The chapter concludes with a discussion of the hidden but strong influences of culture on education.

NOTE: Answer guidelines for all Chapter 12 questions begin on page 184.

Guided Study

The text chapter should be studied one section at a time. Before you read, preview each section by skimming it, noting headings and boldface items. Then read the appropriate section objectives from the following outline. Keep these objectives in mind and, as you read the chapter section, search for the information that will enable you to meet each objective. Once you have finished a section, write out answers for its objectives.

Building on Theory (pp. 307–314)

1. Identify and discuss the logical operations of concrete operational thought, and give examples of how these operations are demonstrated by schoolchildren.

2. Discuss Vygotsky's views regarding the influence of the sociocultural context on learning during middle childhood.

3. Describe the components of the information-processing system, noting how they interact as they enable young children to progress in cognitive functioning.

4. Explain how processing speed increases in middle childhood as a result of advances in automatization and a larger knowledge base.

5. Discuss advances in control processes, especially selective attention and metacognition, during middle childhood.

Language (pp. 314–317)

6. Describe the development of language during the school years, noting changing abilities in vocabulary and pragmatics.

7. Identify several conditions that foster the learning of a second language, and describe the best approaches to bilingual education.

8. (Issues and Applications) Identify the factors that play a role in the relationship between socioenomic status and language learning.

Teaching and Learning (pp. 317–330)

9. Describe cultural and national variations in the academic skills that are emphasized, and explain the concept of a hidden curriculum.

10. (text and Thinking Like a Scientist) Discuss different approaches to the objective assessment of what children have learned, and describe differences between the American and Japanese educational systems.

11. Differentiate several approaches to teaching reading and math, and discuss evidence regarding the effectiveness of these methods.

12. Discuss the controversy over smaller class size and other issues related to improving children's education.

Chapter Review

When you have finished reading the chapter, work through the material that follows to review it. Complete the sentences and answer the questions. As you proceed, evaluate your performance for each section by consulting the answers on page 184. Do not continue with the next section until you understand each answer. If you need to, review or reread the appropriate section in the textbook before continuing.

1. In 2001, Congress passed legislation to improve public education in the United States. This was the _____ _____ _____ _____ Act.

Building on Theory (pp. 307–314)

2. According to Piaget, between ages 7 and 11, children are in the stage of _____ _____ _____ .

3. The concept that objects can be organized into categories according to some common property is _____ .

The logical principle that certain characteristics of an object remain the same even when other characteristics change is _____ . The idea that a transformation process can be reversed to restore the original condition is _____ . The logical principle that two things can change in opposite ways to balance each other out is _____ .

4. Unlike Piaget, Vygotsky regarded instruction by _____ as crucial to cognitive development. In his view, formal education _____ (is/is not) the only context for learning.

5. Vygotsky's emphasis on the _____ context contrasts with Piaget's more _____ approach.

6. Educators', and psychologists', understanding of how children learn is based on the framework that was laid down by _____ and embellished by _____ .

7. The idea that the advances in thinking that accompany middle childhood occur because of basic changes in how children take in, store, and process data is central to the _____-_____ theory.

8. Incoming stimulus information is held for a split second in the _____ _____ , after which most of it is lost.

9. Meaningful material is transferred into _____ _____ , which is sometimes called _____-_____ . This part of memory handles mental activity that is _____ .

10. The part of memory that stores information for days, months, or years is _____-_____ _____ . Crucial in this component of the system is not only storage of the material but also its _____ .

11. One reason for the cognitive advances of middle childhood is _____ maturation, especially the _____ of neural axons.

12. Processing capacity also becomes more efficient through _____ , as familiar mental activities become routine.

13. Memory ability improves during middle childhood in part because of the child's expanded _____ _____ .

14. The knowledge base also depends on _____ , _____ , and _____ .

15. The mechanisms of the information-processing system that regulate the analysis and flow of information are the _____ _____ . These include _____ _____ , _____ , and _____ _____ . Control processes develop spontaneously with _____ , but they are also taught, either _____ or _____ .

16. The ability to evaluate a cognitive task to determine what to do—and to monitor and adjust one's performance—is called _____ . This ability becomes evident by age _____ .

Language (pp. 314–317)

17. During middle childhood, some children learn as many as _____ new words a day. Unlike the vocabulary explosion of the play years, this language growth is distinguished by _____ , _____ , _____ , _____ of thinking, _____ , and the ability to make connections between one bit of knowledge and another and later vocabulary performance in school.

18. The practical application of linguistic knowledge is called the _____ of language.

19. Children are able to change from proper speech, or a _____ _____ , to a colloquial form, or _____ _____ , with their peers.

20. Children who speak a minority language and are learning to speak English are called _____-_____ _____ .

21. Many American children make a _____ _____ as they replace their original language with English. This is especially true of children from _____ _____ backgrounds.

22. The approach to bilingual education in which the child's instruction occurs entirely in the second language is called _____ _____ . In _____ _____ programs, teachers instruct children in both their native language as well as in English. Some programs offer "_____" classes that allow children to connect with their culture while learning academic subjects in the dominant language.

23. In ESL, or _____ _____ programs, children must master the basics of English before joining regular classes with other children.

24. Immersion tends to fail if the child feels _____ , _____ , or _____ because of his or her language.

25. The success of any of these methods seems to depend on the _____ of the home, the warmth and skill of the teacher, the _____ context, and the _____ status of the family.

Teaching and Learning (pp. 317–330)

26. There _____ (is/is not) universal agreement on how best to educate school-children.

27. In the United States, the _____ _____ is a federal law that mandates annual standardized achievement tests for public school children beginning in the third grade. This act implemented the _____ _____ program, reflecting the idea that the primary item of curriculum should be _____ .

28. The _____ is a federal project that measures achievement in reading, mathematics, and other subjects over time.

29. Every culture creates its own _____ _____ , the unofficial rules and priorities that influence every aspect of school learning.

30. (text and Thinking Like a Scientist) Two international approaches to objective assessment of children's achievement are the _____ and the _____ .

Describe several differences between the educational systems in Japan and the United States.

31. Japanese children _____ (score about the same as/outscore) U.S. children in math and science _____ . The recent shift toward greater federal involvement in education in the United States was triggered by passage of the _____ _____ _____ _____ Act.

32. Two distinct approaches to teaching reading are the _____ approach, in which children learn the sounds of letters first, and the _____-_____ approach, in which children are encouraged to develop all their language skills at the same time. Most developmentalists believe that _____ (both approaches/neither approach/only the phonics approach/only the whole-language approach) make(s) sense.

33. In the United States, math was traditionally taught by _____ . A more recent approach replaces this type of learning by making instruction more _____ and _____ .

34. Cross-cultural research reveals that North American teachers present math at a lower level with more _____ but less _____ to other learning. In contrast, teachers in Japan work more _____ to build children's knowledge.

35. Most people assume that children learn best when class size is _____ . Research studies demonstrate that the relationship between class size and student performance is _____ (clear-cut/complex).

Progress Test 1

Multiple-Choice Questions

Circle your answers to the following questions and check them with the answers on beginning on page 184. If your answer is incorrect, read the explanation for why it is incorrect and then consult the appropriate pages of the text (in parentheses following the correct answer).

1. According to Piaget, the stage of cognitive development in which a person understands specific logical ideas and can apply them to concrete problems is called:

   a. preoperational thought.
   b. operational thought.
   c. concrete operational thought.
   d. formal operational thought.

2. Japanese children outscore children in the United States in math. This difference has been attributed to which of the following?
   a. U.S. teachers present math at a lower level.
   b. Japanese teachers encourage more social interaction among groups of children.
   c. Japanese teachers are more collaborative in their teaching.
   d. Each of the above has been offered as an explanation of national differences in math scores.

3. The idea that an object that has been transformed in some way can be restored to its original form by undoing the process is:
   a. identity.
   b. reversibility.
   c. classification.
   d. automatization.

4. Information-processing theorists contend that major advances in cognitive development occur during the school years because:
   a. the child's mind becomes more like a computer as he or she matures.
   b. children become better able to process and analyze information.
   c. most mental activities become automatic by the time a child is about 13 years old.
   d. the major improvements in reasoning that occur during the school years involve increased long-term memory capacity.

5. Cross-cultural research on children's cognition reveals:
   a. the same patterns of development worldwide.
   b. significant variations from country to country.
   c. that children's understanding of classification is unrelated to social interaction.
   d. that children's understanding of reversibility is unrelated to social interaction.

6. Concrete operational thought is Piaget's term for the school-age child's ability to:
   a. reason logically about things and events he or she perceives.
   b. think about thinking.
   c. understand that certain characteristics of an object remain the same when other characteristics are changed.
   d. understand that a thing that has been changed can be returned to its original state.

7. The term for the ability to monitor and adjust one's cognitive performance—to think about thinking—is:
   a. pragmatics.
   b. information processing.
   c. selective attention.
   d. metacognition.

8. Long-term memory is _____ permanent and _____ limited than working memory.
   a. more; less   c. more; more
   b. less; more   d. less; less

9. Passed in 2001, the federal law that mandates annual standardized achievement tests for public school children is the:
   a. Reading First Act.
   b. National Assessment of Educational Progress.
   c. No Child Left Behind Act.
   d. Trends in Math and Science Study.

10. Which theorist believed that cultures (tools, customs, and people) teach children best?
   a. Piaget
   b. Vygotsky
   c. Skinner
   d. Chomsky

11. Which aspect of memory is most likely to change during the school years?
   a. sensory memory
   b. long-term memory
   c. the speed and efficiency of working memory
   d. all of the above

12. Eight-year-old Cho, who recently emigrated from Mayanmar, attends a school in Canada in which all subjects are taught in English. Cho's school is using which strategy to teach English-language learners?
   a. bilingual education
   b. heritage language classes
   c. total immersion
   d. ESL

13. Many American children make a language shift. This means that they:
   a. do not yet speak English well.
   b. are fluent in their first language and in English.
   c. replace their original language with English rather than becoming fluent in both languages.
   d. experience a language explosion in which they learn as many as 20 new words a day.

14. Which theorist emphasized the critical role of maturation in cognitive development?
    a. Piaget
    b. Vygotsky
    c. Skinner
    d. Chomsky

15. Of the following, which was *not* identified as an important factor in the difference between success and failure in second-language learning?
    a. the age of the child
    b. the attitudes of the parents
    c. community values regarding second-language learning
    d. the difficulty of the language

True or False Items

Write T (*true*) or F (*false*) on the line in front of each statement.

_____ 1. A major objection to Piaget's theory is that he underestimated the influence of context, instruction, and culture.

_____ 2. Total immersion is the best strategy for teaching English-language learners.

_____ 3. Vygotsky emphasized the child's own logical thinking.

_____ 4. As a group, Japanese and Korean children outscore children in the United States and Canada in math and science.

_____ 5. Fearing their children were feeling too much academic pressure, the people of Japan recently implemented a more relaxed educational program.

_____ 6. Research evidence consistently demonstrates that children learn best with fewer students in each classroom.

_____ 7. Socioeconomic status does not affect bilingualism.

_____ 8. Most information that comes into the sensory memory is lost or discarded.

_____ 9. Information-processing theorists believe that advances in the thinking of school-age children occur primarily because of changes in long-term memory.

_____ 10. New standards of math education in many nations emphasize problem-solving skills rather than simple memorization of formulas.

Progress Test 2

Progress Test 2 should be completed during a final chapter review. Answer the following questions after you thoroughly understand the correct answers for the Chapter Review and Progress Test 1.

Multiple-Choice Questions

1. According to Piaget, 8- and 9-year-olds can reason only about concrete things in their lives. "Concrete" means:
   a. logical.
   b. abstract.
   c. tangible or specific.
   d. mathematical or classifiable.

2. Research regarding Piaget's theory has found that:
   a. cognitive development seems to be considerably less affected by sociocultural factors than Piaget's descriptions imply.
   b. the movement to a new level of thinking is much more erratic than Piaget predicted.
   c. there is no dramatic shift in the thinking of children when they reach the age of 5.
   d. all of the above are true.

3. The increase in processing speed that occurs during middle childhood is partly the result of:
   a. ongoing myelination of axons.
   b. neurological development in the limbic system.
   c. the streamlining of the knowledge base.
   d. all of the above.

4. When psychologists look at the ability of children to receive, store, and organize information, they are examining cognitive development from a view based on:
   a. the observations of Piaget.
   b. information processing.
   c. behaviorism.
   d. the idea that the key to thinking is the sensory register.

5. The National Assessment of Educational Progress (NAEP):
   a. measures achievement in reading, mathematics, and other subjects over time.
   b. federally mandates annual achievement testing for public school children.
   c. established a five-year cycle of international trend studies in reading ability.
   d. provides states with funding for early reading instruction.

6. The logical operations of concrete operational thought are particularly important to an understanding of the elementary-school subject(s) of:
   a. spelling.
   b. reading.
   c. math and science.
   d. social studies.

7. Which of the following is especially helpful in making it easier to master new information in a specific subject?
   a. a large sensory register
   b. a large knowledge base
   c. unlimited long-term memory
   d. working memory

8. Language "codes" include variations in:
   a. pronunciation.
   b. gestures.
   c. vocabulary.
   d. all of the above.

9. When we refer to a child's improved memory capacity, we are referring to:
   a. the child's ability to selectively attend to more than one thought.
   b. the amount of information the child is able to hold in working memory.
   c. the size of the child's knowledge base.
   d. all of the above.

10. The retention of new information is called:
    a. retrieval.
    b. storage.
    c. automatization.
    d. metacognition.

11. Which of the following terms does *not* belong with the others?
    a. selective attention
    b. metacognition
    c. emotional regulation
    d. knowledge base

12. Which aspect of the information-processing system assumes an executive role in regulating the analysis and transfer of information?
    a. sensory register
    b. working memory
    c. long-term memory
    d. control processes

13. An example of schoolchildren's growth in metacognition is their understanding that:
    a. transformed objects can be returned to their original state.
    b. rehearsal is a good strategy for memorizing, but outlining is better for understanding.
    c. objects may belong to more than one class.
    d. they can use different language styles in different situations.

14. Which of the following most accurately states the relative merits of the phonics approach and the whole-language approach to teaching reading?
    a. The phonics approach is more effective.
    b. The whole-language approach is the more effective approach.
    c. Both approaches have merit.
    d. Both approaches have been discarded in favor of newer, more interactive methods of instruction.

15. Juan attends a school that offers instruction in both English and Spanish. This strategy for teaching English-language learners is called:
    a. bilingual education.
    b. total immersion.
    c. heritage language instruction.
    d. ESL.

Matching Items

Match each term or concept with its corresponding description or definition.

Terms or Concepts

_____ **1.** automatization
_____ **2.** reversibility
_____ **3.** classification
_____ **4.** identity
_____ **5.** information processing
_____ **6.** selective attention
_____ **7.** retrieval
_____ **8.** storage
_____ **9.** metacognition
_____ **10.** total immersion
_____ **11.** concrete operational thought

Descriptions or Definitions

a. the ability to screen out distractions and concentrate on relevant information
b. the idea that a transformation process can be undone to restore the original conditions
c. the idea that certain characteristics of an object remain the same even when other characteristics change
d. developmental perspective that conceives of cognitive development as the result of changes in the processing and analysis of information
e. Piaget's term for the ability to reason logically about direct experiences.
f. an educational technique in which instruction occurs entirely in the second language
g. accessing previously learned information
h. holding information in memory
i. the logical principle that things can be organized into groups
j. process by which familiar mental activities become routine
k. the ability to evaluate a cognitive task and to monitor one's performance on it

Developmental Psychology Applied

Answer these questions the day before an exam as a final check on your understanding of the chapter's terms and concepts.

1. Of the following statements made by children, which best exemplifies the logical principle of identity?

   a. "You can't leave first base until the ball is hit!"
   b. "See how the jello springs back into shape after I poke my finger into it?"
   c. "I know it's still a banana, even though it's mashed down in my sandwich."
   d. "You're my friend, so I don't have to use polite speech like I do with adults."

2. Which of the following statements is the clearest indication that the child has grasped the principle of reversibility?

   a. "See, the lemonade is the same in both our glasses; even though your glass is taller than mine, it's narrower."
   b. "Even though your dog looks funny, I know it's still a dog."
   c. "I have one sister and no brothers. My parents have two children."
   d. "I don't cheat because I don't want to be punished."

3. After moving to a new country, a child's parents are struck by the greater tendency of math teachers in their new homeland to work collaboratively and to emphasize social interaction in the learning process. To which country have these parents probably moved?

   a. the United States   **c.** Japan
   b. Germany   **d.** Australia

4. Dr. Larsen believes that the cognitive advances of middle childhood occur because of basic changes in children's thinking speed, knowledge base, and memory retrieval skills. Dr. Larsen evidently is working from the _____ perspective.

   a. Piagetian
   b. Vygotskian
   c. information-processing
   d. psychoanalytic

5. Some researchers believe that cognitive processing speed and capacity increase during middle childhood because of:
   a. the myelination of neural axons.
   b. repetition and practice
   c. better use of cognitive resources.
   d. all of the above.

6. Mei-Chin is able to sort her Legos into groups according to size. Clearly, she has an understanding of the principle of:
   a. classification.   c. reversibility.
   b. identity.   d. reciprocity.

7. For a 10-year-old, some mental activities have become so familiar or routine as to require little mental work. This development is called:
   a. selective attention.   c. metacognition.
   b. identity.   d. automatization.

8. Lana is 4 years old and her brother Roger is 7. The fact that Roger remembers what their mother just told them about playing in the street while Lana is more interested in the children playing across the street is due to improvements in Roger's:
   a. selective attention.   c. control processes.
   b. automatization.   d. long-term memory.

9. For the first time, 7-year-old Nathan can remember his telephone number. This is probably the result of:
   a. maturation of the sensory register.
   b. increased capacity of working memory.
   c. increased capacity of long-term memory.
   d. improved speed of processing.

10. Nine-year-old Rachel has made great strides in her ability to evaluate and monitor her learning and mastery of specific tasks. In other words, Rachel has shown great improvement in her:
    a. sensory register.
    b. working memory.
    c. long-term memory.
    d. metacognition.

11. Four-year-old Tasha, who is learning to read by sounding out the letters of words, evidently is being taught using which approach?
    a. phonics
    b. whole-word
    c. total immersion
    d. reverse immersion

12. The study of street children in Brazil revealed that:
    a. many never attended school.
    b. many scored poorly on standardized math tests.
    c. many were quite adept at using math practically to sell fruit, candy, and other products to earn their living.
    d. all of the above were true.

13. During the school board meeting, a knowledgeable parent proclaimed that the board's position on achievement testing and class size was an example of the district's "hidden curriculum." The parent was referring to:
    a. the unofficial and unstated educational priorities of the school district.
    b. the political agendas of individual members of the school board.
    c. the legal mandates for testing and class size established by the state board of education.
    d. none of the above.

14. Which of the following best expresses developmentalists' understanding of how children learn?
    a. Children are eager learners, trying to understand the world in ways limited by their maturation.
    b. Children learn from each other.
    c. Children learn from their culture.
    d. Children learn from each other and from their mentors, as long as those mentors know what motivation and understanding the children already have.

15. Andy understands that a ball of clay that is flattened and rolled into a rope hasn't changed in size. Andy's awareness demonstrates an understanding of the logical principle of:
    a. classification.   c. reversibility.
    b. identity.   d. reciprocity.

Key Terms

Writing Definitions

Using your own words, write a brief definition or explanation of each of the following terms on a separate piece of paper.

1. concrete operational thought
2. classification
3. identity
4. reversibility
5. information-processing theory

6. sensory memory
7. working memory
8. long-term memory
9. knowledge base
10. control processes
11. metacognition
12. English-language learner (ELL)
13. total immersion
14. bilingual education
15. ESL (English as a second language)

16. No Child Left Behind Act
17. National Assessment of Educational Progress (NAEP)
18. Reading First
19. hidden curriculum
20. Trends in Math and Science Study (TIMSS)
21. Progress in International Reading Literacy Skills (PIRLS)
22. phonics approach
23. whole-language approach

Cross-Check

After you have written the definitions of the key terms in this chapter, you should complete the crossword puzzle to ensure that you can reverse the process—recognize the term, given the definition.

ACROSS

4. The part of memory that stores unlimited amounts of information for days, months, or years.
5. The ability to evaluate a cognitive task in order to determine what to do.
7. Processes that regulate the analysis and flow of information in memory.
8. According to the theorist in 13 across, cognitive development occurs in _____ .
9. The main characteristic of concrete operational thinking is the ability to use _____ .
12. An approach to teaching a second language in which the teacher instructs the children in school subjects using their native language as well as the second language.
13. Psychologist who developed an influential theory of cognitive development.
14. The principle that objects remain the same even if some characteristics change.
15. The principle that things can return to their original state.

DOWN
1. The part of memory that handles current, conscious mental activity.
2. Process by which familiar mental activities become routine.

3. Ongoing neural process that speeds up neural processing.
6. English as a second language.
10. According to Piaget, the type of cognitive operations that occur during middle childhood.
11. The body of knowledge that has been learned about a particular area.

ANSWERS

CHAPTER REVIEW

1. No Child Left Behind
2. concrete operational thought
3. classification; identity; reversibility
4. others; is not
5. sociocultural; maturational
6. Piaget; Vygotsky
7. information-processing
8. sensory memory (register)
9. working memory; short-term memory; conscious
10. long-term memory; retrieval
11. neurological; myelination
12. automatization
13. knowledge base
14. experience; opportunity; motivation
15. control processes; selective attention; metacognition; emotional regulation; age; explicitly; implicitly
16. metacognition; 9
17. 20; logic; flexibility; memory; speed; metacognition
18. pragmatics
19. formal code; informal code; code-switching
20. English-language learners (ELLs)
21. language shift; Asian American
22. total immersion; bilingual education; heritage
23. English as a second language
24. shy; stupid; lonely
25. literacy; cultural; socioeconomic
26. is not
27. No Child Left Behind Act; Reading First; reading
28. National Assessment of Educational Progress (NAEP)
29. hidden curriculum
30. Trends in Math and Science Study (TIMSS); Progress in International Reading Literacy Skills (PIRLS)

Children in Japan study more than U.S. children and spend more time in school. Teachers are given more respect by students and parents, and they learn from one another. The Japanese government funds and guides education, and the curriculum is universal. Most Japanese children also attend private classes (*juko*).

31. outscore; No Child Left Behind
32. phonics; whole-language; both approaches
33. rote; active; engaging
34. definitions; connection; collaboratively
35. small; complex

PROGRESS TEST 1

Multiple-Choice Questions

1. **c.** is the answer. (p. 307)
   a. Preoperational thought is "pre-logical" thinking.
   b. There is no such stage in Piaget's theory.
   d. Formal operational thought extends logical reasoning to abstract problems.

2. **d.** is the answer. (p. 323)

3. **b.** is the answer. (p. 308)
   a. This is the concept that certain characteristics of an object remain the same even when other characteristics change.
   c. This is the organization of things into groups.
   d. This is the process by which familiar mental activities become routine and automatic.

4. **b.** is the answer. (pp. 310–311)
   a. Information-processing theorists use the mind–computer metaphor at every age.
   c. Although increasing automatization is an important aspect of development, the information-processing perspective does not suggest that most mental activities become automatic by age 13.
   d. Most of the important changes in reasoning that occur during the school years are due to the improved processing capacity of the person's *working memory.*

5. **a.** is the answer. (p. 309)

6. **a.** is the answer. (p. 307)
   b. This refers to metacognition.
   c. This refers to Piaget's concept of identity.
   d. This refers to Piaget's concept of reversiblity.

7. **d.** is the answer. (p. 313)
   a. Pragmatics refers to the practical use of language to communicate with others.

b. The information-processing perspective views the mind as being like a computer.

c. This is the ability to screen out distractions in order to focus on important information.

8. **a.** is the answer. (p. 311)

9. **c.** is the answer. (p. 319)

10. **b.** is the answer. (pp. 309–310)

a. Piaget emphasized the importance of maturation in cognitive development.

c. & d. Skinner and Chomsky each developed a theory of language development.

11. **c.** is the answer. During middle childhood, speed of processing increases and automatization improves, thus improving the efficiency of working memory. (pp. 311–312)

12. **c.** is the answer. (p. 316)

a. In bilingual education, instruction occurs in both languages.

b. Heritage language classes are usually supplemental classes that are held after school.

d. ESL children are taught intensively in English for a few months to prepare them for regular classes. It is not clear that Mei-chin received this type of preparatory instruction.

13. **c.** is the answer. (p. 313)

14. **a.** is the answer. (pp. 307–309)

15. **d.** is the answer. (pp. 315–317)

True or False Items

1. T (pp. 309–310)

2. F   No single approach to teaching a second language is best for all children in all contexts. (p. 316)

3. F   This is true of Piaget. (p. 309)

4. T (pp. 321–322)

5. T (p. 324)

6. F   Research support for this popular assumption is weak. (p. 327)

7. F   The likelihood of parents, school, or culture encouraging bilingualism in children depends on the family's socioeconomic status. (p. 316)

8. T   (p. 311)

9. F   They believe that the changes are due to basic changes in control processes. (p. 312)

10. T (p. 327)

PROGRESS TEST 2

Multiple-Choice Questions

1. **c.** is the answer. (p. 307)

2. **b.** is the answer. (pp. 309–310)

3. **a.** is the answer. (p. 311)

b. Neurological development in the frontal cortex facilitates processing speed during middle childhood. The limbic system, which was not discussed in this chapter, is concerned with emotions.

c. Processing speed is facilitated by *growth*, rather than streamlining, of the knowledge base.

4. **b.** is the answer. (pp. 310–314)

5. **a.** is the answer. (p. 319)

6. **c.** is the answer. (p. 309)

7. **b.** is the answer. (p. 312)

a. The sensory register briefly stores incoming sensations. Its capacity does not change with maturation.

c. & d. Working memory and long-term memory are important in all forms of learning. Unlike a broad knowledge base in a specific area, however, these memory processes do not selectively make it easier to learn more in a specific area.

8. **d.** is the answer. (p. 315)

9. **b.** is the answer. (p. 311)

10. **b.** is the answer. (p. 311)

a. This is the *accessing* of already learned information.

c. Automatization is the process by which well-learned activities become routine and automatic.

d. This is the ability to evaluate a task and to monitor and adjust one's performance on it.

11. **d.** is the answer. (p. 312)

a., b., & c. Each of these is a control process.

12. **d.** is the answer. (p. 312)

a. The sensory register stores incoming information for a split second.

b. Working memory is the part of memory that handles current, conscious mental activity.

c. Long-term memory stores information for days, months, or years.

13. **b.** is the answer. (p. 313)

14. **c.** is the answer. (pp. 324–325)

15. **a.** is the answer. (p. 316)

Matching Items

1. j (p. 312)	5. d (p. 310)	9. k (p. 313)
2. b (p. 308)	6. a (p. 312)	10. f (p. 316)
3. i (p. 308)	7. g (p. 311)	11. e (p. 307)
4. c (p. 308)	8. h (p. 311)	

DEVELOPMENTAL PSYCHOLOGY APPLIED

1. **c.** is the answer. (p. 308)

   a., b., & d. Identity is the logical principle that certain characteristics of an object (such as the shape of a ball) remain the same even when other characteristics change.

2. **a.** is the answer. (p. 308)

   b., c., & d. Reversibility is the logical principle that something that has been changed (such as the height of lemonade poured from one glass into another) can be returned to its original shape by reversing the process of change (pouring the liquid back into the other glass).

3. **c.** is the answer. (p. 323)

4. **c.** is the answer. (pp. 310–314)

   a. This perspective emphasizes the logical, active nature of thinking during middle childhood.

   b. This perspective emphasizes the importance of social interaction in learning.

   d. This perspective does not address the development of cognitive skills.

5. **d.** is the answer. (pp. 311–312)

6. **a.** is the answer. (p. 308)

7. **d.** is the answer. (p. 312)

   a. Selective attention is the ability to focus on important information and screen out distractions.

   b. Identity is the logical principle that certain characteristics of an object remain the same even when other characteristics change.

   c. Metacognition is the ability to evaluate a task and to monitor one's performance on it.

8. **c.** is the answer. (p. 312)

   a. Selective attention *is* a control process, but c. is more specific and thus more correct.

   b. Automatization refers to the tendency of well-rehearsed mental activities to become routine and automatic.

   d. Long-term memory is the part of memory that stores information for days, months, or years.

9. **b.** is the answer. The capacity of working memory increases during middle childhood. (p. 311)

   a., c., & d. These are not limiting factors in remembering the small number of digits in a telephone number.

10. **d.** is the answer. (p. 313)

11. **a.** is the answer. (pp. 324–325)

   b. This approach encourages children to develop all their language skills at the same time.

c. & d. These are approaches to bilingual instruction, not reading instruction, although reverse immersion was not discussed by name.

12. **d.** is the answer. (p. 310)

13. **a.** is the answer. (p. 320)

14. **d.** is the answer. (p. 310)

15. **b.** is the answer. (p. 308)

KEY TERMS

Writing Definitions

1. During Piaget's stage of **concrete operational thought,** lasting from ages 7 to 11, children can think logically about direct experiences and perceptions but are not able to reason abstractly. (p. 307)

2. **Classification** is the process of organizing things into groups according to some common property. (p. 308)

3. In Piaget's theory, **identity** is the logical principle that certain characteristics of an object remain the same even when other characteristics change. (p. 308)

4. **Reversibility** is the logical principle that a transformation process can be reversed to restore the original conditions. (p. 308)

5. **Information-processing theory** models human cognition after the computer, analyzing each component, step by step. (p. 310)

6. **Sensory memory** is the first component of the information-processing system that stores incoming stimuli for a split second, after which it is passed into working memory, or discarded as unimportant; sometimes called the *sensory register.* (p. 311)

7. **Working memory** is the component of the information-processing system that handles current, conscious mental activity; sometimes called short-term memory. (p. 311)

8. **Long-term memory** is the component of the information-processing system that stores unlimited amounts of information for days, months, or years. (p. 311)

9. The **knowledge base** is a broad body of knowledge in a particular subject area that has been learned and on which additional learning can be based. (p. 312)

10. **Control processes** (such as selective attention and metacognition) regulate the analysis and flow of information within the information-processing system. (p. 312)

11. **Metacognition** is the ability to evaluate a cognitive task to determine what to do and to monitor and adjust one's performance on that task. (p. 313)

12. An **English-language learner (ELL)** is a person who is learning English as a second language.(p. 315)

13. **Total immersion** is an approach to bilingual education in which the child's instruction occurs entirely in the new language. (p. 316)

14. **Bilingual education** is a strategy in which school subjects are taught in both the learner's original language and the second (majority) language. (p. 316)

15. **ESL (English as a second language)** is an approach to bilingual education in which children are taught separately, and exclusively in English, to prepare them for attending regular classes. (p. 316)

16. The **No Child Left Behind Act** is a controversial law, enacted in 2001, that uses multiple assessments and achievement standards to try to improve public education in the United States. (p. 319)

17. The **National Assessment of Educational Progress (NAEP)** is an ongoing program of measurement of children's achievement in reading, mathematics, and other subjects. (p. 319)

18. **Reading First** is a federal program that provides states with funding for early reading education. (p. 319)

19. The **hidden curriculum** is the unofficial, unstated, or implicit rules and priorities that influence the academic curriculum and every other aspect of school learning. (p. 320)

20. The **TIMSS (Trends in Math and Science Study)** is an international assessment of math and science skills. (p. 322)

21. **Progress in International Reading Literacy Skills (PIRLS)** is a five-year cycle of trend studies of reading ability among fourth-graders around the world. (p. 322)

22. The **phonics approach** is a method of teaching reading by having children learn the sounds of letters before they begin to learn words. (p. 324)

23. The **whole-language approach** is a method of teaching reading by encouraging children to develop all their language skills simultaneously. (p. 325)

Cross-Check

ACROSS

4. long-term
5. metacognition
7. control
8. stages
9. logic
12. bilingual
13. Piaget
14. identity
15. reversibility

DOWN

1. working
2. automatization
3. myelination
6. ESL
10. concrete
11. knowledge base

13

The School Years: Psychosocial Development

Chapter Overview

This chapter brings to a close the unit on the school years. We have seen that from ages 7 to 11, the child becomes stronger and more competent, mastering the biosocial and cognitive abilities that are important in his or her culture. Psychosocial accomplishments are equally impressive.

Children's interactions with peers and others in their ever-widening social world is the subject of the first section. Because the school years are also a time of expanding moral reasoning, this section also examines Kohlberg's stage theory of moral development as well as current evaluations of his theory. Although the peer group often is a supportive, positive influence on children, some children are rejected by their peers or become the victims of bullying.

The next section explores the ways in which families influence children, including the experience of living in single-parent, stepparent, and blended families. Although no particular family structure guarantees optimal child development, income and harmony and stability are important factors in the quality of family functioning.

The third section explores the growing social competence of children, as described by Freud and Erikson. The section continues with a discussion of the growth of social cognition and self-understanding. The chapter closes with a discussion of the ways in which children cope with stressful situations.

NOTE: Answer guidelines for all Chapter 13 questions begin on page 199.

Guided Study

The text chapter should be studied one section at a time. Before you read, preview each section by skimming it, noting headings and boldface items. Then read the appropriate section objectives from the following outline. Keep these objectives in mind and, as you read the chapter section, search for the information that will enable you to meet each objective. Once you have finished a section, write out answers for its objectives.

The Peer Group (pp. 333–342)

1. Discuss the importance of peer groups to the development of school-age children, focusing on how the culture of children separates itself from adult society.

2. Outline Kohlberg's stage theory of moral development, noting several criticisms.

3. Discuss the plight of two types of rejected children.

4. Discuss how friendships change during the school years.

5. Discuss the special problems of bullies and their victims, and describe possible ways of helping such children.

Families and Children (pp. 342–351)

6. (text and Thinking Like a Scientist) Describe the relative influences of shared and nonshared environmental factors on school-age children.

7. Identify the essential ways in which functional families nurture school-age children.

8. Differentiate 11 family structures.

9. Discuss the impact of the different family structures and functions on the psychosocial development of the school-age child.

10. Explain how low income and high conflict can interfere with good family functioning,.

The Nature of the Child (pp. 351–357)

11. Identify the themes or emphases of psychoanalytic views of the psychosocial development of school-age children.

12. Describe the development of the self-concept during middle childhood and its implications for children's self-esteem.

13. Discuss the concept of resilience, and identify the variables that influence the impact of stresses on schoolchildren.

14. Discuss several factors that seem especially important in helping children cope with stress.

Chapter Review

When you have finished reading the chapter, work through the material that follows to review it. Complete the sentences and answer the questions. As you proceed, evaluate your performance for each section by consulting the answers beginning on page 199. Do not continue with the next section until you understand each answer. If you need to, review or reread the appropriate section in the textbook before continuing.

The Peer Group (pp. 333–342)

1. Getting along with _____ is especially important during middle childhood. Compared to younger children, school-age children are _____ (more/less) deeply affected by others' acceptance or rejection. The inclination to compare themselves with others is called _____ _____ .

2. Peers create their own _____ _____ _____ , which includes the particular rules and rituals that are passed down from older to younger children and that _____ (mirror/do not necessarily mirror) the values of adults.

3. _____ (In some parts of the world/Throughout the world), the culture of children encourages _____ from adults. It may also include _____ _____ , in which children show each other how to avoid adult restrictions.

4. During the school years, children prefer to play with children _____ (of their own sex/of the opposite sex) because _____ stereotypes become more elaborate. _____ and ethnic prejudice is rejected at this time.

5. The theorist who has extensively studied moral development by presenting subjects with stories that pose ethical dilemmas is _____ . According to his theory, the three levels of moral reasoning are _____ , _____ , and _____ .

6. (Table 13.1) In preconventional reasoning, emphasis is on getting _____ and avoiding _____ . "Might makes right" describes stage _____ (1/2), whereas "look out for number one" describes stage _____ (1/2).

7. (Table 13.1) In conventional reasoning, emphasis is on _____ _____ , such as being a dutiful citizen, in stage _____ (3/4), or winning approval from others, in stage _____ (3/4).

8. (Table 13.1) In postconventional reasoning, emphasis is on _____ _____ , such as _____ _____ (stage 5) and _____ _____ _____ (stage 6).

9. One criticism of Kohlberg's theory is that it does not take _____ or _____ differences into account.

10. Research studies of social acceptance among schoolchildren reveal that approximately _____ (what proportion?) are popular, approximately _____ are average in popularity, and approximately _____ are unpopular.

11. Children who are not really rejected but not picked as friends are _____ . Children who are actively rejected tend to be either _____-_____ or _____-_____ .

Briefly explain why rejected children are disliked.

12. The ability to understand human interactions, called _____ _____ , begins in infancy with _____ _____ , continues in early childhood with _____ _____ _____ , and by middle childhood is well established.

13. School children improve in _____ _____ , which is the power to modify their _____ and _____ .

Describe how well-liked children demonstrate their newfound ability to correctly interpret social situations.

14. Having a personal friend is _____ (more/less) important to children than acceptance by the peer group.

15. Friendships during middle childhood become more _____ and _____ . As a result, older children _____ (change/do not change) friends as often and find it _____ (easier/harder) to make new friends.

16. Middle schoolers tend to choose best friends whose _____ , _____ , and _____ are similar to their own.

17. Bullying is defined as _____ efforts to inflict harm through _____ , _____ , or _____ attacks. A key aspect in the definition of bullying is that harmful attacks are _____ . The three types of bullying are _____ , _____ , and _____ .

18. Most bullies usually _____ (have/do not have) friends who admire them, and they are socially _____ but without _____ .

19. Victims of bullying are often _____ -rejected children. Less often, _____ -rejected children become _____ - _____ .

20. Boys who are bullies are often above average in _____ , whereas girl bullies are often _____ - _____ . Boys who are bullies typically use _____ aggression, whereas girls use _____ aggression.

21. The origins of bullying may lie in _____ _____ or _____ predispositions that are present at birth and then strengthened by _____ _____ , a stressful _____ life, hostile _____ , and other problems that intensify _____ impulses rather than teach _____ .

22. One effective intervention in controlling bullying in Norway involved using an _____-_____ approach to change the _____ within schools so that bully-victim cycles are not allowed to persist.

Families and Children (pp. 342–351)

23. No human trait is entirely _____ or entirely _____ .

24. Research demonstrates that _____ (shared/nonshared) influences on most traits are far greater than _____ (shared/non-shared) influences.

25. Family function refers to how well the family _____ _____ .

26. A functional family nurtures school-age children by meeting their basic _____ , encouraging _____ , fostering the development of _____ , nurturing peer _____ , and providing _____ and _____ .

27. (text and Table 13.2) Family structure is defined as the _____ _____ .

Identify each of the following family structures:

a. _____ A family that includes three or more biologically related generations, including parents and children.

b. _____ A family that consists of the father, the mother, and their biological children.

c. _____ A family that consists of one parent with his or her biological children.

d. _____ A family consisting of two parents, at least one with biological children from previous unions and/or of the new couple.

e. _____ In some nations, a family that consists of one man, several wives, and their children.

f. _____ A family that consists of one or more nonbiological children whom adults have legally taken to raise as their own.

g. _____ A family that consists of one or more orphaned, neglected, abused, or delinquent children who are temporarily cared for by an adult to whom they are not biologically related.

h. _____ A family that consists of a parent, his or her biological children, and his or her spouse, who is not biologically related to the children.

i. _____ A family that consists of one or two grandparents and their grandchildren.

j. _____ A family that consists of a homosexual couple and the biological or adopted children of one or both partners.

28. Although the _____ family is still the most common, more than _____ (what percentage?) of all school-age children live in _____-_____ households.

Give several reasons for the benefits of the nuclear family structure.

29. Children in every type of family structure grow up very well and sometimes run into trouble. Thus, family _____ seems more critical than family _____ .

30. Family income _____ (correlates/does not correlate) with optimal child development. Economic distress _____ family functioning. According to the _____-_____ model, economic hardship in a family increases _____ , which often makes adults more harsh and _____ with their children.

31. A second factor that has a crucial impact on children is the _____ and _____ that characterizes family interaction. Children are particularly affected when there are multiple _____ .

The Nature of the Child (pp. 351–357)

32. Freud describes middle childhood as the period of _____ , when emotional drives are _____ and unconscious sexual conflicts are _____ .

33. According to Erikson, the crisis of middle childhood is _____ _____ _____ .

34. As their self-understanding sharpens, children gradually become _____ (more/less) self-critical, and their self-esteem _____ (rises/dips). One reason is that they more often evaluate themselves through

    _____ _____ .

35. Some children are better able to adapt within the context of adversity, that is, they seem to be more _____ . This trait is a _____ process that represents a _____ adaptation to stress.

36. The importance of daily _____ explains why some stressors are so difficult for children.

37. Another element that helps children deal with problems is the _____ _____ they receive.

38. During middle childhood, there are typically _____ (fewer/more) sources of social support. This can be obtained from grandparents or siblings, for example, or from _____ and _____ . In addition, _____ can also be psychologically protective for children in difficult circumstances.

Progress Test 1

Multiple-Choice Questions

Circle your answers to the following questions and check them with the answers on page 200. If your answer is incorrect, read the explanation for why it is incorrect and then consult the appropriate pages of the text (in parentheses following the correct answer).

1. Between 9 and 11 years of age, children are likely to demonstrate moral reasoning at which of Kohlberg's stages?
   a. preconventional
   b. conventional
   c. postconventional
   d. It is impossible to predict based only on a child's age.

2. Which of the following is *not* among the highest values of middle childhood?
   a. protect your friends
   b. don't tell adults what really goes on
   c. try not to be too different from other children
   d. don't depend on others

3. The best strategy for helping children who are at risk of developing serious psychological problems because of multiple stresses would be to:
   a. obtain assistance from a psychiatrist.
   b. increase the child's competencies or social supports.
   c. change the household situation.
   d. reduce the peer group's influence.

4. The culture of children refers to:
   a. the specific habits, styles, and values that reflect the rules and rituals of children.
   b. a child's tendency to assess abilities by measuring them against those of peers.
   c. children's ability to understand social interactions.
   d. all of the above.

5. Girls who are bullies are often above average in _____ , whereas boys who are bullies are often above average in _____ .
   a. size; verbal assertiveness
   b. verbal assertiveness; size
   c. intelligence; aggressiveness
   d. aggressiveness; intelligence

6. As some rejected children get older:
   a. their problems often get worse.
   b. their problems usually decrease.
   c. they may become less rejected and more prosocial.
   d. their peer group becomes less important to their self-esteem.

7. Compared with average or popular children, rejected children tend to be:
   a. brighter and more competitive.
   b. affluent and "stuck-up."
   c. economically disadvantaged.
   d. socially immature.

8. School-age children advance in their awareness of classmates' opinions and accomplishments. These abilities are best described as advances in their:
   a. social comparison.
   b. social cognition.
   c. metacognition.
   d. pragmatic intelligence.

9. Resilience is characterized by all but which of the following characteristics?
   a. Resilience is a stable trait that a child carries throughout his or her life.
   b. Resilience represents a positive adaptation to stress.
   c. Resilience is more than the absence of pathology.
   d. Resilience is the capacity to develop optimally despite significant adversity.

10. With their expanding social world and developing cognition, children may be stressed by a variety of disturbing problems. Which of the following is *not* a means by which children can overcome these problems?
    a. school success
    b. healthy diet
    c. religious faith
    d. after-school achievements

11. Bully-victims are typically children who would be categorized as:
    a. aggressive-rejected.
    b. withdrawn-rejected.
    c. isolated-rejected.
    d. immature-rejected.

12. Bullying during middle childhood:
    a. occurs only in certain cultures.
    b. is more common in rural schools than in urban schools.
    c. seems to be universal.
    d. is rarely a major problem, because other children usually intervene to prevent it from getting out of hand.

13. During the school years, children become _____ selective about their friends, and their friendship groups become _____ .
    a. less; larger   c. more; larger
    b. less; smaller   d. more; smaller

14. Which of the following was *not* identified as a pivotal issue in determining whether divorce or some other problem will adversely affect a child during the school years?
    a. how many other stresses the child is already experiencing
    b. how the child interprets the stress
    c. how much the stress affects the child's daily life
    d. the specific structure of the child's family

15. Erikson's crisis of the school years is that of:
    a. industry versus inferiority.
    b. acceptance versus rejection.
    c. initiative versus guilt.
    d. male versus female.

True or False Items

Write T (*true*) or F (*false*) on the line in front of each statement.

_____ 1. As they evaluate themselves according to increasingly complex self-theories, school-age children typically experience a rise in self-esteem.

_____ 2. During middle childhood, acceptance by the peer group is valued more than having a close friend.

_____ 3. Children from low-income homes often experience more stress.

_____ 4. Bullies and their victims are usually of the same gender.

_____ 5. Children who are labeled "resilient" demonstrate an ability to adapt positively in all situations.

_____ 6. The way a family functions seems to be a more powerful predictor of children's development than the actual structure of the family.

_____ 7. Withdrawn-rejected and aggressive-rejected children both have problems regulating their emotions.

_____ 8. Most aggressive-rejected children clearly interpret other people's words and behavior.

_____ 9. School-age children are less able than younger children to cope with chronic stresses.

_____ 10. Children's ability to cope with stress may depend as much on their appraisal of events as on the objective nature of the actual events.

_____ 11. Friendship circles become wider as children grow older.

Progress Test 2

Progress Test 2 should be completed during a final chapter review. Answer the following questions after you thoroughly understand the correct answers for the Chapter Review and Progress Test 1.

Multiple-Choice Questions

1. Children who are categorized as _____ are particularly vulnerable to bullying.
   a. aggressive-rejected
   b. passive-aggressive
   c. withdrawn-rejected
   d. passive-rejected

2. Environmental influences on children's traits that result from contact with different teachers and peer groups are classified as:
   a. shared influences.
   b. nonshared influences.
   c. epigenetic influences.
   d. nuclear influences.

3. Compared with parents in other family structures, married parents tend to be:
   a. wealthier.
   b. better educated.
   c. healthier.
   d. all of the above.

4. More than half of all school-age children live in:
   a. one-parent families.
   b. blended families.
   c. extended families.
   d. nuclear families.

5. Typically, children in middle childhood experience a decrease in self-esteem as a result of:
   a. a wavering self-theory.
   b. increased awareness of personal shortcomings and failures.
   c. rejection by peers.
   d. difficulties with members of the opposite sex.

6. A 10-year-old's sense of self-esteem is most strongly influenced by his or her:
   a. peers.   c. mother.
   b. siblings.   d. father.

7. Which of the following most accurately describes how friendships change during the school years?
   a. Friendships become more casual and less intense.
   b. Older children demand less of their friends.
   c. Older children change friends more often.
   d. Close friendships increasingly involve members of the same sex, ethnicity, and socioeconomic status.

8. Which of the following is an accurate statement about school-age bullies?
   a. They are socially perceptive but not empathic.
   b. They usually have a few admiring friends.
   c. They are adept at being aggressive.
   d. All of the above are accurate statements.

9. One effective intervention to prevent bullying in the school is to:
   a. change the culture through community-wide and classroom education.
   b. target one victimized child at a time.
   c. target each bully as an individual.
   d. focus on improving the academic skills of all children in the school.

10. Which of the following most accurately describes the relationship between family income and child development?
    a. Adequate family income allows children to own whatever possessions help them to feel accepted.
    b. Because parents need not argue about money, household wealth provides harmony and stability.
    c. The basic family functions are enhanced by adequate family income.
    d. Family income is not correlated with child development.

11. Two factors that most often help the child cope well with multiple stresses are social support and:
    a. social comparison.
    b. religious faith.
    c. remedial education.
    d. referral to mental health professionals.

12. An 8-year-old child who measures her achievements by comparing them with those of her friends is engaging in social:
    a. cognition.   c. reinforcement.
    b. comparison.   d. modeling.

13. Family _____ is more crucial to children's well-being than family _____ is.
    a. structure; SES
    b. SES; stability
    c. stability; SES
    d. function; structure

14. According to Freud, the period between ages 7 and 11 when a child's sexual drives are relatively quiet is the:
    a. phallic stage.
    b. genital stage.
    c. period of latency.
    d. period of industry versus inferiority.

15. Children who are forced to cope with one serious ongoing stress (for example, poverty or large family size) are:
    a. more likely to develop serious psychiatric problems.
    b. no more likely to develop problems.
    c. more likely to develop intense, destructive friendships.
    d. less likely to be accepted by their peer group.

Matching Items

Match each term or concept with its corresponding description or definition.

Terms or Concepts

_____ 1. relational bullying
_____ 2. nuclear family
_____ 3. social comparison
_____ 4. provocative victim
_____ 5. foster family
_____ 6. aggressive-rejected
_____ 7. withdrawn-rejected
_____ 8. physical bullying
_____ 9. effortful control
_____ 10. blended family
_____ 11. extended family

Descriptions or Definitions

a. another term for a bully-victim
b. adults living with their children from previous marriages as well as their own biological children
c. a father, a mother, and the biological children they have together
d. used by boy bullies
e. children who are disliked because of their confrontational nature
f. evaluating one's abilities by measuring them against those of other children
g. three or more generations of biologically related individuals living together
h. children who are disliked because of timid, anxious behavior
i. used by girl bullies
j. a family in which one or more children are temporarily cared for by an adult individual or couple to whom they are not biologically related
k. the ability to regulate one's emotions

Developmental Psychology Applied

Answer these questions the day before an exam as a final check on your understanding of the chapter's terms and concepts.

1. Concluding her presentation on bullying, Olivia notes that one factor in the possible development of bullying is:
   a. an inborn brain abnormality.
   b. insecure attachment.
   c. the presence of hostile siblings.
   d. any of the above.

2. Dr. Ferris believes that skill mastery is particularly important because children develop views of themselves as either competent or incompetent in skills valued by their culture. Dr. Ferris is evidently working from the perspective of:
   a. behaviorism.
   b. social learning theory.
   c. Erik Erikson's theory of development.
   d. Freud's theory of development.

3. The Australian saying that "tall poppies" are cut down underscores the fact that:
   a. older children often ignore their parents and teachers.
   b. culture influences standards of social comparison.
   c. middle childhood is a time of emotional latency.
   d. personal friendships become even more important in middle childhood.

4. Ten-year-old Ramón, who is disliked by many of his peers because of his antagonistic, confrontational nature, would probably be labeled as:
   a. a bully-victim.
   b. withdrawn-rejected.
   c. aggressive-rejected.
   d. resilient.

5. Research regarding factors that contribute to children's problems found the strongest correlation between children's peace of mind and:
   a. marital discord.
   b. income.
   c. illness in the family.
   d. feelings of self-blame and vulnerability.

6. Sandra's family consists of her biological mother, her stepfather, and his two daughters from a previous marriage. Sandra's family would be classified as:
   a. nuclear.
   b. stepparent.
   c. blended.
   d. extended.

7. In discussing friendship, 9-year-old children, in contrast to younger children, will:
   a. deny that friends are important.
   b. state that they prefer same-sex playmates.
   c. stress the importance of loyalty and similar interests.
   d. be less choosy about who they call a friend.

8. Eight-year-old Henry is unpopular because he is a very timid and anxious child. Developmentalists would classify Henry as:
   a. aggressive-rejected.
   b. neglected-rejected.
   c. withdrawn-rejected.
   d. victim-rejected.

9. Concluding her presentation on resilient children, Brenda notes that:
   a. children who are truly resilient are resilient in all situations.
   b. resilience is merely the absence of pathology.
   c. resilience is a stable trait that becomes apparent very early in life.
   d. resilience is a dynamic process that represents a positive adaptation to significant adversity or stress.

10. Of the following children, who is likely to have the lowest overall self-esteem?
    a. Karen, age 5   c. Carl, age 9
    b. David, age 7   d. Cindy, age 10

11. Ten-year-old Benjamin is less optimistic and self-confident than his 5-year-old sister. This may be explained in part by the tendency of older children to:
    a. evaluate their abilities by comparing them with their own competencies a year or two earlier.
    b. evaluate their competencies by comparing them with those of others.
    c. be less realistic about their own abilities.
    d. do both b. and c.

12. Kyle and Jessica are as different as two siblings can be, despite growing up in the same nuclear family structure. In explaining these differences, a developmentalist is likely to point to:
    a. shared environmental influences.
    b. nonshared environmental influences.
    c. genetic differences and shared environmental influences.
    d. genetic differences and nonshared environmental influences.

13. Of the following children, who is most likely to become a bully?
    a. Karen, who is taller than average
    b. David, who is above average in verbal assertiveness
    c. Carl, who is insecure and lonely
    d. Cindy, who was insecurely attached

14. I am an 8-year-old who frequently is bullied at school. If I am like most victims of bullies, I am probably:
    a. obese.
    b. unattractive.
    c. a child who speaks with an accent.
    d. anxious and insecure.

15. The impact of a stressor such as divorce on a child depends on:
    a. how many other stresses the child is experiencing.
    b. how the stress affects the child's daily life.
    c. how the child interprets the stress.
    d. all of the above.

Key Terms

Using your own words, write a brief definition or explanation of each of the following terms on a separate piece of paper.

1. social comparison
2. culture of children
3. deviancy training
4. preconventional moral reasoning
5. conventional moral reasoning
6. postconventional moral reasoning
7. aggressive-rejected
8. withdrawn-rejected
9. social cognition
10. effortful control
11. bullying
12. bully-victim
13. family structure
14. family function
15. nuclear family
16. single-parent family
17. extended family
18. blended family
19. latency
20. industry versus inferiority
21. resilience

ANSWERS
CHAPTER REVIEW

1. peers; more; social comparison
2. culture of children; do not necessarily mirror
3. Throughout the world; independence; deviancy training
4. of their own sex; gender; racial
5. Kohlberg; preconventional; conventional; postconventional
6. rewards; punishments; 1; 2
7. social rules; 4; 3
8. moral principles; social contracts; universal ethical principles
9. cultural; gender
10. one-third; one-half; one-sixth
11. neglected; aggressive-rejected; withdrawn-rejected

Aggressive-rejected children are disliked because of their antagonistic and confrontational behavior, while withdrawn-rejected children are timid, withdrawn, and anxious. Both types often misinterpret social situations, dysregulate their emotions, and are likely to be mistreated at home.

12. social cognition; social referencing; theory of mind
13. effortful control; impulses; emotions

Given direct conflict with another, well-liked children seek compromise in order to maintain the friendship. They assume that social slights are accidental and, in contrast with rejected children, do not respond with fear, self-doubt, or anger. These prosocial impulses and attitudes are a sign of social maturity.

14. more
15. intense; intimate; do not change; harder
16. interests; values; backgrounds

17. systematic; physical, verbal, social; repeated; physical; verbal; relational

18. have; perceptive; empathy

19. withdrawn; aggressive; bully-victims

20. size; sharp-tongued; physical; relational

21. brain abnormalities; genetic; insecure attachment; home; siblings; aggressive; effortful control

22. ecological-systems; culture

23. genetic; environmental

24. nonshared; shared

25. works to meet the needs of its members

26. needs; learning; self-esteem; friendships; harmony; stability

27. genetic and legal relationships among related people living in the same household
    a. extended family
    b. nuclear family
    c. one-parent family
    d. blended family
    e. polygamous family
    f. adoptive family
    g. foster family
    h. stepparent family
    i. grandparents alone
    j. homosexual family

28. nuclear; one-fourth; single-parent

Parents in a nuclear family tend to be wealthier, better educated, psychologically and physically healthier, more willing to compromise, and less hostile than other parents.

29. function; structure

30. correlates; decreases; family-stress; stress; hostile

31. harmony; stability; transitions

32. latency; quiet; submerged

33. industry versus inferiority

34. more; dips; social comparison

35. resilient; dynamic; positive

36. routines

37. social support

38. more; peers; pets; religion

PROGRESS TEST 1

Multiple-Choice Questions

1. **b.** is the answer. (p. 336)

2. **d.** is the answer. (p. 337)

3. **b.** is the answer. (p. 354)

4. **a.** is the answer. (p. 334)
   b. This is social comparison.
   c. This is social cognition.

5. **b.** is the answer. (p. 340)

6. **a.** is the answer. (pp. 340–341)

7. **d.** is the answer. (p. 340)

8. **b.** is the answer. (p. 338)
   a. Social comparison is the tendency to assess one's abilities by measuring them against those of others, especially those of one's peers.
   c. Metacognition, which is not discussed in this chapter, is the ability to monitor and adjust one's cognitive processes.
   d. This term was not discussed in the chapter.

9. **a.** is the answer. Resilience is a dynamic, not a stable, trait. (p. 353)

10. **b.** is the answer. (p. 357)

11. **a.** is the answer. (p. 340)
    b. Withdrawn-rejected children are frequently the victims of bullies, but rarely become bullies themselves.
    c. & d. There are no such categories.

12. **c.** is the answer. (p. 339)
    d. In fact, children rarely intervene, unless a best friend is involved.

13. **d.** is the answer. (p. 339)

14. **d.** is the answer. (p. 348)

15. **a.** is the answer. (p. 351)

True or False Items

1. F In fact, just the opposite is true. (p. 352)

2. F In fact, just the opposite is true. (p. 339)

3. T (p. 348)

4. T (p. 340)

5. F A given child is not resilient in all situations. (p. 353)

6. T (p. 348)

7. T (p. 338)

8. F Just the opposite is true: They tend to misinterpret other people's words and behavior. (p. 338)

9. F   Because of the coping strategies that many school-age children develop, they are better able than younger children to cope with stress. (p. 355)

10. T (p. 350)

11. F   Friendship circles become narrower because friendships become more selective and exclusive. (p. 339)

PROGRESS TEST 2

Multiple-Choice Questions

1. **c.** is the answer. (p. 340)

   a. These are usually bullies.

   b. & d. These are not subcategories of rejected children.

2. **b.** is the answer. (p. 343)

   a. Shared influences are those that occur because children are raised by the same parents in the same home.

   c. & d. There are no such influences.

3. **d.** is the answer. (p. 347)

4. **d.** is the answer. (p. 346)

5. **b.** is the answer. (p. 352)

   a. This tends to promote, rather than reduce, self-esteem.

   c. Only 10 percent of schoolchildren experience this.

   d. This issue becomes more important during adolescence.

6. **a.** is the answer. (p. 352)

7. **d.** is the answer. (p. 339)

   a., b., & c. In fact, just the opposite is true of friendship during the school years.

8. **d.** is the answer. (p. 340)

9. **a.** is the answer. (pp. 341–342)

10. **c.** is the answer. (pp. 348–349)

11. **b.** is the answer. (p. 356)

12. **b.** is the answer. (p. 333)

13. **d.** is the answer. (p. 348)

14. **c.** is the answer. (p. 351)

15. **b.** is the answer. (p. 353)

   c. & d. The text did not discuss how stress influences friendship or peer acceptance.

Matching Items

1. i (p. 340)	**5.** j (p. 346)	**9.** k (p. 338)
2. c (p. 346)	**6.** e (p. 338)	**10.** b (p. 347)
3. f (p. 333)	**7.** h (p. 338)	**11.** g (p. 346)
4. a (p. 340)	**8.** d (p. 340)	

DEVELOPMENTAL PSYCHOLOGY APPLIED

1. **d.** is the answer. (p. 340)

2. **c.** is the answer. The question describes what is, for Erikson, the crisis of middle childhood: industry versus inferiority. (pp. 351–352)

3. **b.** is the answer. (p. 353)

4. **c.** is the answer. (p. 338)

5. **d.** is the answer. (p. 350)

6. **c.** is the answer. (p. 346)

   a. A nuclear family consists of a husband and wife and their biological offspring.

   b. Although Sandra does live with a stepparent, because she also lives with the biological children from his previous marriage, her family would be classified as blended.

   d. An extended family includes children living with one or more of their biological parents, one or more grandparents, and often other relatives as well.

7. **c.** is the answer. (p. 339)

8. **c.** is the answer. (p. 338)

   a. Aggressive-rejected children are antagonistic and confrontational.

   b. & d. These are not classifications used by developmentalists.

9. **d.** is the answer. (p. 353)

10. **d.** is the answer. Self-esteem decreases throughout middle childhood. (p. 352)

11. **b.** is the answer. (p. 352)

   a. & c. These are more typical of preschoolers than school-age children.

12. **d.** is the answer. (p. 353)

13. **d.** is the answer. (p. 340)

   a. & b. It is taller-than-average *boys* and verbally assertive *girls* who are more likely to bully others.

   c. This is a common myth.

14. **d.** is the answer. (p. 340)

   a., b., & c. Contrary to popular belief, victims are no more likely to be fat or homely or to speak with an accent than nonvictims are.

15. **d.** is the answer. (pp. 353–354)

KEY TERMS

1. **Social comparison** is the tendency to assess one's abilities, achievements, social status, and other

attributes by measuring them against those of others, especially those of one's peers. (p. 333)

2. The **culture of children** refers to the specific habits, styles, and values that reflect the rules and rituals of children. (p. 334)

3. **Deviancy training** is the process in which children learn from peers to avoid adult restrictions. (p. 334)

4. **Preconventional moral reasoning** is Kohlberg's first level of moral reasoning, emphasizing rewards and punishments. (p. 336)

5. **Conventional moral reasoning** is Kohlberg's second level of moral reasoning, emphasizing social rules. (p. 336)

6. **Postconventional moral reasoning** is Kohlberg's third level of moral reasoning, emphasizing moral principles. (p. 336)

7. The peer group shuns **aggressive-rejected children** because they are overly confrontational. (p. 338)

8. **Withdrawn-rejected children** are shunned by the peer group because of their timid, withdrawn, and anxious behavior. (p. 338)

9. **Social cognition** is the ability to understand social interactions. (p. 338)

10. **Effortful control** is the ability to regulate one's impulses and emotions through effort, not simply through natural inclination. (p. 338)

11. **Bullying** is the repeated, systematic effort to inflict harm on a child through physical, verbal, or social attacks. (p. 339)

12. A **bully-victim** is a bully who has also been a victim of bullying, also called *provocative victim*. (p. 340)

13. **Family structure** refers to the legal and genetic relationships among relatives in the same household. (p. 344)

14. **Family function** refers to the ways families work to foster the development of children by meeting their physical needs, encouraging them to learn, helping them to develop self-respect, nurturing friendships, and providing harmony and stability. (p. 344)

15. A **nuclear family** consists of two parents and their mutual biological offspring under age 18. (p. 346)

16. A **single-parent family** consists of one parent and his or her biological children. (p. 346)

17. An **extended family** consists of three or more generations of biologically related individuals living in one household. (p. 346)

18. A **blended family** consists of two parents, at least one with biological children from a previous union, and any children the adults have together. (p. 347)

19. In Freud's theory, middle childhood is a period of **latency,** during which emotional drives are quieter, psychosexual needs are repressed, and unconscious conflicts are submerged. (p. 351)

20. According to Erikson, the crisis of middle childhood is that of **industry versus inferiority**, in which children try to master many skills and develop views of themselves as either competent and industrious or incompetent and inferior. (p. 351)

21. **Resilience** is the capacity of some children to adapt positively despite adversity. (p. 353)

14

Adolescence: Biosocial Development

Chapter Overview

Between the ages of 10 and 20, young people cross the great divide between childhood and adulthood. This crossing encompasses all three domains of development—biosocial, cognitive, and psychosocial. Chapter 14 focuses on the dramatic changes that occur in the biosocial domain, beginning with puberty and the growth spurt. The biosocial metamorphosis of the adolescent is discussed in detail, with emphasis on factors that affect the age of puberty, sexual maturation, and brain development.

Although adolescence is, in many ways, a healthy time of life, the text also addresses two health hazards that too often affect adolescence: sex too early and the use of alcohol, tobacco, and other drugs.

NOTE: Answer guidelines for all Chapter 14 questions begin on page 214.

Guided Study

The text chapter should be studied one section at a time. Before you read, preview each section by skimming it, noting headings and boldface items. Then read the appropriate section objectives from the following outline. Keep these objectives in mind and, as you read the chapter section, search for the information that will enable you to meet each objective. Once you have finished a section, write out answers for its objectives.

Puberty Begins (pp. 364–371)

1. Outline the biological events of puberty.

2. Discuss the emotional impact of pubertal hormones.

3. Identify several factors that influence the onset of puberty, and discuss the effects of early and late maturation on male and female adolescents.

4. Discuss the relationship between the poor nutrition of adolescents and their body image concerns.

The Transformations of Puberty (pp. 371–380)

5. Describe the growth spurt in both the male and the female adolescent, focusing on changes in body weight and height.

6. Describe the changes in the body's internal organs that accompany the growth spurt.

7. Discuss the development of the primary sex characteristics in males and females during puberty.

8. Discuss the development of the secondary sex characteristics in males and females during puberty, and describe the role of the social context in the adolescent's sexual behavior.

9. Describe the development of the brain during adolescence.

10. Explain why the brain's immaturity and uneven development partly accounts for adolescent risk taking.

11. Discuss the effects of changing diurnal biorhythms on the adolescent's physical and psychological well-being.

Possible Problems (pp. 380–388)

12. Discuss the potential problems associated with early sexual activity.

13. Discuss sexual abuse, focusing on its prevalence.

14. Discuss drug use and abuse among adolescents today, including their prevalence and significance for development.

Chapter Review

When you have finished reading the chapter, work through the material that follows to review it. Complete the sentences and answer the questions. As you proceed, evaluate your performance for each section by consulting the answers beginning on page 214. Do not continue with the next section until you understand each answer. If you need to, review or reread the appropriate section in the textbook before continuing.

Puberty Begins (pp. 364–371)

1. The period of rapid physical growth and sexual maturation that ends childhood and brings the young person to adult size, shape, and sexual potential is called _____ . The physical changes of puberty typically are complete _____ (how long?) after puberty begins. Although puberty begins at various ages, the _____ is almost always the same.

   List, in order, the major physical changes of puberty in

   Girls: _____

   _____

   Boys: _____

   _____

2. The average girl experiences her first menstrual period, called _____ , at age _____ .

3. The average boy experiences his first ejaculation of seminal fluid, called _____ , at age _____ .

4. Puberty begins when a hormonal signal from the _____ triggers hormone production in the _____ _____ , which in turn triggers increased hormone production by the _____ _____ and by the _____ , which include the _____ in males and the _____ in females. This route is called the _____ _____ .

5. The hormone _____ causes the gonads to dramatically increase their production of sex hormones, especially _____ in girls and _____ in boys.

6. The increase in the hormone _____ is dramatic in boys and slight in girls, whereas the increase in the hormone _____ is marked in girls and slight in boys. Conflict, moodiness, and sexual urges _____ (usually do/do not usually) increase during adolescence. This is due in part to the increasingly high levels of hormones such as

   _____ .

7. During puberty, hormones are quite _____ (consistent from child to child/erratic) in part due to the immaturity of the _____ .

8. Normal children begin to notice pubertal changes between the ages of _____ and _____ . Girls are about _____ (how many?) years ahead of boys in height.

9. Genes are an important factor in the timing of puberty, as demonstrated by the fact that _____ _____ reach puberty at similar ages.

10. Stocky individuals tend to experience puberty _____ (earlier/later) than those with taller, thinner builds.

11. Menarche seems to be related to the accumulation of a certain amount of body _____ .

12. For both sexes, fat is limited by chronic _____ , which therefore delays puberty by several years.

13. The _____ _____ refers to the earlier growth of children over the last two centuries as _____ and _____ _____ have improved.

14. Another influence on the age of puberty is _____ .

15. Research from many nations suggests that family stress may _____ (accelerate/delay) the onset of puberty.

16. Stress may cause production of the hormones that cause _____ . Support for this hypothesis comes from a study showing that early puberty was associated with _____ and _____ .

17. An evolutionary explanation of the stress-puberty hypothesis is that ancestral females growing up in stressful environments may have increased their _____ _____ by accelerating physical maturation.

18. For girls, _____ (early/late) maturation may be especially troublesome.

Describe several common problems and developmental hazards experienced by early-maturing girls.

19. For boys, _____ (early/late/both early and late) maturation may be difficult. _____ (Early/Late) maturing boys may have difficulty, in part because they are likely to befriend _____-_____ , somewhat older boys. _____ (Early/Late) maturing boys may be teased.

20. Most teenagers _____ (do/do not) consume the recommended daily dose of iron. There is a direct link between deficient diets and the availability of _____ _____ in schools.

21. One reason for dietary deficiencies is concern about _____ , defined as a person's idea of how _____ .

The Transformations of Puberty (pp. 371–380)

22. A major _____ spurt occurs in late childhood and early adolescence, during which growth proceeds from the _____ (core/extremities) to the _____ (core/extremities). At the same time, children begin to _____ (gain/lose) weight at a relatively rapid rate.

23. The amount of weight gain an individual experiences depends on several factors, including _____ , _____ , _____ , and _____ .

24. During the growth spurt, a greater percentage of fat is retained by _____ (males/females).

25. About a year after the height and weight changes occur, a period of _____ increase occurs, causing the pudginess and clumsiness of an earlier age to disappear. In boys, this increase is particularly notable in the _____ .

26. Internal organs also grow during puberty. The _____ increase in size and capacity, the _____ doubles in size, heart rate _____ (increases/decreases), and blood volume _____ (increases/decreases). These changes increase the adolescent's physical _____ .

Explain why the physical demands placed on a teenager, as in athletic training, should not be the same as those for a young adult of similar height and weight.

27. During puberty, one organ system, the _____ system, decreases in size, making teenagers _____ (more/less) susceptible to respiratory ailments.

28. One secondary sex characteristic that is mistakenly considered a sign of womanhood and manliness is _____ .

29. Changes in _____

   _____ _____

   involve the sex organs that are directly involved
   in reproduction. By the end of puberty, reproduction _____ (is/is still not) possible.

Describe the major changes in primary sex characteristics that occur in both sexes during puberty.

30. Sexual features other than those associated with
   reproduction are referred to as _____

   _____ _____ .

Describe the major pubertal changes in the secondary
sex characteristics of both sexes.

31. Although sex hormones trigger thoughts about
   sexual intimacy, sexual behavior among teens
   reflects _____ and
   _____ more than biology.

32. Many of the hallmarks of adolescent thinking and
   behavior originate with maturation of the
   _____ . The brain's limbic system,
   which controls _____ and
   _____ _____ , matures
   _____ (before/after) the prefrontal
   cortex.

33. Although adolescents are capable of
   _____ thinking, they do not always
   do so. Myelination and _____ proceed from inside to the cortex and from back to
   front.

34. The limbic system predominates in quick
   _____ reactions, while the prefrontal cortex coordinates _____
   functions, including the capacity for

   _____ _____ .

35. One reason adolescents like intensity and excitement is that the maturing _____
   system is attuned to these strong sensations, as
   yet unchecked by the _____

   _____ .

36. Throughout adolescence, reactions become faster
   because of increased _____ . The
   axons and dendrites that link one neuron to
   another, which make up the brain's _____
   matter, increase, additional _____
   of dendrites occurs, and the _____
   system, neurotransmitters that bring pleasure, is
   very active.

37. The hormones of puberty also affect daily
   rhythms, called _____ rhythms,
   causing, for instance, changes in the level of the
   chemical _____ , which makes peo-
   ple more _____ . Adolescents typically get too _____ (little/much)
   sleep. Among adolescents, _____
   (girls/boys) are particularly likely to be sleep-
   deprived.

Possible Problems (pp. 380–388)

38. A major developmental risk for sexually active
   adolescent girls is _____ . If this
   happens within a year or two of menarche, girls
   are at increased risk of many complications,
   including _____
   _____ . If the baby of a teen
   mother is born healthy, he or she
   _____ (is/is not) likely to experience complications later on, including poor
   _____ , inadequate
   _____ , and low _____ .

39. Worldwide, sexually active teens have higher rates of diseases caused by sexual contact, called

_____ _____

_____ , than any other age group. One reason is that they do not have the natural

_____ _____ that fully developed women have. Another reason is that they are unlikely to seek _____ because they are ashamed and afraid or do not recognize the symptoms.

40. Any sexual activity between a juvenile and an older person is considered _____

_____ _____ .

41. Sexual abuse is more common between the ages of _____ and _____ than at any other time.

42. _____ (Girls/Boys) are more vulnerable to child sexual abuse.

43. Drug use is _____ (up/down) since 1975, but the number of available drugs has _____ (increased/decreased). Worldwide, _____ (girls/ boys) have higher rates of drug use than _____ (girls/boys).

44. One reason teenagers use drugs is that, for many adolescents, _____ are more important than _____ . Another is that adolescents' immature _____ cortex makes them more likely to seek states of excitement.

45. By decreasing food consumption and the absorption of nutrients, tobacco can limit the adolescent _____ _____ .

46. Alcohol impairs _____ and _____ by damaging the brain's _____ and _____ _____ .

47. Many adolescents fail to notice when they move past experimenting with drugs to harmful _____ and then _____ , defined as needing the drug to feel _____ .

48. The idea that each new generation forgets what the previous generation has learned about harmful drugs is referred to as _____

_____ .

Progress Test 1

Multiple-Choice Questions

Circle your answers to the following questions and check them with the answers beginning on page 215. If your answer is incorrect, read the explanation for why it is incorrect and then consult the appropriate pages of the text (in parentheses following the correct answer).

1. Which of the following most accurately describes the sequence of pubertal development in girls?
   a. breasts and pubic hair; growth spurt in which fat is deposited on hips and buttocks; first menstrual period; ovulation
   b. growth spurt; breasts and pubic hair; first menstrual period; ovulation
   c. first menstrual period; breasts and pubic hair; growth spurt; ovulation
   d. breasts and pubic hair; growth spurt; ovulation; first menstrual period

2. Although both sexes grow rapidly during adolescence, boys typically gain more than girls in their:
   a. muscle strength.
   b. body fat.
   c. internal organ growth.
   d. lymphoid system.

3. For girls, the first readily observable sign of the onset of puberty is:
   a. the onset of breast growth.
   b. the appearance of facial, body, and pubic hair.
   c. a change in the shape of the eyes.
   d. a lengthening of the torso.

4. More than any other group in the population, adolescent girls are likely to have:
   a. asthma.
   b. acne.
   c. anemia.
   d. testosterone deficiency.

5. The HPA axis is the:
   a. route followed by many hormones to regulate stress, growth, sleep, and appetite.
   b. pair of sex glands in humans.
   c. cascade of sex hormones in females and males.
   d. area of the brain that regulates the pituitary gland.

6. For males, the secondary sex characteristic that usually occurs last is:
   a. breast enlargement.
   b. the appearance of facial hair.
   c. growth of the testes.
   d. the appearance of pubic hair.

7. For girls, the specific event that is taken to indicate fertility is _____ ; for boys, it is _____ .
   a. the growth of breast buds; voice deepening
   b. menarche; spermarche
   c. anovulation; the testosterone surge
   d. the growth spurt; pubic hair

8. The most significant hormonal changes of puberty include an increase of _____ in _____ and an increase of _____ in _____ .
   a. progesterone; boys; estradiol; girls
   b. estradiol; boys; testosterone; girls
   c. progesterone; girls; estradiol; boys
   d. estradiol; girls; testosterone; boys

9. A child who is chronically malnourished will likely:
   a. begin puberty at a younger-than-average age.
   b. begin puberty later than the normal age range.
   c. never experience menarche.
   d. never experience spermarche.

10. Adolescents' improving ability to plan, reflect, and analyze is partly the result of maturation of the:
    a. hippocampus.
    b. amygdala.
    c. limbic system.
    d. prefrontal cortex.

11. Today, adolescence tends to begin _____ and end _____ .
    a. later biologically; later sociologically
    b. earlier biologically; later sociologically
    c. later sociologically; earlier biologically
    d. earlier sociologically; later biologically

12. Early physical growth and sexual maturation:
    a. tend to be equally difficult for girls and boys.
    b. tend to be more difficult for boys than for girls.
    c. tend to be more difficult for girls than for boys.
    d. are easier for both girls and boys than late maturation.

13. Pubertal changes in growth and maturation typically are complete how long after puberty begins?
    a. one to two years
    b. two to three years
    c. four years
    d. The variation is too great to generalize.

14. The hypothalamus/pituitary/adrenal axis triggers:
    a. puberty.
    b. the growth spurt.
    c. the development of sexual characteristics.
    d. all of the above.

15. One reason adolescents like intensity, excitement, and risk taking is that:
    a. the limbic system matures faster than the prefrontal cortex.
    b. the prefrontal cortex matures faster than the limbic system.
    c. brain maturation is synchronous.
    d. puberty is occurring at a younger age today than in the past.

True or False Items

Write T (*true*) or F (*false*) on the line in front of each statement.

_____ 1. The limbic system matures years before the prefrontal cortex.

_____ 2. During puberty, hormonal bursts lead to quick emotional extremes.

_____ 3. The first indicator of reproductive potential in males is menarche.

_____ 4. Lung capacity, heart size, and total volume of blood increase significantly during adolescence.

_____ 5. Puberty generally begins sometime between ages 8 and 14.

_____ 6. Girls are about two years ahead of boys in height as well as sexually and hormonally.

_____ 7. Each culture and age cohort has its own patterns of drug use and abuse during adolescence.

_____ 8. Only adolescent girls suffer from anemia.

_____ 9. Early-maturing girls tend to have lower self-esteem.

_____ 10. Both the sequence and timing of pubertal events vary greatly from one young person to another.

Progress Test 2

Progress Test 2 should be completed during a final chapter review. Answer the following questions after you thoroughly understand the correct answers for the Chapter Review and Progress Test 1.

Multiple-Choice Questions

1. Which of the following is the correct sequence of pubertal events in boys?
   a. growth spurt, pubic hair, facial hair, first ejaculation, lowering of voice
   b. pubic hair, first ejaculation, growth spurt; lowering of voice, facial hair
   c. lowering of voice, pubic hair, growth spurt, facial hair, first ejaculation
   d. growth spurt, facial hair, lowering of voice, pubic hair, first ejaculation

2. Which of the following statements about adolescent physical development is *not* true?
   a. Hands and feet generally lengthen before arms and legs.
   b. Facial features usually grow before the head itself reaches adult size and shape.
   c. Oil, sweat, and odor glands become more active.
   d. The lymphoid system increases slightly in size, and the heart increases by nearly half.

3. In puberty, a hormone that increases markedly in girls (and only somewhat in boys) is:
   a. estradiol.   c. androgen.
   b. testosterone.   d. menarche.

4. Nutritional deficiencies in adolescence are frequently the result of:
   a. eating red meat.
   b. poor eating habits.
   c. anovulatory menstruation.
   d. excessive exercise.

5. In females, puberty is typically marked by a(n):
   a. significant widening of the shoulders.
   b. significant widening of the hips.
   c. enlargement of the torso and upper chest.
   d. decrease in the size of the eyes and nose.

6. Nonreproductive sexual characteristics, such as the deepening of the voice and the development of breasts, are called:
   a. gender-typed traits.
   b. primary sex characteristics.
   c. secondary sex characteristics.
   d. pubertal prototypes.

7. Puberty is initiated when hormones are released from the _____ , then from the _____ gland, and then from the adrenal glands and the _____ .
   a. hypothalamus; pituitary; gonads
   b. pituitary; gonads; hypothalamus
   c. gonads; pituitary; hypothalamus
   d. pituitary; hypothalamus; gonads

8. If a girl under age 15 becomes pregnant, she is at greater risk for:
   a. a low-birthweight baby.
   b. high blood pressure.
   c. stillbirth.
   d. all of the above.

9. Alcohol impairs memory and self-control by damaging the:
   a. hippocampus and prefrontal cortex.
   b. pituitary gland.
   c. hypothalamus.
   d. gonads.

10. The brain area that predominates in quick, emotional reactions is the:
    a. prefrontal cortex.
    b. limbic system.
    c. dendrite.
    d. axon.

11. The number of substantiated victims of sexual abuse is greatest among children ages:
    a. 12 to 15.   c. 16 to 18.
    b. 4 to 7.   d. 8 to 11.

12. The secular trend refers to:
    a. the complex link between pubertal hormones and emotions.
    b. the effect of chronic stress on pubertal hormones.
    c. earlier growth of children due to improved nutrition and medical care.
    d. effect of chronic malnutrition on the onset of puberty.

13. Puberty is *most accurately* defined as the period:

    a. of rapid physical growth that occurs during adolescence.

    b. during which sexual maturation is attained.

    c. of rapid physical growth and sexual maturation that ends childhood.

    d. during which adolescents establish identities separate from their parents.

14. Which of the following does *not* typically occur during puberty?

    a. The lungs increase in size and capacity.

    b. The heart's size and rate of beating increase.

    c. Blood volume increases.

    d. The lymphoid system decreases in size.

15. Teenagers' susceptibility to respiratory ailments typically _____ during adolescence, due to a(n) _____ in the size of the lymphoid system.

    a. increases; increase

    b. increases; decrease

    c. decreases; increase

    d. decreases; decrease

Matching Items

Match each term or concept with its corresponding description or definition.

Terms or Concepts

    _____ **1.** puberty

    _____ **2.** gonadotropin-releasing hormone (GnRH)

    _____ **3.** testosterone

    _____ **4.** estradiol

    _____ **5.** growth spurt

    _____ **6.** primary sex characteristics

    _____ **7.** menarche

    _____ **8.** spermarche

    _____ **9.** secondary sex characteristics

    _____ **10.** body image

Descriptions or Definitions

    a. onset of menstruation

    b. period of rapid physical growth and sexual maturation that ends childhood

    c. hormone that increases dramatically in boys during puberty

    d. hormone that causes the gonads to enlarge and increase their production of sex hormones

    e. hormone that increases dramatically in girls during puberty

    f. first sign is increased bone length

    g. attitude toward one's physical appearance

    h. physical characteristics not involved in reproduction

    i. the sex organs involved in reproduction

    j. first ejaculation containing sperm

Developmental Psychology Applied

Answer these questions the day before an exam as a final check on your understanding of the chapter's terms and concepts.

1. Concluding her talk on adolescent alcohol use and brain damage, Maya notes that:

    a. studies have shown only that alcohol use is correlated with damage to the prefrontal cortex.

    b. thus far, studies have shown only that alcohol use is correlated with damage to the hippocampus.

    c. animal research studies demonstrate that alcohol does not merely correlate with brain abnormalities; it causes them.

    d. alcohol use causes brain abnormalities only in teens who are genetically vulnerable.

2. I am the hormone that causes the gonads to dramatically increase their production of sex hormones. Who am I?

    a. GnRH   **c.** estradiol

    b. cortisol   **d.** testosterone

3. Twelve-year-old Kwan is worried because his twin sister has suddenly grown taller and more physically mature than he. His parents should:
   a. reassure him that the average boy is about two years behind the average girl in the timing of puberty.
   b. tell him that within a year or less he will grow taller than his sister.
   c. tell him that one member of each fraternal twin pair is always shorter.
   d. encourage him to exercise more to accelerate the onset of his growth spurt.

4. Calvin, the class braggart, boasts that because his beard has begun to grow, he is more virile than his male classmates. Jacob informs him that:
   a. the tendency to grow facial and body hair has nothing to do with virility.
   b. beard growth is determined by heredity.
   c. girls also develop some facial hair and more noticeable hair on their arms and legs, so it is clearly not a sign of masculinity.
   d. all of the above are true.

5. Typically, if an adolescent girl or boy has one problem, such as early and unwanted sexual activity:
   a. he or she also has several other problems.
   b. the problem is isolated and does not adversely impact other areas of development.
   c. the consequences are temporary and not severe.
   d. their earlier development during childhood was also problematic.

6. Which of the following students is likely to be the most popular in a sixth-grade class?
   a. Vicki, the most sexually mature girl in the class
   b. Sandra, the tallest girl in the class
   c. Brad, who is at the top of the class scholastically
   d. Dan, the tallest boy in the class

7. Regarding the effects of early and late maturation on boys and girls, which of the following is *not* true?
   a. Late-maturing boys are more likely to join peer groups that rebel against laws and traditions.
   b. Early puberty that leads to romantic relationships often leads to stress and depression among both girls and boys.
   c. Early-maturing girls may be drawn into involvement with older boys.

   d. Late puberty is often difficult for boys in schools where athletes are the local stars.

8. Teenagers whose parents are divorced and those who live in cities often experience puberty _____ than other teens, perhaps as a result of _____ .
   a. earlier; greater stress
   b. later; greater stress
   c. earlier; poor nutrition
   d. later; poor nutrition

9. Twenty-four-year-old Connie, who has a distorted view of sexuality, has gone from one abusive relationship with a man to another. It is likely that Connie:
   a. has been abusing drugs all her life.
   b. was sexually abused as a child.
   c. will eventually become a normal, nurturing mother.
   d. had attention-deficit disorder as a child.

10. When developmentalists say that hormones have an indirect effect on adolescent moods and emotions, they mean that:
   a. hormones directly affect appetite and nutrition, which dramatically influence emotionality.
   b. the variation in emotionality from teen to teen is too great to state that there is a direct impact.
   c. it is the social responses of others to hormonally triggered changes in appearance that trigger adolescent moods.
   d. all of the above occur.

11. I am the sex hormone that is secreted in greater amounts by females than males. What am I?
   a. GnRH
   b. cortisol
   c. estradiol
   d. testosterone

12. Of the following teenagers, those most likely to be distressed about their physical development are:
   a. late-maturing girls.
   b. early-maturing girls.
   c. early-maturing boys.
   d. girls or boys who masturbate.

13. Thirteen-year-old Kristin is more likely to:
    a. drink too much milk.
    b. eat more than five servings of fruit per day.
    c. choose expensive foods over inexpensive ones.
    d. be iron deficient.

14. I am one of two glands, located above the kidneys, that produce "stress" hormones. What am I?
    a. pituitary gland   c. adrenal gland
    b. ovary   d. testes

15. Eleven-year-old Linda, who has just begun to experience the first signs of puberty, laments, "When will the agony of puberty be over?" You tell her that the major events of puberty typically end about _____ after the first visible signs appear.
    a. 6 years   c. 2 to 4 years
    b. 4 years   d. 1 year

Key Terms

Writing Definitions

Using your own words, write a brief definition or explanation of each of the following terms on a separate piece of paper.

1. puberty
2. menarche
3. spermarche
4. hormone
5. pituitary
6. adrenal glands
7. HPA axis
8. gonads
9. estradiol
10. testosterone
11. secular trend
12. body image
13. growth spurt
14. primary sex characteristics
15. secondary sex characteristics
16. sexually transmitted infections (STIs)
17. child sexual abuse
18. generational forgetting

Cross-Check

After you have written the definitions of the key terms in this chapter, you should complete the crossword puzzle to ensure that you can reverse the process—recognize the term, given the definition.

ACROSS

1. Glands near the kidneys that are stimulated by the pituitary at the beginning of puberty.
7. The first ejaculation of seminal fluid containing sperm.
12. The first menstrual period.
15. The ovaries in girls and the testes or testicles in boys.
16. Gland that stimulates the adrenal glands and the sex glands in response to a signal from the hypothalamus.
17. Event, which begins with an increase in bone length and includes rapid weight gain and organ growth, that is one of the many observable signs of puberty.

DOWN

1. The period of biological, cognitive, and psychosocial transition from childhood to adulthood.
2. Organ system, which includes the tonsils and adenoids, that decreases in size at adolescence.
3. Area of the brain that sends the hormonal signal that triggers the biological events of puberty.
4. A chemical messenger that travels through the bloodstream to influence body tissues.
5. The _____ axis is the route followed by many hormones to trigger puberty.
6. Widely abused drug that loosens inhibitions and impairs judgment.
8. Body characteristics that are directly involved in reproduction.
9. Body characteristics that are not directly involved in reproduction but that signify sexual development.
10. Main sex hormone in males.
11. Drug that decreases food consumption, the absorption of nutrients, and fertility.
13. Main sex hormone in females.
14. Period of rapid physical growth and sexual maturation that ends childhood and brings the young person to adult size.

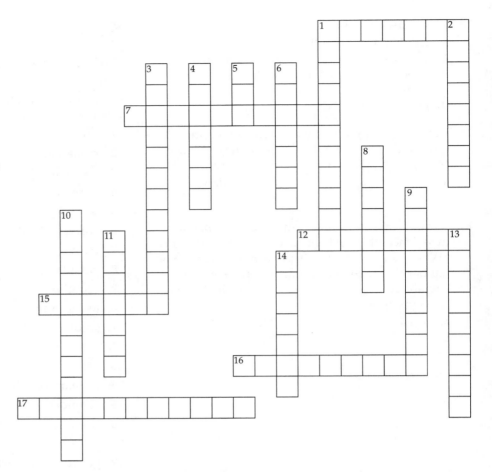

ANSWERS
CHAPTER REVIEW

1. puberty; four years; sequence

Girls: onset of breast growth, initial pubic hair, peak growth spurt, widening of the hips, first menstrual period, completion of pubic-hair growth, and final breast development

Boys: growth of the testes, initial pubic hair, growth of the penis, first ejaculation of seminal fluid, facial hair, peak growth spurt, voice deepening, and completion of pubic-hair growth

2. menarche; 12 years, 8 months
3. spermarche; (just under) 13
4. hypothalamus; pituitary gland; adrenal glands; gonads (sex glands); testes; ovaries; HPA axis
5. GnRH (gonadotropin-releasing hormone); estradiol; testosterone
6. testosterone; estradiol; usually do; testosterone

7. erratic; brain

8. 8; 14; two

9. monozygotic twins

10. earlier

11. fat

12. malnutrition

13. secular trend; nutrition; medical care

14. stress

15. accelerate

16. puberty; conflicted relationships within the family; an unrelated man living in the home

17. reproductive success

18. early

Early-maturing girls may be teased about their big feet or developing breasts. Those who date early may begin "adult" activities at an earlier age, may be pressured by their dates to be sexually active, and may suffer a decrease in self-esteem.

19. both early and late; Early; law-breaking; Late

20. do not; vending machines

21. body image; his or her body looks

22. growth; extremities; core; gain

23. gender; heredity; diet; exercise

24. females

25. muscle; arms

26. lungs; heart; decreases; increases; endurance

The fact that the more visible spurts of weight and height precede the less visible ones of the muscles and organs means that athletic training and weight lifting should match the young person's size of a year or so earlier.

27. lymphoid; less

28. facial and body hair

29. primary sex characteristics; is

Girls: growth of ovaries and uterus and thickening of the vaginal lining

Boys: growth of testes and lengthening of penis; also scrotum enlarges and becomes pendulous

30. secondary sex characteristics

Males grow taller than females and become wider at the shoulders than at the hips. Females take on more fat all over and become wider at the hips, and their breasts begin to develop. About 65 percent of boys experience some temporary breast enlargement. As the lungs and larynx grow, the adolescent's voice (especially in boys) becomes lower. Head and body hair become coarser and darker in both sexes. Facial hair (especially in boys) begins to grow.

31. culture; cohort

32. brain; fear; emotional impulses; before

33. rational; maturation

34. emotional; executive; emotional regulation

35. limbic; prefrontal cortex

36. myelination; white; pruning; dopamine

37. diurnal; melatonin; sleepy; little; girls

38. pregnancy; spontaneous abortion, high blood pressure, stillbirth, cesarean section, and a low-birthweight baby; is; health; education; intelligence

39. sexually transmitted infections; biological defenses; treatment

40. child sexual abuse

41. 10; 15

42. Girls

43. down; increased; boys; girls

44. peers; parents; prefrontal

45. growth rate

46. memory; self-control; hippocampus; prefrontal cortex

47. abuse; addiction; normal

48. generational forgetting

PROGRESS TEST 1

Multiple-Choice Questions

1. **a.** is the answer. (p. 364)

2. **a.** is the answer. (p. 372)

   b. Girls gain more body fat than boys do.

   c. & d. The text does not indicate that these are different for boys and girls.

3. **a.** is the answer. (p. 364)

4. **c.** is the answer. This is because each menstrual period depletes some iron from the body. (p. 370)

5. **a.** is the answer. (p. 365)

   b. This describes the gonads.

   c. These include estradiol and testosterone.

   d. This is the hypothalamus.

6. **b.** is the answer. (p. 364)

7. **b.** is the answer. (p. 364)

8. **d.** is the answer. (p. 365)

9. **b.** is the answer. Worldwide, stocky individuals begin puberty before those with thinner builds. Obviously, a child who is malnourished will be thin. (p. 368)

10. **d.** is the answer. (p. 375)

   a., b., & c. The hippocampus (a) and amygdala (b), which are both part of the limbic system (c), are important in quick emotional reactions.

11. **b.** is the answer. (p. 368)

12. **c.** is the answer. (p. 369)

13. **c.** is the answer. (p. 364)

14. **d.** is the answer. (p. 365)

15. **a.** is the answer. (p. 377)

   c. Brain maturation is asynchronous.

   d. This may be true, but it doesn't explain why adolescents have always liked intensity and excitement.

True or False Items

1. T (p. 377)

2. T (p. 365)

3. F   The first indicator of reproductive potential in males is ejaculation of seminal fluid containing sperm (spermarche). Menarche (the first menstrual period) is the first indication of reproductive potential in females. (p. 364)

4. T (p. 372)

5. T (p. 364)

6. F   Hormonally and sexually, girls are ahead by only a few months. (p. 366)

7. T (p. 385)

8. F   Boys also suffer from anemia, especially if they engage in physical labor or competitive sports. (p. 370)

9. T (p. 369)

10. F   Although there is great variation in the timing of pubertal events, the sequence is very similar for all young people. (p. 364)

PROGRESS TEST 2

Multiple-Choice Questions

1. **b.** is the answer. (p. 364)

2. **d.** is the answer. During adolescence, the lymphoid system *decreases* in size and the heart *doubles* in size. (pp. 372, 373)

3. **a.** is the answer. (p. 365)

   b. Testosterone increases markedly in boys.

   c. Androgen is another name for testosterone.

   d. Menarche is the first menstrual period.

4. **b.** is the answer. (p. 370)

5. **b.** is the answer. (pp. 364, 373)

   a. The shoulders of males tend to widen during puberty.

   c. The torso typically lengthens during puberty.

   d. The eyes and nose *increase* in size during puberty.

6. **c.** is the answer. (p. 373)

   a. Although not a term used in the textbook, a gender-typed trait is one that is typical of one sex but not of the other.

   b. Primary sex characteristics are those involving the reproductive organs.

   d. This is not a term used by developmental psychologists.

7. **a.** is the answer. (p. 365)

8. **d.** is the answer. (p. 380)

9. **a.** is the answer. (p. 386)

10. **b.** is the answer. (p. 377)

   a. The prefrontal cortex is responsible for planning, problem solving, and effortful control.

   c. & d. Dendrites and axons are parts of neurons.

11. **a.** is the answer. (p. 383)

12. **c.** is the answer. (p. 368)

13. **c.** is the answer. (p. 364)

14. **b.** is the answer. Although the size of the heart increases during puberty, heart rate *decreases*. (p. 372)

15. **d.** is the answer. (p. 373)

Matching Items

1. b (p. 364)	5. f (p. 371)	9. h (p. 373)
2. d (p. 365)	6. i (p. 373)	10. g (p. 370)
3. c (p. 365)	7. a (p. 364)	
4. e (p. 365)	8. j (p. 364)	

DEVELOPMENTAL PSYCHOLOGY APPLIED

1. **c.** is the answer. (p. 386)

2. **a.** is the answer. (p. 365)

3. **a.** is the answer. (pp. 364, 366)

   b. It usually takes longer than one year for a prepubescent male to catch up with a female who has begun puberty.

   c. This is not true.

d. The text does not suggest that exercise has an effect on the timing of the growth spurt.

4. **d.** is the answer. (p. 373)

5. **b.** is the answer. (p. 382)

6. **d.** is the answer. (p. 369)

   a. & b. Early-maturing girls are often teased and criticized by their friends.

   c. During adolescence, physical stature is typically a more prized attribute among peers than is scholastic achievement.

7. **a.** is the answer. This is true of early-maturing boys. (p. 369)

8. **a.** is the answer. (pp. 368–369)

9. **b.** is the answer. (p. 382)

10. **c.** is the answer. (p. 366)

11. **c.** is the answer. (p. 365)

    a. GnRH causes the gonads to enlarge and dramatically increase their production of sex hormones in both sexes.

    b. Cortisol is a stress hormone.

    d. Testosterone is secreted in greater amounts in males.

12. **b.** is the answer. (p. 369)

13. **d.** (p. 370)

14. **c.** is the answer. (p. 365)

    a. The pituitary, which is located in the brain, secretes hormones that regulate other glands, including the adrenals.

    b. & d. The ovaries and testes secrete the sex hormones estradiol and testosterone.

15. **b.** is the answer. (p. 364)

KEY TERMS

1. **Puberty** is the period of rapid physical growth and sexual maturation that ends childhood and brings the young person to adult size, shape, and sexual potential. (p. 364)

2. **Menarche,** which refers to the first menstrual period, signals that the adolescent girl has begun ovulation. (p. 364)

3. **Spermarche**, which refers to the first ejaculation of sperm, signals sperm production in adolescent boys. (p. 364)

4. A **hormone** is an organic chemical messenger produced by one body tissue that travels via the bloodstream to another and influences thoughts, emotions, urges, and behaviors. (p. 364)

5. The **pituitary,** a gland in the brain that responds to a biochemical signal from the hypothalamus by producing hormones that regulate growth and control other glands. (p. 365)

6. The **adrenal glands** secrete epinephrine and norepinephrine, hormones that prepare the body to deal with emergencies or stress. (p. 365)

7. The **HPA axis** (hypothalamus-pituitary-adrenal axis) is the route followed by many hormones to trigger puberty and to regulate stress, growth, and other bodily changes. (p. 365)

8. The **gonads** are the paired sex glands in humans—the ovaries in females and the testes or testicles in males. (p. 365)

9. **Estradiol** is a sex hormone that is secreted in greater amounts by females than by males; considered the chief estrogen. (p. 365)

10. **Testosterone** is a sex hormone that is secreted more by males than by females; considered the best-known androgen. (p. 365)

11. The **secular trend** is the tendency toward earlier and larger growth that has occurred among adolescents over the past two centuries. (p. 368)

12. **Body image** is a person's concept of his or her body's appearance. (p. 370)

13. The **growth spurt,** which is the relatively sudden and rapid physical growth of every part of the body, is one of the many observable signs of puberty. (p. 371)

14. During puberty, changes in the **primary sex characteristics** involve those sex organs that are directly involved in reproduction. (p. 373)

15. During puberty, changes in the **secondary sex characteristics** involve parts of the body that are not directly involved in reproduction but that signify sexual development. (p. 373)

16. **Sexually transmitted infections (STIs),** such as syphilis, gonorrhea, herpes, and AIDS, are those that are spread by sexual contact. (p. 381)

17. **Child sexual abuse** is any erotic activity that arouses an adult and excites, shames, or confuses a child—even if the abuse does not involve physical contact. (p. 382)

18. **Generational forgetting** is the idea that each generation forgets what earlier generations had already learned about harmful drugs. (p. 387)

Cross-Check

ACROSS	DOWN
1. adrenal	**1.** adolescence
7. spermarche	**2.** lymphoid
12. menarche	**3.** hypothalamus
15. gonads	**4.** hormone
16. pituitary	**5.** HPA
17. growth spurt	**6.** alcohol
	8. primary
	9. secondary
	10. testosterone
	11. tobacco
	13. estradiol
	14. puberty

15

Adolescence: Cognitive Development

Chapter Overview

Chapter 15 describes the cognitive advances and limitations of adolescence. With the attainment of formal operational thought, the developing person becomes able to think in an adult way, that is, to be logical, to think in terms of possibilities, and to reason scientifically and abstractly.

Even those who reach the stage of formal operational thought spend much of their time thinking at less advanced levels. The discussion of adolescent egocentrism supports this generalization in showing that adolescents have difficulty thinking rationally about themselves and their immediate experiences. Adolescent egocentrism makes them see themselves as psychologically unique and more socially significant than they really are.

The next section of the chapter explores teaching and learning in high school. As adolescents enter secondary school, their grades often suffer and their level of participation decreases. The rigid behavioral demands and intensified competition of most secondary schools do not, unfortunately, provide a supportive learning environment for adolescents.

NOTE: Answer guidelines for all Chapter 15 questions begin on page 227.

Guided Study

The text chapter should be studied one section at a time. Before you read, preview each section by skimming it, noting headings and boldface items. Then read the appropriate section objectives from the following outline. Keep these objectives in mind and, as you read the chapter section, search for the information that will enable you to meet each objective. Once you have finished a section, write out answers for its objectives.

Adolescent Thinking (pp. 391–401)

1. Discuss adolescent egocentrism, and give two examples of egocentric fantasies or fables.

2. Describe evidence of formal operational thinking during adolescence, and provide examples of adolescents' emerging ability to reason deductively and inductively.

3. Explain adolescents' use of illogical, intuitive thought even when they are capable of logical thought.

Teaching and Learning (pp. 401–412)

4. Discuss possible reasons for the slump in academic performance and other problems that often appear during the transition from elementary school to middle school.

5. Discuss the relationship between the technological advances in educational tools and teenage cognition.

6. Evaluate the typical secondary school's ability to meet the cognitive needs of the typical adolescent.

7. Explore some options for improving adolescent engagement in secondary school and for preventing violence.

Chapter Review

When you have finished reading the chapter, work through the material that follows to review it. Complete the sentences and answer the questions. As you proceed, evaluate your performance for each section by consulting the answers on page 227. Do not continue with the next section until you understand each answer. If you need to, review or reread the appropriate section in the textbook before continuing.

1. Adolescents often combine _____ , _____ , and _____ in ways that contrast with the cognitive processes of older people.

Adolescent Thinking (pp. 391–401)

2. The adolescent's belief that he or she is uniquely significant and that the social world revolves around him or her is a psychological phenomenon called _____

_____ .

3. An adolescent's tendency to feel that he or she is somehow immune to the consequences of dangerous or illegal behavior is expressed in the

_____ _____ . Recent research studies have found that many adolescents do not feel _____ .

4. Adolescents, who believe that they are under constant scrutiny from nearly everyone, create for themselves an _____

_____ .

5. Piaget's term for the fourth stage of cognitive development is _____

_____ thought. Adolescent thinking _____ (is/is not) limited by personal experiences.

6. Piaget devised a number of famous tasks to demonstrate that formal operational adolescents imagine all possible _____ of a problem's solution in order to draw the appropriate _____ .

Briefly describe how children reason differently about the "balance beam" problem at ages 7, 10, and 13.

7. The kind of thinking in which adolescents consider unproven possibilities that are logical but not necessarily real is called _____ thought.

8. Adolescents become more capable of _____ reasoning—that is, they can begin with an abstract idea or _____ and then use _____ to draw specific _____ . This type of reasoning is a hallmark of formal operational thought.

9. This kind of reasoning contrasts with reasoning that progresses from particulars to generalities, called _____ reasoning.

10. Most developmentalists _____ (agree/disagree) with Piaget that adolescent thought can be qualitatively different from children's thought. They disagree about whether the change in thinking is _____ (gradual/sudden), whether it results from _____ (sociocultural) or _____ (epigenetic) changes, and whether it occurs in every _____ , as Piaget thought.

11. The fact that adolescents can use _____-_____ reasoning does not necessarily mean that they do use it.

12. In addition to advances in the formal, logical, _____-_____ thinking described by Piaget, adolescents advance in their _____ cognition. Researchers believe that the adult brain has two distinct pathways, called _____-_____ networks.

13. The first mode of thinking, which begins with a prior _____ , is called _____ . The second mode, Piaget's formal hypothetical-deductive reasoning, is called _____ thought.

14. Although intuitive thinking generally is _____ and _____ , it is also often _____ (right/wrong).

15. The belief that if time or money has already been invested in something, then more time or money should be invested is called the _____ _____ _____ .

16. Generally, adolescents use their minds with more _____ than children do. With age, thinking becomes more _____ .

Teaching and Learning (pp. 401–412)

17. The period after primary education and before _____ education is called _____ education. With puberty coming _____ (earlier/later) than in years past, many intermediate _____ schools have been established to educate sixth-graders.

18. During the middle school years, academic achievement often _____ (slows down/speeds up). In addition, behavioral problems become _____ (more/less) common.

19. The "digital divide" that once separated _____ from _____ and _____ from _____ has been bridged. In the United States today, the greatest divide, in terms of technology use, is _____ .

20. One potential danger of the use of computers in education is that teenagers may use technology to distance themselves from _____ .

21. The first year of a new school often correlates with increased _____ , decreased _____ , and the onset of _____ .

22. The curriculum prescribed by a school's educational leaders is called its _____ curriculum. The curriculum that is actually offered is called the _____ curriculum, and the learning that actually occurs is called the _____ curriculum.

23. By high school, curriculum and teaching style are often quite _____ and _____ . Most academic subjects emphasize _____ .

24. Another feature of the secondary school environment is _____-_____

testing, so-called because the consequences of failing are so severe. Whenever this type of testing is a requisite for graduation, there is a potential unintended consequence of more

_____ .

25. A second problem with the high school environment involves student _____ ; many adolescents express _____ and unhappiness with school.

26. Adolescents are more likely to be engaged with school if the school is _____ (small/large). Also, adolescents who are active in school _____ and _____ are more likely to graduate and go to college.

27. The same practices that foster motivation and education can also prevent _____ .

Progress Test 1

Multiple-Choice Questions

Circle your answers to the following questions and check them with the answers beginning on page 227. If your answer is incorrect, read the explanation for why it is incorrect and then consult the appropriate pages of the text (in parentheses following the correct answer).

1. Many psychologists consider the distinguishing feature of adolescent thought to be the ability to think in terms of:
   a. moral issues.
   b. concrete operations.
   c. possibility, not just reality.
   d. logical principles.

2. Piaget's last stage of cognitive development is:
   a. formal operational thought.
   b. concrete operational thought.
   c. universal ethical principles.
   d. symbolic thought.

3. The sunk cost fallacy is the mistaken assumption that
   a. because one has already spent time on something, one should spend more.
   b. analytical thinking works in all situations.
   c. intuitive thinking is generally best.
   d. emotional thinking is sometimes better.

4. The adolescent who takes risks and feels immune to the laws of mortality is showing evidence of the:
   a. invincibility fable.   c. imaginary audience.
   b. sunk cost fallacy.   d. death instinct.

5. Imaginary audiences and invincibility fables are expressions of adolescent:
   a. morality.   c. decision making.
   b. thinking games.   d. egocentrism.

6. The typical adolescent is:
   a. tough-minded.
   b. indifferent to public opinion.
   c. self-absorbed and hypersensitive to criticism.
   d. all of the above.

7. When adolescents enter middle school, many:
   a. experience a drop in their academic performance.
   b. show increased behavioral problems.
   c. lose connections to teachers.
   d. experience all of the above.

8. The psychologist who first described adolescent egocentrism is:
   a. Jean Piaget.
   b. David Elkind.
   c. Lev Vygotsky.
   d. Noam Chomsky.

9. Thinking that begins with a general premise and then draws logical conclusions from it is called:
   a. inductive reasoning.
   b. deductive reasoning.
   c. intuitive thinking.
   d. hypothetical reasoning.

10. Serious reflection on important issues is a wrenching process for many adolescents because of their newfound ability to reason:
    a. inductively.   c. hypothetically.
    b. deductively.   d. symbolically.

11. Hypothetical-deductive thinking is to contextualized thinking as:
    a. rational analysis is to intuitive thought.
    b. intuitive thought is to rational analysis.
    c. experiential thinking is to intuitive reasoning.
    d. intuitive thinking is to analytical reasoning.

12. Many adolescents seem to believe that *their* love-making will not lead to pregnancy. This belief is an expression of the:
   a. sunk cost fallacy.   c. imaginary audience.
   b. invincibility fable.   d. "game of thinking."

13. During middle school, aggressive children are often:
   a. unpopular.
   b. popular.
   c. boys.
   d. girls.

14. One problem with many high schools is that the formal curriculum ignores the fact that adolescents thrive on:
   a. formal operational thinking.
   b. intellectual challenges that require social interaction.
   c. inductive reasoning.
   d. deductive reasoning.

15. (Thinking Like a Scientist) A recent research study investigating teenage religion found that:
   a. most adolescents did not feel close to God.
   b. most adolescents identified with the same tradition as their parents.
   c. few respondents claimed that their beliefs were important to their daily life.
   d. faith was generally not viewed as a personal tool to be used in times of difficulty.

True or False Items

Write T (*true*) or F (*false*) on the line in front of each statement.

_____ 1. The appropriateness of the typical high school's high-stakes testing environment has been questioned, especially for low-income students.
_____ 2. Adolescents are generally better able than younger children at recognizing the sunk cost fallacy.
_____ 3. Adolescents' egos sometimes seem to overwhelm logic.
_____ 4. When high-stakes tests are a requisite for graduation, there is a potential consequence of more high school dropouts.
_____ 5. Adolescents often create an imaginary audience as they envision how others will react to their appearance and behavior.
_____ 6. Thinking reaches heightened self-consciousness at puberty.
_____ 7. Adolescent egocentrism is always irrational.

_____ 8. Inductive reasoning is a hallmark of formal operational thought.
_____ 9. Academic achievement often slows down during the middle school years.
_____ 10. The brain has two distinct processing networks.

Progress Test 2

Progress Test 2 should be completed during a final chapter review. Answer the following questions after you thoroughly understand the correct answers for the Chapter Review and Progress Test 1.

Multiple-Choice Questions

1. Adolescents who fall prey to the invincibility fable may be more likely to:
   a. engage in risky behaviors.
   b. suffer from depression.
   c. have low self-esteem.
   d. drop out of school.

2. Thinking that extrapolates from a specific experience to form a general premise is called:
   a. inductive reasoning.
   b. deductive reasoning.
   c. intuitive thinking.
   d. hypothetical reasoning.

3. Education during grades 7 through 12 is generally called:
   a. primary education
   b. secondary education
   c. tertiary education
   d. analytical education.

4. When young people overestimate their significance to others, they are displaying:
   a. concrete operational thought.
   b. adolescent egocentrism.
   c. a lack of cognitive growth.
   d. immoral development.

5. The imaginary audience refers to adolescents imagining that:
   a. they are immune to the dangers of risky behaviors.
   b. they are always being scrutinized by others.
   c. their own lives are unique, heroic, or even legendary.
   d. the world revolves around their actions.

6. The typical high school environment:
   a. limits social interaction.
   b. does not meet the cognitive needs of the typical adolescent.
   c. emphasizes formal operational thought
   d. is described by all of the above.

7. As compared to elementary schools, most middle schools exhibit all of the following *except*:
   a. a more flexible approach to education.
   b. intensified competition.
   c. inappropriate academic standards.
   d. less individualized attention.

8. Which of the following is true regarding experiential thinking?
   a. It does not advance significantly in most people until adulthood.
   b. It is slower than formal operational thinking.
   c. It is quicker and more powerful than formal operational thinking.
   d. It often deteriorates during early adolescence.

9. In explaining adolescent advances in thinking, sociocultural theorists emphasize:
   a. the sudden change that occurs.
   b. underlying biological changes.
   c. the context in which these changes occur.
   d. the gradual emergence of changes.

10. Analytic thinking is to _____ thinking as emotional force is to _____ thinking.
    a. intuitive; egocentric
    b. egocentric; intuitive
    c. formal; intuitive
    d. intuitive; formal

11. One of the hallmarks of formal operational thought is:
    a. egocentrism.   c. symbolic thinking.
    b. deductive reasoning. d. all of the above.

12. Analytic thinking and experiential thinking:
    a. both use the same neural pathways in the brain.
    b. are really the same type of information processing.
    c. both improve during adolescence.
    d. are characterized by all of the above.

13. The pathways that form the brain's dual-processing networks involve the:
    a. hypothalamus and the amygdala.
    b. cerebellum and the corpus callosum.
    c. prefrontal cortex and the limbic system.
    d. left and right cerebral hemispheres.

14. In the United States, the greatest divide between Internet users and nonusers is now:
    a. gender.   c. ethnicity.
    b. age.   d. income.

15. To avoid a mismatch between its formal curriculum and the needs of adolescents, a middle school should:
    a. minimize group interaction.
    b. discourage role-playing in the classroom.
    c. establish the same goals for every student.
    d. treat students as individual learners.

Matching Items

Match each term or concept with its corresponding description or definition.

Terms or Concepts

_____ **1.** invincibility fable
_____ **2.** imaginary audience
_____ **3.** high-stakes test
_____ **4.** hypothetical thought
_____ **5.** deductive reasoning
_____ **6.** inductive reasoning
_____ **7.** formal operational thought
_____ **8.** sunk cost fallacy
_____ **9.** dual-process model
_____ **10.** adolescent egocentrism

Descriptions or Definitions

a. the tendency of adolescents to focus on themselves to the exclusion of others
b. adolescents feel immune to the consequences of dangerous behavior
c. mistaken belief that if a person has already spent time or money on something, he or she should continue to do so
d. the idea held by many adolescents that others are intensely interested in them, especially in their appearance and behavior
e. the idea that there are two thinking networks in the brain
f. reasoning about propositions that may or may not reflect reality
g. the last stage of cognitive development, according to Piaget
h. thinking that moves from premise to conclusion
i. thinking that moves from a specific experience to a general premise
j. an evaluation that is critical in determining success or failure

Developmental Psychology Applied

Answer these questions the day before an exam as a final check on your understanding of the chapter's terms and concepts.

1. Summarizing her presentation on the mismatch between the needs of adolescents and the traditional structure of their schools, Megan notes that:
   a. most high schools feature intensified competition.
   b. the curriculum of most high schools emphasizes formal operational thinking.
   c. the academic standards of most schools do not reflect adolescents' needs.
   d. all of the above are true.

2. An experimenter hides a ball in her hand and says, "The ball in my hand is either red or it is not red." Most preadolescent children say:
   a. the statement is true.
   b. the statement is false.
   c. they cannot tell if the statement is true or false.
   d. they do not understand what the experimenter means.

3. Fourteen-year-old Monica is very idealistic and often develops crushes on people she doesn't even know. This reflects her newly developed cognitive ability to:
   a. deal simultaneously with two sides of an issue.
   b. take another person's viewpoint.
   c. imagine possible worlds and people.
   d. see herself as others see her.

4. Which of the following is the best example of the sunk cost fallacy?
   a. Adriana imagines that she is destined for a life of fame and fortune.
   b. Ben makes up stories about his experiences to impress his friends.
   c. Kalil continues to work on his old clunker of a car after hours of unsuccessful efforts to get it to run.
   d. Julio believes that every girl he meets is attracted to him.

5. Which of the following is the *best* example of the adolescent's ability to think hypothetically?
   a. Twelve-year-old Stanley feels that people are always watching him.
   b. Fourteen-year-old Mindy engages in many risky behaviors, reasoning that "nothing bad will happen to me."
   c. Fifteen-year-old Philip feels that no one understands his problems.
   d. Thirteen-year-old Josh delights in finding logical flaws in virtually everything his teachers and parents say.

6. Frustrated because of the dating curfew her parents have set, Melinda exclaims, "You just don't know how it feels to be in love!" Melinda's thinking demonstrates:
   a. the invincibility fable.
   b. the personal fable.
   c. the imaginary audience.
   d. adolescent egocentrism.

7. Compared to her 13-year-old brother, 17-year-old Yolanda is likely to:
   a. be more critical about herself.
   b. be more egocentric.
   c. have less confidence in her abilities.
   d. be more capable of reasoning hypothetically.

8. Nathan's fear that his friends will ridicule him because of a pimple that has appeared on his nose reflects a preoccupation with:
   a. the sunk cos fallacy.
   b. the invincibility fable.
   c. an imaginary audience.
   d. preconventional reasoning.

9. Malcolm, a middle schooler who lately is very sensitive to the criticism of others, feels significantly less motivated and capable than when he was in elementary school. Malcolm is probably:
   a. experiencing a sense of vulnerability that is common in adolescents.
   b. a lower-track student.
   c. a student in a school that emphasizes rigid routines.
   d. all of the above.

10. The reasoning behind the conclusion, "if it waddles like a duck and quacks like a duck, then it must be a duck," is called:
    a. experiential thinking.
    b. contextualized thinking.
    c. inductive reasoning.
    d. deductive reasoning.

11. Concluding her presentation on academic achievement during adolescence, LaToya notes that the "low ebb" of learning is the:
    a. last year of primary education.
    b. first year of tertiary education.
    c. first year of middle school.
    d. last year of middle school.

12. Which of the following is an example of deductive reasoning?
    a. Alonza is too lazy to look up an unfamiliar word he encounters while reading.
    b. Brittany loves to reason from clues to figure out "whodunit" crime mysteries.
    c. Morgan, who has enjoyed unscrambling anagrams for years, prefers to follow his hunches rather than systematically evaluate letter combinations.
    d. When taking multiple-choice tests, Trevor carefully considers every possible answer before choosing one.

13. After hearing that an unusually aggressive child has been in full-time day care since he was 1 year old, 16-year-old Keenan concludes that nonparental care leads to behavior problems. Keenan's conclusion is an example of:
    a. inductive reasoning.
    b. deductive reasoning.
    c. hypothetical thinking.
    d. adolescent egocentrism.

14. (Issues and Applications) After studying the results of the Programme for International Student Assessment, Professor Martin is concerned about the performance of students in the United States, which fell below the international average in:
    a. experiential thinking.
    b. intuitive thinking.
    c. problem solving.
    d. all of the above.

15. The dangers of adolescents' increasing use of technology include:
    a. cyberbullying.
    b. distancing from adults.
    c. potential to push them toward risk.
    d. all of the above.

Key Terms

Using your own words, write a brief definition or explanation of each of the following terms on a separate piece of paper.

1. adolescent egocentrism
2. invincibility fable
3. imaginary audience
4. formal operational thought
5. hypothetical thought
6. deductive reasoning
7. inductive reasoning
8. dual-process model
9. intuitive thought
10. analytic thought
11. sunk cost fallacy
12. secondary education
13. middle school
14. high-stakes test

ANSWERS
CHAPTER REVIEW

1. ego; logic; emotion
2. adolescent egocentrism
3. invincibility fable; invincible
4. imaginary audience
5. formal operational; is not
6. determinants; conclusions

Preschoolers have no understanding of how to solve the problem. By age 7, children understand balancing the weights but don't know that distance from the center is also a factor. By age 10, they understand the concepts but are unable to coordinate them. By ages 13 or 14, they are able to solve the problem.

7. hypothetical
8. deductive; premise; logic; conclusions
9. inductive
10. agree; sudden; context; biological; domain
11. hypothetical-deductive
12. hypothetical-deductive; intuitive; dual-processing
13. belief or assumption; intuitive (or contextualized **(per text)** or experiential); analytic

14. quick; powerful; wrong
15. sunk cost fallacy
16. economy; efficient
17. tertiary; secondary; earlier
18. slows down; more
19. boys; girls; rich; poor; age
20. adults
21. bullying; achievement; depression and eating disorders
22. intended; implemented; attained
23. analytic; abstract; logic
24. high-stakes; dropouts
25. motivation; boredom
26. small; clubs; athletics
27. violence

PROGRESS TEST 1
Multiple-Choice Questions

1. **c.** is the answer. (p. 396)
   a. Although moral reasoning becomes much deeper during adolescence, it is not limited to this stage of development.
   b. & d. Concrete operational thought, which *is* logical, is the distinguishing feature of childhood thinking.
2. **a.** is the answer. (p. 395)
   b. In Piaget's theory, this stage precedes formal operational thought.
   c. & d. These are not stages in Piaget's theory.
3. **a.** is the answer. (p. 399)
4. **a.** is the answer. (p. 392)
   b. This concept, which is not discussed in the text, refers to adolescents' tendency to imagine their own lives as unique, heroic, or even legendary.
   c. This refers to adolescents' tendency to fantasize about how others will react to their appearance and behavior.
   d. This is a concept in Freud's theory.
5. **d.** is the answer. These thought processes are manifestations of adolescents' tendency to see themselves as being much more central and important to the social scene than they really are. (pp. 391–394)
6. **c.** is the answer. (pp. 391–392)
7. **d.** is the answer. (p. 402)
8. **b.** is the answer. (p. 392)

9. b. is the answer. (p. 397)

a. Inductive reasoning moves from specific facts to a general conclusion.

c. By its very nature, intuitive thinking does not move logically either from a general conclusion to specific facts or from specific facts to a general conclusion.

d. Hypothetical reasoning involves thinking about possibilities rather than facts.

10. c. is the answer. (pp. 396–397)

11. a. is the answer. (p. 398)

c. Contextualized thinking is both experiential *and* intuitive.

12. b. is the answer. (p. 392)

a. The sunk cost fallacy is the mistaken belief that, because one has invested time and effort in something, one should continue doing so.

d. This concept was not discussed in the text.

c. This refers to adolescents' tendency to fantasize about how others will react to their appearance and behavior.

13. b. is the answer. (p. 402)

c. & d. Gender in relation to middle school aggression was not discussed in the text.

14. b. is the answer. (p. 411)

a., c., & d. Adolescents are more likely to thrive on *intuitive* thinking.

15. b. is the answer. (pp. 400–401)

True or False Items

1. T (pp. 409–410)

2. T (p. 399)

3. T (p. 391)

4. T (p. 410)

5. T (p. 393)

6. T (pp. 391–392)

7. F Adolescents *do* judge each other. (p. 394)

8. F Deductive reasoning is a hallmark of formal operational thought. (p. 397)

9. T (p. 402)

10. T (p. 398)

PROGRESS TEST 2

Multiple-Choice Questions

1. a. is the answer. (p. 392)

b., c., & d. The invincibility fable leads some teens to believe that they are immune to the dan-gers of risky behaviors; it is not necessarily linked to depression, low self-esteem, or the likelihood that an individual will drop out of school.

2. a. is the answer. (p. 397)

b. Deductive reasoning begins with a general premise and then draws logical conclusions from it.

c. By its very nature, intuitive thinking does not move logically either from a general conclusion to specific facts or from specific facts to a general conclusion.

d. Hypothetical reasoning involves thinking about possibilities rather than facts.

3. b. is the answer. (p. 401)

4. b. is the answer. (p. 392)

5. b. is the answer. (p. 393)

a. This describes the invincibility fable.

c. This describes the personal fable, which is not discussed in the chapter.

d. This describes adolescent egocentrism in general.

6. d. is the answer. (p. 411)

7. a. is the answer. (pp. 402–403)

8. c. is the answer. (p. 398)

9. c. is the answer. (p. 397)

a. This reflects Piaget's viewpoint.

b. This reflects epigenetic theory.

d. This reflects information-processing theory.

10. c. is the answer. (p. 398)

11. b. is the answer. (p. 397)

12. c. is the answer. (p. 399)

13. c. is the answer. (p. 398)

14. b. is the answer. (p. 404)

15. d. is the answer. (pp. 403–404)

Matching Items

1. b (p. 392)   **5.** h (p. 397)   **9.** e (p. 398)
2. d (p. 393)   **6.** i (p. 397)   **10.** a (p. 392)
3. j (p. 409)   **7.** g (p. 395)
4. f (p. 396)   **8.** c (p. 399)

DEVELOPMENTAL PSYCHOLOGY APPLIED

1. d. is the answer. (pp. 407, 409–410)

2. c. is the answer. Although this statement is logi-cally verifiable, preadolescents who lack formal operational thought cannot prove or disprove it. (p. 396)

3. **c.** is the answer. (p. 392)

4. **c.** is the answer. (p. 399)

   b. & d. These behaviors are more indicative of a preoccupation with the imaginary audience.

   a. This is an example of a personal fable, which is not discussed in this chapter.

5. **d.** is the answer. (pp. 396–397)

   a. This is an example of the imaginary audience.

   b. This is an example of the invincibility fable.

   c. This is an example of adolescent egocentrism.

6. **d.** is the answer. (pp. 391–392)

7. **d.** is the answer. (p. 396)

8. **c.** is the answer. (p. 393)

   a. In this fable, which is not discussed in the text, adolescents see themselves destined for fame and fortune.

   b. In this fable, young people feel that they are somehow immune to the consequences of common dangers.

   d. This is a stage of moral reasoning in Kohlberg's theory, as discussed in Chapter 13.

9. **a.** is the answer. (p. 403)

10. **c.** is the answer. (p. 397)

    a. & b. Experiential (or contextualized) thinking is more intuitive and less logical.

    d. Deductive thinking moves from a general conclusion to specific principles; this example moves from particulars to a general conclusion.

11. **c.** is the answer. (p. 402)

12. **b.** is the answer. Solving mysteries is an example of deductive reasoning. (p. 397)

    a. This is simply laziness.

    c. This is an example of using insight.

    d. This is an example of analytic thinking.

13. **a.** is the answer. (p. 397)

    b. Keenan is reasoning from the specific to the general, rather than vice versa.

    c. Keenan is thinking about an actual observation, rather than a hypothetical possibility.

    d. Keenan's reasoning is focused outside himself, rather than being self-centered.

14. **c.** is the answer. (pp. 407–408)

15. **d.** is the answer. (p. 405)

KEY TERMS

1. **Adolescent egocentrism** refers to the tendency of adolescents to see themselves as much more socially significant than they actually are. (p. 392)

2. Adolescents who experience the **invincibility fable** feel that they are immune to the dangers of risky behaviors. (p. 392)

3. Adolescents often create an **imaginary audience** for themselves, because they assume that others are as intensely interested in them as they themselves are. (p. 393)

4. In Piaget's theory, the last stage of cognitive development, which arises from a combination of maturation and experience, is called **formal operational thought.** A hallmark of formal operational thinking is more systematic logic and the ability to think about abstract ideas. (p. 395)

5. **Hypothetical thought** involves reasoning about propositions and possibilities that may not reflect reality. (p. 396)

6. **Deductive reasoning** is thinking that moves from the general to the specific, or from a premise to a logical conclusion. (p. 397)

7. **Inductive reasoning** is thinking that moves from one or more specific experiences or facts to a general conclusion. (p. 397)

8. The **dual-process model** is the idea that there are two thinking networks in the human brain, one for emotional thinking and one for analytical thinking. (p. 398)

9. **Intuitive thought** is that which arises from a hunch or emotion, often triggered by past experiences, cultural assumptions, and sudden impulse. (p. 398)

10. **Analytic thought** is logical thinking that arises from rational analysis and the systematic evaluation of consequences and possibilities. (p. 398)

11. The **sunk cost fallacy** is the mistaken belief that, because one has already invested time and effort in something, one should continue doing so. (p. 399)

12. **Secondary education** is education that follows primary education, usually occurring from about age 12 to 18. (p. 401)

13. **Middle school** refers to the years of school between elementary school and high school. (p. 402)

14. **High-stakes tests** are exams and other forms of evaluation that are critical in determining a person's success or failure. (p. 409)

16

Adolescence: Psychosocial Development

Chapter Overview

Chapter 16 focuses on the adolescent's psychosocial development. The first section explores the paths that lead to the formation of identity, which is required for the attainment of adult status and maturity. The next section examines the influences of family and friends on adolescent psychosocial development, including the development of romantic relationships and sexual activity. Depression, self-destruction, and suicide—the most perplexing problems of adolescence—are then explored. The special problems posed by adolescent lawbreaking are discussed, and suggestions for alleviating or treating these problems are given. The chapter concludes with the message that although no other period of life is characterized by so many changes in the three domains of development, for most young people the teenage years are happy ones. Furthermore, serious problems in adolescence do not necessarily lead to lifelong problems.

NOTE: Answer guidelines for all Chapter 16 questions begin on page 240.

Guided Study

The text chapter should be studied one section at a time. Before you read, preview each section by skimming it, noting headings and boldface items. Then read the appropriate section objectives from the following outline. Keep these objectives in mind and, as you read the chapter section, search for the information that will enable you to meet each objective. Once you have finished a section, write out answers for its objectives.

Identity (pp. 415–419)

1. Describe the development of identity during adolescence, and identify the four major identity statuses.

2. Discuss the problems encountered in the formation of religious, gender, ethnic, and vocational identities.

Relationships (pp. 419–427)

3. Describe parental influence on identity formation, including the effect of parent–adolescent conflict and other aspects of parent–teen relationships.

4. Explain the constructive functions of peer relationships and close friendships during adolescence and the unique challenges faced by immigrants.

Sexuality (pp. 427–433)

5. Discuss the development of male–female relationships during adolescence, including the challenges faced by gay and lesbian adolescents.

6. Discuss the various influences on teen sexual behavior, including peers, parents, and schools, and describe current trends in teen sexual behavior. **OK?**

Sadness and Anger (pp. 433–441)

7. Discuss adolescent suicide, noting contributing factors and gender, ethnic, and national variations.

8. Discuss delinquency among adolescents today, noting its incidence and prevalence, causes, and best approaches for prevention or treatment.

Chapter Review

When you have finished reading the chapter, work through the material that follows to review it. Complete the sentences and answer the questions. As you proceed, evaluate your performance for each section by consulting the answers beginning on page 240. Do not continue with the next section until you understand each answer. If you need to, review or reread the appropriate section in the textbook before continuing.

Identity (pp. 415–419)

1. The momentous changes that occur during the teen years challenge adolescents to find their own _____ .

2. According to Erikson, the challenge of adolescence is _____ _____ _____ .

3. The ultimate goal of adolescence is to establish a new identity that involves both rejection and acceptance of childhood values; this is called _____ _____ .

4. The young person who has few commitments to goals or values and is apathetic about defining his or her identity is experiencing _____ _____ .

5. The young person who prematurely accepts earlier roles and parental values without exploring alternatives or truly forging a unique identity is experiencing identity _____ .

6. A time-out period during which a young person experiments with different identities, postponing important choices, is called an identity _____ . An obvious institutional

example of this in North America is attending _____ .

7. Erikson described four aspects of identity: _____ , _____ , _____ , and _____ .

8. Today, a person's identification as either male or female is called _____ _____ , which usually leads to a gender _____ and a sexual _____ .

9. A person's sexual attraction to people of the same sex, other sex, or both sexes constitutes his or her _____ _____ .

10. Since Erikson's time, _____ identity has become more important than _____ identity. The more appropriate term has become _____ _____ .

11. Employment of 20 or more hours during adolescence is likely to impede _____ formation, _____ relationships, _____ achievement, and _____ success.

Relationships (pp. 419–427)

12. Adolescence is often characterized as a time of waning adult influence; this _____ (is/is not) necessarily true. An important aspect of healthy development is supportive relationships with _____ adults.

13. Parent–adolescent conflict peaks during _____ _____ and is particularly notable with _____ (mothers/fathers) and their _____ (sons/daughters). This conflict often involves _____ , which refers to repeated, petty arguments about daily habits.

14. By age 18, increased _____ maturity and reduced _____ bring some renewed appreciation for parents.

15. There _____ (are/are not) cultural differences in parent–adolescent relationships. Some cultures value _____ _____ above all else and avoid

conflict. Thus, the very idea of adolescent rebellion may be a _____ construction in Western culture.

16. Four other elements of parent–teen relationships that have been heavily researched include _____ , _____ , _____ , and _____ .

17. In terms of family control, a powerful deterrent to delinquency, risky sex, and drug abuse is _____ _____ .

Too much interference, however, may contribute to adolescent _____ . Particularly harmful to teens are threats to withdraw love and support, or _____ _____ .

18. Adolescents group themselves into clusters of close friends, called _____ , and larger groups, or _____ , who share common interests.

19. Social pressure to conform to peer activities is called _____ _____ . This pressure is _____ as often as it is _____ . Destructive peer support is called _____ _____ .

20. Two helpful concepts in understanding the influence of peers are _____ , meaning that peers _____ one another; and _____ , referring to the fact that peers encourage one another to do things that _____ .

21. Friends play a special role for adolescents whose parents are _____ . They are particularly important in protecting the adolescent's _____ , especially if the adolescent is of a(n) _____ background.

Sexuality (pp. 427–433)

Briefly outline the four-stage progression of heterosexual involvement.

22. Culture _____ (affects/does not affect) the _____ and _____ of these stages, but the basic _____ seems to be based on _____ factors. In modern developed nations, each stage typically lasts _____ (how long?).

23. Early pairing, especially when it decreases _____-_____ friendships, signifies _____ trouble.

24. For gay and lesbian adolescents, added complications usually _____ (slow down/speed up) romantic attachments.

25. Adolescents who discuss sex openly with their parents take fewer _____ , avoid _____ , and _____ .

26. Most American adults believe that high schools _____ (should/should not) teach sex education.

27. Sexual activity among adolescents _____ (varies/does not vary) from nation to nation.

28. The teen birth rate is _____ (increasing/decreasing). At the same time, contraceptive use has _____ (increased/decreased).

29. In the United Statues, the rate of teen abortions has _____ (increased/decreased) in recent years.

Sadness and Anger (pp. 433–441)

30. Adolescents who have one serious problem _____ (often have/do not usually have) others.

31. The situation in which a person has two or more unrelated illnesses or disorders at the same time is _____ .

32. Cross-sequential research studies show that, from late childhood through adolescence, people generally feel _____ (more/less) competent, on average, each year in most areas of their lives.

33. Clinical depression _____ (increases/decreases) at puberty, especially among _____ (males/females). One explanation is that talking about and mentally replaying past experiences, which is called _____ , is more common among _____ (males/females).

34. Thinking about committing suicide, called _____ _____ , is _____ (common/relatively rare) among high school students.

35. Adolescents are _____ (more/less) likely to kill themselves than adults are.

36. Most suicide attempts in adolescence _____ (do/do not) result in death. A deliberate act of self-destruction that does not result in death is called a _____ .

37. List four factors that affect whether thinking about suicide leads to a self-destructive act or to death.

    a. _____

    b. _____

    c. _____

    d. _____

38. The rate of suicide is higher for adolescent _____ (males/females). The rate of parasuicide is higher for _____ (males/females).

39. Around the world, cultural differences in the rates of suicidal ideation and completion _____ (are/are not) apparent.

40. When a town or school sentimentalizes the "tragic end" of a teen suicide, the publicity can trigger _____ _____ .

(Table 16.2) Briefly describe ethnic differences in suicide rates in the United States.

41. Psychologists influenced by the _____ perspective believe that adolescent rebellion and defiance are normal.

42. Arrests rise rapidly worldwide at about age _____ , peak at age _____ , and then decline slowly. Although statistics indicate that the _____ (incidence/ prevalence) of arrests is highest among this age group, they do not reveal how widespread, or _____ , lawbreaking is among this age group.

Briefly describe data on gender and ethnic differences in adolescent arrests.

43. Developmentalists have found that it _____ (is/is not) currently possible to distinguish children who actually will become career criminals.

List several of the childhood factors that correlate with delinquency.

44. Experts find it useful to distinguish _____-_____ offenders, whose criminal activity stops by age 21, from _____-_____-_____ offenders, who become career criminals.

45. One innovative strategy for helping delinquents is _____ _____ _____ , in which violent youth are assigned to _____ families trained to teach anger management, school achievement, and responsible self-care.

Progress Test 1

Multiple-Choice Questions

Circle your answers to the following questions and check them with the answers beginning on page 241. If your answer is incorrect, read the explanation for why it is incorrect and then consult the appropriate pages of the text (in parentheses following the correct answer).

1. According to Erikson, the primary task of adolescence is that of establishing:
   a. basic trust.   **c.** intimacy.
   b. an identity.   **d.** integrity.

2. According to developmentalists who study identity formation, foreclosure involves:
   a. accepting an identity prematurely, without exploration.
   b. taking time off from school, work, and other commitments.
   c. opposing parental values.
   d. failing to commit oneself to a vocational goal.

3. A large group of adolescents who share common interests is a:
   a. clique.   **c.** crowd.
   b. peer group.   **d.** cluster.

4. The main sources of emotional support for most young people who are establishing independence from their parents are:
   a. older adolescents of the opposite sex.
   b. older siblings.
   c. teachers.
   d. peer groups.

5. For members of minority ethnic groups, identity achievement may be particularly complicated because:
   a. their cultural ideal clashes with the Western emphasis on adolescent self-determination.
   b. peers, themselves torn by similar conflicts, can be very critical.
   c. parents and other relatives tend to emphasize ethnicity and expect teens to honor their roots.
   d. of all of the above reasons.

6. In a crime-ridden neighborhood, parents can protect their adolescents by keeping close watch over activities, friends, and so on. This practice is called:
   a. a moratorium.   **c.** peer screening.
   b. foreclosure.   **d.** parental monitoring.

7. Conflict between adolescent girls and their mothers is most likely to involve:
   a. bickering over hair, neatness, and other daily habits.
   b. political, religious, and moral issues.
   c. peer relationships and friendships.
   d. relationships with boys.

8. Destructive peer support in which one adolescent shows another how to rebel against authority is called:
   a. peer pressure.
   b. deviancy training.
   c. peer selection.
   d. peer facilitation.

9. Adolescents who discuss sex openly with their parents:
   a. take fewer risks.
   b. avoid peer pressure to have unwanted sex.
   c. believe that their parents provide useful information.
   d. are characterized by all of the above.

10. In a recent Disney movie, two high school students encourage each other to participate in the school musical. This type of peer influence is called.
    a. peer pressure.
    b. deviancy training.
    c. selection.
    d. peer facilitation.

11. If the vast majority of cases of a certain crime are committed by a small number of repeat offenders, this would indicate that the crime's:
    a. incidence is less than its prevalence.
    b. incidence is greater than its prevalence.
    c. incidence and prevalence are about equal.
    d. incidence and prevalence are impossible to calculate.

12. Thirteen-year-old Adam, who never has doubted his faith, identifies himself as an orthodox member of a particular religious group. A developmentalist would probably say that Adam's religious identity is:
    a. achieved.
    b. foreclosed.
    c. in moratorium.
    d. oppositional in nature.

13. The early predictors of life-course-persistent offenders include all of the following *except*:
    a. short attention span.
    b. hyperactivity.
    c. high intelligence.
    d. neurological impairment.

14. Regarding gender differences in self-destructive acts, the rate of parasuicide is _____ and the rate of suicide is _____ .
    a. higher in males; higher in females
    b. higher in females; higher in males
    c. the same in males and females; higher in males
    d. the same in males and females; higher in females

15. Conflict between parents and adolescent offspring is:
    a. most likely to involve fathers and their early-maturing offspring.
    b. more frequent in single-parent homes.
    c. more likely between daughters and their mothers.
    d. likely in all of the above situations.

True or False Items

Write T (*true*) or F (*false*) on the line in front of each statement.

_____ 1. Identity achievement before age 18 is elusive.

_____ 2. Most adolescents have political views and educational values that are markedly different from those of their parents.

_____ 3. Peer pressure is inherently destructive to the adolescent seeking an identity.

_____ 4. For most adolescents, group socializing and dating precede the establishment of true intimacy with one member of the opposite sex.

_____ 5. Worldwide, arrests peak at age 16 and then decline slowly with every decade.

_____ 6. Abstinence-only sex education has led to decreased rates of adolescent sex.

_____ 7. Most adolescents break many minor laws.

_____ 8. In finding themselves, teens try to find an identity that is stable, consistent, and mature.

_____ 9. From ages 6 to 18, children feel more competent, on average, each year in most areas of their lives.

_____ **10.** Increased accessibility of guns is a factor in the increased rate of youth suicide in the United States.

Progress Test 2

Progress Test 2 should be completed during a final chapter review. Answer the following questions after you thoroughly understand the correct answers for the Chapter Review and Progress Test 1.

Multiple-Choice Questions

1. Which of the following is *not* one of the arenas of identity formation in Erik Erikson's theory?
   a. religious
   b. sexual
   c. political
   d. social

2. Which of the following is true of gender identity?
   a. It is a person's self-definition as male or female.
   b. It always leads to sexual orientation.
   c. It is a person's biological male/female characteristics.
   d. It is established at birth.

3. Prevalence refers to:
   a. how often a particular behavior occurs.
   b. how widespread a particular behavior is.
   c. the simultaneous occurrence of two or more disorders.
   d. destructive peer pressure.

4. If the various cases of a certain crime are committed by many different offenders, this would indicate that the crime's:
   a. incidence is less than its prevalence.
   b. incidence is greater than its prevalence.
   c. incidence and prevalence are about equal.
   d. incidence and prevalence are impossible to calculate.

5. Thinking about committing suicide is called:
   a. cluster suicide.
   b. parasuicide.
   c. suicidal ideation.
   d. fratracide.

6. Which of the following was *not* noted in the text regarding peer relationships among gay and lesbian adolescents?
   a. Romantic attachments are usually slower to develop.
   b. In homophobic cultures, many gay teens try to conceal their homosexual feelings by becoming heterosexually involved.
   c. Many girls who will later identify themselves as lesbians are oblivious to these sexual urges as teens.
   d. Homosexual men report that they do not become aware of their interests until age 17.

7. The adolescent experiencing identity diffusion is typically:
   a. very apathetic.
   b. experimenting with alternative identities without trying to settle on any one.
   c. willing to accept parental values wholesale, without exploring alternatives.
   d. one who rebels against all forms of authority.

8. Gender identity refers to a person's:
   a. identification as being female or male.
   b. attraction toward a person of the same sex, the other sex, or both sexes.
   c. self-definition as a unique individual.
   d. self-definition in each of the above areas.

9. Crime statistics show that during adolescence:
   a. males and females are equally likely to be arrested.
   b. males are more likely to be arrested than females.
   c. females are more likely to be arrested than males.
   d. males commit more crimes than females but are less likely to be arrested.

10. Which of the following is the most common problem behavior among adolescents?
    a. pregnancy
    b. daily use of illegal drugs
    c. minor lawbreaking
    d. attempts at suicide

11. A time-out period during which a young person experiments with different identities, postponing important choices, is called a(n):
    a. identity foreclosure.
    b. negative identity.
    c. identity diffusion.
    d. identity moratorium.

12. Comorbidity is the situation in which:
    a. one adolescent encourages another to partici-
       pate in a dangerous activity.
    b. feelings of lethargy last two weeks or more.
    c. an overwhelming feeling of sadness disrupts a
       person's normal routine.
    d. two or more unrelated illnesses occur together
       at the same time.

13. Which of the following is *not* true regarding the
    rate of clinical depression among adolescents?
    a. At puberty the rate more than doubles.
    b. It affects a higher proportion of teenage boys
       than girls.
    c. Genetic vulnerability is a predictor of teenage
       depression.
    d. The adolescent's school setting is a factor.

14. Parent–teen conflict tends to center on issues
    related to:
    a. politics and religion.
    b. education.
    c. vacations.
    d. daily details, such as musical tastes.

15. According to a review of studies from various
    nations, suicidal ideation is:
    a. not as common among high school students
       as is popularly believed.
    b. more common among males than females.
    c. more common among females than among
       males.
    d. so common among high school students that
       it might be considered normal.

Matching Items

Match each term or concept with its corresponding
description or definition.

Terms or Concepts

_____ 1. identity
_____ 2. identity achievement
_____ 3. foreclosure
_____ 4. clique
_____ 5. identity diffusion
_____ 6. identity moratorium
_____ 7. peer selection
_____ 8. peer pressure
_____ 9. parental monitoring
_____ 10. parasuicide
_____ 11. cluster suicide

Descriptions or Definitions

a. premature identity formation
b. a group of suicides that occur in the same community, school, or time period
c. the adolescent has few commitments to goals or
   values
d. process by which adolescents choose their friends
   based on shared interests
e. self-destructive act that does not result in death
f. awareness of where children are and what they
   are doing
g. an individual's self-definition
h. a time-out period during which adolescents experiment with alternative identities
i. the adolescent establishes his or her own goals
   and values
j. encouragement to conform with one's friends in
   behavior, dress, and attitude
k. a cluster of close friends

Developmental Psychology Applied

Answer these questions the day before an exam as a final check on your understanding of the chapter's terms and concepts.

1. From childhood, Sharon thought she wanted to follow in her mother's footsteps and be a home-maker. Now, at age 40 with a home and family, she admits to herself that what she really wanted to be was a medical researcher. Erik Erikson would probably say that Sharon:
   a. adopted a negative identity when she was a child.
   b. experienced identity foreclosure at an early age.
   c. never progressed beyond the obvious identity diffusion she experienced as a child.
   d. took a moratorium from identity formation.

2. Eboni repeatedly thinks and talks about past experiences to the extent that her doctor believes it is contributing to her depression. Eboni's behavior is an example of:
   a. comorbidity.
   b. deviancy training.
   c. parasuicide.
   d. rumination.

3. Jennifer has a well-defined religious identity. This is true because she:
   a. self-identifies herself as a religious person.
   b. worships regularly.
   c. reads scripture.
   d. does all of the above.

4. In 1957, 6-year-old Raisel and her parents emigrated from Mexico to the United States. Because her parents hold to the values and customs of their native land, Raisel is likely to have:
   a. an easier time achieving her own unique identity.
   b. a more difficult time forging her identity.
   c. a greater span of time in which to forge her own identity.
   d. a shorter span of time in which to forge her identity.

5. Bill's parents insist on knowing the whereabouts and activities of their son at all times. Clearly, they are very good at:
   a. parental monitoring.
   b. deviancy training.
   c. peer facilitation.
   d. rumination.

6. In our society, obvious examples of institutionalized moratoria on identity formation are:
   a. the Boy Scouts and the Girl Scouts.
   b. college and the military.
   c. marriage and divorce.
   d. bar mitzvahs and baptisms.

7. First-time parents Norma and Norman are worried that, during adolescence, their healthy parental influence will be undone as their children are encouraged by peers to become sexually promiscuous, drug-addicted, or delinquent. Their wise neighbor, who is a developmental psychologist, tells them that:
   a. peers are constructive as often as they are destructive.
   b. research suggests that peers provide a negative influence in every major task of adolescence.
   c. only through authoritarian parenting can parents give children the skills they need to resist peer pressure.
   d. unless their children show early signs of learning difficulties or antisocial behavior, parental monitoring is unnecessary.

8. Padma's parents are concerned because their 14-year-old daughter has formed an early romantic relationship with a boy. You tell them:
   a. not to worry, because boys are more likely to say they have a girlfriend than vice versa.
   b. not to worry; healthy romances are a manifestation of good relationships with parents and peers.
   c. most romantic relationships last throughout high school.
   d. they should do everything they can to break up the relationship.

9. Principal Roberts, who wants to know how many new cases of staph infection occurred this year in the high school, is trying to determine the _____ of this condition.
   a. prevalence
   b. incidence
   c. range
   d. correlation

10. Jill, who has cut herself and engaged in other self-destructive acts, is receiving treatment for these acts of:
    a. suicideal ideation.
    b. comorbidity.
    c. parasuicide.
    d. rumination.

11. Statistically, the person *least* likely to commit a crime is a(n):
    a. African American or Hispanic adolescent.
    b. middle-class White male.
    c. White adolescent of any socioeconomic background.
    d. Asian American.

12. Ray endured severe child abuse, has difficulty controlling his emotions, and exhibits symptoms of autism. These factors would suggest that Ray is at high risk of:
    a. becoming an adolescent-limited offender.
    b. becoming a life-course-persistent offender.
    c. developing an antisocial personality.
    d. foreclosing his identity prematurely.

13. Carl is a typical 16-year-old adolescent who has no special problems. It is likely that Carl has:
    a. contemplated suicide.
    b. engaged in some minor illegal act.
    c. struggled with "who he is."
    d. done all of the above.

14. Statistically, who of the following is *most* likely to commit suicide?
    a. Micah, an African American female
    b. Yan, an Asian American male
    c. James, a American Indian male
    d. Alison, a European American female

15. Coming home from work, Malcolm hears a radio announcement warning parents to be alert for possible cluster suicide signs in their teenage children. What might have precipitated such an announcement?
    a. government statistics that suicide is on the rise
    b. the highly publicized suicide of a teen from a school in his town
    c. the recent crash of an airliner, killing all on board
    d. any of the above

Key Terms

Using your own words, write a brief definition or explanation of each of the following terms on a separate piece of paper.

1. identity
2. identity versus diffusion
3. identity achievement
4. identity diffusion
5. foreclosure
6. moratorium
7. gender identity
8. sexual orientation
9. bickering
10. parental monitoring
11. clique
12. crowd
13. peer pressure
14. deviancy training
15. peer selection
16. peer facilitation
17. comorbidity
18. clinical depression
19. rumination
20. suicidal ideation
21. parasuicide
22. cluster suicide
23. incidence
24. prevalence
25. life-course-persistent offender
26. adolescent-limited offender

ANSWERS

CHAPTER REVIEW

1. identity
2. identity versus diffusion
3. identity achievement
4. identity diffusion
5. foreclosure
6. moratorium; college
7. religion; sex; politics; vocation
8. gender identity; role; orientation
9. sexual orientation
10. ethnic; political; identity politics
11. identity; family; academic; career

12. is not; non-parent

13. early adolescence; mothers; daughters; bickering

14. emotional; egocentrism

15. are; family harmony; social

16. communication; support; connectedness; control

17. parental monitoring; depression; psychological control

18. cliques; crowds

19. peer pressure; constructive; destructive; deviancy training

20. selection; choose; facilitation; none of them would do alone

21. immigrants; self-esteem; Asian

The progression begins with groups of same-sex friends. Next, a loose, public association of a girls' group and a boys' group forms. Then, a smaller, mixed-sex group forms from the more advanced members of the larger association. Finally, more intimate couples peel off.

22. affects; timing; manifestations; sequence; genetic; several years

23. same-sex; social

24. slow down

25. risks; peer pressure to have sex when they do not want to; believe their parents provide useful information

26. should

27. varies

28. decreasing; increased

29. decreased

30. often have

31. comorbidity

32. less

33. increases; females; rumination; females

34. suicidal ideation; common

35. less

36. do not; parasuicide

37. a.   the availability of guns

    b.   the extent of parental supervision

    c.   availability of alcohol and other drugs

    d.   culture

38. males; females

39. are

40. cluster suicides

American Indian and Alaskan Native males have the highest rates, followed by European American males, Hispanic American males, American Indian females, African American males, Asian American males, and so on.

41. psychoanalytic

42. 12; 16; incidence; prevalent

Adolescent males are three times as likely to be arrested as females, and African American youth are three times as likely to be arrested as European Americans, who are three times as likely to be arrested as Asian Americans. However, confidential self-reports find much smaller gender and ethnic differences.

43. is

Among the factors are short attention span, severe child abuse, hyperactivity, inadequate emotional regulation, maternal cigarette smoking, slow language development, low intelligence, early and severe malnutrition, and autistic tendencies.

44. adolescent-limited; life-course-persistent

45. therapeutic foster care; foster

PROGRESS TEST 1

Multiple-Choice Questions

1. **b.** is the answer. (p. 415)

    a. According to Erikson, this is the crisis of infancy.

    c. & d. In Erikson's theory, these crises occur later in life.

2. **a.** is the answer. (p. 416)

    b. This describes an identity moratorium.

    c. This describes a negative identity.

    d. This describes identity diffusion.

3. **c.** is the answer. (p. 422)

4. **d.** is the answer. (p. 422)

5. **d.** is the answer. (pp. 418–419)

6. **d.** is the answer. (p. 421)

    a. A moratorium is a time-out during which adolescents experiment with different identities.

    b. Foreclosure refers to the premature establishment of identity.

    c. Peer screening is an aspect of parental monitoring, but it was not specifically discussed in the text.

7. **a.** is the answer. (p. 420)

8. **b.** is the answer. (p. 423)

9. **d.** is the answer. (p. 430)

10. **d.** is the answer. (p. 424)

11. **b.** is the answer. Incidence is how often a particular circumstance (such as lawbreaking) occurs;

prevalence is how widespread the circumstance is. A crime that is committed by only a few repeat offenders is not very prevalent in the population. (p. 438)

12. b. is the answer. Foreclosed members of a religious group have, like Adam, never really doubted. (p. 416)

   a. Because there is no evidence that Adam has asked the "hard questions" regarding his religious beliefs, a developmentalist would probably say that his religious identity is not achieved.

   c. Adam clearly does have a religious identity.

   d. There is no evidence that Adam's religious identity was formed in opposition to expectations.

13. c. is the answer. Life-course-persistent offenders tend to have low intelligence. (p. 440)

14. b. is the answer. (pp. 435–436)

15. c. is the answer. (p. 420)

   a. In fact, parent–child conflict is more likely to involve mothers and their daughters.

   b. The text did not compare the rate of conflict in two-parent and single-parent homes.

True or False Items

1. T (p. 419)
2. F   Parent–teen conflicts center on day-to-day details, not on politics or moral issues. (p. 420)
3. F   The opposite is just as likely to be true. (p. 423)
4. T (p. 427)
5. T (p. 438)
6. F   Researchers found no significant difference in rates of adolescent sex after abstinence-only sex education. (p. 431)
7. T (p. 439)
8. T (p. 416)
9. F   Just the opposite is true. (p. 433)
10. T (p. 436)

PROGRESS TEST 2

Multiple-Choice Questions

1. **d.** is the answer. (p. 416)
2. **a.** is the answer. (pp. 417–418)
3. **b.** is the answer. (p. 438)

   a. This is prevalence.

   c. This is comorbidity.

   d. This is deviancy training.

4. **c.** is the answer. (p. 438)

   a. This answer would have been correct if the question had stated, "If the majority of cases of a crime are committed by a small number of repeat offenders."

   b. Because it is simply the total number of cases of an event or circumstance (such as a crime), incidence cannot be less than prevalence.

5. **c.** is the answer. (p. 434)

6. **d.** is the answer. Homosexual men report that they become aware at age 11, but don't tell anyone until age 17. (p. 428)

7. **a.** is the answer. (p. 416)

   b. This describes an adolescent undergoing an identity moratorium.

   c. This describes identity foreclosure.

   d. This describes an adolescent who is adopting a negative identity.

8. **a.** is the answer. (p. 418)

   b. This refers to sexual orientation.

   c. This refers to identity in general.

9. **b.** is the answer. (p. 439)

10. **c.** is the answer. (p. 439)

11. **d.** is the answer. (p. 416)

   a. Identity foreclosure occurs when the adolescent prematurely adopts an identity, without fully exploring alternatives.

   b. Adolescents who adopt an identity that is opposite to the one they are expected to develop have taken on a negative identity.

   c. Identity diffusion occurs when the adolescent is apathetic and has few commitments to goals or values.

12. **d.** is the answer. (p. 433)

13. **b.** is the answer. (p. 433)

14. **d.** is the answer. (p. 420)

   a., b., & c. In fact, on these issues parents and teenagers tend to show substantial *agreement*.

15. **d.** is the answer. (p. 434)

Matching Items

1. g (p. 415)	5. c (p. 416)	9. f (p. 421)
2. i (p. 416)	6. h (p. 416)	10. e (p. 434)
3. a (p. 416)	7. d (p. 423)	11. b (p. 436)
4. k (p. 422)	8. j (p. 423)	

DEVELOPMENTAL PSYCHOLOGY APPLIED

1. **b.** is the answer. Apparently, Sharon never explored alternatives or truly forged a unique personal identity. (p. 416)

   a. Individuals who rebel by adopting an identity that is the opposite of the one they are expected to adopt have taken on a negative identity.

   c. Individuals who experience identity diffusion have few commitments to goals or values. This was not Sharon's problem.

   d. Had she taken a moratorium on identity formation, Sharon would have experimented with alternative identities and perhaps would have chosen that of a medical researcher.

2. **d.** is the answer. (p. 434)

3. **d.** is the answer. (p. 417)

4. **b.** is the answer. Ethnic adolescents struggle with finding the right balance between transcending their background and becoming immersed in it. (p. 425)

   c. & d. The text does not suggest that the amount of time adolescents have to forge their identities varies from one ethnic group to another or has changed over historical time.

5. **a.** is the answer. (p. 421)

6. **b.** is the answer. (p. 416)

7. **a.** is the answer. (p. 423)

   b. In fact, just the opposite is true.

   c. Developmentalists recommend authoritative, rather than authoritarian, parenting.

   d. Parental monitoring is important for all adolescents.

8. **b.** is the answer. (p. 428)

   a. In fact, girls are more likely to say they have a boyfriend than vice versa.

   c. This is not true; most teen romantic relationships last about a year.

   d. There's nothing to indicate that the daughter's boyfriend is a negative influence. The relationship may actually be healthy for their daughter, so they shouldn't arbitrarily break it up.

9. **b.** is the answer. (p. 438)

   a. Thi is prevalence.

   c. & d. These statistical concepts were not discussed in this chapter.

10. **c.** is the answer. (p. 434)

11. **d.** is the answer. (p. 439)

12. **b.** is the answer. (p. 440)

13. **d.** is the answer. (pp. 415, 434, 439)

14. **c.** is the answer. (p. 436)

15. **b.** is the answer. (p. 436)

    a., c., & d. Cluster suicides occur when the suicide of a local teen leads others to attempt suicide.

KEY TERMS

1. **Identity,** as used by Erikson, refers to a person's consistent self-definition as a unique individual in terms of roles, attitudes, beliefs, and aspirations. (p. 415)

2. Erikson's term for the psychosocial crisis of adolescence, **identity versus diffusion**, refers to adolescents' need to combine their self-understanding and social roles into a coherent identity. (p. 415)

3. In Erikson's theory, **identity achievement** occurs when adolescents attain their new identities by establishing their own goals and values and abandoning some of those set by their parents and culture and accepting others. (p. 416)

4. Adolescents who experience **identity diffusion**, according to Erikson, have few commitments to goals or values and are often apathetic about trying to find an identity. (p. 416)

5. In **foreclosure**, according to Erikson, the adolescent forms an identity prematurely, accepting parents' or society's roles and values wholesale. (p. 416)

6. According to Erikson, in the process of finding a mature identity, many young people seem to declare an identity **moratorium**, a kind of time-out during which they experiment with alternative identities without trying to settle on any one. (p. 416)

7. **Gender identity** is a person's self-identification of being female or male. (p. 418)

8. **Sexual orientation** refers to a person's sexual attraction toward a person of the other sex, the same sex, or both sexes. (p. 418)

9. **Bickering** refers to the repeated, petty arguing that typically occurs in early adolescence about common, daily life activities. (p. 420)

10. **Parental monitoring** is parental awareness about where one's child is, what he or she is doing, and with whom. (p. 421)

11. A **clique** is a group of adolescents made up of close friends who are loyal to one another. (p. 422)

12. A **crowd** is a larger group of adolescents who have something in common but who are not necessarily friends. (p. 422)

13. **Peer pressure** refers to the social pressure to conform with one's friends in behavior, dress, and attitude. It may be positive or negative in its effects. (p. 423)

14. **Deviancy training** is destructive peer pressure to rebel against authority or social norms. (p. 423)

15. **Peer selection** is the ongoing process in which adolescents choose friends on the basis of shared interests and values. (p. 423)

16. **Peer facilitation** is the encouragement adolescents give one another to engage in behaviors they would not otherwise do alone. (p. 424)

17. **Comorbidity** is the situation in which two or more unrelated disorders occur in a person at the same time. (p. 433)

18. **Clinical depression** describes the syndrome in which feelings of hopelessness and lethargy last in a person for two weeks or longer. (p. 433)

19. **Rumination** is repeatedly thinking and talking about past experiences to the extent of contributing to depression. (p. 434)

20. **Suicidal ideation** refers to thinking about committing suicide, usually with some serious emotional and intellectual or cognitive overtones. (p. 434)

21. **Parasuicide** is a deliberate act of self-destruction that does not result in death. (p. 434)

22. A **cluster suicide** refers to a series of suicides or suicide attempts that are precipitated by one initial suicide and that occur in the same community, school, or time period. (p. 436)

23. **Incidence** is how often a particular circumstance (such as lawbreaking) occurs. (p. 438)

24. **Prevalence** is how widespread within a population a particular behavior or circumstance is. (p. 438)

25. **Life-course-persistent offenders** are adolescent lawbreakers who later become career criminals. (p. 440)

26. **Adolescent-limited offenders** are juvenile delinquents whose criminal activity stops by age 21. (p. 440)

17

Emerging Adulthood: Biosocial Development

Chapter Overview

In this chapter we encounter the developing person in the prime of life. Emerging adulthood is the best time for hard physical labor—because strength is at a peak—and for reproduction—because overall health is good and fertility is high. However, with the attainment of full maturity, a new aspect of physical development comes into play—that is, decline. Chapter 17 takes a look at how people perceive changes that occur as the body ages as well as how decisions they make regarding lifestyle affect the course of their overall development.

The chapter begins with a description of the growth, strength, and health of the individual during emerging adulthood, as well as changes in the efficiency of the body's systems. Sexual-reproductive health, a matter of great concern to young adults, is also discussed, with particular attention paid to trends in sexual responsiveness during adulthood and sexually transmitted infections.

The second section looks at several problems that are more prevalent during young adulthood than at any other period of the life span: eating disorders, drug abuse and addiction, and violence. The section concludes with a discussion of how social norms can reduce risk taking and improve health habits in this age group.

NOTE: Answer guidelines for all Chapter 17 questions begin on page 254.

Guided Study

The text chapter should be studied one section at a time. Before you read, preview each section by skimming it, noting headings and boldface items. Then read the appropriate section objectives from the following outline. Keep these objectives in mind and, as you read the chapter section, search for the information that will enable you to meet each objective. Once you have finished a section, write out answers for its objectives.

Growth, Strength, and Health (pp. 447–456)

1. Describe the changes in growth, strength, and overall health that occur during emerging adulthood.

2. Discuss changes in the efficiency of various body functions, focusing on the significance of these changes for the individual.

3. Identify age-related trends in sexual responsiveness, and discuss changing attitudes about the purpose of sex.

Habits and Risks (pp. 456–468)

4. Discuss trends in exercise and nutrition among emerging adults.

5. Describe the typical victims of anorexia nervosa and bulimia nervosa, and discuss possible explanations for these disorders.

6. Identify the benefits and costs of risk taking among emerging adults, and explain the attraction of "living on the edge."

7. Discuss the causes and consequences of drug abuse during emerging adulthood.

8. (Issues and Applications) Discuss gender differences in violent death.

9. Discuss the social norms approach to reducing risk taking and improving health habits among emerging adults.

Chapter Review

When you have finished reading the chapter, work through the material that follows to review it. Complete the sentences and answer the questions. As you proceed, evaluate your performance for each section by consulting the answers beginning on page 254. Do not continue with the next section until you understand each answer. If you need to, review or reread the appropriate section in the textbook before continuing.

1. The beginning of young adulthood is the best time for _____

_____

_____

(three categories).

2. Complete the following chart. Some developmentalists distinguish the following age groups:

Generation Next, corresponding to ages

_____

Generation X, corresponding to ages

_____

Baby Boomers, corresponding to ages

_____

Seniors, corresponding to ages

_____

Growth, Strength, and Health (pp. 447–456)

3. Girls usually reach their maximum height by age _____ , and boys by age

_____ .

4. Growth in _____ and increases in _____ continue into the 20s.

5. Physical strength _____ (increases/ decreases) during the 20s.

6. Every body system functions optimally at the beginning of _____ . This is true of the _____ , _____ , _____ , and _____- _____ systems.

7. Many diagnostic tests, including _____ , _____ , and _____ are not recommended until age 40.

8. When overall growth stops, _____ , or aging, begins.

9. Many of the body's functions serve to maintain _____ ; that is, they keep physiological functioning in a state of balance. Many of these mechanisms are regulated by the _____ , which is often referred to as the _____ gland. This gland defends the body via various hormonal shifts (the _____ axis).

10. The older a person is, the _____ (less time/longer) it takes for these adjustments to occur. This is one reason emerging adults are less likely to _____ than older adults.

11. The other major reason young adults rarely experience serious illness is _____ _____ , which is defined as _____ .

12. The muscles of the body _____ (do/do not) have the equivalent of an organ reserve. Maximum strength potential typically begins to decline by age _____ .

13. The average maximum heart rate _____ (declines/remains stable/increases) with age. Resting heart rate _____ (declines/remains stable/increases) with age.

Briefly explain why most of the age-related biological changes that occur during the first decades of adulthood are of little consequence to the individual.

Briefly describe sexual activity and the health of the sexual-reproductive system in emerging adulthood.

14. Most emerging adults today _____ (condone/do not condone) premarital sex. Most sexually active adults have _____ (one steady partner/multiple partners) at a time. This pattern of sexual activity is called _____ _____ .

15. Most people in the United States believe that the primary purpose of sex is to _____ _____ _____ . This attitude is especially common among _____ (women/men). About one-fourth of all people in the United States believe that the primary purpose of sex is _____ . This attitude is more common among _____ (women/men) and _____ (younger/older) adults. The remainder believe that the primary purpose of sex is _____ . This attitude is more common among _____ (women/men).

16. One consequence of sexual patterns among today's young adults is that the incidence of _____ _____ _____ is higher today than ever before.

Habits and Risks (pp. 456–468)

17. At every stage of life, _____ protects against serious illness.

State some of the health benefits of exercise.

18. Formerly active adults often quit exercising as the demands of _____ , _____ , and _____ increase. People tend to exercise more if they are part of a _____ network that exercises, and live in a _____ that provides convenient exercise facilities.

19. At every stage of life, _____ affects development.

20. For body weight, there is a homeostatic _____ _____ that is affected by _____ , _____ , _____ , _____ , and _____ .

21. To measure whether a person is too fat or too thin, clinicians calculate his or her _____ _____ _____ , defined as the ratio of _____ (in kilograms) divided by _____ (in meters squared).

22. A BMI of _____ or more is considered obese. Obesity _____ (is/ is not) considered an eating disorder.

23. Most eating disorders are especially prevalent in _____ _____ .

24. One survey of dieters reported that the average woman during early adulthood would like to weigh _____ pounds less, and the average man about _____ pounds more.

25. Dieting may also trigger physiological changes that lead to an eating disorder such as _____ _____ , an affliction characterized by _____ .

26. Anorexia nervosa is diagnosed on the basis of four symptoms:

    a. _____

    b. _____

    c. _____

    d. _____

27. The other major eating disorder is _____ _____ , which is a _____ (more/less) common disorder and involves successive bouts of binge eating followed by purging through vomiting or massive doses of laxatives.

28. Binge-purge eating can cause a wide range of health problems, including damage to the _____ _____ and _____ _____ from the strain of electrolyte imbalance.

Briefly summarize how each of the major theories of development views eating disorders.

Psychoanalytic theory

Behaviorism

Cognitive theory

Sociocultural theory

Epigenetic theory

29. Many emerging adults are attracted to recreational activities and occupations that include _____ , defined as _____ _____ . Other manifestations of the risk-taking impulse are competitive _____ _____ , such as motocross.

30. Drug abuse is defined as using a drug in a manner that is _____ _____ . When the absence of a drug in a person's system causes physiological or psychological craving, _____ _____ is apparent. These destructive behaviors are more common during _____ _____ than at any other stage of life.

31. An important factor in drug use by emerging adults is the tendency to ignore later _____ . This is an example of the logical error called _____ _____ , which is the tendency to undervalue future events.

32. (Issues and Applications) Worldwide, young men are far more likely than women to die a _____ _____ . One reason for this difference may be the fact that higher levels of the hormone _____ correlate with angry reactions to events.

33. Standards for typical behaviors within a given society are called _____ _____ .

Briefly explain the social norms approach to reducing risky behavior.

Progress Test 1

Multiple-Choice Questions

Circle your answers to the following questions and check them with the answers on page 255. If your answer is incorrect, read the explanation for why it is incorrect and then consult the appropriate pages of the text (in parentheses following the correct answer).

1. Senescence refers to:
   a. a loss of efficiency in the body's regulatory systems.
   b. age-related gradual physical decline.
   c. decreased physical strength.
   d. vulnerability to disease.

2. When do noticeable increases in height stop?
   a. at about the same age in men and women
   b. at an earlier age in women than in men
   c. at an earlier age in men than in women
   d. There is such diversity in physiological development that it is impossible to generalize regarding this issue.

3. A difference between men and women during early adulthood is that men have:
   a. a higher percentage of body fat.
   b. lower metabolism.
   c. proportionately more muscle.
   d. greater organ reserve.

4. The majority of young adults rate their own health as:
   a. very good or excellent.
   b. average or fair.
   c. poor.
   d. worse than it was during adolescence.

5. The automatic adjustment of the body's systems to keep physiological functions in a state of equilibrium, even during heavy exertion, is called:
   a. organ reserve.   **c.** stress.
   b. homeostasis.   **d.** muscle capacity.

6. During emerging adulthood:
   a. age signifies cognitive norms and abilities.
   b. age is a more imperfect guide to development than it was during childhood.
   c. social roles become more rigidly determined.
   d. cohort has little effect on behavior.

7. The age of first marriage in the United States today is:
   a. about 25 for women and 27 for men.
   b. about 23 for women and 25 for men.
   c. significantly earlier than it was in the middle of the twentieth century.
   d. has not changed significantly since the middle of the twentieth century.

8. Which of the following is true of every body system?
   a. They all function optimally at the beginning of adulthood.
   b. They all begin to decline at the beginning of adulthood.
   c. They all undergo dramatic changes.
   d. They all begin to show the effects of early lifestyle choices.

9. The decrease in physical strength that occurs over the years of adulthood:
   a. occurs more rapidly in the arm and upper torso than in the legs.
   b. occurs more rapidly in the back and leg muscles than in the arm.
   c. occurs at the same rate throughout the body.
   d. varies from individual to individual.

10. Body mass index is calculated as:
    a. height divided by weight.
    b. weight divided by height squared.
    c. the percentage of total weight that is fat.
    d. the percentage of total weight that is muscle.

11. Diagnostic tests such as mammograms and colonoscopy are not recommended until age:
    a. 25   c. 40
    b. 30   d. 50

12. A 50-year-old can expect to retain what percentage of the muscle reserve he or she had at age 20?
    a. 25   c. 75
    b. 50   d. 90

13. According to epigenetic theory, eating disorders such as anorexia nervosa are more common in young women who:
    a. fear sex and motherhood.
    b. had separation anxiety as toddlers.
    c. abuse alcohol ad drugs.
    d. have divorced parents.

14. Social norms:
    a. are standards of behavior within a given society or culture.
    b. are particularly strong for emerging adults.
    c. change over time.
    d. are characterized by all of the above.

15. Which of the following was *not* suggested as a reason for the high rate of drug use and abuse in emerging adulthood?
    a. Young adults often have friends who use drugs.
    b. Young adults are trying to imitate their parents' behavior.
    c. Young adults may use drugs as a way of relieving job or educational stress.
    d. Young adults often fear social rejection.

True or False Items

Write T (*true*) or F (*false*) on the line in front of each statement.

_____ 1. At least until middle age, declines in homeostasis and organ reserve are usually unnoticed.

_____ 2. Few adults actually use all the muscle capacity that they could develop during young adulthood.

_____ 3. The older a person is, the longer it takes for his or her blood glucose level to return to normal after heavy exertion.

_____ 4. Extreme sports such as motocross have existed since the 1950s.

_____ 5. Emerging adults have the highest rates of heavy drinking and illicit drug use.

_____ 6. The process of aging begins as soon as full growth is reached.

_____ 7. The male/female ratio for violent deaths is about the same throughout the world.

_____ 8. Emerging adult women are at particular risk for eating disorders.

_____ 9. Normal weight is somewhere between 20 and 25 BMI.

_____ 10. Most sexually active young adults have several sexual partners at a time.

Progress Test 2

Progress Test 2 should be completed during a final chapter review. Answer the following questions after you thoroughly understand the correct answers for the Chapter Review and Progress Test 1.

Multiple-Choice Questions

1. The early 20s are the peak years for:
   a. hard physical work.
   b. problem-free reproduction.
   c. athletic performance.
   d. all of the above.

2. Serial monogamy refers to the practice among sexually active adults of:
   a. having more than one partner at a time.
   b. having one steady partner at a time.
   c. engaging in premarital sex.
   d. engaging in extramarital sex.

3. The process of aging, or senescence begins:
   a. after retirement.
   b. during adolescence.
   c. at birth.
   d. as soon as full growth is reached

4. Maximum strength potential typically begins to decline by age:
   a. 30.   c. 50.
   b. 40.   d. 60.

5. Normally, the average resting heart rate for both men and women:
   a. declines noticeably during the 30s.
   b. declines much faster than does the average maximum heart rate.
   c. reaches a peak at about age 30.
   d. remains stable until late adulthood.

6. During emerging adulthood, people follow patterns of development and behavior that vary by:
   a. age.
   b. culture.
   c. cohort.
   d. all of the above.

7. During emerging adulthood, many age differences in behavior and development:
   a. result more from social factors than biological ones.
   b. result more from biological factors than social ones.
   c. are unpredictable.

d. reflect developmental patterns that were established early in childhood.

8. Most people in the United States believe that the main purpose of sex is:
   a. reproduction.
   b. to strengthen pair bonding.
   c. recreation.
   d. different for women than for men.

9. (Issues and Applications) Some experts believe that emerging adults should have priority for bird flu shots because:
   a. their immune systems are less responsive than the systems of older adults.
   b. they are prime disease vectors.
   c. homeostatic mechanisms make them more likely to die than infants and the elderly.
   d. they are rarely prime disease vectors.

10. Many emerging adults engage in risky behaviors because they don't think about future consequences, a tendency called:
    a. senescence.
    b. edgework.
    c. delay discounting.
    d. tertiary thinking.

11. The typical patient with bulimia is a:
    a. college-age woman.
    b. woman who starves herself to the point of emaciation.
    c. woman in her late 40s.
    d. woman who suffers from life-threatening obesity.

12. The social norms approach refers to:
    a. the particular settings of an individual's various homeostatic processes.
    b. an approach to prevention that increases young adults' awareness of social norms for risky behaviors.
    c. the ratio between a person's weight and height.
    d. the average age at which certain behaviors and events occur

13. (Issues and Applications) Relative to all other age groups, young adult males are at increased risk for virtually every kind of:
    a. eating disorder.
    b. violence.
    c. acute disease.
    d. chronic disease.

14. Rates of drug abuse, except when it involves cigarette smoking, often fall:
    a. during adolescence.
    b. in the early 50s.
    c. over the years of adulthood.
    d. during late adulthood.

Matching Items

Match each definition or description with its corresponding term.

Terms

_____ **1.** senescence
_____ **2.** homeostasis
_____ **3.** organ reserve
_____ **4.** set point
_____ **5.** edgework
_____ **6.** drug abuse
_____ **7.** body mass index
_____ **8.** drug addiction
_____ **9.** anorexia nervosa
_____ **10.** bulimia nervosa
_____ **11.** extreme sports

15. Occupations or activities that require a degree of
risk or danger are referred to as:
    a. senescence.
    b. edgework.
    c. homeostasis.
    d. delay discounting.

Definitions or Descriptions

a. using a drug to the extent of impairing one's well-
   being
b. an occupation that requires a degree of risk
c. recreation that includes apparent risk of injury or
   death
d. extra capacity for responding to stressful events
e. a state of physiological equilibrium
f. an affliction characterized by binge-purge eating
g. age-related decline
h. the ratio of a person's weight divided by his or her
   height
i. an affliction characterized by self-starvation
j. the body weight that a person's homeostatic
   processes strive to maintain
k. a condition in which the absence of a drug triggers
   withdrawal symptoms

Developmental Psychology Applied

Answer these questions the day before an exam as a
final check on your understanding of the chapter's
terms and concepts.

1. Emerging adults are more vulnerable than other
   age groups to:
   a. eating disorders.
   b. violent death.
   c. drug abuse.
   d. all of the above.

2. When we are hot, we perspire in order to give off
   body heat. This is an example of the way our body
   functions maintain:
   a. senescence.   c. set point.
   b. homeostasis.   d. BMI.

3. Due to a decline in organ reserve, 28-year-old
   Brenda:
   a. has a higher resting heart rate than she did
      when she was younger.
   b. needs longer to recover from strenuous exer-
      cise than she did when she was younger.

   c. has a higher maximum heart rate than her
      younger sister.
   d. has all of the above.

4. Janine has decided to write her term paper on the
   brain's regulation of homeostatic processes. Her
   research should focus on the:
   a. cortex.
   b. hippocampus.
   c. amygdala.
   d. pituitary.

5. Summarizing her presentation on sexual attitudes
   among emerging adults, Carla notes that most:
   a. believe that physical relationships need not
      involve emotional connections.
   b. condone premarital sex.
   c. no longer believe that marriage is a desirable
      commitment.
   d. believe the primary purpose of sex is repro-
      duction.

6. Elderly Mr. Wilson believes that young adults today have too many sexual partners. Fueling his belief is the fact that:
   a. sexually transmitted infections were almost unknown in his day.
   b. half of all emerging adults in the United States have had at least one sexually transmitted infection.
   c. most sexually active adults have several partners at a time.
   d. all of the above are true.

7. I reduce blood pressure, strengthen the heart and lungs, and make depression less likely. What am I?
   a. a healthy diet
   b. a low-stress lifestyle
   c. an optimistic temperament
   d. exercise

8. Sheila dieted for several weeks until she lost 10 pounds. Upon returning to a normal diet, she is horrified to find that she has gained some of the weight back. It is likely that Sheila's weight gain was caused by:
   a. overconsumption of high-fat foods.
   b. too little exercise in her daily routine.
   c. her homeostatic mechanism returning to her natural set point.
   d. a low body set point.

9. Of the following, who is most likely to suffer from anorexia nervosa?
   a. Bill, a 23-year-old professional football player
   b. Florence, a 30-year-old account executive
   c. Lynn, a 20-year-old college student
   d. Carl, a professional dancer

10. Twenty-year-old Gwynn, who is 9 pounds heavier than the national average for her height and build, should probably:
    a. go on a crash diet, because every additional pound of fat is hazardous to her health.
    b. gradually reduce her weight to slightly below the national average.
    c. realize that because of her high body set point she will be unable to have children.
    d. not worry, because this is probably a healthy weight for her body.

11. As a psychoanalyst, Dr. Mendoza is most likely to believe that eating disorders are caused by:
    a. the reinforcing effects of fasting, bingeing, and purging.
    b. low self-esteem and depression, which act as a stimulus for destructive patterns of eating.
    c. unresolved conflicts with parents.
    d. the desire of working women to project a strong, self-controlled image.

12. Michael is a college freshman who enjoys weekend "booze parties." He has just learned that a survey regarding drinking on campus found that most of his classmates avoid binge drinking. Michael is most likely to:
    a. continue drinking on the weekends.
    b. follow this social norm.
    c. increase his drinking to prove he's not like everyone else.
    d. become more secretive about his drinking.

13. Dr. Ramirez suspects Jennifer may be suffering from anorexia because her BMI is:
    a. lower than 18.
    b. 23.
    c. higher than 25.
    d. higher than 30.

14. Lucretia, who has a BMI of 24, has been trying unsuccessfully to lose 10 pounds. It is likely that her difficulty is due to the fact that:
    a. she has a glandular disorder.
    b. she suffers from bulimia nervosa.
    c. her natural weight set point is higher than she would like.
    d. her obesity is accompanied by a very low metabolic rate.

15. Responding to a question from a reporter, one of the authors of the CARDIA study notes that a key finding of the study was that:
    a. the least fit participants were four times more likely to develop diabetes and high blood pressure.
    b. half of those who were obese as children became normal-weight young adults.
    c. young adults eat more fast food than those of other ages.
    d. people with BMIs under 20 have shorter life expectancies.

Key Terms

Using your own words, write a brief definition or explanation of each of the following terms on a separate piece of paper.

1. senescence
2. homeostasis
3. organ reserve
4. set point
5. body mass index (BMI)
6. anorexia nervosa
7. bulimia nervosa
8. edgework
9. extreme sports
10. drug abuse
11. drug addiction
12. delay discounting
13. social norms
14. social norms approach

ANSWERS

CHAPTER REVIEW

1. hard physical work, reproduction, athletic achievement
2. Generation X: ages 18 to 25
   Generation X: ages 25 to 40
   Baby Boomers: ages 40 to 60
   Seniors: age 60 and older
3. 16; 18
4. muscle; fat
5. increases
6. adulthood; digestive; respiratory; circulatory; sexual-reproductive
7. PSA; mammograms; colonoscopy
8. senescence
9. homeostasis; pituitary; master; HPA
10. longer; get sick, fatigued, or obese
11. organ reserve; the extra capacity that each organ has for coping with stress or physiological extremes
12. do; 30
13. declines; remains stable

The declines of aging primarily affect our organ reserve. In the course of normal daily life, adults seldom have to call on this capacity, so the deficits in organ reserve generally go unnoticed.

The sexual-reproductive system is at its strongest during emerging adulthood. Young adults have a strong sex drive; fertility is greater and miscarriage is less common; orgasm is more frequent; and testosterone is significantly higher in both men and women.

14. condone; one steady partner; serial monogamy
15. strengthen pair bonding; women; reproduction; women; older; recreation; men
16. sexually transmitted infections (STIs)
17. exercise

Exercise reduces blood pressure, strengthens the heart and lungs, and makes depression, osteoporosis, heart disease, arthritis, and some cancers less likely.

18. marriage; parenthood; career; social; community
19. diet (nutrition)
20. set point; genes; diet; age; hormones; exercise
21. body mass index (BMI); weight; height
22. 25; is
23. emerging adulthood
24. 8; 5
25. anorexia nervosa; self-starvation
26. a. refusal to maintain body weight at least 85 percent of normal for age
    b. intense fear of gaining weight
    c. disturbed body perception and denial of the problem
    d. lack of menstruation
27. bulimia nervosa; more
28. gastrointestinal system; cardiac arrest

According to psychoanalytic theory, women with eating disorders have a conflict with their mothers, who provided their first nourishment. According to behaviorism, disordered eating may set up a stimulus–response chain in which self-starvation relieves emotional stress and tension. Cognitive theory suggests that as women enter the workplace, they try to project a strong, self-controlled, "masculine" image. Sociocultural explanations focus on the contemporary cultural pressures to be model-like in appearance. Epigenetic theory suggests that because self-starvation may cause menstruation to cease and sexual hormones to decrease, girls who are genetically susceptible to depression or addiction may resort to this self-destructive behavior to relieve the pressures to marry and reproduce.

29. edgework; occupations and recreational activities that entail a degree of risk or danger; extreme sports

30. harmful to the user's physical, cognitive, or psychosocial well-being; drug addiction; emerging adulthood
31. consequences; delay discounting
32. violent death; testosterone
33. social norms

The social norms approach uses survey responses to make emerging adults more aware of actual social norms for risky behaviors.

PROGRESS TEST 1

Multiple-Choice Questions

1. **b.** is the answer. (p. 450)

   a., c., & d. Each of these is a specific example of the more general process of senescence.

2. **b.** is the answer. (p. 449)

3. **c.** is the answer. (p. 449)

   a. & b. These are true of women.

   d. Men and women do not differ in this characteristic.

4. **a.** is the answer. (p. 449)

5. **b.** is the answer. (p. 450)

   a. This is the extra capacity that each organ of the body has for responding to unusually stressful events or conditions that demand intense or prolonged effort.

   c. Stress, which is not defined in this chapter, refers to events or situations that tax the body's resources.

   d. This simply refers to a muscle's potential for work.

6. **b.** is the answer. (p. 448)

   c. & d. Just the opposite are true.

7. **a.** is the answer. (p. 448)

   c. & d. The age of first marriage is significantly later today than it was in the middle of the twentieth century.

8. **a.** is the answer. (p. 449)

   d. These effects generally do not appear until later in life. Moreover, it is not until early adulthood that most individuals begin making such choices.

9. **b.** is the answer. (p. 449)

10. **b.** is the answer. (p. 458)

11. **c.** is the answer. (p. 450)

12. **d.** is the answer. (p. 450)

13. **a.** is the answer. A bony appearance, lack of menstruation, and food obsession quiet her sexual impulses and preclude pregnancy. (p. 460)

14. **d.** is the answer. (p. 466)

15. **b.** is the answer. In fact, just the opposite is true. Young adults may use drugs to express independence from their parents. (pp. 463–464)

True or False Items

1. T (p. 450)

2. T (p. 450)

3. T (p. 450)

4. F   Extreme sports did not exist before emerging adulthood was identified in the 1990s. (p. 462)

5. T (p. 463)

6. T (p. 450)

7. F   This ratio varies from country to country. (p. 464)

8. T (p. 459)

9. T (p. 458)

10. F   Most sexually active adults have one steady partner at a time. (p. 454)

PROGRESS TEST 2

Multiple-Choice Questions

1. **d.** is the answer. (p. 447)

2. **b.** is the answer. (p. 454)

3. **d.** is the answer. (p. 450)

4. **a.** is the answer. (p. 450)

5. **d.** is the answer. (p. 451)

6. **d.** is the answer. (p. 448)

7. **a.** is the answer. (p. 448)

8. **b.** is the answer. (p. 454)

9. **b.** is the answer. (pp. 451–452)

   a. The immune systems of emerging adults are more responsive than the systems of older adults.

   c. Young adults are less likely to die than infants and the elderly.

   d. Because young adults come in close contact with many others, just the opposite is true.

10. **c.** is the answer. (p. 464)

11. **a.** is the answer. (p. 459)

    b. This describes a woman suffering from anorexia nervosa.

c. Eating disorders are much more common in younger women.

d. Most women with bulimia nervosa are usually close to normal in weight.

12. **b.** is the answer. (p. 467)

   c. This is the body mass index.

13. **b.** is the answer. (pp. 464–466)

   a. Eating disorders are more common in women than men.

   c. & d. Disease is relatively rare at this age.

14. **c.** is the answer. (p. 463)

15. **b.** is the answer. (p. 462)

Matching Items

1. g (p. 450)
2. e (p. 450)
3. d (p. 450)
4. j (p. 458)
5. b (p. 462)
6. a (p. 463)
7. h (p. 458)
8. k (p. 463)
9. i (p. 459)
10. f (p. 459)
11. c (p. 462)

DEVELOPMENTAL PSYCHOLOGY APPLIED

1. **d.** is the answer. (p. 447)

2. **b.** is the answer. (p. 450)

   a. This is age-related gradual physical decline.

   c. This refers to the weight that an individual's homeostatic processes strive to maintain.

   d. This is a measure of weight

3. **b.** is the answer. (p. 450)

   a. Resting heart rate remains stable throughout adulthood.

   c. Maximum heart rate declines with age.

4. **d.** is the answer. (p. 450)

5. **b.** is the answer. (p. 454)

   a. & c. Most emerging adults believe that sexual activity should involve an emotional connection and that marriage is a desirable commitment.

   d. Most believe that the primary purpose of sex is to strengthen pair bonding.

6. **b.** is the answer. (p. 455)

   a. STIs have been part of life since the beginning of time.

   c. Most sexually active adults have one steady partner at a time.

7. **d.** is the answer. (pp. 456–457)

8. **c.** is the answer. (p. 458)

9. **c.** is the answer. (p. 459)

a. & d. Eating disorders are more common in women than men.

b. Eating disorders are more common in younger women.

10. **d.** is the answer. (p. 458)

11. **c.** is the answer. (p. 460)

   a. & b. These explanations would more likely be offered by those who emphasize behaviorism or cognitive theory.

   d. This is a sociocultural explanation of eating disorders.

12. **b.** is the answer. (p. 467)

13. **a.** is the answer. (p. 459)

   b. This is a healthy BMI.

   c., & d. These BMIs are associated with being overweight.

14. **c.** is the answer. (p. 458)

   a. & d. There is no evidence that Lucretia has a glandular disorder or is obese. In fact, a BMI of 24 is well within the normal weight range.

   b. There is no evidence that Lucretia is bingeing and purging.

15. **a.** is the answer. (p. 457)

KEY TERMS

1. **Senescence** is age-related gradual physical decline throughout the body. (p. 450)

2. **Homeostasis** refers to the process by which body functions are automatically adjusted to keep our physiological functioning in a state of balance. (p. 450)

3. **Organ reserve** is the extra capacity of each body organ for responding to unusually stressful events or conditions that demand intense or prolonged effort. (p. 450)

4. **Set point** is the specific body weight that a person's homeostatic processes strive to maintain. (p. 458)

5. The **body mass index (BMI)** is the ratio of a person's weight in kilograms divided by his or her height in meters squared. (p. 458)

6. **Anorexia nervosa** is an affliction characterized by self-starvation that is most common in high-achieving college-age women. (p. 459)

7. **Bulimia nervosa** is an eating disorder that involves compulsive binge eating followed by purging through vomiting or taking massive doses of laxatives. (p. 459)

8. **Edgework** refers to recreational activities and jobs that entail some risk or danger. (p. 462)

9. **Extreme sports** are forms of recreation that include apparent risk of injury or death and are attractive and thrilling as a result. (p. 462)

10. **Drug abuse** is drug use to the extent of impairing the user's physical or psychological health. (p. 463)

11. **Drug addiction** is evident in a person when the absence of a drug in his or her body produces the drive to ingest more of the drug. (p. 463)

12. **Delay discounting** is the tendency to devalue the future consequences of behaviors such as drug use, in favor of more immediate gratification. (p. 464)

13. **Social norms** are standards or rules of behavior within a given culture or society based more on how people should behave than on how they actually behave. (p. 466)

14. The **social norms approach** to reducing risky behaviors uses survey data regarding the prevalence of risky behaviors to make emerging adults more aware of social norms. (p. 467)

18

Emerging Adulthood: Cognitive Development

Chapter Overview

During the course of adulthood, there are many shifts in cognitive development—in the speed and efficiency with which we process information, in the focus and depth of our cognitive processes, perhaps in the quality, or wisdom, of our thinking. Developmental psychologists use three different approaches in explaining these shifts, with each approach providing insights into the nature of adult cognition. This chapter takes a stage approach, describing age-related changes in an attempt to uncover patterns.

The chapter begins by describing how adult thinking differs from adolescent thinking. The experiences and challenges of adulthood result in a new, postformal thought, evidenced by practical, flexible, and dialectical thinking—the dynamic, in-the-world cognitive style that adults typically use to solve the problems of daily life.

The second section explores how the events of early adulthood can affect moral development. Of particular interest are Fowler's six stages in the development of faith.

The third section examines the effect of the college experience on cognitive growth; findings here indicate that years of education correlate with virtually every measure of cognition as thinking becomes progressively more flexible and tolerant.

NOTE: Answer guidelines for all Chapter 18 questions begin on page 268.

Guided Study

The text chapter should be studied one section at a time. Before you read, preview each section by skimming it, noting headings and boldface items. Then read the appropriate section objectives from the following outline. Keep these objectives in mind and, as you read the chapter section, search for the information that will enable you to meet each objective. Once you have finished a section, write out answers for its objectives.

1. Describe three approaches to the study of adult cognition.

Postformal Thought (pp. 472–483)

2. Identify the main characteristics of postformal thought, and describe how it differs from formal operational thought.

3. (text and Thinking Like a Scientist) Describe the contexts and effects of stereotype threat, and discuss findings of research studies aimed at reducing stereotype threat.

4. Define dialectical thought, and give examples of its usefulness.

5. Discuss the effects of culture on cognition.

Morals and Religion (pp. 483–488)

6. Explain Carol Gilligan's view of how moral reasoning changes during adulthood.

7. Explain how the Defining Issues Test helps relate moral development to other aspects of adult cognition and life satisfaction.

8. Describe the six stages of faith outlined by James Fowler.

Cognitive Growth and Higher Education (pp. 488–496)

9. Discuss the relationship between cognitive growth and higher education.

10. Compare college students and institutions today with their counterparts of a decade or two ago, and evaluate the changing college context.

Chapter Review

When you have finished reading the chapter, work through the material that follows to review it. Complete the sentences and answer the questions. As you proceed, evaluate your performance for each section by consulting the answers beginning on page 268. Do not continue with the next section until you understand each answer. If you need to, review or reread the appropriate section in the textbook before continuing.

1. Developmentalists have used three approaches to explain cognitive development: the _____ approach, the _____ approach, and the _____-_____ approach. In this chapter, Kathleen Berger emphasizes the _____ approach.

Postformal Thought (pp. 472–483)

2. Compared to adolescent thinking, adult thinking is more _____ , _____ , and _____ .

3. Reasoning that is adapted to the subjective real-life contexts to which it is applied is called _____ _____ . It is characterized by problem _____ rather than problem _____ .

4. Scholars _____ (agree/do not agree) that there are stages of adult cognition. A recent study found that many adults, but no children or adolescents, achieved a level of _____ that integrated emotions and reason.

5. Developmentalists distinguish between _____ thinking, which arises from the _____ experiences and _____ of an individual, and _____ thinking, which follows abstract _____ .

6. The difference between adolescent and young adult reasoning is particularly apparent for reasoning involving _____ questions.

7. In contrast to adolescent inflexibility regarding personal experiences, adults are more likely to demonstrate _____ _____ when suggesting solutions to real-life problems. One of the hallmarks of post-formal thought is the ability to find _____ _____ to practical problems.

8. This cognitive ability is crucial to countering _____ . Researchers have found that adults have become _____ (more/less) prejudiced about gender, race, and sexuality. When the mere possibility of being negatively stereotyped arouses emotions that disrupt cognition, _____ _____ has occurred. This is especially common when _____ _____ and _____ _____ are being developed, a process that begins in _____ and is complete in emerging adulthood.

9. (Thinking Like a Scientist) Stereotype threat can make _____ and _____ doubt their intellectual ability. As a result, they may become _____ in academic contexts and perform below their _____ . Research studies have shown that intellectual performance among students increases if they _____ the concept that intelligence is plastic and can be changed.

10. Some theorists consider _____ _____ the most advanced form of cognition. This thinking recognizes that every idea, or _____ , implies an opposing idea, or _____ ; these are then forged into a(n) _____ of the two. This type of thinking fosters the view that life-span change is multidirectional, ongoing, and often surprising—that is, a _____ dialectical process. This type of thinking is more often found in _____ -aged people than in _____ adults.

11. Some researchers believe that some _____ encourage flexible, dialectical reasoning more than others. According to this view, ancient _____ philosophy has led Europeans to use _____ _____ , whereas _____ and _____ have led Asians to think more _____ .

Morals and Religion (pp. 483–488)

12. According to many researchers, moral reasoning and religious beliefs are affected by adult _____ , _____ , and _____ . Research by one expert indicates that one catalyst for propelling young adults from a lower moral stage to a higher one is _____ .

13. Carol Gilligan believes that in matters of moral reasoning , _____ (males/females) tend to be more concerned with the question of rights and justice, whereas _____ (males/females) are more concerned with personal relationships. In her view, women are raised to develop a morality of _____ , while men are taught to develop a morality of _____ . Other research _____ (does/does not) support Gilligan's description of gender differences in morality. Other factors, such as education, specific dilemmas, and _____ , correlate more strongly with morality.

14. Other moral issues that contemporary adults are likely to confront arise from increasing _____ and advanced _____ . They also arise from satellite videos, international music, and the _____ .

15. (Issues and Applications) Young, full-time students living on campus are _____ (more/less) likely to accept cheating than are students who commute. Student culture may see cheating as a form of _____ and _____ _____ .

16. The current approach to research on moral reasoning is based on a series of questions about moral reasoning called the _____ _____ _____ . In general, scores on this test increase with _____ and with each year of _____ .

17. The theorist who has outlined six stages in the development of faith is _____ .

18. In the space below, identify and briefly describe each stage in the development of faith.

    Stage 1: _____
    _____
    Stage 2: _____
    _____
    Stage 3: _____
    _____
    Stage 4: _____
    _____
    Stage 5: _____
    _____
    Stage 6: _____
    _____

19. Although Fowler's stage theory of faith _____ (is/is not) totally accepted, the idea that religion plays an important role in human development _____ (is/is not).

Cognitive Growth and Higher Education
(pp. 488–496)

20. Compared to other adults, college graduates tend to be _____ and _____ . In terms of health behaviors, college graduates smoke _____ (more/less), eat _____ (better/ worse), exercise _____ (more/less), and live _____ (longer/shorter). lives. They are also more likely to be spouses, homeowners, and _____ . _____ .

Briefly outline the year-by-year progression in how the thinking of college students becomes more flexible and tolerant.

21. William Perry found that the thinking of students, over the course of their college careers, progressed through _____ levels of complexity.

22. Research has shown that the more years of higher education a person has, the deeper and more _____ that person's reasoning is likely to become.

23. Worldwide, the number of students who receive higher education _____ (has increased/has not increased) since the first half of the twentieth century.

24. Collegiate populations have become _____ (more/less) diverse in recent years. College majors also are changing, with fewer students concentrating on the _____ _____ and more on _____ and the

_____ . The structure of higher education also _____ (has changed/remains the same).

Progress Test 1

Multiple-Choice Questions

Circle your answers to the following questions and check them with the answers on page 269. If your answer is incorrect, read the explanation for why it is incorrect and then consult the appropriate pages of the text (in parentheses following the correct answer).

1. Differences in the reasoning maturity of adolescents and young adults are most likely to be apparent when:
   a. low-SES and high-SES groups are compared.
   b. ethnic-minority adolescents and adults are compared.
   c. ethnic-majority adolescents and adults are compared.
   d. emotionally charged issues are involved.

2. Which of the following is *not* one of the major approaches to the study of adult cognition described in the text?
   a. the information-processing approach
   b. the stage approach
   c. the systems approach
   d. the psychometric approach

3. Compared to adolescent thinking, adult thinking tends to be:
   a. more flexible.
   b. more practical.
   c. more dialectical.
   d. all of the above.

4. A hallmark of mature adult thought is the:
   a. ability to engage in dialectical thinking.
   b. reconciliation of both objective and subjective approaches to real-life problems.
   c. adoption of conjunctive faith.
   d. all of the above.

5. According to James Fowler, the experience of college often is a springboard to:
   a. intuitive-projective faith
   b. mythic-literal faith
   c. individual-reflective faith
   d. synthetic-conventional faith

6. Which approach to adult cognitive development focuses on life-span changes in the efficiency of encoding, storage, and retrieval?
   a. stage
   b. information-processing
   c. psychometric
   d. dialectical

7. Postformal thinking is most useful for solving _____ problems.
   a. science
   b. mathematics
   c. everyday
   d. abstract, logical

8. The term for the kind of thinking that involves the consideration of both poles of an idea and their reconciliation, or synthesis, in a new idea is:
   a. subjective thinking.
   b. postformal thought.
   c. adaptive reasoning.
   d. dialectical thinking.

9. Thesis is to antithesis as _____ is to _____ .
   a. a new idea; an opposing idea
   b. abstract; concrete
   c. concrete; abstract
   d. provisional; absolute

10. Which of the following adjectives best describe(s) cognitive development during adulthood?
    a. multidirectional and dynamic
    b. linear
    c. steady
    d. tumultuous

11. Which of the following most accurately describes postformal thought?
    a. subjective thinking that arises from the personal experiences and perceptions of the individual
    b. objective reasoning that follows abstract, impersonal logic
    c. a form of logic that combines subjectivity and objectivity
    d. thinking that is rigid, inflexible, and fails to recognize the existence of other potentially valid views

12. The Defining Issues Test is a:
    a. standardized test that measures postformal thinking.
    b. projective test that assesses dialectical reasoning.
    c. series of questions about moral dilemmas.
    d. test that assesses the impact of life events on cognitive growth and moral reasoning.

13. According to Carol Gilligan:
    a. in matters of moral reasoning, females tend to be more concerned with the question of rights and justice.
    b. in matters of moral reasoning, males tend to put human needs above principles of justice.
    c. moral reasoning advances during adulthood in response to the more complex moral dilemmas that life poses.
    d. all of the above are true.

14. Colleges today have become:
    a. larger.
    b. more career oriented.
    c. diverse.
    d. all of the above.

15. Research has revealed that a typical outcome of college education is that students become:
    a. very liberal politically.
    b. less committed to any particular values.
    c. more committed to a particular values.
    d. less open-minded.

True or False Items

Write T (*true*) or F (*false*) on the line in front of each statement.

_____ 1. Only about half of all low-income students who enroll in college graduate within 6 years.

_____ 2. Younger adults hold more gender-stereotyped views than older ones.

_____ 3. Most adults are more mature with their use of alcohol by age 25 or 30.

_____ 4. Because they recognize the changing and subjective nature of beliefs and values, dialectical thinkers avoid making personal or intellectual commitments.

_____ 5. Certain kinds of experiences during adulthood—especially those that entail assuming responsibility for others—can propel an individual from one level of moral reasoning to another.

_____ 6. Worldwide, three times as many students are in colleges or universities today than in 1975.

_____ 7. Postformal thought is less absolute and less abstract than formal thought.

_____ 8. Mythic-literal faith, like other "lower" stages in the development of faith, is not generally found past adolescence.

_____ 9. (Thinking Like a Scientist) Students who internalize that intelligence is plastic are less likely to experience stereotype threat.

_____ 10. Moral values are powerfully affected by circumstances.

Progress Test 2

Progress Test 2 should be completed during a final chapter review. Answer the following questions after you thoroughly understand the correct answers for the Chapter Review and Progress Test 1.

Multiple-Choice Questions

1. Which approach to adult cognitive development emphasizes the analysis of components of intelligence?
   a. postformal   c. information-processing
   b. psychometric   d. all of the above

2. Which approach to adult cognitive development "picks up where Piaget left off"?
   a. psychometric
   b. information-processing
   c. postformal
   d. dialectical

3. As adult thinking becomes more focused on occupational and interpersonal demands, it also becomes less inclined toward:
   a. inflexibility.
   b. dialectical thought.
   c. adaptive thought.
   d. all of the above.

4. The result of dialectical thinking is a view that:
   a. one's self is an unchanging constant.
   b. life-span change is dynamic.
   c. "everything is relative."
   d. all of the above are true.

5. The existence of a fifth, postformal stage of cognitive development during adulthood:
   a. is recognized by most developmentalists.
   b. has very little empirical support.
   c. remains controversial among developmental researchers.
   d. is widely accepted in women, but not in men.

6. Formal operational thinking is most useful for solving problems that:
   a. involve logical relationships or theoretical possibilities.
   b. require integrative skills.
   c. involve the synthesis of diverse issues.
   d. require seeing perspectives other than one's own.

7. College seems to make people more accepting of other people's attitudes because it:
   a. boosts self-esteem.
   b. promotes recognition of many perspectives.
   c. promotes extroversion.
   d. does all of the above.

8. The goal of dialectical thinking is forging a(n) _____ from opposing poles of an idea.
   a. thesis
   b. antithesis
   c. synthesis
   d. hypothesis

9. Formal operational thinking is to postformal thinking as _____ is to _____ .
   a. psychometric; information-processing
   b. adolescence; adulthood
   c. thesis; antithesis
   d. self-esteem; extroversion

10. According to James Fowler, which type of faith is typical of middle childhood?
    a. intuitive-projective
    b. mythic-literal
    c. synthetic-conventional
    d. individual-reflective

11. According to James Fowler, individual-reflective faith is marked by:
    a. a willingness to accept contradictions.
    b. a burning need to enunciate universal values.
    c. a literal, wholehearted belief in myths and symbols.
    d. the beginnings of independent questioning of teachers and other figures of authority.

12. (Issues and Applications) Research studies have shown that college students who cheat :
    a. are more likely to believe that the purpose of school is to get good grades rather than to learn.
    b. have a much broader definition of cheating than professors do.
    c. usually have the same value system as their professors regarding academic dishonesty.
    d. are more likely to break social and legal rules throughout their lives.

13. According to James Fowler, the simplest stage of faith is the stage of:
    a. universalizing faith.
    b. intuitive-projective faith.
    c. mythic-literal faith.
    d. conventional faith.

14. Many of the problems of adult life are characterized by ambiguity, partial truths, and extenuating circumstances, and therefore are often best solved using _____ thinking.
    a. formal
    b. reintegrative
    c. postformal
    d. executive

15. A classic study by Perry showed that the thinking of students in college progresses through how many levels of complexity?
    a. 6
    b. 9
    c. 12
    d. 15

Developmental Psychology Applied

Answer these questions the day before an exam as a final check on your understanding of the chapter's terms and concepts.

1. Concluding her comparison of postformal thinking with Piaget's cognitive stages, Lynn notes that:
   a. postformal thinking is characterized by "problem finding."
   b. formal operational thinking is characterized by "problem solving."
   c. intuitive, postformal thinking is used when logical reasoning is too cumbersome.
   d. all of the above are true.

2. Carol Gilligan's research suggests that the individual who is most likely to allow the context of personal relationships to wholly determine moral decisions is a:
   a. 20-year-old man.
   b. 20-year-old woman.
   c. 40-year-old man.
   d. Gilligan does not deal with gender differences in moral thinking.

3. Research suggests that a college sophomore or junior is most likely to have reached a phase in which he or she:
   a. believes that there are clear and perfect truths to be discovered.
   b. questions personal and social values, and even the idea of truth itself.
   c. rejects opposing ideas in the interest of finding one right answer.
   d. accepts a simplistic either/or dualism.

4. (Table 18.4) In his scheme of cognitive and ethical development, Perry describes a position in which the college student says, "I see I'm going to have to make my own decisions in an uncertain world with no one to tell me I'm right." This position marks the culmination of a phase of:
   a. either/or dualism.
   b. modified dualism.
   c. relativism.
   d. commitments in relativism.

5. Which of the following is an example of responding to a stereotype threat?
   a. Because Jessie's older sister teases her for not being as good as she is at math, Jessie protects her self-concept by devaluing math.
   b. Feeling angered that others may think him less capable because of his ethnicity, Liam becomes flustered when trying to solve a problem in front of the class.
   c. Dave writes a scathing criticism of an obviously racist comment made by a local politician.
   d. As an elderly adult, Kathy takes pride in displaying her quick wit and intelligence to others.

6. Dr. Polaski studies how thinking during adulthood is at a different level than that of adolescence. Evidently, Dr. Polaski follows the _____ approach to the study of development.
   a. stage   c. cognitive
   b. psychometric   d. information-processing

7. Jack's uncle believes strongly in God but recognizes that other, equally moral people do not. The openness of his faith places him in which of Fowler's stages?
   a. universalizing faith
   b. conjunctive faith
   c. individual-reflective faith
   d. mythic-literal faith

8. When she was younger, May-Ling believed that "Honesty is always the best policy." She now realizes that although honesty is desirable, it is not *always* the best policy. May-Ling's current thinking is an example of _____ thought.
   a. formal   c. mythic-literal
   b. dialectical   d. conjunctive

9. Who would be the most likely to agree with the statement, "College can be a powerful stimulus to cognitive growth"?
   a. Kohlberg   c. Fowler
   b. Piaget   d. Perry

10. Spike is in his third year at a private, religious liberal arts college, while his brother Lee is in his third year at a public, secular community college. In terms of their cognitive growth, what is the most likely outcome?
    a. Spike will more rapidly develop complex critical thinking skills.
    b. Lee will develop greater self-confidence in his abilities because he is studying from the secure base of his home and family.
    c. All other things being equal, Spike and Lee will develop quite similarly.
    d. It is impossible to predict.

11. In concluding her presentation on "The College Student of Today," Coretta states that:
    a. "The number of students in higher education has increased significantly in virtually every country worldwide."
    b. "There are more low-income and ethnic-minority students today than ever before."
    c. "There are more women and minority instructors than ever before."
    d. all of the above are true.

12. (Thinking Like a Scientist) Research demonstrates that all but which of the following are effective in reducing stereotype threat among college students?
    a. creating educational environments among students who have gender in common
    b. creating educational environments among students who have race in common
    c. interventions that help students internalize the concept that intelligence can change
    d. educational programs that sensitize male ethnic-majority students to the impact of gender and ethnic stereotypes on other students

13. In concluding his paper on postformal thinking, Stanley notes that:
    a. postformal thinking is not the same kind of universal, age-related stage that Piaget described for earlier cognitive growth.
    b. very few adults attain this highest stage of reasoning.
    c. most everyday problems require sensitivity to subjective feelings and therefore do not foster postformal thinking.
    d. all of the above are true.

14. Which of the following would be most helpful to know about a person in predicting whether that individual will go to college and graduate?
    a. age
    b. educational background
    c. household income
    d. Cognitive development is unpredictable from any of these factors.

15. In Fowler's theory, at the highest stages of faith development, people incorporate a powerful vision of compassion for others into their lives. This stage is called:
    a. conjunctive faith.
    b. individual-reflective faith.
    c. synthetic-conventional faith.
    d. universalizing faith.

Key Terms

Writing Definitions

Using your own words, write a brief definition or explanation of each of the following terms on a separate piece of paper.

1. postformal thought
2. subjective thought
3. objective thought
4. stereotype threat
5. dialectical thought
6. thesis
7. antithesis
8. synthesis
9. morality of care
10. morality of justice
11. Defining Issues Test
12. diversity

Cross Check

Cross Check

After you have written the definitions of the key terms in this chapter, you should complete the crossword puzzle to ensure that you can reverse the process—recognize the term, given the definition.

ACROSS

1. Stage of faith in which a person has a powerful vision of compassion, justice, and love that applies to all people.
7. The final stage of dialectical thinking.
8. A proposition or statement of belief.
13. Theorist who believes that as their life experiences expand, both males and females broaden their moral perspectives.
15. Type of thinking that arises from the personal experiences and perceptions of an individual.

DOWN

2. Faith that is magical, illogical, imaginative, and filled with fantasy.
3. Thinking that involves consideration of both poles of an idea simultaneously.
4. Theorist who delineated six stages of faith.
5. Thinking that is suited to solving real-world problems and is less abstract, less absolute, and more integrative and synthetic than formal thought.
6. Test of moral reasoning that consists of a series of questions about moral dilemmas.
9. Approach to adult cognition that analyzes components of intelligence such as those measured by IQ tests.
10. Second stage of dialectical thinking.
11. Thinking that follows abstract, impersonal logic.
12. During early adulthood, the experience that deepens thinking and leads people to become more tolerant of views that differ from their own.
14. Theorist who described the progressive changes in thinking during the college years.

ANSWERS

CHAPTER REVIEW

1. psychometric; information-processing; stage
2. practical; flexible; dialectical
3. postformal thought; finding; solving
4. do not agree; self-acceptance
5. subjective; personal; perceptions; objective; logic
6. emotional
7. cognitive flexibility (or flexible problem solving); multiple solutions
8. stereotypes; less; stereotype threat; ethnic identity; gender identity; adolescence
9. women; minorities; anxious; potential; internalize
10. dialectical thought; thesis; antithesis; synthesis; dynamic; middle; emerging
11. cultures; Greek; analytic logic; Confucianism; Taoism; dialectically
12. responsibilities; experiences; education; college
13. males; females; care; justice
14. globalization; commuication; Internet
15. more; cooperation; mutual support
16. Defining Issues Test; age; education
17. James Fowler
18. Intuitive-projective faith is magical, illogical, filled with fantasy, and typical of children ages 3 to 7.

Mythic-literal faith, which is typical of middle childhood, is characterized by taking the myths and stories of religion literally.

Synthetic-conventional faith is a nonintellectual acceptance of cultural or religious values in the context of interpersonal relationships.

Individual-reflective faith is characterized by intellectual detachment from the values of culture and the approval of significant others.

Conjunctive faith incorporates both powerful unconscious ideas and rational, conscious values.

Universalizing faith is characterized by a powerful vision of universal compassion, justice, and love that leads people to put their own personal welfare aside in an effort to serve these values.

19. is not; is

20. healthier; wealthier; less; better; more; longer; parents of healthy children

First-year students often believe that there are clear and perfect truths to be found. This phase is followed by a wholesale questioning of values. Finally, after considering opposite ideas, students become committed to certain values, at the same time realizing the need to remain open-minded.

21. nine

22. dialectical

23. has increased

24. more; liberal arts; business; professions; has changed

25. helps

PROGRESS TEST 1

Multiple-Choice Questions

1. **d.** is the answer. (p. 474)

a., b., & c. Socioeconomic status and ethnicity do not predict reasoning maturity.

2. **c.** is the answer. (p. 471)

3. **d.** is the answer (p. 472)

4. **b.** is the answer. (p. 474)

5. **c.** is the answer. (p. 487)

6. **b.** is the answer. (p. 471)

a. This approach emphasizes the emergence of a new stage of thinking that builds on the skills of formal operational thinking.

c. This approach analyzes the measurable components of intelligence.

d. This is a type of thinking rather than an approach to the study of cognitive development.

7. **c.** is the answer. (p. 472)

a., b., & d. Because of its more analytical nature, formal thinking is most useful for solving these types of problems.

8. **d.** is the answer. (p. 480)

a. Thinking that is subjective relies on personal reflection rather than objective observation.

b. Although dialectical thinking *is* characteristic of postformal thought, this question refers specifically to dialectical thinking.

c. Adaptive reasoning, which also is characteristic of postformal thought, goes beyond mere logic in solving problems to also explore real-life complexities and contextual circumstances.

9. **a.** is the answer (p. 480)

10. **a.** is the answer. (p. 480)

b. & c. Comparatively speaking, linear and steady are *more* descriptive of childhood and adolescent cognitive development.

11. **b.** is the answer. (p. 472)

12. **d.** is the answer. (p. 486)

13. **c.** is the answer. (p. 484)

a. In Gilligan's theory, this is more true of males than females.

b. In Gilligan's theory, this is more true of females than males.

14. **d.** is the answer. (p. 492)

15. **c.** is the answer. Although they become more committed, they realize they need to remain open-minded. (p. 490)

True or False Items

1. T (p. 493)

2. F Just the opposite is true. (p. 476)

3. T (p. 474)

4. F Dialectical thinkers recognize the need to make commitments to values even though these values will change over time. (p. 480)

5. T (pp. 483–484)

6. T (p. 491)

7. T (p. 472)

8. F   Many adults remain in the "lower" stages of faith, which, like "higher" stages, allow for attaining strength and wholeness. (p. 486)

9. T (pp. 479–480)

10. T (p. 483)

PROGRESS TEST 2

Multiple-Choice Questions

1. **b.** is the answer. (p. 471)

a. This approach emphasizes the possible emergence in adulthood of new stages of thinking that build on the skills of earlier stages.

c. This approach studies the encoding, storage, and retrieval of information throughout life.

2. **c.** is the answer. (p. 472)

3. **a.** is the answer. (p. 475)

b. & c. During adulthood, thinking typically becomes more dialectical and adaptive.

4. **b.** is the answer. (p. 480)

   a. & c. On the contrary, a dialectic view recognizes the limitations of extreme relativism and that one's self evolves continuously.

5. **c.** is the answer. (pp. 472–473)

6. **a.** is the answer. (p. 474)

   b., c., & d. Postformal thought is most useful for solving problems such as these.

7. **b.** is the answer. (p. 490)

   a. & c. The impact of college on self-esteem and extroversion were not discussed. Moreover, it is unclear how such an impact would make a person more accepting of others.

8. **c.** is the answer. (p. 480)

   a. A thesis is a new idea.

   b. An antithesis is an idea that opposes a particular thesis.

   d. Hypotheses, which are testable predictions about behavior, are not an aspect of dialectical thinking.

9. **b.** is the answer. (p. 473)

10. **b.** is the answer. (p. 486)

    a. Intuitive-projective faith is typical of children ages 3 to 7.

    c. & d. Synthetic-conventional faith and individual-reflective faith are more typical of adulthood.

11. **d.** is the answer. (p. 487)

    a. This describes conjunctive faith.

    b. This describes universalizing faith.

    c. This describes mythic-literal faith.

12. **a.** is the answer. (pp. 485–486)

    b. In fact, students who cheat generally have a more limited definition of cheating than their professors do.

    c. The text suggests that students who cheat may have a different value system that encourages cooperation in order to cope with institutions that penalize students who are culturally different or educationally underprepared.

    d. The text does not suggest that students who cheat become lifelong rule breakers.

13. **b.** is the answer. (p. 486)

14. **c.** is the answer. (p. 472)

    a. Formal thinking is best suited to solving problems that require logic and analytical thinking.

    b. & d. These terms are not discussed in the text.

15. **b.** is the answer. (p. 490)

DEVELOPMENTAL PSYCHOLOGY APPLIED

1. **d.** is the answer. (p. 472)

2. **b.** is the answer. (p. 484)

   a. & c. According to Gilligan, males tend to be more concerned with human rights and justice than with human needs and personal relationships, which are more the concern of females.

   d. Just the opposite is true of Gilligan's research.

3. **b.** is the answer. (p. 490)

   a. First-year college students are more likely to believe this is so.

   c. & d. Over the course of their college careers, students become *less* likely to do either of these.

4. **c.** is the answer. (p. 491)

5. **b.** is the answer. (pp. 477–479)

6. **a.** is the answer. (p. 471)

   b. This approach analyzes components of intelligence such as those measured by IQ tests.

   c. Each of these approaches is cognitive in nature.

   d. This approach studies the encoding, storage, and retrieval of information throughout life.

7. **b.** is the answer. (p. 487)

8. **b.** is the answer. May-Ling has formed a synthesis between the thesis that honesty is the best policy and its antithesis. (p. 480)

   a. This is an example of postformal rather than formal thinking.

   c. & d. These are stages in the development of faith as proposed by James Fowler.

9. **d.** is the answer. (p. 490)

10. **c.** is the answer. (p. 490)

11. **d.** is the answer. (p. 492)

12. **d.** is the answer. (pp. 479–480)

13. **a.** is the answer. (p. 473)

    b. Because postformal thinking is typical of adult thought, this is untrue.

    c. It is exactly this sort of problem that *fosters* postformal thinking.

14. **c.** is the answer. (p. 493)

15. **d.** is the answer. (p. 487)

KEY TERMS

Writing Definitions

1. Proposed by some developmentalists as a fifth stage of cognitive development, **postformal thought** is suited to solving real-world problems and is more practical, more flexible, and more dialectical than adolescent thought. (p. 472)

2. **Subjective thought** is thinking that arises from our personal experiences and perceptions. (p. 474)

3. **Objective thought** is thinking that follows abstract, impersonal logic. (p. 474)

4. **Stereotype threat** is the possibility that one's behavior may be misused to confirm another person's prejudiced attitude. (p. 477)

5. **Dialectical thought** is thinking that involves considering both poles of an idea (thesis and antithesis) simultaneously and then forging them into a synthesis. (p. 480)

6. The first stage of dialectical thinking, a **thesis** is a proposition or statement of belief. (p. 480)

7. A statement that contradicts the thesis, an **antithesis** is the second stage of dialectical thinking. (p. 480)

8. The final stage of dialectical thinking, the **synthesis** reconciles thesis and antithesis into a new, more comprehensive level of truth (p. 480)

9. According to Carol Gilligan, women are raised to develop a **morality of care;** they give human needs and relationships highest priority. (p. 484)

10. According to Carol Gilligan, men are raised to develop a **morality of justice;** their emphasis is on distinguishing right from wrong. (p. 484)

11. The **Defining Issues Test (DIT)** is a series of questions developed by James Rest about moral dilemmas used to research moral reasoning. (p. 486)

12. For developmentalists, **diversity** includes differences between people, including differences in culture, age, race, and gender. (p. 494)

Cross-Check

ACROSS

1. universalizing
7. synthesis
8. thesis
13. Gilligan
15. subjective

DOWN

2. intuitive-projective
3. dialectical
4. Fowler
5. postformal
6. Defining Issues
9. psychometric
10. antithesis
11. objective
12. college
14. Perry

19

Emerging Adulthood: Psychosocial Development

Chapter Overview

Biologically mature and no longer bound by parental authority, the young adult typically is now free to choose a particular path of development. Today, the options are incredibly varied. Not surprisingly, then, the hallmark of psychosocial development during emerging adulthood is diversity. Nevertheless, developmentalists have identified several themes or patterns that help us understand the course of development between the ages of 20 and 40.

The chapter begins with a discussion of the two basic identity statuses of adulthood: ethnic identity and vocational identity. Ethnic identity is difficult to achieve for children of immigrants trying to reconcile their parents' background with their new social context. College education is an important stimulus for the development of vocational identity for many emerging adults.

The next section addresses the need for intimacy in adulthood, focusing on the development of friendship, love, and marriage.

The final section of the chapter is concerned with emotional development. During emerging adulthood, both positive and negative emotions are strong. The stresses of this period of life combine with genetic vulnerability in some individuals to trigger substance abuse and the development of mood disorders, anxiety disorders, or schizophrenia.

NOTE: Answer guidelines for all Chapter 19 questions begin on page 282.

Guided Study

The text chapter should be studied one section at a time. Before you read, preview each section by skimming it, noting headings and boldface items. Then read the appropriate section objectives from the following outline. Keep these objectives in mind and, as you read the chapter section, search for the information that will enable you to meet each objective. Once

you have finished a section, write out answers for its objectives.

Identity Achieved (pp. 499–503)

1. Explain how the viewpoint of most developmentalists regarding identity formation has shifted.

2. Discuss the development of ethnic identity.

3. Discuss the development of vocational identity.

Intimacy (pp. 503–516)

4. Review the developmental course of friendship during adulthood, noting factors that promote friendship and gender differences in friendship patterns.

5. Identify Sternberg's three components of love, and discuss the pattern by which they develop in relationships.

6. Discuss the impact of cohabitation on relationships, and identify factors that influence marital success.

7. (Issues and Applications) Describe the different forms of domestic violence.

8. Describe the role of family in the development of the emerging adult, noting both positive and negative effects.

Emotional Development (pp. 516–521)

9. Discuss how the individual's well-being is affected by the independence of emerging adulthood, and explain the diathesis-stress model.

10. Discuss the origins of substance abuse, depression, anxiety disorders, and schizophrenia.

Chapter Review

When you have finished reading the chapter, work through the material that follows to review it. Complete the sentences and answer the questions. As you proceed, evaluate your performance for each section by consulting the answers on page 282. Do not continue with the next section until you understand each answer. If you need to, review or reread the appropriate section in the textbook before continuing.

Identity Achieved (pp. 499–503)

1. Most developmentalists once believed that identity was usually achieved _____ (before/after) adulthood. Today, they believe the identity crisis has been _____ (shortened/lengthened).

2. Of the four identities, two that seem nearly impossible to achieve during adolescence are _____ and _____ .

3. In the United States and Canada, about _____ (what proportion?) of emerging adults are either children of immigrants or native-born adults of African, Asian, Indian, or

Latino descent. Most of them _____ (identify/do not identify) with specific ethnic groups.

4. Identity achievement _____ (is/is not) particularly difficult for immigrants. Briefly explain why this is so. _____

_____

5. Ethnic pride generally _____ (correlates/does not correlate) with self-esteem but not necessarily with _____

_____ .

6. For many emerging adults, attending college is an important step toward achieving _____ identity. The correlation between college education and income is _____ (weaker/stronger) today than in the past. This is because there are fewer _____ jobs and more _____-_____ jobs.

Intimacy (pp. 503–516)

7. In Erikson's theory, the identity crisis of adolescence is followed in Emerging Adulthood by the crisis of _____ _____ _____ . The same need is expressed by other theorists as _____ , _____ , _____ , _____ , _____ , or _____ . The most recent theory notes that an important aspect of close human connections is _____ .

8. As a buffer against stress, as guides to self-awareness, and as a source of positive feelings, _____ are particularly important. Briefly state why this is so.

9. People tend to make more friends during the period of _____ _____ than at any other time.

10. Four factors that promote friendship by serving as _____ _____ _____ are

a. _____

b. _____

c. _____

d. _____

11. When it comes to our close confidants, most of us have two or three basic _____ , and everyone who has those traits is _____ from consideration.

12. Gender differences in friendship _____ (are/are not) especially apparent during adulthood. In general, men's friendships are based on _____ _____ and _____ , whereas friendships between women tend to be more _____ and _____ .

13. More _____ (women/men) than _____ (women/men) are homophobic.

14. Cross-sex friendships are _____ (more/less) common today than in the past.

15. Worldwide, couples today marry _____ (earlier/later) and divorce _____ (more/less) often than earlier cohorts did.

16. (In Person) In most nations, marriage _____ (is/is not) based on romantic love.

17. Robert Sternberg has argued that love has three distinct components: _____ , _____ , and _____ .

18. Sternberg believes that the relative absence or presence of these components gives rise to _____ (how many?) different forms of love.

19. Relationships grow because _____ intensifies, leading to the gradual establishment and strengthening of _____ . Children _____ (do/do not) add stress to a relationship but also make separation _____ (more/less) likely.

20. When commitment is added to passion and intimacy, the result is _____ love.

21. With time, _____ tends to fade and _____ tends to stabilize, even as _____ develops.

22. Arranged marriages are _____ (rare today/still common in many nations).

23. Increasingly common among young adults in many countries is the living pattern called _____ , in which two unrelated adults live together in a committed sexual relationship.

24. Cohabitation _____ (does/does not) seem to benefit the participants. Cohabitants tend to be _____ , _____ , and _____ (more/less) likely to end their relationship than married couples. Research also demonstrates that _____ _____ is more common among cohabitants than among married couples.

25. Marriage between people who are similar in age, SES, ethnicity, and the like is called _____ . Marriage that is outside the group is called _____ . Similarity in interests, attitudes, and _____ , called _____ _____ , is particularly important to long-term commitment.

26. A related factor affecting marriage is marital _____ , the extent to which the partners perceive equality in the relationship. According to _____ _____ theory, marriage is an arrangement in which each person contributes something useful to the other.

27. When couples disagree, _____ _____ is crucial. The destructive interaction pattern called _____ is common in ailing marriages.

28. (Issues and Applications) There are numerous causes of domestic violence, including

_____ .

29. (Issues and Applications) One form of domestic abuse, _____ _____ _____ , entails outbursts of fighting, with both partners sometimes becoming involved.

30. (Issues and Applications) The second type of abuse, _____ _____ , occurs when one partner, almost always the _____ , uses a range of methods to punish and degrade the other. This form of abuse leads to the _____-_____ syndrome and _____ (becomes/does not usually become) more extreme with time.

31. Members of families have _____ lives, meaning that experiences and needs of members at one stage are affected by those at other stages. Although emerging adults strive for independence, family support in the form of _____ aid and gifts of time are important. Family dependence _____ (varies/does not vary) between Western nations and developing nations.

Emotional Development (pp. 516–521)

32. Both positive and negative emotions seem especially strong during the years of _____ . Average well-being _____ (increases/decreases) in emerging adulthood, but so does the incidence of _____ .

33. According to the _____-_____ model, disorders such as schizophrenia are produced by the interaction of _____ with _____ , or an underlying genetic vulnerability.

34. Before age 27, one person in _____ (how many?) is addicted (including alcohol addiction).

35. Before age 30, approximately _____ percent of U.S. residents suffer from a mood dis-

order. The most common of these disorders is

_____ _____ , defined

as the loss of interest in nearly all activities lasting

for _____ (how long?) or more.

36. Another major problem is _____

disorders, which are suffered by _____

(what proportion) of young adults in the United

States. These disorders include

_____-_____

_____ _____ ,

_____-_____

_____ , and _____

_____ .

37. Anxiety disorders are affected by

_____ context. A common anxiety

disorder that keeps some young adults away

from college is _____

_____ . In Japan, a new disorder

called hikikomori is related to anxiety about the

_____ and _____ pres-

sures of high school and college.

38. Schizophrenia is experienced by about

_____ percent of all adults. This dis-

order is partly the result of _____ ,

and partly the result of vulnerabilities such as

_____ when the brain is developing,

and extensive _____ pressure.

Symptoms of this disorder typically begin in

_____ .

Progress Test 1

Multiple-Choice Questions

Circle your answers to the following questions and check them with the answers beginning on page 282. If your answer is incorrect, read the explanation for why it is incorrect and then consult the appropriate pages of the text (in parentheses following the correct answer).

1. According to Erik Erikson, the first basic task of adulthood is to establish:
   a. a residence apart from parents.
   b. intimacy with others.
   c. generativity through work or parenthood.
   d. a career commitment.

2. Most developmental psychologists believe that identity:
   a. takes longer to achieve than in the past.
   b. is usually achieved during adolescence.
   c. is harder for women to achieve than for men.
   d. is no longer a useful concept in developmental science.

3. Which of the following was *not* identified as a gateway to attraction?
   a. physical attractiveness
   b. frequent exposure
   c. similarity of attitudes
   d. apparent availability

4. Which of the following is true of emerging adults who are children of immigrants or native-born adults of African, Asian, Indian, or Latino descent?
   a. Their ethnic pride generally correlates with social adjustment.
   b. Their ethnic identity does not change throughout the life span.
   c. They easily reconcile their parents' background with their new social context.
   d. They tend to identify with very specific ethnic groups.

5. Of the four identities, which now seem almost impossible to achieve during adolescence?
   a. gender and political
   b. ethnic and vocational
   c. religious and ethnic
   d. gender and vocational

6. According to Erikson, the failure to achieve intimacy during Emerging Adulthood is most likely to result in:
   a. generativity.   c. role diffusion.
   b. stagnation.   **d.** isolation.

7. Friendships are important for emerging adults because:
   a. friendship ties are voluntary.
   b. compared to earlier cohorts, they are less likely to be caring for older relatives.
   c. they are likely to postpone marriage.
   d. of all the above reasons.

8. Which of the following statements best characterizes today's job market?
   a. There are more unskilled jobs than in the past.
   b. There are more knowledge-based jobs than in the past.
   c. There are fewer jobs today than in the past.
   d. There are more jobs today than in the past.

9. According to Robert Sternberg, consummate love emerges:
   a. as a direct response to passion.
   b. as a direct response to physical intimacy.
   c. when commitment is added to passion and intimacy.
   d. during the early years of parenthood.

10. An arrangement in which two unrelated, unmarried adults live together in a romantic partnership is called:
    a. cross-sex friendship.
    b. a passive-congenial pattern.
    c. cohabitation.
    d. affiliation.

11. Differences in religious customs or rituals are *most* likely to arise in a:
    a. homogamous couple.
    b. heterogamous couple.
    c. cohabiting couple.
    d. very young married couple.

12. Between ages 18 and 27, the average worker in the United States has how many jobs?
    a. one   c. five
    b. two   d. eight

13. Homogamy is to heterogamy as:
    a. marriage outside the group is to marriage within the group.
    b. marriage within the group is to marriage outside the group.
    c. companionate love is to passionate love.
    d. passionate love is to companionate love.

14. The correlation between college education and income:
    a. is stronger today than ever before.
    b. is weaker today than ever before.
    c. is about the same as it always has been.
    d. is stronger for women than for men.

15. During which period of life do people tend to make the most friends?
    a. early childhood
    b. adolescence
    c. emerging adulthood
    d. adulthood

True or False Items

Write T (*true*) or F (*false*) on the line in front of each statement.

_____ 1. According to Erikson, the adult experiences a crisis of intimacy versus isolation after achieving identity.

_____ 2. There is a positive correlation between college education and income.

_____ 3. According to Sternberg, early in a relationship, companionate love is at its highest.

_____ 4. Cross-sex friendships are rarer today than in the past.

_____ 5. Cohabitation solves all the problems that might arise after marriage.

_____ 6. Most successful couples learn to compromise.

_____ 7. Throughout the world, marriage is generally based on romantic love.

_____ 8. Because of the complexity of the high-tech work world, most young adults can expect to remain at the same job throughout their careers.

_____ 9. Domestic violence is more common among cohabiting couples than among married couples.

_____ 10. According to some research, lust and affection arise from different parts of the brain.

Progress Test 2

Progress Test 2 should be completed during a final chapter review. Answer the following questions after you thoroughly understand the correct answers for the Chapter Review and Progress Test 1.

Multiple-Choice Questions

1. A happy marriage, a stellar college career, good relationships, and a satisfying job are all more likely if young adults have had:
   a. parents who remain married.
   b. excellent teachers.
   c. a wealthy upbringing.
   d. a supportive childhood.

2. (Issues and Applications) The key difference between common couple violence and intimate terrorism is:
   a. the presence of mental illness in the violent partner in intimate terrorism.
   b. the violent control of one partner by the other in intimate terrorism.
   c. the presence of children in intimate terrorism.
   d. the cyclical nature of common couple violence.

3. Kwame and Kendra both enjoy dancing, going to the movies, and working out. Developmentalists would say their marriage is characterized by:
   a. heterogamy.
   b. homogamy.
   c. social homogamy.
   d. b. and c.

4. Which of the following terms does *not* belong with the others?
   a. physical attractiveness
   b. apparent availability.
   c. frequent exposure.
   d. heterogamy.

5. The Western ideal of love is best described in Sternberg's theory as:
   a. romantic.
   b. fatuous.
   c. companionate.
   d. consummate.

6. Which of the following is *not* true today regarding marriage?
   a. Couples are divorcing more often.
   b. Couples are marrying earlier.
   c. Arranged marriage is practiced in one-third of all nations.
   d. In North America and Europe, more than half of those age 18 to 25 have never married.

7. Whereas men's friendships tend to be based on _____ , friendships between women tend to be based on _____ .
   a. shared confidences; shared interests
   b. cooperation; competition
   c. shared interests; shared confidences
   d. finding support for personal problems; discussion of practical issues

8. According to Robert Sternberg, the three dimensions of love are:
   a. passion, intimacy, and consummate love.
   b. physical intimacy, emotional intimacy, and consummate love.
   c. passion, commitment, and consummate love.
   d. passion, intimacy, and commitment.

9. Research on cohabitation suggests that:
   a. there is little variation in why couples cohabit.

b. emerging adults in the United States, Canada, and England cohabit at higher rates than those in Japan, Ireland, and Italy.
   c. adults who cohabit tend to be older and wealthier than married people.
   d. cohabitation leads to a stronger marriage.

10. A homogamous marriage is best defined as a marriage between:
    a. people who are physically similar to each other.
    b. people of similar social backgrounds.
    c. people of dissimilar socioeconomic backgrounds.
    d. two caring people of the same sex.

11. Compared to married adults, cohabiting adults tend to be:
    a. younger.
    b. poorer.
    c. more likely to end the relationship.
    d. all of the above.

12. Today, male–female relationships: O
    a. are more common than in the past.
    b. are not usually preludes to romance.
    c. can last a lifetime.
    d. are characterized by all of the above.

13. The idea that psychopathology is the consequence of the interaction of a genetic vulnerability with challenging life events is expressed in the:
    a. social exchange theory.
    b. diathesis-stress model.
    c. homogamy theory.
    d. heterogamy theory.

14. A loss of interest or pleasure in most activities that lasts for two weeks or more is likely to be diagnosed as:
    a. social phobia.
    b. anxiety disorder.
    c. obsessive-compulsive disorder.
    d. major depression.

15. The disorder characterized by disorganized thoughts, delusions, and hallucinations is:
    a. post-traumatic stress disorder.
    b. anxiety disorder.
    c. schizophrenia.
    d. obsessive-compulsive disorder.

Matching Items

Match each definition or description with its corresponding term.

Terms

_____ **1.** diathesis-stress
_____ **2.** cohabitation
_____ **3.** intimate terrorism
_____ **4.** heterogamy
_____ **5.** equity
_____ **6.** social exchange theory
_____ **7.** social homogamy
_____ **8.** exclusion criteria
_____ **9.** homogamy
_____ **10.** common couple violence

Definitions or Descriptions

a. abusive relationship that leads to battered-wife syndrome
b. a filter in choosing friends
c. the similarity with which a couple regard leisure interests and role preferences
d. a marriage between people with dissimilar interests and backgrounds
e. idea that emotional disorders are caused by genetic vulnerability interacting with challenging life events
f. predicts success in marriages in which each partner contributes something useful to the other
g. arrangement in which two unrelated, unmarried adults live together in a romantic partnership
h. the extent to which partners perceive equality in their relationship
i. a marriage between people with similar interests and backgrounds
j. abusive relationship that tends to improve with time

Developmental Psychology Applied

Answer these questions the day before an exam as a final check on your understanding of the chapter's terms and concepts.

1. Professor Samuels believes that people enlarge their understanding, resources, and experiences through their intimate friends. This idea is called:
   a. interdependence.
   b. affiliation.
   c. communion.
   d. self-expansion.

2. (In Person) Marie notes that her parents have been married for 25 years, even though each seems somewhat unfulfilled in terms of their relationship. Her friends had a similar relationship and divorced after five years. Given the research on divorce, how might Marie explain the differences?
   a. "My parents are just much more patient with and understanding of each other."
   b. "Couples today expect more of each other."

   c. "My parents feel that they must stay together for financial reasons."
   d. "I can't understand what keeps my parents together."

3. Because she is devoutly religious, Concepcion could never develop an intimate friendship with someone of a different faith. Concepcion's choice of friends is obviously limited by:
   a. exclusion criteria.
   b. apparent availability.
   c. exposure frequency.
   d. homogamy.

4. In order to determine ways to lower the high rate of divorce, Dr. Wilson is conducting research on marital satisfaction and the factors that contribute to it. Which of the following would he consider to be important factors?
   a. homogamy
   b. social homogamy
   c. equity
   d. All of the above contribute to marital satisfaction.

5. Rwanda and Rodney have been dating for about a month. Their relationship is most likely characterized by:
   a. strong feelings of commitment.
   b. consummate love.
   c. physical intimacy and feelings of closeness.
   d. all of the above.

6. I am 25 years old. It is most likely that I:
   a. am married.
   b. am divorced.
   c. have never been married.
   d. am divorced and remarried.

7. If asked to explain the high failure rate of marriages between young adults, Erik Erikson would most likely say that:
   a. achievement goals are often more important than intimacy in Emerging Adulthood.
   b. intimacy is difficult to establish until identity is formed.
   c. divorce has almost become an expected stage in development.
   d. today's cohort of young adults has higher expectations of marriage than did previous cohorts.

8. Professor Ryan begins class by asking, "Which disorder is a leading cause of impairment and premature death worldwide?" The correct answer is:
   a. post-traumatic stress disorder.
   b. obsessive-compulsive disorder.
   c. schizophrenia.
   d. depression.

9. Twenty-three-year-old Yoko's anxiety about college has caused her to withdraw from most activities and stay in her room almost all the time. Yoko's problem would likely be diagnosed as:
   a. depression.
   b. hikikomori.
   c. a phobia.
   d. obsessive-compulsive disorder.

10. Which of the following would be the *worst* advice for a young adult entering the job market today?
    a. Seek education that fosters a variety of general abilities and human relations skills.
    b. Expect that educational requirements for work will shift every few years.
    c. To avoid diluting your skills, concentrate your education on preparing for one specific job.
    d. Be flexible and willing to adjust to the varied pacing and timing of today's jobs.

11. Janice was severely malnourished during the early months of her pregnancy. Her child is twice as likely to develop:
    a. schizophrenia.
    b. depression.
    c. a mood disorder.
    d. an anxiety disorder.

12. Our friendships are more intimate, emotional, and tend to share secrets. Who are we?
    a. women
    b. men
    c. adolescents
    d. emerging adults

13. Arthur and Mabel have been married for 5 years. According to Sternberg, if their relationship is a satisfying one, which of the following best describes their relationship?
    a. They are strongly committed to each other.
    b. They are passionately in love.
    c. They are in the throes of establishing intimacy.
    d. They are beginning to wonder why the passion has left their relationship.

14. Philip and Phyllis have an ailing relationship. After dinner, Philip says, "We need to talk about this." In reply, Phyllis says, "I'm too busy." This pattern of interaction is called:
    a. passive-aggressive.
    b. demand/withdraw.
    c. heterogamy.
    d. social homogamy.

15. Your sister, who is about to marry, seeks your advice on what makes a happy marriage. You should mention that all but which one of the following factors contribute to marital happiness?
    a. cohabitation before marriage
    b. the degree to which a couple is homogamous or heterogamous
    c. the degree of marital equity
    d. whether identity needs have been met before marriage

Key Terms

Using your own words, write a brief definition or explanation of each of the following terms on a separate piece of paper.

1. intimacy versus isolation
2. gateways to attraction
3. exclusion criteria
4. cohabitation
5. homogamy
6. heterogamy
7. social homogamy
8. social exchange theory
9. common couple violence
10. intimate terrorism
11. linked lives
12. diathesis-stress model
13. hikikomori

ANSWERS
CHAPTER REVIEW

1. before; lengthened
2. ethnic; vocational
3. half; identify
4. is; Achieving identity is difficult for immigrants because it means reconciling their parents' background with their new social context.
5. correlates; social adjustment
6. vocational; stronger; unskilled; knowledge-based
7. intimacy versus isolation; affiliation; affection; interdependence; communion; belonging; love; self-expansion
8. friends

Friends choose each other, often for the very qualities that make them good sources of emotional support. They are also a source of self-esteem.

9. emerging adulthood
10. gateways to attraction
    a. physical attractiveness
    b. apparent availability
    c. absence of exclusion criteria
    d. frequent exposure

11. filters; excluded
12. are; shared activities; interests; intimate; emotional
13. men; women
14. more
15. later; more
16. is not
17. passion; intimacy; commitment
18. seven
19. intimacy; commitment; do; less
20. consummate
21. passion; intimacy; commitment
22. still common in many nations
23. cohabitation
24. does not; younger; poorer; more; domestic violence
25. homogamy; heterogamy; goals; social homogamy
26. equity; social exchange
27. emotional sensitivity; demand/withdraw
28. youth, poverty, poor impulse control, mental illness, and drug and alcohol addiction
29. common couple violence
30. intimate terrorism; husband; battered-wife; becomes
31. linked; varies
32. emerging adulthood; increases; psychopathology
33. diathesis-stress; stress; diathesis
34. eight
35. 8; major depression; two weeks
36. anxiety; one-fourth; post-traumatic stress disorder; obsessive-compulsive disorder; panic attacks
37. cultural; social phobia; social; academic
38. 1; genes; malnutrition; social; adolescence

PROGRESS TEST 1

Multiple-Choice Questions

1. **b.** is the answer. (p. 503)
2. **a.** is the answer. (p. 499)
   c. Identity formation is equally challenging for women and men.
3. **c.** is the answer. (p. 504)
4. **d.** is the answer. (p. 500)
5. **b.** is the answer. (p. 500)

6. d. is the answer. (p. 503)

   a. Generativity is a characteristic of the crisis following the intimacy crisis.

   b. Stagnation occurs when generativity needs are not met.

   c. Erikson's theory does not address this issue.

7. d. is the answer. (p. 504)

8. b. is the answer. (p. 502)

9. c. is the answer. (p. 508)

   d. Sternberg's theory is not concerned with the stages of parenthood.

10. c. is the answer. (p. 510)

11. b. is the answer. (p. 511)

   a. By definition, homogamous couples share values, background, and the like.

   c. & d. These may or may not be true, depending on the extent to which such a couple is homogamous.

12. d. is the answer. (p. 502)

13. b. is the answer. (p. 511)

14. a. is the answer. (p. 502)

15. c. is the answer. (p. 504)

True or False Items

1. T (p. 503)

2. T (p. 502)

3. F This comes only with time. (p. 508)

4. F Just the reverse is true. (p. 506)

5. F Cohabitation does *not* solve the problems of marriage. (p. 510)

6. T (p. 512)

7. F In about one-third of all nations, marriages are arranged by parents. In another third, parental blessing is required. (p. 507)

8. F Most young adults should learn basic skills so that they have the flexibility to move into different jobs. (pp. 502–503)

9. T (p. 510)

10. T (p. 508)

PROGRESS TEST 2

Multiple-Choice Questions

1. d. is the answer. (p. 504)

2. b. is the answer. (p. 513)

3. c. is the answer. (p. 511)

4. d. is the answer. (p. 504)

   a., b., & c. These factors are all gateways to attraction.

5. d. is the answer. (p. 508)

6. b. is the answer. (pp. 507–508)

7. c. is the answer. (p. 505)

8. d. is the answer. (p. 508)

   a., b., & c. According to Sternberg, consummate love emerges when commitment is added to passion and intimacy.

9. b. is the answer. (p. 510)

   a. Slightly more than half of all women age 25 to 40 in the United States cohabit before their first marriage.

   c. In fact, a large study of adults found that cohabitants were much *less* happy and healthy than married people.

   d. No such finding was reported in the text.

10. b. is the answer. (p. 511)

   a. & d. These characteristics do not pertain to homogamy.

   c. This describes a heterogamous marriage.

11. d. is the answer. (p. 510)

12. d. is the answer. (p. 506)

13. b. is the answer. (p. 518)

14. d. is the answer. (pp. 518–519)

   a. Social phobia is a fear of talking to people.

   b. Depression is a mood disorder.

   c. Obsessive-compulsive disorder is an anxiety disorder.

15. c. is the answer. (p. 520)

Matching Items

1. e (p. 518)	**5.** h (p. 512)	**9.** i (p. 511)
2. g (p. 510)	**6.** f (p. 512)	**10.** j (p. 513)
3. a (p. 513)	**7.** c (p. 511)	
4. d (p. 511)	**8.** b (p. 505)	

DEVELOPMENTAL PSYCHOLOGY APPLIED

1. d. is the answer. (p. 521)

2. b. is the answer. (p. 507)

3. a. is the answer. (p. 505)

4. d. is the answer. The most successful relationships are between people of similar backgrounds and similar interests. The partners' perceptions of marital equity are also important. (pp. 511–512)

5. c. is the answer. (p. 508)

   a. & b. These feelings emerge more gradually in relationships.

6. **c.** is the answer. (p. 511)

7. **b.** is the answer. (p. 503)

   a. In Erikson's theory, the crisis of intimacy *precedes* the need to be productive through work.

   c. & d. Although these items are true, Erikson's theory does not address these issues.

8. **d.** is the answer. (p. 519)

9. **b.** is the answer. (p. 519)

10. **c.** is the answer. (pp. 502–503)

    a., b., & d. These would all be good pieces of advice for new workers today.

11. **a.** is the answer. (p. 520)

12. **a.** is the answer. (p. 505)

13. **a.** is the answer. (p. 508)

14. **b.** is the answer. (p. 512)

15. **a.** is the answer. Cohabitation before marriage does *not* strengthen the relationship. (p. 510)

KEY TERMS

1. According to Erik Erikson, the first crisis of adulthood is **intimacy versus isolation**, which involves the need to share one's personal life with someone else or risk profound loneliness and isolation. (p. 503)

2. **Gateways to attraction** refer to the various qualities, such as physical attractiveness, availability, and frequent exposure, that contribute to the formation of friendships and intimate relationships. (p. 504)

3. **Exclusion criteria** are reasons for omitting certain people from consideration as close friends. (p. 505)

4. Increasingly common among young adults in all industrialized countries is the living pattern called **cohabitation**, in which two unrelated, unmarried adults live together in a committed sexual relationship. (p. 510)

5. **Homogamy** refers to marriage between people who are similar in attitudes, socioeconomic status, interests, ethnicity, religion, and the like. (p. 511)

6. **Heterogamy** refers to marriage between people who are dissimilar in attitudes, interests, SES, religion, ethnic background, and goals. (p. 511)

7. **Social homogamy** is defined as similarity in leisure interests and role preferences. (p. 511)

8. According to social **exchange theory**, social behavior is aimed at maximizing the benefits of a behavior and minimizing the costs. (p. 512)

9. **Common couple violence** is a form of abuse in which one or both partners in a couple engage in outbursts of verbal and physical attack. (p. 513)

10. **Intimate terrorism** is the form of spouse abuse in which the husband uses violent methods of accelerating intensity to isolate, degrade, and punish the wife. (p. 513)

11. Members of a family have **linked lives** in that the success, health, and well-being of one generation in a family are connected to those of another generation. (p. 514)

12. The **diathesis-stress model** is the view that mental disorders are caused by the interaction of a genetic vulnerability with stressful life events. (p. 518)

13. **Hikikomori** is a Japanese word meaning "pull away," referring to a common anxiety disorder in Japan in which emerging adults refuse to leave their rooms. (p. 519)

20

Adulthood: Biosocial Development

Chapter Overview

This chapter deals with biosocial development during the years from 25 to 65. The first section describes changes in appearance and in the functioning of the sense organs and the brain, noting the potential impact of these changes. This section also discusses the changes in the sexual-reproductive system that occur during middle adulthood. The next section discusses the health habits of adults, focusing on smoking, drinking, exercise, and gaining weight. The third section discusses the latest ways in which variations in health are measured to reflect quality of living as well as traditional measures of illness and death rates. The chapter concludes with an exploration of variations in health related to gender and income, emphasizing that, overall, adults are healthier today than in earlier cohorts.

NOTE: Answer guidelines for all Chapter 20 questions begin on page 299.

Guided Study

The text chapter should be studied one section at a time. Before you read, preview each section by skimming it, noting headings and boldface items. Then read the appropriate section objectives from the following outline. Keep these objectives in mind and, as you read the chapter section, search for the information that will enable you to meet each objective. Once you have finished a section, write out answers for its objectives.

The Aging Process (pp. 528–536)

1. Identify the typical physical changes of middle adulthood and discuss their impact.

2. Describe how the functioning of the sense organs and the brain's anatomy and functioning change during middle adulthood.

3. Identify the typical changes that occur in the sexual-reproductive system during middle adulthood.

The Impact of Poor Health Habits (pp. 536–545)

4. Describe the relationship between health and certain lifestyle factors—tobacco and alcohol use, lack of exercise, and overeating—and identify measures for increasing health during middle adulthood.

5. (Issues and Applications) Discuss the concept of resilience as it relates to the body's response to challenging life events.

Measuring Health (pp. 545–548)

6. Differentiate four measures of health.

7. (Issues and Applications) Explain the concepts of quality-adjusted life years and disability-adjusted life years.

Variations in Aging (pp. 548–552)

8. Explain how variations in health are related to gender and socioeconomic status.

Chapter Review

When you have finished reading the chapter, work through the material that follows to review it. Complete the sentences and answer the questions. As you proceed, evaluate your performance for each section by consulting the answers on page 294. Do not continue with the next section until you understand each answer. If you need to, review or reread the appropriate section in the textbook before continuing.

The Aging Process (pp. 528–536)

1. The gradual physical decline that occurs with age is called _____ .

2. Some of the normal changes in appearance that occur during middle adulthood include

    _____

    _____

    _____

3. After age 20, the lens of the eye gradually becomes _____ _____ and the cornea becomes _____ . This contributes to _____ , or difficulty seeing close objects. Difficulty seeing objects at a distance is called _____ .

4. The loss of hearing associated with senescence is called _____ . This often does not become apparent until after age _____ .

5. With normal aging, the ability to hear differences in _____ _____ declines faster than the ability to understand

    _____ .

6. Speech-related hearing losses are first apparent for _____ -(high/low) frequency sounds.

7. With age, neurons in the brain fire more _____ (slowly/rapidly). In addition, by middle adulthood there are fewer _____ and _____ . These changes contribute to a slowing of _____ _____ and make _____ more difficult.

8. Disrupted sleep _____ (is/is not) characteristic of aging.

State several possible causes of dementia that occurs before old age.

9. Two neurological problems that appear in middle age are _____ disease and _____ dementia. Other problems that occur in adulthood that correlate with loss of brain cells include _____ _____ , excessive _____ , poor _____ , and _____ .

10. People who abuse alcohol over decades risk the disease called _____ _____ .

11. Solving crossword puzzles and other _____ challenges may help protect the brain from neurological problems.

12. Adult brains _____ (can/cannot) grow new cells when old ones die. Research with _____ _____ may help answer the question of whether aging of the brain is irreversible.

13. The sexual-reproductive system peaks during _____ _____ . With age, sexual _____ is slower and _____ becomes reduced.

14. Overall in the United States, about _____ percent of all couples are infertile. Male infertility may be the result of specific problems with the _____ _____ or a low _____ . Female infertility may be the result of _____ _____ disease, especially if a _____ _____ infection is not treated.

15. The collective name for the various methods of medical intervention to restore fertility is _____ _____ _____ . The most common method is _____ _____ , in

which _____ are surgically removed and fertilized in a laboratory.

16. At an average age of _____ , a woman reaches _____ , as ovulation and menstruation stop and the production of _____ _____ drops considerably.

17. The psychological consequences of menopause are _____ (variable/not variable). European and North American cultures' perceptions of this aspect of menopause _____ (have/have not) changed over time.

18. Over the past two or three decades, many women used _____ _____ _____ to reduce post-menopausal symptoms.

19. Long-term use of HRT beyond menopause has been shown to increase the risk of _____ and has no proven effects on _____ .

20. Although some experts believe men undergo _____ , most believe that physiologically, men _____ (do/do not) experience anything like menopause.

The Impact of Poor Health Habits (pp. 536–545)

21. Rates of addiction and drug abuse _____ (increase/decrease) sharply by age 30.

22. The addictive drug in tobacco is _____ . In North America today, _____ (fewer/more) people begin smoking than in the past. Today, twice as many women die from _____ cancer as from cancer of the breast, uterus, or ovary combined. Variations in smoking rates from nation to nation, and from one cohort to another, demonstrate that smoking is affected by _____ _____ , laws, and advertisements.

23. Some studies find that adults who drink moderately may live longer, possibly because alcohol increases the blood's supply of

_____-_____

_____ , the "good" cholesterol, and

reduces _____-_____

_____ , the "bad" cholesterol. However, even moderate alcohol consumption poses a health risk if it leads to

_____ or _____ .

List some of the health hazards of excessive alcohol use.

24. Three factors that make it easier to exercise regularly are _____ , _____ , and _____ .

25. The risk of almost every adult disease is reduced by a nutritious diet that consists of

_____ .

26. Overweight, defined as _____

_____ , is present in

_____ (what percent?) of all adults in the United States. Obesity, defined as

_____ , is

a risk factor for _____

_____ and _____ .

27. Throughout much of the world, the rate of obesity is _____ (increasing/decreasing).

28. Between emerging adulthood and late adulthood, a person's metabolism _____ (slows/increases) by about a third, which means that middle-aged people need to eat _____ (more/less) simply to maintain their weight.

29. Current explanations for the trends in overweight and obesity focus on _____ , on _____ , and on _____ factors.

30. (Table 20.2) Although weight loss by _____ usually produces safe results, attempts at weight loss by using

_____-_____

_____ and _____ are controversial.

31. For most conditions and diseases, _____ is less risky than _____ .

32. (Issues and Applications) When stressful challenges are successfully met, the body's damaging response to stress _____ (is/is not) averted. In fact, accumulated stress may lead to increased _____ .

Measuring Health (pp. 545–548)

33. Perhaps the most solid indicator of health of given age groups is the rate of _____ , or death. This rate is often _____-adjusted to take into account the higher death rate among the very old. By this measure, the country with the lowest rate is _____ , and the country with the highest rate is

_____ _____ .

34. A more comprehensive measure of health is _____ , defined as _____ of all kinds.

35. To truly portray quality of life, we need to measure _____ , which refers to a person's inability to perform basic activities, and _____ , which refers to how healthy and energetic a person feels.

36. In terms of quality of life, _____ is probably the most important measure of health.

37. (Issues and Applications) The concept of

_____-_____

_____ indicates how many years of full vitality are lost as a result of a particular disease or disability. The reciprocal of this statistic is known as _____-_____

_____ _____ .

Variations in Aging (pp. 548–552)

38. Worldwide, there are more old _____
(women/men) than _____
(women/men) because at every age, more
_____ (women/men) die. With the
exception of _____ disease before
age 50, _____ (women/men) are
more likely to have every chronic disease.

39. Individuals who are relatively well-educated,
financially secure, and living in or near cities tend
to live _____ (shorter/longer) lives
and have _____ (more/ fewer)
chronic illnesses or disabilities.

Progress Test 1

Multiple-Choice Questions

Circle your answers to the following questions and
check them with the answers beginning on page 294.
If your answer is incorrect, read the explanation for
why it is incorrect and then consult the appropriate
pages of the text (in parentheses following the correct
answer).

1. During the years from 25 to 65, the average adult:
   a. becomes proportionally slimmer.
   b. gains about 5 pounds per year.
   c. gains about 1 pound per year.
   d. is more likely to have pockets of fat settle on
   various parts of the body.

2. Senescence refers to:
   a. the average age at which menopause begins.
   b. the average age at which andropause begins.
   c. age-related physical decline.
   d. premature dementia.

3. Age-related deficits in speech-related hearing are
most noticeable for:
   a. high-frequency sounds.
   b. low-frequency sounds.
   c. mid-range-frequency sounds.
   d. rapid conversation.

4. Regarding age-related changes in vision, most
older adults are:
   a. nearsighted.
   b. farsighted.
   c. nearsighted and farsighted.
   d. neither nearsighted or farsighted

5. As we age:
   a. neurons fire more slowly.
   b. the size of the brain is reduced.
   c. there are fewer synapses.
   d. each of the above occurs.

6. At midlife, individuals who _____
tend to live longer and have fewer chronic illnesses or disabilities.
   a. are relatively well educated
   b. are financially secure
   c. live in or near cities
   d. are or do all of the above

7. The term that refers to diseases of all kinds is:
   a. mortality.   **c.** disability.
   b. morbidity.   **d.** vitality.

8. On average, women reach menopause at age:
   a. 39.   **c.** 46.
   b. 42.   **d.** 51.

9. (Issues and Applications) DALYs is a measure of:
   a. the quality of a person's life.
   b. the impact of disability on the quality of a person's life.
   c. how healthy and energetic a person feels.
   d. long-term difficulty in performing normal
   activities.

10. Among older adults, the need for regular sleep:
   a. is diminished.
   b. increases.
   c. is about the same as it was during early adulthood.
   d. varies widely from individual to individual

11. Mortality is usually expressed as:
   a. the number of deaths each year per 1,000 individuals in a particular population.
   b. the total number of deaths per year in a given
   population.
   c. the average age of death among the members
   of a given population.
   d. the percentage of people of a given age who
   are still living.

12. (Issues and Applications) The concept that indicates how many years of full physical, intellectual, and social health are lost to a particular physical disease or disability is:
   a. vitality.
   b. disability.
   c. morbidity.
   d. quality-adjusted life years.

13. The irreversible brain damage caused by excessive consumption of alcohol over decades is:
    a. Korsakoff's syndrome.
    b. Alzheimer's disease.
    c. Parkinson's disease.
    d. frontotemporal dementia

14. Which of the following is true of all smoking diseases?
    a. They are a natural result of smoking for 10 years or more, whether or not the person eventually quit.
    b. They are related to dosage of nicotine taken in and to length of time the person has smoked.
    c. They are all incurable.
    d. They are all based on the psychological addiction to tobacco.

15. The most common method of treatment for infertile couples is:
    a. assisted reproductive technology.
    b. in vivo fertilization.
    c. in vitro fertilization.
    d. surrogate parenting.

True or False Items

Write T (*true*) or F (*false*) on the line in front of each statement.

_____ 1. Europe is the world leader of the obesity and diabetes epidemics.

_____ 2. During adulthood, back muscles, connecting tissues, and bones lose strength.

_____ 3. Approximately half of all adults in the United States are obese.

_____ 4. Moderate users of alcohol are more likely than teetotalers to have heart attacks.

_____ 5. Those who exercise regularly have lower rates of serious illness than do sedentary people.

_____ 6. Rates of addiction and drug abuse increase markedly by age 30 in every nation.

_____ 7. During middle adulthood, sexual responses slow down.

_____ 8. Senescence refers specifically to the psychological changes that accompany menopause.

_____ 9. Despite popular reference to it, there is no "male menopause."

_____ 10. A woman's culture, expectations, and attitude, more than biology, determine her psychological reaction to menopause.

Progress Test 2

Progress Test 2 should be completed during a final chapter review. Answer the following questions after you thoroughly understand the correct answers for the Chapter Review and Progress Test 1.

Multiple-Choice Questions

1. The first visible age-related changes are seen in the:
   a. hair.   c. teeth.
   b. muscles.   d. skin.

2. Of the following, which is the most costly to society?
   a. disability   c. mortality
   b. morbidity   d. acute illness

3. Two neurological problems that appear during adulthood are:
   a. Alzheimer's disease and Korsakoff's syndrome.
   b. Korsakoff's syndrome and Parkinson's disease.
   c. Parkinson's disease and frontotemporal dementia.
   d. Alzheimer's disease and frontotemporal dementia.

4. Problems that correlate with loss of brain cells in adulthood include:
   a. drug abuse.
   b. excessive stress.
   c. poor circulation.
   d. all of the above.

5. The major reason for infertility among U.S. couples is:
   a. problems with the male's reproductive organs.
   c. a low sperm count.
   b. blockage of the woman's fallopian tubes.
   d. postponing childbearing until they are well past their peak reproductive years.

6. Menopause is caused by a sharp decrease in the production of:
   a. sex hormones.   c. synapses.
   b. neurons.   d. all of the above.

7. To be a true index of health, morbidity rates must be refined in terms of which of the following health measure(s)?
   a. mortality rate
   b. disability and mortality rates
   c. vitality
   d. disability and vitality

8. The term "male menopause" was probably coined to refer to:
   a. the sudden dip in testosterone that sometimes occurs in men who have been sexually inactive.
   b. age-related declines in fertility among men.
   c. men suffering from erectile dysfunction.
   d. age-related declines in testosterone levels in middle-aged men.

9. Which of the following is *not* true regarding hormone replacement therapy (HRT)?
   a. Long-term use (10 years or more) increases the risk of heart disease, stroke, and breast cancer.
   b. HRT reduces hot flashes and decreases osteoporosis.
   c. HRT has no proven effects on dementia.
   d. For most women, the benefits of HRT outweigh the risks.

10. The leading cause of cancer deaths in North America is:
    a. lung cancer.
    b. breast cancer.
    c. prostate cancer.
    d. skin cancer.

11. Which of the following was *not* cited as a possible reason for the high incidence of overweight among children and adults?
    a. genes
    b. parental attitudes
    c. culture
    d. glandular problems

12. Which of the following is *not* true regarding alcohol consumption?
    a. Alcohol decreases the blood's supply of high-density lipoprotein.
    b. Alcohol dependence is more common in middle adulthood.
    c. Alcohol is a major cause of injury and disease worldwide.
    d. Alcohol abuse is the main cause of cirrhosis of the liver.

13. The highest rates of obesity are found during:
    a. adolescence.
    b. early adulthood.
    c. middle adulthood.
    d. late adulthood.

14. Which of the following is true of sexual expressiveness in adulthood?
    a. Menopause impairs a woman's sexual relationship.
    b. Men's frequency of ejaculation increases until approximately age 55.
    c. Signs of arousal in a woman are as obvious as they were at age 20.
    d. The levels of sex hormones gradually diminish and responses slow down.

15. A BMI over 30:
    a. is less harmful among people of African American, Latino, or Asian American ethnicity.
    b. is less harmful among European Americans.
    c. is less harmful to women than men.
    d. is always harmful.

Matching Items

Match each definition or description with its corresponding term.

Terms

_____ **1.** mortality
_____ **2.** morbidity
_____ **3.** vitality
_____ **4.** menopause
_____ **5.** andropause
_____ **6.** ART
_____ **7.** HRT
_____ **8.** osteoporosis
_____ **9.** disability
_____ **10.** quality-adjusted life years

Definitions or Descriptions

a. disease of all kinds
b. collective term for infertility treatments
c. often prescribed to treat the symptoms of menopause
d. a condition of fragile bones
e. death; as a measure of health, it usually refers to the number of deaths each year per thousand individuals
f. the cessation of ovulation and menstruation
g. more important to quality of life than any other measure of health
h. male menopause
i. the inability to perform normal activities
j. number of years of full vitality lost because of disease or disability

Developmental Psychology Applied

Answer these questions the day before an exam as a final check on your understanding of the chapter's terms and concepts.

1. Josef has enjoyed playing football with friends during most of his adult life. He has just turned 45 and notices that he no longer tackles with the same force he had 10 years ago. This is probably because:
   a. his reaction time has slowed.
   b. his Type II muscle fibers have decreased substantially.
   c. his stomach muscles have weakened.
   d. of all of the above reasons.

2. Maureen is British and Maria is Italian. Based on averages, which of the following is most likely true of the two women?
   a. Maria is less obese than Maureen.
   b. Maureen is less obese than Maria.
   c. Both women are equally obese.
   d. Both women are thin.

3. Fifty-five-year-old Dewey is concerned because sexual stimulation seems to take longer and needs to be more direct than earlier in his life. As a friend, you should tell him:
   a. "You should see a therapist. It is not normal."
   b. "See a doctor if your 'sexual prowess' doesn't improve soon. You may have some underlying physical problem."
   c. "Don't worry. This is normal for middle-aged men."
   d. "You're too old to have sex, so just give it up."

4. Female fertility may be affected by:
   a. anorexia.
   b. pelvic inflammatory disease.
   c. smoking.
   d. all of the above.

5. (Issues and Applications) Which of the following would entail the greatest loss of QALYs?
   a. a 70-year-old man dies in an automobile accident.
   b. a 20-year-old woman is permanently disabled and unable to work following an automobile accident.
   c. a 50-year-old man is forced to switch jobs after a skiing accident.
   d. It is impossible to determine from the information given.

6. Summarizing her report on gender differences in aging, Trisha notes that:
   a. at every age, women are more likely than men to have nearly every chronic disease.
   b. at every age, men are more likely than women to have nearly every chronic disease.
   c. the number of years that women outlive men is decreasing.
   d. the number of years that women outlive men is increasing

7. Forty-five-year-old Val is the same weight she has been since college and continues to eat the same types and amounts of food she has always eaten. In order to maintain her weight through middle age, Val should:
   a. continue to eat the same amounts and types of foods.
   b. reduce her caloric intake.
   c. eat more foods high in LDL.
   d. reduce her intake of foods high in HDL.

8. Kirk wants to move to the part of the world that has the lowest annual mortality. You tell him to buy a ticket to:
   a. Germany.   c. France.
   b. Canada.   d. Japan.

9. Mark and Alexis have been trying for two years to have a baby. Before they decide to adopt, they are going to try one more thing—in vitro fertilization. Which of the following should they know about IVF?
   a. It is successful only about half the time.
   b. Birth defects are less likely with IVF.
   c. Low-birthweight twins are born in almost half of all IVF pregnancies.
   d. In some nations, couples may not undergo IVF if the man is over 40.

10. Lung cancer is no longer considered a disease of affluence because:
    a. today, educated people are less likely to smoke.
    b. lung cancer deaths are higher today among the poor.
    c. even poor people today can afford to buy cigarettes.
    d. of all the above reasons.

11. Fifty-year-old Beth has a college degree and a good job and lives near Seattle, Washington. Compared to her sister, who dropped out of high school and is struggling to survive on a dairy farm in rural Wisconsin, Beth is most likely to:
    a. live longer.
    b. have fewer chronic illnesses.
    c. have fewer disabilities.
    d. do or have all of the above.

12. Morbidity is to mortality as _____ is to _____ .
    a. disease; death
    b. death; disease
    c. inability to perform normal daily activities; disease
    d. disease; subjective feeling of being healthy

13. Forty-five-year-old Amber was teaching in New Orleans in 2005 when hurricane Katrina hit. Her home was destroyed, leaving Amber and her roommates homeless. Research suggests that their responses would most likely be to:
    a. get on the first bus out of town.
    b. work together to help themselves and others in similar situations.
    c. curl up in a warm spot and hope the problem will go away.
    d. become so depressed they considered suicide.

14. Jack, who is approaching adulthood, wants to know which health habits have the greatest influence on physical well-being. You point to:
    a. tobacco and alcohol use.
    b. overeating.
    c. exercise.
    d. all of the above.

15. Who of the following is most likely to exercise?
    a. 60-year-old Sam
    b. 55-year-old Jenna
    c. 20-year-old Amy
    d. 45-year-old Jack

Key Terms

Using your own words, write a brief definition or explanation of each of the following terms on a separate piece of paper.

1. senescence

2. presbycusis

3. assisted reproductive technology (ART)

4. in vitro fertilization (IVF)

5. menopause

6. hormone replacement therapy (HRT)

7. andropause

8. mortality

9. morbidity

10. disability

11. vitality

12. quality-adjusted life years (QALYs)

13. disability-adjusted life years (DALYs)

ANSWERS

CHAPTER REVIEW

1. senescence

2. hair turns gray and thins; skin becomes thinner, less flexible, drier, and more wrinkled; middle-age spread occurs; pockets of fat settle on the upper arms, buttocks, and eyelids; back muscles, connecting tissues, and bones lose strength, causing some individuals to become shorter; breathing gets quicker and shallower

3. less elastic; flatter; farsightedness; nearsightedness

4. presbycusis; 60

5. pure tones; conversation

6. high

7. slowly; neurons; synapses; reaction time; multitasking

8. is

The possible causes of early dementia include inheriting a dominant gene for Alzheimer's disease, being born with Down syndrome or another serious genetic disorder, brain damage as a result of trauma, or suffering a massive stroke

9. Parkinson's; frontotemporal; drug abuse; stress; circulation; viruses

10. Korsakoff's syndrome

11. intellectual

12. can; stem cells

13. early adulthood; responsiveness; fertility

14. 15; reproductive organs; sperm count; pelvic inflammatory; sexually transmitted

15. assisted reproductive technology; in vitro fertilization; ova

16. 51; menopause; sex hormones

17. variable; have

18. hormone replacement therapy (HRT)

19. heart disease, stroke, and breast cancer; dementia

20. andropause; do not

21. decrease

22. nicotine; fewer; lung; social norms

23. high-density lipoprotein (HDL); low-density lipoprotein (LDL); smoking; overeating

Heavy drinking is the main cause of liver disease; it also destroys brain cells; contributes to osteoporosis; decreases fertility; is a risk factor for many forms of cancer; and accompanies many suicides, homicides, and accidents.

24. personal commitment; supportive friends; community environment

25. fresh fruits and vegetables, whole grains, fish with omega-3 fatty acids but no toxins, clean water, low-fat milk, and cheese

26. a BMI above 25; 66 percent; a BMI of 30 or more; heart disease; diabetes; stroke; arthritis

27. increasing

28. slows; less

29. genes; parental attitudes and practice; environmental

30. weight-loss drugs; surgery

31. prevention; treatment

32. is; resilience

33. mortality; age; Japan; Sierra Leone

34. morbidity; disease

35. disability; vitality

36. vitality

37. quality-adjusted life years (QALYs); disability-adjusted life years (DALYs)

38. women; men; men; heart; women

39. longer; fewer

PROGRESS TEST 1

Multiple-Choice Questions

1. **d.** is the answer. (p. 528)

   b. & c. Weight gain varies substantially from person to person.

2. **c.** is the answer. (p. 528)

3. **a.** is the answer. (p. 530)

4. **c.** is the answer. (p. 529)

5. **d.** is the answer. (p. 530)

6. **d.** is the answer. (p. 549)

7. **b.** is the answer. (p. 545)

   a. This is the overall death rate.

   c. This refers to a person's inability to perform normal activities of daily living.

d. This refers to how physically, intellectually, and socially healthy an individual feels.

8. **d.** is the answer. (p. 534)

9. **b.** is the answer. (p. 547)

   a. This refers to QALYs.

   c. This refers to vitality.

   d. This refers to the disability itself.

10. **b.** is the answer. (p. 530)

11. **a.** is the answer. (p. 545)

12. **d.** is the answer. (p. 546)

   a. Vitality is a measure of how healthy and energetic a person feels.

   b. Disability measures only the inability to perform basic activities.

   c. Morbidity refers only to the rate of disease.

13. **a.** is the answer. (p. 531)

14. **b.** is the answer. (p. 538)

15. **c.** is the answer. (p. 534)

True or False Items

1. F   The United States is the world leader of the obesity and diabetes epidemics. (p. 541)

2. T (p. 528)

3. F   Approximately two of every three are overweight, and 30 percent are obese. (p. 541)

4. F   Moderate use of alcohol is associated with reduced risk of heart attacks. (p. 538)

5. T (p. 539)

6. F   Rates actually decrease. (p. 537)

7. T (p. 532)

8. F   Senescence is the gradual physical decline that occurs with age. (p. 528)

9. T (p. 535)

10. T (p. 535)

PROGRESS TEST 2

Multiple-Choice Questions

1. **d.** is the answer. (p. 528)

2. **a.** is the answer. When a person is disabled, society not only loses an active contributor but may also need to provide special care. (p. 546)

3. **c.** is the answer. (p. 531)

4. **d.** is the answer. (p. 531)

5. **d.** is the answer. (p. 533)

6. **a.** is the answer. (p. 534)

7. **d.** is the answer. (p. 546)

8. **a.** is the answer. (pp. 535–536)

   b. Most men continue to produce sperm throughout adulthood and are, therefore, theoretically fertile indefinitely.

   c. This disorder was not discussed.

   d For men, there is no sudden drop in hormone levels during middle adulthood.

9. **d.** is the answer. (p. 535)

10. **a.** is the answer. (p. 537)

11. **d.** is the answer. (p. 541)

12. **a.** is the answer. Alcohol increases the blood's supply of HDL, which is one possible reason that adults who drink in moderation may live longer than "teetotalers." (p. 538)

13. **c.** is the answer. (p. 541)

14. **d.** is the answer. (p. 532)

15. **d.** is the answer. (p. 541)

Matching Items

1. e (p. 545)	5. h (p. 535)	9. i (p. 546)
2. a (p. 545)	6. b (p. 534)	10. j (p. 546)
3. g (p. 546)	7. c (p. 535)	
4. f (p. 534)	8. d (p. 535)	

DEVELOPMENTAL PSYCHOLOGY APPLIED

1. **d.** is the answer. (p. 528)

2. **a.** is the answer. (p. 542)

3. **c.** is the answer. (pp. 535–536)

4. **d.** is the answer. (p. 533)

5. **b.** is the answer. Being permanently disabled and unable to work, the 20-year-old woman clearly has lost more years of vitality than either an elderly man, who statistically would be expected to die soon anyway (a.), or a middle-aged man who is simply forced to change jobs following an accident (c.). (pp. 546–547)

6. **a.** is the answer. (p. 549)

7. **b.** is the answer. (p. 541)

   a. As Val ages, her metabolism will slow down, so she should reduce her caloric intake.

   c. & d. Just the opposite is true. She should decrease her intake of foods high in LDL and increase her intake of foods high in HDL.

8. **d.** is the answer. (p. 545)

9. **c.** is the answer. (p. 534)

10. **d.** is the answer. (p. 549)

11. **d.** is the answer. People who are relatively well-educated, financially secure, and live in or near cities tend to receive all of these benefits. (p. 549)

12. **a.** is the answer. (p. 545)

    b. This answer would be correct if the statement was "Mortality is to morbidity."

    c. This answer would be correct if the statement was "Disability is to morbidity."

    d. This answer would be correct if the statement was "Morbidity is to vitality."

13. **b.** is the answer. (p. 544)

14. **d.** is the answer. (pp. 537–542)

15. **c.** is the answer. (p. 539)

KEY TERMS

1. **Senescence** refers to the gradual physical decline that accompanies aging. (p. 528)

2. **Presbycusis** is the loss of hearing associated with aging. (p. 529)

3. **Assisted reproductive technology (ART)** is the collective name for the various medical means of treating infertility. (p. 534)

4. **In vitro fertilization (IVF)** is a fertility treatment in which egg cells are surgically removed from a woman and fertilized in the laboratory. (p. 534)

5. At **menopause,** which usually occurs around age 51, ovulation and menstruation stop and the production of the hormones estrogen, progesterone, and testosterone drops. (p. 534)

6. **Hormone replacement therapy (HRT)** is intended to help relieve menopausal symptoms, especially in women who experience an abrupt drop in hormone level because their ovaries are surgically removed. (p. 535)

7. **Andropause,** or male menopause, refers to age-related changes in sexual desire, muscle mass, and other physical changes that accompany decreases in testosterone levels. (p. 535)

8. **Mortality** means death. As a measure of health, it usually refers to the number of deaths each year per thousand members of a given population. (p. 545)

9. **Morbidity** means disease. As a measure of health, it refers to the rate of diseases of all kinds in a given population, which can be sudden and severe (acute) or extend over a long time period (chronic). (p. 545)

10. **Disability** refers to a person's inability to perform normal activities of daily life. (p. 546)

11. **Vitality** refers to how healthy and energetic—physically, intellectually, and socially—an individual actually feels. (p. 546)

12. **Quality-adjusted life years (QALYs)** is the concept that indicates how many years of full vitality an individual loses due to a particular disease or disability. (p. 546)

13. **Disability-adjusted life years (DALYs),** the reciprocal of QALYs, a measure of the impact that disability has on quality of life. (p. 547)

21

Adulthood: Cognitive Development

Chapter Overview

The way psychologists conceptualize intelligence has changed considerably in recent years. Chapter 21 begins by examining the different methods of measuring intelligence (psychometrics), which may lead to different conclusions regarding increases or decreases in intelligence over the life span. The section then examines the contemporary view of intelligence, which emphasizes its multidimensional nature. Most experts now believe that there are several distinct intelligences rather than a single general entity.

The next section first focuses on the tendency of adults to select certain aspects of their lives to focus on as they age. In doing so, they optimize development in those areas and compensate for declines in others. Each person's cognitive development occurs in a unique context influenced by variations in genes, life experiences, and cohort effects. The section then discusses the cognitive expertise that often comes with experience, pointing out the ways in which expert thinking differs from that of the novice. Expert thinking is more specialized, flexible, and intuitive and is guided by more and better problem-solving strategies.

NOTE: Answer guidelines for all Chapter 21 questions begin on page 305.

Guided Study

The text chapter should be studied one section at a time. Before you read, preview each section by skimming it, noting headings and boldface items. Then read the appropriate section objectives from the following outline. Keep these objectives in mind and, as you read the chapter section, search for the information that will enable you to meet each objective. Once you have finished a section, write out answers for its objectives.

What Is Intelligence? (pp. 556–567)

1. Briefly trace the history of the controversy regarding adult intelligence, including the findings of cross-sectional and longitudinal research and how cross-sequential research compensates for the shortcomings of the other methods.

2. Distinguish between fluid and crystallized intelligence, and explain how each is affected by age.

3. Differentiate the three fundamental forms of intelligence described by Robert Sternberg.

4. Outline Howard Gardner's theory of intelligence.

5. Discuss the roles of age and cultural and historical context in determining which type of intelligence is most valued.

Selective Gains and Losses (pp. 567–574)

6. Explain the concept of selective optimization with compensation.

7. Describe how the cognitive processes of experts differ from those of novices.

Chapter Review

When you have finished reading the chapter, work through the material that follows to review it. Complete the sentences and answer the questions. As you proceed, evaluate your performance for each section by consulting the answers beginning on page 305. Do not continue with the next section until you understand each answer. If you need to, review or reread the appropriate section in the textbook before continuing.

What Is Intelligence? (pp. 556–567)

1. Measuring psychological characteristics such as intelligence is taking a _____ approach to research.

2. Historically, psychologists have thought of intelligence as _____ (a single entity/several distinct abilities).

3. A leading theoretician, _____, argued that there is such a thing as general intelligence, which he called _____ .

4. For the first half of the twentieth century, psychologists were convinced that intelligence peaks during _____ and then gradually declines. During the 1950s, Nancy Bayley and Melita Oden found that on several tests of concept mastery, the scores of gifted individuals _____ (increased/decreased/remained unchanged) between ages 20 and 50.

5. Follow-up research by Bayley demonstrated a general _____ (increase/decrease) in intellectual functioning from childhood through young adulthood. This developmental trend was true on _____ , _____ , and _____ .

6. Bayley's study is an example of a _____ (cross-sectional/longitudinal) research design. Earlier studies relied on _____ (cross-sectional/longitudinal) research designs.

Briefly explain why cross-sectional research can sometimes yield a misleading picture of adult development.

7. Throughout the world, studies have shown a general trend toward _____ (increasing/decreasing) average IQ over successive generations. This trend is called the _____ _____ , and

because of it, IQ tests are _____ every 15 years or so.

8. Cite three reasons that longitudinal findings may be misleading.

   a. _____

   b. _____

   c. _____

9. One of the first researchers to recognize the problems of cross-sectional and longitudinal studies of intelligence was _____ .

10. Schaie developed a new research technique combining cross-sectional and longitudinal approaches, called _____-_____ research.

Briefly explain this type of research design.

11. Using this design, Schaie found that on five _____ _____ _____ , most people improved throughout most of adulthood. The results of this research are known collectively as the _____ _____ _____ .

12. In the 1960s, researchers _____ and _____ differentiated two aspects of intelligence, which they called _____ and _____ intelligence.

13. As its name implies, _____ intelligence is flexible reasoning used to draw inferences and understand relations between concepts. This type of intelligence is also made up of basic mental abilities, including _____ _____ , _____ _____ , and _____ _____ .

14. The accumulation of facts, information, and knowledge that comes with education and experience with a particular culture is referred to as _____ intelligence.

15. During adulthood, _____ intelligence declines markedly, primarily because everything slows down with age. However, if a person's intelligence is simply measured by one _____ score, this decline is temporarily disguised by a(n) _____ (increase/decrease) in _____ intelligence.

16. The theorist who has proposed that intelligence is composed of three fundamental aspects is _____ . The _____ aspect consists of the mental processes that foster academic proficiency by making efficient learning, remembering, and thinking possible. This type of thinking is particularly valued at _____ _____ (what stage of life?).

17. The _____ aspect enables the person to be flexible and innovative when dealing with new situations. This type of thinking is always _____ rather than _____ , meaning that such thinkers frequently find _____ solutions to problems rather than relying on the one that has always been considered correct.

18. The _____ aspect concerns the ability to adapt to the contextual demands of a given situation. This type of thinking is particularly useful for managing the conflicting personalities in a _____ or _____ .

19. Practical intelligence _____ (is/is not) related to traditional intelligence as measured by IQ tests.

20. The researcher who believes that there are eight distinct intelligences is _____ . Evidence from brain-damaged people _____ (supports/does not support) the multidimensional view of intelligence.

21. The value placed on different dimensions of intellectual ability _____ (varies/does not vary) from culture to culture _____ (and/but not) from one stage of life to another. Another factor is the _____ context.

Selective Gains and Losses (p. 567–574)

22. Researchers such as Paul and Margaret Baltes have found that people devise alternative strategies to compensate for age-related declines in ability. They call this _____

_____ _____

_____ .

23. Some developmentalists believe that as we age, we develop specialized competencies, or _____ , in activities that are important to us. In other words, each person becomes a

_____ _____ .

24. There are several differences between experts and novices. First, novices tend to rely more on _____ (formal/informal) procedures and rules to guide them, whereas experts rely more on their _____

_____ and the immediate

_____ to guide them. This makes the actions of experts more _____

and less _____ .

25. Second, many elements of expert performance become _____ , almost instinctive, which enables experts to process information more quickly and efficiently.

26. A third difference is that experts have more and better _____ for accomplishing a particular task.

27. A final difference is that experts are more

_____ .

28. In developing their abilities, experts point to the importance of _____ , usually at least _____ (how long?) before their full potential is achieved. This highlights the importance of _____ in the development of expertise.

29. Research studies indicate that the benefits of expertise are quite _____ (general/specific) and that practice and specialization _____ (can/cannot) always overcome the effects of age.

Progress Test 1

Multiple-Choice Questions

Circle your answers to the following questions and check them with the answers on page 306. If your answer is incorrect, read the explanation for why it is incorrect and then consult the appropriate pages of the text (in parentheses following the correct answer).

Multiple-Choice Questions

1. Most of the evidence for an age-related decline in intelligence came from:
   a. cross-sectional research.
   b. longitudinal research.
   c. cross-sequential research.
   d. random sampling.

2. The major flaw in cross-sectional research is the virtual impossibility of:
   a. selecting subjects who are similar in every aspect except age.
   b. tracking all subjects over a number of years.
   c. finding volunteers with high IQs.
   d. testing concept mastery.

3. Because of the limitations of other research methods, K. Warner Schaie developed a new research design based on:
   a. observer-participant methods.
   b. in-depth questionnaires.
   c. personal interviews.
   d. both cross-sectional and longitudinal methods.

4. Why don't traditional intelligence tests reveal age-related cognitive declines during adulthood?
   a. They measure only fluid intelligence.
   b. They measure only crystallized intelligence.
   c. They separate verbal and nonverbal IQ scores, obscuring these declines.
   d. They yield a single IQ score, allowing adulthood increases in crystallized intelligence to mask these declines.

5. Which of the following is most likely to *decrease* with age?
   a. vocabulary
   b. accumulated facts
   c. working memory
   d. practical intelligence

6. The basic mental abilities that go into learning and understanding any subject have been classified as:
   a. crystallized intelligence.
   b. plastic intelligence.
   c. fluid intelligence.
   d. rote memory.

7. Some psychologists contend that intelligence consists of fluid intelligence, which _____ during adulthood, and crystallized intelligence, which _____ .
   a. remains stable; declines
   b. declines; remains stable
   c. increases; declines
   d. declines; increases

8. Charles Spearman argued for the existence of a single general intelligence factor, which he referred to as:
   a. *g*.
   b. practical intelligence.
   c. analytic intelligence.
   d. creative intelligence.

9. The Flynn effect refers to:
   a. the trend toward increasing average IQ.
   b. age-related declines in fluid intelligence.
   c. ethnic differences in average IQ scores.
   d. the impact of practice on expertise.

10. The shift from conscious, deliberate processing of information to a more unconscious, effortless performance requires:
    a. automatic responding.
    b. subliminal execution.
    c. plasticity.
    d. encoding.

11. Concerning expertise, which of the following is true?
    a. In performing tasks, experts tend to be more set in their ways, preferring to use strategies that have worked in the past.
    b. The reasoning of experts is usually more formal, disciplined, and stereotypic than that of the novice.
    c. In performing tasks, experts tend to be more flexible and to enjoy experimentation more than novices do.
    d. Experts often have difficulty adjusting to situations that are exceptions to the rule.

12. In general, as people age they specialize in activities that are personally meaningful. In other words, each person:
    a. develops fluid intelligence.
    b. develops crystallized intelligence.
    c. develops analytic intelligence.
    d. becomes a selective expert.

13. Which of the following describes the results of Nancy Bayley's follow-up study of members of the Berkeley study?
    a. Most subjects reached a plateau in intellectual functioning at age 21.
    b. The typical person at age 36 improved on 2 of 10 subtests of adult intelligence scales: picture completion and arithmetic.
    c. The typical person at age 36 was still improving on the most important subtests of the intelligence scale.
    d. No conclusions could be reached because the sample of subjects was not representative.

14. Which of the following is *not* one of the general conclusions of research about intellectual changes during adulthood?
    a. In general, most intellectual abilities increase or remain stable throughout early and middle adulthood until the 60s.
    b. Cohort differences have a powerful influence on intellectual differences in adulthood.
    c. Intellectual functioning is affected by educational background.
    d. Intelligence becomes less specialized with increasing age.

15. The psychologist who has proposed that intelligence is composed of analytic, creative, and practical aspects is:
    a. Charles Spearman.   c. Robert Sternberg.
    b. Howard Gardner.   d. K. Warner Schaie.

True or False Items

Write T (*true*) or F (*false*) on the line in front of each statement.

_____ 1. Age impairs processing speed and short-term memory.

_____ 2. A person's IQ is unaffected by school achievement.

_____ 3. To date, cross-sectional research has shown a gradual increase in intellectual ability.

_____ 4. Longitudinal research usually shows that intelligence in most abilities increases throughout early and middle adulthood.

_____ 5. By age 60, most people decline in even the most basic cognitive abilities.

_____ 6. IQ scores have shown a steady upward drift over most of the twentieth century.

_____ 7. All people reach an intellectual peak in adolescence.

_____ 8. Historically, most psychologists have considered intelligence to be comprised of several distinct abilities.

_____ 9. Today, most researchers studying cognitive abilities believe that intelligence is multidimensional.

_____ 10. Compared to novices, experts tend to be more intuitive and less stereotyped in their work performance.

Progress Test 2

Progress Test 2 should be completed during a final chapter review. Answer the following questions after you thoroughly understand the correct answers for the Chapter Review and Progress Test 1.

Multiple-Choice Questions

1. The debate over the status of adult intelligence focuses on the question of its inevitable decline and on:
   a. pharmacological deterrents to that decline.
   b. the accompanying decline in moral reasoning.
   c. its possible continuing growth.
   d. the validity of longitudinal versus personal-observation research.

2. Which of the following generational differences emerged in Schaie's studies of intelligence?
   a. Recent cohorts of young adults were better at math than those who were young in previous decades.
   b. Recent cohorts of young adults were better at reasoning ability, but worse at math, than those who were young in previous decades.
   c. Recent cohorts of young adults were better at all intellectual abilities than those who were young in previous decades.
   d. Recent cohorts of young adults were worse at all intellectual abilities than those who were young in previous decades.

3. The accumulation of facts that comes about with education and experience has been classified as:
   a. crystallized intelligence.
   b. plastic intelligence.
   c. fluid intelligence.
   d. rote memory.

4. According to the text, the current view of intelligence recognizes all of the following characteristics *except*:
   a. multidimensionality.
   b. plasticity.
   c. interindividual variation.
   d. *g*.

5. Thinking that is more intuitive, flexible, specialized, and automatic is characteristic of:
   a. fluid intelligence.
   b. crystallized intelligence.
   c. expertise.
   d. plasticity.

6. The _____ nature of intelligence was attested to by Howard Gardner, who proposed the existence of eight different intelligences.
   a. multidirectional   c. plastic
   b. multidimensional   d. practical

7. Marion Perlmutter's research study of the skills required for successful waitressing discovered that:
   a. experience had little impact on work performance.
   b. expertise required 10 years or more to attain.
   c. younger women outperformed their older counterparts in every area.
   d. age did not make a significant difference in performance.

8. At the present stage of research in adult cognition, which of the following statements has the most research support?
   a. Intellectual abilities inevitably decline from adolescence onward.
   b. Each person's cognitive development occurs in a unique context influenced by variations in genes, life experiences, and cohort effects.
   c. Some 90 percent of adults tested in cross-sectional studies show no decline in intellectual abilities until age 40.
   d. Intelligence becomes crystallized for most adults between ages 32 and 41.

9. Research on expertise indicates that during adulthood, intelligence:
   a. increases in most primary mental abilities.
   b. increases in specific areas of interest to the person.
   c. increases only in those areas associated with the individual's career.
   d. shows a uniform decline in all areas.

10. Research indicates that during adulthood declines occur in:
    a. crystallized intelligence.
    b. fluid intelligence.
    c. both crystallized and fluid intelligence.
    d. neither crystallized nor fluid intelligence.

11. Fluid intelligence is based on all of the following *except*:
    a. working memory.   c. inductive reasoning.
    b. abstract analysis.   d. general knowledge.

12. In recent years, researchers are more likely than before to consider intelligence as:
    a. a single entity.
    b. primarily determined by heredity.
    c. entirely the product of learning.
    d. made up of several abilities.

13. Which of the following is a drawback of longitudinal studies of intelligence?
    a. They are especially prone to the distortion of cohort effects.
    b. People who are retested may show improved performance as a result of practice.
    c. The biases of the experimenter are more likely to distort the results than is true of other research methods.
    d. All of the above are drawbacks.

14. To a developmentalist, an *expert* is a person who:
    a. is extraordinarily gifted at a particular task.
    b. is significantly better at a task than people who have not put time and effort into performing that task.
    c. scores at the 90th percentile or better on a test of achievement.
    d. is none of the above.

15. One reason for the variety in patterns in adult intelligence is that during adulthood:
    a. intelligence is fairly stable in some areas.
    b. intelligence increases in some areas.
    c. intelligence decreases in some areas.
    d. people develop specialized competencies in activities that are personally meaningful.

Matching Items

Match each definition or description with its corresponding term.

Terms

_____ 1. fluid intelligence
_____ 2. crystallized intelligence
_____ 3. analytic intelligence
_____ 4. selective optimization with compensation
_____ 5. general intelligence
_____ 6. creative intelligence
_____ 7. practical intelligence
_____ 8. Seattle Longitudinal Study
_____ 9. selective expert
_____ 10. Flynn effect

Definitions or Descriptions

a. intellectual skills used in everyday problem solving
b. Spearman's idea that intelligence is one basic trait, underlying all cognitive abilities
c. all the mental abilities that foster academic proficiency
d. first study of adult intelligence that used a cross-sequential research design
e. flexible reasoning used to draw inferences
f. the capacity for flexible and innovative thinking
g. the tendency of adults to optimize certain aspects of their lives in order to offset declines in other areas
h. the accumulation of facts, information, and knowledge
i. trend toward increasing average IQ
j. someone who is more skilled than the average person about personally meaningful activities

Developmental Psychology Applied

Answer these questions the day before an exam as a final check on your understanding of the chapter's terms and concepts.

1. In identifying the multiple aspects of intelligence, Gardner explains that:
   a. intelligence appears in three fundamental forms.
   b. a general intelligence can be inferred from these various abilities.
   c. each intelligence has its own neurological network in a particular section of the brain.
   d. fluid intelligence declines with age, while crystallized intelligence increases.

2. In Sternberg's theory, which aspect of intelligence is most similar to the abilities comprising fluid intelligence?
   a. analytic
   b. creative
   c. practical
   d. None of the above is part of Sternberg's theory.

3. Concerning the acquisition of fluid and crystallized intelligence, most experts agree that:
   a. both fluid and crystallized intelligence are primarily determined by heredity.
   b. both fluid and crystallized intelligence are primarily acquired through learning.
   c. fluid intelligence is primarily genetic, whereas crystallized intelligence is primarily learned.
   d. the nature–nurture distinction is invalid.

4. Professor Iglesias is a psychometrician. This means that she specializes in the:
   a. study of intelligence.
   b. study of cognitive development.
   c. measurement of psychological characteristics, especially intelligence.
   d. measurement of age-related psycho-pathologies.

5. Compared to novice chess players, chess experts most likely:
   a. have superior long-term memory.
   b. have superior short-term memory.
   c. are very disciplined in their play, sticking closely to formal rules for responding to certain moves their opponents might make.
   d. are quite flexible in their play, relying on their years of practice and accumulated experience.

6. A psychologist has found that the mathematical ability of adults born in the 1920s is significantly different from that of those born in the 1950s. She suspects that this difference is a reflection of the different educational emphases of the two historical periods. This is an example of:
   a. longitudinal research.   c. a cohort effect.
   b. sequential research.   d. all of the above.

7. Sharetta knows more about her field of specialization now at age 45 than she did at age 35. This increase is most likely due to:
   a. an increase in crystallized intelligence.
   b. an increase in fluid intelligence.
   c. increases in both fluid and crystallized intelligence.
   d. a cohort difference.

8. A contemporary developmental psychologist is most likely to *disagree* with the statement that:
   a. many people show increases in intelligence during middle adulthood.
   b. for many behaviors, the responses of older adults are slower than those of younger adults.
   c. intelligence peaks during adolescence and declines thereafter.
   d. intelligence is multidimensional and multidirectional.

9. Regarding their accuracy in measuring adult intellectual decline, cross-sectional research is to longitudinal research as _____ is to _____ .
   a. underestimate; overestimate
   b. overestimate; underestimate
   c. accurate; inaccurate
   d. inaccurate; accurate

10. Dr. Hatfield wants to analyze the possible effects of retesting, cohort differences, and aging on adult changes in intelligence. Which research method should she use?
    a. cross-sectional   c. cross-sequential
    b. longitudinal   d. case study

11. Joseph has remained associated with interesting and creative people throughout his life. In contrast, James has become increasingly isolated as he has aged. Given these lifestyle differences, which aspect of intelligence will be most affected in Joseph and James?
    a. fluid intelligence
    b. crystallized intelligence

c. overall IQ

d. It is impossible to predict how their intelligence will be affected.

12. When Merle retired from teaching, he had great difficulty adjusting to the changes in his lifestyle. Robert Sternberg would probably say that Merle was somewhat lacking in which aspect of his intelligence?

a. analytic **c.** practical
b. creative **d.** plasticity

13. During World War I, psychologists were convinced that intelligence peaks during:

a. late childhood.
b. adolescence.
c. emerging adulthood.
d. middle adulthood.

14. Compared to her 20-year-old daughter, 40-year-old Lynda is likely to perform better on measures of what type of intelligence?

a. fluid
b. practical
c. analytic
d. none of the above

15. Who would be most likely to agree with the statement, "There are multiple intelligences, each of which is influenced by the individual's genetic heritage and culture?"

a. Schaie
b. Gardner
c. Spearman
d. Perlmutter

Key Terms

Using your own words, write a brief definition or explanation of each of the following terms on a separate piece of paper.

1. general intelligence (*g*)
2. Flynn effect
3. Seattle Longitudinal Study
4. fluid intelligence
5. crystallized intelligence
6. analytic intelligence
7. creative intelligence
8. practical intelligence
9. selective optimization with compensation
10. selective expert

ANSWERS
CHAPTER REVIEW

1. psychometric
2. a single entity
3. Charles Spearman; *g*
4. adolescence; increased
5. increase; vocabulary; comprehension; information
6. longitudinal; cross-sectional

Cross-sectional research may be misleading because each cohort has its own unique history of life experiences and because in each generation, academic intelligence increases as a result of improved education.

7. increasing, Flynn effect; renormed
8. **a.** People who are retested several times may improve their performance simply as a result of practice.
   b. Because people may drop out of lengthy longitudinal studies, the remaining subjects may be a self-selected sample.
   c. Longitudinal research takes a long time.
9. K. Warner Schaie
10. cross-sequential

In this approach, each time the original group of subjects is retested, a new group is added and tested at each age interval.

11. primary mental abilities; Seattle Longitudinal Study
12. Raymond Cattell; John Horn; fluid; crystallized
13. fluid; inductive reasoning; abstract analysis; working memory
14. crystallized
15. fluid; IQ; increase; crystallized
16. Robert Sternberg; analytic; emerging adulthood
17. creative; divergent; convergent; unusual (unexpected, imaginative)
18. practical; family; organization
19. is not
20. Howard Gardner; supports
21. varies; and
22. selective optimization with compensation
23. expertise; selective expert
24. formal; past experiences; context; intuitive; stereotypic
25. automatic

26. strategies

27. flexible (or creative)

28. practice; 10 years; motivation

29. specific; cannot

PROGRESS TEST 1

Multiple-Choice Questions

1. a. is the answer. (p. 556)

b. Although results from this type of research may also be misleading, longitudinal studies often demonstrate age-related *increases* in intelligence.

c. Cross-sequential research is the technique devised by K. Warner Schaie that combines the strengths of the cross-sectional and longitudinal methods.

d. Random sampling refers to the selection of subjects for a research study.

2. a. is the answer. (p. 557)

b. This is a problem in longitudinal research.

c. & d. Neither of these is particularly troublesome in cross-sectional research.

3. d. is the answer. (p. 558)

a., b., & c. Cross-sequential research as described in this chapter is based on *objective* intelligence testing.

4. d. is the answer. (p. 562)

a. & b. Traditional IQ tests measure both fluid and crystallized intelligence.

5. c. is the answer. (pp. 561–562)

a., b., & d. These often increase with age.

6. c. is the answer. (p. 561)

a. Crystallized intelligence is the accumulation of facts and knowledge that comes with education and experience.

b. Although intelligence is characterized by plasticity, "plastic intelligence" is not discussed as a specific type of intelligence.

d. Rote memory is memory that is based on the conscious repetition of to-be-remembered information.

7. d. is the answer. (pp. 561–562)

8. a. is the answer. (p. 556)

b. Practical intelligence refers to the intellectual skills used in everyday problem solving and is identified in Sternberg's theory.

c. & d. These are two other aspects of intelligence identified in Sternberg's theory.

9. a. is the answer. (p. 557)

10. a. is the answer. (p. 570)

b. This was not discussed in the chapter.

c. Plasticity refers to the flexible nature of intelligence.

d. Encoding refers to the placing of information into memory.

11. c. is the answer. (p. 571)

a., b., & d. These are more typical of *novices* than experts.

12. d. is the answer. (p. 568)

a. & b. Women and men do not differ in their tendencies toward emotion- or problem-focused coping.

13. c. is the answer. (p. 557)

b. The text does not indicate that they improved on those tests.

d. No such criticism was made of Bayley's study.

14. d. is the answer. In fact, intelligence often becomes *more specialized* with age. (p. 568)

15. c. is the answer. (p. 562)

a. Charles Spearman proposed the existence of an underlying general intelligence, which he called *g*.

b. Howard Gardner proposed that intelligence consists of eight autonomous abilities.

d. K. Warner Schaie was one of the first researchers to recognize the potentially distorting cohort effects on cross-sectional research.

True or False Items

1. T (p. 562)

2. F Intellectual functioning as measured by IQ tests is powerfully influenced by school achievement. (p. 564)

3. F Cross-sectional research shows a decline in intellectual ability. (p. 556)

4. T (p. 557)

5. F Many adults show intellectual improvement over most of adulthood, with no decline, even by age 60. (p. 559)

6. T (pp. 557–558)

7. F Psychologists now agree that intelligence does *not* peak in adolescence and decline thereafter. (p. 555)

8. F Historically, psychologists have conceived of intelligence as a single entity. (p. 556)

9. T (p. 559)

10. T (p. 569)

PROGRESS TEST 2

Multiple-Choice Questions

1. **c.** is the answer. (p. 556)

2. **b.** is the answer. (pp. 558–559)

3. **a.** is the answer. (p. 562)

   b. Although intelligence is characterized by plasticity, "plastic intelligence" is not discussed as a specific type of intelligence.

   c. Fluid intelligence consists of the basic abilities that go into the understanding of any subject.

   d. Rote memory is based on the conscious repetition of to-be-remembered information.

4. **d.** is the answer. This is Charles Spearman's term for his idea of a general intelligence, in which intelligence is a single entity. (p. 556)

   a. Multidirectionality simply means that abilities follow different trajectories with age, as explained throughout the chapter.

   b. Plasticity simply refers to the ability to change.

   c. Interindividual variation is a way of saying that each person is unique.

5. **c.** is the answer. (pp. 569–571)

6. **b.** is the answer. (p. 564)

   a., c., & d. Gardner dealt with the multidimensionality of intelligence, not its direction, plasticity, or practicality.

7. **a.** is the answer. (p. 573)

   b. Expertise at waiting on tables took far less than 10 years to attain.

   c. & d. Older women outperformed younger women in the number of customers served.

8. **b.** is the answer. (p. 564–566)

   a. There is agreement that intelligence does *not* peak during adolescence.

   c. Cross-sectional research usually provides evidence of *declining* ability throughout adulthood.

   d. Crystallized intelligence refers to the accumulation of knowledge with experience; intelligence does not "crystallize" at any specific age.

9. **b.** is the answer. (p. 568)

10. **b.** is the answer. (p. 562)

    a., c., & d. Crystallized intelligence typically *increases* during adulthood.

11. **d.** is the answer. This is an aspect of crystallized intelligence. (p. 561)

12. **d.** is the answer. (pp. 561–564)

    a. Contemporary researchers emphasize the different aspects of intelligence.

    b. & c. Contemporary researchers see intelligence as the product of both heredity and learning.

13. **b.** is the answer. (p. 558)

    a. This is a drawback of cross-sectional research.

    c. Longitudinal studies are no more sensitive to experimenter bias than other research methods.

14. **b.** is the answer. (p. 568)

15. **d.** is the answer. (pp. 567–568)

Matching Items

1. e (p. 561)   5. b (p. 556)   9. i (p. 568)
2. h (p. 562)   6. f (p. 563)   10. j (p. 557)
3. c (p. 562)   7. a (p. 563)
4. g (p. 567)   8. d (p. 558)

DEVELOPMENTAL PSYCHOLOGY APPLIED

1. **c.** is the answer. (p. 564)

   a. This is Sternberg's theory.

   b. This refers to Spearman's view of a *g* factor.

   d. While this is true, it is not part of Gardner's theory.

2. **a.** is the answer. This aspect consists of mental processes fostering academic proficiency by making efficient learning, remembering, and thinking possible. (p. 562)

   b. This aspect enables the person to accommodate successfully to changes in the environment.

   c. This aspect concerns the extent to which intellectual functions are applied to situations that are familiar or novel in a person's history.

3. **d.** is the answer. This is so in part because the acquisition of crystallized intelligence is affected by the quality of fluid intelligence. (p. 562)

4. **c.** is the answer. (p. 555)

5. **d.** is the answer. (p. 571)

   a. & b. The text does not suggest that experts have special memory abilities.

   c. This describes the performance of novice rather than experts.

6. **c.** is the answer. (p. 559)

   a. & b. From the information given, it is impossible to determine which research method the psychologist used.

7. **a.** is the answer. (p. 562)

   b. & c. According to the research, fluid intelligence declines markedly during adulthood.

d. Cohort effects refer to generational differences in life experiences.

8. **c.** is the answer. (p. 555)

9. **b.** is the answer. (pp. 556–557)

   c. & d. Both cross-sectional and longitudinal research are potentially misleading.

10. **c.** is the answer. (pp. 558–559)

    a. & b. Schaie developed the cross-sequential research method to overcome the drawbacks of the cross-sectional and longitudinal methods, which were susceptible to cohort and retesting effects, respectively.

    d. A case study focuses on a single subject and therefore could provide no information on cohort effects.

11. **b.** is the answer. Because the maintenance of crystallized intelligence depends partly on how it is used, the consequences of remaining socially involved or of being socially isolated become increasingly apparent in adulthood. (p. 568)

12. **b.** is the answer. Creative intelligence enables the person to accommodate successfully to changes in the environment, such as those accompanying retirement. (p. 563)

    a. This aspect of intelligence consists of mental processes that foster efficient learning, remembering, and thinking.

    c. This aspect of intelligence concerns the extent to which intellectual functions are applied to situations that are familiar or novel in a person's history.

    d. Plasticity refers to the flexible nature of intelligence; it is not an aspect of Sternberg's theory.

13. **a.** is the answer. (p. 556)

14. **b.** is the answer. (p. 563)

15. **b.** is the answer. (p. 564)

    a. Schaie developed the cross-sequential research method.

    c. Spearman proposed that there is a single entity, which he called general intelligence.

    d. Perlmutter conducted research studies on expertise.

KEY TERMS

1. **General intelligence (*g*)** is the idea that intelligence is one basic trait, underlying all cognitive abilities, according to Spearman. (p. 556)

2. The **Flynn effect** refers to the trend toward increasing average IQ over successive generations. (p. 557)

3. The **Seattle Longitudinal Study** was the first study of adult intelligence that used a cross-sequential research design. (p. 558)

4. **Fluid intelligence** is made up of those basic mental abilities—inductive reasoning, abstract thinking, short-term memory, speed of thinking, and the like—required for understanding any subject matter. (p. 561)

5. **Crystallized intelligence** is the accumulation of facts, information, and knowledge that comes with education and experience within a particular culture. (p. 562)

6. In Robert Sternberg's theory, **analytic intelligence** includes all the mental processes that foster academic proficiency by making efficient learning, remembering, and thinking possible. (p. 562)

7. In Sternberg's theory, **creative intelligence** involves the capacity for flexible and innovating thinking. (p. 563)

8. According to Sternberg, **practical intelligence** involves the capacity to adapt one's behavior to the demands of the situation. This type of intelligence includes the intellectual skills used in everyday problem solving. (p. 563)

9. **Selective optimization with compensation** describes the tendency of adults to select certain aspects of their lives to focus on, and optimize, in order to compensate for declines in other areas. (p. 567)

10. A **selective expert** is someone who is notably more skilled and knowledgeable than the average person about whichever activities are personally meaningful. (p. 568)

22

Adulthood: Psychosocial Development

Chapter Overview

Chapter 22 is concerned with adulthood, which was commonly believed to be a time of crisis and transition. Today, researchers realize the fluidity of age boundaries and that good and bad events may occur at any age. The chapter begins by examining the concept of stages during adulthood, then identifies five basic clusters of personality traits that remain fairly stable throughout adulthood. One personality trend that does occur during middle age, as gender roles become less rigid, is the tendency of both sexes to take on characteristics typically reserved for the opposite sex.

The second section explores changes in relationships with friends and relatives and in the marital relationship in adulthood. It also depicts the effects of divorce and remarriage on family interaction.

The final section of the chapter examines the importance of generativity in the individual's life during adulthood. As many women and men begin to balance their work lives with parenthood, caring for parents, and other concerns, the motivation for many adults shifts from extrinsic rewards to intrinsic ones.

NOTE: Answer guidelines for all Chapter 22 questions begin on page 318.

Guided Study

The text chapter should be studied one section at a time. Before you read, preview each section by skimming it, noting headings and boldface items. Then read the appropriate section objectives from the following outline. Keep these objectives in mind and, as you read the chapter section, search for the information that will enable you to meet each objective. Once you have finished a section, write out answers for its objectives.

Ages and Stages (pp. 578–585)

1. Describe the psychosocial tensions and goals of adulthood, as described by Erikson and other social scientists.

2. Explain how the social clock influences the timing of important events during adulthood, and discuss problems with the concept of the midlife crisis.

3. Describe the Big Five cluster of personality traits, and explain the concept of an ecological niche, noting how it interacts with personality.

4. Explain the tendency toward gender role convergence during adulthood.

Intimacy (pp. 585–595)

5. Discuss the importance of the social convoy in protecting adults against the effects of stress, and describe two methods of coping with stress.

6. Describe how and why marital relationships tend to change during adulthood, and discuss whether these patterns apply to same-sex couples.

7. Discuss the impact of divorce and remarriage during adulthood.

Generativity (pp. 596–607)

8. Explain how caregiving helps meet the mature adult's need for generativity.

9. Discuss whether middle-aged adults are accurately described as the "sandwich generation," focusing on their caring for their elderly parents.

10. Describe how the balance among work, family, and self often shifts during adulthood.

Chapter Review

When you have finished reading the chapter, work through the material that follows to review it. Complete the sentences and answer the questions. As you proceed, evaluate your performance for each section by consulting the answers beginning on page 318. Do not continue with the next section until you understand each answer. If you need to, review or reread the appropriate section in the textbook before continuing.

Ages and Stages (pp. 578–585)

1. In Erikson's theory, the identity crisis of adolescence is followed in early adulthood by the crisis of _____ _____ _____ , and then later by the crisis of _____ _____ _____ .

2. Today, most social scientists regard adult lives as less _____ and more _____ than stage models suggest.

3. Although most developmentalists _____ (take/do not take) a strict stage view of adulthood, they do recognize that development is influenced by the _____ _____ , which is defined as _____ .

4. The social clock is affected by national and _____ norms. A powerful influence on the social clock is_____ _____ . The lower a person's SES, the _____ (younger/older) the age at which he or she is expected to leave school, begin work, marry, have children, and so forth.

5. The influence of SES is particularly apparent with regard to the age at which _____ (men/women) are expected to finish _____ .

6. The notion of a midlife crisis _____ (is/is not) accepted by most developmentalists as an inevitable event during middle age.

7. The major source of developmental continuity during adulthood is the stability of _____ .

8. List and briefly describe the Big Five personality factors.

   a. _____
   _____

   b. _____
   _____

   c. _____
   _____

   d. _____
   _____

   e. _____
   _____

9. The stability of personality results in large part from the fact that beginning in early adulthood most people have settled into an _____ _____ .

10. Although personality certainly begins with _____ and is manifested in the decisions that form the person's lifestyle, it may shift if the _____ shifts.

11. Of the Big Five traits, _____ and _____ tend to increase slightly with age, while _____ and _____ tend to decrease. The most stable trait seems to be _____ .

12. A sixth trait, known as _____ on others, is significant in _____ .

13. During middle age, gender roles _____ (loosen/become more rigid). Some researchers even believe that there is a _____ _____ of personality traits.

14. The psychoanalyst who believed that everyone has both a masculine and feminine side is _____ . According to this theory, adults begin to explore the _____ _____ of their personalities.

Intimacy (pp. 585–595)

15. The group of people with whom we form relationships that guide us through life constitutes our _____ _____ .

16. The most supportive members of the social convoy tend to be _____ .

17. The total burden of stress and disease that an individual must cope with is called _____ _____ . When this load is large, there is increased risk of major _____ , premature _____ , and even _____ .

18. In _____-_____ coping, people try to cope with stress by tackling the problem directly. In _____-_____ coping, people cope with stress by trying to change their emotions. Generally speaking, _____ (younger/older) adults are more likely to be emotion-focused and _____ (younger/older) adults to be more problem-focused. Women may be more _____-focused than men, as their bodies produce the hormone _____ that triggers _____-_____ behaviors.

19. Family members tend to have _____ lives, in which triumphs and tragedies are shared. A group of people who live together in one dwelling is a _____ , but not necessarily a _____ .

20. The belief that family members should care for and support one another is called _____ .

21. Someone who becomes accepted as part of a fam-

ily to which he or she is unrelated is called
_____ _____ .

22. Generally, married people are somewhat
_____ , _____ , and
_____ than unmarried ones of the
same age and background.

23. Couples who wed as teenagers are likely to be
more _____ , more
_____ , and less _____
than those who marry later.

24. The time in parents' lives when grown children
leave the family home is called the
_____ _____ .

25. Older couples have less _____-
_____ stress, fewer _____ ,
higher _____ , and more time
together than younger couples.

26. Research findings on marital success and satisfaction generally _____ (apply/do not
apply) to homosexual partners.

27. In the United States, nearly one out of every
_____ marriages ends in divorce, a
rate that _____ (is/is not) matched
by other nations. Divorce is most likely to occur
within _____ (how many?) years of
marriage.

28. Divorce following a long-term marriage is typically _____ (more/less) difficult
than divorce early in a marriage.

29. Second marriages end in divorce _____
(more/less) often than first marriages.

Generativity (pp. 596–607)

30. According to Erikson, after intimacy comes
_____ versus _____ .

31. Because of their role in maintaining the links
between the generations, mature adults become
the _____ . This role tends to be
filled most often by _____ (women/
men); with today's smaller families, however,
gender equity in this role _____
(is/is not) more apparent.

32. For most adults, the chief form of generativity
involves caring for _____ .
Although the intimacy and satisfaction of mar-

riage often _____ (increase/
decrease) with parenthood, the level of commitment _____ (increases/decreases).
In the ideal situation, two parents form a
_____ _____ in raising
children.

33. Proportionately, about _____ of all
North American adults will become stepparents,
adoptive parents, or foster parents at some point
in their lives.

34. Strong bonds between parent and child are particularly hard to create when a child has already
formed _____ _____
to other caregivers.

35. Because they are legally connected to their children for life, _____ (adoptive/
step/foster) parents have an advantage in establishing bonds with their children.

36. Middle-aged people are sometimes called the
_____ generation because they feel
pressured to fulfill the needs of both younger and
older generations.

37. Care for elderly parents tends to tilt toward the
_____ (husband's/wife's) parents.
Caregiving is determined not only by need but
also by _____ and
_____ .

38. As people age, the _____ (intrin-
sic/extrinsic) rewards associated with working
tend to become more important than the
_____ (intrinsic/extrinsic) rewards.

39. Job change _____ (is/is not) common after emerging adulthood.

40. State three reasons that losing a job is more devastating the older a worker is.

a. _____

b. _____

c. _____

41. Today, shift work is increasingly _____
(common/rare) in the workplace.

42. One solution to potential conflict between work and family roles is _____ .

43. In the United States, _____ (what proportion?) of the mothers are dependent children are employed.

Progress Test 1

Multiple-Choice Questions

Circle your answers to the following questions and check them with the answers beginning on page 319. If your answer is incorrect, read the explanation for why it is incorrect and then consult the appropriate pages of the text (in parentheses following the correct answer).

1. The most important factor in how a person adjusts to adulthood is his or her:
   a. gender.
   b. developmental history.
   c. age.
   d. race.

2. The Big Five personality factors are:
   a. emotional stability, openness, introversion, sociability, locus of control.
   b. neuroticism, extroversion, openness, emotional stability, sensitivity.
   c. extroversion, agreeableness, conscientiousness, neuroticism, openness.
   d. neuroticism, gregariousness, extroversion, impulsiveness, openness.

3. Concerning the prevalence of midlife crises, which of the following statements has the *greatest* empirical support?
   a. Virtually all men, and most women, experience a midlife crisis.
   b. Virtually all men, and about 50 percent of women, experience a midlife crisis.
   c. Women are more likely to experience a midlife crisis than are men.
   d. Few contemporary developmentalists believe that the midlife crisis is a common experience.

4. Shifts in personality during adulthood often reflect:
   a. increased agreeableness, conscientiousness, and generativity.
   b. rebellion against earlier life choices.
   c. the tightening of gender roles.
   d. all of the above.

5. During middle age, gender roles tend to:
   a. become more distinct.
   b. reflect patterns established during early adulthood.
   c. converge.
   d. be unpredictable.

6. Regarding the concept of the "sandwich generation," most developmentalists agree that:
   a. middle-aged adults often are burdened by being pressed on one side by adult children and on the other by aging parents.
   b. women are more likely than men to feel "sandwiched.'
   c. men are more likely than women to feel "sandwiched."
   d. this concept is largely a myth.

7. In the United States and other Western countries, the lower a person's socioeconomic status:
   a. the younger the age at which the social clock is "set" for many life events.
   b. the older the age at which the social clock is "set" for many life events.
   c. the more variable are the settings for the social clock.
   d. the less likely it is that divorce will occur.

8. In families, one member tends to function as the _____ , celebrating family achievements, keeping the family together, and staying in touch with distant relatives.
   a. sandwich generation
   b. nuclear bond
   c. intergenerational gatekeeper
   d. kinkeeper

9. According to Erikson, the failure to achieve intimacy during early adulthood is most likely to result in:
   a. generativity.   c. role diffusion.
   b. stagnation.   d. isolation.

10. For Freud, a healthy adult is one who can:
   a. love and work.
   b. make money.
   c. have many children.
   d. have authority over others.

11. Erikson theorized that if generativity is not attained, the adult is most likely to experience:
    a. lack of advancement in his or her career.
    b. infertility or childlessness.
    c. feelings of emptiness and stagnation.
    d. feelings of profound aloneness or isolation.

12. Concerning the degree of stability of personality traits, which of the following statements has the greatest research support?
    a. There is little evidence that personality traits remain stable during adulthood.
    b. In women, but less so in men, there is notable continuity in many personality characteristics.
    c. In men, but less so in women, there is notable continuity in many personality characteristics.
    d. In both men and women, there is notable continuity in many personality characteristics.

13. People who exhibit the personality dimension of _____ tend to be outgoing, active, and assertive.
    a. extroversion   c. conscientiousness
    b. agreeableness   d. neuroticism

14. According to Jung's theory of personality:
    a. as men and women get older, gender roles become more distinct.
    b. to some extent, everyone has both a masculine and a feminine side to his or her character.
    c. the recent blurring of gender roles is making adjustment to midlife more difficult for both men and women.
    d. gender roles are most distinct during childhood.

15. Which of the following personality traits was *not* identified in the text as either increasing or decreasing slightly during adulthood?
    a. neuroticism   c. openness
    b. introversion   d. conscientiousness

True or False Items

Write T (*true*) or F (*false*) on the line in front of each statement.
_____ 1. At least 75 percent of American men experience a significant midlife crisis between ages 38 and 43.
_____ 2. Better than age as a predictor of whether a midlife crisis will occur is an individual's developmental history.
_____ 3. The Big Five personality traits remain quite stable throughout adulthood.

_____ 4. Younger adults tend to be more emotion-focused when responding to stress.
_____ 5. In the United States in most cases, several generations live together.
_____ 6. A prime influence on the cultural clock-setting is socioeconomic status.
_____ 7. Husbands tend to be more pleased with marriage than are wives.
_____ 8. The younger the bride and groom, the more likely their marriage is to succeed.
_____ 9. As adults mature, personality tends to improve slightly.
_____ 10. There is no evidence that the stability of personality traits is influenced by heredity.

Progress Test 2

Progress Test 2 should be completed during a final chapter review. Answer the following questions after you thoroughly understand the correct answers for the Chapter Review and Progress Test 1.

Multiple-Choice Questions

1. An individual's social convoy is most likely to be made up of:
   a. older relatives.
   b. younger relatives.
   c. people of the same gender.
   d. members of the same generation.

2. Which of the following would be a good example of an ecological niche?
   a. an extrovert marries an introvert
   b. a conscientious person cohabits with someone who is disorganized
   c. a sculptor marries a canvas artist
   d. a workaholic marries a homebody

3. The prime effect of the social clock is to make an individual aware of:
   a. his or her socioeconomic status.
   b. the diversity of psychosocial paths during early adulthood.
   c. the means of fulfilling affiliation and achievement needs.
   d. the "right" or "best" time for assuming adult roles.

4. Allostatic load refers to:
   a. the combined burden of stress and disease that an individual must cope with.
   b. the idea that family members share all aspects of each other's lives.
   c. the idea that family members should support one another.
   d. the difficulty stepparent sometimes have in forming strong bonds with stepchildren.

5. Whether a person ranks high or low in each of the Big Five personality factors is determined by:
   a. heredity.
   b. temperament.
   c. his or her lifestyle.
   d. the interaction of genes, culture, and early experiences.

6. Regarding the strength of the contemporary family bond, most developmentalists believe that:
   a. family links are considerably weaker in the typical contemporary American family than in earlier decades.
   b. family links are considerably weaker in the typical contemporary American family than in other cultures.
   c. both a. and b. are true.
   d. despite the fact that families do not usually live together, family links are not weaker today.

7. Your brother, who became a stepparent when he married, complains that he can't seem to develop a strong bond with his 9-year-old stepchild. You tell him:
   a. strong bonds between parent and child are particularly hard to create once a child is old enough to have formed attachments to other caregivers.
   b. the child is simply immature emotionally and will, with time, warm up considerably.
   c. most stepparents find that they eventually develop a deeper, more satisfying relationship with stepchildren than they had ever imagined.
   d. he should encourage the child to think of him as the child's biological father.

8. Which of the following statements explains why couples in long-term marriages are particularly likely to report an increase in marital satisfaction?
   a. Marital satisfaction is closely tied to financial security, which tends to improve throughout adulthood.
   b. The successful launching of children is a source of great pride and happiness.

c. There often is improvement in marital equity during this period.
d. All of the above statements are correct.

9. Which of the following are typically the most supportive members of a person's social convoy?
   a. parents
   b. children
   c. coworkers
   d. friends

10. Which of the following is *not* true concerning divorce and remarriage during adulthood?
    a. Divorce is most likely to occur within the first five years of a wedding.
    b. Women with children are less likely to re-marry.
    c. Remarriages break up more often than first marriages.
    d. Remarried people report higher average levels of happiness than people in first marriages.

11. Jan has been so much a part of her best friend's life that she effectively has been "adopted" by her family. In other words, Jan has become:
    a. a kinkeeper.
    b. fictive kin.
    c. part of the sandwich generation.
    d. part of the social convoy.

12. Which of the following personality traits tends to remain quite stable throughout adulthood?
    a. agreeableness
    b. neuroticism
    c. openness
    d. all of the above

13. Which of the following factors make divorce more likely?
    a. either partner is under age 21.
    b. substance abuse.
    c. cohabitation before marriage.
    d. All of the above factors make divorce more likely.

14. The belief that family members should care for each other, sacrificing personal freedom and success to do so, is called:
    a. familism.
    b. kinkeeping.
    c. empty nest syndrome.
    d. gender convergence.

15. Even decades after divorce, which of these factors still tend(s) to be lower for divorced adults than for nondivorced adults?
    a. income
    b. family welfare
    c. self-esteem
    d. all of the above

Matching Items

Match each definition or description with its corresponding term.

Terms

_____ 1. kinkeepers
_____ 2. sandwich generation
_____ 3. extroversion
_____ 4. agreeableness
_____ 5. conscientiousness
_____ 6. neuroticism
_____ 7. social convoy
_____ 8. ecological niche
_____ 9. familism
_____ 10. openness

Definitions or Descriptions

a. tendency to be outgoing
b. tendency to be imaginative
c. tendency to be organized
d. those who focus more on the family
e. tendency to be helpful
f. those pressured by the needs of the older and younger generations
g. tendency to be moody
h. the belief that family members should remain close and supportive of one another
i. a chosen lifestyle and context
j. "a protective layer of social relations"

Developmental Psychology Applied

Answer these questions the day before an exam as a final check on your understanding of the chapter's terms and concepts.

1. Forty-five-year-old Ken, who has been single-mindedly climbing the career ladder, now feels that he has no more opportunity for advancement and that he has neglected his family and made many wrong decisions in charting his life's course. Ken's feelings are probably signs of:
   a. normal development during middle age.
   b. an unsuccessful passage through early adulthood.
   c. neuroticism.
   d. his being in the sandwich generation.

2. For her class presentation, Christine plans to discuss the Big Five personality factors. Which of the following is *not* a factor that Christine will discuss?
   a. extroversion   c. independence
   b. openness   d. agreeableness

3. It has long been assumed that, for biological reasons, I will inevitably experience a midlife crisis. I am:
   a. a middle-aged man.
   b. a middle-aged woman.
   c. either a middle-age man or a middle-aged woman.
   d. neither a. nor b.

4. Manuel is 50 years old. Although he is financially independent, he continues to work. Which of the following was *not* mentioned as a way that work helps meet his generativity needs?
   a. It helps Manuel with his need to accumulate personal wealth.
   b. It helps him express creative energy.
   c. It helps him support the health of his family.
   d. It helps him contribute to the community.

5. Compared to when they were younger, middle-aged Sarah is likely to become more _____ , while middle-aged Donald becomes more _____ .
   a. introverted; extroverted
   b. assertive; emotionally expressive
   c. disappointed with life; satisfied with life
   d. extroverted; introverted

6. The parents of Rebecca and her adult twin, Josh, have become frail and unable to care for themselves. It is likely that:
   a. Rebecca and Josh will play equal roles as caregivers for their parents.
   b. Rebecca will play a larger role in caring for their parents.
   c. Josh will play a larger role in caring for their parents.
   d. If Rebecca and Josh are well educated, their parents will be placed in a professional caregiving facility.

7. Forty-five-year-old Elena has been working for the telephone company for 20 years. Because of technological advances, she has been laid off. According to the text, this job loss is devastating to her because:
   a. she can't work the long hours new jobs require.
   b. she doesn't have the knowledge needed to perform available jobs.
   c. she wants to spend time with her grandchildren and all new jobs are 9 A.M. to 5 P.M.
   d. her husband planned on retiring as long as she was still bringing in a paycheck.

8. Ben and Nancy have been married for 10 years. Although they are very happy, Nancy worries that with time this happiness will decrease. Research would suggest that Nancy's fear:
   a. may or may not be reasonable, depending on whether she and her husband are experiencing a midlife crisis.
   b. is reasonable, because marital discord is most common in couples who have been married 10 years or more.
   c. is unfounded, because after the first 10 years or so, the longer a couple has been married, the happier they tend to be.
   d. is probably a sign of neuroticism.

9. Concluding her presentation on culture and personality, Jaya notes that a sixth personality dimension, known as dependence on others, is significant in:
   a. Western Europe.   c. Scandinavia.
   b. Africa.   d. Asia.

10. Cathy's life is stress-filled because she is unemployed, a single parent, and the primary caregiver for her ailing mother. A developmentalist would say Cathy:
   a. has a high allostatic load.
   b. needs more problem-focused coping.
   c. needs more emotion-focused coping.
   d. has a low allostatic load.

11. Jack doesn't plan to retire as long as his job continues to be satisfying and boosts his self-esteem. Jack is clearly motivated by:
   a. extrinsic rewards of work.
   b. intrinsic rewards of work.
   c. familism.
   d. generativity.

12. Compared to his sister, Melvin is more likely to respond to stress:
   a. in a problem-focused manner.
   b. in an emotion-focused manner.
   c. in a tend-and-befriend manner.
   d. with lower arousal of his sympathetic nervous system.

13. After a painful phone call with her unhappy mother, your college roommate confides her fear that she will not be able to handle the burdens of children, career, and caring for her aging parents. Your response is that:
   a. she's right to worry, because women who juggle these roles simultaneously almost always feel unfairly overburdened.
   b. her mother's unhappiness is a warning sign that she herself may be genetically prone toward developing a midlife crisis.
   c. Both a. and b. are true.
   d. If these roles are important to her, if her relationships are satisfying, and if the time demands are not overwhelming, filling these roles is likely to be a source of satisfaction.

14. All his life, Bill has been a worrier, often suffering from bouts of anxiety and depression. Which personality cluster best describes these traits?
   a. neuroticism   c. openness
   b. extroversion   d. conscientiousness

15. Jan and her sister Sue have experienced similar frequent changes in careers, residences, and spouses. Jan has found these upheavals much less stressful than Sue and so is probably characterized by which of the following personality traits?
   a. agreeableness   c. openness
   b. conscientiousness   d. extroversion

Key Terms

Writing Definitions

Using your own words, write a brief definition or explanation of each of the following terms on a separate piece of paper.

1. social clock
2. midlife crisis
3. Big Five
4. ecological niche
5. gender convergence
6. social convoy

7. allostatic load
8. linked lives
9. household
10. familism
11. fictive kin

12. empty nest
13. kinkeeper
14. sandwich generation
15. extrinsic rewards of work
16. intrinsic rewards of work

Cross Check

After you have written the definitions of the key terms in this chapter, you should complete the crossword puzzle to ensure that you can reverse the process—recognize the term, given the definition.

ACROSS

2. A person who becomes part of a family to which he or she has no blood ties is considered _____ kin.
7. Clusters of personality traits that remain quite stable throughout adulthood.
9. The family, friends, acquaintances, and even strangers who move through life with a person.
11. Because they are often squeezed by the needs of the younger and older generations, middle-aged adults are often referred to as the _____ generation.
12. The extent to which a person is anxious, moody, and self-punishing.
13. A person who celebrates family achievements, gathers the family together, and keeps in touch with family members who have moved away.

DOWN

1. A period of unusual anxiety and radical reexamination that is widely associated with adulthood.
3. The belief that family members should be close and supportive of one another.
4. The extent to which a person is kind, helpful, and easy-going.
5. The extent to which a person is organized, deliberate, and conforming.
6. The total burden of stress and disease that an individual must cope with is called the _____ load.
8. The lifestyle and social context into which adults settle that are compatible with their individual personality needs and interests.

10. The extent to which a person is outgoing, assertive, and active.

ANSWERS

CHAPTER REVIEW

1. intimacy versus isolation; generativity versus stagnation
2. rigid; fluid
3. do not take; social clock; a timetable for behaviors set by social norms

4. historical; socioeconomic status; younger
5. women; childbearing
6. is not
7. personality
8. **a.** extroversion: outgoing, assertive
   b. agreeableness: kind, helpful
   c. conscientiousness: organized, conforming
   d. neuroticism: anxious, moody
   e. openness: imaginative, curious
9. ecological niche
10. genes; context
11. agreeableness; conscientiousness; openness; neuroticism
12. dependence; Asia
13. loosen; gender convergence
14. Carl Jung; shadow side
15. social convoy
16. friends
17. allostatic load; illness; aging; death
18. problem-focused; emotion-focused; older; younger; emotion; oxytocin; tend-and-befriend
19. linked; household; family
20. familism
21. fictive kin
22. happier; healthier; wealthier
23. depressed; violent; educated
24. empty nest
25. child-rearing; arguments; incomes
26. apply
27. two; is; five
28. more
29. more
30. generativity; stagnation
31. kinkeepers; women; is
32. children; decrease; increases; parental alliance
33. one-third
34. strong attachments
35. adoptive
36. sandwich
37. wife's; personality; familism
38. intrinsic; extrinsic
39. is
40. **a.** Older workers may never have learned the skills required for a new job.
    b. Older workers are paid more.
    c. Older workers find relocation more difficult.
41. common
42. telecommuting
43. two-thirds

PROGRESS TEST 1

Multiple-Choice Questions

1. **b.** is the answer. (p. 581)
2. **c.** is the answer. (p. 581)

3. **d.** is the answer. (p. 580)

   a. & b. Recent studies have shown that the prevalence of the midlife crisis has been greatly exaggerated.

   c. The text does not suggest a gender difference in terms of the midlife crisis.

4. **a.** is the answer. (p. 583)

   b. This answer reflects the notion of a midlife crisis—a much rarer event than is popularly believed.

   c. Gender roles tend to loosen in middle adulthood.

5. **c.** is the answer. (p. 583)

   a. Gender roles become *less* distinct during middle adulthood.

   b. Gender roles often are most distinct during early adulthood, after which they tend to loosen.

   d. Although there *is* diversity from individual to individual, gender-role shifts during middle adulthood are nevertheless predictable.

6. **d.** is the answer. (pp. 599–600)

   b. & c. Women are no more likely than men to feel burdened by the younger and older generations.

7. **a.** is the answer. (p. 580)

   d. Low SES is actually a risk factor for divorce.

8. **d.** is the answer. (p. 596)

   a. This was a term used to describe adult women and men who are pressured by the needs of both the younger and older generations.

   b. & c. These terms are not used in the text.

9. **d.** is the answer. (p. 578)

   a. Generativity is a characteristic of the crisis following the intimacy crisis.

   b. Stagnation occurs when generativity needs are not met.

   c. Erikson's theory does not address this issue.

10. **a.** is the answer. (p. 579)
11. **c.** is the answer. (p. 596)

    a. Lack of career advancement may prevent generativity.

    b. Erikson's theory does not address these issues.

    d. Such feelings are related to the need for intimacy rather than generativity.

12. **d.** is the answer. (p. 581)
13. **a.** is the answer. (p. 581)

    b. This is the tendency to be kind and helpful.

c. This is the tendency to be organized, deliberate, and conforming.

d. This is the tendency to be anxious, moody, and self-punishing.

14. **b.** is the answer. (pp. 583–584)

a. Jung's theory states just the opposite.

c. If anything, the loosening of gender roles would make adjustment easier.

d. According to Jung, gender roles are most distinct during adolescence and early adulthood, when pressures to attract the other sex and the "parental imperative" are highest.

15. **b.** is the answer. (p. 581)

True or False Items

1. F   Studies have found that crises at midlife are not inevitable. (pp. 580–581)

2. T (p. 581)

3. T (p. 581)

4. F   Younger adults are more problem-focused. (p. 586)

5. F   This is no longer true in the United States. (p. 587)

6. T (p. 580)

7. T (p. 591)

8. F Just the opposite is true.(p. 591)

9. T (p. 583)

10. F The stability of personality is at least partly attributable to heredity. (p. 581)

PROGRESS TEST 2

Multiple-Choice Questions

1. **d.** is the answer. (p. 585)

2. **c.** is the answer. (p. 581)

3. **d.** is the answer. (p. 579)

4. **a.** is the answer. (p. 586)

b. This refers to linked lives.

c. This is familism.

5. **d.** is the answer. (p. 581)

6. **d.** is the answer. (p. 587)

7. **a.** is the answer. (p. 598)

b. Many stepchildren remain fiercely loyal to the absent parent.

c. Most stepparent actually have unrealistically high expectations of the relationship they will establish with their stepchildren.

d. Doing so would only confuse the child and, quite possibly, cause resentment and further alienation.

8. **d.** is the answer. (p. 591)

9. **d.** is the answer. (p. 585)

10. **d.** is the answer. (pp. 594–595)

11. **b.** is the answer. (p. 589)

12. **d.** is the answer. (p. 581)

13. **d.** is the answer. (p. 595)

14. **a.** is the answer. (p. 588)

15. **d.** is the answer. (pp. 593–594)

Matching Items

1. d (p. 596)
2. f (p. 599)
3. a (p. 581)
4. e (p. 581)
5. c (p. 581)
6. g (p. 581)
7. j (p. 585)
8. i (p. 581)
9. h (p. 588)
10. b (p. 581)

DEVELOPMENTAL PSYCHOLOGY APPLIED

1. **a.** is the answer. (p. 581)

b. & c. Ken's feelings are common in middle-aged male workers, and not necessarily indicative of neuroticism.

d. The sandwich generation refers to middle-aged adults being squeezed by the needs of the younger and older generations.

2. **c.** is the answer. (p. 581)

3. **d.** is the answer. Researchers have found no evidence that a midlife crisis is inevitable in middle adulthood. (p. 580)

4. **a.** is the answer. (p. 601)

5. **b.** is the answer. This is an example of the convergence of gender roles during middle adulthood. (p. 583–584)

a. & d. Extroversion is a relatively *stable* personality trait. Moreover, there is no gender difference in the developmental trajectory of this trait.

c. There is no gender difference in life satisfaction at any age.

6. **b.** is the answer. Because women tend to be kinkeepers, Rebecca is likely to play a larger role than her brother. (p. 596)

d. The relationship of education to care of frail parents is not discussed in the text.

7. **b.** is the answer. (p. 603)

8. **c.** is the answer. (p. 591)

a. Marital satisfaction can be an important buffer against midlife stress.

d. There is no reason to believe Nancy's concern is abnormal, or neurotic.

9. **d.** is the answer. (p. 583)

10. **a.** is the answer. (p. 586)

11. **b.** is the answer. (p. 601)

12. **a.** is the answer. (p. 586)

   b., c., & d. Each of these is more typical of women.

13. **d.** is the answer. (pp. 599–600)

14. **a.** is the answer. (p. 581)

   b. This is the tendency to be outgoing.

   c. This is the tendency to be imaginative and curious.

   d. This is the tendency to be organized, deliberate, and conforming.

15. **c.** is the answer. Openness to new experiences might make these life experiences less threatening. (p. 581)

KEY TERMS

Writing Definitions

1. The **social clock** represents the culturally set timetable that establishes when various events and behaviors in life are appropriate and called for. (p. 579)

2. A once-popular myth, the **midlife crisis** is a period of unusual anxiety, radical reexamination, and sudden transformation that is widely associated with middle age but has more to do with developmental history than with chronological age. (p. 580)

3. The **Big Five** are clusters of personality traits that remain quite stable throughout adulthood. (p. 581)

4. **Ecological niche** refers to the lifestyle and social context adults settle into that are compatible with their individual personality needs and interests. (p. 581)

5. **Gender convergence** is the tendency of the sexes to become more similar as women and men age. (p. 583)

6. A **social convoy** is a group of people of the same generation who guide, encourage, and socialize with each other as they move through life. (p. 585)

7. **Allostatic load** refers to the total burden of stress and illness that a person must cope with. (p. 586)

8. **Linked lives** refers to the idea that family members tend to share all aspects of each other's lives. (p. 587)

9. A **household** is a group of people who live together. (p. 587)

10. **Familism** is the idea that family members should support each other because family unity is more important than individual freedom and success. (p. 588)

11. **Fictive kin** refers to a person who becomes accepted as part of an unrelated family. (p. 589)

12. The **empty nest** refers to the time in the lives of parents when their grown children have left the home to pursue their own lives. (p. 591)

13. Because women tend to focus more on family than men do, they are the **kinkeepers,** the people who celebrate family achievements, gather the family together, and keep in touch with family members who have moved away. (p. 596)

14. Middle-aged adults were once commonly referred to as the **sandwich generation** because of the false belief that they are often squeezed by the needs of the younger and older generations. (p. 599)

15. The **extrinsic rewards of work** include salary, pension, and other tangible benefits. (p. 601)

16. The **intrinsic rewards of work** include job satisfaction, self-esteem, and other intangible benefits. (p. 601)

Cross-Check

ACROSS	DOWN
2. fictive	1. midlife crisis
7. Big Five	3. familism
9. social convoy	4. agreeableness
11. sandwich	5. conscientiousness
12. neuroticism	6. allostatic
13. kinkeeper	8. ecological niche
	10. extroversion

23

Late Adulthood: Biosocial Development

Chapter Overview

Chapter 23 covers biosocial development during late adulthood, discussing the myths and reality of this final stage of the life span. In a society such as ours, which glorifies youth, there is a tendency to exaggerate the physical decline brought on by aging. In fact, the changes that occur during the later years are largely a continuation of those that began earlier in adulthood, and the vast majority of the elderly consider themselves to be in good health.

Nonetheless, the aging process is characterized by various changes in appearance, by an increased incidence of impaired vision and hearing, and by declines in the major body systems. These are all changes to which the individual must adjust. In addition, the incidence of life-threatening diseases becomes more common with every decade.

Several theories have been advanced to explain the aging process. The most useful of these focus on our genetic makeup and cellular malfunctions, which includes declining immune function. However, environment and lifestyle factors also play a role, as is apparent from studies of those who live a long life.

NOTE: Answer guidelines for all Chapter 23 questions begin on page 334.

Guided Study

The text chapter should be studied one section at a time. Before you read, preview each section by skimming it, noting headings and boldface items. Then read the appropriate section objectives from the following outline. Keep these objectives in mind and, as you read the chapter section, search for the information that will enable you to meet each objective. Once you have finished a section, write out answers for its objectives.

Prejudice and Predictions (pp. 615–620)

1. Define *ageism*, and explain the contributions of gerontology to changing views about old age.

2. Describe ongoing changes in the age distribution of the American population, noting the current shape of the "demographic pyramid."

3. Explain the current state of the dependency ratio, and distinguish among three categories of the aged.

Senescence (pp. 620–635)

4. Discuss primary and secondary aging in relation to diseases in old age, and describe the adjustments older adults may have to make in various areas of life in order to maintain optimal functioning.

5. Discuss the importance of good health habits for successful aging.

6. List several characteristic effects of aging on the individual's appearance, noting how the aged see themselves.

7. Describe age-related problems in vision and hearing.

8. Explain the concept of compression of morbidity.

Theories of Aging (pp. 635–643)

9. Briefly describe the wear-and-tear theory of aging.

10. Discuss the genetic theory of senescence, focusing on an epigenetic theory explanation.

11. Discuss the cellular aging theory, focusing on free radicals as sources of aging.

12. Describe an alternative cellular aging theory centering on the deterioration of the immune system.

The Centenarians (pp. 643–645)

13. Identify lifestyle characteristics associated with the healthy, long-lived adult.

Chapter Review

When you have finished reading the chapter, work through the material that follows to review it. Complete the sentences and answer the questions. As you proceed, evaluate your performance for each section by consulting the answers beginning on page 334. Do not continue with the next section until you understand each answer. If you need to, review or reread the appropriate section in the textbook before continuing.

Prejudice and Predictions (pp. 615–620)

1. The prejudice that people tend to feel about older people is called _____ .

2. Sometimes, younger adults automatically lapse into _____ when they talk to older adults.

Describe this form of speech.

3. The multidisciplinary study of aging is called _____ . The traditional medical specialty devoted to aging is _____ .

Most doctors in this field see patients who are _____ , which leads them to consider aging as an _____ .

4. The cultural bias that labels older people as infirm and ill _____ (is/is not) weakening.

5. The study of the characteristics of human populations is called _____ . Today, because of changes in the proportions of the population in various age groups, we are witnessing a _____ _____ .

6. The fastest-growing age group today is the _____ , defined as people over age _____ .

7. In the past, when populations were sorted according to age, the resulting picture was a(n) _____ , with the youngest and _____ (smallest/largest) group at the bottom and the oldest and _____ (smallest/largest) group at the top.

List three reasons for this picture.

a. _____

b. _____

c. _____

8. Today, because of _____ _____ and increased _____ , the shape of the population is becoming closer to a(n) _____ .

9. The shape of the demographic pyramid _____ (varies/is the same) throughout the world.

10. The ratio of self-sufficient, productive adults to dependent children and elderly adults is called the _____ _____ . Because of the declining _____ rate and the small size of the cohort just entering _____ _____ , this ratio is _____ (lower/higher) than it has been for a century. As people live longer, the ratio will _____ .

11. There is an inverse relationship between birth rates and _____ . Most people over age 65 _____ (are/are not) "dependent."

12. Approximately _____ percent of the elderly live in nursing homes.

13. Older adults who are healthy, relatively well-off financially, and integrated into the lives of their families and society are classified as _____-_____ .

14. Older adults who suffer physical, mental, or social deficits are classified as _____-_____ . The _____-_____ are dependent on others for almost everything; they are _____ (the majority/a small minority) of those over age 65. Age _____ (is/is not) an accurate predictor of dependency. For this reason, some gerontologists prefer to use the terms _____ aging, _____ aging, and _____ aging.

Senescence (pp. 620–635)

15. In discussing the aging process, or _____ , gerontologists distinguish between the irreversible changes that occur with time, called _____ _____ , and _____ _____ , which refers to changes caused by particular _____ influences or _____ . This latter category of age-related changes _____ (is/is not) inevitable with the passage of time. The distinction between these categories of age-related changes _____ (is/is not) clear-cut.

16. The leading cause of death for both men and women is _____ _____ . This disease is more _____-related than _____-related.

17. Most elderly people _____ (have/do not have) any particular disease.

18. During late adulthood, all the major body systems become _____ and less _____ . Older people take _____ (less/more) time to recover from illnesses and are _____ (less/more) likely to die of them.

19. A key factor in how people age is how well they respond with _____ _____ _____ _____ , choosing activities they can do well as their adjustment to aging.

20. A frequent sleep complaint among older adults is _____ , which is often treated with prescription _____ drugs.

Explain why this medical intervention may be particularly harmful in late adulthood.

21. Frequent waking during the night becomes more common during late adulthood because the decrease in the brain's _____ _____ with advancing age means sleep is not as deep and _____ are not as long.

22. Elderly drivers have _____ (fewer/more) auto accidents than younger adults.

23. As people age, they need _____ (more/fewer) daily calories because bodies become _____ (more/less) efficient at digesting food and using its nutrients.

24. Among health habits, both _____ and _____ may be even more important in later life than earlier.

25. Elders are likely to be healthier if they drink no more than _____ glasses of wine or beer a day.

26. One cognitive change that everyone experiences is that with age, we think more _____ . In addition, the brain _____ as it ages. Even so, older adults use _____ (fewer/more) parts of the brain when thinking than younger adults.

27. As people age, the skin becomes _____ , _____ , and _____ (more/less) elastic, which produces wrinkling and makes blood vessels and pockets of fat more visible. Dark patches of skin known as "_____ _____" also become visible. Many men experience the genetic condition called _____ _____ _____ .

28. Most older people are _____ than they were in early adulthood, because their _____ have settled closer together.

29. With age, body fat tends to collect more in the _____ and _____ _____ than in the arms, legs, and upper face.

30. Body weight is often _____ (higher/lower) in late adulthood, particularly in _____ (men/women), who have more _____ and less body _____ than the other sex.

31. For many of the healthy elderly, the most troubling part of aging is loss of _____ ability.

32. Approximately _____ percent of those older than 75 have one of the three major eye diseases of the elderly. The first of these, _____ , involves a thickening of the _____ of the eye. The second, _____ , involves the _____ of the eyeball because of a buildup of _____ within the eye. The disease _____ _____ involves deterioration of the _____ .

33. Age-related hearing loss, or _____ , affects about _____ percent of those age 65 and older. The hard-of-hearing are often mistakenly thought to be _____ or _____ _____ , and are more subject to _____ , _____ , and even _____ symptomatology.

34. Fortunately, _____ is available for every sensory loss.

35. A goal of many researchers is a limiting of the time any person spends ill, that is, a(n) _____ _____ _____ .

Theories of Aging (pp. 635–643)

36. The oldest theory of aging is the _____-_____-_____ theory, which compares the human body to a(n) _____ . Overall, this analogy _____ (is a good one/doesn't hold up).

State three facts that support the wear-and-tear theory.

37. Some theorists believe that, rather than being a mistake, aging is incorporated into the _____ of all species in a kind of _____ .

38. The oldest age to which members of a species can live, called the _____ _____ _____ , which in humans is approximately _____ years, is quite different from _____ _____ _____ , which is defined as _____ _____ .

39. Life expectancy varies according to

    _____ , _____ ,

    and _____ factors that affect fre-

    quency of _____ in childhood, ado-

    lescence, or middle age. In the United States

    today, average life expectancy at birth is about

    _____ for men and

    _____ for women.

40. In ancient times, average life expectancy was only

    about _____ years, due to the fact

    that _____ .

    In 1900, in developed nations, the average life

    expectancy was about age _____ .

    This increase was due largely to better

    _____ _____ mea-

    sures, including _____ ,

    _____ , and _____ .

Briefly state one possible explanation for primary
aging according to epigenetic theory.

41. The leading causes of death in early adulthood

    are _____ (genetic/nongenetic)

    events. Among the genetic diseases that the evo-

    lutionary process would have no reason to select

    against are _____

    _____ .

42. Another theory of aging suggests that some

    occurrence in the _____ themselves,

    such as the accumulation of accidents that occur

    during _____ _____ ,

    causes aging. According to this theory, toxic envi-

    ronmental agents and the normal process of

    _____ repair result in

    _____ that damage the instructions

    for creating new cells.

43. Another aspect of the cellular theory of aging is

    that metabolic processes can cause electrons to

separate from their atoms, resulting in atoms

called _____ _____

_____ that scramble DNA mole-

cules or produce errors in cell maintenance and

repair.

44. Free radical damage may be slowed by certain

    _____ that nullify the effects of free

    radicals. These include vitamins

    _____ , _____ ,

    and _____ , and the mineral

    _____ .

45. A variant of the cellular theory suggests that the

    body's _____ system becomes

    weaker as we age.

46. The "attack" cells of the immune system include

    the _____ _____ from

    the bone marrow, which create _____

    that attack invading _____ and

    _____ , and the _____

    _____ from the _____

    gland, which produce substances that attack any

    kind of infected cells.

47. Over the course of adulthood, the power, produc-

    tion, and efficiency of T and B cells

    _____ (increases/decreases/

    remains constant).

48. Individuals with stronger immune systems tend

    to live _____ (longer/shorter) lives

    than their contemporaries. This has led some

    researchers to conclude that the

    _____ of the immune system is the

    cause of aging.

49. Females tend to have_____

    (weaker/stronger) immune systems than males,

    as well as _____ (smaller/larger)

    thymus glands. However, as a result, women are

    more vulnerable to _____ diseases

    such as rheumatoid arthritis.

50. When human cells are allowed to replicate out-

    side the body, the cells stop replicating at a cer-

    tain point, referred to as the _____

    _____ .

51. The very ends of chromosomes, called the

_____ , are much

_____ (longer/shorter) in older

cells.

52. (Thinking Like a Scientist) One promising strategy for slowing the aging process is

_____ _____ .

The Centenarians (pp. 643–645)

53. Three places famous for long-lived people are

_____ , _____ , and

_____ . Because of the absence of

_____

_____ , some

researchers believe the people in these regions are
lying about their true age.

List four characteristics shared by long-lived people
in these regions.

a. _____

b. _____

c. _____

d. _____

Progress Test 1

Multiple-Choice Questions

Circle your answers to the following questions and
check them with the answers beginning on page 335.
If your answer is incorrect, read the explanation for
why it is incorrect and then consult the appropriate
pages of the text (in parentheses following the correct
answer).

1. Ageism is:
   a. the study of aging and the aged.
   b. prejudice or discrimination against older peo-
      ple.
   c. the genetic disease that causes children to age
      prematurely.
   d. the view of aging that the body and its parts
      deteriorate with use.

2. The U.S. demographic pyramid is becoming a
   square because of:
   a. increasing birth rates and life spans.
   b. decreasing birth rates and life spans.
   c. decreasing birth rates and increasing life
      spans.
   d. rapid population growth.

3. Primary aging refers to the:
   a. changes that are caused by illness.
   b. changes that can be reversed or prevented.
   c. irreversible changes that occur with time.
   d. changes that are caused by poor health habits.

4. Geriatrics is the:
   a. medical specialty devoted to aging.
   b. study of secondary aging.
   c. multidisciplinary study of old age.
   d. study of optimal aging.

5. Which disease involves the hardening of the eyeball due to the buildup of fluid?
   a. cataracts
   b. glaucoma
   c. macular degeneration
   d. myopia

6. As a result of the slowdown and loss of efficiency
   in the body's major systems, which of the following is more common in late adulthood?
   a. coronary heart disease
   b. strokes
   c. most forms of cancer
   d. All of the above are equally common.

7. A direct result of damage to cellular DNA is:
   a. errors in the reproduction of cells.
   b. an increase in the formation of free radicals.
   c. decreased efficiency of the immune system.
   d. the occurrence of a disease called progeria.

8. Which theory explains aging as due in part to
   mutations in the cell structure?
   a. wear and tear
   b. immune system deficiency
   c. cellular aging
   d. genetic clock

9. According to the genetic adaptation theory of a
   genetic clock, aging:
   a. is actually directed by the genes.
   b. occurs as a result of damage to the genes.
   c. occurs as a result of hormonal abnormalities.
   d. can be reversed through environmental
      changes.

10. Laboratory research on the reproduction of cells
    cultured from humans and animals has found
    that:
    a. cell division cannot occur outside the organ-
       ism.
    b. the number of cell divisions was the same
       regardless of the species of the donor.

c. the number of cell divisions was different depending on the age of the donor.

d. under the ideal conditions of the laboratory, cell division can continue indefinitely.

11. Presbycusis refers to age-related:
   a. hearing losses.
   b. decreases in ability of the eyes to focus on distant objects.
   c. changes in metabolism.
   d. changes in brain activity during sleep.

12. Highly unstable atoms that have unpaired electrons and cause damage to other molecules in body cells are called:
   a. B cells.   c. free radicals.
   b. T cells.   d. both a. and b.

13. In triggering our first maturational changes and then the aging process, our genetic makeup is in effect acting as a(n):
   a. immune system.
   b. secondary ager.
   c. demographic pyramid.
   d. genetic clock.

14. Age-related changes in the immune system include all of the following except:
   a. shrinkage of the thymus gland.
   b. loss of T cells.
   c. reduced efficiency in repairing damage from B cells.
   d. reduced efficiency of antibodies.

15. Women are more likely than men to:
   a. have stronger immune systems.
   b. have smaller thymus glands.
   c. be immune to autoimmune diseases such as rheumatoid arthritis.
   d. have all of the above traits.

True or False Items

Write T (*true*) or F (*false*) on the line in front of each statement.

_____ 1. The dependency ratio is higher than it has been for a century.

_____ 2. People with stronger immune systems tend to live longer than their contemporaries.

_____ 3. Because of demographic changes, the majority of America's elderly population is now predominantly old-old rather than young-old.

_____ 4. Gerontologists focus on distinguishing aging in terms of the quality of aging, that is, in terms of young-old versus old-old.

_____ 5. Although the production of T cells declines with age, the efficiency of the immune system is not affected.

_____ 6. The immune system helps to control the effects of cellular damage.

_____ 7. A decline in the number of free radicals may accelerate the aging process.

_____ 8. Although average life expectancy is increasing, maximum life span has remained unchanged.

_____ 9. Although older people are more susceptible to disease, they tend to recover faster from most illnesses.

_____ 10. The importance of lifestyle factors in contributing to longevity is underscored by studies of the long-lived.

Progress Test 2

Progress Test 2 should be completed during a final chapter review. Answer the following questions after you thoroughly understand the correct answers for the Chapter Review and Progress Test 1.

Multiple-Choice Questions

1. People tend to view late adulthood more negatively than is actually the case because:
   a. they are afraid of their own impending death.
   b. of the tendency to categorize and judge people on the basis of a single characteristic.
   c. of actual experiences with older people.
   d. they were taught to do so from an early age by their parents.

2. An important demographic change in America is that:
   a. ageism is beginning to diminish.
   b. population growth has virtually ceased.
   c. the median age is falling.
   d. the number of older people in the population is increasing.

3. Changes in appearance during late adulthood include all of the following except a:
   a. slight reduction in height.
   b. significant increase in weight.
   c. redistribution of body fat.
   d. marked wrinkling of the skin.

4. Heart disease and cancer are:
   a. caused by aging.
   b. genetic diseases.
   c. examples of secondary aging.
   d. all of the above.

5. As a result of the _____ birth rate, the population dependency ratio in most industrialized countries is _____ than it was at the turn of the twentieth century.
   a. increasing; higher
   b. increasing; lower
   c. decreasing; higher
   d. decreasing; lower

6. Regarding the body's self-healing processes, which of the following is *not* true?
   a. Women have a larger thymus and a stronger immune system.
   b. Given a healthy lifestyle, cellular errors accumulate slowly, causing little harm.
   c. Aging makes cellular repair mechanisms less efficient.
   d. Women who postpone childbirth have less efficient cellular repair mechanisms.

7. In ancient times, the average life expectancy was only about 20 years primarily because:
   a. so many babies died.
   b. there were few effective treatments for serious illnesses.
   c. accidents and warfare took scores of lives in most parts of the world.
   d. people did not understand the importance of a healthy diet to longevity.

8. The oldest age to which a human can live is ultimately limited by:
   a. cellular aging.
   b. the maximum life span.
   c. the average life expectancy.
   d. the Hayflick limit.

9. Cardiovascular disease is the leading cause of death for:
   a. men.
   b. women.
   c. both men and women.
   d. neither men nor women; cancer is the leading cause of death.

10. Each time a cell duplicates:
    a. the genetic clock is reset.
    b. the telomere is shortened.
    c. the Hayflick limit is reached.
    d. telomerase is released.

11. In studies of three regions of the world known for the longevity of their inhabitants, the long-lived showed all of the following characteristics *except*:
    a. their diets were moderate.
    b. they were spared from doing any kind of work.
    c. they interacted frequently with family members, friends, and neighbors.
    d. they engaged in some form of exercise on a daily basis.

12. In defending itself against internal and external invaders, the immune system relies on two kinds of "attack" cells: _____, manufactured in the bone marrow, and _____, manufactured by the thymus gland.
    a. B cells; T cells
    b. T cells; B cells
    c. free radicals; T cells
    d. B cells; free radicals

13. The view of aging that the body and its parts deteriorate with use and with accumulated exposure to environmental stresses is known as the _____ theory.
    a. programmed senescence
    b. genetic clock
    c. cellular aging
    d. wear-and-tear

14. Worldwide, the fastest-growing age group are those:
    a. under 5 years of age.
    b. between 20 and 30 years of age.
    c. between 60 and 70 years of age.
    d. over age 100.

15. In humans, average life expectancy varies according to all of the following *except*:
    a. historical factors.
    b. ethnic factors.
    c. cultural factors.
    d. socioeconomic factors.

Matching Items

Match each term or concept with its corresponding description or definition.

Terms or Concepts

_____ 1. young-old
_____ 2. old-old
_____ 3. glaucoma
_____ 4. cataracts
_____ 5. B cells
_____ 6. T cells
_____ 7. compression of morbidity
_____ 8. oxygen free radicals
_____ 9. Hayflick limit
_____ 10. primary aging
_____ 11. secondary aging

Descriptions or Definitions

a. the universal changes that occur as we grow older
b. limiting the time a person is ill
c. the number of times a cell replicates before dying
d. unstable atoms with unpaired electrons that damage cells
e. attack infected cells and strengthen other aspects of the immune system's functioning
f. the majority of the elderly
g. thickening of the lens of the eye
h. the minority of the elderly
i. create antibodies that attack bacteria and viruses
j. age-related changes that are caused by health habits, genes, and other conditions
k. hardening of the eyeball due to the buildup of fluid

Developmental Psychology Applied

Answer these questions the day before an exam as a final check on your understanding of the chapter's terms and concepts.

1. Which of the following is *most* likely to be a result of ageism?
   a. the participation of the elderly in community activities
   b. laws requiring workers to retire by a certain age
   c. an increase in multigenerational families
   d. greater interest in the study of gerontology

2. Loretta majored in psychology at the local university. Because she wanted to serve her community, she applied to a local agency to study the effects of aging on the elderly. Loretta is a:
   a. developmental psychologist.
   b. behaviorist.
   c. gerontologist.
   d. demographer.

3. An 85-year-old man enjoys good health and actively participates in family and community activities. This person is best described as being:
   a. ageist.
   b. young-old.
   c. old-old.
   d. a gerontologist.

4. Concluding her presentation on demographic trends in the United States, Marisa states that, "By the year 2050:
   a. there will be more people age 60 and older than below age 30."
   b. there will be more people age 30 to 59 than below age 30."
   c. there will be more people below age 30 than above age 60."
   d. people over age 65 will make up 16 percent of the world's population.

5. Renne has to spend time at a nursing facility because of a broken kneecap. Although the facility contains a large dining room for residents, she prefers to eat alone in her room. The *most* likely reason for this is:
   a. her failed hearing.
   b. that she has digestive problems and does not want anyone to know.
   c. she does not want to be with other old people.
   d. all of the above.

6. Professor Wilson believes that primary aging occurs because there is no reason for "mother nature" to waste resources on adults who are no longer able to produce the next generation. Professor Wilson is evidently a proponent of:
   a. wear-and-tear theory.
   b. cellular aging theory.
   c. epigenetic theory.
   d. free radical theory.

7. In summarizing research evidence concerning the causes of aging, you should state that:
   a. "Errors in cellular duplication cannot explain primary aging."
   b. "Impairments of the immune system are closely involved in aging."
   c. "Aging is simply a mistake; species are not genetically programmed to die."
   d. a., b., and c. are equally accurate.

8. A flu from which younger adults readily recover can prove fatal to older adults. The main reason for this is that older adults:
   a. are often reluctant to consult doctors.
   b. have a greater genetic predisposition to the flu.
   c. have diminished immunity.
   d. are often weakened by inadequate nutrition.

9. The wear-and-tear theory might be best suited to explain:
   a. the overall process of aging.
   b. the wrinkling of the skin that is characteristic of older adults.
   c. the arm and shoulder problems of a veteran baseball pitcher.
   d. the process of cell replacement by which minor cuts are healed.

10. With regard to nutrition, most elderly should probably be advised to:
    a. take large doses of vitamins and, especially, antioxidants.
    b. eat foods that are high in calories.
    c. consume a varied and healthy diet.
    d. eat large meals but eat less often.

11. I am a cell that is produced in the bone marrow that creates antibodies to destroy bacteria and viruses. Who am I?
    a. B cell
    b. T cell
    c. thymus cell
    d. free radical

12. Extrapolating from the results of research studies of human and animal health and longevity, Shelly suggests that human life could potentially be extended by:
    a. careful diet.
    b. social respect.
    c. regular exercise.
    d. all of the above.

13. Mary and Charlie are both 50. As they advance through adulthood, it is likely that:
    a. Charlie will be healthier than Mary.
    b. Charlie is more likely to be incapacitated by a cold.
    c. Mary's immune responses will be weaker.
    d. all of the above are true.

14. Because age is not an accurate predictor of dependency, some gerontologists prefer to use the term _____ to refer to the *young-old*, and the term _____ to refer to the *oldest-old*.
    a. optimal aging; usual aging
    b. usual aging; impaired aging
    c. impaired aging; optimal aging
    d. optimal aging; impaired aging

15. In concluding her presentation on human longevity, Katrina states that:
    a. current average life expectancy is about twice what it was at the turn of the century.
    b. current maximum life span is about twice what it was at the turn of the century.
    c. both average life expectancy and maximum life span have increased since the turn of the century.
    d. although maximum life span has not increased, average life expectancy has, because infants are less likely to die.

Key Terms

Writing Definitions

Using your own words, write a brief definition or explanation of each of the following terms on a separate piece of paper.

1. ageism
2. elderspeak
3. gerontology
4. geriatrics
5. demography
6. centenarian
7. dependency ratio
8. young-old
9. old-old
10. oldest-old
11. primary aging
12. secondary aging
13. cardiovascular disease
14. compression of morbidity

15. wear-and-tear theory
16. genetic clock
17. maximum life span
18. average life expectancy
19. oxygen free radicals
20. antioxidants
21. B cells
22. T cells
23. Hayflick limit
24. telomeres
25. calorie restriction

Cross Check

After you have written the definitions of the key terms in this chapter, you should complete the crossword puzzle to ensure that you can reverse the process—recognize the term, given the definition.

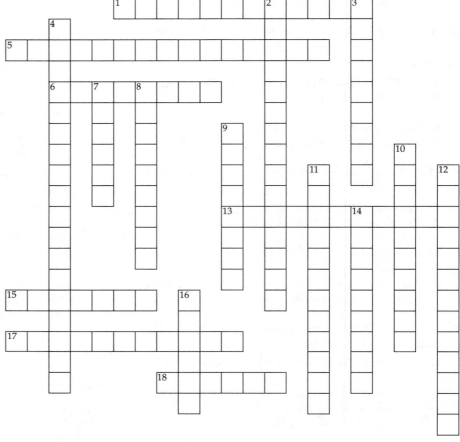

ACROSS

1. Compounds such as vitamins A, E, and C that nullify the effects of oxygen free radicals.
5. Maximum number of years that a particular species is genetically programmed to live.
6. Eye disease that can destroy vision, caused by the hardening of the eyeball due to the buildup of fluid.
13. The study of old age.
15. The universal and irreversible physical changes that occur as people get older is referred to as _____ aging.
17. Theory of aging that the parts of the human body deteriorate with use as well as due to accumulated exposure to pollution and radiation, toxic foods, drugs, disease, and various other stresses.
18. Older people who suffer physical, mental, or social deficits in later life.

DOWN

2. Ratio of self-sufficient, productive adults to children and the elderly.
3. The changes that occur with age that are caused by health habits, genes, and other influences that vary from person to person are referred to as _____ aging.
4. Highly unstable atoms with unpaired electrons that are capable of reacting with other molecules in the cell, tearing them apart and possibly accelerating aging.
7. Prejudice against older people.
8. Common eye disease involving the thickening of the lens that, left untreated, can distort vision.
9. Elderly people who are healthy and vigorous.
10. The study of populations and social statistics associated with these populations.
11. Theory of aging that the regulatory mechanism in the cells' DNA controls cellular processes and "times" aging and the moment of death.
12. Maximum number of times that cells cultured from humans and animals divide before dying.
14. Elderly adults who are dependent on others for almost everything.
16. Immune system cells that are manufactured in the bone marrow and create antibodies that attack specific invading bacteria and viruses.

ANSWERS

CHAPTER REVIEW

1. ageism
2. elderspeak

Like babytalk, elderspeak uses simple and short sentences, exaggerated emphasis, slower talk, higher pitch, and repetition.

3. gerontology; geriatrics; ill; illness

4. is

5. demography; demographic shift

6. centenarians; 100

7. pyramid; largest; smallest

   a. Each generation of young adults gave birth to more than enough children to replace themselves.

   b. About half of all children died before age 5.

   c. Those who lived to be middle-aged rarely survived diseases like cancer or heart attacks.

8. fewer births; survival; square

9. varies

10. dependency ratio; birth; late adulthood; lower; reverse (from 2:1 to 1:2)

11. longevity; are not

12. 4

13. young-old

14. old-old; oldest-old; a small minority; is not; optimal; usual; impaired

15. senescence; primary aging; secondary aging; environmental; illnesses; is not; is not

16. cardiovascular disease; risk; age

17. do not have

18. slower; efficient; more; more

19. selective optimization with compensation

20. insomnia; narcotic

Prescription doses are often too strong for an older person, overwhelming the person's capacity for homeostasis and causing confusion, nausea, depression, impaired cognition, and unsteadiness.

21. electrical activity; dreams

22. fewer

23. fewer; less

24. diet; exercise

25. one or two

26. slowly; shrinks; more

27. dryer; thinner; less; age spots; male pattern baldness

28. shorter; vertebrae

29. torso; lower face

30. lower; men; muscle; fat

31. sensory

32. 26; cataracts; lens; glaucoma; hardening; fluid; macular degeneration; retina

33. presbycusis; 40; retarded; mentally ill; depression; demoralization; psychotic

34. compensation

35. compression of morbidity

36. wear-and-tear; machine; doesn't hold up

Each body has a certain amount of energy and strength; for example, women who have never been pregnant tend to live longer than other women. People who are overweight tend to sicken and die at younger ages. One breakthrough of modern medical technology is replacement of worn-out body parts.

37. DNA; genetic clock

38. maximum life span; 122; average life expectancy; the number of years the average newborn in a population group is likely to live

39. historical; cultural; socioeconomic; death; 75; 81

40. 20; so many babies died; 50; public health; sanitation, immunizations, and antibiotics

One explanation is that because reproduction is essential for the survival of our species, it was genetically important for deaths to occur either very early in life or after childbearing and child rearing.

41. nongenetic; Parkinson's disease, Huntington's disease, Alzheimer's disease, type 2 diabetes, coronary heart disease, and osteoporosis

42. cells; cell reproduction; DNA; mutations

43. oxygen free radicals

44. antioxidants; A; C; E; selenium

45. immune

46. B cells; antibodies; bacteria; viruses; T cells; thymus

47. decreases

48. longer; decline

49. stronger; larger; autoimmune

50. Hayflick limit

51. telomeres; shorter

52. calorie restriction

53. Georgia (Republic of); Pakistan; Ecuador; verifiable birth or marriage records

   a. Diet is moderate, consisting mostly of fresh vegetables.

   b. Work continues throughout life.

   c. Families and community are important.

   d. Exercise and relaxation are part of the daily routine.

PROGRESS TEST 1

Multiple-Choice Questions

1. **b.** is the answer. (p. 615)

   a. This is gerontology.

   c. This is progeria.

   d. This is the wear-and-tear theory.

2. **c.** is the answer. (p. 617)

3. **c.** is the answer. (p. 620)

   a., b., & d. These are examples of secondary aging.

4. **a.** is the answer. (p. 616)

5. **b.** is the answer. (p. 630)

   a. Cataracts are caused by a thickening of the lens.

   c. This disease involves deterioration of the retina.

   d. Myopia, which was not discussed in this chapter, is nearsightedness.

6. **d.** is the answer. (p. 622)

7. **a.** is the answer. (p. 639)

   b. In fact, free radicals damage DNA, rather than vice versa.

   c. The immune system compensates for, but is not directly affected by, damage to cellular DNA.

   d. This genetic disease occurs too infrequently to be considered a *direct* result of damage to cellular DNA.

8. **c.** is the answer. (p. 639)

9. **a.** is the answer. (p. 636)

   b. & c. According to the genetic clock theory, time, rather than genetic damage or hormonal abnormalities, regulates the aging process.

   d. The genetic clock theory makes no provision for environmental alteration of the genetic mechanisms of aging.

10. **c.** is the answer. (pp. 640–641)

11. **a.** is the answer. (p. 631)

12. **c.** is the answer. (p. 639)

    a. & b. These are the "attack" cells of the immune system.

13. **d.** is the answer. (p. 636)

    a. This is the body's system for defending itself against bacteria and other "invaders."

    b. Secondary aging is caused not only by genes but also by health habits and other influences.

    c. This is a metaphor for the distribution of age groups, with the largest and youngest group at the bottom, and the smallest and oldest group at the top.

14. **c.** is the answer. B cells create antibodies that *repair* rather than damage cells. (p. 640)

15. **a.** is the answer. (p. 640)

b. & c. Women have *larger* thymus glands than men. They are also *more* susceptible to autoimmune diseases.

True or False Items

1. F   The ratio is lower than it has ever been, with fewer people who are dependent on others for care. (p. 618)

2. T (p. 640)

3. F   Although our population is aging, the terms *old-old* and *young-old* refer to degree of physical and social well-being, not to age. (p. 620)

4. T (p. 616)

5. F   The declining production of T cells contributes to diminished immunity. (p. 640)

6. T (p. 640)

7. F   Inasmuch as free radicals damage DNA and other molecules, it is their *presence* that may contribute to aging. (p. 639)

8. T (pp. 636–637)

9. F   Older people tend to recover more slowly from illnesses than younger people do. (p. 622)

10. T (p. 645)

PROGRESS TEST 2

Multiple-Choice Questions

1. **b.** is the answer. (p. 615)

2. **d.** is the answer. (pp. 616–617)

   a. Ageism is prejudice, not a demographic change.

   b. Although birth rates have fallen, population growth has not ceased.

   c. Actually, with the "squaring of the pyramid," the median age is rising.

3. **b.** is the answer. Weight often decreases during late adulthood. (p. 630)

4. **c.** is the answer. (pp. 620–621)

   a. & b. Over time, the interaction of accumulating risk factors with age-related weakening of the heart and relevant genetic weaknesses makes the elderly increasingly vulnerable to heart disease.

5. **d.** is the answer. (p. 618)

6. **d.** is the answer. The text does not discuss the impact of age of childbearing on a woman's cell repair mechanisms. However, it does note that women who have never been pregnant may *extend* life. (pp. 635–636)

7. **a.** is the answer. (p. 637)

   b. Serious illnesses are more likely among older adults.

   c. & d. Although both of these may be true, neither is the primary reason for an average life expectancy of only 20 years.

8. **b.** is the answer. (p. 636)

   a. This is a theory of aging.

   c. This statistic refers to the number of years the average newborn of a particular species is likely to live.

   d. This is the number of times a cultured cell replicates before dying.

9. **c.** is the answer. (p. 621)

10. **b.** is the answer. (p. 641)

11. **b.** is the answer. In fact, just the opposite is true. (p. 643)

12. **a.** is the answer. (p. 640)

13. **d.** is the answer. (p. 635)

   a. & b. According to these theories, aging is genetically predetermined.

   c. This theory attributes aging and disease to the accumulation of cellular errors.

14. **d.** is the answer. (p. 617)

15. **b.** is the answer. (p. 637)

Matching Items

1. f (p. 620)   5. i (p. 640)   9. c (p. 641)
2. h (p. 620)   6. e (p. 640)   10. a (p. 620)
3. k (p. 630)   7. b (p. 633)   11. j (p. 620)
4. g (p. 630)   8. d (p. 639)

DEVELOPMENTAL PSYCHOLOGY APPLIED

1. **b.** is the answer. (p. 615)

2. **c.** is the answer. (p. 616)

   a. Although Loretta is probably a developmental psychologist, that category is too broad to be correct.

   b. Behaviorism describes her *approach* to studying, not *what* she is studying.

   d. Demographics is the study of populations.

3. **b.** is the answer. (p. 620)

   a. An ageist is a person who is prejudiced against the elderly.

   c. People who are "old-old" have social, physical, and mental problems that hamper their successful aging.

   d. A gerontologist is a person who studies aging.

4. **d.** is the answer. (p. 617)

5. **a.** is the answer. Most older adults suffer from hearing loss, and this often makes them more likely to want to remain socially isolated. (p. 632)

   b. & c. There is no indication that she has digestive problems or that she does not want to associate with other older people.

6. **c.** is the answer. (p. 638)

7. **b.** is the answer. (p. 640)

   a. Errors in cellular duplication *do*, in part, explain primary aging.

   c. For each species, there *does* seem to be a genetically programmed maximum life span.

8. **c.** is the answer. (p. 622)

   a. In fact, older adults are more likely to consult doctors.

   b. There is no evidence that this is true.

   d. Most older adults are adequately nourished.

9. **c.** is the answer. In this example, excessive use of the muscles of the arm and shoulder has contributed to their "wearing out." (p. 635)

10. **c.** is the answer. (p. 624)

   a. Large doses of vitamins can be harmful.

   b. Older adults need fewer calories to maintain body weight.

   d. This is an unhealthy dietary regimen.

11. **a.** is the answer. (p. 640)

   b. T cells are manufactured in the thymus gland.

   c. There is no such thing.

   d. Free radicals are unstable atoms that may accelerate aging.

12. **d.** is the answer. (p. 645)

13. **b.** is the answer. (p. 640)

   a. At that age, women tend to be healthier than men.

   c. Throughout life, women generally have *stronger* immune systems than men do.

14. **d.** is the answer. (p. 620)

15. **d.** is the answer. (pp. 636–637)

   a. Current average life expectancy is 28 years more than it was at the turn of the century.

   b. & c. Maximum life span has not changed since the turn of the century.

KEY TERMS

1. **Ageism** is prejudice against older people. (p. 615)

2. **Elderspeak** is a babyish way of speaking to older adults, using simple sentences, a slower rate, higher pitch, and repetition. (p. 615)

3. **Gerontology** is the study of old age. (p. 616)

4. **Geriatrics** is the medical specialty devoted to aging. (p. 616)

5. **Demography** is the study of the characteristics of human populations. (p. 616)

6. A **centenarian** is a person who is 100 years of age or older. (p. 617)

7. The **dependency ratio** is the ratio of self-sufficient, productive adults to children and elderly adults. (p. 618)

8. Most of America's elderly can be classified as **young-old,** meaning that they are "healthy and vigorous, relatively well-off financially, well integrated into the lives of their families and communities, and politically active." (p. 620)

9. Older people who are classified as **old-old** are those who suffer severe physical, mental, or social problems in later life. (p. 620)

10. Elderly adults who are classified as **oldest-old** are dependent on others for almost everything. (p. 620)

11. **Primary aging** refers to the universal and irreversible physical changes that occur as people get older. (p. 620)

12. **Secondary aging** refers to changes that are more common as people age but are caused by health habits, genes, and other influences that vary from person to person. (p. 620)

13. **Cardiovascular disease** refers collectively to the various diseases that affect the heart and the circulatory system. (p. 621)

14. Researchers who are interested in improving the health of the elderly focus on a **compression of morbidity,** that is, a limiting of the time any person spends ill. (p. 633)

15. According to the **wear-and-tear theory** of aging, the parts of the human body deteriorate with use as well as with accumulated exposure to pollution and radiation, toxic foods, drugs, disease, and various other stresses. (p. 635)

16. According to one theory of aging, our genetic makeup acts, in effect, as a **genetic clock,** triggering hormonal changes, regulating cellular reproduction and repair, and "timing" aging and the moment of death. (p. 636)

17. The **maximum life span** is the maximum number of years that a particular species is genetically programmed to live. For humans, the maximum life span is approximately 122 years. (p. 636)

18. **Average life expectancy** is the number of years the average newborn of a particular species is likely to live. (p. 636)

19. **Oxygen free radicals** are highly unstable atoms with unpaired electrons that are capable of reacting with other molecules in the cell, tearing them apart and possibly accelerating aging. (p. 639)

20. **Antioxidants** are compounds such as vitamins A, E, and C that nullify the effects of oxygen free radicals. (p. 639)

21. **B cells** are immune system cells that are manufactured in the bone marrow and create antibodies that attack specific invading bacteria and viruses. (p. 640)

   Memory aid: The B cells come from the *bone* marrow and attack *bacteria.*

22. **T cells** are immune system cells that are manufactured in the thymus and produce substances that attack infected cells of the body. (p. 640)

23. The **Hayflick limit** is the maximum number of times that cells cultured from humans and animals divide before dying. (p. 641)

24. **Telomeres** are the ends of chromosomes; their length seems correlated with longevity. (p. 641)

25. **Calorie restriction** is the practice of limiting dietary energy intake in an effort to slow down aging. (p. 642)

Cross-Check

ACROSS

1. antioxidants
5. maximum life span
6. glaucoma
13. gerontology
15. primary
17. wear-and-tear
18. old-old

DOWN

2. dependency ratio
3. secondary
4. oxygen free radicals
7. ageism
8. cataracts
9. young-old
10. demography
11. genetic clock
12. Hayflick limit
14. oldest-old
16. B cells

24

Late Adulthood: Cognitive Development

Chapter Overview

This chapter describes the changes in cognitive functioning associated with late adulthood. The first section reviews usual changes associated with the information-processing system, providing experimental evidence that suggests declines in older adults' control processes, including their retrieval strategies. It also describes neurological and other reasons for impaired cognitive development during late adulthood. Despite some inevitable decline, real-life conditions provide older adults with ample opportunity to compensate for the pattern of decline observed in the laboratory. It appears that, for most people, cognitive functioning in daily life remains essentially unimpaired.

The main reason for reduced cognitive functioning during late adulthood is dementia, the subject of the second section. This pathological loss of intellectual ability can be caused by a variety of diseases and circumstances; risk factors, treatment, and prognosis differ accordingly.

The final section of the chapter makes it clear that cognitive changes during late adulthood are by no means restricted to declines in intellectual functioning. For many individuals, late adulthood is a time of great aesthetic, creative, philosophical, and spiritual growth.

NOTE: Answer guidelines for all Chapter 24 questions begin on page 350.

Guided Study

The text chapter should be studied one section at a time. Before you read, preview each section by skimming it, noting headings and boldface items. Then read the appropriate section objectives from the following outline. Keep these objectives in mind and, as you read the chapter section, search for the information that will enable you to meet each objective. Once

you have finished a section, write out answers for its objectives.

The Usual: Information Processing After Age 65
(pp. 649–662)

1. Summarize research findings regarding changes in both sensory and working memory during late adulthood.

2. Summarize research findings regarding changes in the older adult's ability to access the knowledge base and to use control processes efficiently.

3. Discuss how the distinction between explicit and implicit memory explains older adults' problems with certain kinds of memories.

4. (text and Thinking Like a Scientist) Explain how noninvasive neuroimaging techniques have changed neuroscientists' understanding of how the brain works, and describe age-related changes in the brain.

5. Discuss secondary aging as a cause of cognitive decline.

6. Characterize and explain discrepancies between how the elderly perform on memory and problem-solving tasks in the laboratory, on the one hand, and in daily life, on the other.

The Impaired Dementia (pp. 662–670)

7. Discuss the problem with identifying the cause of dementia in an older adult.

8. Identify and describe the two most common organic causes of dementia.

9. Describe the causes of subcortical dementias, and explain how symptoms of dementia can sometimes be reversed or slowed through proper treatment.

The Optimal: New Cognitive Development (pp. 670–675)

10. Discuss the claims of developmentalists regarding the possibility of positive cognitive development during late adulthood, and cite several areas of life in which such development may occur.

Chapter Review

When you have finished reading the chapter, work through the material that follows to review it. Complete the sentences and answer the questions. As you proceed, evaluate your performance for each section by consulting the answers beginning on page 350. Do not continue with the next section until you understand each answer. If you need to, review or reread the appropriate section in the textbook before continuing.

The Usual: Information Processing After Age 65 (pp. 649–662)

1. Most intellectual abilities _____
(change little/change a lot) throughout early and middle adulthood. In Schaie's longitudinal study, beginning at about age _____ ,
older adults began to show significant declines in the five "primary mental abilities":

_____ _____ ,

_____ _____ ,

_____ _____ ,

_____ _____ , and

_____ _____ .

2. Researchers agree, however, that there are significant _____ (differences/similarities) in intellectual ability in later life.

3. In order for stimuli to become information that is perceived, they must cross the _____ _____ .

4. One study found that _____ _____ accounted for nearly one-third of the variance in cognitive scores for older adults.

5. Some experts believe that the simplest way to predict how much an older person has aged intellectually may be to measure _____ , _____ , or _____ .

6. Reduced sensory input impairs cognition because some information is simply _____ , and because less important information _____ by capturing attention.

7. Once information is perceived, it must be placed in _____ _____ .

8. Working memory has two interrelated functions: to temporarily _____ information and then to _____ it.

9. Older adults are particularly likely to experience difficulty in multitasking, because it requires screening out _____ and _____ irrelevant thoughts.

10. The difficulty older adults have in multitasking is called the _____-_____ _____ .

11. The _____ _____ consists of the storehouse of information held in _____-_____ memory. This storehouse is far from perfect, because _____ _____ allows most material to be forgotten, never reaching this part of memory. And those memories that do are still subject to _____ .

12. Long-term memory for _____ remains unimpaired over the decades, and typically increases at least until age _____ . Also unimpaired are specific areas of _____ . Events that are

_____ in nature and based on _____ rather than factual details are also remembered better.

13. A common memory error is _____ _____ , not remembering who or what was the source of a specific piece of information.

14. (Thinking Like a Scientist) One way of investigating long-term memory and aging has been to compare memories of public events or facts in different _____ . Another has been to probe memory of _____ _____ learning.

15. (Thinking Like a Scientist) Overall, how much of their knowledge base is available to older adults seems to depend less on _____ _____ and more on _____ _____ .

16. The _____ _____ of the information-processing system help people think clearly and well and include _____ mechanisms, _____ strategies, _____ _____ , and _____ _____ . These processes depend on activity in the brain's _____ _____ , which shrinks with age.

17. Older adults are more likely to rely on prior _____ , general _____ , _____ , and _____ _____ .

18. Use of _____ strategies also worsens with age.

19. Research indicates that impaired cognition in older adults is less a function of _____ declines and more a result of declines in the _____ _____ .

20. (Thinking Like a Scientist) Although brains become _____ with age, older adults tend to use _____ (more/fewer) areas of the brain than younger

adults do. Age-related decreases in brain activity _____ (are/are not) inevitable. Today's noninvasive techniques involve neuroimaging that is _____, i.e., in living brains.

21. (Thinking Like a Scientist) Neuroscience has demonstrated that the brain has _____ (one or two/many) language areas. Imaging studies have also shown that _____ and _____ can be formed in adulthood, that intellectual ability _____ (correlates/does not correlate) with brain size, and that people use their brains differently as they age.

22. (Thinking Like a Scientist) Older brains sometimes show more brain activity, perhaps because their brains compensate for intellectual slowdown by _____ . Another possible explanation is that the brain "_____" and no longer uses a different region for each function.

23. Memory benefits when a person is given a clue before being asked to remember something, called _____ .

24. Memory takes two forms: _____ memory is "automatic" memory involving _____ , _____ responses, _____ procedures, and the _____ . This type of memory is _____ (more/less) vulnerable to age-related deficits than is _____ memory. This latter type of memory involves _____ , _____ , _____ , and the like, most of which was _____ (consciously/unconsciously) learned.

25. As people get older, differences in implicit and explicit memory might be reflected in their remembering how to _____ a particular task but not being as able to _____ its actions.

26. One universal change is a _____ in brain processes. This can be traced to reduced

production of _____ , including _____ , _____ , _____ , and _____ . It is also due to reductions in the volume of _____ _____ , the slower speed of the _____ _____ _____ , and a smaller prefrontal cortex.

27. According to some experts, the slowing of brain processes means that thinking becomes _____ , _____ , and _____ with advancing age. Using memory strategies and reminders, however, older adults often are able to _____ for slower processing.

28. The overall slowdown of cognitive abilities that often occurs in the days or months before death is called _____ _____ .

29. Declines in cognitive functioning may be caused by _____ _____ , _____ _____ , or _____ .

30. Declines in cognitive functioning may also be associated with systemic conditions that affect the brain and other organs such as _____ , _____ , _____ , and _____ . Several factors contribute to these diseases, including _____ _____ .

31. Declines in cognitive functioning may also be associated with ageism, including disparaging _____ .

32. Older adults may _____ (overestimate/underestimate) their memory skills when they were younger; consequently, they tend to _____ (overestimate/underestimate) their current memory losses. As a result of this misperception, older adults may lose _____ in their memory.

33. The impact of ageist stereotypes on cognitive functioning is revealed in a study in which the memory gap between old and young _____ (deaf/hearing) _____ (Chinese/North Americans) was twice as great as that for _____ (deaf/hearing) _____ (Chinese/North Americans) and five times as great as that for _____ .

34. Laboratory tests of memory may put older persons at a disadvantage because they generally use _____ material, which reduces motivation in older adults.

35. Most older adults _____ (do/do not) consider memory problems a significant handicap in daily life.

The Impaired: Dementia (pp. 662–670)

36. Although pathological loss of intellectual ability in elderly people is often referred to as _____ , a more precise term for this loss is _____ , which is defined as _____ .

37. Traditionally, when dementia occurred before age _____ , it was called _____ _____ ; when it occurred after this age, it was called _____ _____ . This age-based distinction is arbitrary, however, because the same _____ may occur at any age.

38. Dementia, which can be caused by more than 70 diseases and circumstances, is characterized by _____ _____ and _____ . Dementia lasts a long time; that is, it is _____ . This is unlike the acute, severe memory loss that lasts only hours or days, called _____ .

39. The most common form of dementia is _____ _____ . This disorder is characterized by abnormalities in the _____ _____ , called _____ and

_____ , which destroy normal brain functioning.

40. Plaques are formed from a protein called _____ ; tangles are twisted masses of threads made of a protein called _____ within the neurons. Plaques and tangles usually begin in the _____ of the brain.

41. Physiologically, the brain damage that accompanies this disease _____ (does/does not) vary with the age of the victim.

42. With age, Alzheimer's disease (AD) becomes _____ (more/no more/less) common, affecting about _____ percent of adults age 65 and _____ percent of those age 85.

43. When Alzheimer's disease appears in middle adulthood, the person either has _____ or has inherited one of three genes: _____ , _____ , or _____ . However, this is quite _____ (common/rare), and the disease usually progresses _____ (less/more) quickly, reaching the last phase within _____ years.

44. About _____ (what proportion?) of the population inherits the gene _____ , which increases the risk of Alzheimer's disease. The protective _____ allele of the same gene may dissipate the _____ that cause the formation of plaques.

45. The first stage of Alzheimer's disease is marked by _____ about recent events. Most people _____ (recognize/do not recognize) that they have a memory problem during this stage, which is often indistinguishable from the normal decline in _____ memory.

46. In the second stage, there are noticeable deficits in the person's _____ and _____-_____

_____ . Changes in _____ are common in this stage. The third stage begins when memory loss becomes dangerous and _____ because the person can no longer manage _____

_____ _____ . People in the fourth stage require _____-_____ _____ . In the fifth stage, people no longer_____ and do not respond with any action or emotion at all. In general, death comes _____ (how many years?) after stage one.

47. The second major type of dementia is _____ _____ . This condition occurs because a temporary obstruction of the _____ _____ , called a(n) _____ , prevents a sufficient supply of blood from reaching the brain. This causes destruction of brain tissue, commonly called a(n) _____ .

48. Unlike the person with Alzheimer's disease, the person with VaD shows a _____ (gradual/sudden) drop in intellectual functioning. The prognosis for a person with VaD is generally quite _____ (good/poor).

49. Another category of dementias, called

_____ _____ , originates in brain areas that do not directly involve thinking and memory. These dementias cause a progressive loss of _____ control. Causes of these dementias include_____ disease, _____ disease, and _____ _____ .

50. The most common of these dementias results from _____ _____ , which produces muscle tremors or rigidity. This disease is related to the degeneration of neurons that produce the neurotransmitter _____ .

51. In a related form of dementia, round deposits of protein are found throughout the brain. The main symptom of this dementia, called

_____ _____ , is loss of _____ .

52. Many AIDS and syphilis patients develop a brain _____ that causes dementia.

53. Chronic alcoholism can lead to _____ syndrome, the chief symptom of which is severely impaired _____-_____ _____ .

54. Oftentimes, the elderly are thought to be suffering from brain disease when, in fact, their symptoms are a sign of _____ dementia caused by some other factor such as

_____ , _____

_____ , _____

_____ , _____ ,

or other _____ _____ .

55. The most common cause of reversible dementia is _____ . Symptoms of dementia can result from drug _____ that occur when a person is taking several different medications. This problem is made worse by the fact that many of the drugs prescribed to older adults can, by themselves, slow down _____ _____ .

56. In general, psychological illnesses such as schizophrenia are _____ (more/less) common in the elderly than in younger adults. Approximately _____ percent of the elderly who are diagnosed as demented are actually experiencing psychological illness.

57. Generally speaking, depression _____ (is/is not) very treatable in late adulthood. However, many older adults who are depressed _____ (are/are not) treated.

58. One consequence of untreated depression among the elderly is that the rate of _____ is higher for those over age _____ than for any other group.

59. The incidence of dementia can be cut in half through regular _____ .

The Optimal: New Cognitive Development
(pp. 670–675)

60. According to Erik Erikson, older adults are more interested in _____

_____

than younger adults and, as the "social witnesses" to life, are more aware of the

_____ of the generations.

61. According to Abraham Maslow, older adults are more likely to achieve _____ .

62. Many people become more appreciative of _____ and _____ _____ as they get older.

63. Many people also become more _____ and _____ than when they were younger.

64. One form of this attempt to put life into perspective is called the _____ _____ , in which the older person connects his or her own life with the future.

65. One of the most positive attributes commonly associated with older people is _____ , which Baltes defines as expert knowledge in the _____ _____ of life.

Progress Test 1

Multiple-Choice Questions

Circle your answers to the following questions and check them with the answers beginning on page 351. If your answer is incorrect, read the explanation for why it is incorrect and then consult the appropriate pages of the text (in parentheses following the correct answer).

1. The information-processing component that is concerned with the temporary storage of incoming sensory information is:
   a. working memory.   c. the knowledge base.
   b. long-term memory.   d. sensory memory.

2. (Thinking Like a Scientist) Neuroimaging studies have demonstrated each of the following *except*
   a. the human brain has dozens of areas that are activated when language is used.
   b. intellectual ability does not correlate with brain size.
   c. people use their brains differently as they age.
   d. most people, most of the time, only use about 10 percent of their brain capacity.

3. The two basic functions of working memory are:
   a. storage that enables conscious use and processing of information.
   b. temporary storage and processing of sensory stimuli.
   c. automatic memories and retrieval of learned memories.
   d. permanent storage and retrieval of information.

4. Memory for skills is called:
   a. explicit memory.   c. episodic memory.
   b. declarative memory.   d. implicit memory.

5. Strategies to retain and retrieve information in the knowledge base are part of which basic component of information processing?
   a. sensory register   c. control processes
   b. working memory   d. explicit memory

6. The plaques and tangles that accompany Alzheimer's disease usually begin in the:
   a. temporal lobe.
   b. frontal lobe.
   c. hippocampus.
   d. cerebral cortex.

7. Secondary aging factors that may explain some declines in cognitive functioning include:
   a. fewer opportunities for learning in old age.
   b. disparaging self-perceptions of cognitive abilities.
   c. difficulty with traditional methods of measuring cognitive functioning.
   d. all of the above.

8. When using working memory, older adults have particular difficulty:
   a. performing several tasks at once.
   b. picking up faint sounds.
   c. processing blurry images.
   d. recalling the meaning of rarely used vocabulary.

9. The most common cause of reversible dementia is:
   a. a temporary obstruction of the blood vessels.
   b. genetic mutation.
   c. overmedication.
   d. depression.

10. Dementia refers to:
    a. pathological loss of intellectual functioning.
    b. the increasing forgetfulness that sometimes accompanies the aging process.
    c. abnormal behavior associated with mental illness and with advanced stages of alcoholism.
    d. a genetic disorder that doesn't become overtly manifested until late adulthood.

11. Which of the following diseases does *not* belong with the others?
    a. Huntington's disease
    b. Parkinson's disease
    c. multiple sclerosis
    d. multi-infarct dementia

12. Alzheimer's disease is characterized by:
    a. a proliferation of plaques and tangles in the cerebral cortex.
    b. a destruction of brain tissue as a result of strokes.
    c. rigidity and tremor of the muscles.
    d. an excess of fluid pressing on the brain.

13. Multi-infarct dementia and Alzheimer's disease differ in their progression in that:
    a. multi-infarct dementia never progresses beyond the first stage.
    b. multi-infarct dementia is marked by sudden drops and temporary improvements, whereas decline in Alzheimer's disease is steady.
    c. multi-infarct dementia leads to rapid deterioration and death, whereas Alzheimer's disease may progress over a period of years.
    d. the progression of Alzheimer's disease may be halted or slowed, whereas the progression of multi-infarct dementia is irreversible.

14. Medication has been associated with symptoms of dementia in the elderly for all of the following reasons *except*:
    a. standard drug dosages are often too strong for the elderly.
    b. the elderly tend to become psychologically dependent upon drugs.
    c. drugs sometimes have the side effect of slowing mental processes.
    d. the intermixing of drugs can sometimes have detrimental effects on cognitive functioning.

15. The primary purpose of the life review is to:
    a. enhance one's spirituality.
    b. produce an autobiography.
    c. give advice to younger generations.
    d. put one's life into perspective.

True or False Items

Write T (*true*) or F (*false*) on the line in front of each statement.

_____ 1. As long as their vision and hearing remain unimpaired, older adults are no less efficient than younger adults at inputting information.

_____ 2. Reduced sensory input impairs cognition by increasing the power of interference.

_____ 3. Cultural attitudes are unrelated to impaired thinking in the elderly.

_____ 4. A majority of the elderly feel frustrated and hampered by memory loss in their daily lives.

_____ 5. In studies of problem solving in real-life contexts, the scores of older adults were better than those of younger adults.

_____ 6. The majority of cases of dementia are organically caused.

_____ 7. Alzheimer's disease is partly genetic.

_____ 8. Cognition that is unaffected by speed is usually unaffected by primary aging.

_____ 9. Late adulthood is often associated with a narrowing of interests and an exclusive focus on the self.

_____ 10. According to Maslow, self-actualization is actually more likely to be reached during late adulthood.

Progress Test 2

Progress Test 2 should be completed during a final chapter review. Answer the following questions after you thoroughly understand the correct answers for the Chapter Review and Progress Test 1.

Multiple-Choice Questions

1. Research suggests that aging results in:
   a. increased sensitivity of sensory memory.
   b. a significant decrease in the sensitivity of the sensory register that cannot usually be compensated for.
   c. declines in memory for events.
   d. no noticeable changes in sensory memory.

2. Which of the following most accurately characterizes age-related changes in working memory?

   a. The ability to screen out distractions and inhibit irrelevant thoughts declines.
   b. Storage capacity declines while processing efficiency remains stable.
   c. Storage capacity remains stable while processing efficiency declines.
   d. Both storage capacity and processing efficiency remain stable.

3. Information remembered for years or decades is stored in:

   a. sensory register.
   b. working memory.
   c. long-term memory.
   d. short-term memory.

4. Conscious memory for words, data, and concepts is called _____ memory.

   a. sensory
   b. implicit
   c. explicit
   d. knowledge base

5. In general, with increasing age the control processes used to remember new information:

   a. become more efficient.
   b. become more complex.
   c. become more intertwined.
   d. become simpler and less efficient.

6. Which type of memory is most vulnerable to age-related deficits?

   a. sensory memory
   b. implicit memory
   c. explicit memory
   d. knowledge base

7. Regarding the role of genes in Alzheimer's disease, which of the following is *not* true?

   a. Some people inherit a gene that increases their risk of developing the disease.
   b. Some people inherit a gene that lowers their risk of developing the disease.
   c. Most people inherit either the protective or the destructive gene.
   d. Alzheimer's disease is a multifaceted disease that involves multiple genetic and environmental factors.

8. One study tested memory in different age groups by requiring younger and older adults to remember to make telephone calls at a certain time. It was found that:

   a. older adults did worse than younger adults because their memories were not as good.
   b. older adults did better than younger adults because they were able to trust their memories.
   c. older adults did better than younger adults because they didn't trust their memories and therefore used various reminders.
   d. older adults did worse than younger adults because they were less accustomed to having to do things at a certain time.

9. Laboratory studies of memory in late adulthood often fail to take into account the effects of:

   a. the knowledge base of older adults.
   b. lack of practice in taking tests under pressure.
   c. the explicit memory that is central to the functioning of older adults.
   d. the ability of older adults to rely on their long-term memories.

10. Dementia:

    a. is more likely to occur among the aged.
    b. has no relationship to age.
    c. cannot occur before the age of 60.
    d. is an inevitable occurrence during late adulthood.

11. The most common form of dementia is:

    a. Alzheimer's disease.
    b. multi-infarct dementia.
    c. Parkinson's disease.
    d. alcoholism and depression.

12. Organic causes of dementia include all of the following *except*:

    a. Parkinson's disease.
    b. multiple sclerosis.
    c. Huntington's disease.
    d. leukemia.

13. The psychological illness most likely to be misdiagnosed as dementia is:

    a. schizophrenia.
    b. anxiety.
    c. personality disorder.
    d. depression.

14. On balance, it can be concluded that positive cognitive development during late adulthood:
    a. occurs only for a small minority of individuals.
    b. leads to thought processes that are more appropriate to the final stage of life.
    c. makes older adults far less pragmatic than younger adults.
    d. is impossible in view of increasing deficits in cognitive functioning.

15. A key factor underlying the older adult's cognitive developments in the realms of aesthetics, philosophy, and spiritualism may be:
    a. the realization that one's life is drawing to a close.
    b. the despair associated with a sense of isolation from the community.
    c. the need to leave one's mark on history.
    d. a growing indifference to the outside world.

Matching Items

Match each definition or description with its corresponding term.

Terms

_____ 1. delirium
_____ 2. working memory
_____ 3. knowledge base
_____ 4. control processes
_____ 5. subcortical dementias
_____ 6. dementia
_____ 7. Alzheimer's disease
_____ 8. multi-infarct dementia (MID)
_____ 9. Parkinson's disease
_____ 10. source amnesia
_____ 11. life review

Definitions or Descriptions

a. the inability to remember the origins of a specific piece of information
b. temporarily stores information for conscious processing
c. strategies for retaining and retrieving information
d. severely impaired thinking, memory, or problem-solving ability
e. memory loss and confusion that disappears in hours and days
f. caused by a temporary obstruction of the blood vessels
g. stores information for several minutes to several decades
h. caused by a degeneration of neurons that produce dopamine
i. putting one's life into perspective
j. characterized by plaques and tangles in the cerebral cortex
k. brain disorders that do not directly involve thinking and memory

Developmental Psychology Applied

Answer these questions the day before an exam as a final check on your understanding of the chapter's terms and concepts.

1. Leland's parents are in their 70s, and he wants to do something to ensure that their cognitive abilities remain sharp for years to come. As a friend, what would you encourage Leland to suggest that his parents do?
   a. They should take long walks several times a week.
   b. They should spend time reading and doing crossword puzzles.
   c. They should go to a neurologist for regular checkups.
   d. They should do a. and b.

2. Summarizing her presentation on aging and cognitive decline, Martina states that many researchers believe that the simplest way to predict how much an older person has aged intellectually is to measure his or her:
   a. reaction time.
   b. cerebral blood volume.
   c. vision, hearing, or smell.
   d. working memory capacity.

3. Although 75-year-old Sharonda remembers a relative once telling her that her ancestors were royalty in their native country, she can't recall which relative it was. Like many older adults, Sharonda is evidently displaying signs of:
   a. multi-infarct dementia.
   b. Alzheimer's disease.
   c. subcortical dementia.
   d. source amnesia.

4. Depression among the elderly is a serious problem because:
   a. rates of depression are far higher for the elderly than for younger adults.
   b. in late adulthood depression becomes extremely difficult to treat.
   c. depression in the elderly often goes untreated, contributing to a higher rate of suicide than for any other age group.
   d. organic forms of dementia cause depression.

5. Because she has trouble screening out distractions and inhibiting irrelevant thoughts, 70-year-old Lena is likely to:
   a. have suffered a mini-stroke.
   b. be at increased risk of developing dementia.
   c. experience typical age-related declines in her working memory.
   d. have some type of reversible dementia.

6. Developmentalists believe that older people's tendency to reminisce:
   a. represents an unhealthy preoccupation with the self and the past.
   b. is an underlying cause of age segregation.
   c. is a necessary and healthy process.
   d. is a result of a heightened aesthetic sense.

7. A patient has the following symptoms: blurred vision, slurred speech, and mental confusion. The patient is probably suffering from:
   a. Alzheimer's disease.
   b. vascular dementia
   c. Huntington's disease.
   d. Parkinson's disease.

8. Because of deficits in sensory input, older people may tend to:
   a. forget the names of people and places.
   b. be distracted by irrelevant stimuli.
   c. miss details in a dimly lit room.
   d. reminisce at length about the past.

9. Holding material in your mind for a minute or two requires which type of memory?
   a. working memory   c. long-term memory
   b. explicit memory   d. sensory register

10. Marisa's presentation on "Reversing the Age-Related Slowdown in Thinking" includes all of the following points *except*:
    a. regular exercise.
    b. avoiding the use of anti-inflammatory drugs.
    c. cognitive stimulation.
    d. consumption of antioxidants.

11. Which type of material would 72-year-old Jessica probably have the greatest difficulty remembering?
    a. the dates of birth of family members
    b. a short series of numbers she has just heard
    c. the first house she lived in
    d. technical terms from her field of expertise prior to retirement

12. Sixty-five-year-old Lena is becoming more reflective and philosophical as she grows older. A developmental psychologist would probably say that Lena:
    a. had unhappy experiences as a younger adult.
    b. is demonstrating a normal, age-related tendency.
    c. will probably become introverted and reclusive as she gets older.
    d. feels that her life has been a failure.

13. Concerning the public's fear of Alzheimer's disease, which of the following is true?
    a. A serious loss of memory, such as that occurring in people with Alzheimer's disease, can be expected by most people once they reach their 60s.
    b. From 65 to 85, the incidence of Alzheimer's disease rises from 1 in 100 to 1 in 5.
    c. Alzheimer's disease is much more common today than it was 50 years ago.
    d. Alzheimer's disease is less common today than it was 50 years ago.

14. At the present stage of research into cognitive development during late adulthood, which of the following statements has the greatest support?
    a. There is uniform decline in all stages of memory during late adulthood.
    b. Long-term memory shows the greatest decline with age.
    c. Working memory shows the greatest decline with age.
    d. The decline in memory may be the result of the failure to use effective encoding and retrieval strategies.

15. Lately, Wayne's father, who is 73, harps on the fact that he forgets small things such as where he put the house keys and has trouble eating and sleeping. The family doctor diagnoses Wayne's father as:
    a. being in the early stages of Alzheimer's disease.
    b. being in the later stages of Alzheimer's disease.
    c. suffering from senile dementia.
    d. possibly suffering from depression.

Key Terms

1. dual-task deficit
2. control processes

3. priming
4. explicit memory
5. implicit memory
6. terminal decline
7. dementia
8. delirium
9. Alzheimer's disease
10. vascular dementia (VaD)/multi-infarct dementia (MID)
11. subcortical dementias
12. Parkinson's disease
13. life review
14. wisdom

ANSWERS
CHAPTER REVIEW

1. change little; 60; verbal meaning; spatial orientation; inductive reasoning; number ability; word fluency
2. differences
3. sensory threshold
4. sensory impairment
5. vision; hearing; smell
6. missed; interferes
7. working memory
8. store; process
9. distractions; inhibiting
10. dual-task deficit
11. knowledge base; long-term; selective memory; alteration
12. vocabulary; 80; expertise; happy; emotions
13. source amnesia
14. cohorts; high school
15. how long ago information was learned; how well it was learned
16. control processes; storage; retrieval; selective attention; logical analysis; prefrontal cortex
17. knowledge; principles; familiarity; rules of thumb
18. retrieval
19. memory; control processes
20. smaller; more; are not; in vivo
21. many; neurons; dendrites; does not correlate
22. recruiting extra brain areas; dedifferentiates
23. priming
24. implicit; habits; emotional; routine; senses; less; explicit; words; data; concepts; consciously

25. perform; describe
26. slowdown; neurotransmitters; dopamine; glutamate; acetylcholine; serotonin; neural fluid; cerebral blood flow
27. slower; simpler; shallower; compensate
28. terminal decline
29. primary aging; secondary aging; ageism
30. hypertension; diabetes; arteriosclerosis; emphysema; poor eating habits, smoking, and lack of exercise
31. stereotypes
32. overestimate; overestimate; confidence
33. hearing; American; deaf; American; Chinese
34. meaningless
35. do not
36. senility; dementia; severely impaired judgment, memory, or problem-solving ability
37. 60; presenile dementia; senile dementia (or senile psychosis); symptoms
38. mental confusion; forgetfulness; chronic; delirium
39. Alzheimer's disease; cerebral cortex; plaques; tangles
40. B-amyloid; tau; hippocampus
41. does not
42. more; 1; 20
43. trisomy-21; APP; presenilin 1; presenilin 2; rare; more; three to five
44. one-fifth; ApoE4; ApoE2; proteins
45. absentmindedness; recognize; explicit
46. concentration; short-term memory; personality; debilitating; basic daily needs; full-time care; talk; 10 to 15
47. vascular dementia or multi-infarct dementia; blood vessels; infarct; stroke (or ministroke)
48. sudden; poor
49. subcortical dementias; motor; Parkinson's; Huntington's; multiple sclerosis
50. Parkinson's disease; dopamine
51. Lewy body; inhibition
52. infection
53. Korsakoff's; short-term memory
54. reversible; medication; inadequate nutrition; alcohol abuse; depression; mental illness
55. overmedication; interactions; mental processes
56. less; 10
57. is; are not
58. suicide; 85
59. exercise
60. arts, children, and the whole of human experience; interdependence

61. self-actualization
62. nature; aesthetic experiences
63. reflective; philosophical
64. life review
65. wisdom; fundamental pragmatics

PROGRESS TEST 1

Multiple-Choice Questions

1. **d.** is the answer. (p. 650)
   a. Working memory deals with mental, rather than sensory, activity.
   b. & c. Long-term memory, which contains the knowledge base, includes information that is stored for several minutes to several years.

2. **d.** is the answer. (pp. 656–657)

3. **a.** is the answer. (p. 651)
   b. These are the functions of sensory memory.
   c. This refers to long-term memory's processing of implicit and explicit memories, respectively.
   d. This is the function of long-term memory.

4. **d.** is the answer. (p. 657)
   a. & b. Explicit memory is memory of facts and experiences, which is why it is often called declarative memory.
   c. This type of memory, which is a type of explicit memory, was not discussed.

5. **c.** is the answer. (p. 654)

6. **c.** is the answer. (p. 663)

7. **d.** is the answer. (pp. 659–660)

8. **a.** is the answer. (pp. 651–652)
   b. & c. These may be true, but they involve sensory memory rather than working memory.
   d. Memory for vocabulary, which generally is very good throughout adulthood, involves long-term memory.

9. **c.** is the answer. (p. 667)

10. **a.** is the answer. (p. 662)

11. **d.** is the answer. Each of the other answers is an example of subcortical dementia. (p. 666)

12. **a.** is the answer. (p. 663)
    b. This describes multi-infarct dementia.
    c. This describes Parkinson's disease.
    d. This was not given in the text as a cause of dementia.

13. **b.** is the answer. (p. 666)
    a. Because multiple infarcts typically occur, the disease *is* progressive in nature.

c. The text does not suggest that MID necessarily leads to quick death.

d. At present, Alzheimer's disease is untreatable.

14. **b.** is the answer. (pp. 667–668)

15. **d.** is the answer. (p. 672)

True or False Items

1. F   The slowing of perceptual processes and decreases in attention associated with aging are also likely to affect efficiency of input. (pp. 650–651)

2. T (p. 650)

3. F   In fact, cultural attitudes can lead to impaired thinking in the elderly. (p. 660)

4. F   Most older adults perceive some memory loss but do not feel that it affects their daily functioning. (p. 661)

5. T (pp. 661–662)

6. T (pp. 663–667)

7. T (p. 664)

8. T (p. 658)

9. F   Interests often broaden during late adulthood, and there is by no means exclusive focus on the self. (pp. 671–672)

10. T (p. 671)

PROGRESS TEST 2

Multiple-Choice Questions

1. **c.** is the answer. (p. 650)

2. **a.** is the answer. (p. 651)

3. **c.** is the answer. (p. 652)

   a. The sensory register stores information for a split second.

   b. Working memory stores information briefly.

   d. Short-term memory is another name for working memory.

4. **c.** is the answer. (p. 657)

   a. Sensory memory, or the sensory register, stores incoming sensory information for only a split second.

   b. This is unconscious, automatic memory for skills.

   c. Explicit memory *is* only one part of the knowledge base. Another part—implicit memory—is unconscious memory for skills.

5. **d.** is the answer. (p. 654)

6. **c.** is the answer. (p. 658)

a. & b. Age-related deficits in these types of memory are minimal.

d. Although explicit memory *is* part of the knowledge base, another part—implicit memory—shows minimal age-related deficits.

7. **c.** is the answer. Only one-fifth of all people inherit the destructive gene. The text does not indicate that everyone else inherits the protective gene. (p. 665)

8. **c.** is the answer. (p. 662)

9. **b.** is the answer. Laboratory experiments test explicit memory, not implicit memory. (p. 661)

10. **a.** is the answer. Although age is not the key factor, it is true that dementia is more likely to occur in older adults. (p. 663)

11. **a.** is the answer. (p. 663)

    b. MID is responsible for about 15 percent of all dementia.

    c. & d. Compared to Alzheimer's disease, which accounts for about 70 percent of all dementia, these account for a much lower percentage.

12. **d.** is the answer. (p. 666)

13. **b.** is the answer. (p. 669)

    a. & c. These psychological illnesses are less common in the elderly than in younger adults, *and* less common than depression among the elderly.

    d. This disorder was not discussed in association with dementia.

14. **b.** is the answer. (pp. 671–672)

    a. & d. Positive cognitive development is *typical* of older adults.

    c. Pragmatism is one characteristic of wisdom, an attribute commonly associated with older people.

15. **a.** is the answer. (p. 672)

    b. & c. Although these may be true of some older adults, they are not necessarily a *key* factor in cognitive development during late adulthood.

    d. In fact, older adults are typically *more* concerned with the whole of human experience.

Matching Items

1. e (p. 663)	5. k (p. 666)	9. h (p. 666)
2. b (p. 651)	6. d (p. 662)	10. a (p. 653)
3. g (p. 652)	7. j (p. 663)	11. i (p. 672)
4. c (p. 654)	8. f (p. 666)	

DEVELOPMENT PSYCHOLOGY APPLIED

1. **d.** is the answer. While c. might be something they should do, the most important things are for them to get exercise and maintain activities that promote cognitive stimulation. (p. 659)

2. **c.** is the answer. (p. 650)

3. **d.** is the answer. (p. 653)

a., b., & c. Sharonda's inability to recall the source of this information is a common form of forgetfulness among older adults; it is not necessarily a sign of dementia.

4. **c.** is the answer. (p. 669)

a. In general, psychological illnesses are less common in the elderly than in younger adults.

b. Depression is quite treatable at any age.

d. Symptoms of *depression* are often mistaken as signs of *dementia*.

5. **c.** is the answer. (pp. 650–651)

a., b., & d. Lena's symptoms are not indicative of any type of dementia.

6. **c.** is the answer. (pp. 672–673)

d. This would lead to a greater appreciation of nature and art, but not necessarily to a tendency to reminisce.

7. **b.** is the answer. (pp. 665–666)

8. **c.** is the answer. (p. 650)

a. & d. The sensory register is concerned with noticing sensory events rather than with memory.

b. Age-related deficits in the sensory register are most likely for ambiguous or weak stimuli.

9. **a.** is the answer. (p. 651)

b. Explicit memory involves words, data, concepts, and the like. It is *a part of* long-term memory.

c. Long-term memory includes information remembered for years or decades.

d. The sensory register stores information for a split second.

10. **b.** is the answer. In fact, *use* of anti-inflammatory drugs may help sustain cognitive functioning in old age. (p. 659)

11. **b.** is the answer. Older individuals are particularly likely to experience difficulty holding new information in mind, particularly when it is essentially meaningless. (p. 661)

a., c., & d. These are examples of long-term memory, which declines very little with age.

12. **b.** is the answer. (pp. 672–673)

13. **b.** is the answer. (p. 664)

c. & d. The text does not indicate the existence of cohort effects in the incidence of Alzheimer's disease.

14. **d.** is the answer. (p. 654)

a. Some aspects of information processing, such as long-term memory, show less decline with age than others, such as working memory.

b. & c. The text does not indicate that one particular subcomponent of memory shows the *greatest* decline.

15. **d.** is the answer. (p. 669)

a., b., & c. The symptoms Wayne's father is experiencing are those of depression, which is often misdiagnosed as dementia in the elderly.

KEY TERMS

1. The **dual-task deficit** involves impaired performance of one task due to interference from the simultaneous performance of another task. (p. 651)

2. Memory **control processes,** which include strategies for retaining information, retrieval strategies for reaccessing information, selective attention, and rules or strategies that aid problem solving, tend to become simpler and less efficient with age. (p. 654)

3. **Priming** involves the use of a clue, or some other form of preparation, to jog one's memory. (p. 657)

4. **Explicit memory** is memory of consciously learned words, data, and concepts. This type of memory is more vulnerable to age-related decline than implicit memory. (p. 657)

5. **Implicit memory** is unconscious or automatic memory involving habits, emotional responses, routine procedures, and the senses. (p. 657)

6. **Terminal decline** is the overall slowdown of cognitive abilities that often occurs in the days or months before death. (p. 659)

7. **Dementia** is severely impaired judgment, memory, or problem-solving ability that is irreversible and caused by organic brain damage or disease. (p. 662)

8. **Delirium** refers to acute, severe memory loss and confusion that disappears in hours or days. (p. 663)

9. **Alzheimer's disease (AD),** a progressive disorder that is the most common form of dementia, is characterized by plaques and tangles in the cerebral cortex that destroy normal brain functioning. (p. 663)

10. **Vascular dementia (VaD)/multi-infarct dementia (MID),** which accounts for about 15 percent of all dementia, occurs because an infarct, or tempo-

rary obstruction of the blood vessels (often called a stroke), prevents a sufficient supply of blood from reaching an area of the brain. It is characterized by sporadic and progressive loss of brain functioning. (p. 666)

11. **Subcortical dementias,** such as Parkinson's disease, Huntington's disease, and multiple sclerosis, cause a progressive loss of motor control, which initially does not directly involve thinking or memory. (p. 666)

12. **Parkinson's disease,** which produces dementia as well as muscle rigidity or tremors, is related to the degeneration of neurons that produce dopamine. (p. 666)

13. In the **life review,** an older person attempts to put his or her life into perspective by recalling and recounting various aspects of life to members of the younger generations. (p. 672)

14. As used in this context, **wisdom** refers to expert knowledge in the fundamental pragmatics of life. (p. 673)

25

Late Adulthood: Psychosocial Development

Chapter Overview

There is great variation in development after age 65. Certain psychosocial changes are common during this stage of the life span—retirement, the death of a spouse, and failing health—yet people respond to these experiences in vastly different ways.

Individual experiences may help to explain the fact that theories of psychosocial aging, discussed in the first section of the chapter, are often diametrically opposed. The second section of the chapter focuses on the challenges to generativity that accompany late adulthood, such as finding new sources of achievement once derived from work. In the third section, the importance of marriage, friends, neighbors, and family in providing social support is discussed, as are the different experiences of married and single older adults. The final section focuses on the frail elderly—the minority of older adults, often poor and/or ill, who require extensive care.

NOTE: Answer guidelines for all Chapter 25 questions begin on page 366.

Guided Study

The text chapter should be studied one section at a time. Before you read, preview each section by skimming it, noting headings and boldface items. Then read the appropriate section objectives from the following outline. Keep these objectives in mind and, as you read the chapter section, search for the information that will enable you to meet each objective. Once you have finished a section, write out answers for its objectives.

Theories of Late Adulthood (pp. 680–691)

1. Explain the central premises of self theories of psychosocial development during late adulthood.

2. Discuss Erikson's stage of integrity versus despair, and describe how the search for identity continues into old age.

3. (text and Issues and Applications) Describe how older adults use selective optimization to cope with aging, and explain how the positivity effect contributes to their coping ability.

4. Identify and describe the stratification theories of psychosocial development during late adulthood.

5. Discuss dynamic theories of late adulthood.

10. Describe relationships between older adults and their adult children, and differentiate three patterns of grandparent–grandchild relationships.

Coping with Retirement (pp. 691–696)

6. Discuss how retirement from work is viewed during late adulthood, and describe some activities chosen by retired people.

The Frail Elderly (pp. 706–712)

11. Describe the frail elderly, and explain why their number is growing.

7. Discuss volunteerism, religious involvement, and political activism among the elderly.

12. Identify and discuss factors that may protect the elderly from frailty.

13. Describe the typical case of elder abuse.

Friends and Relatives (pp. 696–705)

8. Describe the components of the social convoy, and explain this convoy's increasing importance during late adulthood.

14. Discuss alternative care arrangements for the frail elderly, identifying some of the potential advantages and disadvantages of each.

9. Discuss how, and why, marriage relationships tend to change as people grow old, and describe gender differences in the experience of losing a spouse.

Chapter Review

When you have finished reading the chapter, work through the material that follows to review it. Complete the sentences and answer the questions. As you proceed, evaluate your performance for each section by consulting the answers on page 366. Do not continue with the next section until you understand each answer. If you need to, review or reread the appropriate section in the textbook before continuing.

Theories of Late Adulthood (pp. 680–691)

1. Theories of psychosocial development in late adulthood include _____ theories, _____ theories, and _____ theories.

2. Theories that emphasize the active part that individuals play in their own psychosocial development are _____ theories. As one such theorist, _____ , described it, people attempt to _____ .

3. The most comprehensive theory is that of _____ , who called life's final crisis _____ versus _____ .

4. Another version of self theory suggests that the search for _____ is lifelong. This idea originates in Erikson's crisis of _____ versus _____ _____ .

5. Partly as a result of changes in _____ , _____ , and _____ , maintaining identity during late adulthood is particularly challenging. In the strategy of _____ , new experiences are incorporated unchanged. This strategy involves _____ reality in order to maintain self-esteem. It leads to _____ .

6. The opposite strategy is _____ , in which people adapt to new experiences by changing their self-concept. This process can be painful, because it may cause people to abandon their _____ , leading to _____ and hastening mortality.

7. Paul Baltes emphasizes _____ _____ _____ , which is the idea that

individuals set their own _____ , assess their own _____ , and then figure out how to accomplish what they want to achieve despite the _____ and _____ of later life.

8. (Issues and Applications) Dramatic changes in personality in late adulthood are _____ (common/rare).

9. (Issues and Applications) The general personality shift known as the _____ _____ refers to the tendency of elderly people to perceive, prefer, and remember positive experiences more than negative ones. In addition, the trait of _____ on others may increase over time.

10. Theorists who emphasize _____ maintain that _____ forces and _____ influences limit individual and direct life at every stage. One form of this theory focuses on _____ _____ , reflecting how industrialized nations segregate the oldest generation.

11. According to _____ theory, in old age the individual and society mutually withdraw from each other. This theory is _____ (controversial among/almost universally accepted by) gerontologists.

12. The opposite idea is expressed in _____ theory, which holds that older adults remain socially active. According to this theory, if older adults do disengage, they do so _____ (willingly/unwillingly).

13. The dominant view is that the more _____ the elderly play, the greater their _____ _____ and the longer their lives.

14. The most recent view of age stratification is that disengagement theory and activity theory may be too _____ . According to this view, older adults become more _____ in their social contacts.

15. Two other categories of stratification that are especially important in late adulthood are _____ and _____ . Another stratification theory, which draws attention to the values underlying the gender divisions promoted by society, is _____ theory. According to this theory, _____ policies and _____ values make later life particularly burdensome for women.

16. Currently in the United States, the ratio of women to men reaches nearly two to one by age _____ . This ratio is reached worldwide by age _____ .

17. According to the _____ _____ theory, race is a _____ _____ , and racism and racial discrimination shape the experiences and attitudes of both racial _____ and racial _____ .

18. Some theorists believe that stratification theory may distort reality. They point out that compared to European Americans, elderly _____ and _____ Americans are more often nurtured and respected by their families. Non-European elders are benefited by _____ , large family size, and strong _____ _____ . Similarly, elderly women are less likely than elderly men to be _____ and _____ because they tend to be _____ and _____ .

19. According to _____ theory, each person's life is an active, changing, self-propelled process occurring within ever-changing _____ contexts.

20. According to _____ theory, people experience the changes of late adulthood in much the same way they did earlier in life. Thus, the so-called _____ _____ personality traits are maintained throughout old age.

Coping with Retirement (pp. 691–696)

21. Social scientists have generally assumed that older adults _____ (wanted/did not want) employment. Recent research has found that most older adults _____ (do/do not) want to stop working as soon as they are eligible to do so.

22. If both spouses are employed, it _____ (is/is not) best for them to retire together. A major problem with retirement is inadequate _____ , especially for how to spend _____ .

23. Many older adults stay busy by maintaining their _____ and _____ . This reflects the desire of most elderly people to _____ (relocate when they retire/age in place). One result of this is that many of the elderly live _____ .

24. Rather than moving, many elderly people prefer to remain in the neighborhoods in which they raised their children, thus creating _____ _____ retirement communities.

25. Many of the elderly use the time they once spent earning a living to pursue _____ interests.

26. The eagerness of the elderly to pursue educational interests is exemplified by the rapid growth of _____ , a program in which older people take short courses on college campuses while students are on vacation.

27. Compared to younger adults, older adults are _____ (more/less) likely to feel a strong obligation to serve their communities.

28. Religious faith _____ (increases/remains stable/decreases) as people age. Religious involvement correlates with _____ and _____ health, as well as with long _____ .

29. By many measures, the elderly are more _____ active than any other age group. Compared to younger people, the elderly are more likely to _____ _____ . The idea that the political concerns of the elderly clash with those of the young _____ (is/is not) confirmed by the data.

30. The major United States organization affecting the elderly is the _____ .

Friends and Relatives (pp. 696–705)

31. The phrase _____ _____ highlights the fact that the life course is traveled in the company of others.

32. Elderly Americans who are married tend to be _____ , _____ , and _____ than those who are unmarried.

33. Although research on older homosexual couples has not been done, studies involving younger couples suggest that they _____ (do/do not) benefit from an intimate relationship.

Give two possible reasons that marriages may improve with time.

34. Poor health generally has a _____ (major/minor) impact on the marital relationship.

35. The average married woman experiences about _____ (how many?) years of widowhood. After age 74, there are many more _____ (widows/widowers) than _____ (widows/widowers).

36. The death of a mate usually means not only the loss of a close friend and lover but also lower _____ , _____ , _____ , and _____ .

37. In general, living without a spouse is somewhat easier for _____ (widows/widowers).

State several reasons for this being so.

38. Because more people are living longer, more older people are part of _____ families than at any time in history. Sometimes, this takes the form of a _____ family, in which there are more _____ than in the past but with only a few members in each generation.

39. Today, when one generation needs help, assistance typically flows from the _____ (younger/older) generation to their _____ (parents/children) instead of vice versa.

40. While intergenerational relationships are clearly important to both generations, they also are likely to include _____ and _____ . The _____–_____ relationship is an example of this.

41. The idea that adult children are obligated to care for their aging parents is called _____ _____ This idea _____ (is/is not) found in every culture.

42. Grandparenthood often begins in _____ _____ . By age 70, _____ (what percent?) of all people are grandparents.

43. Grandparent–grandchild relationships take one of three forms: _____ , _____ , or _____ . In the past, grandparents adopted a _____ role. The _____ pattern is sometimes not undertaken by choice. One reason is _____ ; another is that the elder lives with the grandchildren.

44. Most contemporary grandparents seek the _____ role as they strive for the love and respect of their grandchildren while maintaining their own _____ .

45. Grandparents who take over the work of raising their children's children are referred to as _____ _____ . This role is more common when parents are _____ _____ .

46. Grandparents are most likely to provide surrogate care for infants who are _____-_____ or school-age boys who are _____ , for example. If the relationship is the result of a legal decision that the parents were _____ or _____ , it becomes _____ _____ .

47. Approximately _____ percent of adults over age 65 in the United States have never married. This _____ (is/is not) the most married cohort in history. Those who have never married tend to be _____ (quite content/lonely and unsupported).

48. Having a partner and children _____ (is necessary/is not necessary) for happiness in old age.

49. In buffering against stress, having at least one close _____ is crucial.

50. Successful aging requires that people keep themselves from becoming _____ _____ .

The Frail Elderly (pp. 706–712)

51. Elderly people who are physically infirm, very ill, or cognitively impaired are called the _____ _____ .

52. The crucial sign of frailty is an inability to perform the _____ _____ , which comprise five tasks: _____ , _____ , _____ , _____ , and _____ _____ .

53. Actions that require some intellectual competence and forethought are classified as _____ _____ . These include such things as _____ _____ .

54. The number of frail elderly is _____ (increasing/decreasing). One reason for this trend is that _____

_____ . A second reason is that medical care emphasizes _____ _____ more than _____ _____ . A third reason is that adequate nutrition, safe housing, and other preventive measures often don't reach those who _____ _____ .

55. The dynamic perspective reminds us that some people enter late adulthood with protective _____ in place. These include _____ .

56. An especially helpful form of caregiver support is _____ _____ , in which a professional caregiver takes over to give the family caregiver a break.

57. The frail elderly are particularly vulnerable to _____ _____ . Most cases of elder maltreatment _____ (involve/do not involve) family members.

58. Many older Americans and their relatives feel that _____ _____ should be avoided at all costs. An intermediate form of care is _____ _____ , which provides some privacy and independence, along with some _____ supervision.

Progress Test 1

Multiple-Choice Questions

Circle your answers to the following questions and check them with the answers on page 367. If your answer is incorrect, read the explanation for why it is incorrect and then consult the appropriate pages of the text (in parentheses following the correct answer).

1. According to disengagement theory, during late adulthood people tend to:
  a. become less role-centered and more passive.
  b. have regrets about how they have lived their lives.
  c. become involved in a range of new activities.
  d. exaggerate lifelong personality traits.

2. The intermediate form of elder care that provides some of the privacy and independence of living at home, along with some medical supervision, is:
   a. Elderhostel.
   b. a naturally occurring retirement community.
   c. respite care.
   d. assisted living.

3. Elderhostel is:
   a. a special type of nursing home in which the patients are given control over their activities.
   b. a theory of psychosocial development advocating that the elderly can help each other.
   c. an agency that allows older people of the opposite sex to live together unencumbered by marriage vows.
   d. a program in which older people take short courses on college campuses while students are on vacation.

4. (Issues and Applications) Longitudinal studies of monozygotic and dizygotic twins have found evidence that:
   a. genetic influences weaken as life experiences accumulate.
   b. strongly supports disengagement theory.
   c. some traits seem even more apparent in late adulthood than earlier.
   d. all of the above are true.

5. A former pilot, Eileen has always been proud of her 20/20 vision. Although to the younger members of her family it is obvious that her vision is beginning to fail, Eileen denies that she is having any difficulty and claims that she could still fly an airplane if she wanted to. An identity theorist would probably say that Eileen's distortion of reality is an example of:
   a. assimilation.
   b. accommodation.
   c. selective optimization.
   d. disengagement.

6. Because women tend to be caregivers, as older adults they are:
   a. more likely than men to be depressed.
   b. more likely than men to be lonely.
   c. more likely than men to be depressed and lonely.
   d. less likely than men to be lonely or depressed.

7. The idea that individuals set their own goals, assess their abilities, and figure out how to accomplish what they want to achieve during late adulthood is referred to as:
   a. disengagement.
   b. selective optimization with compensation.
   c. dynamic development.
   d. age stratification.

8. After retirement, the elderly are likely to:
   a. pursue educational interests.
   b. become politically involved.
   c. do volunteer work because they feel a particular commitment to their communities.
   d. do any of the above.

9. Which of the following theories does *not* belong with the others?
   a. disengagement theory
   b. feminist theory
   c. critical race theory
   d. continuity theory

10. Respite care is best described as:
    a. an intermediate form of elder care between a person's residence and a nursing home.
    b. long-term care.
    c. an arrangement in which a professional caregiver relieves a frail elderly person's usual caregiver.
    d. an activity of daily life (ADL).

11. On average, older widows:
    a. live about 6 years after their husband dies.
    b. almost always seek another husband.
    c. find it more difficult than widowers to live without a spouse.
    d. experience all of the above.

12. In general, during late adulthood the *fewest* problems are experienced by individuals who:
    a. are married.
    b. have always been single.
    c. have long been divorced.
    d. are widowed.

13. Which of the following is true of adjustment to the death of a spouse?
    a. It is easier for men in all respects.
    b. It is initially easier for men, but over the long term it is easier for women.
    c. It is emotionally easier for women but financially easier for men.
    d. It is determined primarily by individual personality traits, and therefore shows very few sex differences.

14. According to dynamic theories:

   a. self-integrity is maintained throughout life.

   b. adults make choices and interpret reality in such a way as to express themselves as fully as possible.

   c. people organize themselves according to their particular characteristics and circumstances.

   d. each person's life is largely a self-propelled process, occurring within ever-changing social contexts.

15. Which of the following most accurately expresses the most recent view of developmentalists regarding stratification by age?

   a. Aging makes a person's social sphere increasingly narrow.

   b. Disengagement is always the result of ageism.

   c. Most older adults become more selective in their social contacts.

   d. Older adults need even more social activity to be happy than they did earlier in life.

True or False Items

Write T (*true*) or F (*false*) on the line in front of each statement.

_____ **1.** Preschool girls are more likely to live with grandparents than rebellious school-age boys are.

_____ **2.** As one of the most disruptive experiences in the life span, losing a spouse tends to have similar effects on men and women.

_____ **3.** Continuity theory stresses how people adjust to aging and circumstances.

_____ **4.** Religious faith increases with age.

_____ **5.** Older adults do not understand the social concerns of younger age groups.

_____ **6.** Most developmentalists support the central premise of disengagement theory.

_____ **7.** In the United States, the rate of volunteering decreases with age, but older volunteers put in more hours.

_____ **8.** Most older people suffer significantly from a lack of close friendships.

_____ **9.** Nearly one in two older adults makes a long-distance move after retirement.

_____ **10.** Financial and emotional assistance typically flows from the younger generation to the older generation.

Progress Test 2

Progress Test 2 should be completed during a final chapter review. Answer the following questions after you thoroughly understand the correct answers for the Chapter Review and Progress Test 1.

Multiple-Choice Questions

1. Critics of disengagement theory point out that:

   a. older people want to substitute new involvements for the roles they lose with retirement.

   b. disengagement usually is not voluntary on the part of the individual.

   c. disengagement often leads to greater life satisfaction for older adults.

   d. disengagement is more common at earlier stages in the life cycle.

2. A beanpole family is one that consists of:

   a. fewer generations with fewer members than in the past.

   b. fewer generations with more members than in the past.

   c. more generations than in the past but with only a few members in each generation.

   d. more generations with more members than in the past.

3. According to continuity theory, during late adulthood people:

   a. become less role-centered.

   b. become more passive.

   c. become involved in a range of new activities.

   d. cope with challenges in much the same way they did earlier in life.

4. Developmentalists who believe that stratification theory unfairly stigmatizes women and minority groups point out that:

   a. African Americans often outlive European Americans.

   b. elderly women are less likely than men to be lonely and depressed.

   c. multigenerational families and churches often nurture Hispanic Americans.

   d. all of the above are true.

5. Following retirement, most elderly people:

   a. relocate to sunny climate.

   b. spend less time on housework and unnecessary chores.

   c. prefer to age in place.

   d. move in with their children.

6. (Issues and Applications) Protective factors that act as buffers for the elderly include:
   a. personality and social setting.
   b. financial resources and age.
   c. attitude and social network.
   d. none of the above.

7. The major United States organization affecting the elderly is:
   a. Elderhostel.
   b. the AARP.
   c. Foster Grandparents.
   d. Service Corps of Retired Executives.

8. Younger non-Europeans are less often married, have fewer children, and are less often church members than their elders. For this reason, it is likely that:
   a. they are more likely to be disengaged.
   b. this cohort shift could change the meaning of ethnicity.
   c. they would not need to engage in selective optimization with compensation.
   d. they will be more active in adulthood.

9. Which of the following would *not* be included as an instrumental activity of daily life?
   a. grocery shopping   c. making phone calls
   b. paying bills   d. taking a walk

10. One of the most important factors contributing to life satisfaction for older adults appears to be:
    a. contact with friends.
    b. contact with younger family members.
    c. the number of new experiences to which they are exposed.
    d. continuity in the daily routine.

11. Of the three approaches to grandparenting, which of the following is often forced upon the elder because of circumstances?
    a. involved grandparenting
    b. remote grandparenting
    c. companionate grandparenting
    d. natural grandparenting

12. In general, the longer a couple has been married, the more likely they are to:
    a. be happier with each other.
    b. have frequent, minor disagreements.
    c. feel the relationship is not equitable.
    d. do all of the above.

13. Which of the following is *not* true regarding long-term marriages?
    a. Married elders tend to be healthier than those who never married.
    b. Absolute levels of conflict and emotional intensity drop over time.
    c. Marriages generally change for the better in late adulthood.
    d. Marriages improve in late adulthood, unless one spouse becomes seriously ill.

14. Which of the following is *not* a major factor contributing to an increase in the number of frail elderly?
    a. people are living longer
    b. medical care's focus on preventing death rather than enhancing life
    c. inadequate expenditures on social services
    d. those who are already somewhat frail tend to be excluded from receiving help

15. According to Erikson, achieving integrity during late adulthood above all involves:
    a. the ability to perceive one's own life as worthwhile.
    b. being open to new influences and experiences.
    c. treating other people with respect.
    d. developing a consistent and yet varied daily routine.

Matching Items

Match each definition or description with its corresponding term.

Terms

_____ 1. disengagement theory
_____ 2. self theories
_____ 3. continuity theory
_____ 4. positivity effect
_____ 5. activity theory
_____ 6. stratification theories
_____ 7. activities of daily life (ADLs)
_____ 8. instrumental activities of daily life (IADLs)
_____ 9. dynamic theories
_____ 10. Elderhostel

Definitions or Descriptions

a. theories such as Erik Erikson's that emphasize self-actualization
b. an educational program for the elderly
c. eating, bathing, toileting, walking, and dressing
d. theory that a person's life is an active, largely self-propelled process that occurs within ever-changing social contexts.
e. theory that people become less role-centered as they age
f. actions that require intellectual competence and forethought
g. tendency for elderly people to perceive, prefer, and remember positive experiences
h. theories such as feminist theory and critical race theory that focus on the limitations on life choices created by social forces
i. theory that elderly people become socially withdrawn only involuntarily
j. theory that each person copes with late adulthood in the same way he or she did earlier in life

Developmental Psychology Applied

Answer these questions the day before an exam as a final check on your understanding of the chapter's terms and concepts.

1. Which of the following statements *most* accurately describes psychosocial development in late adulthood?
   a. Many leading gerontologists believe that people become more alike as they get older.
   b. Older adults generally fit into one of two distinct personality types.
   c. Many gerontologists believe that the diversity of personalities and patterns is especially pronounced among the elderly.
   d. Few changes in psychosocial development occur after middle adulthood.

2. An advocate of which of the following theories would be most likely to agree with the statement, "Because of their more passive style of interaction, older people are less likely to be chosen for new roles"?
   a. disengagement   c. self
   b. continuity   d. dynamic

3. An advocate for feminist theory would point out that:
   a. because most social structures and economic policies have been established by men, women's needs are devalued.
   b. women in the United States make up the majority of the elderly and the elderly poor.
   c. many elderly women are expected to care for frail relatives even if it strains their own health.
   d. all of the above are true.

4. Professor Martin states that "membership in certain groups can place the elderly at risk for a number of dangers." Professor Martin evidently is an advocate of which theory of psychosocial development?
   a. self theories   c. dynamic
   b. stratification   d. continuity

5. When they retire, most older adults:
   a. immediately feel more satisfied with their new way of life.
   b. engage in a variety of social activities.
   c. have serious, long-term difficulties adjusting to retirement.
   d. disengage from other roles and activities as well.

6. The one *most* likely to agree with the statement, "Older adults have an obligation to help others and serve the community," is:
   a. a middle-aged adult.   c. an older man.
   b. an older woman.   d. an older adult.

7. (Issues and Applications) When elderly Mr. Flanagan reflects on his life, he remembers mostly good times and experiences. This selectivity in thinking is called:
   a. the positivity effect.
   b. respite care.
   c. aging in place.
   d. disengagement.

8. Research indicates that the primary perpetrators of elder abuse are:
   a. professional caregivers.
   b. mean-spirited strangers.
   c. another relative.
   d. middle-aged children.

9. Beyonce's mother wishes to age in place. This means that she:
   a. plans to continue working as long as possible.
   b. wishes to remain in her home even after her health begins to decline.
   c. plans to move back to her childhood home.
   d. will do each of the above.

10. Of the following older adults, who is most likely to be involved in a large network of intimate friendships?
    a. William, a 65-year-old who never married
    b. Darrel, a 60-year-old widower
    c. Florence, a 63-year-old widow
    d. Kay, a 66-year-old married woman

11. Following a heated disagreement over family responsibilities, Sidney's grandson stormed away shouting, "Why should I listen to you?" Afterward, Sidney is filled with despair and feels that all his years of work to build a strong family were wasted. An identity theorist would probably say that Sidney is demonstrating:
    a. assimilation.
    b. accommodation.
    c. selective optimization.
    d. a healthy identity that is firm but flexible.

12. Claudine is the primary caregiver for her elderly parents. The amount of stress she feels in this role depends above all on:
    a. how frail her parents are.
    b. her subjective interpretation of the support she receives from others.

    c. her relationship to her parents prior to their becoming frail.
    d. her overall financial situation.

13. Wilma's elderly mother needs help in taking care of the instrumental activities of daily life. Such activities would include which of the following?
    a. bathing
    b. eating
    c. paying bills
    d. all of the above

14. In concluding her presentation on the frail elderly, Janet notes that "the number of frail elderly is currently _____ than the number who are active, financially stable, and capable; however, the frail elderly are _____ in absolute number."
    a. greater; decreasing
    b. less; increasing
    c. greater; increasing
    d. less; decreasing

15. Jack, who is 73, looks back on his life with a sense of pride and contentment; Eleanor feels unhappy with her life and that it is "too late to start over." In Erikson's terminology, Jack is experiencing _____ , while Eleanor is experiencing _____ .
    a. generativity; stagnation
    b. identity; emptiness
    c. integrity; despair
    d. completion; termination

Key Terms

Using your own words, write a brief definition or explanation of each of the following terms on a separate piece of paper.

1. self theories
2. integrity versus despair
3. positivity effect
4. stratification theories
5. disengagement theory
6. activity theory
7. dynamic theories
8. continuity theory
9. age in place
10. AARP
11. social convoy
12. filial responsibility

13. frail elderly
14. activities of daily life (ADLs)
15. instrumental activities of daily life (IADLs)
16. respite care
17. assisted living

ANSWERS

CHAPTER REVIEW

1. self; stratification; dynamic
2. self; Abraham Maslow; self-actualize
3. Erik Erikson; integrity; despair
4. identity; identity; role confusion
5. appearance; health; employment; assimilation; distorting; rigidity
6. accommodation; identity; deterioration
7. selective optimization with compensation; goals; abilities; limitations; declines
8. rare
9. positivity effect; dependence
10. stratification; social; cultural; choice; age stratification
11. disengagement; controversial among
12. activity; unwillingly
13. roles; life satisfaction
14. extreme; selective
15. gender; ethnicity; feminist; social; cultural
16. 70; 80
17. critical race; social construct; minorities; majorities
18. African; Hispanic; familism; religious faith; lonely; depressed; caregivers; kinkeepers
19. dynamic; social
20. continuity; Big Five
21. wanted; do
22. is; planning; time
23. home; yard; age in place; alone
24. naturally occurring
25. educational
26. Elderhostel
27. more
28. increases; physical; emotional; life
29. politically; vote in elections and lobby for their interests; is not
30. AARP (formerly the American Association of Retired Persons)
31. social convoy

32. healthier; wealthier; happier
33. do

One reason may be traced to the effects of their children, who were a prime source of conflict when they were younger but are now a source of pleasure. Another is that all the shared contextual factors tend to change both partners in similar ways, bringing them closer together in memories and values.

34. minor
35. six; widows; widowers
36. status; income; activities; identity
37. widows

One reason is that elderly women often expect to outlive their husbands and have anticipated this event. Another is that in most communities, widows can get help from support groups. A third is that many elderly men were dependent on their wives to perform the basic tasks of daily living.

38. multigenerational; beanpole; generations
39. older; children
40. tension; conflict; mother–daughter
41. filial responsibility; is
42. middle age; 85
43. remote; involved; companionate; remote; involved; cultural
44. companionate; independence (autonomy)
45. surrogate parents; poor, young, ill, drug- or alcohol-addicted
46. drug-affected; rebellious; abusive; neglectful; kinship care
47. 4; is; quite content
48. is not necessary
49. confidant
50. socially isolated
51. frail elderly
52. activities of daily life (ADLs); eating; bathing; toileting; dressing; transferring from a bed to a chair
53. instrumental activities of daily life (IADLs); shopping, paying bills, driving a car, taking medications, and keeping appointments
54. increasing; more people are reaching old age; death postponement; life enhancement; need them the most
55. buffers; family members and friends, past education and creative problem solving, adequate pensions and work opportunities, good health habits
56. respite care
57. elder abuse; involve
58. nursing homes; assisted living; medical

PROGRESS TEST 1

Multiple-Choice Questions

1. **a.** is the answer. (p. 685)

   b. This answer depicts a person struggling with Erikson's crisis of integrity versus despair.

   c. This answer describes activity theory.

   d. Disengagement theory does not address this issue.

2. **d.** is the answer. (p. 711)

3. **d.** is the answer. (p. 693)

4. **c.** is the answer. (p. 684)

   a. Such studies have found that genetic influences do not weaken with age.

   b. This research provides support for self theories rather than disengagement theory.

5. **a.** is the answer. (p. 682)

   b. Accommodating people adapt to new experiences (such as failing vision) by changing their self-concept.

   c. People who selectively optimize are more realistic in assessing their abilities than Eileen evidently is.

   d. There is no sign that Eileen is disengaging or withdrawing from her social relationships.

6. **d.** is the answer. (p. 688)

7. **b.** is the answer. (p. 682)

   a. This is the idea that the elderly withdraw from society as they get older.

   c. This is the theory that each person's life is a self-propelled process occurring within ever-changing social contexts.

   d. According to this theory, the oldest generation is segregated from the rest of society.

8. **d.** is the answer. Contrary to earlier views that retirement was not a happy time, researchers now know that the elderly are generally happy and productive, spending their time in various activities. (pp. 693–696)

9. **d.** is the answer. Each of the other theories can be categorized as a stratification theory. (p. 690)

10. **c.** is the answer. (p. 709)

11. **a.** is the answer. (p. 699)

    b. & c. In fact, just the opposite is true.

12. **a.** is the answer. (p. 697)

13. **c.** is the answer. (pp. 698–700)

14. **d.** is the answer. (p. 689)

    a. This expresses continuity theory.

    b. This expresses self theory.

    c. This expresses stratification theory.

15. **c.** is the answer. (p. 685)

    a. This is the central idea behind disengagement theory.

    b. & d. These ideas are expressions of activity theory.

True or False Items

1. F (p. 703)

2. F Women tend to be more prepared and have more friends to sympathize with them. Men, who tend to depend on their wives for basic needs and emotional support, find it hard to turn to others for help. (pp. 695–700)

3. T (p. 690)

4. T (p. 695)

5. F In fact, older adults are willing to vote against the interests of their own group if a greater good is at stake. (p. 696)

6. F In fact, disengagement theory has *few* serious defenders. (p. 685)

7. T (p. 693)

8. F Most older adults have at least one close friend and, as compared with younger adults, are less likely to feel a need for more friendships. (pp. 704–705)

9. F A minority of older adults moves to another state. (p. 692)

10. F Aid flows in the opposite direction. (p. 701)

PROGRESS TEST 2

Multiple-Choice Questions

1. **a.** is the answer. (p. 685)

   b. If disengagement were *not* voluntary, this would not be a choice of the elderly.

   c. & d. Neither of these answers is true, nor a criticism of disengagement theory.

2. **c.** is the answer. (p. 700)

3. **d.** is the answer. (p. 690)

   a. & b. These answers describe disengagement theory.

   c. This answer pertains to activity theory.

4. **d.** is the answer. (p. 688)

5. **c.** is the answer. (p. 692)

6. **c.** is the answer. (pp. 683–684)

7. **b.** is the answer. (p. 696)

a. Elderhostel is an educational program for older adults.

c. & d. These service organizations affect a much smaller percentage of the elderly.

8. **b.** is the answer. (p. 689)

a. & d. This finding does not bear directly on disengagement, activity level, or selective optimization.

9. **d.** is the answer. (p. 706)

10. **a.** is the answer. (p. 704)

b., c., & d. The importance of these factors varies from one older adult to another.

11. **a.** is the answer. Elders often become involved grandparents for cultural reasons and sometimes because they live with the grandchildren. (p. 702)

b. Remote grandparenting is rare today.

c. Companionate grandparenting is the preferred approach.

d. There is no such term as natural grandparenting.

12. **a.** is the answer. (p. 697)

b. & c. The longer a couple has been married, the *less* likely they are to have frequent disagreements or feel that the relationship is not equitable.

13. **d.** is the answer. Generally, older spouses accept each other's frailties and tend to each other's needs with feelings of affection. (pp. 697–698)

14. **c.** is the answer. Many nations spend substantial money on services for the elderly. (p. 707)

15. **a.** is the answer. (p. 680)

Matching Items

1. e (p. 685) 5. i (p. 685) 8. f (p. 706)
2. a (p. 680) 6. h (p. 684) 9. d (p. 689)
3. j (p. 690) 7. c (p. 706) 10. b (p. 693)
4. g (p. 683)

DEVELOPMENTAL PSYCHOLOGY APPLIED

1. **c.** is the answer. (p. 679)

2. **a.** is the answer. (p. 685)

b. Continuity theory, a type of dynamic theory, maintains that older adults cope with aging in much the same ways as when they were younger.

c. Self theories emphasize the quest for self-actualization.

d. Dynamic theories emphasize that life is a self-propelled, ever-changing process within an ever-changing social context.

3. **d.** is the answer. (p. 686)

4. **b.** is the answer. "Groups" are the social "strata" that this theory focuses on. (p. 684)

a. & c. These theories emphasize the efforts of the individual to reach his or her full potential (self theories) by interpreting experiences in the face of ever-changing social contexts (dynamic theories, of which continuity theory is one [d.]).

5. **b.** is the answer. (pp. 693–696)

a. Although the text does not say this specifically, the discussion of the many activities engaged in by elderly people suggests a strong level of satisfaction.

d. There is much evidence that *conflicts* with disengagement theory.

6. **d.** is the answer. (p. 693)

a. Middle-aged adults tend to be more focused on individual and family needs.

b. & c. The text does not suggest that there is a gender difference in older adults' sense of obligation to serve others.

7. **a.** is the answer. (p. 683)

8. **d.** is the answer. (p. 710)

9. **b.** is the answer. (p. 692)

10. **c.** is the answer. (p. 699)

a. & b. At every age, women have larger social circles and more intimate relationships with their friends than men.

d. Widows tend to be more involved in friendship networks than married women.

11. **b.** is the answer. (p. 682)

a. People who assimilate are *unlikely* to doubt their values or beliefs.

c. Selective optimization, which has no direct bearing on Sidney's response, refers to adults who structure their lives so that they can do what they want, despite the physical and cognitive losses of late adulthood.

d. On the contrary, Sidney's self-doubt is an unhealthy sign of crumbling too easily in the face of this circumstance.

12. **b.** is the answer. (p. 709)

13. **c.** is the answer. (p. 706)

a. & b. These are examples of "activities of daily life."

14. **b.** is the answer. (p. 707)

15. **c.** is the answer. (p. 680)

a. This is not the crisis of late adulthood in Erikson's theory.

b. & d. These are not crises in Erikson's theory.

KEY TERMS

1. **Self theories** such as Erik Erikson's theory focus on how adults make choices, confront problems, and interpret reality in such a way as to express themselves as fully as possible. (p. 680)

2. The final stage of development, according to Erik Erikson, is **integrity versus despair,** in which older adults seek to integrate the unique experiences with their vision of community. (p. 680)

3. The **positivity effect** is the tendency for elderly people to perceive, prefer, and remember positive experiences and images more than negative ones (p. 683)

4. **Stratification theories** emphasize that social forces limit individual choices and affect the ability to function. (p. 684)

5. According to **disengagement theory,** aging results in role relinquishment, social withdrawal, and passivity. (p. 685)

6. **Activity theory** is the view that older people remain active in a variety of social spheres and become withdrawn only unwillingly. (p. 685)

7. According to **dynamic theories**, each person's life is an active, ever-changing, largely self-propelled process that occurs within ever-changing social contexts. (p. 689)

8. According to the **continuity theory** of aging, each person copes with late adulthood in much the same way that he or she coped with earlier periods of life. (p. 690)

9. Many elderly people prefer to **age in place** by remaining in the same home and community, even after their health declines. (p. 692)

10. The **AARP** is the major organization representing elderly adults in the United States. (p. 696)

11. The **social convoy** is the network of people with whom we establish meaningful relationships as we travel through life. (p. 696)

12. **Filial responsibility** is the idea that adult children are obligated to care for their aging parents. (p. 701)

13. The **frail elderly** are the minority of adults over age 65 who are physically infirm, very ill, or cognitively impaired. (p. 706)

14. In determining frailty, gerontologists often refer to the **activities of daily life (ADLs),** which comprise five tasks: eating, bathing, toileting, dressing, and transferring from a bed to a chair. (p. 706)

15. The **instrumental activities of daily life (IADLs)** are actions that require some intellectual competence and forethought, such as shopping for food, paying bills, and taking medication. (p. 706)

16. **Respite care** is an arrangement in which a professional caregiver takes over to give a family caregiver a break from caring for a frail elderly person. (p. 709)

17. **Assisted living** is an intermediate form of elder care that provides some of the privacy and independence of living at home, along with some medical supervision. (p. 711)

Epilogue

Death and Dying

Epilogue Overview

Death marks the close of the life span—a close individuals must come to terms with, both for themselves and for their loved ones. Indeed, an understanding and acceptance of death is crucial if life is to be lived to the fullest.

The first section focuses on how dying is viewed throughout the life span, in different cultures and religions, and at different points in history. The next section discusses hospice and other forms of palliative care designed to help the terminally ill patient to die "a good death."

Although the concept of an unvarying sequence of stages among the dying is not universally accepted, the pioneering work of Elisabeth Kübler-Ross was instrumental in revealing the emotional gamut of terminally ill patients and the importance of honest communication.

The final section deals with changing expressions of bereavement and how people can be aided in the process of recovery.

NOTE: Answer guidelines for all Epilogue questions begin on page 378.

Guided Study

The text Epilogue should be studied one section at a time. Before you read, preview each section by skimming it, noting headings and boldface items. Then read the appropriate section objectives from the following outline. Keep these objectives in mind and, as you read the Epilogue section, search for the information that will enable you to meet each objective. Once you have finished a section, write out answers for its objectives.

Death and Hope (pp. Ep-1–Ep-10)

1. Discuss the various meanings of death over the life span.

2. Describe some religious and cultural variations in how death is viewed and treated.

Dying and Acceptance (pp. Ep-10–Ep-18)

3. Identify Kübler-Ross's stages of dying, and discuss these stages in light of more recent research.

4. Explain the concept of palliative care, focusing on the advantages and disadvantages of hospices.

5. Discuss the steps that patients, family members, and medical personnel can take to plan for a swift, pain-free, and dignified death.

6. Discuss issues surrounding euthanasia.

Bereavement (pp. Ep-18–Ep-24)

7. Describe recent changes in the mourning process, and identify several specific problems that may become pathological.

8. Suggest steps that can be taken in helping someone to recover from bereavement.

Epilogue Review

When you have finished reading the Epilogue, work through the material that follows to review it. Complete the sentences and answer the questions. As you proceed, evaluate your performance for each section by consulting the answers beginning on page 378. Do not continue with the next section until you understand each answer. If you need to, review or reread the appropriate section in the textbook before continuing.

1. The study of death and dying is _____ . Customs and rituals related to dying, death, and bereavement function to bring _____ in death, _____ of dying, and then _____ of life through bereavement.

Death and Hope (pp. Ep-1–Ep-10)

2. (Table Ep.1) Briefly describe four changes in death over the past 100 years.

3. Children as young as _____ have some understanding of death. Dying children often fear that death means _____ _____ . For this reason, telling children that the deceased person is sleeping or in heaven _____ (is/is not) helpful.

4. Adolescents and emerging adults die in _____ , _____ , and _____ , partly because they may _____ death.

5. A major shift in attitudes about death occurs when adults become responsible for _____ and _____ . From age 25 to 60, terminally ill adults worry about _____ .

6. During late adulthood, anxiety about death _____ (increases/decreases). Many developmentalists view acceptance of one's own mortality during late adulthood as a sign of _____ _____ .

7. Belief in life after death is directly related to people's estimate of _____

_____ .
For this reason, the aged tend to be
_____ (more/less) religious than the young.

8. Among Buddhists, disease and death are inevitable sufferings, which may bring
_____ . Among _____ ,
helping the dying to relinquish their ties to this world and prepare for the next is considered an obligation for the immediate family.

9. Native American traditions consider death an affirmation of _____ and
_____ .

10. Preparations for death are not emphasized in the _____ tradition because hope for _____ should never be extinguished.

11. Many _____ believe that death is the beginning of eternity in _____ or _____ ; thus, they welcome or fear it.

12. In many _____ nations, death affirms religious faith, and caring for the dying is a holy reminder of mortality.

13. In most _____ and _____ traditions, adults take on an important new status through death.

14. Some people who survive a serious illness report having had a _____-_____ _____ in which they left their bodies. These experiences often include _____ elements.

Dying and Acceptance (pp. Ep-10–Ep-18)

15. A *good death* is one that is _____ , _____ , and _____ and that occurs at _____ , surrounded by _____ and _____ . Because of modern medical techniques, a swift and peaceful death is _____ (more/less) difficult to ensure today than in the past. **but also more likely because of improved sanitation, etc.??**

16. A major factor in our understanding of the psychological needs of the dying was the pioneering work of _____ .

17. Kübler-Ross's research led her to propose that the dying go through _____ (how many?) emotional stages. In order, the stages of dying are _____ , _____ , _____ , _____ , and _____ .

18. Another set of stages of dying is based on _____ hierarchy of needs, which are _____ needs, _____ , _____ and _____ , _____ , and _____ .

19. Other researchers typically _____ (have/have not) found the same five stages of dying occurring in sequence.

20. The institution called the _____ provides care to terminally ill patients. The first modern institution of this type was opened in London by _____ .

21. Medical care that is designed not to treat an illness but to relieve pain and suffering is called _____ _____ .

22. The least tolerable physical symptom of fatal illness is _____ . Physicians once worried about causing _____ if pain relievers such as _____ were given too freely. Pain medication for dying patients may have the _____ _____ of reducing pain while _____
_____ .

23. All competent individuals have the legal right to control decisions related to life-prolonging treatments, including _____ _____ , in which a seriously ill person is allowed to die naturally, and _____ _____ , in which someone intentionally acts to terminate the life of a suffering person. Usually, if a patient prefers to die naturally, the order _____ is placed on that person's hospital chart.

24. Active euthanasia is _____ (legal/illegal) in most parts of the world. When a doctor provides the means for someone to end his or her own life, it is referred to as _____-_____ _____ .

25. In the United States, the state of _____ has allowed physician-assisted suicide since 1994 but under very strict guidelines. Many critics note that legalizing euthanasia or physician-assisted **OK?** suicide will create a _____ _____ in which societies begin hastening death. Since that time, concerns that physician-assisted suicide might be used more often with the old and the poor _____ (have/have not) been proven to be well-founded.

26. Some people make a _____ _____ to indicate what medical intervention they want if they become incapable of expressing those wishes. To avoid complications, each person should also designate a _____ _____ _____ , someone who can make decisions for them if needed. Proxies _____ (do/do not) guarantee a problem-free death. One problem is that _____ members may disagree with the proxy; another is that proxy directives may be _____ by hospital staff.

Bereavement (pp. Ep-18–Ep-24)

27. The sense of loss following a death is called _____ . An individual's emotional response to this sense of loss is called _____ .

28. The ceremonies and behaviors that comprise the public response to a death are called _____ . These ceremonies are designed by _____ to channel _____ toward _____ of life.

29. A crucial factor in mourning is people's search for _____ in death. The normal reaction at first is intense, with a strong desire to assess _____ . Emotions gradually ease as the person engages in _____ _____ .

30. In recent times, mourning has become more _____ , less _____ , and less _____ .

31. As rituals diminish, problems such as _____ _____ may become more common. This is a situation in which a bereaved person is _____ _____ .

32. Modern life also increases the incidence of _____ _____ , in which the bereaved are _____ .

33. Another problem is _____ _____ , in which circumstances such as _____ and _____ interfere with the grief process.

34. List two steps that others can follow to help a bereaved person.

    a. _____

    b. _____

Progress Test 1

Circle your answers to the following questions and check them with the answers on page 379. If your answer is incorrect, read the explanation for why it is incorrect and then consult the appropriate pages of the text (in parentheses following the correct answer).

Multiple-Choice Questions

1. Passive euthanasia is most accurately described as:
   a. care designed to relieve pain and suffering.
   b. a situation in which treatment relieves pain while at the same time hastening death.
   c. a situation in which a person is allowed to die naturally.
   d. a situation in which someone takes action to bring about another person's death.

2. Children as young as _____ (what age?) have some understanding of death.
   a. 4   c. 2
   b. 7   d. 9

3. Kübler-Ross's stages of dying are, in order:
   a. anger, denial, bargaining, depression, acceptance.
   b. depression, anger, denial, bargaining, acceptance.
   c. denial, anger, bargaining, depression, acceptance.
   d. bargaining, denial, anger, acceptance, depression.

4. Most adults hope that they will die:
   a. with little pain.
   b. with dignity.
   c. swiftly.
   d. in all of the above ways..

5. *Hospice* is best defined as:
   a. a document that indicates what kind of medical intervention a terminally ill person wants.
   b. mercifully allowing a person to die by not doing something that might extend life.
   c. an alternative to hospital care for the terminally ill.
   d. providing a person with the means to end his or her life.

6. Palliative care refers to:
   a. heroic measures to save a life.
   b. conservative medical care to treat an illness.
   c. efforts to relieve pain and suffering.
   d. allowing a terminally ill patient to die naturally.

7. Adolescents and emerging adults are more likely than other age groups to die in suicides, accidents, and homicides in part because they:
   a. are easily influenced by others.
   b. romanticize death.
   c. have poor relationships with their parents.
   d. cannot establish an identity.

8. Which of the following is a normal response in the bereavement process?
   a. experiencing powerful emotions
   b. culturally diverse emotions
   c. a lengthy period of grief
   d. All of the above are normal responses.

9. A double effect in medicine refers to a situation in which:
   a. the effects of one drug on a patient interact with those of another drug.
   b. medication relieves pain and has a secondary effect of hastening death.

   c. family members disagree with a terminally ill patient's proxy.
   d. medical personnel ignore the wishes of a terminally ill patient and his or her proxy.

10. Near-death experiences:
    a. often include angels and other religious elements.
    b. occur more often following serious injuries than serious illnesses.
    c. occur in most people who come close to dying.
    d. are characterized by each of the above.

True or False Items

Write T (*true*) or F (*false*) on the line in front of each statement.

_____ 1. Hospice care is affordable to all who need it.

_____ 2. Subsequent research has confirmed the accuracy of Kübler-Ross's findings regarding the five stages of dying.

_____ 3. Studies have found that doctors spend less time with patients who are known to be dying.

_____ 4. Following the death of a loved one, the bereaved can best ensure their psychological health and well-being by increasing their social contacts and the number of activities in which they are involved.

_____ 5. To help a bereaved person, one should ignore the person's depression.

_____ 6. Researchers agree that the hospice is beneficial to the dying person and his or her family.

_____ 7. Physician-assisted suicide is legal almost everywhere in the world.

_____ 8. Hospices administer pain-killing medication but do not make use of artificial life-support systems.

_____ 9. In the long run, the bereavement process may have a beneficial effect on the individual.

_____ 10. Fear of death increases in late adulthood.

Progress Test 2

Progress Test 2 should be completed during a final review of the Epilogue. Answer the following questions after you thoroughly understand the correct answers for the Epilogue Review and Progress Test 1.

Multiple-Choice Questions

1. Kübler-Ross's primary contribution was to:
   a. open the first hospice, thus initiating the hospice movement.
   b. show how the emotions of the dying occur in a series of clear-cut stages.
   c. bring attention to the psychological needs of dying people.
   d. show the correlation between people's conceptualization of death and their developmental stage.

2. In recent times, mourning has become all of the following *except*:
   a. more private.
   b. less emotional.
   c. more likely to lead to social isolation.
   d. more religious.

3. Which of the following is *not* a limitation of hospices?
   a. Most insurance plans will not pay for hospice care unless the patient has been diagnosed as terminally ill.
   b. Hospice care can be very expensive.
   c. Almost no hospices serve children.
   d. The dying typically do not receive skilled medical care.

4. A health care proxy is most accurately described as a(n):
   a document that indicates what medical intervention an individual wants if he or she becomes incapable of expressing those wishes.
   b. person chosen by another person to make medical decisions if the second person becomes unable to do so.
   c. situation in which, at a patient's request, someone else ends his or her life.
   d. indication on a patient's chart not to use heroic, life-saving measures.

5. As a result of ongoing police investigations, the bereaved members of a murder victim's family may be at increased risk of experiencing:
   a. absent grief.
   b. disenfranchised grief.
   c. incomplete grief.
   d. a good death.

6. Research reveals that Kübler-Ross's stages of dying:
   a. occur in sequence in virtually all terminally ill patients.
   b. do not occur in hospice residents.
   c. are typical only in Western cultures.
   d. make feelings about death seem much more predictable and universal than they actually are.

7. Living wills are an attempt to:
   a. make sure that passive euthanasia will not be used in individual cases.
   b. specify the extent of medical treatment desired in the event of terminal illness.
   c. specify conditions for the use of active euthanasia.
   d. ensure that death will occur at home rather than in a hospital.

8. Many _____ welcome or fear death because they believe it is the beginning of eternity in heaven or hell.
   a. Buddhists
   b. Muslims
   c. Christians
   d. Jews

9. Ritual is to emotion as:
   a. grief is to mourning.
   b. mourning is to grief.
   c. affirmation is to loss.
   d. loss is to affirmation.

10. Healing after the death of a loved one is most difficult when:
    a. the death is a long, protracted one.
    b. the bereaved is not allowed to mourn in the way or she wishes.
    c. a period of grief has already elapsed.
    d. no other mourners are present.

Matching Items

Match each term or concept with its corresponding description or definition.

Terms or Concepts

_____ **1.** DNR
_____ **2.** hospice
_____ **3.** living will
_____ **4.** passive euthanasia
_____ **5.** double effect
_____ **6.** physician-assisted suicide
_____ **7.** palliative care
_____ **8.** grief
_____ **9.** bereavement

Definitions or Descriptions

a. hospice treatment that relieves suffering and safeguards dignity

b. an alternative to hospital care for the terminally ill

c. hospital chart order to allow a terminally ill patient to die naturally

d. a document expressing a person's wishes for treatment should he or she become terminally ill and incapable of making such decisions

e. providing the means for a terminally ill patient to end his or her life

f. an individual's response to the loss of a loved one

g. the sense of loss following a death

h. allowing a seriously ill person to die naturally by withholding medical intervention

i. situation in which a pain-relieving drug also hastens the death of a terminally ill patient

Developmental Psychology Applied

Answer these questions the day before an exam as a final check on your understanding of the chapter's terms and concepts.

1. Among my people, elders take on an important new status through death as they join the ancestors who watch over our entire village. I am:
   a. African.   **c.** Hindu.
   b. Muslim.   **d.** Native American.

2. Among my people, family members have an obligation to help the dying to relinquish their ties to this world and prepare for the next. I am:
   a. African.   **c.** Hindu.
   b. Muslim.   **d.** Native American.

3. The terminally ill patient who is convinced his laboratory tests must be wrong is probably in which of Kübler-Ross's stages?
   a. denial
   b. anger
   c. depression
   d. bargaining

4. Dr. Aziz, who specializes in the study of death, would most likely describe himself as a(n):
   a. palliative care specialist.
   b. thanatologist.
   c. geriatric specialist.
   d. euthanist.

5. Following 30-year-old Ramón's unexpected and violent death, which of the following individuals is most likely to experience disenfranchised grief?
   a. Kent, his unmarried partner
   b. Janet, the younger sister with whom he has not been in touch for years
   c. his father, who divorced Kent's mother two years earlier
   d. his biological mother, who put Kent up for adoption when he was a baby

6. Dr. Welby writes the orders DNR (do not resuscitate) on her patient's chart. Evidently, the patient has requested:
   a. a living will.
   b. passive euthanasia.
   c. active euthanasia.
   d. an assisted suicide.

7. Armand has directed his lawyer to prepare a document specifying that he does not what to be kept alive by artificial means. His lawyer is creating:
   a. a health care proxy.
   b. grief work.
   c. a double effect.
   d. a living will.

8. The doctor who injects a terminally ill patient with a lethal drug is practicing:
   a. passive euthanasia.
   b. active euthanasia.
   c. an assisted suicide.
   d. an act that became legal in most countries in 1993.

9. Which of the following statements would probably be the most helpful to a grieving person?
   a. "Why don't you get out more and get back into the swing of things?"
   b. "You're tough; bear up!"
   c. "If you need someone to talk to, call me any time."
   d. "It must have been his or her time to die."

10. Dr. Robins is about to counsel her first terminally ill patient and his family. Research suggests that her most helpful strategy would be to:
   a. keep most of the facts from the patient and his family in order not to upset them.
   b. be truthful to the patient but not his family.
   c. be truthful to the family only, and swear them to secrecy.
   d. honestly inform both the patient and his family.

Key Terms

Using your own words, write a brief definition or explanation of each of the following terms on a separate piece of paper.

1. thanatology
2. near-death experience
3. good death
4. hospice
5. palliative care
6. double effect
7. passive euthanasia
8. DNR (do not resuscitate)
9. active euthanasia
10. physician-assisted suicide
11. slippery slope
12. living will
13. health care proxy
14. bereavement
15. grief
16. mourning
17. absent grief
18. disenfranchised grief
19. incomplete grief

ANSWERS
EPILOGUE REVIEW

1. thanatology; acceptance; hope; reaffirmation
2. Death occurs at a later age, takes longer, and more often occurs in hospitals. The major causes of death have also shifted, from infectious diseases to chronic illnesses such as cardiovascular disease and cancer.
3. 2; being abandoned by the people they love; is not
4. suicides; accidents; homicides; romanticize
5. work; family; leaving something undone
6. decreases; mental health
7. how likely they are to die; more
8. enlightenment; Hindus
9. nature; community
10. Jewish; life
11. Christians; heaven; hell
12. Muslim
13. African; Asian
14. near-death experience; religious
15. swift; painless; dignified; home; friends; family; more
16. Elisabeth Kübler-Ross
17. five; denial; anger; bargaining; depression; acceptance
18. Maslow's; physiological needs; safety; love; acceptance; respect; self-actualization
19. have not
20. hospice; Cecily Saunders
21. palliative care
22. pain; addiction; morphine; double effect; speeding up death
23. passive euthanasia; active euthanasia; DNR (do not resuscitate)

24. illegal; physician-assisted suicide

25. Oregon; slippery slope; have not

26. living will; health care proxy; do not; family; ignored

27. bereavement; grief

28. mourning; cultures; grief; reaffirmation

29. meaning; blame; grief work

30. private; emotional; religious

31. absent grief; not expected or allowed to go through a mourning period

32. disenfranchised grief; not allowed to mourn publicly

33. incomplete grief; suicides; murders

34. **a.** Be aware that powerful, complicated, and culturally diverse emotions are likely.

    b. A friend should listen and sympathize, never implying that the person is too grief-stricken or not grief-stricken enough.

PROGRESS TEST 1

Multiple-Choice Questions

1. **c.** is the answer. (p. Ep-13)

    a. This describes palliative care.

    b. This is the "double effect" that sometimes occurs with morphine and other opiate drugs.

    d. This is active euthanasia.

2. **c.** is the answer. (p. Ep-2)

3. **c.** is the answer. (p. Ep-11)

4. **d.** is the answer. (p. Ep-10)

5. **c.** is the answer. (p. Ep-12)

    a. This is a living will.

    b. & d. These are forms of euthanasia.

6. **c.** is the answer. (p. Ep-13)

7. **b.** is the answer. (p. Ep-4)

8. **d.** is the answer. (pp. Ep-18–Ep-19)

9. **b.** is the answer. (p. Ep-13)

10. **a.** is the answer. (p. Ep-9)

    b. & c. Near-death experiences, which occur in some people who are dying, are no more likely to occur following a serious injury than an illness.

True or False Items

1. F   Hospice care is too expensive for most. (p. Ep-12)

2. F   Later research has not confirmed Kübler-Ross's findings that the emotions of an individual faced with death occur in orderly stages. (p. Ep-11)

3. T (p. Ep-10)

4. F   The psychological well-being of the bereaved depends above all on their being able to openly express their grief. (p. Ep-21)

5. F   A friend should listen, sympathize, and not ignore the mourner's pain. (p. Ep-23)

6. F   Hospices have significant benefits, but some people are critical of them in part because they deny hope to the dying and because they are expensive. (p. Ep-12)

7. F   These practices are *illegal* throughout most of the world. (p. Ep-14)

8. T (p. Ep-12)

9. T (p. Ep-23)

10. F   Just the opposite is true. (p. Ep-5)

PROGRESS TEST 2

Multiple-Choice Questions

1. **c.** is the answer. (p. Ep-11)

2. **d.** is the answer. In recent times, mourning has become less religious than formerly. (p. Ep-20)

3. **d.** is the answer. Hospices generally *do* provide patients with skilled medical care. (p. Ep-12)

4. **b.** is the answer. (p. Ep-16)

    a. This is a living will.

    c. This is voluntary euthanasia.

    d. This refers to "DNR."

5. **c.** is the answer. (p. Ep-21)

    a. Absent grief occurs when people cut themselves off from the community and customs of grief and mourning.

    b. Disenfranchised grief occurs when bereaved people are not permitted to mourn publicly.

    d. A good death is one that is swift and painless and that occurs in the company of loved ones.

6. **d.** is the answer. (p. Ep-11)

    b. & c. There is no evidence that hospice residents experience different emotional stages than others who are dying or that these stages are a product of Western culture.

7. **b.** is the answer. (p. Ep-16)

8. **c.** is the answer. (p. Ep-7)

9. **b.** is the answer. Mourning refers to the ceremonies and rituals that a religion or culture prescribes for bereaved people, and grief refers to an individual's emotional response to bereavement. (p. Ep-18)

10. **b.** is the answer. (p. Ep-21)

a. & c. In such situations, death is expected and generally easier to bear.

d. This issue was not discussed.

Matching Items

1. c (p. Ep-13)   5. i (p. Ep-13)   9. g (p. Ep-18)
2. b (p. Ep-12)   6. e (p. Ep-14)
3. d (p. Ep-16)   7. a (p. Ep-13)
4. h (p. Ep-13)   8. f (p. Ep-18)

DEVELOPMENTAL PSYCHOLOGY APPLIED

1. **a.** is the answer. (p. Ep-8)

b. The text notes that in many Muslim nations, death serves to affirm religious faith.

d. Native Americans consider death an affirmation of nature and community.

2. **c.** is the answer. (p. Ep-6)

3. **a.** is the answer. (p. Ep-11)

4. **b.** is the answer. (p. Ep-1)

a. Palliative care is care aimed at relieving the suffering of a dying person.

c. Such a person would study elderly people, but not necessarily those who are dying.

d. There is no such term.

5. **a.** is the answer. (p. Ep-21)

b., c., & d. Because each of these individuals is biologically related to Ramón, none is likely to be excluded from mourning his death.

6. **b.** is the answer. (p. Ep-13)

a. A living will is a document expressing how a person wishes to be cared for should he or she become terminally ill.

c. This is when a person *intentionally acts* to end another's life.

d. In this situation, a person provides the means for another to take his or her own life.

7. **d.** is the answer. (p. Ep-16)

a. A health care proxy is a person chosen to make decisions for a person unable to do so.

b. Grief work is the experience and expression of strong emotions on the death of a loved one.

c. In the double effect, pain is eased but death is hastened.

8. **b.** is the answer. (p. Ep-14)

9. **c.** is the answer. (p. Ep-23)

a., b., & d. These statements discourage the bereaved person from mourning.

10. **d.** is the answer. (p. Ep-11)

KEY TERMS

1. **Thanatology** is the study of death and dying. (p. Ep-1)

2. A **near-death experience** is an episode in which a person comes close to dying and reports having left his or her body, while feeling peacefulness and joy. (p. Ep-9)

3. A **good death** is one that is peaceful, quick, painless, and that occurs at the end of a long life, in the company of family and friends. (p. Ep-10)

4. A **hospice** is an institution in which terminally ill patients receive palliative care. (p. Ep-12)

5. **Palliative care,** such as that provided in a hospice, is care that relieves suffering while safeguarding the person's dignity. (p. Ep-13)

6. A **double effect** is a situation in which medication has the intended effect of relieving a dying person's pain and the secondary effect of hastening death. (p. Ep-13)

7. **Passive euthanasia** involves allowing a seriously ill person to die naturally by withholding medical interventions. (p. Ep-13)

8. **DNR (do not resuscitate)** is a written order from a physician that no attempt should be made to revive a dying patient if he or she suffers cardiac or respiratory arrest. (p. Ep-13)

9. **Active euthanasia** involves a person taking action to end another person's life in order to relieve suffering. (p. Ep-14)

10. A **physician-assisted suicide** is one in which a doctor provides the means for a person to end his or her life. (p. Ep-14)

11. A **slippery slope** is an argument that a given action will start a chain of events that will end in an undesirable outcome. (p. Ep-15)

12. A **living will** is a document that specifies what medical intervention a person wants if he or she becomes incapable of expressing those wishes. (p. Ep-16)

13. A **health care proxy** is a person chosen to make medical decisions for someone else if the second person becomes unable to do so. (p. Ep-16)

14. **Bereavement** is the sense of loss people feel following a death. (p. Ep-18)

15. **Grief** refers to an individual's emotional response to bereavement. (p. Ep-18)

16. **Mourning** refers to the ceremonies and rituals that a religion or culture prescribes for bereaved people. (p. Ep-18)

17. **Absent grief** occurs when people cut themselves off from the community and customs of grief and mourning. (p. Ep-21)

18. **Disenfranchised grief** occurs when bereaved people are not permitted to mourn publicly. (p. Ep-21)

19. **Incomplete grief** occurs when circumstances, such as a criminal investigation, interfere with grieving. (p. Ep-21)

Appendix B

More About Research Methods

Appendix B Overview

The first section describes two ways of gathering information about development: library research and using the Internet. The second section discusses the various ways in which developmentalists ensure that their studies are valid.

NOTE: Answer guidelines for all Appendix B questions begin on page 393.

Guided Study

Appendix B should be studied one section at a time. Before you read, preview each section by skimming it, noting headings and boldface items. Then read the appropriate section objectives from the following outline. Keep these objectives in mind and, as you read the appendix section, search for the information that will enable you to meet each objective. Once you have finished a section, write out answers for its objectives.

Make It Personal (pp. B-1)

1. Explain how observing ethical standards guides a properly conducted interview.

Read the Research (pp. B-1–B-3)

2. Identify several helpful resources for conducting library research on development.

3. Discuss the advantages and disadvantages of using the Internet to learn more about development.

Additional Terms and Concepts (pp. B-3–B-5)

4. Differentiate populations and samples, and the concept and selection of a representative sample.

5. Explain how researchers use hypotheses and operational definitions to guide their research.

6. Discuss the importance of meta-analyses , statistical significance, and effect size in reporting results.

Appendix B Review

When you have finished reading Appendix B, work through the material that follows to review it. Complete the sentences and answer the questions. As you proceed, evaluate your performance for each section by consulting the answers beginning on page 393. Do not continue with the next section until you understand each answer. If you need to, review or reread the appropriate section in the textbook before continuing.

Make It Personal (p. B-1)

1. Before asking questions as part of a research assignment, remember that observing _____ _____ comes first.

2. Before interviewing someone, you should _____ the person of your purpose and assure him or her of _____ .

3. Research studies that may be published require that you inform the college's _____ _____ _____ .

Read the Research (pp. B-1–B-3)

4. Four journals that cover development in all three domains are _____ , _____ , _____ , and _____ .

5. The best journals are _____-_____ , which means that scientists other than an article's authors decide if it is worthy of publication.

6. Two good handbooks in development are _____ , and _____ .

7. Two advantages of using the Internet to learn about development are
   a. _____
   b. _____

8. Two disadvantages of using the Internet are
   a. _____
   b. _____

9. To help you select appropriate information, use general topic lists, called _____ , and _____ _____ , which give you all the sites that use a particular word or words.

Additional Terms and Concepts (pp. B-3–B-5)

10. To make statements about people in general, called a _____ , scientists study a group of research _____ , called a _____ .

11. When a sample is typical of the group under study—in gender, ethnic background, and other important variables—the sample is called a(n) _____ _____ .

12. Ideally, a group of research participants constitute a _____ _____ , which means that everyone in the population is equally likely to be selected. To avoid _____ _____ , some samples are _____ , and trace development of some particular characteristic in an entire cluster.

13. In a _____ study, researchers begin with a group of participants that already share a particular characteristic and then look "backward" to discover other characteristics of the group.

14. Every researcher begins by formulating a

_____ .

15. When the person carrying out research is unaware of the purpose of the research, that person is said to be _____ to the hypothesized outcome.

16. Researchers use _____

_____ to define variables in terms of specific, observable behavior that can be measured precisely.

17. Journal articles that summarize past research are called _____ .

18. A study that combines the findings of many studies to present an overall conclusion is a

_____ .

19. Researchers often report quantitative analyses that measure _____

_____ , which indicates whether or not a particular result could have occurred by chance.

20. The statistic that indicates how much of an impact the independent variable had on the dependent variable is _____

_____ .

Progress Test

Circle your answers to the following questions and check them with the answers on page 394. If your answer is incorrect, read the explanation for why it is incorrect and then consult the appropriate pages of the text (in parentheses following the correct answer).

1. A journal article that summarizes past research is:
   a. *Psycscan: Developmental Psychology.*
   b. *Child Development Abstracts and Bibliography.*
   c. *Developmental Psychology.*
   d. a review article.

2. Which of the following is *not* one of the journals that publish research on all three domains of development ?
   a. *The Developmentalist*
   b. *Developmental Psychology*
   c. *Human Development*
   d. *Child Development*

3. Which of the following is a disadvantage of conducing Internet research?
   a. You can spend hours sifting through information that turns out to be useless.
   b. Anybody can put anything on the Internet.
   c. There is no evaluation of bias on Internet sites.
   d. Each of the above is a disadvantage of Internet research.

4. To say that the study of development is a science means that developmentalists:
   a. use many methods to make their research more objective and more valid.
   b. take steps to ensure that a few extreme cases do not distort the overall statistical picture.
   c. recognize the importance of establishing operational definitions.
   d. do all of the above.

5. The entire group of people about whom a scientist wants to learn is called the:
   a. reference group.
   b. sample.
   c. representative sample.
   d. population.

6. A researcher's conclusions after conducting a study are not valid because a few extreme cases distorted the results. In designing this study, the researcher evidently failed to pay attention to the importance of:
   a. sample size.
   b. "blindness."
   c. representativeness.
   d. all of the above.

7. Rachel made a study of students' opinions about different psychology professors. She took great care to survey equal numbers of male and female students, students who received high grades and students who received low grades, and members of various minorities. Clearly, Rachel wished to ensure that data were obtained from a:
   a. population.
   b. "blind" sample.
   c. representative sample.
   d. comparison group.

8. A person who gathers data in a state of "blindness" is one who:
   a. is unaware of the purpose of the research.
   b. is allowing his or her personal beliefs to influence the results.
   c. has failed to establish operational definitions for the variables under investigation.
   d. is basing the study on an unrepresentative sample of the population.

9. Which of the following is an example of a good operational definition of a dependent variable?
   a. walking
   b. aggression
   c. 30 minutes of daily exercise
   d. taking steps without support

10. The technique of combining the results of many studies to come to an overall conclusion is:
    a. meta-analysis.
    b. effect size.
    c. a prospective study.
    d. a retrospective study.

11. For a psychologist's generalizations to be valid, the sample must be representative of the population under study. The results must also be:
    a. statistically significant.
    b. derived from participants who are all the same age.
    c. large enough.
    d. none of the above.

12. The particular individuals who are studied in a specific research project are called the:
    a. independent variables.
    b. dependent variables.
    c. participants.
    d. population.

13. A research study that begins with participants who share a certain characteristic and then "looks backward" is a:
    a. prospective study.
    b. retrospective study.
    c. meta-analysis.
    d. representative sample.

14. A research study that begins with participants who share a certain characteristic and then "looks forward" is a:
    a. prospective study.
    b. retrospective study.
    c. meta-analysis.
    d. representative sample.

15. Summarizing the results of his research study, Professor Schulman notes that "the effect size was zero." By this she means that the:
    a. independent variable had no impact on the dependent variable.
    b. independent variable had a large impact on the dependent variable.
    c. dependent variable had no impact on the independent variable.
    d. dependent variable had a large impact on the independent variable

Key Terms

Using your own words, write a brief definition or explanation of each of the following terms on a separate piece of paper.

1. population
2. participants
3. sample
4. representative sample
5. blind
6. operational definition
7. meta-analysis
8. effect size

ANSWERS
APPENDIX B REVIEW

1. ethical standards
2. inform; confidentiality
3. Institutional Review Board (IRB)
4. *Developmental Psychology; Child Development; Developmental Review; Human Development*
5. peer-reviewed
6. *Handbook of Child Psychology; Handbook of Aging*
7. a. Virtually everything you might want to know is on the Internet.
   b. The Internet is quick and easy to use, any time of the day or night.
8. a. There is so much information available on the Internet that it is easy to waste time.
   b. Anybody can put anything on the Internet.
9. directories; search engines
10. population; participants; sample
11. representative sample
12. random sample, selection bias; prospective

13. retrospective
14. hypothesis
15. blind
16. operational definitions
17. reviews
18. meta-analysis
19. statistical significance
20. effect size

PROGRESS TEST

1. **d.** is the answer. (p. B-4)
2. **a.** is the answer. (p. B-1)
3. **d.** is the answer. (p. B-2)
4. **d.** is the answer. (pp. B-3–B-5)
5. **d.** is the answer. (p. B-3)
6. **a.** is the answer. (p. B-3)

   b. "Blindness" has no relevance here.

   c. Although it is true that a distorted sample is unrepresentative, the issue concerns the small number of extreme cases—a dead giveaway to sample size.

7. **c.** is the answer. Rachel has gone to great lengths to make sure that her student sample is typical of the entire population of students who takes psychology courses. (p. B-3)

8. **a.** is the answer. (p. B-4)

9. **d.** is the answer. (p. B-4)

   a., b., & c. Each of these definitions is too ambiguous to qualify as an operational definition.

10. **a.** is the answer. (p. B-4)

11. **a.** is the answer. (p. B-4)

12. **c.** is the answer. (p. B-3)

    a. These are the factors that a researcher manipulates in an experiment.

    b. These are the outcomes that a researcher measures in an experiment.

d. It is almost always impossible to include every member of a population in an experiment.

13. **b.** is the answer. (p.4)
14. **a.** is the answer. (p. 4)
15. **a.** is the answer. (p. 4)

    b. In this case, the effect size would be a number close to 1.0.

    c. & d. Independent variables impact dependent variables, and not vice versa.

KEY TERMS

1. The **population** is the entire group of individuals who are of particular concern in a scientific study. (p. B-3)

2. **Participants** are the people who are studied in a research project. (p. B-3)

3. A **sample** is a subset of individuals who are drawn from a specific population. (p. B-3)

4. A **representative sample** is a group of research subjects who accurately reflect key characteristics of the population being studied. (p. B-3)

5. **Blind** is the situation in which data gatherers and sometimes their research participants are deliberately kept unaware of the purpose of the study in order to avoid unintentionally biasing the results. (p. B-4)

6. An **operational definition** is a precise description of a behavior or variable being studied so that another person will know whether it occurred, and how it is measured. (p. B-4)

7. **Meta-analysis** is a research technique in which the results of many studies are combined to produce one overall result (p. B-4)

8. **Effect size** is a statistical measure of how much impact an independent variable had on a dependent variable in a research study. (p. B-4)